# AFRICAN AMERICAN LIFE IN THE POST-EMANCIPATION SOUTH, 1861–1900

*A Twelve-Volume Anthology of Scholarly Articles*

Series Editor

## DONALD G. NIEMAN

*Clemson University*

A GARLAND SERIES

# SERIES CONTENTS

VOLUME

**10**

# AFRICAN AMERICANS AND EDUCATION IN THE SOUTH, 1865–1900

Edited with an introduction by

## DONALD G. NIEMAN

GARLAND PUBLISHING, Inc.
New York & London
1994

**Library of Congress Cataloging-in-Publication Data**

African Americans and education in the South, 1865–1900 / edited
with an introduction by Donald G. Nieman.
    p.    cm. — (African American life in the Post-Emancipa-
tion South ; v. 10)
    Includes bibliographical notes.
    ISBN 0–8153–1447–7 (alk. paper)
    1. Afro-Americans—Education—Southern  States—History—
19th century—Case studies.   2. Freedmen—Education—Southern  States—History—19th century—Case studies.   3. Education—Southern  States—History—19th century—Case studies.
4. Reconstruction.   I. Nieman, Donald G.   II. Series.
LC2802.S9A47   1994
371.8'296073—dc20                                    93–38436
                                                        CIP

Printed on acid-free, 250-year-life paper
Manufactured in the United States of America

# CONTENTS

# INTRODUCTION

The Civil War and its aftermath brought about dramatic changes in the lives of African Americans. Among these, few were more important to the freedpeople than the opportunities for education opened to them. During slavery, every southern state except Tennessee had prohibited teaching slaves to read and write. Although some slaves had learned to read and write (either surreptitiously or with the assistance of their owners), well over 90 percent of African Americans emerged from slavery illiterate. With the destruction of slavery, however, northern benevolent societies, the federal government, and black southerners themselves created a system of schools for the freedpeople. While far from adequate to meet the needs of the black community, this system—which by the 1870s included grammar schools, normal schools, colleges, law schools, and medical schools—afforded many former slaves and their descendants important opportunities and had a significant impact on African American life in the post-emancipation South.

Among the forces shaping black education, none was more important than blacks' passion for education. When northern teachers first opened freedmen's schools in occupied areas of the South during the Civil War, former slaves—adults as well as children—responded enthusiastically. Teachers typically taught packed classes of youngsters during the day and offered classes for adults in the evening. African Americans' thirst for knowledge deeply impressed their teachers. "I never before saw children so eager to learn, although I had several years' experience in New England schools," remarked Charlotte Forten, a black teacher who left Salem, Massachusetts in 1862 to open a school on South Carolina's St. Helena Island. "Coming to school is a constant delight and recreation to them."[1]

Although most of the early black schools were started by northern freedmen's aid societies, often with the assistance of the Freedmen's Bureau, African Americans often took the initiative in establishing schools. In 1862, when a band of Yankee teachers arrived on St. Helena Island, they found that a literate black artisan had already opened a school.[2] Nor was this an isolated instance. In many communities, former slaves—the vast majority of whom were desperately poor—started their own schools. In early 1867, for example, the Freedmen's Bureau agent at Brenham, Texas reported that local blacks would soon "have a small building ready . . . for a school which will accommodate about twenty scholars—also a place provided for the teacher to live in." Moreover, bigger plans were in the works, according to the agent: "they are building a schoolhouse capable of holding a large number of scholars, but as it is being done by contributions of labor and material it . . . progresses slowly."[3]

Despite their poverty, African Americans generously supported schools. Between 1865 and 1870, they paid almost $700,000 in tuition to Freedmen's Bureau schools and contributed another $500,000 through their churches to assist education.[4] In addition to their support for primary education, black churches played an important role in opening the doors of higher education to former slaves and their children. The African Methodist Episcopal Church established a half-dozen colleges in the South in the 1870s and 1880s, including Allen University in Columbia, South Carolina, Paul Quinn College in Waco, Texas, and Morris Brown College in Atlanta. The other principal black Methodist organizations were also active supporters of higher education. The African Methodist Episcopal Zion Church founded Lane College in Jackson, Tennessee, and the Colored Methodist Episcopal Church established Livingstone College in Salisbury, North Carolina.

Black teachers figured prominently in the growth of black education. During the war and its immediate aftermath, many of those who taught in the freedmen's schools were northern blacks, drawn to the South by a sense of mission, and southern blacks, many of whom had only recently learned to read and write. By 1869, a majority of the 3,000 teachers in schools supervised by the Freedmen's Bureau were African Americans.[5] Moreover, with the development of black normal schools and colleges, there was steady growth in the number of black teachers, who held most of the jobs in the black schools opened by the Republican-controlled state governments during the late 1860s and early 1870s. In many localities, Democrats replaced black teachers with whites when they drove the Republicans from power in the mid–1870s. However, protests by black parents and teachers ultimately forced Southern Democrats to relent, restoring black teachers to the classrooms in black schools.

Northern whites also exercised an important influence on black education in the post-emancipation South. Early in the war, as the Union Army occupied sections of the Virginia Tidewater and the South Carolina Sea Islands, northern freedmen's aid societies sent teachers to the South to open schools. During the war and its aftermath, their ranks swelled as several thousand northerners, most of them white women from New England, came South to teach the former slaves. The Freedmen's Bureau, a War Department agency established in 1865 to supervise blacks' transition from slavery to freedom, buttressed this effort. Although it did not establish schools, it provided financial assistance to schools established by the northern societies and by southern blacks. In 1870, over 4,000 schools employing 9,300 teachers and teaching almost 250,000 students operated under the Bureau's supervision. Although its educational program was suspended in 1870, the Bureau's activities had far-reaching consequences. The schools it nurtured formed the basis of the black public school system created by southern Republicans in the late 1860s and early 1870s.

Northern churches and philanthropists also supported black education. Most of the major northern Protestant denominations sent teachers to the South during the 1860s. They also played a major role in supporting black higher education. The American Missionary Association, an arm of the Congregationalist Church, helped establish Fisk University, Atlanta University, Hampton Institute, and Tougaloo College, institutions that would educate generations of African Americans. Other northern denominations, including the Baptists, Methodists, Presbyterians, and Episcopalians, also helped found black colleges in the South. Northern philanthropic institutions supplemented the work of the churches. In 1867, the George Peabody Education Fund began making substantial grants to support black education in the South. Fifteen years later, it was joined by the John F. Slater Fund, which also became a major contributor to black schools.

For all the good they did, northern whites left an ambiguous legacy. Most northern educators viewed their task as civilizing a backward, albeit educable, people. For them, education went well beyond teaching African Americans to read, write, and compute; they also thought it imperative to inculcate in the freedpeople diligence, punctuality, respect for authority, sobriety, thrift, and devotion to family, lest they confuse liberty with license. Despite their heavy-handed paternalism, most of the teachers who went to the South during and after the Civil War believed that former slaves had the capacity for self-improvement, independence, and citizenship. After the end of Reconstruction, however, an increasing number of influential northern supporters of black education took a dim view of African Americans' potential for advancement.

This was especially true of officials at the Peabody and Slater Funds, the two major philanthropies which supported black education in the decades following Reconstruction. Reflecting the pseudo-scientific racism popular in the 1880s and 1890s, they assumed that blacks were ill-suited for higher learning and directed their largesse to schools like Hampton and Tuskegee that emphasized industrial education and manual training. As a result, black liberal arts schools suffered, making access to higher learning and the professions more difficult for black southerners.

Northern whites also bequeathed a legacy of segregated schools that would haunt the South for more than a century. Although many Bureau officials believed in integrated schools in principle, they sought to assuage southern whites' opposition to race mixing by establishing segregated schools. When southern Republicans created systems of public education, they followed the Bureau's lead. Southern Republicans did not mandate segregation by law. Except in a few isolated instances, however, they operated separate schools for blacks and whites. Although black schools generally received equal resources while the Republicans were in power, segregation had unfortunate consequences. With black and white children in separate schools, public officials could diminish the resources available for educating black children while increasing public support for white schools, something that was not lost on Democrats when they returned to power after the end of Reconstruction.

In addition to northern whites and African Americans themselves, southern whites also had a profound effect on black education. In the aftermath of the Civil War, many white southerners remained deeply opposed to black education. On the one  hand, they asserted that blacks were ineducable; on the other, they feared that education would make blacks discontented with their subordinate status, encourage black assertiveness, and give former slaves the tools to challenge white dominance. The white-controlled state governments created under President Andrew Johnson's conservative program of Reconstruction in 1865–1866 excluded blacks from the public schools and generally made no provision for separate black schools. Moreover, whites sometimes burned schools established by northern benevolent societies and southern blacks and attacked the teachers who taught in them. A black preacher who established a church and school in Aberdeen, Alabama shortly after the war was severely beaten and run out of town by a mob of whites who informed him that "the land belonged to them and no d____ nigger would preach or teach school there."[6]

During the late 1860s and early 1870s, southern Republicans **responded** to their black constituents' demand for education, creating the first systems of public schools for blacks in the region. Redemption and the return of white Democrats to power in the mid–1870s, however, created formidable new obstacles to black education. Although Southern Democrats left in place the black schools that their Republican opponents had created, they slashed state support for them. Moreover, they shifted most of the resources that were available for education to the white schools, creating a system of public education that was not only separate (as it had been under the Republicans) but grossly unequal. In South Carolina, for example, per pupil expenditures for whites increased from $2.75 to $3.11 between 1880 and 1895. During the same period, per pupil expenditures for African Americans declined from $2.51 to $1.05.[7]

A final factor shaping black education was former slaves' poverty. Despite African Americans' enthusiasm for education, poverty placed limits on opportunities for educational advancement. The vast majority of black southerners lived in the countryside and were tenant farmers, sharecroppers, and agricultural laborers. Vulnerable to exploitation by white employers and merchants and tied to the production of commodities (most notably cotton) whose prices steadily declined, most rural blacks experienced unremitting poverty. Those who held non-agricultural jobs fared little better. Relegated mainly to unskilled, low-paying jobs, most remained desperately poor. As a result, many black children had to work to help support their families and received very little formal education or, worse yet, never saw the inside of a classroom. The grim realities of black life also worked to discourage many blacks from attending or remaining in school. Aware of the sharply restricted economic opportunities open to them, too many fatalistically concluded that schooling would do little to improve their economic prospects.

Black initiative, northern white assistance, and southern white resistance combined with the reality of black poverty to establish the parameters of black educational advancement during the decades following emancipation. On the one hand, there was significant progress. A system of black public and private schools took shape, offering African Americans a range of educational opportunites that had been unimaginable under slavery. On the other hand, the resources devoted to black schools were never adequate, and after the end of Reconstruction, the disparity between expenditures on white and black schools steadily widened. This mix of progress and poverty was reflected in the statistics on black literacy: between 1860 and 1900, the rate of illiteracy among southern blacks was nearly halved, falling from over 90 percent to about 50 percent. Still, despite this very real progress, one-half of black adults remained illiterate, unable to read a labor contract or a ballot or to examine a store account or a wage settlement with an employer.

The essays that follow explore the complex factors shaping black education in the post-emancipation South, focusing both on the progress African Americans enjoyed and the very real barriers they faced. They examine the growth of black elementary schools, normal schools, colleges, and professional schools; curricula and pedagogy in black schools; the growing emphasis on industrial education; the role of black educators; and shifts in public and private support for black education. The essays highlight the role blacks themselves played in overcoming poverty, racism, and indifference to open the doors of educational opportunity and explore the impact of education on the lives of black southerners and their communities. Taken together, they treat a vital aspect of the black experience, illuminating both the triumph and tragedy of African American life in the post-emancipation South.

## NOTES

[1] Forten quoted in James M. McPherson, ed., *The Negro's Civil War: How American Negroes Thought and Acted During the War for the Union* (New York: Pantheon, 1965), 116–17.

[2] Eric Foner, *Reconstruction: America's Unfinished Revolution, 1863–1877* (New York: Harper & Row, 1988), 97.

[3] Capt. Edward Collins (Brenham) to Lt. T.J. Kirkman, March 24, 1867, Freedmen's Bureau Records, Texas, Letters Received, Record Group 105, National Archives.

[4] Arnold H. Taylor, *Travail and Triumph: Black Life and Culture in the South Since the Civil War* (Westport, Conn.: Greenwood Press, 1976), 118.

[5] Robert C. Morris, *Reading, 'Riting, and Reconstruction: The Education of Freedmen in the South, 1861–1870* (Chicago: University of Chicago Press, 1981), 58.

[6] Affadavit by B. Alexander, June 16, 1866, Freedmen's Bureau Records, Alabama, Letters Received, Record Group 105, National Archives.

[7] Taylor, *Travail and Triumph*, 123.

## SUGGESTED READING

Horace Mann Bond. *Negro Education in Alabama: A Study in Cotton and Steel*. Washington, D.C.: Associated Publishers, Inc., 1939.

Henry Allen Bullock. *A History of Negro Education in the South from 1619 to the Present*. Cambridge, Mass.: Harvard University Press, 1967.

Ronald E. Butchart. *Northern Schools, Southern Blacks, and Reconstruction: Freedmen's Education in the South, 1865–1875*. Westport, Conn.: Greenwood Press, 1980.

Louis R. Harlan. *Booker T. Washington: The Making of a Black Leader, 1858–1901*. New York: Oxford University Press, 1973.

———. *Booker T. Washington: The Wizard of Tuskegee, 1901–1915*. New York: Oxford University Press, 1983.

———. *Separate and Unequal: Public School Campaigns and Racism in the Seabord South, 1901–1915*. Chapel Hill: University of North Carolina Press, 1958.

Jacqueline Jones. *Soldiers of Light and Love: Northern Teachers and Georgia Blacks, 1865–1873*. Chapel Hill: University of North Carolina Press, 1980.

Robert C. Morris. *Reading, 'Riting, and Reconstruction: Freedmen's Education, 1862–1875*. Chicago: University of Chicago Press, 1980.

Donald Spivey. *Schooling for the New Slavery: Black Industrial Education, 1868–1915*. Westport, Conn.: Greenwood Press, 1978.

William Preston Vaughn. *Free Schools for All: Blacks and Public Education in the South, 1865–1877*. Lexington, Ky.: University of Kentucky Press, 1974.

# Suspicion Versus Faith: Negro Criticisms of Berea College in the Nineteenth Century

*by Jacqueline G. Burnside*

Racial coeducation, in nineteenth-century America, referred to the education of white students with black students. In the post-bellum South, this type of mixing was a bold experiment rarely sustained except at one private college in Berea, Kentucky. Berea College, reopening in 1866 after the Civil War, admitted several blacks into its primary and secondary grades. It was to be the only school in the South to maintain racial coeducation on a large scale for any length of time, a period of almost four decades.[1]

This article focuses on the mid-1890s, a formative period when Berea began experiencing a phenomenal rate of growth, largely due to the vision and impetus of President William Goodell Frost. Frost's new policies aroused the suspicions of several Negro critics who perceived dangerous consequences resulting from these changes. Thus, controversy about President Frost's policies served to alienate a faction of the black citizens whom Berea was chartered to serve. Subsequently, the passage of Kentucky's Day Law in 1904 prohibited coeducation of the races, and Berea College's compliance with this law resulted in further criticisms of President Frost by people who believed he had been responsible for changing the college into a white institution.

In recent years, this view has been presented by historian Dave Nelson in a *Journal of Negro History* article (1974). Nelson concluded that Frost had been interested only in increasing the number of white students, while discouraging the attendance of black students, and so "thwarted the purposes of the founders."[2] How-

---

The author holds a baccalaureate degree from Berea College and is a doctoral candidate in sociology at Yale University.

Accompanying photographs appear courtesy of the Berea College Archives.

[1]Maryville College in Tennessee admitted black men, but not black women, together with white men and women. Its enrollments of blacks were always small. See Ralph Waldo Lloyd's *Maryville College: A History of 150 Years, 1819-1969* (Maryville, Tenn., 1969).
[2]See Paul David Nelson's "Experiment in Interracial Education at Berea College, 1858-1908," *Journal of Negro History* 59 (1974): 13-27. Nelson's interpretation of some documents differs considerably from the one I present.

ever, in contrast to Nelson's view, this article examines criticisms of Berea College by its Negro alumni, critiques that permit a more balanced analysis of the historical controversies surrounding the college's existence as an interracial institution. By describing Berea's social setting in the postbellum South, these Negro criticisms can be placed in proper perspective so as to broaden the debate on *how* Berea College changed from a racially mixed institution into a segregated one.

I

Where the foothills of the Cumberland Mountains slope downward to meet the central plains of Kentucky's bluegrass lies the institution known as Berea College. Originally founded by the Reverend John G. Fee in 1855, the school was dedicated to Christian principles of antirum, anticaste prejudice, and antisectarianism. Although some care had been taken by its abolitionist founders to select a friendly site, Berea was often regarded with suspicion by many neighboring residents. In the aftermath of John Brown's raid on Harper's Ferry in 1859, local antiabolition sentiments grew so hostile that Berea school families were forced (by armed escorts) out of the state of Kentucky altogether. They went into exile in Ohio. After the Civil War, most of the original families returned to start a school "for all persons of good character."[3]

The newly reopened school received its first young black pupils in spring 1866.[4] They were children of freed slaves who had been among the first to flock to Berea. The school's principal, J.A.R. Rogers, later recalled that historic moment when these children of freed slaves made Berea a mixed school:

[3]When confronted with the mob's ultimatum to leave the state, the families banded together to pray while some of their members hurried to the capitol in Frankfort to seek protection from the governor. The governor refused to render any means of protection, disavowing responsibility for the group's safety. When the group heard this news, they decided the wiser course of action would be to leave. See John G. Fee's *Autobiography* (Chicago, 1891), 146-55, and *American Missionary* 4 (1860): 13-14, 39-46, 63-65.

[4]See Richard Drake's *One Apostle was a Lumberman* (Berea, 1975), which notes that the first blacks who were taught at Berea were a group of ministers; however, this group did not matriculate through the school.

> That was a memorable day when the first came. The colored pupils were admitted to the lowest department, the only one they were prepared to enter but a panic struck the whole school. Soon scholars from every department began to leave. For a time I tried to have the departments move on as usual without paying any attention to the defection, but students were leaving so rapidly, that I addressed them and showed them the folly and guilt of such prejudice. I remember at last turning to those who were left and saying "Will ye also go away?"[5]

Many white students who left eventually returned to school. Mostly children of local residents, these students realized that the Berea school offered the best education available in the area. Within its first year, Berea's mixed enrollment grew from less than a hundred to over one hundred sixty, one-half of whom were black.[6] By the end of its first decade, the "school" had been formally organized into a "college" consisting of primary, secondary, and college departments, complete with two dormitories and a boarding hall. The board of trustees and the college's first president, E. Henry Fairchild, formerly a professor at racially mixed Oberlin College in Ohio, formed the governing body. Under Fairchild's presidency (1869-89), total enrollments grew to approximately 450 students, one-half to two-thirds of them black.[7]

The seemingly peaceful character of racial coeducation that some alumni later described can be explained by three reasons. One is the small size of the college and the relative minority of white students. Whites had to interact with blacks in order to participate in school; nearly all school activities, such as baseball teams, the brass band, and the literary societies, were racially mixed, as were both male and female dormitories, where it was not uncommon for whites to room with blacks.[8]

The second reason for racial harmony on campus resulted from the strong organizational ties between Berea College and Oberlin College. Located in the "free" state of Ohio, Oberlin College had begun racial coeducation shortly after its founding in 1833. However, Oberlin served not just as a source of person-

[5] J.A.R. Rogers to William G. Frost, February 17, 1893, Frost Papers (hereinafter cited as FP), Box 4, Berea College Archives (hereinafter cited as BCA).

[6] See *Berea College Catalogue, 1866-67* (Cincinnati, 1867).

[7] *Ibid.*

[8] From black alumni, see Elgetha Brand Bell to Elizabeth Peck, May 14, 1956, BCA Record Group (hereafter RG) 8, Box 2, and the file on Angus A. Burleigh, Box 3. From a white alumnus and faculty member, see E.G. Dodge to Frost, April 11, 1925, Box 13, FP.

nel for Berea (Rogers, Fairchild, and most of Berea's teachers had been associated with Oberlin); it also was a link to financial support, since members of the same group of Congregationalists in Oberlin had provided money through the American Missionary Association (AMA) to help establish Berea.

Third, the religious zeal of former abolitionists like Fee, Rogers, and Fairchild provided moral support for the college's commitment to overcome caste prejudice by coeducation of the races. President Fairchild explained this guiding philosophy in his inaugural address:

> How soon will [white] people be prepared to give equal rights and protection to colored people, if from childhood they are taught that colored children are not fit to be near them as equals, but as inferiors may be all about them? If as children they are not allowed to meet in the same schools and Sabbath-schools, how, as men, will they be able to meet at the polls, sit on juries . . . and testify in all cases on an equal footing with them?[9]

## II

Fairchild's statement captured the essence of the "Berea Spirit" which opposed conventional race relations in the South. The unconventionality of Berea College, in most cases, limited the type of financial support it received. School fees, paid by students, provided a small part of operating expenses. In addition to thousands of dollars donated from the Freedman's Fund and the AMA, Berea received the bulk of its funds from wealthy philanthropists in Ohio and New England. Having distant funding sources meant Berea could afford to be independent of local constraints imposed by wealthy southerners, many of whom disdained the education at Berea College merely because blacks were educated there with whites. Berea's wealthy donors remained a steady money source until the late 1880s, when most of these former antislavery supporters became a vanishing breed. The younger generation of benefactors proved less interested in contributing to racially mixed or all-black schools. As a result, by the latter years of E. Henry Fairchild's presidency the college was

---

[9]See E. Henry Fairchild's inaugural address, *Berea College Catalogue, 1870* (Cincinnati, 1870), 12-13.

4

**"Racial coeducation was a bold experiment rarely sustained except at one private college in Berea, Kentucky." Photograph ca. 1887.**

experiencing a gradual decline in donations; the institution delayed new developments because of demands to meet current operating expenses.

Berea's financial deficits were still increasing two years after Fairchild had been succeeded by President William B. Stewart. Financial deficits were not Stewart's only problems, however. Some of Berea's staff and trustees called for Stewart's resignation after they obtained information about his allegedly improper conduct at his previous job in an all-black Baptist academy in Tennessee. Stewart resigned, although he retained a seat on Berea's Board of Trustees.[10]

After the board accepted Stewart's resignation, it promptly offered the position to Oberlin professor of Greek William Goodell Frost. Frost, on leave from Oberlin, was living in Germany in 1892 with his three young sons by a former marriage and his new bride, Eleanor Marsh. After much deliberation and discussion with Eleanor, he accepted the invitation to assume the

[10]See William B. Stewart Papers, Box 1, BCA. See also the President's Report of June 24, 1891. There is some speculation that Stewart's resignation was manipulated by certain persons who wanted Frost as president.

office of president.[11]


## III


Prior to leaving Germany, Frost wrote to the Board of Trustees addressing those key factors which influenced his decision of acceptance:

> The peculiar work of Berea for years to come, that which secures for her the support of men and the blessing of heaven is for the colored race. And her work for this race is a work for fundamental morality and the welfare of the whole country. It is a principle of absolute righteousness that every man should be regarded according to his worth and not according to any accident of birth. Character is more than color.

> How shall Berea do most for this cause: (a) By actually elevating to the level of cultured manhood as many members of the race as possible. But many other schools are doing this work. Berea's peculiar opportunity is (b) to do this in connection with the education of white students, thus teaching the races to live and work together, and (c) to afford an object lesson to the whole country, making it possible for advocates of justice everywhere to say

>> "There is Berea with hundreds of white and colored students working together in friendly relations on the soil of slavery . . ."

> We must get more students, and especially more white students.[12]


This letter by Frost to the brethren at Berea contains two very important points. One is the indication of Frost's optimistic attitude about Berea's peculiar work for blacks; he thinks it is work that will be supported by men and blessed by heaven. The second point is Frost's definition of Berea's work. He emphasizes that many schools are educating black students, but Berea has a special opportunity to educate blacks with whites in a way that would teach the "races to live and work together." These points are the very basis of Frost's later disappointments, even though his sentiments echo the spirit of Fairchild's inaugural address.

[11]See Frost to his mother, Maria Goodell Frost, November 20, 1892, Box 2, Folder 1, FP. Frost, born in 1854, grew up with the Oberlin influence of evangelism and social reforms; his mother was the daughter of abolitionist William Goodell, while his father, the Reverend Lewis P. Frost, had graduated from Oberlin in 1848. Frost followed suit in 1876. See his autobiography, *For the Mountains* (New York, 1937).

[12]Frost to the "Brethren at Berea," July 16, 1892, Box 4, FP.

Nevertheless, Frost's policies to increase white enrollments and obtain new funding sources coincided with an increase in racial hostility in the South and the rest of the nation. Berea's work may have been blessed by heaven but it was not supported by enough generous white men to meet even the college's payroll.

Frost had studied Berea's current operations prior to accepting the presidency, so he knew about the decline in black and white enrollments and about the college's budget deficits.[13] Recognizing the urgent need for more money, Frost arrived at Berea College eager to commence work, but spent most of the first year recovering from typhoid fever. While convalescing, he sought accounts of the college's history from retired Berea workers and included these details into speeches and newspaper articles to tell potential benefactors about the great changes their donations could work. On numerous occasions when writers criticized Berea for being a mixed school, Frost would emphasize its unique heritage, one made possible by missionary pioneers like the Reverend Fee, Principal Rogers, and President Fairchild.[14]

## IV

This energetic, thirty-eight-year-old president expanded the scope of his duties by assuming both the admissions and development functions. In his admissions travel, he visited adjacent counties to see the mountain communities from which Berea could draw more white students. Here he made speeches about Berea and met poor families living in conditions he thought reminiscent of his ancestors from the eighteenth century. Often he described these Anglo-Saxon mountaineers to eastern philanthropists as "our contemporary ancestors."[15]

In his development travel, Frost went with Berea's financial agent Fairchild to the North and the East soliciting funds for Berea's expansion. Frost needed money to meet Berea's current operating expenses, but he also wanted more money for the long-

[13]Berea College's treasurer's report, June 23, 1892, Board of Trustees Annual Reports, RG 2, Box 1, BCA. It was several years before Frost chose to accept his full presidential salary.

[14]For Frost's historical sketch of Berea College, see Box 3, Folder 6, FP.

[15]Frost to Maria G. Frost, August 29, 1893, Box 2, FP.

term security of endowments. What Frost first encountered awakened him to the dismal aspects of fundraising. Writing from Boston (1894) to Eleanor Marsh in Berea, he shared his discouragements:

> Well, I have had a good cry! Have been working for today's interview a long time, and the last of old friends of Berea prove, like all the rest, to be no special friend after all. So it simply comes to this: We must build up a new constituency from the bottom. *Not one* of all the donors who were on the list has increased his subscription at Fairchild's solicitation, and scarcely one new one has been enlisted by him.[16]

Equal lack of success by Berea's financial agent, Eugene Fairchild, clearly indicated the need for a different strategy. Prospective donors had to be instructed, not merely told, about Berea's peculiar work in educating black and white youths. In addition to Eleanor Marsh's fundraising trips, Frost was assisted in his fundraising endeavors by several alumni, chief among them being the Reverend William E. Barton, a white alumnus (class of 1885) and a newly elected trustee then living in Boston. A close friendship developed as both men shared a kinship of ideas in working together. In fact, one of Barton's early letters to Frost contains two clues concerning the direction of Berea's proposed expansion:

> If Berea were simply a preparatory school for colored youth, . . . it would not pay.
> If we can reach a larger number of young people from the mountains, if we can reach out toward the North and pick out of many communities the very best of their young people, who without the help of Berea would never obtain an education, and give them the mental and moral and spiritual development that will make them a power for good in the world, there is a net gain — it is all net gain — to the kingdom of God that justifies a good deal of work.[17]

Barton's emphasis on educating students from the North with the southern mountaineers would later appear to donors as Berea's attempt to "efface sectional lines" between the North and the South. Also, the inability of students to acquire an education if it were not for Berea's help emerged as official admis-

---

[16]Frost to Eleanor Marsh Frost (hereinafter EMF), November 26, 1894, Box 1, FP.
[17]William E. Barton to Frost, October 4, 1893, Box 4, FP. Barton's interests in Berea led him to write several articles about the Cumberland Mountain people and about black spirituals (which he collected). Most of his articles appeared in the *Berea Quarterly*, a public relations organ edited by Frost from 1895 to 1916.

sions policy. Both issues — erasing sectionalism and educating poor students — became Berea's specialties as Barton's assistance proved instrumental in Frost's wooing new donors in the Boston area. This assistance included arranging special hotel dinners (expenses paid by Barton's colleagues) and public meetings with Frost as featured speaker. In his speeches, Frost introduced the wealthy Americans to their "contemporary ancestors" who were living in the Appalachian Mountains. By telling interesting anecdotes and describing colorful dialects, Frost captured the romantic imaginations of his listeners. Donors who had been reluctant to contribute to a "colored" school were delighted to contribute to a Berea College that served the educational needs of their "contemporary ancestors."[18]

## V

Among his achievements of 1894, Frost listed the purchase of new equipment, a small increase in white students' enrollment (there was also a small increase in black enrollment), the selection of a sound board of trustees, and the early retirement of Tutor James Hathaway.[19] While Frost described Hathaway's leaving Berea as an "achievement," some members of the black Berean community considered it manipulation by Frost and Berea's white faculty to rid the college of any black teachers. When President Frost arrived in Berea, there had been approximately eighteen members on the college's faculty, only one of whom was black — James Hathaway.

To analyze Hathaway's case fully requires an examination of earlier Negro criticisms of the school. Berea's most outspoken black critic, an alumnus of the class of 1874, lawyer John T. Robinson, wrote a private letter to Frost responding to Frost's questions about a news article on Berea College, Negro rights, and Christianity.[20] Robinson wanted to clarify the wrong impres-

[18]See Frost to EMF, November 13, 1894, Box 1; excerpts from the Diary of EMF, March 18, 1898, Box 43, both in FP.

[19]See Box 2, Folder 7. Frost also served as president of the Board of Trustees, a position which Fee had held during Fairchild's tenure.

[20]See J.T. Robinson, "His Alma Mater - Mr. J.T. Robinson, a Former Student of Berea College Takes that Institution to Task," in Lexington *Standard*, October —, 1893,

sion that Frost had of Robinson's interests in publishing the 1893 article, "His Alma Mater — a Former Student of Berea College Takes that Institution to Task." The attorney asserted that he wrote in the interest of truth and justice and not solely in the special interest of the Negro. By writing the article, he wanted to focus public attention on important concerns about Berea's interracial policies which, he noted to Frost, "Date all the way back over twenty years, under this same *calm surface* you now describe."[21]

Attempting to diminish the importance of Robinson's opinions, Frost had implied that they were based on hearsay. However, Robinson described his vigilance of Berea College through the years by visits to the school and by keeping aware of current policies, though at a distance. In his "Alma Mater" article, he questioned Berea's practice of its Christian principle that "God Hath Made of One Blood All Nations of Men." He cited examples of caste prejudice among the Berea workers that had occurred during President Fairchild's administration. Robinson emphasized to Frost that he was not criticizing the *"present management"* but the *"general principle"* of racial brotherhood which he believed some whites associated with Berea had not practiced.

The appearance of the Robinson article started an intermittent debate published on the front pages of the weekly Lexington *Standard*, a black newspaper whose staff included Berea alumnus James Hathaway.[22] By publishing Robinson's article, the *Standard*'s staff was initiating a debate about Berea College interracial policies that had never been addressed publicly.

Robinson's "Alma Mater" article (and his letter to Frost) listed three criticisms of Berea College's practice of racial brotherhood. The first involved interracial dating: Robinson described the Board of Trustees' 1872 policy which formalized their cautious attitude toward interracial dating, though not prohibiting such

---

clipping in Vertical Files, RG 13.7 Series Blacks, BCA (hereinafter Black Series Files). Not much is known about John T. Robinson. He was a black man who enrolled at Berea around 1869. He once listed Germantown (Bracken County) as his home.

[21]J.T. Robinson to Frost, December 15, 1893, Box 4, FP.

[22]The *Standard* was published from 1892 to 1895 by an association of black citizens. Staff members included James Hathaway (Berea College tutor), J.C. Jackson (a Berea trustee, 1879-95), A.W. Titus (former Berea student), and Benjamin Tibbs.

dating among students.[23] Yet to Robinson, the policy statement represented a "shameful compromise" because it was interpreted as the college's affirmation against social equality of white and black students. Although the Board rescinded its interracial dating regulations in 1889, Robinson believed their impact on social relations remained. Thus, President Fairchild, and later President Frost, could insist publicly that coeducation of the races did not lead to intimate social relations; slavery and ignorance had resulted, however, in "almost unlimited amalgamation."[24]

Robinson's second criticism indicates why Berea College's racial coeducation became the center of controversy. Berea College offered its Christian principles of brotherhood as a practical way for a sorely divided nation to learn to live and work together again. This was possible within the "secluded associations" formed on campus; harmony and cordiality among the races were said to be almost everywhere in evidence. Outside the immediate area, though, Berea's anticaste influences on some white students seemed to be of short duration, argued Robinson.

This short-term effect on anticaste prejudice caused the most concern for Robinson. He asserted that few white students from Berea would "publicly make it known" that they went to a mixed school or defend it; nor would they treat their Negro classmates with ordinary civility outside the school. Those who adhered to this attitude (if they had the means) would usually take a few months at some other school in order to finish, and never mention Berea, unless compelled to do so, and then would be likely to say, "We had nothing to do with the 'coons' or 'darkies.' "[25]

[23]While not prohibiting social relations between the races (as long as both parties were discreet), the resolution stated the trustees' preference that "under existing circumstances" it was not desirable "for those of the other sex and a different race, especially when the differences in is quite marked." Berea College Board of Trustees' Minutes, Series V (1858-1905): 81-82, RG 2, Box 2, Book A, BCA. For a more positive view of the Board's resolution, see Drake's *One Apostle* and Richard Sears' "Day of Small Things" (1984, unpublished manuscript, BCA). Sears presents evidence that the trustees were intending to preempt the faculty's efforts to prohibit interracial dating by approving certain conditions for permission to date. Though this be true, it is also true that, in Robinson's opinion, the board's policy mitigated against mixed dating by fostering inequality against black men. Robinson eventually married a cousin of John Fee, a sister of his original fiancée who died.

[24]See Fairchild's inauguration address in *Berea College Catalogue, 1869* (Cincinnati, 1870), 11-13.

[25]Robinson, "His Alma Mater," 1.

*11*

Robinson, urging no silent consent from black people, warned that proponents of these attitudes were people who would make Berea a white school if they could. His third criticism concerned an

> . . . impression [which] prevails that education of the colored people at Berea was not contemplated at the start, but by concession on part of the whites they were admitted, (as a gracious favor) therefore, they owe their presence in the school to the forebearance of the whites. This is a serious mistake.[26]

Robinson believed this mistake could undermine Berea's efforts to change a caste society into one of equality and brotherhood. He urged Berea's new president, Frost, to heed these criticisms, for Berea College's future.[27]

The future of blacks throughout the South was under discussion at that time, for although Robinson wrote specifically about the college and the attitudes of its students, the racial attitudes he described mirrored images of the growing racist mood of the nation. During the 1880s and the 1890s, the political rights of black people were revoked systematically, as state after state enacted laws designed to prevent blacks from voting, from living where they pleased and could afford, from sitting or standing where they chose, and from marrying whom they loved — if the partner-to-be belonged to a different race.

This racial ostracism of "Jim Crow" laws and customs was intended to destroy the political power of black voters; it also was designed to keep black and white laborers, sharecroppers, and factory workers from uniting to demand fair treatment from their employers. Racial segregation controlled not only black men and women but also poor white men and women, for it encouraged all whites to think they were superior to blacks, simply because of the color of their skins.

VI

Such was the public mood when Berea College, under Presi-

[26]*Ibid.*, 2.
[27]*Ibid.*

dent Frost, began to gain more and more national attention. The forced "retirement" of Berea's sole black faculty member, Hathaway, served as one catalyst for critical public perceptions about the college's new president. Another catalyst was Berea's increased enrollments of white students, while black enrollments stayed virtually the same. These two issues lay at the heart of the controversy about President Frost's management of Berea College.

James S. Hathaway was twenty-five when he graduated from Berea in 1884. He was hired immediately as a tutor in math and Latin. In addition to his regular duties, he was paid to travel around Kentucky and make speeches to promote the virtues of morality and industry among his black audiences. Hathaway, after working almost ten years without promotion at the faculty's lowest rank of tutor, asked the Board of Trustees in 1893 to grant leave for a year of study. The board granted him the customary year's leave without salary. Upon consultation with President Frost, Hathaway realized that a strong possibility existed that he could return after a year's absence only to discover he no longer had a position. For that reason, he resigned and accepted a professorship at the State Normal School at Frankfort.[28]

Officially, Frost did not dismiss Hathaway for any deficiencies as a teacher; in fact, he wrote a complimentary letter of recommendation when Hathaway resigned. This letter testified to Hathaway's "satisfactory service" as a tutor in Latin and mathematics and described his attributes as a "man of reliable Christian character and a gentleman of good natural abilities as well as of most pleasing manners and address."[29] As an additional measure, the faculty designated a representative to express to Professor Hathaway their "appreciation of his service as tutor in Berea College."[30] All this was done in spite of the fact that Hathaway was not generally well received at Berea by his faculty colleagues. Frost may have heard the opinions expressed among some faculty members that Hathaway was a "zealous and wily"

[28]Board of Trustees Annual Reports (1890-94): 4, 9. Hathaway eventually became president of the State Normal School (later Kentucky State University) in Frankfort, for 1900-07 and 1910-12.

[29]See John H. Jackson to Frost, July 10, 1895, which enclosed a copy of Hathaway's recommendation from Frost, Box 4, FP. Also see W.P. Johnson, *Biographical Sketches of Prominent Negro Men and Women* (Lexington, 1897), 39-41, 56.

[30]Faculty Minutes, Vol. IV (September 1893), RG 6.1, Box 6, BCA.

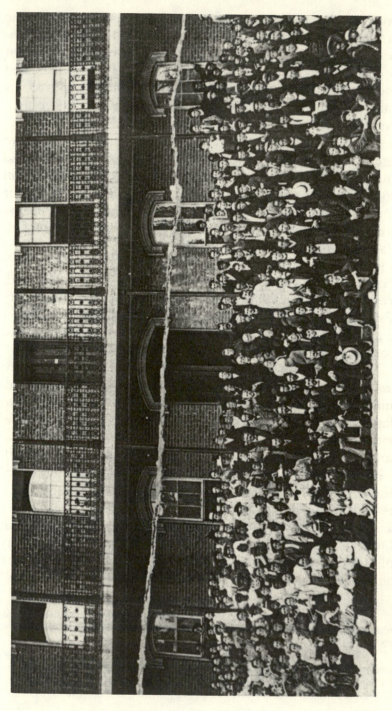

Berea students and faculty, ca. 1897. President Frost is standing in front of the doors.

personality. Hathaway's inclusion in faculty meetings was met with private concerns that "the faculty secrets would . . . leak out to the colored community."[31]

President Frost, adamant in his belief that Hathaway was a competent tutor but would be incompetent as a professor, never visited Hathaway's classroom. He formed his opinion based on information from several faculty members who voted nay on the question of Hathaway's promotion to the rank of professor.[32] Frost's view of Hathaway's competence stemmed also from Frost's attitude that "not many men of any race are born to be professors." President Frost preferred to think that a college professor ought to be of rare timbre, descending from generations of culture — in other words, a man like himself.[33]

J.T. Robinson, in his *Standard* article, "Defence of Hathaway and the Negro," charged that the case of Hathaway, a victim of prejudice, evidenced Berea's inconsistency. Robinson now believed Frost was revising Berea's image from one of a "mere colored school" to that of a predominantly white, albeit mixed, school.[34] This theme echoed in the *Standard* when it printed Hathaway's reply to a Frost letter. Contending that the college president "was bent upon the subordination of the Negro in Berea College," Hathaway remembered the occasion when Frost remarked to him the presence of a black instructor kept some whites from attending Berea. To support his contention that Frost was doing away with Negro instruction "by fair means or foul," Hathaway referred to Frost's explanation to white applicants about the minimal association required with blacks at Berea. In addition, Hathaway drew upon his own experience to cite the lack of blacks deemed qualified as professors; he also felt social

[31]E.G. Dodge to Frost, April 11, 1925, Box 13, FP. See also Faculty Minutes, Vol. II (1880-89): 201, 232; Vol. III (1889-92): 20, 86, Box 5. There are various entries noting permission for Hathaway's absences from Berea provided he arranged for a substitute teacher. Hathaway was one of the organizers of the Intelligence Publishing Company, which printed the *Standard.*

[32]See Frost's letter addressed to "Dear Friend," September 10, 1895, Box 4, FP.

[33]See Frost's "An Answer Made," in the Lexington *Standard,* 1894, clipping in Black Series Files. Frost held an opinion that the black race (and poor mountain whites) would produce great and useful men such as orators, statesmen, inventors, and authors long before they would produce the rare professional men qualified to be college professors. Frost felt secure being the son of educated parents. See Frost's *For the Mountain.*

[34]J.T. Robinson, "Defense of Hathaway and the Negro," in Lexington *Standard,* 1893 or 1894, clipping in Black Series Files.

*15*

slights had been made toward his family when President Frost failed to visit their home except on the day they were moving out of Berea.[35] The Louisville *New South* also accused Frost of manipulation in securing Hathaway's "voluntary resignation" in order to cater to the prejudice of some whites against a Negro teacher. The newspaper charged Frost with being fearful lest the presence of a black professor interfere with his goal to obtain more white students.[36]

Meanwhile, at the same meeting where the trustees accepted Hathaway's resignation, they appointed a new professor of pedagogics, John H. Jackson, a black alumnus (class of 1874, A.M. '83) and a trustee. Dividing his time between his duties in Frankfort at the State Normal Institute and teaching in Berea, Jackson held the Berea position for one year. President Frost began to proclaim the Jackson appointment when he wrote a response to some of the accusations that were appearing in the Lexington *Standard* in 1894.[37]

Frost's explanatory responses netted little other than a caustic rejoinder from J.T. Robinson, now unconvinced that the Jackson appointment was anything more than a hollow gesture. Feeling the tone of Frost's article to be personal and patronizing, Robinson reported that Frost's answers had been evasive and misleading. Rather, the important question pertained to Frost's interpretation of Berea's principles: "What is President Frost's policy calculated to do . . . for the cause of justice and equality in America; is it encouraging or discouraging the public sentiment which is now grinding the life out of the colored people?"[38]

Highly sensitive that these grievances could affect adversely Berea's new image, Frost declined to continue the debate in the *Standard*. Instead, he composed a public statement to clarify

[35]James Hathaway, "The Berea Question," in Lexington *Standard*, circa 1893, clipping in *ibid*. For his part, Frost rationalized that his convalescence from typhoid fever had restricted his social engagements.

[36]"Berea College and the Colored Professorship," Louisville *New South*, November 24, 1894, in *ibid*.

[37]Frost, "An Answer Made," in Lexington *Standard*, n.d., in *ibid*. Jackson served as trustee, 1892-96.

[38]See Robinson, "The B.C.Q. Is Still Agitating the Mind of Brother Robinson," in Lexington *Standard*, May 4, 1894, in *ibid*. Robinson's exposition on the "public sentiment" can be found in the article "A Killing Frost," in Lexington *Standard*, December 7, 1894, in *ibid*.

the objectives of his new policies for Berea College. With Trustee Barton's help, this statement was printed as a supplement to the Berea College *Reporter* with special distribution to all Negro newspapers.[39] Entitled "Berea's Invitation is to All," the *Supplement* carried pictures of the Reverend Fee and President Frost. In a historical overview, Frost attempted to show that his policies were congruent with the principles of Berea's founders. For example, one policy concerned the formula to increase Berea's enrollment to approximate Kentucky's population ratio of six whites to one black. The *Supplement* article contended that everyone had been invited to send new students, but some people, like Trustee Barton, had been more active than others in promoting Berea's enrollments. Nevertheless, black students were encouraged to attend Berea College in order to take advantage of every educational opportunity within their reach.[40]

When Robinson reviewed the *Supplement* in his *Standard* article, "The Real Berea Bomb," he contended that black people did not receive the same considerations as white people at Berea; he perceived the real Berea "Bomb" to be the color line drawn by Frost's proposed 6 percent plan for student enrollments. Said Robinson:

> It should make no difference whether white or colored students are in the majority if the Berea idea [mixed school] is to be promoted, and no distinction made on account of color or station in life, but there is where we and the president part company. . . .
>
> Berea received its right to existence by reason of the fact that it is a "mixed school," and not its adaptability for accommodating the greater number of any class, by diminishing the importance of the lesser class; therefore, if setting the Negro out is the price to be paid for a larger white attendance [and it is], the germinal principle [equality] which gives the school a right to exist ends.[41]

There were other black alumni whose perspectives of Berea's new development under President Frost seemed different from Robinson's. J.W. Hughes (class of 1895) expressed his view in the *New South:*

[39]Frost to EMF, December 13, 1894, Box 1, FP.

[40]"Berea's Invitation is to All," Berea College *Reporter Supplement*, in Black Series Files.

[41]Robinson, "The Real Berea Bomb," in Lexington *Standard*, circa December 1894, in *ibid.*

Whatever may be the attitude of President Frost toward the colored students at Berea, it is their privilege to come and receive the benefit of that which was given as much to them as to any other people. They owe their presence here as an appreciation for what the founder and donors have placed within their reach.

I do not attempt to interpret the President's actions or sayings; but if his intentions are what some think them to be, then a withdrawal on the part of the Colored students will only favor his plans. On the other hand, if he means to adhere to the principles on which the institution was founded, then he will be glad to welcome you in large numbers.[42]

This pragmatic theme was reflected also in a letter the Reverend James Bond (class of 1892) sent to the *Standard*. In Bond's opinion, Frost was "intending to do right" by the principles of Berea College and the mistakes he had made were "of the head and not the heart." Bond suggested that people with grievances or suggestions could meet with the faculty and trustees at Berea's annual commencement.[43]

## VII

The Board of Trustees did receive a formal petition at their next meeting.[44] Twenty black former and current students had signed a petition asking the trustees to hire a Negro professor, Frank L. Williams (class of 1889), and his wife, Fannie Miller Williams (class of 1888). The trustees replied to this petition by stating that they would not appoint a Negro professor in response to pressure from the black students. Such reaction, they said, would create a perception of Berea's being subject to control by its black constituency and that image would hinder Berea's success in obtaining more white students.

The trustees' denial of the petition reflected Berea's "cautious" regard for hiring Negro professors. Their caution may have been due to organizational concerns to hire the most competent professors but there was also a political desire to avoid arousing

[42]J.W. Hughes, "Contributed — Berea Question, " in Louisville *New South*, November 24, 1894, in *ibid*.

[43]See James Bond, "The Other Side of the Berea Question Heard From in the Person of a Former Student, " in Lexington *Standard*, circa April 1894, in *ibid*. At Frost's urging, Bond was elected as a trustee in 1896.

[44]"Petition of 1894, " Board of Trustees, General correspondence, RG 2, Series IV, Box 1.

racial hostility from the college's white constituency:

> In the first place the standards at Berea are high and competent colored candidates are still few. It is often true that there is not a single colored person obtainable who is prepared to fill a vacancy which occurs.
>
> In the next place, the appointment of a colored person in response to a petition, or in a way which causes him to be regarded as a special representative of the colored element, is wrong in principle, and detrimental to the interests of the Cause. It is drawing a color line . . . when we appoint a colored professor he is to be a professor of the white as much as of the colored. . . . The only reason for appointing a man must be that he can do the whole work required better than anyone else who can be secured.
>
> In the third place, we are now trying to establish the principle that white and colored young people may mingle as students without detriment to either, and with mutual advantage, and we should not be justified in taking any action which would imperil our position as a mixed school. We ought to take no action which will needlessly inflame the feelings of those whose views are different from ours.[45]

This third consideration indicates clearly the trustees' refusal to risk a white flight similar to that experienced by Principal Rogers on the first day Berea received black students. Such a risk could hinder the current success of Berea in maintaining its principles:

> As stated already we are fighting for the principle that white and colored students may meet in the classroom without harm, and with mutual respect and profit.
>
> To us this is self-evident, but no other southern school has been able to demonstrate it. Colored people can receive instruction at Camp Nelson and a hundred other colored schools, but there is only one Berea. Our success is measured largely by the number of white people who can be brought to accept this principle. In bringing white students to Berea we are doing a work against caste which Fisk and Hampton have not even had a chance to attempt.[46]

The trustees' statement is a prime example of Frost's assumption that the large number of white students now coming to Berea were in fact being "brought to accept" the principle of racial coeducation. Despite some of the contrary examples presented by the Negro critics, it is fairly clear that the trustees would hardly have changed their decision about hiring black faculty. As long as a substantial portion of their new donors seemed to approve, the

[45]See Board of Trustees' "Response to Petition of 26," 1894, RG 2, Box 1.
[46]Ibid.

trustees maintained the college's direction. So they did not appoint either of the Williamses as a professor. When the issue threatened to surface again the next year, Frost previewed the probabilities in letters to certain trustees prior to the annual meeting and found official sentiments had not changed. Trustee Barton offered his opinion that a mixed faculty would lead Berea ultimately toward being a black school:

> It is much for a Mountain boy to overcome generations of prejudices and meet colored people on a level; it is too much to expect that now they will not be deterred if a colored man, unless he be a giant in intellectual and moral qualities, be set over them . . . Both as a matter of principle and of expediency, it appears to me unwise to appoint at this turn a colored professor.[47]

Thus it happened that racial equality became secondary to expediency for Berea's new growth. The faculty later registered their support for Frost and the trustees when they disapproved the student literary society's selection of Professor F.L. Williams as a speaker for the 1895 commencement exercises. They charged that Williams had made public statements which created false impressions about Berea. The society's officers remained unconvinced, however, and believed the true basis of the faculty's action was President Frost's negative "attitude toward colored people."[48]

The question of President Frost's attitude toward blacks formed the central topic of a critical pamphlet published by J.T. Robinson, F.L. Williams, J.S. Hathaway, and J.W. Hughes. This thirty-two-page document, "Save Berea College for Christ and Humanity," was a final appeal by the Negro critics to focus public scrutiny on the management policies at their alma mater.[49] In one regard, the pamphlet simply reviewed earlier controversies between Robinson and Frost, between Hathaway and Frost, and finally between Williams and Frost. Hughes' moderate opinion appeared on the last page. In another regard, the pamphlet evoked a critical defense from Frost, who quickly circulated a form letter among Berea's benefactors. Addressing such issues as the direction of Berea's growth and the lack of Negro professors,

[47]William E. Barton to Frost, June 15, 1895, Box 4, FP.

[48]Pharis A. White, "A Protest Made by some of the Students of Berea," in Lexington *Standard*, circa June 1895, clipping in Black Series Files.

[49]See Robinson, Williams, Hathaway, and Hughes, "Save Berea College for Christ and Humanity — Elements of Danger, " in *ibid*.

Frost justified his policies by noting that the Board of Trustees had concurred (with the exception of the Reverend Fee) with his decisions.[50] He denounced the pamphlet as being full of "capital misrepresentations" and declared that the college had never made greater progress than over the past two years. As evidence he highlighted student enrollment figures (more than two-sevenths Negro enrollment while Kentucky's Negro population was only one-seventh) and the successful fundraising for Berea's endowment. True to his temper, Frost tried to discredit three of the pamphlet's writers by making disparaging contentions about their motives.[51]

Although the newspaper debates subsided, the controversy itself was never resolved. The basic claim made by the Negro critics was that black people were not receiving the same considerations as white people at Berea College. As the Board's official actions revealed, that criticism was valid. From the college's viewpoint, there were extenuating circumstances, however, including the fact that new donors were less likely to help educate black youth than to help white youth, and that the board sought to maintain black enrollments at a percentage high enough to retain commitment to their cause, yet not so high as to risk another "white flight" from the college. Neither Frost nor the trustees responded to Robinson's statement that enrollment numbers ought not to be the basis of policy if the college was really practicing racial brotherhood.

On the other hand, even Berea College's inconsistencies indicate the strength of its founding commitments, in the face of adverse pressures to become all-white. The college did have a suspect record on hiring black faculty, yet black alumni always held one or more seats on the Board of Trustees, seats that were not merely symbolic positions.

## VIII

With Negro criticisms fading from the public's view, Frost concentrated on Berea's unique sectional appeal (reuniting North and South) and on raising funds for a second endowment. Aided

[50]See Frost's letter to "Dear Friend," September 10, 1895, Box 4, FP.
[51]*Ibid.* Frost did not question Hughes' motives since he was potentially an ally.

## "A PREFERRED BENEVOLENCE"

### BEREA COLLEGE

Asks assistance in its unique and promising work for a vigorous but isolated people (Lincoln's Kin).

#### Of National Concern!

These robust, capable people are **Americans**—many " Sons of the Revolution"—were loyal to the Union; but lack of water-ways and railways has kept them in pioneer conditions. They lack the educated leaders and con-nections with more advanced communities, which the West possessed.

By well adapted **Normal** and **Industrial Work, "Exten-sion Lecturers" on Horse-back, etc.,** Berea is saving them from corrupting influences, and fitting them to reinforce the **best elements of the Nation.**

Non-sectarian.  Largely dependent on individual gifts.
Special need for new buildings and "extension work."
A gift of $100 constitutes an "effective helper "
Every "sustaining scholorship" of $40 opens the way for one more student.
Send gifts or inquiries to the President,

WM. GOODELL FROST, PH.D., Berea, Ky.

*GEO. W. CABLE*—I have seen Berea * * It is in a better position than any other school to assist in the solution of the whole southern problem.
*N. S SHALER*—Excellent work for the young people of the mountains, I know them well.  None are more needy or more capable.
*DR. FIELD*—President Frost is better fitted for this great work than any other man in the country.

Make money-orders payable to T. J. Osborne, *Treasurer*, Berea, Madison County, Ky.

In bequests use the corporate name BEREA COLLEGE.

Berea Quarterly *(1906)*

**"Aided by the publication of the *Berea Quarterly*, Frost shifted Berea's image as a 'mixed' school to a school whose national mission was to erase sectional lines and educate America's 'contemporary ancestors.'"**

by the publication of the *Berea Quarterly*, Frost shifted Berea's image as a "mixed" school to a school whose national mission was to erase sectional lines and educate America's "contemporary ancestors."[52]

Frost made one of his first "Sectional Lines" speeches at a Richmond, Kentucky, dinner given in his honor; he also wanted to promote Berea College's appeal to Kentuckians. Addressing the small crowd of lawyers, bankers, and wealthy farmers, he spoke about what he perceived as the one common problem resulting from emancipation, namely, that a large slave population was now freed from any guidance by master or mistress.[53] Sympathetic to how changing conditions brought difficulties for everyone including the freedman, Frost concluded that the provision for public schools was society's best method for building anew. However, attaining enough schools would be difficult because of teacher shortages, but Berea was contributing to the solution by training competent teachers and developing good leaders for the masses of freedmen. In words similar to those Booker T. Washington would use,[54] Frost expressed the need for industrial education: "Only the few need high book education, but all need an incentive and training for industry, and instruction in the art of living. . . ."[55]

Then turning to Berea's mission for coeducation of the races, Frost sought to allay his audience's fears about the consequences of social equality. "We have tried our simple plan for twenty-nine years," he said, "and the evil consequences have not come; and our way is the way of the Christian world at large."[56] Concluding his appeal, Frost called for continuance of the harmony essential to the accomplishment of Berea's great work: "We do

---

[52]Frost edited the *Berea Quarterly*, which was published from May 1895 to October 1916 with primary distribution to donors. Recently, one historian analyzed the historical trends that led to the redirection of missionary zeal from the social uplift of southern blacks toward preservation of mountain whites. See James C. Klotter, "The Black South and White Appalachia," *Journal of American History* 66 (1980): 832-49.

[53]See Frost, "Sectional Lines" (a speech delivered in Richmond, Kentucky, August 1895), in Vertical Files, RG 13.7, Day Law (hereinafter Day Law Files).

[54]For a humorous assessment of the East's penchant for popular Negro causes, see A.D. Mayo to Frost, December 3, 1896, Box 5, FP. For an account on the Frosts' visit to Booker T. Washington's Tuskegee Institute, see EMF Diary, April 1901.

[55]Frost, "Sectional Lines."

[56]*Ibid.*

not ask you to agree with us. We only ask you to notice that the relations of the races are as wholesome and pure in Berea as in any town in the state, and that this is only a matter of etiquette and conventionality after all."[57]

Those Kentuckians in Frost's audience, like most of their contemporaries in the state, did not agree with Berea's ideas of coeducation; few maintained publicly, however, that they wanted to see the college abolished. But soon Berea's experiment would be challenged by outside political forces, while inside the college there continued the serious problem of declining black enrollments. Frost's struggles had just begun.

## IX

During Frost's first year, enrollment of blacks as well as whites increased. Thereafter, black enrollments declined slightly to an average of two hundred students, while white enrollments continued to increase dramatically. The increased availability of black schools accounts for part of this decline. However, blacks who sought a higher education beyond Normal training would find Berea, with its improved facilities, to be the best institution available in the state. For those blacks who perceived an educational advantage in associating with whites, they could receive that particular advantage nowhere in the South other than at Berea.[58]

While Robinson's warning of the real Berea bomb was somewhat exaggerated, it is clear that the phenomena he described were based on a combination of real factors. One factor was the controversies between President Frost and the Negro professors, Hathaway and Williams. They, and a substantial number of other Berea-educated teachers, were members of the State Association of Teachers in Colored Schools. After the college's refusal to hire Negro professors, a faction of the association's members became disillusioned about the future for blacks at Berea College and thoroughly suspicious of President Frost's attitude toward Negro

[57]*Ibid.*
[58]See James White's speech, recorded in "Three Speeches at Richmond Meeting," a meeting held prior to a petition drawn for passage of the Day Law. Box 27, FP.

Figure 1:   BEREA STUDENT ENROLLMENT   1866-1904

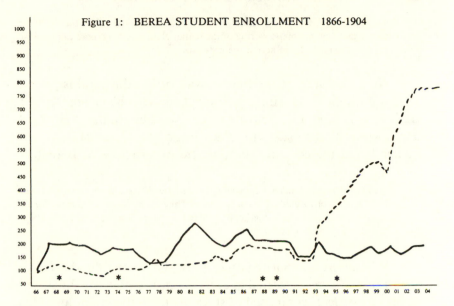

*No Catalogues.     — — — White Students.     —— Black Students.
Source: Berea College *Catalogues* 1866-88 and 1891-1904.

equality. As a result, several teachers throughout the region began urging their black youth to attend instead the State Normal School at Frankfort.[59] Ironically, by refusing to encourage black youth to attend Berea, some of the black teachers were facilitating the white conversion of the total student enrollment. In terms of percentages, blacks in 1892 represented a declining one-fourth of the total enrollment.[60]

Black people who had been wary of these rapid changes found their suspicions substantiated by their observations of conditions in campus life. During Fairchild's administration, when black enrollment peaked at a two-thirds majority at Berea, the campus environment reflected the social interaction of a selective community. One white student noted:

> Any white man or woman coming to Berea knew in advance that he must be willing to recite, eat and worship with a majority of students of another race. They

[59]H.C. Tinsley to Frost, July 13, 1899, Box 5, FP. Berea-trained teachers were working in approximately twenty-two Kentucky counties by 1900.
[60]These figures and the graph are based on enrollment data from Berea College *Catalogues* between 1866 and 1888 and between 1891 and 1904, published variously at Cincinnati and at Berea.

must find for themselves a school life as partners with the colored majority or do without any school life worthy of the name. Naturally only those came whose minds were made up to accept the conditions.[61]

An acceptance of the Berean way of life during this period meant a minority of whites participating with blacks in student activities. Berea's two boarding halls, Ladies Hall and Howard Hall, were filled mostly with black boarders. One black student remembered the cordial relations she experienced at Berea:

Many of my school mates were white girls and boys. We did not room together, while it was not forbidden. We were free to choose our own roommates. We ate together, walked to class together and there was never any unpleasantness about the situation while I was there.[62]

When Berea embarked on its period of growth under President Frost, changes occurred in every facet of school life. Increased white enrollment, composed of students from the mountains plus from the North, occurred so rapidly that the Berea principle of anticaste prejudice seemed to be stressed less and less. The white person who previously came to Berea willing to accept interaction with a black majority now had a different choice with a black minority. As one white alumnus and faculty member wrote:

The white man who came in the years just before the Day Law [1904] was more likely to have said within himself, "I am willing to go to that school because, little as I wish to treat niggers as equals and friends, I think I can to a great extent ignore the majority of them who are there, and keep [them] pretty nearly outside the circle of my real school life."[63]

It was exactly this increase in caste prejudice that contributed to a lack of confidence in Berea's management and the subsequent decline in black enrollment. Whites who adhered to caste prejudice perceived the influx of more white students as reinforcement for their attitudes. At the same time, President Frost interpreted the influx to be a positive sign of *decreasing* caste prejudice. In his letter to a prospective white student, he explained

[61]See Dodge to Frost, April 11, 1925, Box 13, FP.

[62]Elgetha Brand Bell to Berea Alumni Association's Birmingham Chapter, 1956, RG 8, Box 2.

[63]See Dodge to Frost, April 11, 1925. See also "White Students' Petition," circa 1898, Day Law Files, Peck's Notes 2.

Berea's arrangement for blacks and whites:

> We intend to give every human being a fair and equal chance because he is a human being, made in the image of God. . . .
>
> We do not, however, compel other people to think as we do nor to associate with our colored students more than they please. It is quite possible for people to attend Berea and have no more to do with the colored people than at their home. White and colored students never room together and seldom board at the same places. It is no more for white and colored people to meet in the same recitation room than it is for them to work together in the same field or in the same house. . . .
>
> We are sorry that some white people stay away because the colored are here. You will notice, however, that these white people who stay away from Berea are unable to give any good reason for doing so. It is only because they have a kind of prejudice about it.
>
> And we are glad to say that every year more and more white people give up these prejudices. . . .[64]

Frost could certainly be hopeful that more whites were learning to free themselves from their prejudices, although he was away on fundraising trips too often to check personally the effectiveness of that learning process. These absences, combined with frequent staff turnovers, resulted in Frost's being caricatured and his attitudes often misrepresented by whites and blacks.[65]

By far the most popular misrepresentation about Frost (and one that still persists to this day) concerned his attitude toward blacks. While some of Frost's actions, such as the decision on black faculty, seemed indicative of an anti-Negro attitude, other actions, such as the defense of Berea's being a "mixed" school, seemed indicative of a humanistic attitude which was congruent with Berea's principles of brotherhood.

On the issue of the black faculty member, Frost may have been considering character more than color when he appointed Jackson rather than Hathaway to a professorship. Yet, some of his black critics *and* white supporters were motivated to consider color more than character, especially after no other black faculty

[64]Frost to Melissa Parkerson, March 5, 1901, Box 6, FP. A smaller excerpt of this letter has been interpreted more negatively by Nelson in his article on interracial education at Berea.

[65]Frost to EMF, February 28, 1899, Box 1, FP. For an example, see the case of the college's washerwoman in Frost's letter to George Fairchild, February 14, 1899, Box 5, FP.

was hired when Jackson resigned a year later. On a similar note, Frost's manner of inviting more white students to Berea, by telling them that they would not have to associate with black students more than they pleased, has been (and continues to be) criticized. Still, Frost was making a truthful assessment of Berea's campus life. Moreover, that same assessment could be made about Berea's current situation with a black minority.[66]

While fundraising, Frost became adept at analyzing the particular moods of the wealthy northerners and easterners. As he and Eleanor Marsh experienced rejections to their donation appeals for racial coeducation, they observed how these wealthy donors were affected by (and in turn affected) the popularity of anti-Negro sentiments across the nation.[67] Rather than risk Berea's fading into mediocrity in the face of racist conditions, Frost carefully cultivated the donors' interests toward personally supporting their "contemporary ancestors." In his public relations about Berea's mission, he exercised discretion in choosing methods that would be very appealing to donors and thus most expedient for Berea's service to all its students. Frost observed how the needs of the white majority from the mountains and the needs of the black minority were very similar.[68] The students were different, but in mingling at Berea they could learn to respect each other's differences, since they were taught there that "God hath made of one blood all nations of men."

This was the ideal with which Berea had experimented for over three decades; this was the ideal that became more and more difficult to achieve. As Berea's size increased very rapidly, new white Bereans were not interested in associating very much with the black Bereans and they could easily avoid doing so. As for the black Bereans, the college's principles of equality retained a firm appeal to many who still believed that in the Berea community a Negro would be regarded as an American citizen the same as anyone else. Disregard of Negro rights was growing ram-

[66]Berea College's black student enrollment was approximately 12 percent in 1980.

[67]See various entries from the Diary of EMF, e.g. March 18, 1898, and January 2, 1899.

[68]Klotter presents a comparison of parallel stereotypes depicting southern blacks and Appalachian whites that were adhered to by northern reformers, historians, and journalists. Such similiarities, he noted, tend to occur whenever members of a self-styled superior class evaluate behaviors and attitudes of members of what they view as a lower class. See Klotter, "Black South and White Appalachia," 835-37.

pant across the nation while Berea College persisted as the only institution in the South to symbolize racial equality by remaining unsegregated.

## X

In summary, it is clear that some inconsistencies in the college's practices of racial brotherhood existed before President Frost assumed office. The Frost administration exacerbated those inconsistencies. However, people other than Frost shared the responsibility for shaping the way Berea College emerged. Evidence of this fact is borne out in the nonsupportive actions of the white faculty toward their black colleague, and in the attitudes of some white students. They seized the opportunity of an expanding campus, not to embrace racial equality, but to subvert it by minimizing their associations with blacks. It is further borne out in the suspicions of some black alumni and teachers who refused to encourage black youth to attend Berea College.

Despite such detractions, it is readily conceivable that Berea College could have maintained its mixed enrollment trend of two-sevenths black and five-sevenths white students indefinitely. Yet, this was not to be the college's fate. In 1904, the Berea symbol was challenged by the Kentucky legislature when it enacted a law to prohibit coeducation of the races in *all* private institutions, namely Berea College.[69] The creation and passage of Kentucky's so-called Day Law reflected the South's racial segregationist attitudes, attitudes which gave credence to the popular misconception that racial coeducation would lead to serious evils because black people were taught to be the social equals of white people.[70] Berea, under the leadership of President Frost, spent years in litigation to contest the constitutionality of the Day Law, but to no avail. Thus, Berea's peculiar work for the "fundamental

[69]For an interesting account of the Day Law and Berea's recourse through the high courts, see Richard A. Heckman and Betty J. Hall's "Berea College and the Day Law," *Register of the Kentucky Historical Society* 66 (1968): 35-52.

[70]In 1895, the Florida legislature enacted a law to prohibit coeducation of the races in public, private, or parochial schools. Within a few years Tennessee also enacted a similar law, one that affected Maryville College. Day Law Files; A.D. Mayo to Frost, February 12, 1898, Box 5, FP.

morality and welfare of the whole country'' was brought to an immoral end.

When the college opened its doors for the fall session of 1904, only white students could enroll. Black students were provided scholarships by Berea College so they could continue their education at black institutions like Fisk, Knoxville College, and the State Normal School at Frankfort.

Due to their previous suspicions of President Frost, some of his critics believed he personally aided in the drafting and passage of the Day Law. However, correspondence between Frost, trustees, and alumni does not lend support to this claim. On the contrary, Frost was highly distressed at the state's interference with Berea, and it was largely at his urging that Berea's trustees pursued the law's appeal through the courts.[71] That process consumed four years, during which time Eleanor Marsh and Frost, assisted by some trustees, began raising hundreds of thousands of dollars for an ''adjustment'' fund. Besides paying the legal expenses, the new funds were also to be used to construct a primary school in Berea for black youth, as well as to establish Lincoln Institute, a school that was organized according to the Berea model.[72]

The forced segregation of Berea College remained in existence for almost fifty years, a period spanning two generations of students.

[71]See William E. Barton to Frost, September 25, 1901; James Bond to Frost, February 5, 1904; President's Address to Trustee, March 30, 1904; "Berea's Course Under Adverse Legislation," all in FP. Also see "Hostile Legislation against Berea — A Ruthless Hand Stayed by Appeal to the Constitution," *Berea Quarterly* 8 (1904): 12-17, and Frost to EMF, January 22, 1905, Box 2, FP.

[72]See George C. Wright, "The Founding of Lincoln Institute," *Filson Club History Quarterly* 49 (1975): 57-70.

# "WE BEST CAN INSTRUCT OUR OWN PEOPLE"

# NEW YORK AFRICAN AMERICANS IN THE

# FREEDMEN'S SCHOOLS, 1861 - 1875

*Ronald E. Butchart*

The story of the education of America's freedmen is a familiar, if not often told, tale. Within weeks of the bombardment of Fort Sumter, northern groups organized to aid the Civil War's human contraband, the fleeing slaves. In the next decade, over four dozen organizations raised millions of dollars to send thousands of teachers into the ravaged South to establish schools for a people who had been systematically denied access to formal education. "Behind the mists of ruin and rapine waved the calico dresses of women who dared," wrote W.E.B. DuBois, "and after the hoarse mouthings of the field guns rang the rhythm of the alphabet."[1]

Much of the effort to tell this tale has centered on the teachers. Who were these "women who dared"? Why did they go into that hostile land, many while the war yet raged? The answers to those and other questions have ranged across the spectrum. For southern contemporaries and their later apologists, the teachers were arrogant meddlers, misguided zealots, foolish romantics at best, vicious agents of an abolitionist craze to destroy the South at worst.[2] For northern supporters and recent historians, they were an army of civilization, "soldiers of light and love," naive and insufficiently abolitionist, yet still "the real heros of their age."[3]

Despite this focus on the freedmen's teachers, our understanding of this remarkable group remains partial. The work to this point has been impressionistic and hence extremely selective in its use of evidence, or narrowly focused on atypical groups.[4] As a result, we can hear the voices of some teachers, but the image we gain of them is unfocused and occasionally distorted.

To begin to sharpen our picture of the freedmen's educators, I began several years ago a quantitative and qualitative project aimed at identifying and gathering information on as large a sample

Ronald E. Butchart is a member of the faculty at the State University College at Cortland.

The research for this article was supported by a grant from the State University of New York's NEW YORK AFRICAN AMERICAN INSTITUTE.

**Afro-Americans in New York Life and History** (January 1988)
P.O. Box 1663
Buffalo, New York 14216

of freedmen's teachers as possible.  My file now includes 5,350 individuals with a wide range of prosopographic information.  Much work remains before I can speak confidently about all aspects of the group, But I have reported a number of preliminary findings in an earlier essay. [5]

One of the most intriguing groups among the freedmen's teachers were the northern black teachers who went south to teach among their kindred.  They have also been the most neglected group. [6]  Yet here may be found the greatest heroism.  Disadvantaged as a group, if not always as individuals, they gave years out of their lives for meager salaries.  Limited educationally by their social circumstances, they gave knowledge from their own store for incalculable rewards.  Yet what fear and loathing must have attended many of them as they traveled into that region, so recently the scene of black slavery.

The purpose of the project reported here, then, was to begin to repair that neglect, to give this important but obscure group of nineteenth century African Americans its due.  The project attempted to accomplish that task by selecting a sample of the black teachers who taught in the South, and uncovering all that could be learned about that group.  The sample comprised all of the black teachers known to be from New York State.  The result has been, I think, not only to tell the story of this group, but also to extend our understanding of the black community in nineteenth century New York, and to alter in important ways what we know about the freedmen's teachers more generally.  But before turning to those findings, allow me to make a few comments about the sample and some of the research.

Of that large file of teachers mentioned earlier, I can now identify the homes of only slightly more than half.  About ten percent have been identified as black, though, as we shall see, the project reported here suggests that the actual percentage of blacks was much higher.  The file originally yielded 348 teachers from New York State.  Initially, thirty of those were identified as black.  To create a profile comparable to the data I had accumulated on other teachers, I especially sought the teachers' ages, marital status, gender, length of service to the freedmen, occupations before and after their service, educational background, and, at least roughly, their social class.  I sought qualitative material as well, the traditional sources of narrative history.

The initial group shrank slightly when I discovered an earlier error in coding, and when what appeared to be two individuals turned out to be the same woman; C. Mary Hicks, a widowed teacher from Albany, became Catherine Mary Williams of Albany after she married while teaching in the South. [7]  But then the sample mushroomed, growing from 28 to 51 black New Yorkers, and pushing the total number of teachers from New York to 368. [8]  That happened as racial identifications were made for some, and New York residence was established for others. With that as background, let us turn to the findings.

One of the most significant findings is the number of black New Yorkers who went south. At a time when African Americans accounted for slightly over one percent (1.2%) of the population of New York State, blacks accounted for over fourteen percent of the total teaching force from New York.[9]    In other words, they participated in freedmen's education at better than ten times the rate of their white counterparts. That compares favorably with my earlier finding that 10.4 percent of the larger national sample of freedmen's teachers were black.[10]    Further, the fact that this small research sample turned up seventeen individuals who had not previously been identified as black suggests that this finding is conservative. It is likely that many more individuals in the file are black, and that further research focused on all teachers from one state or region would show black participation even higher than this rate suggests.

There was a significant gender difference in the New York African American teaching corps, as there was in the national movement. Leaders of the freedmen's aid societies complained incessantly about the difficulty in getting and holding male teachers.[11] That difficulty was reflected in the number of black men from New York who taught. Only 35 percent of the teachers were men, a percentage that slips to 32 when we look at those who spent more than one year in the South. That is below the percentage of black men in the national sample, which was just about evenly divided between black males and females, but is slightly higher than the percentage of white males, who made up 30.2 percent of the white teachers. One-third of the black women teachers from the state were married, four of whom were widows. One-quarter (26.4%) of all women in the larger sample are known to have been married.[12]

One measure of the commitment of teachers to the task is the amount of time they were willing to devote to it. Going south for five or six months, the usual tenure in many freedmen's schools, was significant, but required less commitment and created less disruption in one's life course than spending two or more years in the work. It seemed significant in the larger file, then, to find that women not only were more likely to engage in freedmen's education, but were even more likely to return for multiple terms. Further, black teachers served longer terms than their white colleagues. Nationally, all blacks averaged 2.25 terms, higher than the 1.95 terms averaged by all whites. New York's black teachers showed even greater commitment, moreover, averaging 3.13 terms. Of those spending more than one year in the South, the national group averaged 3.33 years; among the New York African American teachers, the average was 4.51 years.[13]

TABLE 1

New York's Black Teachers Who Taught
In the South, 1861-1875

| Name | Sex | MStat | BYr | Home | Education | Occup1 | YrsS | Occup2 | ParentOccup |
|---|---|---|---|---|---|---|---|---|---|
| Anderson, Celinda D. | F | S | | Brooklyn? | High School | | 3 | Teacher | |
| Anderson, Matilda C. | F | S | 43 | Brooklyn | Common School | Teacher | 6 | Principal | Porter |
| Ball, Mason C. | M | S | 49 | NYC | Common School | Carrier | 1 | | Barber |
| Cardozo, Laura J. | F | M | | Brooklyn | | Teacher | 5 | Wife | |
| Cardozo, Thomas W. | M | M | 38 | Flushing | Newburg Coll. | Teacher | 4 | Politics | Gov clerk |
| Condol, Nathan T. | M | S | 43 | Geneva | Oberlin Prep. | Teacher | 10 | Teacher | Day Laborer |
| Douglass, Charles R. | M | S | 44 | Rochester | | Clerk | 1 | Gov service | Editor |
| Freeman, Edwin H. | M | M | 18 | Troy | | Clrgy,tchr | 5 | | |
| Freeman, Sophia | F | M | 20 | Troy | | Wife | 4 | | |
| Groves, Carrie W. | F | W? | | NYC | | Principal | 9 | | |
| Groves, Phoebe C. | F | S | | NYC | | Teacher | 6 | | Teacher |
| Hall, Alice C. | F | S | 48 | Lansingburgh | | Student? | 6 | | Baker |
| Hall, James D.S. | M | M? | | Brooklyn | | Minister | 3 | | |
| Highgate, Caroline M. | F | S | 49 | Syracuse | | Student? | 1 | | Barber |
| Highgate, Edmonia G. | F | S | 44 | Syracuse | High School | Teacher | 6 | Died 1870 | Barber |
| Highgate, Hannah F. | F | M | 21 | Syracuse | | Wife | 2 | | |
| Highgate, Willella C. | F | S | 52 | Syracuse | | Student? | 1 | | Barber |
| Hoffman, Harriet W. | F | S | | NYC | Common School | Teacher | 1 | | |
| Hoy, Martha L. | F | S | 48 | Brooklyn | | | | | |
| Hunter, Hezekiah H. | M | M | 35 | Brooklyn | Common School | Teacher | 6 | | Tchr,pol,clrgy |
| Hunter, Lizzie R. | F | M | | Brooklyn | | Wife | 1 | Wife | |
| Jacobs, Harriet B. | F | S | 15 | NYC | Informal | Nurseaid | 4 | | Slave |

| Name | Sex | M.S. | Age | Residence | Education | Occupation | No. | Occupation | Occupation |
|---|---|---|---|---|---|---|---|---|---|
| Jacobs, Louisa | F | S | 36 | NYC | Boarding School | | 7 | | Nurseaid |
| Johnson, Kitty | F | S | | NYC | Normal School | | 1 | | Waiter |
| Lapene, Mary C. | F | S | 45 | NYC | | | 2 | | |
| McKinney, Christopher | M | M | | Flushing | Common school | Teacher | 1 | | |
| McKinney, E. L. | F | M | | Flushing | | Teacher | 1 | | |
| Mobley, Hardy | M | M | | Brooklyn | | Porter | 6 | Clergy | Slaves |
| Mobley, M. Catherine | F | S | 13 | Brooklyn | | Student? | 1 | | Porter |
| Mobley, Martha E. | F | S | 51 | Brooklyn | | Student? | 1 | | Porter |
| Mobley, Sarah J. | F | S | 55 | Brooklyn | | Tailoress | 1 | | Porter |
| Mobley, Susan | F | M | 43 | Brooklyn | | Wife | 1 | Wife | Slaves |
| Paul, Thomas | M | M | 17 | Albany | Dartmouth | Principal | 1 | | Clergy |
| Payne, George F. | M | ? | | NYC | | Carman, expr | 1 | | |
| Payne, Sebastian | M | S | | NYC | | Minister | 3 | | Seaman |
| Payne, William O. | M | ? | 48 | NYC | Common School | Principal | 2 | Professor | Seaman |
| Reeve, John B. | M | ? | | Long Island | Post-graduate | Teacher | 1 | | |
| Smith, Charlotte S. | F | S | 31 | NYC | Normal School | Teacher | 2 | | |
| Snowden, Georgiana M. | F | S | 25 | NYC | Normal School | | 4 | | |
| Snowden, T. B. | M | S | | NYC | Normal School | | 4 | | |
| Stewart, Maria W. | F | W | 63 | NYC, Wmsburg | | Teacher | 5 | Matron | |
| Swails, Sarah | F | M | 36 | Elmira | | Wife | 1 | Wife | |
| Swails, Stephen A. | M | M | 32 | Elmira | Common School | Boatman | 1 | Pol, news | Boatman |
| Thompson, William H. | M | ? | 44 | Yonkers | | Principal | 2 | | |
| Usher, Charlotta V. | F | S | 42 | Albany | Normal School | Porter | 1 | Clerk | Steward |
| Vogelsang, Peter | M | M | 15 | Brooklyn | | | 1 | Teacher | |
| West, Harriet J. | F | S | | Brooklyn? | | Teacher | 4 | | |
| Williams, Catherine M. | F | W | 32 | Albany | | Student? | 4 | | Barber |
| Wilson, Anna M. | F | S | 46 | Brooklyn | | Wife | 5 | Wife | Principal |
| Wilson, Mary A. G. | F | M | 19 | Brooklyn | | Wife | 4 | | |
| Wilson, William J. | M | M | 15 | Brooklyn | | Principal | 3 | Cashier | |

Key to Table 1:

MStat      Marital Status; not known for all men in this study
BYr        Birth Year; included only if confirmed
Home       Residence prior to work in South
Education  Highest schooling attained
Occup1     Primary occupation before working in freedmen's schools
YrsS       Number of years spent teaching in freedmen's schools
Occup2     Primary occupation after working in freedmen's schools
ParentOcc  Occupation of parent, usually father

Note:

In Table 1 the designation "student" was given to those for whom the sources gave no occupation, and whose age suggested that they may not have yet established a vocation. The designation "wife" was given to married women for whom the census and other sources gave no other occupation, a common occurrence in the nineteenth century even for women who may have contributed directly to the family income through sale of domestic production, sale of services such as washing or childcare, or taking in boarders. The designation here is intended to convey the likelihood that these women were active in the family economy, not to suggest marginality.

Biographical sketches of the individuals in this file are available from the author.

One of the factors I have been studying has been kin and acquaintance networks among those working in the South. Over one-fifth (22%) of the total group of teachers served in the South within a family or close acquaintance group. Those networks seem to have been important, for those in such groups were more likely to stay in the South for more than one term; 28.6% of those teaching for two or more terms were affiliated with such a network. Among New York's black teachers, networks assumed an even greater role. Nearly three-fifths (58%) of the teachers went south in some form of familial group. That included eight married couples, two with children who also taught; two widows with one or more teaching offspring; at least two brothers; and two sisters. The same proportion of those serving more than one year were also members of families.[14]

As a group, the teachers from New York were not young people free to engage in an adventure because they did not yet have major obligations. That is clear from the family data above, but is reinforced by what we know about their average age. New York blacks for whom year of birth has been confirmed averaged 31.7 years of age when they first went into the work.[15]

One of the more difficult factors to discover about obscure people living in the nineteenth century is their level of educational attainment. Manuscript census schedules and other traditional prosopographic sources do not include such information. Few school records date back that far, except in more elite institutions. As a result, we tend to find educational level primarily for the more unusual historical actors, and consequently obtain an inflated educational level in collective biographies. That seems to be the case with the data collected so far on the national file. Over half of those for whom educational level is known (only 2.8% of the large file) acquired at least some higher education, obviously an absurdly high figure for the entire teacher corps.

While black teachers may not have enjoyed as much education as white teachers, the results of this project may still give us a more accurate picture of the amount of schooling shared by those taking charge of southern black schools. I have been able to find information on the educational level of 37 percent of the New York African American teachers. Nearly one-sixth of those (15.8%) had some college, including attendance at Dartmouth College, Newburgh Collegiate Institute, New York Central College, and Union Theological Seminary. Over two-fifths (42.1%) had some form of secondary education. If typical of the entire sample, this level of education would have compared well with teachers anywhere in the country, many of whom had only a common school education in this era.[16]

Both the educational attainments and the subsequent careers of these New York African Americans were above nineteenth century expectations for their class of origin, judging from what we know of the occupations of the parents of 25 of them.[17] The parents of seventeen were laborers or performed service occupations. These included barbers, day laborers, porters, slaves, seamen, a nursemaid, a waiter and a steward. Two of them were skilled workers (a journeyman baker and a boatman). Five parents held higher status positions, including a clergyman, a government clerk, and an editor; two of them, who were also freedmen's teachers themselves, were educators.[18]

The occupations held by the New York teachers themselves before they went into the South were somewhat higher in status than their parents, and higher than was usual for the race at that time. Whereas the majority of their parents had worked in manual and service occupations, a majority of teachers had worked in non-manual occupations as clergymen, teachers, and clerks.[19] Only seven of the 29 teachers whose occupations are known worked in manual or service occupations, including two porters, a tailoress, nursemaid, carrier, expressman, and boatman. Among them was Stephen Swails, who had followed in his father's footsteps as a boatman in Elmira, New York. He had a distinguished military career before moving his family to South Carolina and teaching the freedmen with his wife for one year. In the next year he moved into South Carolina politics as a state senator.[20] Charles Douglass, Rochester, son of the illustrious Frederick Douglass, also served in the Civil War. He received an appointment as clerk in the War Department before teaching for a year in Washington DC.[21] Sarah J. Mobley worked as a tailoress; her father, Hardy Mobley, was a porter, agent, and minister before he moved his wife and daughters back to their native Georgia to teach. His cabinetmaker sons remained in Brooklyn.[22]

A remarkably high percentage (65%) of those whose occupations are known had been educators; five of them had been principals in black schools in New York State. These nineteen teachers had an average of nearly seven years of teaching each in northern schools before engaging in the freedmen's education work.[23]

Among the experienced teachers were people such as William J. Wilson, an active abolitionist, talented writer, and black leader. He held the post of principal of Brooklyn Colored School No. 1 from at least 1842 to 1863, before taking up teaching duties in Washington DC, along with his wife and daughter.[24]

Caroline W. Groves was principal of a public school for six years in a sparsely settled area of Manhattan that would later become Harlem. Few black children lived in the vicinity of Colored School No. 4, so school officials gave permission for the school to be opened to any white children who wished to attend. Groves, a popular teacher in a pleasant location, "soon had twice as many white as colored pupils, and had to turn away twenty more whites." She and her daughter Phoebe, who had assisted her for at least two years in New York City, moved to Washington DC in 1863, where they taught for several years.[25]

Less is known at this time about Charlotte S. Smith. She taught in New York City from 1850 to 1862, at least. She received her training between 1853 and 1856 at New York City's Colored Normal School, which met on Saturdays during the school year. In 1855 she was promoted to principal of Colored School No. 1 where she remained until 1863. Although I do not have a record of her teaching among the freedmen until 1866, she apparently left New York in 1863. It is possible that she taught for a minor organization whose papers I have not yet located. I lost track of her in St. Augustine, Florida, where she taught for two years for the National Freedmen's Relief Association, the New York Branch of the American Freedmen's Union Commission.[26]

In contrast to those older teachers with years of experience, Edmonia Highgate finished high school in Syracuse in about 1860, taught for a year in Montrose, Pennsylvania, and then moved into a position as principal of the colored school in Binghamton for three years. At the age of twenty she devoted an energetic but short life to freedmen's education. She taught in Maryland, Louisiana, and Mississipppi, spending some summers scouring New York for donations. In October, 1870, as she prepared to take a position at Tougaloo Normal School, she died suddenly. Her widowed mother and two sisters taught with her at various times in the 1860s.[27]

Similarly, Nathan T. Condol, son of a day laborer, taught in his native Geneva, New York, for three years before leaving to spend "a few terms in academical training" at Oberlin College's preparatory department in anticipation of teaching in the South. But after only one term, "feeling intensely" that he was called to teach immediately, he took an appointment with the American Missionary Association at the age of 23. By January 1866 he was teaching a school of 166 freedmen in Mississippi, the heart of the Black Belt. He dedicated his life to the freedmen, remaining among them as a teacher until felled by yellow fever in 1878.[28]

It is a good deal more difficult to trace these individuals after their work in the South. Many may have stayed in the South, as did Wilson, Douglass, Condol, Swails, and Hezekiah Hunter. Others may have returned to different places in the North than the home towns from which I have traced them. Some of the single women doubtlessly married, taking their husbands' names; even if they returned to the cities and towns in which I expected to find them, they would be invisible to me. Thus far, I can account for only 19 of the 51 New York teachers after their sojourn. I know the vocations of thirteen of those (I know the whereaboutgs, but not the occupations, of five wives; as noted, Highgate died while in the freedmen's work). If we can hazard some generalizations about the teachers from the experiences of these thirteen it would appear that the freedmen's teachers did well for themselves. Six of them remained in education. Six more moved into the nineteenth century equivalent of white collar work: two in southern politics, two in government service, one in the ministry, and one' with the ill-fated Freedmen's Savings and Trust Company. Maria W. Stewart, ardent anti-colonizationist and abolitionist, perhaps the first woman to speak in public in the United States, and at 63 years of age the oldest of the New York teachers, moved from her teaching post to matron at Freedmen's Hospital in Washington. [29]

Traditional historians of freedmen's education could see nothing but base motives in the decisions of northern teachers to leave the comfort of their homes to work in a hostile region among a despised people. Fanaticism, intolerance, hatred of southern society, venality, vengeance and bigotry top the list of motives attributed to these workers. The teachers were accused of abolitionism, of rank political motives, of being incompentent and hence seeking work where incompetence would not be noticed. Teaching the southern blacks was an adventure for many, those historians claimed, or a well-paying sinecure. [30]

Those charges have been refuted in recent years.[31] What we have learned from this research adds weight to that refutation. We can explore motivation by looking at the charges of abolitionism, political motivation, and the search for adventure and high pay.

I have remarked elsewhere that few of the freedmen's teachers professed any interest in abolitionism. In making that argument I was defining an abolitionist quite strictly to include only those who were known to have spoken out against slavery or racial injustice generally, who belonged to some abolitionist organization, or who in other ways took a clear political stand in favor of black rights in the North or the abolition of slavery in the South. Abolitionism in this definition is distinct from the more general anti-slavery sentiment found rather generally diffused throughout the North in the 1850s. While even in its best moments abolitionism could, by twentieth century standards, embrace a paternalistic racism, it remained more committed to racial justice, and was actuated more by a sense of moral imperative, than the anti-slavery impulse. My argument holds that, if anything, the freedmen's aid movement was insufficiently abolitionist. [32]

Clearly, that definition is also distinct from the implicit definition of abolitionism embraced by earlier historians of the freedmen's education movement. For them, abolitionism amounted to little more than fanatical hatred of the South and all of its institutions and culture. Its commitment to black liberty was foolishly visionary, these historians argued, and its efforts on behalf of African Americans were transparent manipulations aimed at destroying the South.

In arguing that little abolitionism touched the education movement, I pose two tests. One is to look closely at the ideology and practice of the aid societies and their agents. What one finds is accommodationism and paternalism, not abolitionism. The other test is to look at the teachers themselves to find evidence of abolitionist sentiments. The quantitative project of which this study is a part is intended, among other things, to advance that second test.

To this point, that second test has been disappointing. Few abolitionists chose to engage in teaching the freedmen; few freedmen's teachers reflected even vaguely abolitionist concerns in their activities before engaging in the work, in their letters of application, or in their reports from the field. Approximately one percent of the larger group of teachers have thus far been identified as abolitionists. Significantly, nearly two-fifths of those are black.[33]

The black teachers from New York present a much more positive picture. At least seven, or nearly fourteen percent, were active in various struggles for black freedom. For example, Maria W. Stewart spoke out against slavery in public and through the pages of William Lloyd Garrison's *Liberator*.[34] Thomas Paul, Jr., attended the short-lived, abolitionist-sponsored Noyes Academy, along with men who would become leading black spokesmen.[35] John B. Reeve, a graduate of the abolitionist New York Central College, was vice-president of a black convention held in Syracuse, October 1864, called to take a forceful stand on the clouded political scene and the stalemated Civil War.[36] A speaker at that convention, urging unwavering commitment to its goals, was Edmonia G. Highgate, then twenty years old and one of very few women ever to speak before the mid-century black conventions.[37]

Likewise, William J. Wilson contributed frequent essays on political and social issues to *Frederick Douglass' Weekly* and the *Anglo-African Magazine*. He was active in the Negro convention movement, and a founding member of the Committee of 13 against Colonization, formed in 1851.[38] Born in the same year as Wilson, and perhaps a compatriot in many struggles in the New York City and Brooklyn area, was Peter Vogelsang. He was involved in the national colored convention movement in the 1830s, was a leader in an abolition-tinged self-improvement society, the Phoenix Society, was prominent in an organization to raise money for a black college in New Haven, and in other ways made his political convictions clear.[39] Harriet Jacobs, author of *Incidents in the Life of a Slave Girl*, intended for her slave narrative to have an abolitionist impact. She also wrote to New York papers on antislavery issues, assisted in launching an antislavery reading room, and engaged in quiet protests against discrimination.[40] Others lived in intimate proximity to the stimulation of abolitionist discourse and activity—Mary A.G. and Anna M. Wilson, Charles R. Douglass, Nathan T. Condol, C.M. Hicks (later Catherine Williams)—but the evidence so far does not indicate whether they embraced the discourse or the activity.[41]

A few of the New York teachers became involved in politics while in the South, though it appears that only Thomas W. Cardozo had political ambitions before he engaged in the southern work. As noted earlier, Stephen A. Swails was elected to the South Carolina state legislature after teaching in the state one year. From 1872 to 1874 he served as president pro tem of the state senate, attended the National Republican Convention in 1872, and was appointed to the board of trustees of the University of South Carolina. He became a newspaper editor and a dominant political force in his county. Joel Williamson, a careful historian, judges Swails and four of his political compatriots as "remarkably effective managers in view of their sudden elevation to their posts." Hezekiah H. Hunter also dabbled briefly in South Carolina politics, serving in the state senate for two years. [42]

On the other hand, another of New York's teachers, Thomas W. Cardozo, turned out to be a scoundrel. The brother of the noted South Carolina politician, Francis L. Cardozo, and member of Charleston's black elite, Thomas W. Cardozo seemed constantly to seek offices of one sort or another, almost always with disaster for himself and those around him. A pattern of corruption first appeared when he began teaching in New York. He held teaching positions on Staten Island and Flushing, but sought to unseat William J. Wilson, Brooklyn's long-time principal. Though married to one of Wilson's teachers (who apparently retained her maiden name, Laura J. Williams, throughout the attack on Wilson), he spread rumors, created dissension among patrons, and approached members of the board of education saying "he had heard that Mr. Wilson would be discharged, and [seeking] his position for himself." Wilson resigned, for reasons that went beyond the problems with Cardozo, and took a position teaching the freedmen in Washington D.C. The gambit netted Cardozo nothing but opprobrium.[43]

Two years later Cardozo moved with his wife back to Charleston as Superintendent of the American Missionary Association's work there. That was a short-lived office, however, for news of his dalliance with a student in New York led to his abrupt dismissal and his replacement by his brother, Francis, who would build his own political fortunes on the position. After a brief stint in ] business in Charleston and teaching in Baltimore, the Cardozos lived for a time in Syracuse while they raised money for an educational venture in

North Carolina. According to Euline Brock, while at Syracuse Cardozo was already "considering the political opportunities" available in the South, and when his "prospects for a political career in North Carolina" turned out to be bleak, he and his wife left the normal school they had begun in Elizabeth City and moved to Vicksburg. They began teaching there in early 1871. He moved into politics as soon as his six-month residency had been satisfied, eventually winning the state superintendency of education in 1874. It was not long, however, before his past, and apparently some current corruption, caught up with him. He resigned his office and fled the state in the face of impeachment. [44]

It appears, then, that only one of fifty-one teachers had political motives before going into the freedmen's work, and three at most took advantage of the political situation in the Reconstruction South.

Finally, it is clear that none of the New York teachers were attracted to freedmen's education for the salary or for the mere adventure. They were all aware that the aid societies paid minimal wages, well below what most could make teaching in the North. The American Freedmen's Union Commission paid between $20 and $30 a month depending on experience. The American Missionary Association (AMA) paid between $15 and $25, depending on gender. Others paid similarly. Some urged prospective teachers to donate their time. For a group which was, as we have seen, moderately upwardly mobile, the financial prospects of freedmen's education held no promise. Unless, like Cardozo, they saw freedmen's education as providing other financial advantages—and there is no evidence that any did except for him—taking the position meant only sacrifice.

The candidates knew that. Matilda C. Anderson wrote, "If my circumstances should allow me to do so, I would heartily engage in this work without compensation. But being poor and dependent upon my own exertions for a livelihood, I regret that I cannot serve from motives of pure benevolence . . . ." She requested salary sufficient to meet expenses and assist her widowed mother. Edmonia G. Highgate similarly regretted not being one of those who could engage in the work without compensation, but added, "I am willingly making some sacrafice [sic] by leaving a situation that yields me twice the salary which I hope for in my new field." [46]

As for adventure, it was well known from the beginning of the freedmen's education movement that the South was a dangerous place for a northern teacher to be. A few were killed, many were harassed, most were ostracized by white southern society. Nor was the work itself easy. Nathan T. Condol, for instance, working with a white friend from Geneva and a freedman assistant, was teaching a day school of over 170, a night school of 56 (every evening and Saturday), and Sunday School, within three months of reaching Mississippi. Two years later his Sunday School numbered 203. He closed a one page description of his work graphically: "Excuse brevity, we write during recess." While black teachers may have found comfort among their own people, the work can hardly be described as a casual southern vacation or a hospitable adventure.[47]

What is needed is a new interpretation of the reasons women and men chose to engage in the work. If our traditional understanding of the motives of the freedmen's teachers do not work., how do we explain them? It is likely that the thinking of blacks and of whites diverged on that subject, for racial identification and one's sense of self and vocation in relation to issues of racial justice were necessarily different. What follows, then, applies to the motivation of black teachers.

A powerful sense of calling impelled some of these men and women. After speaking to Oberlin President Charles G. Finney, Nathan T. Condol returned to his room to write, "I am called upon by the Supreme Being, working within, to go immediately south and work in His vineyard." He had earlier asked to be sent to the Washington DC area, but now asked for any appointment, "so long as I know I am working not for myself." Edmonia G. Highgate's motivation flowed out of "a desire to be a pioneer in trying to raise [the freedmen] up to the stature of manhood and womanhood in " 'Christ Jesus.' "[48] Yet few of the black New York teachers spoke of their calling in these religious terms. Though doubtlessly all religious people, they spoke most clearly about race as their commitment, even to sponsors known to be concerned about evangelizing the freedmen before all other objectives.

New York's African American teachers identified racially with the freedmen. The sense of racial identification was clear in the words of Hezikiah Hunter. "I believe *we* best can instruct our own people," he wrote to the American Missionary Association in 1865, "knowing our own peculiarities—needs—necessities. Further—I believe, we, that are competent owe it to *our people* to teach them as our *specialty*." Edmonia Highgate likewise spoke explicitly of her "intense interest in the education of my freed brethren South...." Nathan T. Condol wrote of being "desirous of assisting in the edification of my race...." Matilda C. Anderson expressed a more modest humanitarianism: "Being naturally fond of teaching I feel still more interested in engaging in this good work, and to labor with many others in dividing my small store of knowledge with those of my fellow creatures who have been deprived of the privileges which I have enjoyed."[49]

For a significant number of New York's African American freedmen's teachers, the sense of racial identification was compounded by their own direct roots in southern soil. Many were returning home. Harriet and Louisa Jacobs had escaped from slavery many years earlier. They returned to the South in 1863, serving in Virginia and Georgia.[50] Hardy Mobley, his wife and several of his children, had been born in slavery in Georgia. He purchased his and their freedom in the 1850s for $3,000, and moved to Brooklyn. As he prepared to return to his native state, he declared he was going to encourage "the improvement of his old neighbors" who had not been as fortunate as he. Likewise, Thomas W. Cardozo and his sister and brother-in-law, E.L. and Christopher C. McKinney, had grown up in the ambivalent milieu of Charleston, South Carolina's free black elite. The McKinneys had spent several years in Ohio and New York; Cardozo had moved to New York City with his mother in 1857, and married a teacher from Brooklyn in the early 1860s. The Cardozos went to Charleston in April, 1865. Christopher McKinney spoke of his "earnest desire to return to my native home in Charleston," wishing "to labor for the intellectual advancement of my people." He arrived in Charleston with his wife in January 1866. Edmonia G. Highgate's mother, Hanna Francis Highgate, a widow by 1862, was born in Virginia. She taught in nearby Maryland in 1864-1865, and returned to the South again in 1868 to teach with her daughters in Mississippi.[51]

Another sizable group had roots only somewhat less directly planted in southern soil. These were the children of southern black men and women, some of whom may once have been slaves themselves. Were they drewn back to their parents' native soil, touched by family stories of life in the slave South? We may never know directly, yet it is interesting to note that of the seven teachers one or both of whose parents were born in a southern state, all taught in that or an adjoining state. Both of Mason C. Ball's parents were born in Virginia: he taught in Maryland. Frederick Douglass escaped from slavery in Maryland; Charles R. Douglass worked and taught in the District of Columbia. Alice C. Hall taught for several years in the cities and villages of Maryland, the state of her father's birth. Edmonia G. Highgate taught in her mother's native Virginia. Peter Lapene was born in South Carolina in 1809; his daughter, Mary Caroline Lapene, taught in North Carolina from 1869-1871, many years after his death. Lewis and Rachel Payne (or Paine) were born in Virginia and the District of Columbia, respectively; Sebastian and George F. Payne taught in Maryland.[52]

Quantitative research such as primarily pursued here does not definitively answer the question of the motives of the freedmen's teachers. It does, however, provide some important clues. There is little in this data to give comfort to the traditional interpretation. These women and men were clearly not fanatics, mindless zealots, nor vengeful bigots. Many were abolitionists, but those struggling for black freedom have come to appreciate that label in ways traditional historians could not understand. Neither political aspiration nor high salaries, incompetence nor superficial adventurism, impelled them into that cauldron of racial oppression. A commitment to do good, however, and contribute their mite to changing the fortunes of their race, were clearly at work.

There was heroism in these people. They did not seek fame or fortune. They did not walk the corridors of power. They only sought to make a difference. There can be no nobler aspiration.

## NOTES

I wish to extend a special acknowledgement to Dr. Carleton Mabee, Professor Emeritus, SUNY College at New Paltz, for his generosity in sharing his notes on black teachers in New York State. Mr. Jerry Porter, East Greenbush, New York, provided crucial information about Mrs. C.M. Williams, his great-grandmother.

,1 W.E.B. DuBois, **The Souls of Black Folk** (1903; rpt. New York: New American Library, 1969), 65. The most recent treatments of freedmen's education are Ronald E. Butchart, **Northern Schools, Southern Blacks, and Reconstruction: Freedmen's Education, 1862 - 1875** (Westport CT: Greenwood Press, 1980); Robert C. Morris, **Reading, 'Riting, and Reconstruction: The Education of Freedmen in the South, 1861-1870** (University of Chicago Press, 1981).

2 The most complete statement of the southern view of freedmen's teachers is contained in Henry L. Swint, **The Northern Teacher in the South, 1862-1870** (Nashville: Vanderbilt University Press, 1941).

3 Jacqueline Jones, **Soldiers of Light and Love:Northern Teachers and Georgia Blacks, 1865-1873** (Chapel Hill: University of North Carolina Press, 1980); Morris, **Reading, 'Riting, and Reconstruction**; Sandra E. Small, "The Yankee Schoolmarm in Freedmen's Schools: An Analysis of attitudes," **Journal of Southern History,** 45 (1979): 381-402; Sylvia D. Hoffert, "Yankee Schoolmarms and the Domestication of the South," **Southern Studies,** 24 (Summer 1985): 188-201. James M. McPherson, **The Struggle for Equality: Abolitionists and the Negro in the Civil War and Reconstruction** (Princeton: Princeton University Press, 1964); and Butchart, **Northern Schools, Southern Blacks, and Reconstruction,** focus primarily on aspects of the freedmen's education movement beyond the teachers, but do include chapters on the teachers.

4 Jones, **Soldiers of Light and Love,** is an example of the dangers of a narrow focus. Although hers is a valuable book at some levels, many of her generalizations about the teachers, their experiences, and the movement in general are mistaken. She used Georgia as her case study, a state dominated by the American Missionary Association. She incorrectly assumes that, as the largest aid organization, the AMA was a typical aid organization. Some of her data is in error, compounding the books difficulties.

5 Ronald E. Butchart, "An Interim Report of a study of Teachers in Nineteenth Century Amerca: Freedmen's Teachers, 1862-1875," unpublished paper presented to the History of Education Society, 1985.

6 A splendid exception is Morris, **Reading, 'Riting, and Reconstruction,** 85-130, although he deals more with southern blacks than with the large number of northern blacks who ventured into the South.

7 I began suspecting that these were the same invividuals when one disappeared from the Albany **Directory** in 1866, while the other could not be found before 1867, and both lived at 5 Lark Street. She seems to have gone by C. Mary before her second marriage, but by Catherine later, which added to the confusion. Through pure happenstance, I was working on this problem in the New York State Archives where I met Mr. Jerry Porter, the great-grandson of Mrs. Williams, who was able to confirm through relatives that the widow of Rev. Henry Hicks met and married Robert Williams while in the South. Mrs. Hicks taught in Albany's Wilberforce School from 1852 to 1856, and 1859-60. She appears to have been widowed in 1854, shortly after the birth of her first child. See **Albany Directory** (Albany: Adams, Sampson & Co.), 1860-1875: Albany Board of Education, **Annual Report of the Board of Education, City of Albany** (Albany, 1861-62); New York State census manuscript schedules, 1855: City of

Albany, 10th Ward, p. 39, Michael Douge; City of Albany, 8th ward, p. 69, Michael Douge.

8 To be included in the file, an individual had to have lived in New York state for a year or more. Three of the teachers included in the final file were no longer in the state by 1861, but had made the state their residence for several years prior to the beginning of the freedmen's education movement. Edwin H. and Sophia Freeman had lived in Troy, New York, for several years in the 1840s and 1850s, but were in Newark, New Jersey, before leaving for the freedmen's work. Maria W. Stewart taught in New York City and Williamsburg between 1837 and 1852, but moved to Baltimore in the later year. It is thus problematic whether we can legitimately consider these three as New Yorkers. I have chosen to do so because of the length of their stay in the state, and their teaching and promotion of black education in the state.

Four of the 51 have not yet been definitively identified: T. B. Snowden, Celinda D. Anderson, Harriet J. West, and Kitty Johnson. It is possible that one or more of them were not New Yorkers.

Miss T.B. Snowden has yet to be located in state or city records. However, she appears to be the sister of Georgiana M. Snowden, who taught in New York City Colored School No. 6 from 1862 to 1866, and moved directly into freedmen's education, teaching in Maryland from 1866 to 1870. The presumption of a relationship between these women is based on the fact that Miss T.B. Snowden also taught in Maryland during the same four years, and, for three of those years, for the same organization. See New York, N.Y., Board of Education, **Twenty-first Annual Report of the Board of Education** (New York: 1862):102, and subsequent reports to 1866; **Trow's New York City Directory for 1863** (H. Wilson, comp., New York: John F. Trow, 1863); and manuscript reports, 1866-1870, from Baltimore Association for the Moral and Educational Improvement of the Colored People, and Pennsylvania Freedmen's Relief Association, in Bureau of Refugees, Freedmen, and Abandoned Lands, Records of the Education Division, 1865-1872, National Archives (hereafter: BRFAL Records).

Celinda D. Anderson taught in Delaware from 1867 to 1870, and then appeared in Brooklyn, teaching in Brooklyn Colored School No. 4, in 1874. I cannot yet establish that she was from New York prior to her service in Delaware. See ms. reports from Delaware Association for the Moral Improvement and Education of the Colored People, in BRFAL Records; Brookly, N.Y., City Superintendent of Schools, **Nineteenth Annual Report of the City Superintendent of Schools of the Consolidated City of Brooklyn** (Brooklyn:1874) 56.

Harriet J. West likewise taught in Brooklyn after her efforts in the South. She taught in Maryland for a Quaker organization from 1865 to 1869, moving directly from the work to Brooklyn Colored School No. 1 in 1869. See Friends' Association of Philadelphia and Vicinity for the Relief of Colored Freedmen, **Third Report of the Executive Board of the Friends' Association of Philadelphia and Its Vicinity, for the Relief of Colored Freedmen** (Philadelphia: C. Sherman, 1866); ms. reports of Friends' Freedmens Association, BRFAL Records; and Brooklyn Supt. of Schools, **15th Annual Report**, (1870): 127.

Most problematic is Miss Kitty Johnson, who taught for the Methodist Episcopal Freedmen's Aid Society in Georgia in the late 1860s. A Kitty Johnson attended New York City Colored Normal School in 1856-57; these might. be the same person. At this point I have no evidence that they are beyond the fact that "Kitty"is an unusual name in the nineteenth century, so there is some probability that they are the same (there is only one Kitty in the entire file of 5,350 names, for example). See New York Board of Education, **15th Annual Report** . . . (1856), appendix, p. 22; BRFAL Records.

9  Blacks made up 1.3% of New York State's population in 1860, 1.2% in 1870. U.S. Dept. of Commerce, Bur. of the Census, **Negro Population, 1790-1915** (Washington: Government Printing Office, 1918), Table 5, p. 51.

10  Butchart, "Interim Report: Freedmen's Teachers," 5-6.

11  Butchart, **Northern Schools, Southern Blacks, and Reconstruction**, 124; Morris, **Reading, 'Riting and Reconstruction**, 58.

12  Butchart, "Interim Report: Freedmen's Teachers," 4-5.

13  Butchart, "Interim Report: Freedmen's Teachers," 6.  Gender is again implicated in interesting ways.  Among the black New York teachers, women averaged 3.30 terms, versus 2.83 terms for men.  Among those New Yorkers devoting more than one year to the service, women averaged a high 4.62 years, compared to a respectable 4.3 years for men.  Both averages are still much higher than any other group identified so far.

14  Two possible family groups have not yet been confirmed: George F., Sebastian, and William Oscar Payne (or Paine); and Georgianna and T.B. Snowden.  The results reported here assume that George F. and Sebastian Payne were brothers, though William Oscar Payne was not; and that the Snowdens were sisters.  See also Butchart, "Interim Report: Freedmen's Teachers," 7.  Celinda D. and Matilda C. Anderson, both from Brooklyn, were not sisters.

15  Birth year is now known for 68% of the New York black teachers.  It is not yet possible to make meaningful comparisons with the larger file, since birth year is known for only 4.1% of that group, but it appears that these black teachers were somewhat older than their white counterparts.

16  Butchart, "Interim Report: Freedmen's Teachers," 9-10.  College graduates include Thomas Paul, Jr., among Dartmouth College's first African American graduates; John B. Reeve, New York Central College, Union Theological Seminary, and, later, D.D., Lincoln Univ.  Thomas W. Cardozo is said to have attended Newburgh Collegiate Institute, though it is not clear whether he graduated.  BRFAL Records; J. Carleton Hayden, "Paul, Thomas, Sr.," in **Dictionary of American Negro Biography**, ed. by Rayford W. Logan and Michael R. Winston (New York: W.W. Norton and Co., 1982): 482-483; William J. Simmons, **Men of Mark: Eminent, Progressive and Rising** (1887; rpt. New York: Arno Press, 1968): 199-201;  William Wells Brown, **The Rising Son; or, Antecendents and Advancement of the Colored Race** (Boston: A.G. Brown, 1874), 495-96.

17  The parents of 25 teachers consisted of only 20 different couples.  Eight individuals shared four parents: Edmonia, Caroline, and Willela Highgate, whose father, Charles Highgate, was a barber; M. Catherine, Martha E., and Sarah J. Mobley, whose father, Hardy Mobley, was a porter and one of the freedmen's teachers himself; and (perhaps) George F. and Sebastian Payne, whose father, Lewis Payne, was a seaman.  In most cases, parental occupation was determined by manuscript census schedules

18  See Table 1.

19  This discussion excludes those listed as wives or students in the Table 1. The designation "wife" was given to married women for whom the census and other sources gave no other occupation, a common occurrence in the nineteenth century even for women who may have contributed to the family income through the sale of domestic production, services such as washing or childcare, or taking in boarders.  The designation here is intended to convey the likelihood that these women were active in the family economy, not to suggest marginality.  The designation "student" was given to those for whom the sources gave no occupation, and whose age suggested that they may not have yet established a vocation.

20  **Boyd's Elmira Directory** (Elmira: Hall Bros., 1863); New York State

census manuscript schedules, 1865: Chemung County, Town of Elmira, Ward 3, p. 59; **Freedmen's Record** 3 (March 1867): 47; Robert Ewell Greene, **Black Defenders of America, 1775-1973: A Reference and Pictorial History** (Chicago: Johnson Publishing, 1974): 92-93; Thomas Holt, **Black over White: Negro Political Leadership in South Carolina during Reconstruction** (Urbana: University of Illinois Press, 1977): 77-78, Table 5, [240]; Joel Williamson, **After Slavery: The Negro during Reconstruction in South Carolina, 1861-1877** (Chapel Hill: University of North Carolina Press, 1965), 28, 30, 379.

21 **Rochester Daily Union City Directory** (Rochester: Cutis, Butts, & Co., 1860); **Boyd's Rochester and Brockport Directory** (Rochester: Dewey, Darrow & Brother, 1864); **Crisis** 21 (March 1921): 215; Benjamin Quarles, **Frederick Douglass** (1948; rpt. New York: Atheneum, 1968):110.

22 "Documents:Letters to the American Colonization Society," **Journal of Negro History** 10 (1925): 298-99; **The Brooklyn City Directory**, J. Lain, comp. (Brooklyn: J. Lain and Co., 1860-1875); New York State census manuscript schedules, 1865: King County, City of Brooklyn, Ward 16, 2nd District, dw. 68, fam. 156, Hardy Mosly [sic]; **American Missionary** 9 (April 1865): 90; American Missionary Association, **Twentieth Annual Report of the American Missionary Association and the Proceedings at the Annual Meeting** (New York: AMA, 1866): 29.

23 This is a conservative estimate. It is unclear how many years Edwin H. Freeman taught in Troy, how many years Christopher McKinney may have taught in Ohio before moving to Flushing, whether the wife of either man taught before going South, and exactly how long Thomas Paul, Jr., taught in Boston and elsewhere before going to Albany as principal.

24 Brooklyn, N.Y., Board of Education, **Annual Report of the Brooklyn Board of Education** (Brooklyn, 1850-1854); Brooklyn Supt. of Schools, **Annual Reports,** (1855-1864); Federal census manuscript schedules, 1860: King County, City of Brooklyn, Ward 11, 3rd District, dw. 1350, fam. 1595, William Wilson; Brown, **Rising Son**, 444-45; Carleton Mabee, **Black Education in New York State: From Colonial to Modern Times** (Syracuse: Syracuse University Press, 1979): 129-130; AMA, 18th Annual Report (1864): 26; U.S. Education Office, **Special Report of the Commissioner of Education on the Condition and Improvement of Public Schools in the District of Columbia** (Washington DC: Government Printing Office, 1871): 225.

25 Mabee, **Black Education in New York State**, 86; New York Board of Education, **16th Annual Report . . .** (1857): 108, and subsequent reports through 1863; **American Freedman** (December 1866): 141; **Pennsylvania Freedmen's Bulletin** (June 1867): inside front cover; Lillian Dabney, **The History of Schools for Negroes in the District of Columbia, 1807-1947** (Washington DC: Catholic University of America Press, 1949): 77.

26 Federal census manuscript schedules, 1850: New York City, Ward 5, dw. 193, fam. 274, Charlotte Smith; New York City Board of Education, **12th Annual Report** (1853): 74, and subsequent reports; New York, N.Y., Board of Education, **Documents of the Board of Education of the City of New York for the Year 1855** (New York: 1855), Document No. 19, p. 21, and other **Documents** from 1853, 1854, and 1856; **American Freedman**, (December 1866): 141; BRFAL Records.

27 Federal census manuscript schedules, 1860: Onondaga County, City of Syracuse, Ward 7, dw. 430, fam. 552, Charles Highgate; **New York Weekly Anglo-African,** 28 December 1861; **Binghamton Standard,** 31 December 1862, 30 March 1864; recommendation to AMA by D. H. Cruttenden, 26 January 1864, American Missionary Association Archives, item #86795, Amistad Research Center, New Orleans (hereafter: AMA #); Dorothy Sterling, ed., **We Are Your Sisters: Black Women in the Nineteenth Century** (New York: W.W. Norton and Co., 1984), 274-304.

28 M.H. Goodwin to Whom it May Concern, and M. Wheeler, endorsement, 12

September 1864, AMA #87609; Nathan Tappan Condol to George Whipple, 10 October 1865, AMA #112724; Condol to Thomas K. Beecher, 20 January, 1866, AMA #72146; Condol to M.E. Strieby, 7 September 1869, AMA # 72333; **Geneva Gazette**, 27 September 1878. Condol was supported at Oberlin, and his salary and expenses in Mississippi were covered, by the black Freedmens and Soldiers Aid Society of Geneva, and Thomas K. Beecher's church in Elmira: see Harriet M. Gayton and others to American Missionary Association, [May 1865], AMA #89565; Condol to Strieby, 12 September 1865, AMA #112659; and Thomas K. Beecher to [AMA], 24 October 1865, AMA #89307.

29 The teachers include Celinda D. Anderson, Brooklyn; Nathan T. Condol, Aberdeen, Miss.; Hezekiah Hunter, who also dabbled in politics and held a pastorate in South Carolina; Harriet J. West, Brooklyn; Matilda C. Anderson, who became a principal in Brooklyn; and John B. Reeve, who created the Theology Department at Howard University. See Brooklyn City Superintendent of Schools, **Annual Reports**, 1870 through 1878; **Geneva Gazette**, 27 September 1878; Holt, **Black over White**, Table 5 [234]; Rayford Logan, **Howard University: The First Hundred Years** (New York: New York University Press, 1969), 51.

Stephen Swails and Thomas W. Cardozo both devoted themselves to state politics, the former more successfully than the latter. See note 20; and Euline W. Brock, "Thomas W. Cardozo: Fallible Black Reconstruction Leader," **Journal of Southern History** 47 (May 1981): 183-206.

Charles R. Douglass spent his last fifty years in Washington in government service; Hardy Mobley moved to New Iberia, Louisiana, where he served as a minister; and William J. Wilson worked as a cashier for the savings and trust. See **Crisis**, 21 (March 1921): 215; **American Missionary** 19 (February 1875): 34; recommendation of Louis A. Bell by William J. Wilson, 23 October 1867, Antislavery Collection, Cornell University (hereafter:CU); Brown, **Rising Son**, 444-45. Concerning Stewart, see Eleanor Flexnor, "Maria W. Stewart," in **Notable American Women, 1607-1950: A Biographical Dictionary**, v. 3 (Cambridge MA: Belknap Press, 1971): 377-78; Dabney, **Schools for Negroes in D.C.**, 27.77.

30 See especially Swint, **Northern Teacher**, 35-68; George R. Bentley, **A History of the Freedmen's Bureau** (1955; rpt. New York: Octagon, 1970): 169-84; Edgar W. Knight, "The 'Messianic' Invasion of the South after 1865," **School and Society** 57 (5 June 1943): 645-51.

31 Butchart, **Northern Schools, Southern Blacks, and Reconstruction**, 115-34 and passim.

32 Butchart, review essay, **Educational Studies** 14 (Spring 1983): 31-36; and Butchart, **Northern Schools, Southern Blacks, and Reconstruction**, 130-34.

33 Butchart, "Interim Report: Freedmen's Teachers," 9, 18.

34 Flexnor, "Maria W. Stewart," 377-78; Benjamin Quarles, **Black Abolitionists** (New York: Oxford University Press, 1969), 7, 192; Mabee, **Black Education in New York State**, 123; Dabney, **Schools for Negroes in D.C.**, 77.

35 Hayden, "Paul, Thomas, Sr.," 482-83; Quarles, **Black Abolitionists**, 90.

36 **Proceedings of the National Convention of Colored Men Held in the City of Syracuse, N.Y., October 4, 5, 6, and 7, 1864** (Boston: J.S. Rock and George L. Ruffin 1864), 49; Simmons, **Men of Mark**, 199-201; Quarles, **Black Abolitionists**, 114.

37 **Proc. of the Nat. Colored Conv., Syracuse, 1864**, 15; Howard Holman Bell, ed., **Minutes of the Proceedings of the National Negro Conventions, 1830-1864** (New York: Arno Press and the New York Times, 1969), iv; Sterling, 294-304.

38 **Proceedings of the Colored National Convention, Held in Rochester, 1853** (Rochester: Frederick Douglass' Paper, 1853), 5, 20-25; **Proceedings of the Colored National Convention, Held in Philadelphia, 1855** (Salem, NJ: The Convention, 1856), 5, 6; **Proc. of the Nat. Colored Conv., Syracuse, 1864**, 6, 29;

Brown, **Rising Son**, 444-45; Joan R. Sherman, **Invisible Poets: Afro-Americans of the Nineteenth Century** (Urbana: University of Illinois Press, 1974), 244; Mabee, **Black Education in New York State**, 129-130; Quarles, **Black Abolitionists**, 87, 212, 229.

39 **Anglo-African Magazine** 1 (October 1859): n.p.; **Minutes and Proceedings of the First Annual Convention of the People of Colour, Held in Philadelphia, 1831** (Philadelphia: Committee of Arrangements, 1831), 7, 8; **Minutes and Proceedings of the Second Annual Convention, for the Improvement of the Freed Peiple of Color, Held in Philadelphia, 1832** (Philadelphia: the Convention, 1832), 24, 25; **Minutes of the Fourth Annual Convention, for the Improvement of the Free People of Colour, in the United States, New York, 1834** (New York: the Convention, 1834), 8; Quarles, **Black Abolitionists**, 102, 107; Herbert Aptheker, ed., **Documentary History of the Negro People** (New York: Citadel Press, 1951), 140-41.

40 Harriet Brent Jacobs, **Incidents in the Life of a Slave Girl, Written by Herself** (ed. Lydia Maria Child; Boston: by the author, 1861), passim; Sterling, 73-4. The authenticity of Jacob's book has been recently established; see Jean Fagan Yellin, "Written by Herself: Harriet Jacobs' Slave Narrative," **American Literature** 53 (November 1981): 479-86.

41 The Wilsons were wife and daughter of William J. Wilson; Douglass was son of Frederick Douglass; Condol attended preparatory school at Oberlin College, the leading abolitionist college in the country; Hicks was the widow of Henry Hicks, black activist of Albany. On the latter, see Mabee, **Black Education in New York State**, 123. It should be recalled that the younger Wilson, Douglass, and Condol were all still in their late teens when the Civil War started.

42 Williamson, **After Slavery**, 379, 30; Holt, **Black over White**, 109; Greene, **Black Defenders of America**, 92-93; Morris, **Reading, 'Riting, and Reconstruction**, 106, 240. Morris calls Swails one of "several prominent Northern politicos of dubious integrity," a judgement not found elsewhere in the literature. On Hunter, see Holt, Table 5, [234].

43 **Brooklyn Daily Times**, 8 July 1863; James McCune Smith, testimonial for William J. Wilson, 2 June 1864, AMA Archives; Mabee, **Black Education in New York State**, 129-30, 314. I am indebted to Professor Mabee for sharing his original material on Cardozo with me.

44 Brown, **Rising Son**, 495; Brock, "Thomas W. Cardozo," 183-206; Morris, **Reading, 'Riting, and Reconstruction**, 86-88. Hezekiah H. Hunter also dabbled in politics in South Carolina for a brief time; see Holt, **Black over White**, Table 5, [234].

45 Butchart, **Northern Schools, Southern Blacks, and Reconstruction**, 122-23.

46 Matilda Anderson to AMA, 24 March 1864, AMA #87066; Edmonia G. Highgate to S.S. Jocelyn, 30 January 1864, AMA #86810.

47 N.T. Condol to M.E. Strieby, 26 March 1867, AMA #72248; see also Butchart, **Northern Schools, Southern Blacks, and Reconstruction**, 115-18, 181-95.

48 N. Tappan Condol to George Whipple, 10 October 1865, AMA #112724; Edmonia G. Highgate to S.S. Jocelyn, 30 January 1864, AMA #86810.

49 Hezekiah H. Hunter and Lizzie R. Hunter to Executive Committee of the American Missionary Association, 25 February 1865, [emphasis in original] AMA #88340; Edmonia G. Highgate to S.S. Jocelyn, 30 January 1864, AMA #87616; Matilda Anderson to AMA, 24 March 1864, AMA #87066.

50 Jacobs, passim; **Freedmen's Record** (December 1865).

51 **American Missionary** 9 (April 1865): 90; **Quarterly Journal of the Library of Congress** (October 1977): 354-55; Brock, "Thomas W. Cardozo," 186-188; Morris, **Reading, 'Riting, and Reconstruction**, 88: C.C. McKinney to Gentlemen the American Missionary Association, 11 December 1865, AMA #87474;

Teacher's Monthly Report, January 1866, AMA #45934; Federal census manuscript schedules, 1860: Onondaga County, Syracuse, Ward 7, dw. 430, fam. 552, Charles Highgate; AMA, **19th Annual Report** (1865): 17; **American Freedman** (April 1869) : 15; Pennsylvania Freedmen's Relief Association, "Monthly Reports of Schools for Freedmen," February 1869, BRFAL Records.

52 Federal census manuscript schedules, 1850: New York City, Ward 14, dw. 248, fam. 817, W.S. Ball; American Freemen's Union Commission, "Commission Book," n.p., CU; Quarles, **Frederick Douglass**, 2; Federal census manuscript schedules, 1860: Rensselaer County, Town of Lansingburgh, dw. 570, fam. 696, ms. p. 87, James Hall; **American Freedman** (December 1866): 139; AFUC, "Commission Book," n.p.; Federal census manuscript schedules, 1860: Onondago County, Syracuse, Ward 7, dw 430, fam. 552, Charles Highgate; AMA, **18th Annual Report** (1864): 25; Federal census manuscript schedules, 1850: New York City, Ward 8, dw. 83, fam. 254, Peter Lapane [sic]; AFUC, "Commission Book," n.p.; Federal census manuscript schedules, 1850: New York City, Ward 5, dw. 220, fam. 572, Lewis Paine; AFUC, "Commission Book," n.p.

# Schools for Blacks:

# J. Milton Turner

# in

# Reconstruction Missouri

BY LAWRENCE O. CHRISTENSEN*

Organized efforts to educate black children in Missouri began
during the Civil War. The American Missionary Association, an
organization committed to Christianizing and educating blacks, cooperated with the Western Sanitary Commission, the United States
Army and black leaders in establishing a system of free schools in

*Lawrence O. Christensen, associate professor of History at the University
of Missouri-Rolla, presented this address at the annual meeting of the State
Historical Society of Missouri, Columbia, October 17, 1981. Dr. Christensen
received the B.S. Ed. and M.A. degrees from Northeast Missouri State University, Kirksville, and the Ph.D. from the University of Missouri-Columbia. Research for this paper was supported by a University of Missouri-Rolla Summer
Research Grant and by a grant from the Weldon Spring Research Fund.

St. Louis during 1864.[1] After the Civil War, the AMA continued to support black schools in various towns across the state.[2]

In 1867, the AMA secretary, J. R. Shipherd, asked Colonel F. A. Seely, chief disbursing officer for Missouri for the Bureau of Refugees, Freedmen, and Abandoned Lands, "to immediately supervise the schools and other interests of the AMA in Missouri." Shipherd offered to pay Seely's traveling expenses and to "add any other equitable compensation agreed upon for services rendered." The secretary assured Seely that similar arrangements had been made with other Freedmen Bureau officials.[3]

Whether Seely made a formal agreement with the AMA is unclear, but he and the bureau cooperated with that organization in improving the educational opportunities for blacks in Missouri. During the same month that Shipherd made his offer, Seely requested that the bureau pay the travel expenses of AMA teachers to staff black schools in Sedalia, Mexico, Washington and St. Louis. They came from Indianola, Muscatine and Oskaloosa, Iowa.[4] In October 1868, Shipherd requested that Seely prepare a quitclaim deed for a school site purchased in Fulton and forward it for his signature.[5] A few months later, the bureau transferred certain buildings in Missouri and Kansas to the AMA in an effort to reduce its educational commitments in those states.[6]

Seely's interest in black education continued, and his critique of a report on the condition of Missouri's schools for blacks came to the attention of Bureau Commissioner Oliver Otis Howard. Howard asked him to "draw up a letter for his signature" in which he would "state clearly and strongly the condition of the freedmen's schools with a view to rousing the local authorities to some vigorous action." He instructed Seely to address the letter to the state superintendent of education. The bureau favored public schools, and although it had little to spend in Missouri, and there was "some doubt about the legality of any expenditures for Education in that

---

[1] Lawrence O. Christensen, "Black St. Louis: A Study in Race Relations, 1865-1916" (unpublished Ph.D. dissertation, University of Missouri-Columbia, 1972), 38-50.

[2] Joe M. Richardson, "The American Missionary Association and Black Education in Civil War Missouri," MISSOURI HISTORICAL REVIEW, LXIX (July, 1975), 448.

[3] J. R. Shipherd to F. A. Seely, December 2, 1867, Record Group 105 Bureau of Refugees, Freedmen, and Abandoned Lands, Missouri Chief Disbursing Officer, Letters Received, Registered Vol. 2, 1867-1869 E-W, National Archives, Washington, D. C.; hereafter cited BFRA Letters.

[4] F. A. Seely to Gen. Geo. W. Bullock, December 19, 1867, *ibid.*

[5] J. R. Shipherd to F. A. Seely, October 17, 1868, *ibid.*

[6] Oscar C. Gabin to F. A. Seely, January 18, 1869, *ibid.*

State," Howard encouraged Seely to exert every effort "in favor of the colored people."[7]

Within a month, Seely had asked J. Milton Turner to investigate the condition of black education in Missouri.[8] State law required boards of education to establish and maintain schools for blacks if at least fifteen of them between the ages of five and twenty-one lived in a township. Even if fewer than fifteen resided there, they had to be counted in school censuses. If a school board failed to carry out its responsibilities, the law conferred upon the state superintendent of schools authority to establish and operate black schools.[9]

Seely could not have made a better choice. Turner was the most prominent black in the state. After the Civil War, he helped organize and served as secretary of the Missouri Equal Rights League. Later, he established and taught in black schools in Kansas City and Boonville.[10] After being approached by Seely, the native St. Louisan consulted State Superintendent of Schools Thomas A. Parker. Parker promised to issue Turner a commission delegating to him "all necessary power." He informed Turner about immediate problems in Randolph County.[11]

Armed with the cooperation of Superintendent Parker, Turner accepted the bureau's offer of one hundred dollars a month and started work on August 1, 1869.[12] During the next seven months, J. Milton investigated educational conditions across the state, pushed for the establishment of black schools, secured teachers, risked his life in hostile environments and reported what he found in twenty-nine letters to his immediate superior, Colonel Seely. Those letters allow us to see conditions in Reconstruction Missouri from a unique perspective, through the eyes of a very perceptive black observer.

Throughout this correspondence one is struck by the cooperation among the state superintendent, the American Missionary As-

---

[7] E. Whittlesey to F. A. Seely, June 22, 1869, *ibid.*

[8] J. Milton Turner to F. A. Seely, July 17, 1869, *ibid.*

[9] William E. Parrish, *Missouri Under Radical Rule, 1865-1870* (Columbia, Mo., 1965), 125-126.

[10] Lawrence O. Christensen, "J. Milton Turner, An Appraisal," Missouri Historical Review, LXX (October, 1975), 3; Gary R. Kremer, "A Biography of James Milton Turner" (unpublished Ph.D. dessertation, The American University, Washington, D. C., 1978) is the most thorough study of Turner's life.

[11] J. Milton Turner to F. A. Seely, July 17, 1869, BFRA, Letters Received, Registered Vol. 3, 1869 T-Z.

[12] J. Milton Turner to F. A. Seely, August 3, 1869, *ibid.*

**Oliver Otis Howard,
Bureau Commissioner**

sociation and the bureau. Turner served as the point man and liaison for these groups. For example, in late August Turner wrote to the county superintendent of schools of Madison County concerning the opening of a black school and the building of a schoolhouse in Fredericktown. He identified himself as an agent of the bureau but said he wrote on behalf of Professor Parker.[13] Turner often threatened recalcitrant school directors with the state superintendent's power to take over the administration of a school district that failed to comply with the law.[14] The American Missionary Association contributed many of the teachers for the schools established by Turner.[15]

J. Milton began his work near Boonville, his current home. He wrote Seely that there were three or four places within a few miles of there that needed his attention. He asked Seely to send a teacher identified as "Female Brown," but, if she did not want the position, Seely should send "the English woman." Turner needed a teacher for one school immediately. He also urged Seely to hasten his travel money so that he could visit Huntsville and Saline County.

---

[13] J. Milton Turner to Daniel Peterson, August 27, 1869, *ibid.*
[14] See for example, J. Milton Turner to F. A. Seely, October 23, 1869, *ibid.*
[15] See for example, J. Milton Turner to F. A. Seely, October 21, 1869, *ibid.*

Prodding Madison County directors had resulted in schools being opened in Fredericktown and Mine La Motte.[16]

Ten days later Turner described conditions in the Huntsville area. "I have succeeded in . . . frightening the Rebel Bd. of Ed. at this place to reopen the Colored School in Oct. But have not permission to supply them teachers." Turner expressed concern about what he might find in Roanoke, just ten or twelve miles south in Howard County. Both blacks and whites had warned him about going there. Undaunted, he wrote, "I shall know all its dangers in about 2 hours."[17] He survived the experience but failed to open a school. Two months later, Superintendent Parker still had the case before him.[18]

Ever on the move, Turner next investigated circumstances at Tipton. He found the board of education willing to open a school,

> . . . but quite anxious to employ an incompetent and very ignorant Negro man as teacher. I protested against him being employed, found the address of the Co. Supt. and wrote him a protest against granting this man a certificate. After some trouble the Bd. of Ed. consented to employ Mr. Thorn, a very good teacher and a white man.

At Sedalia, a competent teacher named Carter ran "a very poorly organized School." Turner observed, "I found him useing a cowhide quite liberally and requested him to banish it. He promised he would."[19]

While in the Pettis County city, Turner visited George P. Beard's normal school. Turner offered him "colored pupils." "I found him true blue and very willing to take them but his business is in poor condition, and I refused to send them because I knew it would effectivally stop the Normal School," he noted.[20]

Turner found black education "sadly neglected at Otterville" in Cooper County. The board of education claimed that fewer than fifteen blacks lived there. Turner counted more than the needed number and threatened to report the board to the state superintendent. The board chairman suggested that blacks must have moved into the township after the original count and asked for time to conduct another enumeration. Turner granted the re-

---

16 J. Milton Turner to F. A. Seely, September 7, 1869, *ibid.*

17 J. Milton Turner to F. A. Seely, September 17, 1869, *ibid.* Punctuation in quotes has been standardized; spelling has been unchanged.

18 J. Milton Turner to F. A. Seely, November 12, 1869, *ibid.*

19 J. Milton Turner to F. A. Seely, October 15, 1869, *ibid.*

20 *Ibid.*

quest. He described one member of the board as a Massachusetts man, a "practical Yankee and much more radical than I am but in the minority of the Bd. of Ed." Named E. D. Bailey and postmaster at Otterville, the Massachusetts man urged Turner to be firm with the board.[21]

Boards frequently failed to accurately count the black children in a township to avoid organizing schools for them. In a township south of Boonville Turner found thirty-two eligible students, whereas the board had counted fewer than fifteen. He ordered the township clerk to open a school within thirty days and threatened to report the situation to the state superintendent if he failed to comply.[22]

Difficulty in securing teachers for black schools probably frustrated Turner more than faulty township enumerations. He readily corrected the latter; he had less success with the former. At one point he observed that many districts would open schools if they could find teachers. He requested that Seely place a notice in a St. Louis newspaper that teaching positions were available through

---

[21] *Ibid.*
[22] J. Milton Turner to F. A. Seely, October 20, 1869, *ibid.*

*Lincoln Univ., Jefferson City, Mo.*

**J. Milton Turner**

him.[23] To support his contention, the Keytesville board in Chariton County opened a school when Turner supplied Jessee Newsome as a teacher.[24] Moreover, his letters are replete with requests to C. H. Howard of the AMA for teachers and the frustration of awaiting their arrival.[25]

He returned to Otterville on October 20. A new count revealed that forty black children lived in the township. Turner confronted the clerk of the school board with these figures, and the school official lamely explained that membership on the board had changed and that the books were in chaos. Perceptively, Turner evaluated the argument, "I saw quite easily that this statement was merely that of a man caught in an overt act but seemed not to see this fact." Turner also checked the township school fund and discovered plenty of money to operate a school. Caught, the clerk asked Turner to supply a teacher.[26]

Problems were not so easily resolved in Callaway County. The Fulton Board of Education agreed to open a school if it could "be furnished with a colored teacher who is also a minister." Turner promised to locate someone and wrote to the AMA. After consulting with a Major Clarke, however, he concluded that neither the town nor the county wanted competent teachers for black schools. County Superintendent Thomas A. Russell poisoned the atmosphere, according to Turner. He called Russell an "old idiot [who] should be in the Fulton lunatic Asylum instead of the Fulton Schools." When Turner protested against his policy, Russell informed him "that he would examine no negro applicant for a School nor would he grant any such applicant [a] certificate . . . ." Russell told Turner that a township board could employ anyone it chose to teach in a black school. So far as he was concerned, such a teacher need not know the English alphabet. When Turner asked the clerk of the county court for an enumeration, that "ungentlemanly" fellow asked to be paid for making the count and said that he would send the result directly to Professor Parker. Turner summarized his view of the town when he wrote, "Fulton is the meanest place and people I have ever seen."[27]

---

23 J. Milton Turner to F. A. Seely, October 16, 1869, *ibid.*
24 J. Milton Turner to F. A. Seely, October 20, 1869, *ibid.*
25 *Ibid.;* J. Milton Turner to F. A. Seely, October 23, 25, November 2, 5, 1869, BFRA, Letters Received, Registered Vol. 3, 1869 T–Z.
26 J. Milton Turner to F. A. Seely, October 21, 1869, *ibid.*
27 J. Milton Turner to F. A. Seely, October 23, 1869, *ibid.* In this instance and each instance hereafter, underlined words appear in the original.

After leaving hostile Callaway County, Turner stopped in Boonville on his way to Kansas City. Arriving home, he found his wife
suffering from a "congestive chill" that a physician thought would
turn into typhoid fever. Since Mrs. Turner taught in a black school
in Boonville, Turner wrote to C. H. Howard of the AMA for a
replacement.[28] In the crowded railroad coach on the way to Kansas
City, Turner lost his pocketbook containing $65.00.[29] He wired
Seely to please send him a check for $50.00 and to charge it against
his salary.[30] On a brighter note, upon arriving in Kansas City,
Turner registered at the Broadway Hotel; in his words, "a thing
I did not think possible."[31] A contemporary newspaper described
the hotel as "a splendid structure and an ornament to the city."
It contained 150 rooms and cost $100,000.00, and apparently did
not make it a practice to rent rooms to blacks.[32]

State Superintendent Parker had directed Turner to visit the
western part of the state, even though citizens of Liberty and In-

---

[28] J. Milton Turner to F. A. Seely, October 25, 1869, *ibid.*
[29] J. Milton Turner to F. A. Seely, October 27, 1869, *ibid.*
[30] Telegram, J. Milton Turner to F. A. Seely, October 27, 1869, *ibid.*
[31] J. Milton Turner to F. A. Seely, October 27, 1869, *ibid.*
[32] Columbia *Missouri Statesman,* November 12, 1869.

dependence had threatened to lynch him. At least that is what he wrote to Seely, and while in that area, he made no mention of visiting either of those communities.[33]

Instead, he attempted to reopen a school in Westport. After delays in finding the appropriate officials, Turner discovered a tangle in the school fund. The board claimed to have financed an earlier school for black children with funds designated for the support of white schools. Turner questioned that allegation. He had a white woman prepared to teach in the black school, but he doubted that the members of the board would accept her or any white teacher. He assured Seely that if the board failed to reopen the school he would recommend interference by the state superintendent.[34]

The problem of too few black teachers for black schools prompted Turner to stop in Sedalia on his way home. He discussed with Professor George Beard the conversion of his school into a normal school for blacks.[35] Failing to persuade Beard, Turner later helped to create a petition drive that resulted in a legislative appropriation to establish a normal department in the Lincoln Institute.[36]

Back in Cooper County, Turner encountered an unusual problem at Lone Elm Prairie. In that township the fifty black students lived in such a scattered pattern that the board of education had trouble choosing a building site "sufficiently central to be accessible to the greatest number of colored children in the Township."

---

33 J. Milton Turner to F. A. Seely, October 27, November 2, 1869, BFRA, Letters Received, Registered Vol. 3, 1869 T-Z.

34 J. Milton Turner to F. A. Seely, November 2, 1869, *ibid*.

35 J. Milton Turner to F. A. Seely, November 5, 1869, *ibid*.

36 J. Milton Turner to F. A. Seely, February 28, 1870, BFRA, Letters Received, Registered Vol. 4, 1870 L-Z.

**Black Homes**

Turner extracted a promise from the board of education that it would make arrangements for opening a school.[37]

Two days later, Turner took an English woman named Mrs. Emma Dodwell, probably the English woman mentioned earlier, to a consolidated school in rural Cooper County. Taking care of Mrs. Dodwell interrupted Turner's plan to drive to Arrow Rock. Blacks in that Saline County community had requested his presence. The energetic investigator decided to drive a buggy to Arrow Rock the next day and to take a night train to Jefferson City where he had scheduled a meeting with Parker. Turner had ten or twelve cases prepared for Parker's official interference.[38]

Turner's subtlety in dealing with people is illustrated in his approach to securing a black school in Arrow Rock. A Mr. Wilhelm represented the board of education, and he alleged that the board had been defrauded of money raised for the black school. As a consequence, the board could not build a schoolhouse, but it was willing to use funds belonging to white children to open a school for blacks in a black church that was under construction. Turner described his actions:

> I called a meeting of colored people and made them promise to complete the House in 15 days.
>
> I think old man Wilhelm talks most too kind to be relied upon, and I shall ask Mr. Parker to send him a 20 day notice . . . . I have told the colored people to tease old man Wilhelm untill he gives them a school that he may be rid of them. I think the school will be in operation in about 25 or 30 days.[39]

Other places shared the attitudes of Fulton rather than Arrow Rock and failed to yield to Turner's wiles. As planned he met with Parker in early November. "I have just concluded a very satisfactory interview with Prof. Parker," he wrote. "He is preparing to move on Fulton, Fayette, Roanoke and Rocheport and all such places."[40]

Conditions in New Madrid County in Southeast Missouri intrigued Turner. The teacher of a black school in the county accompanied him on the steamboat trip south and sought Turner's support for his school. Robert W. Stokes impressed Turner with his effort.

37 J. Milton Turner to F. A. Seely, November 6, 1869, BFRA, Letters Received, Registered Vol. 3, 1869 T-Z.
38 J. Milton Turner to F. A. Seely, November 8, 1869, *ibid.*
39 J. Milton Turner to F. A. Seely, November 9, 1869, *ibid.*
40 J. Milton Turner to F. A. Seely, November 12, 1869, *ibid.*

> From examination of his school house and grounds to-
> gether with such of his labors as I have had success of
> seeing during today, I have no hestitancy in pronouncing
> him <u>by far</u> the most enterprising and generally useful
> colored man I have met in all Missouri,

was his comment to Seely. The blacks in the area also impressed
Turner. He called them a "<u>highly intelligent</u>" set of men and noted
their prosperity. Blacks had erected their school building without
any assistance, but according to Turner "they do not seem as
thoroughly imbued with the importance of educating the children
among them as what their surroundings would bespeak." Still blacks
had the "very <u>best</u> school building in the county . . ." even though
it was unfinished and humble.[41]

After spending five days in the area, Turner failed to discover
any public school organization except for two directors, one "a
rabid Democrat" and one described as "ignorant." He visited the
towns of New Madrid and Point Pleasant, "which by the way,"
he remarked, "is the most <u>unpleasant</u> point I have visited since
the war." He continued, "There are other places I would like to
visit but my life has been threatened several times, and I fear
to go too far into the interior." He counted about four hundred
black children, noting that schools should be established at New
Madrid and Point Pleasant, "but judging from personal observance
I question the practicability of their being established at present . . . . It would be impossible for Stokes' school to exhist were
it not for the determination of the number of colored people in
its immediate neighborhood."

He proceeded to detail the history of the school:

> It was organized in Nov., 1867 by Robert W.
> Stokes. . . . In 1868 a number of colored citizens by united
> effort built a box school house . . . . In size the house is
> 22 x 30; it is unfinished within and without. It has no
> furniture and no apparatus for teaching. These colored men
> formed themselves into a school society. They elected from
> their number a local school board and assumed the sup-
> port and direction of the school . . . .

But the school currently shouldered a $645.00 debt that in Turner's
estimation the black population could not remove. He urged Seely
to provide funds for the school, "To give permanence to this school

---

41 J. Milton Turner to F. A. Seely, February 5, 1870, BFRA, Letters Received, Registered Vol. 4, 1870 L-Z. There is an unexplained gap in the correspondence between November 12, 1869, and this letter.

or to plant it firmly as the germ of a new life for this <u>anti-progressive</u> region does seem to me an indispensable necessity of the public safety." He wrote to both Parker and Oliver Otis Howard, Commissioner of the Freedmen's Bureau, soliciting their support for the school. Finally, Turner advised New Madrid blacks to organize the county school system by electing members of their race as school directors the next year.

As an aside, he alerted Seely to the practice of certain people, a Judge Riley, Louey Cline, Mark Sherwood and others, of visiting St. Louis's House of Refuge and taking "colored boys . . . and virtually enslaving them on their farms—without compensation."[42]

On his way back to St. Louis, Turner organized schools across the Mississippi River from Cairo, Illinois, and at Commerce in Scott County. He recruited a black named Mr. Lee from Cairo to conduct the former, describing him as having "<u>some</u> ability but not much proficiency."[43] In Commerce, Turner found the "children . . . so numerous and so very immoral" that he asked some of the leading blacks to sustain a school until a public supported one could be organized. They agreed and Turner recruited a black woman named Miss Reed as the teacher.[44]

Not long after his trip to Southeast Missouri, Turner received notice of his dismissal from Secretary of War W. W. Belknap. Why he lost his job is unclear, but he acknowledged being "abruptly discharged."[45] Within a few weeks he had accepted a teaching position at Lincoln University in Jefferson City, but when the possibility of his reemployment by the bureau surfaced, Turner wrote that he would accept it because, "I can accomplish more good in such a position than in the one I now occupy." Neither a twenty dollar per month reduction in pay nor a great sacrifice in personal comfort would deter him from returning to the bureau. A concrete offer failed to materialize, however, and he continued teaching at Lincoln.[46]

Turner summarized his work on behalf of black education in a long report to Seely. During his seven month tenure he traveled between eight and ten thousand miles, and prodded boards of education to spend between seven and nine thousand dollars "be-

---

42 J. Milton Turner to F. A. Seely, February 9, 1870, *ibid.*
43 J. Milton Turner to F. A. Seely, February 12, 1870, *ibid.*
44 J. Milton Turner to F. A. Seely, February 15, 1870, *ibid.*
45 J. Milton Turner to F. A. Seely, March 17, 1870, *ibid.*
46 J. Milton Turner to F. A. Seely, March 14, 17, May 9, 1870, *ibid.*

longing to the colored children as their <u>pro rata</u> share of the common school fund . . . ." He continued, "I have caused directly and indirectly the erection of Seven or Eight school houses and opened thirty-two schools in various parts of the state." Turner asserted, "Compared with other formerly slaveholding states, I find the general disposition of the community in this favorable to the education of colored children . . . ."

He noted, however,

> . . . that in such sections where the largest number of colored people are found there is a preponderance of disloyal and former slave holding people, who in most cases are opposed to the establishment of these schools. While this class of opponents do not openly and unreservedly declare their opposition to the establishment of such schools, they in various ways evade and impede the execution of the law providing for the educational interests of colored children. More intense disloyal neighborhoods rather than organize colored schools frequently render the law ineffectual by refusing to create in their school district any school organization whatever. In such cases I have found Hon. T. A. Parker, State Superintendent of Public Schools, ready to assume and exercise whenever possible the power delegated by the 25th section of the State School

Law.[47] The want of a cordial cooperation on the part of subordinate officers has frequently rendered his efforts ineffectual.

In many localities positive objections are raised by both white and colored inhabitants to the appointment of white teachers in colored schools. Whenever practicable I have respected this prejudice but owing to the scarcity of efficient teachers of my own color, [and] the opposition to white teachers being insurmountable the establishing of schools has been considerably hindered.

Without egotism I must in conclusion say that my duties in many sections of the state have been rendered arduous by the unyielding distaste evinced by those opposed to colored schools. A remedy for this condition of things I am at a loss to suggest unless it be the daily spread of more enlightened ideas as a permeating ingredient of an advancing civilization.

Turner concluded,

I take pleasure in being able to announce that the colored people generally are frugal and temperate, very anxious to be taught for which they are apparently ready to make considerable sacrifice. . . .[48]

---

47 This refers to the provision that allowed the state superintendent to take over school districts.

48 J. Milton Turner to F. A. Seely, February 28, 1870, BFRA, Letters Received, Registered Vol. 4, 1870 L-Z.

**Burning Freedmen's Schoolhouse**

Turner's letters provide students with the best contemporary treatment of the problems in establishing black schools in Missouri during Reconstruction. They show Turner to be an articulate, courageous, skilled and committed worker in the cause of black education. They also reveal that his personal efforts were complemented by the cooperation and commitment of T. A. Parker, C. H. Howard of the AMA and Colonel F. A. Seely of the Freedmen's Bureau. Unfortunately that team broke up in 1870. Turner, of course, left the bureau; Ira Divoll replaced Parker as state superintendent of schools; and the Freedmen's Bureau ceased its educational work.[49]

A sad letter from Robert Stokes, the New Madrid teacher, illustrated that the team had disbanded before the work was finished. On August 2, 1870, Stokes's school burned, and he received a warning in writing that he would be "treated in the same way." He described the blacks in New Madrid County as "disheartened" but desirous of rebuilding. Stokes pleaded,

> To do this however they need the encouragement of an extraneous friendly influence—a substantial helping hand, shewing to them that altho' dwelling in the midst of designs inimical to their rightful advancement, they are yet cared for by the forces of the progressive spirit of the age in which we live.[50]

Seely asked permission to appropriate $500.00 to rebuild the school.[51] That was the last Missouri letter in the file.

---

[49] David D. March, *The History of Missouri* (New York, 1967), II, 1082; John Hope Franklin, *Reconstruction After the Civil War* (Chicago, 1961), 38.

[50] Robert W. Stokes to F. A. Seely, August 25, 1870, BFRA, Letters Received, Registered Vol. 5, 1870 G-Z.

[51] F. A. Seely to E. Whittlesey, August 27, 1870, *ibid.*

---

# 'Our Little Circle': Benevolent Reformers, The Slater Fund, and The Argument For Black Industrial Education, 1882-1908

ROY E. FINKENBINE

The events of the Civil War years transformed some four million Black slaves into free men and women. Yet, ninety-six percent of them remained illiterate. The vast majority lacked any working knowledge of the American political process or the southern economy beyond the rudiments required to complete the day-to-day tasks of plantation agriculture. Immediately after the war, the Freedmen's Bureau and several northern Protestant missionary organizations embarked on the business of creating an educational system for the freedmen's community. A concern for Black literacy and a rudimentary education in the liberal arts dominated these initial efforts. But by the time the last federal troops left the South in 1877, this early movement for freedmen's education had become moribund —the Freedmen's Bureau was defunct, northern missionary enthusiasm was waning, and southern state and local governments were rapidly abandoning their responsibilities for freedmen's education. In this less than fertile ground, northern white philanthropy soon represented one of the few remaining avenues of hope.[1]

After Reconstruction ended, both southern white leaders and northern philanthropists sought a curriculum for Black schools that would help alleviate racial tension, encourage sectional harmony, and prepare the freedmen for their role in the emerging New South society. The industrial education model advocated by accommodationist Black leader Booker T. Washington appeared to be designed to meet those ends. As a result, the aforementioned leaders generalfy encouraged the movement toward industrial education that occurred in Black schools during the last two decades of the nineteenth century. Foremost among the northern philanthropic funds championing this change was the Slater Fund for the Education of Freedmen.

John Fox Slater, a Connecticut industrialist, established the Slater Fund in 1882. Motivated by a belief that education was vital if recently-emancipated southern Blacks were to become responsible participants in the political process, convinced that support for Black education could not be expected from southern whites, and aroused by the moderate success of the Peabody Fund — which had been created in 1867 to assist southern schools—Slater donated one million dollars

6

*The exterior of a Freedmen's school in Vicksburg, Mississippi. (from June 23, 1866* Harper's Weekly)

"for uplifting the lately emancipated population of the Southern states." To implement this goal, he named a distinguished board to administer his endowment and he allowed the members a free hand in setting the policies and practices of the Fund. Slater asked only that the monies of the Fund be distributed "in no partisan, sectional, or sectarian spirit."[2]

Anxious to meet their charge, members of the board met in late 1882 to establish objectives and procedures for the Slater Fund. This original board included a former president of the United States, the chief justice of the United States Supreme Court, a leading southern politician, two prominent Protestant clergymen, one of the foremost temperance advocates, two wealthy bankers, a university president, and Slater's son. Among their initial actions, members of the board selected Methodist clergyman Atticus G. Haygood of Georgia to be their general agent. A noted author, editor, preacher, and the president of Emory College, Haygood had written *Our Brother in Black,* a prescriptive discussion of southern race relations, the year before. As

agent, he was charged with distributing monies to various Black schools and colleges throughout the South, with visiting and inspecting the programs of recipients, and with making recommendations to the board.[3]

The board quickly determined to support Black industrial education, and continued to do so throughout its first two decades. Prior to an early board meeting, former President Rutherford B. Hayes, a board member, confided to his diary:

A few ideas seem to be agreed upon. Help none but those who help themselves. Educate only at schools which provide in some form for industrial education. These two points should be insisted upon. Let the normal instruction be that men must earn their own living, and that by the labor of their hands as far as may be. This is the gospel of salvation for the colored man. Let not the labor be servile, but in manly occupations like those of the carpenter, the farmer, and the blacksmith.[4]

7

The board resolved in 1883 to give preferential treatment in appropriations to institutions which provided instruction in agriculture, industrial skills, and other occupations which would "enable colored youth to make a living, and to become useful citizens."[5]

Largely due to the support of the Slater board, industrial education became the dominant curriculum in Black schools during the 1880s and 1890s. These institutions instructed Blacks in a variety of manual skills and occupations, including agriculture, the mechanical arts, domestic science, carpentry and other construction trades, leatherworking, and metalworking. Most of the industrial education offered by Black institutions in the decades following Reconstruction would be considered low-level "vocational" training today. There was little or no industrial training in the sense of preparing students to work or assume leadership roles in modernized industries. To many proponents of the industrial education curriculum, such manual training was more important as a means of teaching morals and work discipline than in preparing skilled artisans. But industrial education did offer many Blacks their first real educational opportunities.[6]

Between 1883 and 1886, the Slater board distributed over $100,000 to Black schools and colleges in the southern states, primarily to equip and operate manual training programs. Although Haygood noted extensive opposition to industrial education in his report to the board in 1883, by 1886 he observed that there were few Black schools and colleges that did not offer it in some form. By the 1887-88 academic year, the fund was spending more than $40,000 per year to aid industrial training programs in some forty-one schools. Under Haygood's guidance, the board used the promise of Slater funds to persuade reluctant institutions to adopt the curriculum. He admitted that it was the policy of the board to "bring all the best schools into line, in industrial education." And he used his influence in the division of Slater monies to control, punish, or rebuke recalcitrant schools. As a result, a shift from liberal arts to industrial education took place at many Black schools throughout the South during the 1880s. After Curry assumed the agency of the Slater Fund

*Hampton Institute as it appeared around 1870 shortly after its founding. (Hampton University's Archival and Museum Collection, Hampton University, Hampton, Virginia)*

8

*The books of Dr. Atticus G. Haygood, particularly* Our Brother in Black, *gave focus to the philosophy of the Slater Fund Trustees.*

in 1891, he convinced the board to turn its resources to funding a few model industrial schools like Hampton Institute in Virginia and Booker T. Washington's Tuskegee Institute in Alabama. By 1900 these two influential schools received one-half of the annual Slater appropriations.[7]

Historians have recognized the importance of the Slater Fund to the development of Black industrial education. August Meier declared that the Slater Fund was "the chief impetus in advancing the cause of industrial education during the 1880s."[8] In his study of Black education in postbellum Alabama, Robert G. Sherer demonstrated that the Slater Fund "was primarily responsible for the rise of industrial education in Alabama."[9] But no studies have concerned themselves with the personal motivations and ideologies responsible for fostering the Black industrial educa-

tion movement in the postbellum South, particularly the control wielded over the Slater Fund by a clique of five individuals: former President Rutherford B. Hayes, industrialist Morris K. Jesup, university president Daniel Coit Gilman, and southern educational spokesmen Atticus G. Haygood and Jabez L.M. Curry. In abbreviated form, this clique would influence Black industrial education in the South to 1908.

This circle emerged from Hayes's relationships with Curry, Gilman, Haygood, and Jesup, and its beginnings preceded the formation of the Slater Fund. Hayes and Curry had been roommates at Harvard Law School in the early 1840s. Just as Curry remembered Hayes as one of his "most valued friends and intimate associates while in law school," Hayes recalled that he had "loved" Curry during their Cambridge years. The friendship, temporarily dampened by geographic distance and the emotional strain generated by the sectional conflict, was rekindled in 1876-77 with Hayes's election to the presidency. Although a southern Democrat, Curry rejoiced at his former roommate's ascent to that high office, and Hayes reciprocated by offering Curry a place in his administration. Curry never served under Hayes, although he did advise him on certain political matters, including federal policy toward the South. But the association also had a distinctly personal side — Hayes and Curry were frequent confidential correspondents and occasional visitors during the years that Hayes was in the White House. Curry admitted that he "rejoice[d] with special vigor" whenever Hayes was able to break away from the duties of state to visit his Richmond home and reweave memories of college days at Harvard.[10]

Hayes and Gilman became close friends during the late 1870s. Although their relationship lacked the emotional intensity of the Hayes-Curry friendship, they frequently corresponded and Gilman advised Hayes on a few federal appointments. Hayes was an occasional guest at the Gilman home in Baltimore during his presidential years. Hayes's

9

friendships with Haygood and Jesup rapidly developed as a result of their philanthropic work for the Slater Fund. By the late 1880s, Hayes was able to refer to this cadre of friends on or around the fund as "our little circle" or "our circle." With Hayes as the hub, this circle functioned as an intellectual, emotional, and policymaking network.[11]

This circle controlled Slater Fund decision-making from the Fund's formation to 1908. Although small, it underwent a few changes in membership during that period. Curry, who was not a member of the Slater board until 1890, participated informally in the circle until 1885 when he accepted a diplomatic appointment to Spain. Upon his return three years later, he resumed his informal influence over Slater Fund affairs. Hayes eventually maneuvered his formal appointment to the board. Haygood grudgingly abandoned the circle for a California bishopric in 1891. Hayes died in 1893. Despite these departures, the "rump" clique of Curry, Gilman, and

*Dr. Jabez Lamar Monroe Curry, Hayes's roommate at Harvard Law School, served as the general agent both for the Peabody Educational Fund and the John F. Slater Fund. (from Edwin Anderson Alderman,* J. L. M. Curry *[1911])*

Jesup continued to function effectively for another decade. After Curry's death, Gilman and Jesup directed Slater Fund affairs for another five years.[12]

Significant discrepancies in background divided members of the Slater circle. Jesup and Gilman had been reared in urban Connecticut, Haygood and Curry in rural Georgia, and Hayes in a small Ohio town. Jesup and Gilman were the sons of northern businessmen, Haygood and Curry were the sons of southern slaveholders. Prior to Appomattox, the members of the circle had held opposing views on the major issues of the era — slavery and secession. Curry had owned slaves and defended slavery in Congress. Both Curry and Haygood had been rabid secessionists and had fought for the Confederacy. Jesup and Hayes had opposed the 'peculiar institution.' Jesup abandoned business dealings in Virginia during the 1850s because of

*Rutherford B. Hayes served as president of the board of trustees of the Slater Fund from its inception until his death in 1893.*

10

his distaste for slavery and slaveholders. As a young lawyer in antebellum Cincinnati, Hayes defended fugitive slaves. During the Civil War, he served as a general in the Union army.

Yet, members of the Slater circle shared several common characteristics. All came from strict evangelical Protestant family backgrounds and continued to be religiously active during their adult years. All except Jesup had a college education, were trained in one of the professions, and had participated in politics or the diplomatic service. All shared a deep interest in various national reform causes, including prison reform, civil service reform, conservation, education, juvenile delinquency, the poor, temperance, the suppression of 'indecent' literature, and the problems of American Indians and Blacks. These similarities of background, together with members' considerable occupational and geographical mobility during the postwar period, suggests the cosmopolitanism of those whom Hayes described as "our little circle."[13]

Despite the dissimilarity of their antebellum backgrounds and the geographic distance that separated them, this cosmopolitanism of members of the circle allowed them to function as an 'invisible college' or intellectual network. They penned frequent letters to each other, often sharing books, pamphlets, printed sermons, and newspaper clippings of mutual interest. These letters are filled with discussions of attitudes, beliefs, and policies regarding Black industrial education and a host of other national interests. In time, certainly by the late 1880s, the circle began to use a common benevolent language adopted from Haygood's *Our Brother in Black* to describe their efforts for Black industrial education. The freedmen were generally referred to as "our brother in black," while Black industrial education was commonly termed "uplift." The shift from liberal arts to industrial education in Black institutions was called a "revolution." These and other "code words" colored the speeches, letters, publications, and personal discussions of circle members. Both their intellectual network and their common

benevolent language helped them to function as a cohesive clique.[14]

The circle also functioned as an emotional support network, based upon male homosocial preferences. It was not unlike the nineteenth-century networks identified and studied by Drew Gilpin Faust, Lawrence J. Friedman, and Carroll Smith-Rosenberg.[15] Letters written between members of this "little circle" demonstrate the deep emotional attachment, intense mutual respect and concern, and desire for proximity that these men shared. Numerous letters tell of their "love" and "affectionate regards" for each other. Although these letters performed a major function in group life, members also endeavored to visit each other whenever they could. This emotional closeness was also manifested in other ways. Hayes worried about Curry's tendency to "overwork," and loaned Haygood significant sums of money. In 1903 Jesup hurried to the bedside of the dying Curry in order to comfort him. Hayes and Haygood exchanged personal photographs and valued them highly. Hayes assisted Curry in his hobby of collecting autographed letters written by prominent public figures. Such rituals encouraged group cohesiveness.[16]

More importantly, the circle functioned as a policymaking network. Circle members occupied the crucial leadership positions that allowed them to control the direction of the Slater board. Hayes served as president of the board from its inception until his death in 1893. Gilman, who had been the secretary of the board during the Fund's first twelve years, replaced him. He served until 1908, as did Jesup, the Fund's treasurer throughout its first twenty-seven years. The agents of the Fund — Haygood (1882-91) and Curry (1891-1903) — executed the policies of the board. Hayes clearly functioned as both the formal and informal leader of the circle. An unobtrusive leader, he advised and coordinated, sharing actual policymaking with other circle members. A skilled mediator, he was primarily responsible for keeping Haygood as Slater agent until 1891, then maneuvered the selection of Curry to succeed him. He evoked a high degree of genuine respect within the circle, ranging from the deep affection of Haygood to the dependable friendship of Gilman. His tolerance, personal involvement, commitment to group harmony, and rare but subtle chastisements promoted stable group relations. After Hayes's death, the "rump" clique of Curry, Gilman, and Jesup retained control of the policymaking process on the Slater board. As Curry noted to Gilman in 1894, "it seems that you and Mr. Jesup and myself will have as usual all the work to do." Clique size, intimacy, shared decisionmaking, and cohesiveness allowed Curry, Gilman, and Jesup to function together harmoniously after Hayes's death.[17]

As the agents of the Slater Fund, Haygood and Curry were largely responsible for its direction. An examination of their beliefs about Blacks demonstrates a consistent pattern of racial stereotyping. Often cast as a moderate on racial matters, Haygood's numerous books, articles, and speeches betray a strong belief in Black inferiority. Haygood was appalled by the "barbarous moral debasement" of Blacks. "Elements of evil and superstition," he asserted, characterized Black religion. He posited that Blacks had only a vague notion of religious dogma. Black liturgies, he observed, were "attended with many follies and extravagances, many mistakes and wastes of power, in some cases with exhibitions of fanatical superstition." Such "extravagances," Haygood believed, also dominated Black family life. He was particularly troubled by the marital and sexual attitudes and activities he observed in the freedmen's community. "Loose notions and looser practices as to the marriage relation," he alleged, exemplified Black family life, which was hampered by immodesty, infidelity, sexual depravity, and licentiousness. To Haygood, Black family life clearly lacked "domestic virtue and family purity." Compounding this problem, he argued, was the excessive use of ardent spirits by Black males. Drunken Blacks, he alleged, created problems in the Black family and menaced white womanhood. This prompted him to justify the practice of

*Daniel Coit Gilman, one of the original trustees of the Slater Fund, was the first president of Johns Hopkins University. (from Franklin Fabian,* The Life of Daniel Coit Gilman *[1910])*

lynching in the South.

Haygood did note a few positive qualities among southern Blacks, but these tended to reinforce the corollary image of Blacks as kind-hearted, good-tempered, happy-go-lucky Sambos. Yet, most of the traits that Haygood observed in Blacks simply supported his stereotype of Blacks as savages. To him, the freedmen's community appeared to be ignorant, immoral, indolent, improvident, wasteful, and given to base, instinctual desires. Even Black professionals, including teachers and preachers, were not exempted from this image. According to Haygood, Blacks were by their very nature "crude," primitive, and tending toward savagery. Although Haygood took solace in the belief that the Black apprenticeship in slavery had formed a "habit of submission" and a fear of "white man's vengeance" in the race, he feared that schooling Blacks in the liberal arts would

12

breed discontent among them, just as he perceived that it had among northern urban immigrants "whose murmurings hint of suppressed earthquakes." The wrong kind of education, Haygood argued, would destroy Black docility and loose Black savagery upon the South.[18]

Curry shared Haygood's stereotypical view of Blacks. He characterized Black workers as "stupid, indolent, shiftless . . . with a low tone of morality." He asserted that Blacks had "loose notions of piety and morality and with strong racial peculiarities and proclivities . . . had not outgrown the feebleness of the moral sense which is common to all primitive races." Throughout his writings and speeches, Curry stereotyped Black behavior again and again as ignorant, immoral, superstitious, wasteful, and lacking in foresight. Of Black religion, he wrote:

> The discipline of virtue, the incorporation of creed into personal life, is largely wanting, and hence physical and hysterical demonstrations, excited sensibilities, uncontrolled emotions, transient outbursts of ardor, have been confounded with the graces of the Spirit and of faith based on knowledge. Contradiction, negation, paradox and eccentricity are characteristics of the ignorant and the superstitious, especially when they concern themselves with religion.[19]

To Curry, Blacks were immoral, irrational, instinctual beings. On occasion, this belief prompted him to view the moral and economic uplift of southern Blacks as "hopeless" and to express doubts as to the feasibility of Black industrial education. Certainly, he believed, that the race problem was the greatest issue that Western civilization had encountered and this made the curricular choice for Black education one of vital importance.[20]

Haygood's and Curry's fear of Black savagery and desire for docile Black behavior was confirmed by what they believed to have occurred during the era of Reconstruction. They accepted the myth that the decade following the Civil War was a period in which northern Radicals and southern Blacks successfully collaborated to dominate and exploit southern whites. Although both remembered slavery as too repressive, they observed that the social system which had replaced it was insufficiently repressive. As a result, this Black-Radical coalition had wreaked "incalculable mischief" on the white South. The end result of this travail had been temporary white "subordination to the black race." Both Haygood and Curry argued that Blacks must be strictly controlled. Curry even implicitly justified efforts at intimidating Blacks, such as those employed by the Ku Klux Klan during Reconstruction. He noted that when "negro dominancy" occurred, whites could use "no measures too . . . severe."[21]

Although less overtly concerned with Black savagery, Hayes, Jesup, and Gilman shared Haygood and Curry's stereotyped image of southern Blacks. Hayes concluded that Blacks lacked "the thrift, the education, the morality, and the religion required to make a prosperous and intelligent citizenship." He once characterized Black oratory as their singular talent as a race. Gilman claimed that Black culture was fraught with "error" — lacking acceptable social and sexual mores and attitudes toward work. But despite their ethnocentrism and accompanying paternalism, Hayes and Gilman differed from their southern colleagues in their willingness to credit Blacks with the ability for improvement as a race. Both believed that the freedmen's racial attributes might be altered through proper education. On the other hand, Jesup, like Haygood and Curry, seems to have accepted Black inferiority as innate and irreversible. Labelling Blacks as ignorant, improvident, thriftless, and imitative, he argued that, separated from the "refining influence" of whites, they would revert to their "native condition" of savagery.[22]

But because they shared an ethnocentric and stereotypical view of southern Blacks, and a common craving for a solution to the race question, members of the Slater circle endorsed the movement toward legal segrega-

13

*The foundation for a new building at Tuskegee is laid by workmen, most of whom were students at this industrial school. (from Booker T. Washington,* Tuskeegee and Its People: Their Ideals and Achievements *[1906])*

*Hampton students of various ages learn tailoring skills during the late 19th century. (Hampton University's Archival and Museum Collection, Hampton University, Hampton, Virginia)*

14

tion of the races that occurred throughout the South in the decades after Reconstruction. Fifteen years before Booker T. Washington's Atlanta Exposition speech, which accepted the segregated nature of southern life, Hayes declared:

> We would not undertake to violate the laws of nature, we do not wish to change the purpose of God in making these differences of nature. We are willing to have these elements of our population [whites and blacks] separate as the fingers are, but we rejoice to see them united for every good work, for National defense, one, as the hand.[23]

Historians George Sinkler and Rayford W. Logan have employed Hayes's defense of segregation as an explanation of his willingness to abandon Reconstruction upon ascending to the Presidency. Like Hayes, the rest of his "little circle" also sought segregation along racial lines. None of the members demonstrated a commitment to social equality between Blacks and whites. Haygood used the analogy of oil's insolubility in water to explain and defend southern segregation. He argued that segregation was a social device which both Blacks and whites desired. Blacks, he perceived, wanted to be separate from whites due to "instinct." Hayes, Haygood, and the other members of the circle believed that laws enforcing segregation protected both races from those who sought to alter radically race relations in the South.[24]

Haygood and Curry reflected the circle's advocacy of segregation in their administration of the fund. From the beginning of his agency, Haygood exhibited a preference for segregated schools, arguing that they were "best for all parties." He found it inconceivable that coracial education could prove successful in uplifting southern Blacks. Nor did Blacks favor the prospect, he argued, claiming that "black children . . . don't want to sit at the same desks with white children." For this reason, he used his influence in the division of the monies of the fund to punish Blacks who defied southern segregation prac-

tices. The clearest example was Haygood's reaction to William Hooper Councill's violation of the prevailing racial code. Councill had first obtained Slater subsidies in 1884 while serving as principal of the Huntsville (Alabama) Normal School. Councill had later resigned his position under pressure after two separate incidents in which he and his students attempted to sit in the "white" car on a train and had been ejected. When the Alabama Black was restored to the principalship in 1888, Haygood refused additional grants to the school. He advised Hayes that "we can make better use of the $600. Councill's use of the money in his day was not satisfactory." After Curry accepted the agency of the fund in 1891, he continued his predecessor's *de facto*

*William Cooper Councill, president of Alabama's Huntsville Normal School, incurred the displeasure of Atticus Haygood by openly demonstrating against segregation. As a result, the school lost grant money from the Slater Fund. (from G. F. Richings,* Evidences of Progress Among Colored People *[1897])*

15

policy of not funding coracial schools.[25]

Circle members believed the physical separation of the races to be a natural phenomenon. Haygood spoke for the others when he asserted:

> There never was in this world, in any nation or community, such a thing as social equality, and there never will be. The social spheres arrange themselves to suit themselves, and no laws promulgated by State or church will change the special affinities and natural selections of men. Men choose the circles for which they have affinity, seek companionships they prefer, and find the places that are suited to them.[26]

Segregation, according to Haygood, was a predictable result of human interaction. Like the other members of the circle, he posited that the structure of southern segregation had developed as it did because of the inferiority of the Black race. Whites, according to this line of reasoning, were the natural leaders of southern society. As Curry told southern educators at the Capon Springs Conference in 1899, "The white people are to be the leaders to take the initiative, to have the directive control in all matters pertaining to civilization and the highest interests of our beloved land. History demonstrates that the Caucasian will rule. He ought to rule." He went on to note in his speech that white supremacy did not mean "hostility to the negro, but friendship for him." Curry's advocacy of white supremacy, the most radical of any of the members of the circle, was sufficiently extreme to allow him to develop a close friendship with Ben Tillman, the Negrophobe governor of South Carolina during the 1890s. But the other members of the circle must also be categorized as white supremacists.[27]

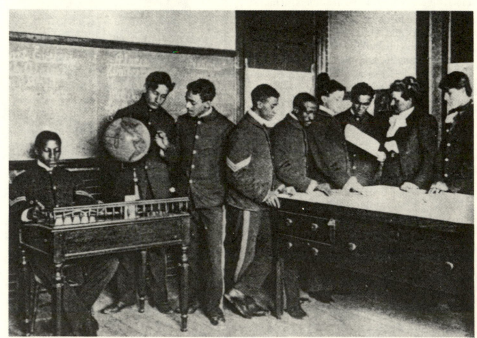

*In addition to Black students, Native Americans, several of whom can be seen in this social studies class from the 1880s, also attended Hampton Institute. (Hampton University's Archival and Museum Collection, Hampton University, Hampton, Virginia)*

16

White supremacy was not a rationale used by circle members to justify abandoning southern Blacks. Rather, they argued, it created a set of paternalistic obligations for white leaders — whites should ostensibly oversee Black institutions in order to provide proper direction. This was especially true of Black education. Haygood expressed concern that "the Negroes show so marked a desire to control the colleges built for their benefit that their friends are anxious lest the impatience of the very people they labor for should mar their best planned efforts to help them." The accommodationist Booker T. Washington's management of Tuskegee Institute seems to have been the sole exception to the circle's desire for white control of Black schools. Only during Washington's extended absence from Tuskegee in 1896 did Curry observe that the institution was "showing the effect of exclusive negro management and of the constant absence of Mr. Washington." But whenever possible, members of the circle determined, Black students should be taught by southern whites. It seemed to them to be divinely ordained. It was, in Hayes's view, the "grave and indispensable duty" of "every [white] Christian" to assist southern Blacks. In good biblical tone, Haygood asserted that southern whites were to be "the keepers of our 'brothers in black.'" He even suggested that "Providence" had placed Blacks in the South so that they might learn the lessons of western civilization from the superior white race. For these white reformers, Black education was a mandated stewardship, not a matter of choice.[28]

The degradation of slavery, Black cultural differences, and the events of the Reconstruction years had produced in the minds of circle members a fear of Black savagery. As benevolent paternalists, they favored the approach of educating and socializing Blacks for their role in southern society. Haygood, Curry, and Jesup sought a curriculum designed to ensure Black docility. Hayes and Gilman envisioned the uplifting of the Black race. Whatever the approach, they all agreed that Black savagery posed a serious threat to

*Dynamic and purposeful, Booker T. Washington presided over Tuskegee Institute for 34 years. (from Mary Helm,* The Upward Path *[1909])*

southern white culture. Hayes voiced the fear that "reconstruction has not yet been finished . . . while millions of freemen, with votes in their hands, are left without education." Something needed to be done. The solution they agreed upon, in the words of Gustavus R. Glenn, Georgia commissioner of education, was to find and encourage a curriculum designed to "educate the beast out of the negro." Like Glenn, members of the circle soon supported the industrial education curriculum developed at Hampton Institute and Tuskegee Institute and argued that the solution to the race question and the salvation of southern society lay in the extension of the Hampton-Tuskegee method. To their mind, no other form of schooling would suffice in restraining southern Blacks. Black education in the liberal arts would merely breed discontent among members of the race and ill prepare them for their role. Only industrial

17

education would fit Blacks for the "responsibilities of citizenship, and save them and our institutions from the perils of ill understood liberty and ignorant and reckless use of the franchise." Curry perhaps stated the circle rationale best when he warned the Alabama legislature in 1885 that Blacks must be educated properly "or they will drag us down."[29]

The industrial education model provided an answer to this dilemma. Hayes's "little circle" soon voiced an unmitigated preference for the education model developed by Samuel Chapman Armstrong at Hampton and copied by Tuskegee and sister institutions. Armstrong's curriculum, Hayes proclaimed, "hits the nail on the head. It solves the whole negro problem." Circle members were attracted by the twin emphasis on industrial **and** moral education that characterized the curriculum at the Virginia school. As Slater educational theory developed during the 1880s, it became clear to circle members that industrial education could employ objectives that included proper personal discipline and moral improvement, in addition to training in agricultural, industrial, and domestic skills. And it did not challenge the underlying tenets of segregation or white supremacy. Such an education could train a future generation of conservative Black leaders. It would fit them "for the places they are to fill in life."[30] It is particularly instructive to note that the curriculum prepared students to become farmers, industrial laborers, construction workers, and domestic servants. Even Black leaders were not to be trained for careers beyond traditional Black roles.

Circle members shared a belief in the positive ends that Black industrial education would achieve. Like many postbellum educators, they claimed that manual training would foster orderly and docile Black behavior. In his speeches on the subject, Hayes frequently argued that industrial education would promote conservative tendencies in students. Gilman observed that it would have a modifying, sobering influence on Blacks and create order and discipline in the Black

community. Haygood assured educators of both races that the industrial education curriculum "fosters good discipline." Curry was even more direct. In 1892 he reported to the Slater Board that industrial education was proving "advantageous in restraining appetites and preventing vicious indulgences" among Blacks. But all of the members of the circle hoped that the discipline gained by Black students in manual labor schools would eventually assist in restraining the supposed savagery of the entire race. Hayes suggested that a major benefit of Black industrial education would be its usefulness in preventing criminal behavior within the Black community. This notion took on increasing importance, he noted, as ever greater numbers of Blacks flocked to southern cities. Hayes spoke to many of the same fears of unrestrained urban Black communities that had troubled antebellum whites and ultimately led to the development of residential segregation in many southern cities during the opening decades of the twentieth century.[31]

Foremost among the elements of personal discipline that circle members hoped to develop in Black students was a proper attitude toward work. They theorized that the industrial education curriculum would teach Blacks the value of labor and develop appropriate work habits. This training was necessary, they believed, to destroy the characteristic indolence that Blacks had allegedly manifested during slavery times and after. In 1890 Curry outlined for the Louisiana legislature the work discipline that industrial educators valued. This included training "the will into habits of industry and temperance, in the virtues of punctuality, order, and good behavior." By this means, industrial education would mold Blacks into "more useful members of society." What circle members desired from Blacks was nothing less than a thorough acceptance of the Protestant work ethic and the complete abandonment of traditional African work rhythms. They assumed that providing southern Blacks with the proper work discipline would limit racial discord in the South, develop a tractable Black labor

*Students learn millinery skills at Tuskegee. (from Booker T. Washington,* Tuskegee and Its People: Their Ideas and Achievements *[1906])*

force, encourage sectional harmony, attract northern capital, and cause southern industries and railroads to flourish. Their advocacy of Black industrial education harmonized easily with the philosophy of the New South movement.[32]

A corollary of the circle's emphasis on Black work discipline was the belief that something needed to be done for the "moral uplifting of the negroes." Curry summarized the Slater philosophy in 1894 when he wrote to Gilman that a "model" industrial education curriculum must encourage "good order, discipline, a healthy moral atmosphere." Circle members believed that educating Blacks in the dominant Euro-American moral code would help ensure docile Black behavior, provide an underlying philosophical basis for Black work discipline, and eliminate undesirable Black cultural practices and values. They recognized that moral education was a crucial component of the Hampton model. Hayes typified the thought of circle members

when he suggested that Black industrial education should include the "proper cultivation . . . of . . . the heart." He and the "little circle" believed that this moral "cultivation" must encourage Black honesty, respect for property, thrift, accumulation, orderly family life, strict sexual mores and behavior, and proper notions of religion. Jesup observed that if Blacks internalized these dominant white values, they could learn to "imitate" white behavior, thus tempering the savage instincts of their race.[33] Black students, then, were to be trained as Victorian moralists, albeit with a black skin and a southern accent.

Despite their racial stereotyping and desire for docile Black behavior, the members of the Slater circle can be characterized as benevolent reformers. This matches their own perceptions. Circle members consistently couched their discussions of Black industrial education in a rhetoric of missionary endeavor, referring to themselves as "missionaries" and their efforts as a "mission," "moral reform," and a

19

"sacred" venture. Haygood compared their work to that of American missionaries abroad, including the career of his sister Laura Askew Haygood in China. And Hayes's "little circle" seems to have functioned as a reform community. Through the intimacy born of the intellectual and emotional support provided by the clique, the leadership of Hayes and Gilman, a common benevolent language, and a common commitment to Black industrial education, this reform community endured from 1882 to 1908. Yet like Mr. Norton, the white philanthropist in Ralph Ellison's *Invisible Man,* the language of "innocent words" that they fashioned masked their true, if unconscious, motives.[34] Unlike Ben Tillman and other virulent racists, they clothed their acceptance of white supremacy in benevolent trappings. But like these Negrophobes, they feared Black savagery and craved docile Black behavior. These fears motivated their argument for Black industrial education. From our late twentieth-century perspective, their claims as benevolent reformers have a hollow ring.

The Slater Fund, which began contributing money to Tuskegee Institute in 1883, would have probably helped to furnish this science building upon its completion. (from Max Bennett Thrasher, Tuskegee: Its Story and Its Work [1901])

20

# Footnotes

[1] For an overview of freedmen's education in the South during Reconstruction, see Robert C. Morris, *Reading, 'Riting, and Reconstruction: The Education of Freedmen in the South, 1861-1870* (Chicago, 1981); Ronald E. Butchardt, *Northern Schools, Southern Blacks, and Reconstruction: Freedmen's Education, 1862-1875* (Westport, Conn., 1980); and Joe M. Richardson, *Christian Reconstruction: The American Missionary Association and Southern Blacks, 1861-1890* (Athens, 1986).

[2] Louis D. Rubin, *Teach the Freeman: The Correspondence of Rutherford B. Hayes and the Slater Fund for Negro Education, 1881-1893*, 2 vols. (Baton Rouge, 1959), 1:xx; Merle Curti and Roderick Nash, *Philanthropy in the Shaping of American Higher Education* (New Brunswick, N.J., 1965), 173.

[3] Rubin, *Teach the Freeman*, 1:xviii-xix, xxi.

[4] Charles R. Williams, ed., *Diary and Letters of Rutherford B. Hayes*, 5 vols. (Columbus, 1922-26), 4:88.

[5] *Proceedings of the John F. Slater Fund for the Education of Freedmen, 1883* (Baltimore, 1883), 7.

[6] August Meier, *Negro Thought in America, 1880-1915: Racial Ideologies in the Age of Booker T. Washington* (Ann Arbor, 1964), 87-89.

[7] *Report of the Commissioner of Education for the Year 1885-86* (Washington, 1887), 651; *Proceedings of the Slater Fund, 1883*, 14; Meier, *Negro Thought in America*, 90; Rubin, *Teach the Freeman*, 1:xxviii, 92; *Twentieth Annual Report of the Freedmen's Aid Society of the Methodist Episcopal Church for 1887* (Cincinnati, 1887), 14; *Twenty-Second Annual Report of the Freedmen's Aid Society of the Methodist Episcopal Church* (Cincinnati, 1889), 14; Elam Frank Dempsey, *Atticus Greene Haygood* (Nashville, 1940), 291-92; Harold W. Mann, *Atticus Greene Haygood: Methodist Bishop, Editor, and Educator* (Athens, 1965), 185, 187; Dwight O. Holmes, *The Evolution of the Negro College* (College Park, Md., 1934), 170.

[8] Meier, *Negro Thought in America*, 98.

[9] Sherer, *Subordination or Liberation?: The Development and Conflicting Theories of Black Education in Nineteenth Century* (Alabama University, 1977), 64.

[10] J. L. M. Curry, "Recollections and Reflections: Rutherford B. Hayes," *Religious Herald* (9 January 1902), 2; Notes for Autobiography, Book 1, 43, J. L. M. Curry Papers, Library of Congress (hereafter referred to as JLMCP); Curry to Rutherford B. Hayes, 9 August, 26 September, 10 October, 1877; 15 February, 11 March, 1879, Rutherford B. Hayes Papers, Rutherford B. Hayes Presidential Center (hereafter referred to as RBHP); Jessie Pearl Rice, *J. L. M. Curry: Southerner, Statesman, and Educator* (New York, 1949), 83.

[11] Daniel Coit Gilman to Hayes, 23 January, 1879; 4 December, 1880; 27 January, 1881, RBHP; Hayes to Gilman, 15 February, 1881, Daniel Coit Gilman Papers, Milton S. Eisenhower Library, Johns Hopkins University (hereafter referred to as DCGP); *Proceedings of the Slater Fund, 1888*, 4; *Proceedings of the Slater Fund, 1889*, 4.

[12] Biographical information on members of the Slater circle can be found in the hundreds of letters in JLMCP, RBHP, and DCGP. Many of these are reprinted in Rubin, *Teach the Freeman*. Additional information can be gleaned from the clippings, letters, and miscellaneous items in the Atticus G. Haygood Papers, Robert W. Woodruff Library, Emory University (hereafter referred to as AGHP). Helpful printed sources include Kenneth E. Davison, *The Presidency of Rutherford B. Hayes* (Westport, Conn., 1972); Harry Barnard, *Rutherford B. Hayes and His America* (Indianapolis, 1954); David P. Thelen, "Rutherford B. Hayes and the Reform Tradition in the Gilded Age," *American Quarterly* 22 (Summer 1970), 150-65; Mann, *Atticus Greene Haygood*; Rice, *J. L. M. Curry*; Fabian Franklin, *The Life of Daniel Coit Gilman* (New York, 1910); and Abraham Flexner, *Daniel Coit Gilman: Creator of the American Type of University* (New York, 1946). The best available source on Jesup is "Jesup, Morris Ketchum," *Dictionary of American Biography* (1964), 5:61-62.

[13] Geoffrey Blodgett convincingly employs occupational and geographic mobility as indices of cosmopolitanism in studying another nineteenth-century reform circle. See Blodgett, "Reform Thought and the Genteel Tradition," in *The Gilded Age*, ed. H. Wayne Morgan (Syracuse, 1970), 55-76.

[14] For a detailed discussion of the Slater circle as an intellectual, emotional, and policymaking network, see Roy E. Finkenbine, "A Little Circle: White Philanthropists and Black Industrial Education in the Postbellum South" (Ph.D. diss., Bowling Green State University, 1982), 74-94.

[15] Faust, *A Sacred Circle: The Dilemma of the Intellectual in the Old South, 1840-1860* (Baltimore, 1977); Friedman, "Confidence and Pertinacity in Evangelical Abolitionism: Lewis Tappan's Circle," *American Quarterly* 31 (Spring 1979), 81-106; Smith-Rosenberg, "The Female World of Love and Ritual: Relations Between Women in Nineteenth-Century America," *Signs* 1 (Autumn 1975), 1-29.

[16] Hayes to Curry, 8 January, 1891; 12 November, 1892, JLMCP; Rubin, *Teach the Freeman*, 1:105, 2:151; Rice, *J. L. M. Curry*, 180.

[17] Rubin, *Teach the Freeman*, 1:xxxi-xxxii; Morris K. Jesup to Gilman, 24 August [1890], DCGP.

21

[18]Morton Sosna, *In Search of the Silent South: Southern Liberals and the Race Issue* (New York, 1977), 7; Haygood, address delivered at the Gammon School of Theology, Atlanta, Georgia, 27 October, 1886, AGHP; Haygood, *Our Brother in Black: His Freedom and His Future* (Miami, 1969), 11-15, 29, 221; Haygood, *Sermons and Speeches* (Nashville, 1883), 356; Haygood, *Pleas for Progress* (Nashville, 1889), 28, 37, 49; Haygood, "How He Makes His Way," in *Speeches Delivered at Monteagle and Chautauqua* (1883), n.p.; Haygood, "Hand as Well as Head and Heart Training," address delivered at Holly Springs, Mississippi, 10 March, 1885, 1, 7, AGHP; Haygood to Gilman, 10 August, 1887, RBHP; Mann, *Atticus Greene Haygood,* 156; Isabel C. Barrows, ed., *First Mohonk Conference on the Negro Question* (Boston, 1890), 85; *Proceedings of the Slater Fund, 1883,* 12-13; Haygood, "The Negro Pulpit," *Wesleyan Christian Advocate* 54, n.s. 12 (8 January, 1890), 1.

[19]Curry, *Address Delivered to the General Assembly of Georgia* (Atlanta, 1889), 9-10; Curry, *Difficulties, Complications, and Limitations Connected With the Education of the Negro,* Slater Fund Occasional Papers, no. 5 (Baltimore, 1895), 5.

[20]Harvey Wish, "Negro Education and the Progressive Movement," *Journal of Negro History* 49 (July 1964), 185; Curry to Robert Winthrop, 18 June, 1894, JLMCP; Curry, *Difficulties Connected With Negro Education,* 5.

[21]Curry, speech to Pennsylvania Society of New York, 31 October, 1899, JLMCP; Curry to Hayes, 7 November, 1879, RBHP; Rice, *J. L. M. Curry,* 83; Curry, address delivered to the Senate and House of Representatives of Alabama, 1 February, 1889, 13, JLMCP.

[22]Barrows, *First Mohonk Conference,* 10, 54-55; Hayes, speech delivered at Hampton Institute, 23 May, 1878 (reprinted in *Southern Workman* 7 [June 1878], 46); Wish, "Negro Education," 15; Gilman, *A Study in Black and White,* Slater Fund Occasional Papers, no. 10 (Baltimore, 1897), 5.

[23]Hayes, speech delivered at Hampton Institute, 20 May, 1880 (reprinted in *Southern Workman* 9 [June 1880], 68).

[24]Sinkler, "Race: Principles and Policies of Rutherford B. Hayes," *"Ohio History* 77 (Winter-Spring-Summer 1968), 166; Logan, *The Negro in American Life and Thought: The Nadir, 1877-1901* (New York, 1954), 29-36; Haygood, *Our Brother in Black,* 232-33.

[25]Haygood, *Our Brother in Black,* 144; Sherer, *Subordination or Liberation?,* 10, 37-38; Rubin, *Teach the Freeman,* 2:19-20; Rice, *J. L. M. Curry,* 104.

[26]Haygood, "The Education of the Negro," in *Speeches Delivered at Monteagle and Chautauqua,* n.p.

[27]*Proceedings of the Second Capon Springs Conference for Education in the South* (Raleigh, N.C., 1899), 38; Curry to Gilman, 20 February, 5 December, 1894, DCGP. Several letters from the Curry-Tillman correspondence are in the JLMCP.

[28]Barrows, *First Mohonk Conference,* 9, 85; Curry to Gilman, 9 March 1896, DCGP; Hayes to Curry, 11 February 1891, JLMCP; Haygood, *Our Brother in Black,* 148; Haygood, "The Southern Church and the Negro," *Cumberland Presbyterian Review* 1 (April, 1889), 140-41.

[29]Haygood, *Pleas for Progress,* 11-12; Hayes speech delivered at Springfield, Ohio, 30 May, 1884, RBHP; Gustavus R. Glen to Curry, [January 1892], JLMCP; Curry, *Address Delivered to the Senate and House of Representatives of Alabama, February 6, 1885* (Montgomery, 1885), 9.

[30]Hayes, speech delivered at Hampton Institute, 20 May, 1880, 68; *Proceedings of the Slater Fund, 1883,* 14; Haygood, "Industrial Education for the Negro," in *Twenty-First Annual Report of the Freedmen's Aid and Southern Education Society of the Methodist Episcopal Church* (Cincinnati, 1888), 61; Hayes, speech delivered before the Education Convention, Toledo, Ohio, 5 December, 1885, RBHP.

[31]Hayes, speech delivered at the Toledo Manual Training School, 7 October, 1884, RBHP; Gilman, *Study in Black and White,* 8, 12; Isabel C. Barrows, ed., *Second Mohonk Conference on the Negro Question* (Boston, 1891), 16; *Proceedings of the Slater Fund, 1892,* 9; Hayes, speech delivered at Vanderbilt University, 17 November, 1889, RBHP; Hayes, speech delivered at the Toledo High School, 22 March, 1888, RBHP. For a discussion of southern white fears of unrestrained urban Black communities, see Richard C. Wade, *Slavery in the Cities: The South, 1820-1860* (New York, 1964), 243-81; and Lawrence J. Friedman, *The White Savage: Racial Fantasies in the Postbellum South* (Englewood Cliffs, N.J., 1970), 119-20.

[32]Hayes, speech delivered before the Findlay Conference, 14 November, 1888, RBHP; Curry, *Address Delivered Before the General Assembly of Alabama* (n.p.), 5; *Proceedings of the Slater Fund, 1891,* 19. For a discussion of the thought of circle members on southern economic development and sectional harmony, see Finkenbine, "A Little Circle," 135-45.

[33]Haygood, *Our Brother in Black,* 129, 157, 182, 189, 243; Curry to Gilman, 8 November, 1894, DCGP; Hayes, speech delivered at Vanderbilt University, 18 November, 1889; Barrows, *Second Mohonk Conference,* 55; Curry, *Difficulties Connected With Negro Education,* 22-23; Haygood, *Sermons and Speeches,* 390.

[34]Hayes to Curry, 4 December, 1891, JLMCP; *proceedings of the Slater Fund, 1891,* 16, 18; Haygood, "The Gospel Among the Slaves," *Wesleyan Christian Advocate* 58, n.s. 16 (12 July, 1894), 3; Ellison, *Invisible Man* (New York, 1972), 110.

22

# Stability and Change in Discrimination Against Black Public Schools: Birmingham, Alabama, 1871–1931

By CARL V. HARRIS

EVERYWHERE IN THE POSTBELLUM SOUTH THE BLACK PUBLIC schools were separate and inferior, but the rate of discrimination against black students varied significantly from place to place and from decade to decade. Most studies of the chronology of school discrimination have dealt with entire states and have focused on rural areas, where the majority of southerners, black and white, lived. But recent scholarship has called notice to the postbellum southern city as a crucial arena for setting the twentieth-century pattern of southern race relations,[1] and this article focuses on the chronological pattern of stability and change in school discrimination in one major New South city – Birmingham, Alabama – from Reconstruction to the Great Depression. It seeks also to explore the array of political, organizational, economic, financial, and ideological factors that shaped

[1] Both Richard C. Wade and C. Vann Woodward, in separate forewords to the two editions of Howard N. Rabinowitz's recent study, *Race Relations in the Urban South, 1865-1890* (New York, 1978; Urbana, Ill., 1980), have called attention to the crucial role of the city in postbellum southern race relations. Wade pointed out that after emancipation the southern cities had to cope with numerous new issues of dealing with their increasing numbers of black citizens, and he observed, "The countryside had no such crisis. Space maintained racial distance; local governments had modest responsibilities, largely confined to education, alms and roads; scattered populations prevented the development of cohesive black communities. Cities, then, would necessarily define the new racial relations in the South" (pp. ix–x, 1978 edition). Also John W. Cell in *The Highest Stage of White Supremacy: The Origins of Segregation in South Africa and the American South* (Cambridge, Eng., and other cities, 1982) has argued that the emergence of the social system and the ideology of segregation that would characterize the twentieth-century South was correlated with the emergence of industrialization and urbanization, and that the new towns of the Piedmont led in the development of the system. I want to thank W. Elliot Brownlee, Joseph H. Cartwright, David C. Hammack, J. Morgan Kousser, Lester C. Lamon, Karen K. Miller, Howard N. Rabinowitz, and Peter Wallenstein for helpful comments on earlier drafts of this article.

MR. HARRIS is an associate professor of history at the University of California at Santa Barbara.

the chronological pattern of school discrimination.

For the black community of Birmingham, public education was the most important of all government services. Blacks, emerging from slavery to freedom, were stung by white allegations that their race was inherently inferior; they were anxious to prove that under freedom they could achieve and advance like any other race; and they looked to the school as potentially the most powerful of all agencies of racial uplift. But they realized that the necessary numbers of schoolteachers, unlike the smaller leadership staffs of black churches and fraternal associations, could not be sustained with the voluntary resources that the black community could generate from within itself. Schools depended upon tax revenue collected and allocated by the white-dominated state and local governments, and thus black school progress inevitably involved difficult bargaining with white officials. Black leaders hoped, as slavery receded into the past, as blacks demonstrated their eagerness and capacity for education, and as blacks advanced economically, culturally, and politically, that white officials would steadily increase their investment in black education, placing it on a persistent upward trajectory.[2]

But the reality was to be far more complex and frustrating. Blacks would continually encounter debilitating constraints that rendered progress intermittent at best, that often produced long periods of frustrating stagnation at unacceptably severe levels of discrimination, and that all too often imposed disheartening setbacks.

A persuasive historical interpretation, exemplified in valuable studies of the postbellum South by Horace Mann Bond, Louis R. Harlan, Eric Anderson, J. Morgan Kousser, and Robert A. Margo, has been that increases in discrimination against black public schools were closely associated with one major causative factor: decline in black voting, particularly the conclusive disfranchisement of blacks around 1900. Several historians add that the discrimination became even worse during the ensuing "Progressive Era" when school funds increased significantly but were distributed in a more inequitable manner. For example, J. Morgan Kousser, analyzing county-level data for North Carolina, showed that immediately after the disfranchisement of most blacks in 1900, blacks suffered a dramatic intensification of discrimination in school expenditures. Moreover, after 1900 in North Carolina the poorer whites, many but not all of whom had also lost the vote, suffered a significant but lesser discrimina-

[2] Peter Kolchin, *First Freedom: The Responses of Alabama's Blacks to Emancipation and Reconstruction* (Westport, Conn., 1972), 84–87; Birmingham *Weekly Pilot* (Negro), September 8, 1883; August 2, 1884; Birmingham *Weekly Iron Age*, October 4, November 22, December 20, 1883; Huntsville *Gazette* (Negro), August 29, 1883.

tion, in relation to wealthy whites. Thus Kousser concluded that "In North Carolina education at least, 'progressivism' was, as a consequence of disfranchisement, for middle-class whites only." [3]

The Birmingham story confirms in part the long-run negative impact of disfranchisement upon black education relative to white, but it also qualifies the emphasis on disfranchisement as the exclusive force shaping the chronological pattern of discrimination, and it suggests that the impact of "progressivism" on black schools was not entirely negative. In Birmingham the impact of disfranchisement and of electoral politics generally was less profound than in the rural areas that have been studied. Other factors that have not been systematically analyzed for rural or for urban areas actually had a greater impact on patterns of discrimination than did electoral politics. First, general economic conditions, particularly changes in the business cycle and related changes in the availability of school revenue, sharply affected rates of discrimination. Nineteenth-century depressions severely diminished black school allocations, absolutely and in relation to white schools. Prosperity and revenue growth always boosted black schools absolutely and under some conditions advanced them relatively but under other conditions caused them to fall relatively further behind the whites. Second, the ideology of the dominant white interest groups in Birmingham—the commercial, professional, and industrial groups—affected the rate of discrimination, primarily because those white groups, for their own reasons, tended to view black education more favorably than did dominant white groups in rural areas. Third, organizational changes in school and city governance affected the rate of discrimination. In particular, black schools benefited from a shift during the 1880s to a centralized, bureaucratized, and professionalized urban school system that was able to isolate itself somewhat from electoral politics. And the professionalization and political independence of schools were supported and intensified by municipal and state reform efforts that have typically been labeled "progressive." Thus in some ways local and state progressivism fostered progress in urban black schools, even though progressive officials also sustained many longstanding racial

---

[3] Kousser, "Progressivism—For Middle-Class Whites Only: North Carolina Education, 1880-1910," *Journal of Southern History*, XLVI (May 1980), 169-94 (quotation on p. 192); Margo, "Race Differences in Public School Expenditures: Disfranchisement and School Finance in Louisiana, 1890-1910," *Social Science History*, VI (Winter 1982), 9-33; Rabinowitz, *Race Relations in the Urban South*, 329-30; Anderson, *Race and Politics in North Carolina, 1872-1901: The Black Second* (Baton Rouge and London, 1981), 315, 325-30; Harlan, *Separate and Unequal: Public School Campaigns and Racism in the Southern Seaboard States, 1901-1915* (Chapel Hill, 1958), 39-44; Bond, *Negro Education in Alabama: A Study in Cotton and Steel* (New York, 1969), 148-63, 178-94; Bond, *The Education of the Negro in the American Social Order* (New York, 1934), 84-115, 151-71.

FIGURE 1

Black/White Ratios of Expenditures for Teachers' Salaries per School-age Child in the Population for North Carolina, Alabama, and Birmingham, 1874–1931

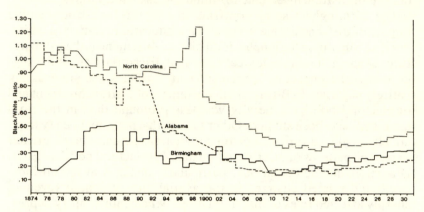

constraints that kept blacks from moving toward equality with whites.

Figure 1 begins to place the Birmingham pattern in the context of patterns in North Carolina and in rural Alabama. The dotted top line of the figure traces for North Carolina a precipitous drop, immediately after the disfranchisement of 1900, in the black/white ratio of expenditures for teachers' salaries per school-age child in the population. The dashed middle line traces the comparable black/white ratio for rural Alabama, where the most precipitous decline occurred during the 1890s, when black voting was declining but before the conclusive disfranchisement of Alabama blacks by a new constitution adopted in 1901.[4]

Historian Horace Mann Bond has argued that in rural Alabama the crucial turning point was the enactment, in 1891, of a state law that revised the rules for apportioning the annual school allocation of the state legislature. The new law continued a long-established process

[4] The figures in this article were drafted by Walter R. Gamboa, graphic illustrator. Alabama and North Carolina data in Figures 1, 2, and 3 are taken from Horace Mann Bond's tabulations, based upon annual and biennial reports of state departments of education. See Bond, *Education of the Negro in the American Social Order*, 153–56. Following a suggestion by Professor J. Morgan Kousser, I completed Bond's Alabama series for 1893 to 1907 from partial information published in Alabama, Department of Education, *Annual Reports* from 1893 through 1907. Bond's Alabama data and my additions cover only expenditures by rural county school systems but not expenditures by separate urban districts. On the decline of Alabama black voting during the 1890s, particularly after passage of the 1893 Sayre secret ballot act, see J. Morgan Kousser, *The Shaping of Southern Politics: Suffrage Restriction and the Establishment of the One-Party South, 1880-1910* (New Haven and London, 1974), 132–38.

of distributing the state allocation among counties on a strict per capita basis, according to total school-age population. But for the first time the new law gave local authorities complete discretion in dividing the fund between the races within their localities. This law permitted local white leaders in the Black Belt counties (the southern Alabama plantation counties whose population was predominately black) to divert to their local white schools much of the state allocation that came to their counties on the basis of their black population. This diversion process began immediately after passage of the 1891 law and by 1894 had caused the rural Alabama black/white ratio of per capita expenditures for teachers' salaries to drop from .81 to .46 (see Figure 1), a drop that reflected a 26 percent decline in the rural black per capita expenditure and a 30 percent increase in the rural white per capita expenditure.[5]

In both North Carolina and Alabama the period of near-equality in the rural black/white ratio had been characterized by a low rural level of funding for both races—a level of roughly $1.00 per year per child—a level that sustained only traditional one-room country schools for three months a year. In each state the sharp drop in the rural black/white ratio occurred when white authorities found a way to boost rural white funding well above the $1.00 per student level, so as to sustain better schools for six to nine months a year, while allowing the black rural schools to stagnate at or below the old $1.00 per child level. The drop was more devastating in Alabama, where it occurred before disfranchisement, because Alabama actually cut the per capita expenditure per black child in half and diverted substantial sums from black to white schools. North Carolina, on the other hand, allowed the black per capita expenditure to rise slightly, but not nearly so rapidly as the white per capita expenditure, which after 1900 was boosted dramatically by new school taxes instituted by "progressive" political leaders.

The solid line in Figure 1 traces the more stable black/white ratio of expenditures for teachers' salaries per school-age child in Birmingham, where blacks consistently composed approximately 40 percent of the population.[6] During all of the late nineteenth century Birmingham blacks lagged further behind Birmingham whites than rural Alabama blacks lagged behind the minimally funded rural

[5] Bond, *Negro Education in Alabama*, 148–63.

[6] I compiled the Birmingham data in all the figures that accompany this article from the following sources: Alabama, Department of Education, *Annual Reports*; Birmingham, Board of Education, *Annual Reports*; Birmingham, Board of Education, Minutes (Birmingham Board of Education Building, Birmingham, Ala.); Birmingham, Minutes of the Mayor and Board of Aldermen (Birmingham City Hall, Birmingham, Ala.).

FIGURE 2

Expenditures for Teachers' Salaries per School-age Child in the Population for Birmingham Blacks, Birmingham Whites, Rural Alabama Blacks, and Rural Alabama Whites, 1874–1931 (1913 Dollars)

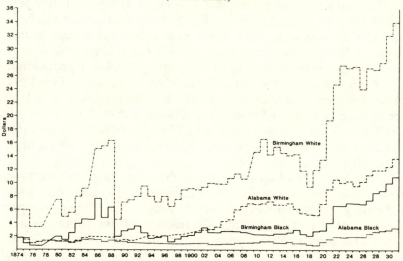

whites. But Figure 2, which presents absolute expenditures for teachers' salaries for each race in Birmingham and in rural Alabama, shows that Birmingham blacks received much more absolutely per child and consequently had much better schools than did rural Alabama blacks. Indeed, as Figure 2 shows, during most of the 1880s and 1890s the expenditure per *black* child in Birmingham was higher than the average expenditure per *white* child in the Alabama countryside. Only during the twentieth century did rural white absolute expenditures surpass the level of $2.00 per child and move steadily above the Birmingham black level. Even then the rural white average remained far below the standard set by the Birmingham white level. (Since these figures are in constant 1913 dollars, the variations over time represent not simply episodes of inflation and deflation but rather fluctuations in the actual level of resources provided for each child of school age. Only one fluctuation—the sharp peak in Birmingham expenditures between 1886 and 1888—was a statistical fluke, caused by an inconsistency in school census procedures.)

In Figure 1 the trend of the solid line, the Birmingham black/white ratio of expenditures for teachers' salaries per school-age child, confirms that disfranchisement, in 1901, had a long-run negative impact; generally the ratio was lower after disfranchisement. But disfranchisement in Birmingham was not accompanied by such a sharp immediate drop in the ratio as was disfranchisement in North Carolina. And in Birmingham, as in rural Alabama, the black/white ratio suffered its greatest decline during the mid-1890s, well before disfranchisement. In the years immediately following disfranchisement the Birmingham ratio actually reversed directions and climbed slightly. The drop in 1910 occurred when Birmingham annexed a dozen small, surrounding towns into Greater Birmingham, doubling its population from 60,000 to 132,685, increasing its area sixfold, and forcing its school system to digest a large suburban population for which black school facilities had been far less developed than had those for whites.[7] And finally, after the 1910 annexation the Birmingham black/white ratio climbed modestly but steadily.

The configurations in Figure 1 suggest that in the urban setting of Birmingham disfranchisement had a less profound impact on the ratio of discrimination in expenditures for teachers' salaries than did disfranchisement in the countryside. They also suggest that in the city, at least, and perhaps also in the countryside, several factors other than disfranchisement helped to shape the chronological pattern of discrimination.

One factor that deserves attention is change in the black role in determining local election results during the late nineteenth century when blacks were still voting. In North Carolina, for example (see Figure 1), a Fusionist (Populist-Republican) coalition dominated state politics from 1894 to 1900, and the black/white school expenditure ratio responded sharply and positively to the increased black electoral leverage. Then in 1900 the Democrats regained complete political control of North Carolina and disfranchised the blacks, and the black/white ratio plummeted immediately, sank steadily for years, and stayed down for decades.[8]

In Birmingham, by contrast, throughout the period 1874 to 1901 black voters experienced significant variations in their participation in town elections and in their leverage upon election results, but seldom did the black/white ratio of school expenditures move in concert with changes in black electoral leverage.

The pattern of variation in nineteenth-century black leverage upon the results of Birmingham elections is indicated by the rows of information along the bottom of Figure 3 and of subsequent figures. The row labeled "Years of Black Voting" is shaded for the years in which

[7] Carl V. Harris, *Political Power in Birmingham, 1871-1921* (Knoxville, Tenn., 1977), 32, 104-12; Birmingham, Board of Education, *Annual Report, 1910*, pp. 1-32.

[8] Kousser, "Progressivism — For Middle-Class Whites Only," 177-79; Kousser, *Shaping of Southern Politics*, 183-95.

FIGURE 3

Black/White Ratios of Expenditures for Teachers' Salaries per School-age Child in the Population for Birmingham, 1874-1931

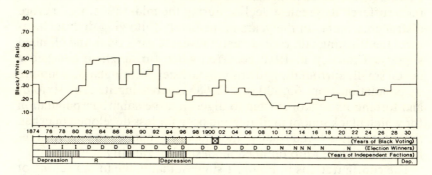

blacks were able to vote in the decisive elections. The black-bordered "X" at 1901 in this row indicates the conclusive disfranchisement of blacks by the Alabama Constitution of 1901. The row labeled "Years of Independent Factions" is shaded for years in which blacks not only voted but also enjoyed the leverage provided by the existence of an organized independent faction that challenged the Democrats. In the row labeled "Election Winners" the initials — "D" for Democrats, "I" for Independents, and "C" for Citizen Reformers — indicate the winning parties or factions in town elections. After 1910 all city elections are marked with the initial "N" to indicate that they were technically nonpartisan, even though all the victors continued to be Democrats. The bottom row indicates with the word "Depression" the years of the major economic depressions, and indicates with the letter "R" the year of a major school reorganization.[9]

During the years that blacks voted, black leverage upon election results rose when whites quarreled politically among themselves, particularly when an organized white dissident faction challenged the dominant Democrats, but black leverage on the results fell when most whites united behind the Democrats and no organized opposition appeared. In the years marked with the letter "I" (1876, 1878, and 1880), a dissident white Independent faction, linked with the statewide Greenback-Independent movement, fielded opposition slates against the local Democrats, who typically in those years held all-white town conventions to nominate Democratic slates. Blacks took advantage of the organized white challenge to the Democrats, voted heavily for the Independents, and played a decisive role in helping them win. As Figure 3 shows, two of the three black-

[9] Harris, *Political Power in Birmingham*, 59-89.

supported Independent victories were not immediately followed by positive movements in the black/white ratio of per capita school expenditures. Indeed, the Independent regimes presided over some of the lowest years for the black/white ratio.[10]

By 1882 the white Independent movement had faded, and the incumbent Independent mayor ran a distant third in the general election. During the 1882 campaign the Democrats, for the first time in years, made no attempt to hold an all-white convention to nominate a single Democratic slate, and in the general election they confidently conducted a contest between two Democratic factions, each of which outpolled the dying Independent faction. The victorious Democratic faction was led by Alexander O. Lane, a prominent young Democratic attorney, a staunch Presbyterian, a supporter of strong law enforcement, and, most important, a vigorous civic reform leader and a successful advocate of heavy investment in civic improvement projects, including schools. Lane became a highly popular mayor, built a large white majority for his faction, and in 1884 and 1886 was overwhelmingly reelected. Thus during the 1880s electoral competition was weak, and whites were largely united behind Lane.[11]

But large numbers of blacks continued to vote; indeed, during the early 1880s an influx of black laborers temporarily boosted the black proportion of the registered voters from the 30 percent level of the 1870s to a peak of 48 percent in 1884, after which the proportion declined rapidly to 32 percent again by 1888. Lane sought and received endorsement from several black leaders, enlarging his coalition and hastening the decline of the Independents, but rival black leaders endorsed Lane's Democratic opponents. In 1884 and 1886, when Lane won two-to-one general election victories over lackluster Democratic opponents, he probably had the support of a majority of blacks as well as a majority of whites.[12]

Thus as the black percentage of the electorate expanded in 1882 and 1884, potential black leverage grew, but without an Independent anti-Democratic focus blacks lost their political unity and found themselves dividing their votes among white Democrats. During the mid-1880s the black Lane voters exercised the leverage that came from being one component of the broad Lane coalition. But after 1884 the percentage of black voters declined again, and blacks were

[10] *Ibid.*, 64; Birmingham *Weekly Iron Age*, November 15, December 6, 1876; August 8, 1877; October 23, 30, November 13, 20, 1878; Birmingham *Weekly Independent*, February 1, 1879; December 4, 11, 1880.

[11] Birmingham *Weekly Iron Age*, November 30, December 7, 14, 1882; December 4, 1884; November 25, December 2, 1886.

[12] *Ibid.*, November 23, 1882; December 4, 1884; November 25, December 9, 1886; Birmingham *News*, November 28, 1888; Huntsville *Gazette*, November 10, 1888.

ultimately less crucial to the Lane Democrats, who had the support of a solid majority of whites and could triumph even if the black vote were eliminated. Black voters had been more important to the Independents, who had had the support of only a minority of whites and could never hope to triumph without solid black support. During the Lane years the black/white ratio of expenditures for teachers' salaries made a sharp gain, rising above .40 for the first time, and twice reaching .50 (see Figure 3). While the role of black voters in the Lane coalition no doubt helped blacks achieve the gain, other factors, to be discussed later, helped to account for the gain in the face of some actual decline in the decisiveness of black electoral leverage.

In 1888 Mayor Lane voluntarily stepped down, and the Democratic leaders, with Lane's support, moved abruptly to terminate black electoral leverage by establishing an all-white, city Democratic primary to choose the Democratic nominee to succeed Lane. Thus the Democratic leaders revealed a lack of commitment to their erstwhile black supporters and, indeed, an eagerness to be rid of them. The white primary was hotly contested, but in the general election the Democratic leaders, assisted vigorously by outgoing Mayor Lane, rallied nearly all whites behind the primary winner. The Republican Party, for the first and last time, nominated a mayoral candidate, Thomas G. Hewlett. He received a solid black vote, but the blacks were overwhelmed, two-to-one, by a solid white vote for the Democratic primary winner.[13]

The Democratic white primary, thus established in 1888, held sway in 1890 and 1892 when the Democratic primary winners (Lane himself in 1890) ran unopposed in general elections, and blacks found themselves completely shut out of any opportunity to cast meaningful ballots. During those years, however, the black/white school expenditure ratio recovered from an 1887 dip and until 1893 remained near .40, though not again reaching the .50 level.[14]

Then in 1894 and 1896 an independent white faction refused to accept the Democratic primary nominees and organized Citizens' Reform tickets to oppose the Democrats in general elections, once again providing blacks a chance to vote in city elections. In the 1894 general election the Citizens, receiving overwhelming black support, defeated the Democrats and took control of city hall for two years, but in 1896 the Democrats regained control in a close general election in which both sides courted the black vote and in which a

[13] Birmingham *News*, November 2, 9, 15, 16, 24, 28, December 1, 4, 1888; Birmingham *Age-Herald*, December 5, 1888.

[14] Harris, *Political Power in Birmingham*, 66–67; Birmingham *Age-Herald*, November 7, 1890; March 29, November 15, 17, 1892; November 18, 1894.

crucial minority of blacks voted Democratic. Ironically, during the mid-1890s when blacks briefly held the balance of power in town elections, the black/white school expenditure ratio dropped sharply. After 1896 the Citizens movement faded, and the Democratic white primary again held sway until 1901 when a new constitution disfranchised blacks. During these years the black/white school expenditure ratio recovered slightly, though never regaining the .40 level.[15]

Thus before 1900 black voters played an electoral role in three city administrations: a decisive role in electing the Independent slates of 1876 to 1882 and the Citizen slate of 1894 to 1896 and a less decisive but still substantial role in sustaining the broad Lane coalition, 1882–1888. But the black/white ratio of Birmingham per capita school expenditures fell to low points during the Independent and Citizen regimes, hit its high point during the Lane regime, and persisted at its second-highest level during the 1888 to 1893 period, when blacks were excluded from meaningful voting by the all-white Democratic primary system. The pattern suggests that the black/white ratio of school expenditures did not respond solely to changes in black electoral leverage and that the ratio was responding to other factors as well.

This does not suggest that disfranchisement and the other constraints on black voting were insignificant in Birmingham. It reflects, rather, the reality that even when blacks were able to vote, they suffered massive and persistent political disadvantages. Most important was a pervasive belief by whites that blacks should remain permanently in a lower-caste status, a status that whites considered utterly inconsistent with black voting or black political leverage of any kind. Thus officials who owed their election to black votes were quite squeamish about acknowledging any dependence on blacks, were quite reluctant to grant black requests, and were extremely careful to avoid even the appearance of providing favors to blacks. Moreover, in most years the impact of the black vote was minimized by devices such as at-large elections, gerrymandered wards, and informal economic and social pressures. In Birmingham and in most southern cities after Reconstruction such devices excluded blacks from holding local political office, from distributing or receiving political patronage, or from functioning as accepted components of local government coalitions, and political exclusion severely limited

---

[15] Harris, *Political Power in Birmingham*, 66–70. Evidence provided by black poll-tax payments in Birmingham (recorded in city and state education reports) indicates that the constitution of 1901 did indeed sharply curtail black voting in Birmingham. From 1898 through 1901 nearly 1,000 Birmingham blacks paid the poll tax annually, but beginning in 1902 typically fewer than 50 blacks paid it. The evidence also suggests that some factor other than the poll tax was the active ingredient in disfranchisement.

FIGURE 4

Alabama State Allocation for Black Schools in Birmingham per School-age Child in the Population and per Student Based on Average Daily Attendance and Expenditures from Government Revenue for Black Teachers' Salaries per student in Birmingham Based on Average Daily Attendance, 1874–1931 (1913 Dollars)

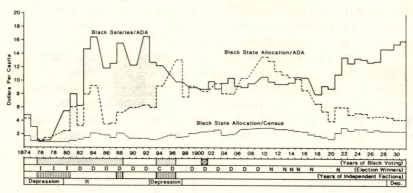

the ability of black voters to influence local school allocations. Such political disadvantages meant that often factors other than electoral activity played a major role in determining patterns of allocations to blacks.[16]

Since the Birmingham black/white ratio of expenditures for teachers' salaries dropped sharply and permanently in the mid-1890s, the question arises: did Birmingham's local officials, like the Black Belt's local officials, begin taking advantage at that time of the discretionary authority granted them in the state law of 1891 to divert to the white schools a large portion of the state allocation that they received on the basis of the black population?

Figure 4 demonstrates that Birmingham officials did not in fact resort to persistent diversion of state black funds to white schools. The dotted bottom line traces the annual state black school allocations to Birmingham per *school-age child*, measured in constant 1913 dollars.[17] The dashed middle line converts the state black allocations to per capita figures based upon the actual black *average*

[16] *Ibid.*, 78; Birmingham *Weekly Iron Age*, November 16, December 7, 1882; December 4, 1884; see also the political polemics in Birmingham *Weekly Independent*, August 11, 18, 25, September 1, November 17, December 22, 1877; Montgomery *Advertiser and Mail*, January 26, 1879.

[17] For each year the bottom line of Figure 4 represents the sum of two state school allocations, derived from separate taxes and distributed according to different principles: (1) The larger portion — typically one-half to three-fourths of the total state allocation to Birmingham — was the state legislature's annual education allocation, derived from the state property tax and distributed among counties and towns according to school-age population; and (2) The smaller portion came from the poll tax, levied by the state and then returned to the

daily attendance (ADA) in Birmingham. (Sharp fluctuations in the middle line occurred whenever there was a major change in the relationship between the average daily attendance and the census of school population. Such changes occurred in 1888, when a new, more thorough school census procedure significantly raised the tally of the school-age population; in 1894 when the depression drastically reduced the daily attendance in relation to the school census; and in 1910 when the annexation of suburbs with few black schools increased Birmingham's school-age black population far more than it increased her black daily attendance.) The solid top line traces the total expenditure for black teachers' salaries per capita (ADA). For each year the shaded area between the top and middle lines represents the *local* governmental allocation to salary expenditures for black schools per student in attendance.[18] Although the per capita salary for teachers in Birmingham's black schools varied widely, the state allocation for blacks provided a floor beneath which that salary seldom fell. (Even in years like 1897, 1899, 1903, 1907, and 1910-1914, when the black salaries did fall below the state black allocation, no black state money was in fact diverted to Birmingham's white schools, because the small black janitorial expenditures used the remainder of the state's black allocations.)

But why did the white officials of Birmingham refrain from the Black Belt practice of diverting the state black fund to the white schools? The blacks of Birmingham had no more electoral leverage on their local officials after the disfranchisement of 1901 than did the blacks in the Black Belt, and Birmingham whites clamored as persistently as did rural whites for more money for white schools.

The factors that influenced the Birmingham officials were no doubt complex, but one key factor was that the white interest groups that dominated local government in Birmingham had a more favorable perspective on the value of eduction for blacks than did the planters who dominated local government in the Black Belt. Birmingham's local officeholders (mayors and aldermen before 1911, city commissioners thereafter) were predominately representatives of the large and prosperous local downtown business and professional community — attorneys, merchants, realtors, investment brokers, contractors, and grocers. The appointed board of education, established in 1884, was even more uniformly composed of middle-class business and professional men. The city's elite industrial and

---

locality of origin, where exactly the portion paid by each race was to be spent on the schools of that race.

[18] For 1883 through 1887 black elementary students paid tuition that pushed the actual per capita black salary expenditures approximately three or four dollars higher than shown by the top line in Figure 4.

financial firms—the banks, utilities, coal and iron corporations, and railroads—were less likely to be represented among officeholders, but their economic power translated into significant influence on most local governmental issues.[19]

The business and professional men who dominated Birmingham city government were vigorous city boosters. In general they believed that improvement in civic services fostered local economic development and population growth, which would in turn, they believed, enhance the prosperity of all. In particular they sought to build a strong public education system because they believed that such a system would attract a higher-quality population, would improve the productivity of the rising generation, and would socialize the young to the disciplines and values needed to maintain good social order in a densely populated city.[20]

Although the dominant white civic boosters placed a much higher priority on white public education than on black, they did see positive value in black public schools since white businessmen employed blacks in many subservient capacities and white middle-class families relied heavily on blacks to perform domestic service. Such white employers believed that black schools would improve the deportment, the health, the morals, and the service of their black employees.[21]

Industrialists also tended to throw their influence strongly behind public education. Those industrialists who foresaw using blacks as skilled or semiskilled labor believed that black schools could help to upgrade labor productivity. Even those iron and steel industrialists who foresaw using blacks only for unskilled common labor came to believe that attractive black schools would help them solve a persisting problem—the high rate of turnover among their unskilled black laborers. Since black parents placed a high value on being near a good black school, industrialists believed that such schools were useful in attracting and holding black workers.[22]

Out in the countryside, on the other hand, many white planters considered blacks fit only for the physical drudgery of unskilled farm labor and believed that education inappropriately tended to raise blacks' aspirations and to ruin them as plantation laborers. Black Belt

---

[19] Harris, *Political Power in Birmingham*, 57–89, 273–75.

[20] Birmingham *News*, October 12, 1900; Birmingham *Age-Herald*, September 22, 1894; testimony of Mayor Alexander O. Lane in U. S. Congress, Senate, *Report Upon Relations Between Labor and Capital, and Testimony Taken by Committee, 48th Congress* (4 vols., Washington, 1885), IV, 371.

[21] Birmingham, Board of Education, *Annual Report, 1899*, pp. 11–12.

[22] U. S. Congress, Senate, *Report upon Relations Between Labor and Capital*, IV, 371; Birmingham *Age-Herald*, June 6, 1901, January 7, 1910.

FIGURE 5

Black/White Ratios of Expenditures from Local Birmingham Tax Revenue for Teachers' Salaries per Student Based on Average Daily Attendance, 1874–1930

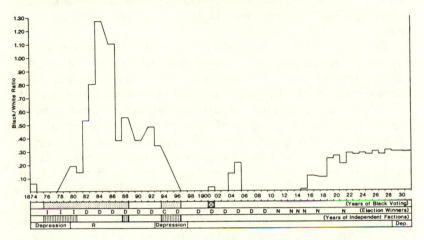

local governments dominated by planters with such views might well consider the diversion of state school funds from black schools to white schools beneficial not only because it aided the white schools but also because it undermined the black schools.[23]

By contrast, the white, middle-class civic boosters and industrialists of Birmingham saw enough positive value in black schooling to refrain from diverting the state black school allocation to the white schools and, indeed, in times of local revenue growth, to supplement the state black fund with local revenue.

But if the Birmingham city officials, for such reasons, persistently channeled all the growing state black allocation to the black schools, over the years they nonetheless produced wide variations in their allocations to black schools from the *local* revenue that they themselves raised through local tax levies and over which they had complete discretion. This is indicated by the bulging and shrinking of the shaded area in Figure 4 and by the sharp ups and downs in the black/white ratio of local per capita expenditures, as traced in Figure 5. As Figure 4 shows, these variations caused total per capita payments to black teachers to fluctuate dramatically, from a low of $1.03 in 1876 to peaks above $15.00 during the 1880s and 1890s, peaks that were not reached again until the late 1920s. Moreover, as Figure 5 shows, the variation in the black/white ratio of local school expenditures per

[23] U. S. Congress, Senate, *Report upon Relations Between Labor and Capital*, IV, 23–28, 150–54.

capita, with the highest points in the mid-1880s, with the next highest in the late 1880s and early 1890s, and with an upward movement after 1916, did not correlate closely with variation in the black role in electing the local regimes, with high points in the 1870s and mid-1890s.

But the variation in the local black/white ratio did respond sharply to another important factor—changes in the general economic situation and related changes in the availability of local school revenue. The low ratios of the 1870s occurred in the midst of a nationwide depression, a depression that hit Birmingham with devastating force. The town had been founded in 1871 at the intersection of two new railroads and had boomed for two years as people rushed in to participate in the "magic" industrial expansion envisioned because of the unique confluence of coal, iron ore, and limestone in the hills surrounding Birmingham. But in 1873 a cholera epidemic and then the depression had burst Birmingham's first boom, causing the new town to languish in the doldrums until 1879, limiting revenue and stifling any local support the Independent regime might have wished to give black schools.[24]

Recovery came in 1879 as the national economic picture brightened and as local developers solved technological problems, raised capital, dug coal mines, and built iron furnaces, launching a dramatic second Birmingham boom. During the 1880s Birmingham experienced prodigious growth, its population jumping from 3,000 to 26,000, and its real estate values skyrocketing. The boom produced sufficient local general tax revenue to improve all general city services and to expand school expenditures enormously. It was in the midst of such local revenue growth that Mayor Lane and his regime of white Democratic civic boosters, who received helpful but not decisive political support from black voters, became willing and able to supplement the state black school allocation with significant local appropriations to the black schools.[25]

The boom continued until 1893, when another nationwide depression hit Birmingham, halting growth, closing industries, decimating city revenue, and forcing deep retrenchment in all city services, particularly in education. Indeed, in the year 1897–1898 school officials reimposed elementary school tuition for the first time in a decade, forcing many students, particularly blacks, to drop out of school. This cruel depression setback to black education is indicated in Figure 5 by the elimination, in the mid-1890s, of all local allocations to

[24] Harris, *Political Power in Birmingham*, 12–14.
[25] *Ibid.*, 15–24; Ethel Armes, *The Story of Coal and Iron in Alabama* (Birmingham, 1910), 238–41, 265–85.

FIGURE 6

Total Local Support for Birmingham Teachers' Salaries per Student Based on Average Daily Attendance of Black and White Students and Local Support for Black Teachers' Salaries per Student Based on Average Daily Attendance, 1874–1931 (1913 Dollars)

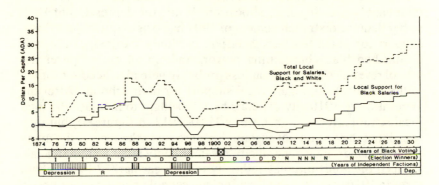

black schools, despite the electoral leverage exercised by black voters during the 1894 and 1896 Citizen challenges to the Democrats.[26]

The impact of the depressions of the mid-1870s and the mid-1890s is further indicated in Figure 6, the top line of which shows the total local support for teachers' salaries per student (black and white combined) that the city officials could make available, and the bottom line of which shows Birmingham's local support for teachers' salaries per black student. At the low points of the depressions of the 1870s and 1890s the sharp decline in the total local salary support squeezed the local support for black salaries down to nothing.

The depression of the 1890s hit the Birmingham schools particularly hard because the Alabama Constitution permitted no earmarked local school taxes, and thus it forced schools to compete with other city services for general city revenue, revenue that was in turn severely constrained by low constitutional limits on general city tax rates. The severe retrenchment forced upon the schools by the 1893 depression convinced Birmingham school officials that they must acquire an independent source of local school revenue that they could count on even when hard times tempted the aldermen to place other priorities first. Educators throughout the state agreed and launched a series of campaigns for state constitutional amendments to authorize earmarked local school taxes. But rural conservatives opposed all tax increases and not until 1916 did the state approve an amendment

[26] Birmingham, Board of Education, *Annual Report, 1899*, pp. 25–34; Harris, *Political Power in Birmingham*, 99–103.

allowing significant earmarked city and county school taxes.[27]

Thus the return of prosperity after 1900 brought only a modest increase in Birmingham's total local allocation to schools, and it restored no local revenue to the black schools, leaving them with only their slowly growing state allocation. While the depression of 1893 rather than the disfranchisement of 1901 had originally stopped local support for black teachers' salaries, certainly the loss of the vote diminished black bargaining power, and, in an era of perennial school revenue shortage, that loss probably helped to account for the failure of blacks to regain local support for their schools. After the annexation of 1910 city officials briefly sought to increase the total local school allocation (see years 1910–1912 in Figure 6), but they found that they could not sustain the increase in the face of the many other demands upon general city revenue. Only after school officials attained the constitutional authority to levy earmarked local school taxes in 1916 and 1917 did Birmingham school officials experience a new era of steadily expanding local school resources.[28] (The rise of local school revenue after 1917 was temporarily offset by steep wartime inflation, and in Figure 6, which is expressed in constant dollars, the increases first appear clearly in 1921 and continue in the years immediately thereafter.) And only in the 1920s, when the new earmarked school taxes finally pushed local school revenue above 1880 levels, did Birmingham school officials feel they had the leeway to again allocate significant amounts of local revenue to black schools.

From the 1890s onward the persistent shortage of school revenue prompted some white spokesmen to demand that only tax revenue paid directly by blacks be spent on black schools, so that white tax payments would not subsidize black education. Historian Robert A. Margo has reported that data from Louisiana suggest that, after disfranchisement in that state, the racial distribution of school expenditures in fact did come to reflect the racial distribution of taxes paid, and he points out that such an interpretation is consistent with the findings of Kousser for North Carolina.[29]

In Birmingham, however, disfranchisement did not reduce the black schools to only the tax money paid directly by blacks. In 1876 blacks owned no taxable property in Birmingham, and in 1884 they

---

[27] Some authorizations for minor increases in city and school taxes were achieved, but John Herbert Phillips, the superintendent of Birmingham schools, and other educators considered them totally inadequate. See Harris, *Political Power in Birmingham*, 99–104, 138–44.

[28] *Ibid.*, 140–44; Birmingham, Board of Education, *Annual Report, 1920*, pp. 44–51.

[29] Birmingham *Age-Herald*, December 5, 1890; January 29, 1899; Birmingham, *Negro American Press*, February 17, 1894; Margo, "Race Differences in Public School Expenditures," 26, 29, 32.

owned only 0.5 percent of the taxable property. Estimates based on systematic samples of tax returns indicate that in 1893 blacks owned 0.4 percent of the property, in 1904, 1.4 percent, and after 1910 and the annexation of the suburbs, slightly more than 2 percent.[30] Thus Birmingham blacks, who comprised roughly 40 percent of Birmingham's population, paid directly only a miniscule percentage of the state and local property taxes used to finance schools. Before 1901 blacks also paid poll taxes, but even when the poll tax is included, the best estimates indicate that during the 1880s the direct black payment of taxes that were used to finance education covered only 10 percent of the black teachers' salaries. During the depression of the 1890s direct black tax payments covered 30 percent of black teachers' salaries, from 1900 to 1910 covered 10 percent, and after 1910 covered 15 to 20 percent. Thus despite disfranchisement and despite strident white demands that no white tax money support black schools, white taxes continued to pay the largest portion of black school salaries.[31]

A key factor in Birmingham's overall pattern of school discrimination, and in its long struggle to expand local school revenue, was the advent in 1883, at the beginning of a period of prosperity and hectic growth, of a full-time professional school superintendent who rigorously reorganized the entire school system. The new superintendent, appointed upon the initiative of civic-reform mayor Alexander O. Lane, was John Herbert Phillips: born in Kentucky, descended from a long line of prominent Welsh Presbyterian preachers, educated in Ohio, and rapidly achieving prominence among young educators as a dynamic advocate of centralized, professionalized, bureaucratic

[30] Jefferson County, Assessment of Taxes on Real and Personal Property in the County of Jefferson for the Year 1876; Jefferson County, Concise Form of Amount of Taxes Due by Each Taxpayer of Jefferson County, Alabama, for the Year 1884; and Jefferson County, Concise Form of Amount of Taxes Due by Each Taxpayer of Jefferson County for the Tax Year 1893; (all in the Department of Archives and Manuscripts, Birmingham Public Library, Birmingham, Ala.) and Jefferson County, Tax Assessment Volumes, 1904, 1910, 1916, and 1928 (Tax Assessor's Office, Jefferson County Courthouse, Birmingham, Ala.). For 1876 and 1884 I made exact tabulations. For all other years I drew systematic samples of 400 taxpayers to determine the proportion of property owned by blacks. Since the few very large businesses and corporations with assessments of over $100,000 (all owned by whites) could not be properly sampled, they were excluded from the samples, which means that the reported percentages of property owned by blacks are based upon property owned in blocks of less than $100,000. They thereby exclude considerable white property, and thus they represent upper-bound estimates of the percentage of taxable property owned by blacks.

[31] Black leaders asserted that black renters in fact paid, through their rent, the property tax on the houses they rented. And under some conditions the property tax on such houses would indeed have been passed through to the renters. If for 1910 one assumes that indeed all the property tax on all the houses rented by Negroes was passed through to the renter, then one can estimate that the proportion of 1910 black teachers' salaries covered by black direct and indirect payments of the property tax used to finance schools would have been closer to 30 percent than to the 15 to 20 percent estimated here for direct taxes only.

school systems built on the model created by Superintendent William T. Harris of St. Louis.[32]

Upon his arrival in Birmingham in the summer of 1883 Superintendent Phillips found four small uncoordinated schools—two white and two black. Each school had been initiated not by city authorities but by volunteer efforts of citizens. Each had applied for and had received funding from the town board of aldermen, but each was governed by its own set of trustees, the black schools by black trustees. The white schools were far better funded and organized, but all the schools had haphazard curriculums and classroom procedures, all charged tuition, and none had regular examinations or systematic records.[33]

In 1883, marked with an "R" for "Reorganization" on the lowest row at the bottom of Figure 6 and other figures, Superintendent Phillips undertook a thoroughgoing reorganization, arranging for the board of aldermen to delegate school matters to a single appointed board of education, centralizing in the superintendent's office the administrative authority over all schools, prescribing a standard sequential graded curriculum for all schools, instituting a rigorous system of examination and selection of teachers, systematizing teachers' salary scales, and launching an ambitious, centrally planned school construction program. In short, Superintendent Phillips accomplished in Birmingham, in an unusually rapid and thoroughgoing fashion, in the midst of a period of booming prosperity and growth, a school reorganization featuring the sort of professionalization, bureaucratization, and centralization of authority that historian David Tyack has seen in many late-nineteenth-century cities and which he has aptly labeled "the transformation from village school to urban system." [34]

The school reorganization of 1883, the accompanying achievement of political independence by a board of education composed of prominent citizens who enthusiastically supported Superintendent Phillips, and the population growth and prosperity that made possible a rapid infusion of local tax revenue into the local school system, as shown in Figure 6, were major factors in the dramatic increase during the 1880s and early 1890s in local appropriations for black education.

Superintendent Phillips presided over the Birmingham public

[32] Elizabeth Mason Ware, "John Herbert Phillips, Educator" (M.A. thesis, Birmingham-Southern College, 1937), 2–9.

[33] Birmingham, Board of Education, *Annual Report, 1887*, pp. 39–41, 45.

[34] *Ibid.*, *1884, 1887, passim*; David B. Tyack, *The One Best System: A History of American Urban Education* (Cambridge, Mass., 1974), 5.

school system from 1883 until his death in 1921, effectively implementing there many of the goals of a broad national school reform campaign, a campaign that David Tyack has called "part and parcel of urban 'progressivism' generally." Certainly, in Birmingham and Alabama, Superintendent Phillips effectively allied himself with political efforts of the sort that historians have typically labelled "progressive," efforts that emphasized order, efficiency, expertise, expansion of government services, intensification of government regulation, centralization of authority, separation of administration and politics, the adaptation of the corporate model to municipal government, the application of middle-class ethical standards to government, and the fostering of greater influence by people in the upper socio-economic levels while giving some attention to justice for people in the lower levels.[35]

After the revenue crunch of the 1890s the need to increase city tax revenue, particularly to obtain constitutional authority to levy local school taxes, united Superintendent Phillips and the local municipal reform leaders. The goal of broadening the tax base and relieving the persistent revenue crunch was one motivation of the civic boosters who promoted the 1910 annexation of many surrounding suburbs into Greater Birmingham. But after initial exhilaration at the increased tax revenue, city officials discovered that the cost of municipal services for the suburbs balanced out the new tax revenue, leaving the city as strapped as ever. Municipal reformers and civic boosters also campaigned successfully to change in 1911 from the mayor-alderman form of government to the progressive and purportedly more efficient city commission form. The new city commission, dominated by Birmingham's leading progressive politicians — Alexander O. Lane (the mayor of the 1880s), James M. Weatherly, and George B. Ward — was eager to upgrade all civic services, particularly education, but during its first few years it was stymied by the continuing revenue shortage, which the commission's more orderly accounting procedures served only to reveal more vividly. The commissioners therefore worked vigorously at the local and state levels to expand their taxing authority through constitutional amendments. Superintendent Phillips built crucial support for this effort through a growing statewide network of professional educators and municipal reform leaders, and in 1916 it was a combination of such progressive

---

[35] Dewey W. Grantham, *Southern Progressivism: The Reconciliation of Progress and Tradition* (Knoxville, Tenn., 1983), xv–xxii, 279–85, 290, 301–302; Tyack, *The One Best System*, 7; George B. Tindall, *The Emergence of the New South, 1913–1945* (Baton Rouge, 1967), 32, 223–28, 254–63; Samuel P. Hays, "The Politics of Reform in Municipal Government in the Progressive Era," *Pacific Northwest Quarterly*, LV (October 1964), 157–69.

forces that mounted the statewide campaign that finally produced referendum approval of a constitutional amendment allowing earmarked city and county school taxes.[36]

Meanwhile, Phillips's fame as a progressive urban school administrator had spread far beyond Birmingham, bringing him professional recognition as president of the Alabama Education Association in 1892, as president of the Southern Education Association in 1905, as frequent speaker at annual meetings of the National Education Association, as longtime member of the NEA's most prestigious body, the Council of Education, and as president of that council in 1902.[37]

On racial questions Superintendent Phillips held attitudes quite typical of most southern urban progressives, and the elaborate records that he kept of black and white school allocations in Birmingham make it possible to delineate the advantages and the constraints that progressivism brought to black education in one key New South city.

Phillips held to the general southern white belief, shared by most southern white progressives, that Negroes were a backward or adolescent people, inherently inferior, possessing less mental capacity, and many centuries behind whites in cultural evolution. But the Negro was also an integral component of southern life and economy, said Phillips, and he believed that the "enlightened selfishness" of white southerners, as well as "their sense of right, justice and patriotism," should lead them to invest significant resources in Negro education. Phillips had a deep faith in the powerful capacity of education to uplift the children of any race, building character, overcoming cultural backwardness, and enhancing economic productivity by preparing children for efficient service in occupational niches that he considered appropriate. The school alone, he believed, could make blacks an asset instead of a burden to the South.[38]

---

[36] The issues surrounding these campaigns were complex, and to some extent city officials exploited a popular enthusiasm for more school revenue to increase city general revenue as well. See Harris, *Political Power in Birmingham*, 81–89, 104–12, 126–45; Birmingham *News*, May 25, 1911; March 11, November 16, 1913; October 4, 1914; November 16, December 29, 30, 1915; Birmingham *Age-Herald*, November 11, 1916, January 31, 1917; John H. Phillips, "Local Taxation" (Typescript, Research Department, Birmingham Board of Education, Birmingham, Ala.); John H. Phillips, "Alabama's First Question: Local Taxation for Schools," (Typescript, Research Department, Birmingham Board of Education); Birmingham, Board of Education, *Annual Report, 1920*, 35–51; Edward S. Lamonte, *George B. Ward: Birmingham's Urban Statesman* (Birmingham, 1974).

[37] *Who's Who in America, 1906–1907* (Chicago and London, 1906), 1405.

[38] John Herbert Phillips, "Educational Needs of the South," in *Journal of Proceedings and Addresses of the Forty-Third Annual Meeting of the National Education Association, 1904*, pp. 94–100; Phillips, "Character-Building—The Foundation of Education," *ibid., 1909*, 936–38; Phillips, "The Essential Requirements of Negro Education" (Typescript, Research Department, Birmingham Board of Education), 1–12; and Phillips, "The Education of the

FIGURE 7

Distribution of Birmingham Teachers on Monthly Pay Scale, by Race, 1881–1907

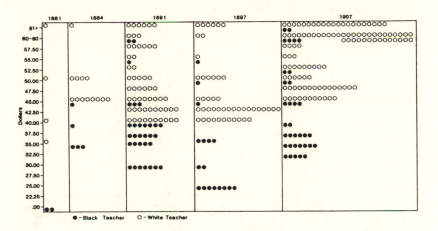

● – Black Teacher   O – White Teacher

Thus Phillips, when he took charge of the Birmingham school system in 1883, immediately pulled the struggling and largely ignored black schools firmly under the authority of the city and of his office and, while maintaining strict racial segregation, exercised firm, central supervision over them. He insisted upon a basic floor of decency or adequacy that was far above the level at which the black schools had languished before 1883 under the decentralized village school system, though it was still far below the level of the white schools.

For example, before the arrival of Superintendent Phillips, the board of aldermen, who had elected teachers and set salaries, had decreed that no black teacher should be paid more than $20 per month—lower than the typical wage of an unskilled black laborer and far lower than the $35-a-month salary of the lowest white teacher (see Figure 7). Soon after his arrival Phillips acquired the major voice in selecting teachers and in setting salaries. The Birmingham schools had always employed only blacks to teach in black schools, and Phillips continued that practice. He established a formal salary schedule with $2.50 intervals between the monthly salary steps, and, as Figure 7 shows, he immediately raised the lowest black salary to the previous white floor, and by 1891 he had created some overlap in the two distributions, with the top black teachers above the white floor and with the black principals (the top three blacks in 1891)

Southern Negro" (Typescript, Research Department, Birmingham Board of Education) 1–13 (quotations from p. 2).

FIGURE 8

Average Salary Steps per Rehired Faculty Member in Birmingham, by Race, 1885–1910

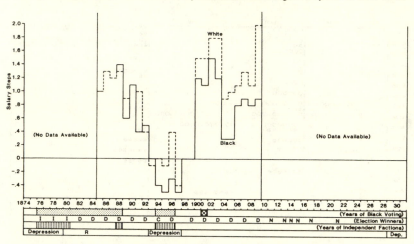

above the vast majority of the white teachers.[39]

But by 1897 the depression of the mid-1890s had pushed the black salary schedule down much below the white, even though the years 1894 through 1896 were years of renewed black electoral leverage. During the depression Phillips and the school board held the white floor salary constant at $40 per month, saving money by holding many white teachers at that level for several consecutive years, but they actually pushed the black floor down two steps, to $25, and they cut the salaries of many experienced black teachers, shoving them down the salary scale and creating a gap of several steps between the majority of black and of white teachers. Only the three black principals stood above any white teacher. Phillips deplored the adverse effect of the depression on both salary schedules, considering it an aberration, and when prosperity returned he brought about considerable reconvergence of the black and white scales, as shown by the 1907 data in Figure 7.[40]

Not only did Superintendent Phillips establish a systematic salary schedule, but he sought to use the prospect of regular upward steps at rehiring time each summer as an incentive to promote discipline and to improve professional performance by the teachers. To that end he

[39] Birmingham, Minutes of the Mayor and Board of Aldermen, C, 111–12 (April 6, 1881); Birmingham, Board of Education, *Annual Report, 1887*, pp. 145–51; Birmingham Board of Education, Minutes, I, 30 (June 25, 1885).

[40] Birmingham, Board of Education, *Annual Report, 1899*, pp. 31–37.

and the principals regularly evaluated teachers, and at the conclusion of each year he wrote a confidential report concerning "the average standing of each teacher in the schools as regards ability to teach and govern, progress of class, and punctuality in attendance at school or teachers' meetings," and he believed that his reports, and not any political considerations, should be the major factor determining the teachers' rates of advancement.[41]

Figure 8 records annually from 1884 through 1909 the average number of $2.50 salary steps per rehiring for both black and white teachers. During Phillips's first years in the 1880s the teachers of both races averaged roughly one step per year, but during the depression of the 1890s Phillips eliminated step increments for whites and imposed negative steps on blacks. With recovery from the depression Phillips was able to grant whites slightly more than one step increase per year as he sought to help them make up for the ground they had lost, and he also resumed giving steps to most blacks, some years indeed more than one step per black teacher. Typically, average black increments lagged behind white, but rather closely behind. Probably Phillips generally judged the professional performance of black teachers to be lower than the performance of whites, and no doubt race prejudice itself was a factor in those judgments. But the chronological pattern, in which black and white advancement rates showed similar profiles that clearly reflected economic conditions, suggests that Phillips, with his emphasis on professional criteria, stabilized the relationship between black and white salaries and reduced the impact that short-run political events might have on the rate of discrimination.[42]

The pattern of salary discrimination is summarized in Figure 9, which shows black and white average salaries. In 1883 the new salary schedule and procedures instituted by Superintendent Phillips immediately boosted the average black salary from $20 to $40 per month, a new level much nearer equality with the white level, and a new level at which the black average salary then persisted for years. During the depression of the mid-1890s the black average sank from $40 to $30, but with the return of prosperity it climbed back to $40, despite the disfranchisement of 1901. The $40 level then persisted until the inflationary World War I period, when both black and white average salaries began to climb steadily.[43] Figure 10, which shows the ratios

[41] Quotation, *ibid.*, *1884*, p. 50; see also *ibid.*, *1907*, p. 26.

[42] *Ibid.*, *1887*, p. 15; *ibid.*, *1891*, pp. 69–70.

[43] The average salary figures are shown in current dollars to make clear the rather remarkable stability of the salary schedules between 1883 and 1910. If the figures were converted to constant 1913 dollars to erase the effects of wartime inflation, the postwar increases would remain, but they would be slightly later and less steep.

FIGURE 9

Average Salary per Month of Birmingham Teachers, by Race, in Current Dollars, 1874–1931

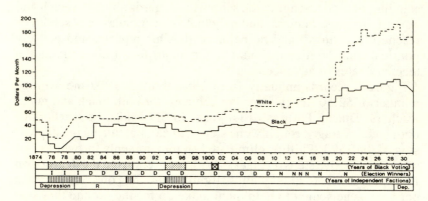

between black and white average salaries, roughly repeats the chronology already sketched, with the low point in the 1870s, the high point in the 1880s, and thereafter relative stability with a slight long-run downward trend.

The analysis of salary discrimination in Figures 7, 8, 9, and 10 suggests that Superintendent Phillips and the school board had rather persistent notions about the proper relation between black and white salaries, notions that incorporated prejudicial calculations of the future role of blacks in the society and the economy, calculations of the appropriate level of investment in black education in light of the projected black roles, calculations of the differential market situations of black and white teachers, and calculations of the relative qualifications and teaching capabilities of black and white teachers. Those notions and prejudicial calculations were expressed quite explicitly in such a differential salary schedule as that of 1891, which placed the bulk of the black salaries immediately below the bulk of the white, with some slight overlap, which provided whites some greater range between floor and ceiling salaries, and which allowed whites to climb the steps with slightly greater speed and regularity. Major departures from the basic salary schedule arrangement and from the typical $40-a-month average black salary came not with black political victories or defeats, but rather with economic depression, while economic recovery tended to bring restoration.[44]

Discrimination in salaries per teacher was only one component in the overall discrimination in expenditures for black education;

[44] Birmingham, Board of Education, *Annual Report, 1891*, pp. 69–70; *ibid., 1899*, pp. 31–36.

FIGURE 10

Black/White Ratios of Average Salaries of Birmingham Teachers, 1874–1931

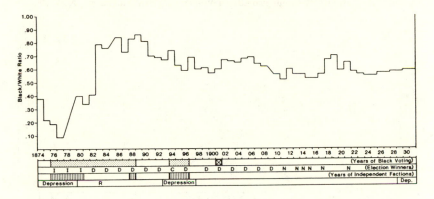

FIGURE 11

Number of Pupils per Teacher in Birmingham Based on Average Daily Attendance, by Race, 1874–1931

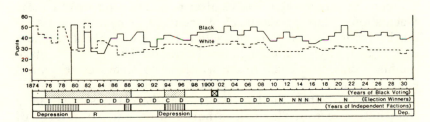

equally important was discrimination in the number of pupils assigned to each teacher. Superintendent Phillips was quite attentive to pupil/teacher ratios and sought to keep the ratios at levels that he could justify according to professional standards. Figure 11, showing pupils per teacher by race, presents a discriminatory pattern of considerable long-run stability, a pattern that after the mid-1880s shows rough adherence to a rule of thumb that the white daily attendance per teacher should be held near thirty students, if possible, and the black near forty students. Black class size crept above forty students primarily during periods of robust enrollment growth that severely outran construction of new black schools (the late 1880s, the early 1900s, and the 1920s). When enrollment growth leveled off (the early 1890s, the late 1920s), officials sought to bring black class size down again.[45]

[45] *Ibid.*, *1884*, pp. 12–13; *ibid.*, *1887*, pp. 34–35. No data are shown for blacks during the 1870s because their school met only three months a year, with highly irregular attendance.

FIGURE 12

Black Teachers as Percentage of Number Needed for Pupil/Teacher Ratio Equal to the White Pupil/Teacher Ratio in Birmingham Based on Average Daily Attendance, 1874–1931

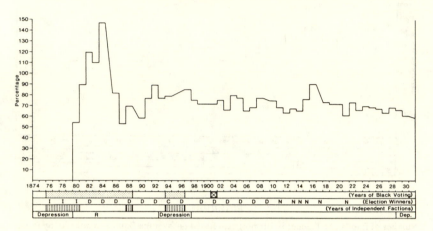

Figure 12 presents the relative discrimination produced by these fluctuations, showing the black percentage of equality in pupil/teacher ratios (technically the actual number of black teachers divided by the hypothetical number of black teachers needed to make the black class size equal to the white). The blacks came nearest equality in the early 1880s, lost ground during a period of dramatic attendance growth in the late 1880s, and thereafter settled into a long-run pattern of fluctuation between 60 and 80 percent of equality.

Though Phillips at times sought to justify the racial differential in his salary schedule, pointing to alleged racial differences in teacher preparation, in teacher qualifications, and in teacher competence, he never attempted any public justification for the discrimination involved in placing forty black students in each classroom, but only thirty white students, and clearly there were no professional criteria that could justify it. Phillips perceived lower competence among black teachers and greater attendance and discipline problems among black students, but, according to purely professional criteria, both perceptions should have suggested smaller rather than larger class sizes for blacks. Thus the discrimination in pupil/teacher ratios probably reflected Phillips's own implicit prejudicial calculations of the relative value of investment in black and white education as well as the more political factor of Phillips's assessment of the level of support for black education that white taxpayers would tolerate.[46]

[46] *Ibid.*, *1891*, pp. 69–70; *ibid.*, *1887*, pp. 34–35.

The patterns in relative class sizes suggest that once Superintendent Phillips had established his centralized and professionalized school regime, and once his professional rules of thumb had been sanctioned by community acceptance, those rules played a major role in determining racial allocation patterns and causing them to persist. At times the rules acted as buffers protecting blacks from even deeper cuts, but at other times they acted as constraints, perpetuating venerable patterns of discrimination.

Since the criteria and rules of thumb of the professional administrators were so important in shaping routine allocation decisions, black leaders found that if they could through lobbying with the administrators and board of education achieve a breakthrough on a pattern or rule of thumb, that breakthrough would be likely to persist far into the future.

Such a breakthrough was the establishment in 1901 of a black high school with a level of financial support well above the traditional black level. In 1883 Superintendent Phillips had established a white high school, grades 8 through 11, as soon as he had arrived in Birmingham, but for the blacks he had provided only elementary and grammar schools, advancing only through grade 7. Middle-class blacks disliked this glaring discrimination, and in the late 1890s, under the leadership of Dr. W. R. Pettiford, a black Baptist pastor and savings bank president, they launched a campaign for a black high school. The black leaders won the crucial support of the president of the school board, a prominent Jewish merchant and civic leader named Samuel Ullman, and in 1900, despite the political disfranchisement campaign going on at the time, despite the opposition of key white political leaders, and even despite reservations on the part of Superintendent Phillips, they gained approval for a black high school. The black leaders finally persuaded Phillips primarily by guaranteeing the enrollment of a sufficient number of *tuition-paying* black students to cover the entire cost of the black high school. In the white high school at that time tuition covered roughly 70 percent of the cost.[47]

The black high school was established in 1901 under the principalship of Arthur H. Parker, Pettiford's protege, and it proved to be a great success, developing quickly into the cultural center of Birmingham's black middle-class community. At first tuition in fact provided roughly 70 percent of the financial support of the black high school, as in the white high school, but by 1910 that percentage had dropped

[47] Arthur Harold Parker, *A Dream That Came True: Autobiography of Arthur Harold Parker* (Birmingham, 1932–33), 34–39; Birmingham *News*, January 18, May 3, June 11, September 4, 1900.

FIGURE 13

Comparison by Race of Birmingham High School and Elementary School Salary Expenditures per Student Based on Enrollment, 1900–1931

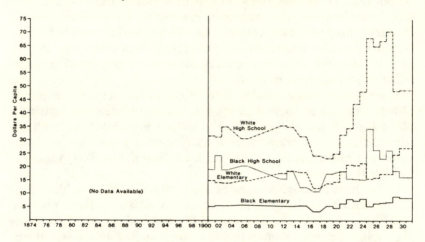

below 50 in both schools, and in 1910 the city abolished the tuition in both high schools.[48]

As Figure 13 shows, by 1910 the black patrons and the board of education had established a level of per capita expenditures for the black high school that was about the same as the level in the white elementary schools. That level was two to three times higher than the level in the black elementary schools but was only half the level in the white high school. That rough pattern, supported in the early years through black and white high school tuition payments, was firmly established by 1910 and was perpetuated with government revenue for decades after the abolition of high school tuition.

The black experience with the high school suggests not only the important role of professional allocation criteria in perpetuating established patterns, but also the crucial role played by the large middle-class black community that had emerged by 1900, a community whose leaders commanded substantial resources and understood how to appeal to the standards and rationalizations of professional educators.

All discriminatory allocations analyzed thus far have been annual operating expenditures, primarily for teachers' salaries, but blacks suffered greater discrimination in capital outlays for school build-

[48] Parker, *Dream That Came True*, 41–57; Birmingham, Board of Education, *Annual Report, 1902*, p. 13; *ibid., 1907*, p. 12; *ibid., 1910*, p. 78.

ings, which were politically much more difficult to obtain. Whereas decisions about salaries and class sizes involved slight annual incremental shifts and were made behind the scenes by an appointed school board according to internal professional recommendations of the superintendent, decisions to construct school buildings involved major monetary outlays that always inspired widely publicized debates among the elected aldermen or city commissioners and that after 1905 always required major campaigns to obtain referendum approval by the voters, campaigns in which the proportion of the funds to be spent on the black and the white schools became a topic of discussion. Moreover, the black and white schoolhouses themselves were quite visible public buildings, and white voters who found their own school buildings crowded and inadequate saw in every new building for blacks dramatic evidence of the diversion of tax dollars that could have upgraded white schools. Not surprisingly, the voters and the city officials frequently refused to construct all the buildings for blacks recommended by Superintendent Phillips. Consequently, the black/white ratios in value of school buildings per student in daily attendance were always much lower than the black/white ratios of teachers' salaries per student in daily attendance.[49]

Black leaders looked upon the inadequacy of black school buildings and upon the great difficulty of obtaining new buildings as crucial bottlenecks holding back the progress of black education generally, and black petitions to city officials devoted far more attention to buildings than to any other aspect of education. The light-frame schoolhouses for blacks were perennially dilapidated, unsanitary, vulnerable to fire, and severely overcrowded, and in the midst of such conditions black leaders found it terribly difficult to induce the many black children who were not in school to enroll. In most years only a very low proportion—about one-fourth—of the school-age black children were in daily attendance. Moreover, the shortage of black classrooms often prevented the hiring of more black teachers even when black enrollment did grow. Thus the space shortage led to discriminatory increases in the black pupil/teacher ratio. The black quest for new school buildings was almost continual, but progress came in a few exciting spurts, between which lay long periods of stagnation.[50]

[49] Birmingham, Board of Education, *Annual Report, 1911*, Exhibit B; *ibid., 1920*, pp. 35–44; Birmingham, Board of Education, *The Birmingham School Survey, 1923* (Birmingham, 1923), 110–56; Birmingham *News*, May 27, 1923.
[50] Birmingham, Board of Education, Minutes, III, 162 (November 6, 1905); *Annual Report, 1899*, p. 18; *ibid., 1902*, pp. 11, 19; Birmingham, *News*, January 18, May 2, 1900; March 7, 1905; U. G. Mason, M.D., *An Appeal to the White Citizens for Better Negro*

The first period of stagnation stretched from 1874 to 1882. During those years the board of aldermen sold city bonds to build a handsome $5,000 four-room brick school building for whites, and they used local revenue to finance ten-month school sessions for white children. But during the 1870s the board of aldermen, ignoring black petitions, took no responsibility for providing schoolhouses for blacks and provided no local revenue for black schools. Black parents had to arrange to use the state black allocation, which was meager in those days, to finance three-month sessions that met in churches and rented cabins. Thus in the matter of local governmental provision of school buildings, the earliest years in Birmingham conformed closely with the pattern found by historian Howard N. Rabinowitz in five other New South cities — a pattern of exclusion of blacks as cities began to provide services, followed after a few years by a shift to the provision of segregated and inferior facilities.[51]

In Birmingham, which was not founded until 1871 when Radical Reconstruction was already fading, the shift from exclusion to government provision of segregated black school buildings came not with the advent of Radical Republicans but rather in 1883 with the advent of the progressive school superintendent, John H. Phillips. Under Phillips the city finally assumed responsibility for black as well as white schoolhouses, and during the first phase of Phillips's construction program, from 1883 through 1887, the city built creditable frame schoolhouses for both races, moving black children from rented churches and renovated cottages into four commodious two-story institutional structures that had been designed for school use. (This is reflected in Figure 14.) The improvement of black physical facilities promoted an encouraging increase in black enrollment and attendance, and briefly it raised the black/white ratio of the value of school buildings per capita to more than .40 (see Figure 15).[52]

During the second phase of Phillips's construction program, 1887 through 1891, the city began to build stately brick structures for white schools, while continuing to build frame structures for black schools. (This is reflected in Figure 14.) As the value of the white

Schools in the City of Birmingham (Birmingham, 1909); Birmingham Reporter (Negro), October 15, 1915; August 18, 1917; March 3, 1923.

[51] Rabinowitz, Race Relations in the Urban South, 152–81; Birmingham, Minutes . . . Aldermen, B, 29 (December 23, 1873); 43 (February 4, 1874); 70 (April 10, 1874); 93 (July 15, 1874); 113 (September 11, 1874); 208–10 (August 4, 1875); 401 (September 6, 1876); 412–13 (October 4, 1876); Birmingham, Board of Education, Annual Report, 1887, pp. 39–42; Alabama, Department of Education, Annual Reports, 1876–1880.

[52] Birmingham, Board of Education, Annual Report, 1884, pp. 15–16; ibid., 1887, pp. 29–47; Birmingham, Board of Education, "The Superintendent's Report, 1884–1885" in Minutes, I, 38–39 (July 27, 1885).

FIGURE 14

Value of Birmingham School Buildings per Student Based on Average Daily Attendance, 1874–1931 (1913 Dollars)

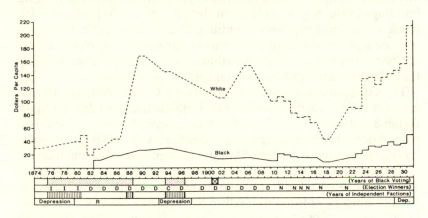

FIGURE 15

Black/White Ratio of the Value of Birmingham School Buildings per Student Based on Average Daily Attendance, 1874–1931

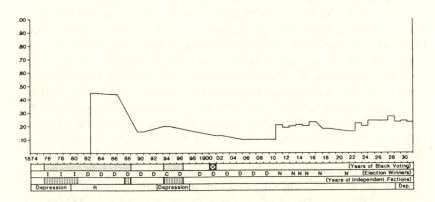

school structures surged upwards, the black/white ratio of the per capita value of school buildings sank to .16, even though from 1887 to 1891 the absolute per capita value of buildings for blacks rose from $13 to $19 (see Figures 14 and 15).[53]

A northern visitor who talked with Phillips about the large discrepancies in black and white buildings reported that Phillips and other southern urban progressive educators typically asserted that "the

[53] Birmingham, Board of Education, *Annual Report, 1891*, pp. 11–17, 39.

Negro school buildings compare as favorably with average Negro homes as the white school buildings do with white people's homes," and that, in fact, the Negro schools were "generally the best-looking buildings in the Negro sections of the city . . . ." To Phillips, such black school buildings were "creditable" and "sufficient"; they could provide a physical school environment superior to the physical surroundings in the black home, and thus they could help the school in its task of exercising uplifting leverage upon its students.[54]

The depression of the mid-1890s halted all school construction for a decade and reduced expenditures for maintenance, so that the light-frame buildings for black students deteriorated severely, and one burned down under mysterious circumstances. In 1899, as prosperity returned, Superintendent Phillips recommended the construction of four white schools and one large black school, but from 1900 to 1907 the mayor and aldermen constructed only the white schools. Phillips deeply deplored the failure to build new black schools, and he and the school board pointed out forcefully that the three surviving frame school buildings for blacks had deteriorated so severely that they were no longer creditable or sufficient, that they provided a depressing rather than an uplifting environment for their students, and that they were therefore utterly unfit for school use.[55]

After 1905 Phillips collaborated closely with a new self-styled "progressive" mayor, George B. Ward, in linking the need for new black school buildings with a broader progressive campaign to upgrade the sanitation and health of the city. Said Mayor Ward, "The colored people are so intertwined in the life and conditions of the South that they must either be elevated by the whites or the whites will be affected injuriously by them through bad health and sanitary conditions." Mayor Ward's new progressive emphasis on the possible citywide impact of bad conditions in the black community, including the black schools, helped him to achieve passage, in 1908, of a new bond issue that included money for Birmingham's first brick school for blacks. By 1911 the city had completed the "plain substantial" brick building with twenty-four classrooms, and the $46,000 cost of that one structure more than doubled the per capita value of school buildings for blacks for the entire Greater Birmingham area (see Figure 14). Ward and Phillips advocated more brick structures for blacks, but intensifying revenue shortages curtailed all school construction, black and white, until the post–World War I era, and until

[54] *Ibid.*, *1887*, p. 37; *ibid.*, *1891*, p. 70; A. J. McKelway, "Conservation of Childhood," *Survey*, XXVII (January 6, 1912), 1526.

[55] Birmingham, Board of Education, *Annual Report*, *1907*, pp. 23–26; *ibid.*, *1910*, pp. 3–8.

then most black students remained in dilapidated frame buildings.[56]

During World War I black leaders acquired greater leverage on city officials because those officials and Birmingham's leading industrialists became apprehensive about the loyalty of blacks in wartime and because labor shortages made Birmingham industrialists increasingly dependent upon black labor at the very time that opportunities in northern industry were causing many blacks to migrate to northern cities. Black leaders shrewdly used the wartime leverage to extract promises for construction of new black schools, and most of those promises were kept in the early 1920s, when the sudden influx of new earmarked local school revenue financed a new school construction program that finally achieved a broad upgrading of black school structures.[57]

In the 1920s the school board had a freer hand because in 1919 "progressive" forces in the state legislature had enacted a new state education code that for the first time removed all local elected officials from boards of education (the mayor had been sitting ex-officio on the Birmingham board) and that gave school boards independent legal and financial authority to construct buildings without seeking the approval of the elected city officials.[58] In 1921 Superintendent Phillips died suddenly, at the height of his powers and on the eve of forward steps for which he had long been laying groundwork, but he was succeeded by his protege, Charles B. Glenn, who continued his policies and emphases. After 1922 the school board built several large concrete and brick buildings for blacks despite protests by white labor organizations and by a vociferous Ku Klux Klan. Year by year the board moved large numbers of black students out of rickety, dangerous, old frame structures into plain but substantial concrete, brick, and stucco buildings. As of 1923, 70 percent of the enrolled black students studied in old, wooden buildings, but by 1931 only 33 percent did.[59]

The dramatic improvement in black buildings encouraged black

[56] Ibid., 1907, pp. 25–26; ibid., 1910, p. 5; ibid., 1913, p. 129; Birmingham School Survey, 1923, p. 157; Mayor Ward quoted in Birmingham News, May 1, 1909.

[57] Birmingham Age-Herald, April 7, 9, May 12, July 21, 28, 30, 1917; Birmingham Reporter (Negro), April 7, June 30, July 14, August 4, 11, 18, September 1, 15, 1917, March 16, 30, April 27, 1918; Birmingham, Board of Education, Report of Progress: Birmingham Public Schools, September 1, 1921 to August 31, 1931 (Birmingham, 1931), 184–99.

[58] Birmingham Age-Herald, February 19, 1920; Birmingham, Board of Education, Annual Report, 1920, p. 10; ibid., 1925, pp. 12–23, 51–53; Alabama, Department of Education, Annual Report, 1919, pp. 11–57.

[59] Birmingham, Board of Education, Birmingham School Survey, 1923, p. 33; Birmingham Board of Education, Annual Report, 1925, pp. 12–23, 51–53; Birmingham, Board of Education, Report of Progress, 1931, p. 187; Birmingham Labor Advocate, May 19, June 23, 1923; Birmingham News, May 26, 1923; May 13, 1927; Parker, Dream That Came True, 79–87.

leaders not only because it finally placed most black students in a school environment that met a minimum standard of decency but also because they believed the more attractive new buildings helped to stimulate an upsurge in black enrollment and attendance. As of 1916 only one-fourth of the black school-age children had been in daily attendance, a proportion that had held quite steady for more than twenty years, but by 1931 fully two-thirds of black school-age children were in daily attendance, and black leaders rejoiced that such an increased portion of young blacks were being brought into the uplifting milieu of the schools.[60]

Black leaders also attributed the attendance surge in part to the enactment, in 1915, of Alabama's first compulsory school attendance law, sponsored by progressives and professional educators, led by Superintendent Phillips. At first the law was not vigorously enforced among blacks, but Phillips and Glenn, his successor, took steps to provide increasingly effective enforcement of the law in both black and white areas, bringing a larger portion of Birmingham's school-age population, white and black, within the ambit and the responsibility of the schools. During the 1920s the compulsory attendance policy and the construction of more attractive school buildings for blacks reinforced each other in promoting an upsurge in black attendance. Thus did white, progressive, professional administrators purposefully stimulate black attendance growth that would, they knew, necessitate steady augmentations in the allocations for black education.[61]

As Figure 14 indicates, in only two periods—the expansionary 1880s and the expansionary 1920s—did blacks experience sustained augmentations to the per capita value of their school buildings. (The 1911 augmentation, reflecting the completion of the first brick school for blacks, was not sustained because revenue shortage abruptly halted all construction until 1919.) In both expansionary periods the augmentations provided significant advancements over the old black standard: in the 1880s from rented churches and shacks into creditable wooden institutional structures; and in the 1920s from worn-out, unsanitary, wooden buildings into substantial concrete and brick structures.

Both expansionary periods gave promise not only of *absolute* black

[60] Birmingham *Reporter*, December 21, 1929; September 13, 1930; November 28, 1931; Ambrose Caliver, "The Largest Negro High School," *School Life*, XVII (December 1931), 73–74.

[61] Birmingham, Board of Education, *Annual Report, 1920*, pp. 60–65; Birmingham *News*, September 7, 1910; John Herbert Phillips, "Conditions of Compulsory Education in the South" (Typescript, Research Department, Birmingham Board of Education).

advancement over old black levels, but also of *relative* black advancement upward toward the standard set by the white level. But such promise was usually only partially and temporarily fulfilled, since in both periods the expanding revenue provided resources to raise the white level also, placing it, in the end, approximately as far above the black level as before.

In the early 1880s, when the school board first began building wooden schools for blacks, while they were still building wooden schools for whites, the cost per square foot was roughly 50 percent as much for the more cheaply constructed wooden structures for black students as for those built for whites. And since the value of city-owned black buildings had started at zero in 1883, the new construction for use by blacks quickly produced a large relative gain—from .00 to .45—in the black/white ratio of the per capita value of school buildings (see Figure 15). But when the city in 1887 shifted to brick for new white schools, while continuing to use wood for new black schools, the relative construction cost per square foot dropped to only 17 percent as much for new black structures as for new white, and that was quickly reflected in a permanent drop in the black/white ratio of the per capita value of buildings.[62]

In the 1920s, when the progressive, white, professional administrators and the school board shifted from wood to brick, concrete, and stucco construction for new black schools, they tacitly adopted a rule of thumb that black construction costs would be roughly 50 percent of white costs per cubic foot—a rule to which they were to adhere for some years, and a rule that provides insight into the level of investment in physical plant that the progressives thought appropriate for black education. The new 50 percent rule of thumb, if sustained over time, portended long-run gains in the black/white ratio of the overall value of school buildings per capita. But, as Figure 15 shows, by 1931 the black/white ratio had not yet risen, largely because the dramatic black attendance surge continually outran the completion of new structures for black students, and because the white administrators, sliding away from rules of thumb regarding congestion, continually packed far more children into black classrooms than into white, and also continually resorted to the use of old frame structures that had almost no remaining monetary value. Thus by 1931 the overall black/white ratio of per capita value of buildings continued to stagnate at roughly .20.[63]

[62] Birmingham, Board of Education, *Annual Report, 1887*, p. 29; *Annual Report, 1891*, p. 39.

[63] Birmingham, Board of Education, *Birmingham School Survey, 1923*, pp. 20, 33, 36; Birmingham, Board of Education, *Report of Progress, 1931*, pp. 184–93.

FIGURE 16

Expenditures for Birmingham Teachers' Salaries per Student Based on Average Daily Attendance, by Race, 1874–1931 (1913 Dollars)

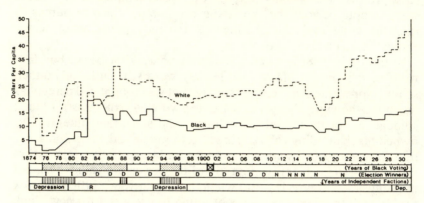

   As delineated in the first portion of this article, and as summarized in Figure 16, in the matter of expenditures for teachers' salaries, as in the matter of school buildings, blacks experienced *absolute* gains over old black levels only during the two periods of steadily expanding local school revenue—the 1880s and the 1920s. In the early 1880s the black salary expenditure per black student in daily attendance jumped from the $5 level to the $20 level and back down to the $15 level, where it hovered until the depression of the 1890s. The depression dragged it down to the $10 level (in constant dollars), where it stagnated until the 1920s. During the 1920s the school authorities used the local revenue growth to nearly double black salary expenditure per student in attendance, pushing them to $18.52 by 1932, even as the black daily attendance itself was surging upward. But during the 1920s the school administrators also used the local revenue growth to more than double white salary expenditures per student in attendance, pushing them from the pre–World War I level of $25 to a 1932 level of $54 (see Figure 16).

   What then was the *relative* pattern of black expenditures in the 1920s, in comparison with the white? Figure 17 measures the relative position of black salary expenditures according to two different black/white ratios—one ratio for all school-age children in the population and the other ratio only for children in daily attendance. Each ratio highlights significant aspects of the reality of the 1920s.

   The top line in Figure 17 measures the relative position of the races according to the black/white ratio of salaries *per child in attendance*.

FIGURE 17

Black/White Ratios of Expenditures for Birmingham Teachers' Salaries per Capita Based on Average Daily Attendance and on the Number of School-age Children in the Population, 1874-1931

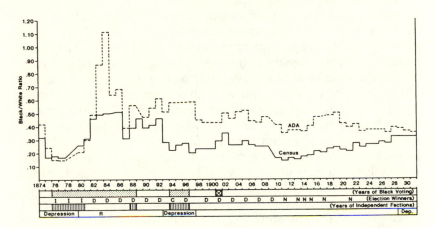

This ratio held rather steady at roughly 40 percent from 1910 through 1931, with a brief relative black gain during the world war years and with a relative black loss after the Great Depression descended in 1929. This highlights the fact that black increases per child in attendance were more than matched by white increases per child in attendance, so that at the end of the 1920s each black child in school suffered relative racial discrimination just as severe as at the beginning of the 1920s.

The bottom line in Figure 17 traces the black/white ratio based on *school-age children in the population*, as counted by the school census. This ratio, which repeats a line sketched in Figures 1 and 3, rose steadily during the 1920s. This reflected the fact that during these years the percentage of black school-age children who actually attended school increased from 24 percent of the black school-age population to 68 percent, an increase much steeper than the corresponding increase among white school-age children, from 54 percent to 74 percent. Thus, during the 1920s, black people, by sending such a dramatically increasing portion of their children to school, where each could lay claim to the rising expenditure per black child in attendance, managed to get white officials to enlarge the black school expenditure per child in the population more rapidly than they enlarged the white. The moderate relative gain in expenditures per school-age child, which blacks thus earned by bringing their rate of attendance almost up to the white rate, was significant, and blacks applauded it. Even after this gain, however, discrimination remained severe, with expenditure per black child in the population only one-third as much as per white child.[64]

Despite the sharp discrimination that remained and persisted, most black educators saw both expansionary periods—the 1880s and the 1920s—as periods of genuine progress in black education. They were encouraged by the absolute gains over old black levels, and they considered the attainment of certain minimal absolute levels of salaries and facilities to be crucial. During both periods black teachers' salaries climbed above a bare subsistence level, and during both periods black children moved out of dreadfully obsolete facilities into facilities that were spartan but that at least stood above a minimum decency threshold. In each period black leaders urged parents to hasten to take advantage of the new facilities, and in each period they were pleased to find that the improvements did foster new black pride in the schools and did help to inspire significant enrollment and attendance growth, thereby spreading the influence of the schools to a larger portion of young blacks. In each period black leaders hoped that the professional educators would regularly provide additional progressive steps, particularly as blacks demonstrated the good use they made of the new resources. Said Negro principal B. H. Hudson in 1884, after Superintendent Phillips had begun to move black children into city-owned institutional structures, "Now if the people want more and better schools, let those which you have be crowded to their utmost capacity, and I believe that you will find our city Fathers ready and willing to give them." The black educators hoped that if the city officials did regularly give "more and better schools," the schools could become agencies truly capable of uplifting the entire race, bringing it closer to the educational standard and the skill level seen in the white race.[65]

Black leaders typically phrased their requests to white leaders cautiously, asking for specific programs or buildings or for specific improvements needed to maintain basic standards of decency but not explicitly requesting relative advancement toward the white level.[66] Still, realization of the deepest black hopes for elevating the race through education would require a steady upward trajectory of black/white ratios, signifying persistent relative gains toward the white

[64] Report by Dr. Carol W. Hayes, supervisor of Birmingham Negro elementary schools, in Birmingham *Reporter*, November 28, 1931.

[65] Birmingham *Pilot* (Negro), March 22, 1884; Birmingham *Reporter*, October 19, December 21, 1929; January 17, 1930; November 28, December 19, 26, 1931.

[66] Birmingham *Reporter*, May 8, June 5, September 4, 1926, April 7, 1928.

level of school facilities and expenditures. But in each expansionary period black gains were finally more than matched by white gains, so that, as Figure 17 shows, over the course of half a century the black/white ratios of school expenditures, whether based on total school-age population or on average daily attendance, followed long-run downward trends that by 1930 left the black per capita expenditures at roughly one-third the white, in contrast to earlier periods when the ratio had been roughly one-half.

Clearly one of the factors that influenced the downward trajectory was the weakness of black leverage upon elections. Before 1901 strong antiblack attitudes and elaborate exclusionary devices undermined the effectiveness of the black vote, and in 1901 the new constitution disfranchised blacks, eliminating their electoral leverage completely. But in the urban center of Birmingham neither the black electoral gains and losses before 1901 nor the conclusive disfranchisement in 1901 translated as directly into immediate and commensurate gains and losses in relative school allocations as those that J. Morgan Kousser found for North Carolina or as Horace Mann Bond found for rural Alabama.

Several factors other than variations in electoral leverage helped to account for this pattern. In the plantation area of rural Alabama politically powerful white groups believed that rural investment in black education was already above the optimal absolute level and that it should be reduced. Consequently, when black electoral leverage declined and disappeared and when rural progressive education campaigns increased school revenue, the rural authorities distributed the increase almost entirely to whites. In the Alabama Black Belt they even reduced absolutely the allocation to blacks, thus sharply intensifying racial discrimination.

In Birmingham, by contrast, the politically dominant white interest groups and the progressive, professional administrators believed that the existing level of investment in local black education was below an optimal absolute level. Consequently, when prosperity and progressive reorganization enhanced local school revenue and placed control over school revenues and budgets more completely in the hands of professional school administrators, who were not as vulnerable as were elected officials to the strong antiblack views of the masses of white voters, those administrators proceeded to share some of the new revenue with blacks. By so doing they marginally increased the local absolute investment in black education, bringing black facilities and expenditures up to minimal levels that progressives considered essential. As a result, the black/white ratio of school expenditures was more stable in Birmingham than in rural Alabama or in North Carolina, and urban progressivism, as manifested in the school allocation patterns of the 1880s and the 1920s, brought blacks substantial absolute gains over old black levels.

Still, the urban, white, professional educators and the dominant urban, white, interest groups, while placing a higher value on black education than did most rural whites, nonetheless shared to a large degree the common white belief that black human beings were inherently less capable and less worthy, deserving a lesser educational investment from society. This belief strictly delimited the absolute educational gains and the educational thresholds that they prescribed for blacks. Accordingly, even in the best of times in the progressive urban South, when black education's most sympathetic white friends had maximum independence from white political pressures and maximum leeway to use new resources to increase black allocations, the black schools, though achieving urgently needed progress over debilitating old black levels, sank ever further below the more rapidly rising white level.

# The Anatomy of Failure: Medical Education Reform and the Leonard Medical School of Shaw University, 1882–1920

Darlene Clark Hine, *Vice Provost and Professor of History, Purdue University*

The Leonard Medical School of Shaw University, one of a dozen black medical schools established in the late nineteenth-century South,[1] operated for close to forty years. Leonard's development was affected by the transformation of the medical profession and by the emergence of philanthropic foundations as powerful benefactors of medical schools.[2] The reform impulse in American medicine was embodied in its most public form in Abraham Flexner's *Medical Education in the United States and Canada* financed by the Carnegie Foundation.[3] In this report, Flexner provided a critical evaluation of 155 medical schools, including those which were

---

[1]Some good recent studies of the American Medical profession which fail to address adequately the history of blacks in medicine include: Martin Kaufman, *American Medical Education: The Formative Years, 1765–1910* (Westport, Conn., Greenwood Press, 1976); John Duffy, *The Healers: A History of American Medicine* (Urbana: University of Illinois Press, 1976); E. Richard Brown, *Rockefeller Medicine Men: Medicine and Capitalism in America* (Berkeley: University of California Press, 1979); Paul Starr, *The Social Transformation of American Medicine* (New York: Basic Books, 1982).

[2]Howard Waitzkin, "Medical Philanthropies: The Band-Aid Treatment?" *The Sciences*, (July–August, 1980), 25–28; Howard S. Berliner, "Philanthropic Foundations and Scientific Medicine," Doctor of Science Thesis, School of Hygiene and Public Health, The Johns Hopkins University, 1977), pp. 143–45, 158.

[3]Abraham Flexner, *Medical Education in the United States and Canada* (New York: Carnegie Foundation, 1910); Berliner, "Philanthropic Foundations," pp. 147–49; Berliner, "A Larger Perspective on the Flexner Report," *International Journal of Health Services*, 5 (1975), 573–92; Robert P. Hudson, "Abraham Flexner in Perspective: American Medical Education, 1865–1910," *Bulletin of the History of Medicine*, 46 (Fall 1972), 545–61; Stephen Kunitz, "Professionalism and Social Control in the Progressive Era: The Case of the Flexner Report," *Social Problems*, 22 (October 1974), 16–27. See also Gerald E. Markowitz and David Karl Rosner, "Doctors in Crisis: A Study of the Use of Medical Education Reform to Establish Modern Professional Elitism in Medicine," *American Quarterly*, 25 (March, 1973), 83–107.

*Journal of Negro Education*, Vol. 54, No. 4 (1985)
Copyright © 1985, Howard University

512

responsible for training the vast majority of early black physicians. Perhaps because they survived, the larger and more resourceful institutions—Howard University Medical School in Washington and Meharry Medical School in Nashville—have received some scholarly attention.[4] Little is known, however, about the Leonard Medical School in Raleigh, North Carolina, which existed from 1882 to 1920. Leonard was one of the many schools which Flexner deemed "beyond repair."

Among the other black institutions which Flexner designated inadequate were: Flint Medical College in New Orleans, Knoxville Medical College in Knoxville, the Medical Department of the University of West Tennessee in Memphis; and the National Medical College in Louisville. This brief history of the Leonard Medical School examines the responses of the school's white administrators to the vortex of convergent nineteenth- and twentieth-century reform impulses within the medical profession. There is yet another reason for investigating the rise and fall of this obscure medical school for blacks. An examination of the Leonard failure provides deeper understanding of the reasons why Howard and Meharry survived to become the institutional anchors of the black medical education system in America.

The Flexner Report sent shock waves throughout the medical profession. Flexner's observations stimulated an already reform-minded American Medical Association (AMA) to intensify efforts to upgrade medical education and health care delivery. His critique of medical education gave to the AMA ideological hegemony in the field of medicine and made it the dominant professional organization.[5] His trenchant diagnosis of ills that afflicted the medical profession and prescriptive suggestions rested upon the ideology that a higher socioeconomic status for physicians could best be achieved by a significant reduction in the numbers of undertrained doctors. Toward this end, Flexner advocated the closing of dozens of inadequate medical schools, on the one hand, and the simultaneous adoption of higher admission standards for those remaining. He

---

[4]Darlene Clark Hine, "The Pursuit of Professional Equality: Meharry Medical College, 1921–1938, A Case Study," in Vincent P. Franklin and James D. Anderson, eds., *New Perspectives on Black Educational History* (Boston: G. K. Hall, 1978), pp. 173–92; Leslie A. Falk, "Meharry Medical College: A Century of Service," *Southern Exposure*, 6 (Summer 1978), 14–17; Leslie A. Falk and N. A. Quaynor-Malm, "Early Afro-American Medical Education in the United States: The Origins of Meharry Medical College in the Nineteenth Century," *Proceedings of the XXIII Congress of the History of Medicine* (London: September 2–9, 1972), pp. 346–56; James Summerville, *Educating Black Doctors: A History of Meharry College* (University: University of Alabama Press, 1983), pp. 31–32; and Rayford W. Logan, *Howard University: The First Hundred Years, 1867–1967* (New York: New York University Press, 1969), pp. 42, 47.

[5]Berliner, "Philanthropic Foundations," pp. 83–107.

argued that a good medical school should possess well-equipped laboratories, a comprehensive library affiliated with a teaching hospital, and, perhaps most important, should employ a full-time faculty of research scientists and clinical instructors. Higher admission standards and the need for large-scale capital outlay for new laboratory and library facilities and faculties meant a corresponding increase in tuition fees and selection of better educated students. The consequences of implementing these changes were predictable. Less competitive, academically inferior, and unendowed medical schools—precisely those institutions which attracted lower-class white males, blacks, and women students—were endangered.

Actually, the medical schools established for blacks, with the exception of Meharry and Howard, were an endangered species long before Flexner's evaluation appeared. As early as the 1890s the Association of American Medical Colleges (AAMC) and various state licensing boards of examiners had already adopted significant reforms including higher admission standards, a more rigorous curriculum, and tougher requirements for graduation.[6] Thus, the winds of reform within the medical profession were already evolving into gusty gales spelling doom for the ill-equipped and financially unstable institutions, both black and white, long before the publication of the Flexner Report. Beginning in 1912, however, Flexner was appointed to the influential position of general secretary of the Rockefeller Foundation's General Education Board (GEB). Now in control of almost unlimited financial resources, Secretary Flexner, could employ Rockefeller millions to create and shape his vision of a medical education system appropriate to the needs of black and white Americans.

Decades before the GEB and other philanthropic foundations would become interested in black medical education, northern white Baptist and Methodist missionaries had attempted to address the need for more, and better, trained black physicians by establishing three black medical schools: Meharry, Leonard, and the Medical Department of New Orleans University (renamed in 1901 the Flint Medical College). Moreover, the absence of adequate hospital facilities and black health care personnel, which undoubtedly contributed to the poor health that black southerners endured in the post-Civil War years, had aroused the concern of the United States government. The forty-seven hospitals established by the Freedmen's Bureau during the Civil War, however, were by the 1880s a distant memory. Of this number, only Freedmen's Hospital in

[6]Kaufman, *American Medical Education*, pp. 155.

Washington, D.C., survived into the twentieth century. In 1868, the United States Congress appropriated funds to establish the Howard University School of Medicine in order to provide competent hospital personnel and to train black physicians.[7] The black medical schools created and managed by white missionaries, and those headed by black and white physicians, lacking the government support which Howard enjoyed, existed on a precarious economic foundation, as did many of their white counterparts. As long as Howard received support from the U.S. government its survival was ensured. This was not the case with Leonard and Meharry. But, Meharry still exists and Leonard does not. Thus, the question to be explored is why Leonard failed.

The origins and early history of Leonard and Meharry are strikingly similar. Both medical schools originated as special departments within black colleges which owed their existence to white missionary organizations. In 1875 the American Baptist Home Society donated the initial funds for the establishment of Shaw University, subsequent home of the Leonard Medical School. Likewise, the Freedman's Aid Society of the Methodist Episcopal Church bore the financial responsibility for Central Tennessee College and its medical department, later renamed the Meharry Medical College.[8]

White Civil War veterans administered both institutions. Leonard's first president was Henry Martin Tupper (1831–1893), a native of Monson, Massachusetts, and graduate of Amherst College (1859) and the Newton Theological Institute (1862). Moving to Raleigh, North Carolina, in 1865, Tupper established Shaw College, a theological seminary devoted to the training of "a colored ministry." Tupper convinced potential benefactors of the connection between medicine and ministry by arguing that the "colored Christian physician" would represent the highest achievement of the black race. Meharry's founder, George W. Hubbard, like Tupper, decided to remain in the South following the War and to make his life among the freedmen of Nashville, Tennessee. Hubbard earned a medical degree from the Nashville (later renamed the Vanderbilt) Medical

[7]Thomas Holt, Cassandra Smith-Parker and Rosalyn Terborg-Penn, *A Special Mission: The Story of Freedmen's Hospital, 1862–1962* (Washington, D.C.: Academic Affairs Division of Howard University, 1975), pp. 1–9; and Logan, *Howard University.*

[8]Charles Victor Roman, *Meharry Medical College, A History* (Nashville, Tenn.: Sunday School Publishing Board of the National Baptist Convention, Inc., 1934), pp. 24–33. In 1900 the name was changed from the Medical Department of Central Tennessee to the Meharry Medical College of Walden University. On October 13, 1915, Meharry was granted a separate corporate existence. Clara Barnes Jenkins, "An Historical Study of Shaw University, 1865–1963." (Ed. D. diss., University of Pittsburgh, 1965), pp. 36–60.

School, and in 1876 accepted the position of dean of the newly formed medical department of the Central Tennessee College.[9]

The transformation of dreams of a good medical school into a going concern required a great deal of money, and Tupper and Hubbard enjoyed some initial success in fund-raising. In part, to repay those who contributed substantial sums during these formative years, both medical schools were named after white benefactors. In 1882 Tupper received a $6,000 contribution from his brother-in-law, Judson Wade Leonard of Hampden, Massachusetts, along with a small grant from the newly created John F. Slater Fund.[10] Hubbard received start-up funds from Samuel Meharry, a white farmer living in Shawnee Mound, Indiana. Meharry donated $500 and thereupon persuaded his brothers, Alexander, Hugh, David, and Jesse to give even more. The Meharry family eventually contributed over thirty thousand dollars to the institution which bears their name.[11]

Parallels in the early history of Leonard and Meharry persisted throughout the closing decades of the nineteenth century. Both schools, operating on miniscule budgets, lacked decent equipment, libraries, and clinical facilities. At each school students received instruction from part-time faculties comprised of white southern physicians. Leonard's six faculty members were all residents of Raleigh and were either ex-slaveholders themselves or the sons of former slaveholders. Dr. James McKee, the superintendent of the Insane Asylum for White People, served as dean of the Leonard Medical School for over twenty years. Initially, Meharry relied on the services of seven local white physicians. One of the earliest faculty members was W. G. Snead, a former Confederate army surgeon.[12] In the absence of a pool of black physicians, Tupper and Hubbard were left with no other recourse than to depend upon white physicians. Actually, there were advantages to having a faculty made up of local white physicians. Tupper, for one, was quite pleased that one member of the Leonard's faculty served on the North Carolina Medical Board. This particular faculty member, in preparing students to take the examination, was apparently responsible for the large number of Leonard graduates who successfully

[9]Jenkins, "Shaw University," pp. 49–59; Henry M. Tupper, *Twentieth Annual Report of Shaw University, 1886–1887.* Copies of all Annual Reports were found at the Shaw University Library, Raleigh, North Carolina. A copy of the original Charter of Shaw University was discovered in the General Education Board (GEB) Papers, Box 103, Folder 929, Rockefeller Archive and Research Center, Pocantico Hills, New York. Also see Hine, "Meharry Medical College," p. 175.

[10]Jenkins, "Shaw University," pp. 49–59.

[11]Hine, "Meharry Medical College," p. 175.

[12]Falk, "Meharry Medical College," p. 15; Jenkins, "Shaw University," p. 60.

earned their licenses. Tupper often related the anecdote that during the course of one state board examination in which several Leonard students performed admirably, a bewildered examiner rhetorically muttered, "What does it mean that the colored young men are passing a better examination than the white young doctors?"[13]

The advent of the twentieth century, however, found the two institutions embarking on divergent paths, one heading toward success and the other toward failure. That Meharry continued to develop and to receive adequate support from the Methodists and other white philanthropists is well known. Leonard was not so fortunate and as the years passed it was handicapped by decreasing financial support and plagued by well-intentioned but inadequate management. To his credit, Tupper, throughout his reign, struggled valiantly to keep Leonard's doors open and to increase the school's operating budget. He used student labor to construct a building for the medical school; he organized fairs and other social events to solicit private donations from black and white Baptists. In 1890 he received a timely gift of $12,000 from John D. Rockefeller. Yet, in spite of his best efforts the medical school's continuing drain on the resources of the university led trustees and others to question the wisdom of keeping it afloat. Undaunted, Tupper refused to abandon the school, insisting that "no class of laborers will be more useful to the colored race than the educated Christian doctor."[14] As financial pressures mounted, however, Tupper collapsed under the strain; he died in the fall of 1893.

Charles F. Meserve, also white and a native of Plymouth County, Massachusetts, who had served as superintendent and special disbursing agent at Haskell Institute (an Indian Industrial Training School) in Lawrence, Kansas, became the second president of Shaw University. He was equally as determined as his predecessor to continue operating the Leonard Medical School. Meserve occupied the presidency until 1919, overseeing the graduation of 438 black doctors.[15]

Meserve had been in office only a short time before the full realization of Leonard's financial problems set in. He soon acknowledged that the medical school had never been placed on a sound economic foundation. After reviewing Tupper's records, Meserve noted that, "My predecessor was enabled to keep the institution going only by devoting all the money he could possibly collect from

[13]*19th Annual Report of Shaw University, 1884–1885;* also see the 21st and 22nd Annual Reports, 1887–1889, Raleigh, North Carolina.
[14]Jenkins, "Shaw University," pp. 49–60; 29th Annual Report, May 31, 1894.
[15]Jenkins, "Shaw University," pp. 49–60.

the students and other sources to paying the salaries of the medical professors." Meserve observed that even this practice proved insufficient: "For year by year he (Tupper) was obliged to transfer funds from other departments to the medical, and after this was done, there was a large deficiency, which he met by borrowing from banks."[16]

Perennial economic difficulties amounted to only a part of Meserve's myriad dilemmas. Just as he was beginning to discover the extent of the financial problems he also had to grapple with the necessity of implementing the higher admission requirements, extensive curriculum revisions, and the more demanding graduation reform policies promulgated by the AAMC. According to new rules, students seeking admission to medical schools now had to possess high school diplomas and/or to demonstrate proficiency in Latin, arithmetic, and elementary physics. All AAMC member institutions had to institute a new three-year curricula, extending each academic year to six months. In addition, the AAMC made oral and written examinations and completion of laboratory work in chemistry, histology and pathology prerequisites for graduation. Many southern white physicians applauded the reforms, and indeed a significant group of them worked to make them even stronger. In 1892 these reform-minded physicians met to organize the Southern Medical College Association (SMCA). The group thereupon adopted a resolution requiring all potential students to have completed, at minimum, the first year of high school. In the mid-1890s the organization voted to extend the three-year curriculum an additional year, effective in 1899.[17]

Leonard's white faculty readily endorsed the four-year course reform. In fact, from its inception, Leonard had adopted a four-year course as one measure to overcome the tremendous deficiences in the prior academic preparation of black students seeking admission. Many students entered the school without high school diplomas. An early catalogue read, "while a two to three year's course would doubtless at first have secured a larger attendance, yet in the end, a four year's course will ensure thoroughness that will give confidence and confer lasting benefits."[18] Occasionally there were exceptions, and some students were allowed to earn a medical

---

[16]Charles F. Meserve to J. L. M. Curry, January 9, 1895, Charles F. Meserve Letters, Shaw University Library, Raleigh, North Carolina. Unprocessed File. (Hereinafter, Meserve will be referred to by surname only.)

[17]Kaufman, *American Medical Education*, p. 155; G. C. Savage, "Medical Education in the South," *Bulletin of the American Academy of Medicine*, 4 (October 1899), pp. 358–75; Duffy, *The Healers*, p. 362.

[18]*The 16th Annual Catalogue of the Officers and Students of Leonard Medical School*, 1896, Shaw University Library.

degree without completing the full four years. Responding to a potential applicant, Meserve declared that, "if a student, at the end of three years, is able to pass an examination in all branches of medicine, he will be allowed to graduate and receive his diploma."[19]

It was easier for Leonard to enforce the four-year curriculum requirement than it was to raise admission standards, improve instruction, and provide adequate clinical facilities. Leonard's student body came from the most impoverished and under-educated sector of southern black society. Thus, higher admission standards would have severely restricted the eligible population of students. Not only did the students lack suitable academic skills, they also found it difficult to secure funds with which to pay for tuition and fees, room and board, and books. To ease the financial strain on incoming students, Tupper had granted each student a $60 renewable tuition scholarship. Actually, this scholarship was little more than a paper transfer, for students never received any money. Instead, the funds were used to pay faculty salaries.[20] This strategy of awarding paper scholarships proved to be an effective recruitment technique and an attractive fund raising device. Donors were more inclined to contribute to scholarships than to give money for faculty salaries.

Meserve continued Tupper's scholarship aid program and instituted a work-study plan. He assisted students in finding summer employment as Pullman car porters, waiters, and handymen around the college and in town, or as office assistants to local white physicians. Although the costs of room, board, and books rarely exceeded $8.00 per month, Meserve was frequently unable to collect even this nominal sum. As the financial pressures mounted, Meserve lamented to Tupper's widow that student debts from 1889 to 1895 amounted to over $9,000. Meserve and his predecessor's fiscal policies subsidized virtually the entire cost of the medical education of the student body. When the Trustees and benefactors suggested an increase in room and board fees, Meserve resisted, asserting that while the fees were "so low as to seem almost ridiculous . . . the means of the students are so slender that the charge cannot be increased."[21]

Without adequate fees, tuition, and income from benefactors, the school's laboratories and clinical facilities steadily deteriorated.

[19]Meserve to E. C. Merchant, March 16, 1898, Meserve Letters.
[20]*16th Annual Catalogue, 1896;* Meserve to J. B. Bennett, March 15, 1898, Meserve Letters.
[21]Meserve to Mrs. H. M. Tupper, January 4, 1895; Meserve to Mrs. A. S. Leonard, February 18, 1898; Meserve to Reverend D. S. Sanders, October 4, 1895; Meserve to Curry, January 9, 1895; Meserve to General T. J. Morgan, January 20, 1895. All are located in Meserve letters.

Because all of the money was deployed to pay faculty salaries, little remained for rehabilitating the physical plant. By the late 1890s Meserve privately despaired over the future of the institution. His relationship with the institution remained, at best, ambivalent. He never wavered in his commitment to the necessity of providing blacks with medical education. Yet he knew that the quality of such instruction and training as provided by Leonard was inadequate. He was trapped in a classic dilemma of his time. Where else were poor, academically lacking black farm youths to go for a medical education? All of the better-equipped white schools stringently adhered to segregationist doctrines. At the beginning of one school term he wrote, "We opened last Tuesday although we were hardly in condition to do so on account of our building operations and extensive repairs." Elaborating, he added that "all charts, skeletons, models, manikins, etc., that are indispensable to good work are in nearly every instance almost worthless." He confided that the library and reading room existed in name only while the hospital, established to provide clinical experience for the students, needed massive and immediate renovation. Finally, he noted that the medical school buildings were "cold, damp, dark fire traps" and remained unconnected to sewer lines.[22]

Meserve's attempts to raise funds to refurbish Leonard's delapidated physical plant and his appeals to the Baptist Home Mission Society for increased allocations met a cool reception. Leaders of the Society were reluctant to support the medical apparatus at Shaw. Many considered more realistic the Booker T. Washington philosophy of concentrating on industrial education as the type of learning most suitable for blacks. Meserve and his white medical school faculty futilely tried to persuade Society members to their point of view. In one jointly signed letter the faculty maintained that, "from a wide acquaintance with the colored people and a careful observation of their home life, it has come to be, not merely an opinion, but a strong conviction, that the educated Christian physician is doing more to directly and immediately improve the home life of the colored people than the educated teacher, the educated minister, the educated businessman, the educated lawyer or the educated mechanic." The physicians argued, "The home life and sanitary surroundings of the colored people of this city have been materially improved since one of our graduates, ten years ago, entered upon the practice of medicine."[23] The Baptist Home Mission

[22]Meserve to Reverend D. S. Sanders, October 4, 1895. Meserve Letters.
[23]Leonard Medical School Faculty to E. O. Silver, Chairman of the Board of Trustees, February 16, 1897, Meserve Letters.

Society members were unmoved. Frustrated, Meserve threatened, "It will be utterly impossible to continue this department unless something is done, and right soon."[24]

Unable to raise money from the Baptists, Meserve turned northward only to confront growing indifference. When his numerous solicitations to scores of prospective northern white donors, church organizations, and philanthropic foundations netted little return, he declared, "the younger generations are not imbued with the ideas and enthusiasm of the old anti-slavery agitators, workers and friends. The fact must not be overlooked that as the years go by, the North is taking less and less interest in this work in the South." Unwilling to abandon his quest for capital, Meserve next appealed to southern whites. After the white faculty of Leonard agreed to forego portions of their salary, Meserve proudly proclaimed that, "these white physicians, men who were born and bred in the South, by their scholarly instruction and daily example, are in my judgment, doing more to break down any prejudice that may have existed and to build up education for the colored people in the South, than could be done in any other way."[25] In fact, the white physicians had little choice but to make these contributions, for Meserve simply did not have the money with which to pay all of their salaries.

Meanwhile, as Leonard existed on the brink of disaster, powerful and wealthy philanthropic foundations were becoming much more interested in all aspects of black education. In the opening years of the twentieth century, John D. Rockefeller created and endowed the General Education Board (GEB).[26] The GEB quickly became the major philanthropic foundation concerned with upgrading the quality of black medical education. The GEB's attention soon focused on Leonard. As a result of Meserve's 1904 appeal to the John F. Slater Fund for assistance, W. T. B. Williams, a general field agent, visited Leonard. Williams shared his optimistic evaluation of the school with the officers of the GEB. Mindful of the major shortcomings, Williams nevertheless filed a favorable report and declared that Leonard should continue its work. He wrote, "After looking at them [the students], and taking into consideration the grade of school from which most of them have come, I am of the opinion that they are fairly well prepared for such work . . . I

[24]Meserve to Reverend J. L. Richardson, Deacon Gutterson and Samuel Colgate, January 3, 1895; Meserve to Anna Leonard, February 18, 1898; Meserve Letters.

[25]Meserve to Curry, January 9, 1895, Meserve to Leonard, February 18, 1898. Meserve Letters.

[26]In 1903 John D. Rockefeller gave Shaw University $1500. The gift was duly recorded in the Secretary's Minutes of the Shaw University Board of Trustees Meeting, April 30, 1903. Copy of Minutes book found in the Shaw University Library. Unprocessed files.

should like to see this school strengthened as much as possible, especially in the way of science equipment for laboratory work."[27] On the basis of Williams's report, the GEB granted $13,000 to the American Baptist Home Mission Society for use at Shaw University. The GEB stipulated, however, that North Carolina blacks had to raise a matching sum of five thousand dollars before January 1, 1907.[28]

The GEB award was welcomed, but Leonard's complex array of problems eluded easy resolution. In May, 1907, Meserve again appealed to the GEB for a grant of $12,493.95 with which he promised to place "the Medical School on its feet." After delineating the significant reforms in American medicine, he concluded, "A crisis has come in the life of the Leonard Medical School." He elaborated, "The requirements for admission to Medical Schools have been raised and the examinations for licenses before the State Medical Examining Boards have become much more severe than formerly. Better equipment and a large teaching force are, therefore, demanded." In pointing out the impact on Leonard of the higher standards and medical education reforms, Meserve asserted that, "This lack of equipment prevents us from receiving recognition from some of the State Medical Examining Boards, and from obtaining membership in the American Association of Medical Colleges."[29]

Meserve's intense concentration on fund-raising ill prepared him for the shock of the Flexner Report. With the appearance of the published evaluation of the Leonard Medical School, Meserve's chances for procuring major philanthropic grants all but disappeared. In a straightforward, damning, albeit accurate, portrayal, Flexner described Leonard as, "A philanthropic enterprise that has been operating for well-nigh thirty years and has nothing in the way of plant to show for it." He deemed the laboratory and clinical facilities "hardly more than nominal," consisting of an "exceedingly well-kept dissecting room, a slight chemical laboratory, and a still slighter equipment of pathology." He counted three patients at the school's sixteen-bed hospital and observed that the school lacked a library, museum, dispensary, and teaching accessories.[30]

---

[27]W. T. B. Williams, Summary of Visit to Shaw University, Raleigh, North Carolina. No exact date was on the document. GEB Papers, Box 103, Folder 929.

[28]Williams made subsequent visits in 1906 and 1907. The summaries of his reports are dated March 17, 1906 and January 13, 1907 respectively. A memorandum regarding Shaw University, approved by the GEB Executive Committee, detailing stipulations of the grant was dated November 7, 1904. GEB Papers, Box 103, Folder 929.

[29]Meserve to Wallace Buttrick, May 25, 1907. GEB Papers, Box 103, Folder 929.

[30]Flexner, *Medical Education*, Chapter 14, pp. 280–282, 303–305; Also see Herbert M. Morais, *The History of the Negro in Medicine* (New York, 1967), pp. 60–61, 228.

Flexner did not restrict his critical assessment of Leonard merely to deficiencies in instruction. Moving beyond the obvious flaws, Flexner attacked the managerial and fiscal policies pursued by Tupper and Meserve as constituting the paramount reason for the poor quality of the Leonard Medical School. He observed that, "It is evident that the policy of paying practitioners has absorbed the resources of a school that exists for purely philanthropic objects." In Flexner's opinion, the "income ought to have been spent within; it has gone outside to reimburse practitioners who supposed themselves assisting in a philanthropic work."[31]

Although Leonard possessed a few redeeming characteristics, namely its missionary zeal and emphasis on sanitation training, Flexner advised that philanthropists desiring to aid the cause of black medical education would do well to spend their money elsewhere. Of the eight existing black medical schools, Flexner considered only Meharry and Howard worthy of salvation. He declared the remaining schools "in no position to make any contribution of value" and asserted that they were "wasting small sums annually sending out undisciplined men, whose lack of real training is covered up by the imposing M.D. degree." Flexner recommended that since Howard's future was virtually assured because of the support of the Federal Government, private benefactors should funnel their money to support and upgrade Meharry. In arguing for the strengthening of Meharry, Flexner declared, "It is in management, location and other essential factors considered the most important school for the training of Negro physicians in the country."[32]

In spite of Flexner's negative assessment of Leonard, Meserve held fast to his dreams and convictions. He refused to acquiesce to the charted fate and searched desperately for a solution whereby the institution could be saved. It is ironic that Flexner and Meserve shared many of the same values and assumptions concerning the role and place of the black physician in American medicine. Flexner had asserted that, "the Negro needs good schools rather than many schools—schools to which the more promising of the race can be sent to receive a substantial education in which hygiene rather than surgery, for example, is strongly accentuated." He added, "If at the same time these men can be imbued with the missionary spirit so that they will look back upon the diploma as a commission to serve their people humbly and devotedly, they may play an impor-

[31]Flexner, *Medical Education*, pp. 281–82.
[32]Ibid.; Abraham Flexner to William C. Graves, The Julius Rosenward Fund, March 19, 1917, quoted in Hine, "Meharry Medical College," p. 176.

tant part in the sanitation and civilization of the whole nation."[33] The major difference between Flexner's and Meserve's views on black medical education concerned the number of schools needed to train the black sanitation expert physician. Flexner believed two such schools sufficient to meet the black need while Meserve desired that the number be increased to three, with Leonard being the third school worthy of white philanthropic support.

In spite of Flexner's criticisms, Meserve again tried to preserve Leonard by appealing to the Board of Trustees of Shaw University. He reasoned that if he could secure membership in the AAMC, philanthropic foundations would look upon requests for funds with more favor. His efforts met with partial success. As a compromise solution, in 1914 the Board of Trustees instructed Meserve to try to work out a plan whereby Leonard could serve as a two-year preparatory school for those black students who wished to enter Meharry or Howard. Accordingly, Meserve contacted administrators of both schools and for a moment it seemed that there was a chance that Leonard would survive to fill this intermediary position in the black medical education system. Officers of the three institutions agreed to cooperate on the condition that the GEB grant them two million dollars, with eight hundred thousand going to Meharry and Howard respectively and four hundred thousand going to Leonard. They submitted a proposal to the funding agency, arguing that "Shaw, being in close proximity to the raw material from which physicians are made, can at much less cost carry on the preparatory work for Howard University (and Meharry), and through this medium our output of graduates can be doubled."[34]

Officers of the GEB reviewed the proposal and voted against it. Flexner's view, that two black medical schools were sufficient and that the problems afflicting Leonard were beyond redress, prevailed. By 1919 all of the philanthropic foundations concentrated on providing funds to strengthen Howard and Meharry. In February of that year Meharry received a $150,000 grant toward a permanent endowment from the Carnegie Foundation. A month later, the GEB appropriated an identical amount to the same institution. Howard University, too, benefited from foundation largess, receiving a $250,000 award from the GEB. The grant stipulated that the money be used to improve clinical instruction and to pay the salaries of several fulltime clinical assistants. Having exhausted

[33]Flexner, *Medical Education*, pp. 281–82.
[34]Secretary's Minutes—Shaw University Board of Trustees Meeting, February 4, 1910, April 6, 1911; Petition Proposal prepared by Dr. A. M. Moore, March 27, 1918. Copy found among notes of the Board of Trustees Meeting minutes.

524  *The Journal of Negro Education*

every strategy, unable to secure adequate funds with which to keep abreast of new techniques, equipment, and facilities, the Leonard Medical School closed officially in 1920.[35]

A confluence of several interrelated factors contributed to the failure of the Leonard Medical School. From the outset the school existed on a precarious financial foundation. The fiscal policies pursued by the school's administrators which channeled all funds raised into faculty salaries left nothing for the repair and rehabilitation of a woefully inadequate and delapidated physical plant. The school's inability to inaugurate higher admission standards, improve instruction, and secure membership in professional accreditation organizations spelled doom even before the Flexner Report appeared. This is not to say that the report held no significance for Leonard. In revealing the institution's internal structural and administrative inadequacies to the larger philanthropic community, it sealed Leonard's fate. To be sure, both Meharry and Howard suffered many deficiencies, but the pivotal factor was that Flexner deemed them both worth saving.

On the strength of Flexner's subsequent recommendations, the major white philanthropic foundations poured money into Meharry, thus enabling it to construct new buildings, purchase up-to-date equipment and supplies, and hire a full-time faculty. Howard's survival was never really in question, for as long as it received funds from the United States government the school could implement the reforms required by the AMA. No such support was forthcoming to Leonard. The closing of Leonard in an era when all white southern medical schools and many northern ones excluded blacks helped to determine the future availability of black physicians and severely restricted the opportunities for blacks desirous of entering the medical profession.

[35]Henry S. Pritchett to Bishop Thomas Nicholson, February 24, 1919; Wallace Buttrick to Nicholson, March 3, 1919, GEB Papers, Box 133, Folder 1228; Flexner to J. Stanley Durkee, February 28, 1920, GEB Papers, Box 28, Folder 257.

# A Black Teacher and Her School
# in Reconstruction Darien:
# The Correspondence of Hettie Sabattie and
# J. Murray Hoag, 1868-1869

By WHITTINGTON B. JOHNSON

The education of blacks was one of the most sudden and significant changes wrought in the South during Reconstruction. Much of this achievement was due to northern white benevolent societies, such as the American Missionary Association, the Methodist Freedmen's Aid Society and the American Freedmen's Union Commission, each of which was instrumental in making educational efforts a function of the Freedmen's Bureau, contrary to the initial intent of Congress when it created that agency in March 1865.[1] Much credit should also go to the pioneer black teachers—freedmen as well as southern and northern free persons of color—who established schools throughout the South for African-Americans who had been prohibited from learning how to read or write under slavery. In some communities, white benevolent societies and local black groups simultaneously operated separate schools, which often led to rancorous rivalries. Blacks were usually distrustful of whites, while whites were disdainful of black teachers and dismayed at the popularity of black-controlled schools among black families who preferred them to the white-managed counterparts, even when the latter were free and the former charged tuition.[2]

---

[1]Ronald E. Butchart, *Northern Schools, Southern Blacks, and Reconstruction: Freedmen's Bureau Education, 1862-1875* (Westport, Conn., 1980), 98. The author would like to thank his colleague Janet Martin for helpful suggestions.

[2]Jacqueline Jones, *Soldiers of Light and Love: Northern Teachers and Georgia Blacks, 1865-1873* (Chapel Hill, 1980), 69-70; James D. Anderson, *The Education of Blacks in the South, 1865-1935* (Chapel Hill, 1988), 12; Robert C. Morris, *Reading, 'Riting and Reconstruction: The Education of Freedmen in the South, 1861-1870* (Chicago, 1976), 90-91.

---

MR. JOHNSON is associate professor of history at the University of Miami.

THE GEORGIA HISTORICAL QUARTERLY
VOL. LXXV, No. 1, SPRING 1991

Thoughout the South and almost without exception, black schools were established in areas promptly after their occupation by Union troops, and freedmen received them enthusiastically.[3] Most teachers were white females from New England and the Midwest. They generally had similar family and religious backgrounds, had been trained in recently established normal schools, and had journeyed south to spread Yankee work ethics, moral values, and religious tenets among the newly emancipated populace. Their stories are those of triumph and defeat, joy and sadness, ease and hardship, sincerity and hypocrisy, commitment and indecision.[4]

Although less numerous than their white counterparts, black teachers were predominantly male and their backgrounds more diverse. According to Robert C. Morris, "Their ranks included former slaves and free blacks. They varied widely with respect to academic competence. They came from all social classes. Some had extensive teaching experience; some had none at all. There were radicals among them, but there were also teachers closely allied with conservative Southern whites."[5] In Georgia, about two hundred native black men and women taught in freedmen schools in at least seventy counties. Men outnumbered women by almost two to one, and most of the latter were single and very young, in their teens and twenties. The efforts of those Georgia blacks were supplemented by eighteen New England African-Americans sponsored by freedmen's aid societies.[6]

Black teachers were sent primarily to rural areas of the South, which were considered unsafe for white northerners. Apparently the difference in hostility manifested toward white and black teachers was inconsequential. Both encountered difficulty securing housing, faced hostility from southern whites, and discipline problems in their classrooms.[7] Nevertheless,

[3]Anderson, *The Education of Blacks in the South*, 6; Morris, *Reading, 'Riting, and Reconstruction*, 119.
[4]All the works cited in notes 1-3 have sections on AMA teachers, but Jones devotes the most attention to this topic.
[5]Morris, *Reading, 'Riting, and Reconstruction*, 129.
[6]Jones, *Soldiers of Light and Love*, 63-65.
[7]Joe M. Richardson, *Christian Reconstruction: The American Missionary Association and Southern Blacks, 1861-1890* (Athens, Ga., 1986), 202.

black teachers were more effective in the classroom. Joe M. Richardson maintains that, "by 1870 the association [AMA] admitted that most effective teachers of freedmen came from among themselves. They have the readiest access to their own race, and can do a work for them no teachers sent from the North can accomplish."[8]

Freedmen were not ideal students by almost any measurement. Most had never seen the inside of a school and even though some of these students were in their teens, they were simply unprepared for the rigors of a classroom.[9] Facilities were poor in many instances and the situation was compounded by crowded classroom conditions where different age groups and grade levels were taught in the same room.[10] Moreover, "throughout the South the refusal to rent buildings for black education," writes Ronald Butchart, "banished schools to barns and sheds that were often floorless, poorly lighted, drafty, cold and nearly always without the aids teachers had come to rely on."[11]

In addition to the students' weak educational background, which was often compensated for by their high motivation, and woefully inadequate facilities, the textbooks, published mainly by the American Tract Society (ATS), were not those used in northern schools. Rather, they were designed specifically for freedmen with the intent "to produce a safe working class for the South and a pious and moral membership for" the churches which were closely allied with those northern benevolent societies. *The Freedmen's Primer, The Freedmen Spelling Book, The Lincoln Primer*, and the first, second and third *Freedmen Readers*, among the more popular texts, used anecdotes from the lives of Abraham Lincoln, Paul Cuffee, and Toussaint L'Ouverture to emphasize the importance of hard work, loyalty, philanthropy, and thrift.[12] Furthermore, those texts "contained social values designed," writes James Anderson, "to inculcate in ex-slaves an acceptance of economic and racial subordination."[13]

[8]*Ibid.*, 190.
[9]Leon F. Litwack, *Been in the Storm so Long: The Aftermath of Slavery* (New York, 1979), 451.
[10]Richardson, *Christian Reconstruction*, 46.
[11]Butchart, *Northern Schools, Southern Blacks*, 116-17.
[12]Richardson, *Christian Reconstruction*, 42.
[13]Anderson, *The Education of Blacks in the South*, 30.

The desire for education among newly freed slaves was suggested as early as January 1863 in this Thomas Nast cartoon on "The Past and the Future of Emancipation of the Negroes." *Sketch from* Harper's Weekly, *January 24, 1863*.

The correspondence between J. (John) Murray Hoag, a Freedmen's Bureau official, and Hettie E. Sabattie, a black teacher, sheds light on an early effort to introduce education to blacks in a single community, Darien, Georgia. Located in McIntosh County near the mouth of the Altamaha River just over fifty miles south of Savannah, Darien served as a coastal outlet for cotton shipped from the central Georgia black belt. By 1860, this county seat had 315 white residents and 255 blacks (including 36 free blacks). The Civil War took its toll on local whites, however, due to high casualties among its Confederate officers and soldiers, and the fact that many other residents fled inland when Union gunboats appeared off the coast.[14]

As a result of those losses, blacks outnumbered whites after the war (the black-white ratio was 4 to 1 in 1870) which paid immediate dividends to an ambitious New Jersey-born African-American, Tunis Campbell, who migrated to McIntosh County from St. Catherines Island in December 1866, and later moved to Darien in early 1868. In April of that year, he was elected to the offices of both state senator and justice of the peace; his son was elected to the Georgia assembly. The elder Campbell, a strong advocate of black education, had attended the Georgia Education Convention in May 1867, where a resolution to promote education and to employ qualified local black teachers was adopted. He may have been instrumental, therefore, in establishing the school in which Hettie Sabattie taught since it was in operation before the Freedmen's Bureau repaired a local church and hired her to move the school there.[15]

The correspondence between Hoag and Sabattie reveals some disappointing aspects of opening a school in Darien. Circumstances certainly were not promising. The educational level of black children in Darien was very low, as one would have expected since none had been exposed to any schooling before the war. Whites in the town offered no assistance and apparently were unwilling to house other members of their race who came into their community to teach African-Americans. Federal authorities failed to provide adequate funds for the school and appear to have been more interested in the teachers submitting bureaucratic paperwork than in providing the school with proper facilities and sufficient materials.

[14]Russell Duncan, *Freedom's Shore: Tunis Campbell and the Georgia Freedmen* (Athens, Ga., 1986), 2-3, 55-56; for the free black figures see *Population of the United States in 1860* (Washington, D.C., 1864), 74; Richard R. Wright, *A Brief Historical Sketch of Negro Education in Georgia* (Savannah, 1894), 21.

[15]Duncan, *Freedom's Shore*, see the introduction and first two chapters.

Hoag, an Irish-American wheelwright from New York City, was forty years old when he enlisted as a private in the New York Artillery in August 1862. He subsequently received a quick promotion to corporal, and in September 1863 was promoted to second lieutenant and assigned to a company in the Fourth United States Colored Infantry. At the Battle of New Market Heights near Richmond in September 1864, where the victorious black troops suffered heavy casualties, Hoag was wounded twice after leaving his sickbed to lead his troops. As a result of this heroic display of leadership, Hoag was promoted to captain in November 1864. He left the army temporarily in January 1867, but soon returned and was assigned to Savannah as an assistant superintendent of education in the Freedmen's Bureau, a position he held until May 1869. He retired from the army in January 1870 as a captain. While based in Savannah, Hoag was responsible for supervising schools in southeast Georgia—hiring construction workers, assigning teachers, establishing the tuition rate, and opening and closing Freedmen's Bureau schools in Savannah, the Sea Islands, and nearby counties. He served under the Freedmen's Bureau state superintendent of education in Atlanta who was responsible for all black schools in Georgia. In 1868 Hoag's immediate supervisor was Edmund Asa Ware, a civilian professional educator and the first president of Atlanta University (founded in 1865). Ware was succeeded by John Lewis, a field grade Union officer who subsequently became Georgia's first state superintendent of education after the assembly created the position in October 1870.[16]

The other correspondent and central figure in the establishment of Darien's school was Hettie Sabattie. A very light-skinned mulatto, Sabattie had been born in Darien in 1836 to free mulatto parents: Mary Garey Sabattie, a Darien native, and Clemente Sabattie, a barber who had migrated to the town from Santo Domingo in 1795. Clemente moved with his wife,

[16]*Seventh Census*, 1850, New York. Microfilm, M-432, roll 554, p. 203; F. B. Heitman, *Historical Register of The United States Army, 1789-1889* (Washington, 1890), 343; *The War of The Rebellion: A Compilation of the Official Records of the Union and Confederate Armies*, series 1, volume 42, part 3 (Washington, 1893), 169; Jones, *Soldiers of Light and Love*, 33, 90, 96.

son (Clemente, Jr.), and daughter to Savannah when Hettie was young. He joined the Independent Presbyterian Church in the early 1840s, and by 1854, owned land assessed at five hundred dollars and two slaves. His wife was a prominent member of Christ Episcopal Church before her death in the mid-1840s.[17]

The Sabatties were among a small group of African-American slaveholders in antebellum Savannah. While some of that select group had considerable holdings in black property, most, like the Sabatties, owned fewer than four slaves.[18] Despite their elite status, there was no meaningful social stratification among Savannah's black community and social interaction between slaves and free blacks was actually more common than that between free blacks and mulattoes. Unlike Charleston or New Orleans though, there was no mulatto aristocracy in Savannah, despite the preponderance of non-white property holdings they claimed.[19]

Growing up in this environment, Hettie Sabattie may have received the first two years of her formal education at a school

[17]Chatham County Register of Free Person of Colour, 1837-1849, Georgia Historical Society, Savannah, Georgia; Chatham County Tax Digest, 1854. Microfilm, Georgia Department of Archives and History, Atlanta, Georgia (hereinafter cited as GDAH); "List of Colour Members," Independent Presbyterian Church Sessional Minutes, 1828-1851, microfilm, GDAH; Christ Episcopal Church Parish Register, 1822-1851. Microfilm, GDAH; *Journal of the Proceedings of The Episcopal Diocese of Georgia* (Savannah, 1856), 45.

[18]City of Savannah Tax Digest 1837, 1850, 1860; see also *Seventh Census on the United States, 1850* (Washington, D.C., 1850), and *Eighth Census of the United States, 1860*. The tax digests, however, have the more reliable information. In 1850, for instance, the census listed Andrew Marshall, the venerable pastor of the First African Baptist Church, as the owner of eight slaves, but he did not own any slaves. He apparently rented dwellings to slaves whom the census taker listed as his.

[19]Southern Claims Case Files, Chatham County Georgia, Record Group 217 (National Archives, Washington, D.C.), contains numerous instances of mixed marriages, i.e., free African-Americans and slaves, in the depositions which blacks, who had sustained property damages at the hands of Union soldiers, filed. This suggests that the practice was quite common; *Seventh Census of the United States, 1850*; *Eighth Census of the United States, 1860*. The number of mixed marriages, i.e., black and mulatto, was much smaller than either the number of mulatto or black marriages. Moreover, in 1860 although free mulattoes slightly outnumbered free blacks among Savannah's African-American population (410 to 395), only 1 of the 16 African-Americans who owned real estate in the $1000 range was black, and only 17 of the 101 homeowners in the $100 to $1000 range were black; John Blassingame, *Black New Orleans, 1860-1880* (Chicago, 1973) contains an excellent discussion on the mulatto aristocracy of the Crescent City; see also Ira Berlin, *Slaves Without Masters: The Free Negro in the Antebellum South* (New York, 1974), 214-15. The "three caste system" to which the author alludes did not exist in Savannah.

operated by Mary Woodhouse (who, like her mother, worshipped at Christ Episcopal Church), and continued her education at another unidentified school.[20] It is obvious from her letters that Hettie attended school beyond the first two grades. Although her spelling was less than perfect, a common shortcoming of literate people of that time, she expressed herself well in writing and exhibited signs of intelligence and discernment. Her letters indicate that, despite the best efforts of the antebellum Savannah city council, Sabattie, like other blacks in the city, had become literate.

At the age of thirty-two, Hettie Sabattie returned to Darien from Savannah after the war and had begun to teach in a black-controlled school there. (Whether she had previous teaching experience is not known.) In October 1868, Hoag took an interest in the community and requested of the state superintendent in Atlanta an appropriation of $100 to repair a church in Darien in order that it might be converted into a school that he felt could accommodate from seventy-five to a hundred students.[21] He visited Darien later that month, where he met Sabattie and another black teacher, a Miss Thorpe, but was apparently not impressed. "The resident teachers," he wrote, "are not competent as I wish." He applied to the American Missionary Association for "two ladies," but acknowledged that "should I not succeed in obtaining these ladies we must fall back upon the local teachers before alluded to and do the best

[20]A fellow black Episcopalian, James Porter, organist at St. Stephen's, operated a school which taught academy-level courses, but he did not arrive in Savannah until the mid-1850s, by which time Hettie Sabattie had probably completed her schooling. Jean Fromantin, a fellow countryman of her father, was one of the first free blacks to operate a school in Savannah, but he closed his school in 1844 after fifteen years of operation. Since Sabattie was only eight at the time, she probably did not attend Fromantin's school either. *Savannah Tribune*, November 13, 1895; Charles C. Coffin, *Four Years of Fighting* (Boston, 1866), 420; Robert Perdue, *The Negro in Savannah, 1865-1900* (Garden City, N.Y., 1973), 124-26; and Joseph Frederick Waring, *Cerveau's Savannah* (Savannah, 1973), 66-67.

[21]J. Murray Hoag to Hon. E. A. Ware, October 1, 1868. This and all the letters that follow are located in Record Group 105, Bureau of Refugees, Freedmen, and Abandoned Lands, Savannah, Georgia. National Archives, Washington, D.C. J. Murray Hoag's letters are found in Box 27 under the heading Press Copies of Letters Sent from February 18, 1867 to March 11, 1869. Hettie E. Sabattie's letters are found in Box 28 under the heading Letters Received, 1865-72.

we can."[22] When, by December, the AMA failed to grant his request, his correspondence with Sabattie began.

Savannah, Georgia                    December 10, 1868
Miss Hetty Sabatti
Darien, Georgia
      Will you please open a school in the church building recently repaired and as far as you may be make the school pay you. Enclosed find a School Registry . . .[23] Also a few blank school reports. I wish you to fill one of these blank reports promptly on the last day of each month and mail the same to me. Be sure and answer carefully all questions. I will be down as soon as I find time and will then make needful arrangements from your pay, provided the school does not support you. Anything you need or wish and know, write and ask for at any time.
      Please answer this and say if you will begin the school as I desire.

Very respectfully

J. Murray Hoag
Bvt. Capt. U.S.A.h

---

Savannah, Georgia                    December 25, 1868
Miss Hettie E. Sabatti
Darien Georgia
      Enclosed please find a Circular Letter from Mr. Ware Superintendent of Education requesting teachers to forward their reports to Col. Lewis U.S.A. direct instead of to Agents as heretofore.
      Please make your December Report to him as directed—Also please make application to him for necessary books—Your report should include Miss Thorpe school if you both taught but one school. If separate, please ask her to report to Mr. Ware also.

Very respectfully
Your obedient servant

J. Murray Hoag
Bvt Capt. U.S.

---

[22]J. Murray Hoag to Bt. Col. J. R. Lewis, October 23, 1868. Sabattie [referred to as Labbattie] and Thorpe are identified as the two teachers Hoag referred to in Giles Pease to George Whipple, March 4, 1868, "Letters from Georgia," AMA Archives, microfilm, no. 21333 (cited in Duncan, *Freedom's Shore*, 136, n47).
      [23]This and subsequent deletions are either repetitious or unrelated to black education. The original spelling, grammar, and syntax of the letters have been retained. This letter and the enclosed Circular Letter are not in the collection.

Darien, Georgia                          December 31, 1868

Capt. J. M. Hoag
Sir:
    Youre note of December 20th[24] had been received and I am
truly sorry the answer has been delayed until this date, but sickness prevented me writing. Hoping this may reach you safely. I
will send it by the next oppertunity that presents itself. I also
send you a report of my school. I cannot say anything of Miss
Thorpe's as she is out of the city. You may probably see her in
Savannah. You will please let me hear from you soon concearning the books as I cannot get along without them for there are
no books to be bought in this place. Hoping to hear from you
soon.

                          I am very respectfully your,

                          Hettie E. Sabattie

---

Darien                                   January 4th, 1869

Capt. J.M. Hoag
Sir:
    Youre letter of December 25th has been received, also the
Circular letter of Mr. Ware, State Supetend you requested me
to forward my December Report to Col. Lewis. I had already
sent it to you. Miss Thorpe and myself taught in the same building but seperate school[25] so I cannot tell anything about the
Report of her school and she want to have until tomorrow night.
I opened the school today had a great many children come but
they have no books.

                          Youres Very Truly

                          Hettie E. Sabattie

---

Savannah, Georgia                        January 6, 1869

Miss Hattie E. Sabattie
Darien, Ga.
    Your favor of the 4th Instant is just at hand and contents
noted. Your school report forwarded to me. I sent on to Col.
Lewis as required.
    Have this day sent you by Express a supply of such Books
as I have viz—

    [24]This letter to Hettie Sabattie and the enclosed Circular Letter are not in the
collection.
    [25]Sometimes grade levels were referred to as schools; therefore the two black ladies
probably taught different grades in that school.

Educational efforts for black children continued in Darien and surrounding areas long after Hettie Sabattie gave up her school there. This photograpn is of a black school and its white teacher in neighboring Liberty County in the 1880s. *Photograph from William E. Wilson Photographic Archive, Hargrett Rare Book and Manuscript Library, University of Georgia Libraries.*

30     Lincoln Primers and First Readers
15 do Spelling Books
15 do Second Readers

You must charge those able to pay enough for these books to repay you for express charges.

Very Respectfully

J. Murray Hoag
Bvt. Capt. U.S.A.

---

Darien                                      January 10, 1869
Capt. J. M. Hoag
Savannah, Ga.

Your letter of January 6th have been received. I am glad to know that you have received my Letter and Report. I am also glad to hear of your sending books for the use of the school. Though I have not received them yet. I am hoping to get them this coming week. I am sorry to have to say to you that we have lost Miss Thorpe in our school. She expects to be married on the 20th of this month and leave for Savannah whare she will reside. So by this I am compelle to apply to you for another teacher as I find it is almost useless for me to make the attempt to carry on the school alone as the number has already got so large that I find it Dificult for me to controle the children. Thursday and Friday I closed the school as the number increased to 125 and they kept coming. I am trying to secure the services of a young man hare untill another teacher can be got. If I can get him we will open tomorrow morning. I think it will be best to send a colored male teacher as there are great many large boys and girls who I think need a man to controle them it was for this reason—that I found it necessary to close the school untill I could get someone to assist me. My reason for saying a colored teacher is because it is so hard to get Board for a white teacher and I Earnestly ask you to send one as soon as posible for the school. Cannot go on as it ought without propper persons to carry it on. I think I can get Board for one in a very nice family. Mr. L. Jackson has promised me to do all he can to help me.[26] I am sory to troble you so mutch but it cannot be avoided at the present time.

Hoping to hear from you soon.

I am Very
Respectfully Youres

Hattie E. Sabattie

---

Savannah, GA.                                    January 19, 1869
Bvt. Col. John R. Lewis, U.S.Army
Asst. Command Chief Supt. of Schools
Atlanta, Ga.
Colonel

I have the honor to report having just returned from Darien and to submit the following facts for your consideration—Darien as has before been reported, has a large colored population with at least three hundred children that should be at school. Miss Thorpe and Miss Sabattie two col'd girls have done more or less toward teaching for some time past—The former is about being married and leaving town—and the latter is suffering with chills to such an extent as renders school more than half the time impossible—finding such to be the condition of affairs I rented a small house for teachers and placed it under repairs— the actual rent is but $5.00 per month and yet the necessary repairs will for a time, at least, make it about $20.00. Two ladies from the AMA will leave here for said field on Friday 22nd Inst. The people are pledged to their support—Bureau paying

---

[26]Apparently the newly created black leadership of Darien supported the school because Lewis Jackson, a forty-three year old native Georgian, was the McIntosh County ordinary (judge), the first black to hold that position. A property owner, his real estate was valued at $800; he was also a carpenter. *Population Schedules, 1870. Georgia.* No. M-593, roll 164.

House rent. I shall from my private means advance the little furniture necessary trusting to tuition over and above teachers expenses for my pay.[27] Miss Sabattie talks of leaving for Savannah on account of her health—I told her if after the teachers arrived she was able and desired to remain I would secure her as appointment from the AMA and I doubt not there will be work enough for all—I hope and long tuition will pay house rent as well as other demands but until such time I trust you will feel authorized to pay a monthly rent of $20.00—I will bear the same upon my returns as Home or School House as you direct.

> I am Colonel
> Very Respectfully Your Obedient Servant
> J. Murray Hoag
> Bvt. Capt. U.S. Army Bounty Officer
> and Asst. Supt. of Schools

---

Savannah, Georgia           February 18, 1869
Miss Hettie E. Sabattie
Darien, Ga.

Have seen several of the people from South End Sapelo Island all of whom express great desire for a school at that point and from what they say I am led to conclude a good paying school could be there established.

If you think you could do as well there and wish to try it I should be very much pleased to have you do so. I will send you books as at Darien and aid you to the 25% from the Peabody Fund.[28]

> I am as Ever
> Your Obedient Servant
>
> J. Murray Hoag
> Bvt. Capt. U.S.A. Bounty Officer
> and Asst. Supt. of Schools

---

Darien           Feb. 22nd, 1869
Capt. J.M. Hoag
Sir:

Yours of the 18th instant has been Received. I will be glad to take the offer which you made me of a school on Sapelo Island providing it will support me. I am in hopes to see some of the people in a few days when I think I will be able to make all necessary arrangements for my going to the Island.

[27] As assistant superintendent, Hoag was authorized to set tuition rates.

[28] George Peabody, a northern philanthropist, established this fund in 1867 to provide financial support for southern schools.

You will please if it is convenient let me know something about my pay for the time that I had the school here as I am mutch in want of means to get such articles as I may want, if I should go to the Island.

I took the school on the first of January and kept it until the other teachers came and not one person ever gave me a cent I wrote to Colonel Lewis when I sent my Report concearning the pay for the time that I taught and I never recieved any answer please let me hear from you by return mail if you should send me any money please send it by express and I will be ceartain to get it.

The books which you will send for the school I would like to have them of the national series that is primmer in First readers and a few Second Readers.[29] I think the people are able to pay something for books so if you can get those. I would rather them send me the price of each. You had better send them heare as I can take them with me.

Yours Very Respectfully
Hettie E. Sabattie

---

Savannah Ga.                          Feby 23d, 1869
Bvt. Col. J.R. Lewis U.S. Army
Asst. Comm. and Chief Supt of Schools

Atlanta, Ga.
Colonel

I have the honor to report having visited Sapelo Island on the 5th Inst. for the purpose of establishing a school at the south end.

I went under the impression that Miss Miller a former teacher there had not left, but finding that in this I was mistakened I recommended Miss Hattie E. Sabattie of Darien to them and have since written her myself—I particularly desired this change since a feeling of jealousy is growing up between the Mission School and that kept of Miss Sabattie at Darien[30]—Yesterday I rec'd a call from Lieut Reily[31] who informed me that

---

[29]The *National* Series, the most widely used series, was published in New York by A. S. Barnes and Company. Richard Greene Parker and James Madison Watson wrote the two volumes: the *National*, used in grades 1-5, and the *Reader*, sometimes referred to as "Parker and Watson." See Jones, *Soldiers of Light and Love*, 226.

[30]Jealousies and rivalries between AMA schools and those established by local African-Americans occurred frequently in Georgia cities. Much of this stemmed from the haughty attitude of the AMA which required its teachers to belong to an evangelical church, attempted to indoctrinate African-Americans with "Yankee virtues," and generally did not have a high regard for local black teachers.

[31]The state superintendent of education probably had authorized Lieutenant Reily to establish that school and ordered him to apprise Hoag once his mission had been

he was authorized to established a school at Sapelo So. End and had already left the teachers there—Please inform me of the result of this effort that I may not cause Miss sabattie useless trouble and expense.

Respectfully

J. Murray Hoag
Bvt. Capt. USA B. O.
and A. Supt. of S.

---

Savannah, Georgia             February 23, 1869
Miss Hettie E. Sabattie
Darien, Georgia

I have just learned indirectly that Col. Lewis had sent a teacher to Sapelo South End. Should this be so it would of course render your going there useless—You can learn the facts by asking some of the people.

Do you see any of the people from Harris Neck[32]—I learn there are many children and a general desire for a school there.

Intend going there soon—but in the meantime should you find it a good opening and wish to try it go ahead and I will aid you as far as is in my power.

Col. Lewis makes all payments from Peabody Fund hence you must look to him for your January pay.

Respectfully Yours

J. Murray Hoag
Bvt. Capt. U.S.A.

The correspondence between Hettie Sabattie and J. Murray Hoag ended abruptly after the latter's letter above, and it is likely that Sabattie's association with the school ended just as abruptly. At some point after her short-lived teaching career in Darien, she returned to Savannah.[33] In 1871 she lived in a house on the corner of Perry and Harris Streets with her teen-age daughter Mary and worked as a seamstress, the occupation she had usually listed on the Registration of Free Persons of Color before the war.[34]

---

accomplished. The lieutenant probably was not stationed in Savannah; hence he called Hoag to give him the information.

[32]Harris Neck is located north of Darien on St. Catherines Island.

[33]Sabattie's whereabouts after receiving this letter are unknown since she does not appear in 1870 census reports for either Darien or Savannah. See *Population Schedules of the Ninth Census of the United States, 1870*. Microfilm no. 593, rolls 140, 141, and 164.

[34]Account #6028, Registers of Signatures of Depositors In Branches of Freedmen's Savings and Trust Company, 1865-1874, Savannah, Georgia. National Archives,

The relationship between the mulatto teacher and the Freedmen's Bureau agent reveals much about the developmental pattern of black education in Darien, and illuminates how a similar process going on throughout the South actually functioned. The J. Murray Hoags within the Freedmen's Bureau and the Hettie Sabatties among black teachers were clearly key players in the phenomenal growth of black education in the region.

Hoag is an excellent example of dedicated bureau officials who generally remained nameless while their superiors are often listed in accounts of the period.[35] He appears to have been a perceptive, conscientious, and able administrator who was genuinely interested in establishing black schools in his jurisdiction. The bureau could not have functioned efficiently without Hoag and fellow assistant superintendents of his caliber.

Hettie Sabattie represents an even more anonymous entity in the drama of Reconstruction education efforts. Historians have dealt with other schools in McIntosh County that operated during the same period—an AMA-sponsored school operated by a northern black male teacher and a school run by a local white resident, Harriet Atwell Newell, on her husband's plantation and supported by northern Presbyterian aid.[36] But none of their accounts make mention of Sabattie's school.

There were no doubt dozens of other native black women whose teaching experiences in their communities resembled that of Hettie Sabattie and whose efforts were equally as significant in paving the way for universal public school education in the South. If their names and faces remain obscured, they gain visibility through the revealing case study Sabattie's correspondence provides.

---

Washington, D. C. This source lists her as Hetty E. Sabatty and states that she was born in Darien. She has also been listed in the Registers of Free Persons of Color as Hetty Sabatte, and in there Savannah is listed as her birthplace.

[35]For example, in her well-documented study, *Soldiers of Light and Love* (pp. 76, 78-79), Jacqueline Jones identifies Hoag's superiors in the educational hierarchy of Georgia and describes the duties of the assistant superintendents, but never identifies Hoag or any other assistant superintendent by name; nor do any of the other works cited in this article.

[36]*Ibid.*

# THE ROLE OF TUSKEGEE INSTITUTE IN THE EDUCATION OF BLACK FARMERS

## ALLEN W. JONES

While the economically depressed white farmers of the South sought solutions to their problems in the 1880's and 1890's through the Grange, the Agricultural Wheel, and the Farmers' Alliance, numerous industrial schools and institutes were established throughout the South in an effort to help the landless, uneducated, and deprived mass of black farmers. Founded on July 4, 1881, in the heart of Black Belt Alabama by an act of the state legislature, Tuskegee Institute emerged rapidly under the leadership of Booker T. Washington and his formula of self-help into a center for educating and uplifting more than 1,000,000 black farmers in the South.[1]

In 1890, with approximately fifty-seven per cent of the race illiterate and only 121,000 of the 1,689,000 blacks engaged in agriculture owning the land they tilled, Booker T. Washington concluded "that the great body of the Negro population must live in the future as they have done in the past, by the cultivation of the soil, and the most helpful service now to be done is to enable the race to follow agriculture with intelligence and diligence."[2] To this end he devoted much of his life and the work of his school at Tuskegee.

Agriculture was emphasized at Tuskegee Institute from its very beginning. Since employment was needed for students and more provisions were needed than the school was able to buy, students were put to work in 1882 on the school's small farm raising food for the boarding department and feed for the horses and other animals needed to carry on the work of the institution. The teaching of agriculture evolved from the school farm which expanded from a few acres in 1882 to over 2300 acres in 1915.[3] Professor Charles W. Greene, a graduate of Hampton

---

Allen W. Jones is Associate Professor of History and Archivist at Auburn University, Auburn, Alabama.

[1] Theodore Saloutos, *Farmer Movements in the South, 1865-1933* (Lincoln, Neb.: 1964), 31-43; John D. Hicks, *The Populist Revolt* (Lincoln, Neb.: 1961), 96-127; August Meier, *Negro Thought in America, 1880-1915* (Ann Arbor, Mich.: 1969), 85-99; *Acts of the General Assembly of Alabama, 1880-1881* (Montgomery, 1881), 395-396.

[2] Francis B. Simkins, *A History of the South* (New York: 1958), 506; Booker T. Washington, *Working With the Hands* (New York, 1904), 135.

[3] "How Tuskegee Helps the Farmer," typescript, *ca.* 1910, Box 979, Booker T. Washington Papers, Library of Congress, Washington, D.C. Hereafter cited as BTW Papers. See also Anson Phelps Stokes, *Tuskegee Institute, The First Fifty Years* (Tuskegee Institute: 1931), 65.

Institute, was brought to Tuskegee by Washington in 1888 to serve as superintendent of the school's farm. In this position "Farmer Greene," as he was known around Tuskegee, found an opportunity to teach students and local black farmers lessons in the best methods of farming and to develop a number of ideas in farming methods and techniques. He taught the students to put out onion sets in the fall, introduced some important forage plants among local farmers, and was the first to put out Bermuda sod as a pasture at Tuskegee Institute.[4] His work laid the foundation for the establishment of a definite "Course of Study in Agriculture" in 1893, and the Department of Agriculture in 1896. By the time Washington died in 1915, the School of Agriculture had eighteen instructors who directed the study and work of 325 students.[5] Those students who received agricultural training were expected to return to the farms and share their newly acquired knowledge of farming methods with other black farmers. But the number of graduates who returned to the farm was small, and the real success of Tuskegee Institute's agricultural program came primarily from its graduates and former students who took the lead in teaching agriculture to black farmers and who founded industrial institutes and normal schools throughout the South.[6]

On his many buggy trips into the rural areas of Black Belt Alabama during the 1880's, Booker T. Washington witnessed the extreme poverty and ignorance of the black farmers who had never enjoyed the benefits of education. Washington was impressed, however, by "the unusual amount of common sense displayed . . . [by] the uneducated black man in the South, especially the one living in the country dis-

---

[4] J. H. Palmer, "Farmer Greene," typescript, March 1940, Box 15, Thomas M. Campbell Papers, Tuskegee Institute Archives, Tuskegee, Alabama. Hereafter cited as TMC Papers. Greene was instrumental in the organization of the Farmers Conferences, the Macon County Farmers' Institute, the Macon County Fair Association, and the Farmers Short Course in Agriculture. He held various positions in the Agriculture Department until 1915 when he was appointed Demonstration Agent for Macon County. Tuskegee *News*, November 11, 1915. See also Louis R. Harlan, ed., *The Booker T. Washington Papers* (Urbana, Ill.: 1972), II, 54.

[5] *Catalogue of the Tuskegee Normal and Industrial Institute at Tuskegee, Alabama, 1893-94* (Tuskegee Institute: 1894), 46-47; *Catalogue of the Tuskegee Normal and Industrial Institute at Tuskegee, Alabama 1895-96 (Tuskegee Institute: 1896)*, 41-42; *Tuskegee To Date, 1915* (Tuskegee Institute, 1915), 3-4.

[6] Monroe N. Work, "Agricultural Training at Tuskegee Institute," typescript, *ca.* 1915, Box 3, Monroe N. Work Papers, Tuskegee Institute Archives, Tuskegee, Alabama. Hereafter cited as MNW Papers. For a list of Tuskegee graduates who became teachers and leaders in the field of agriculture, see Montgomery *Journal*, May 31, 1915; George F. King, *King's Agricultural Digest*, 1923, *passim;* Monroe N. Work, *Industrial Work of Tuskegee Graduates and Former Students during the Year 1910* (Tuskegee Institute: 1911), 6-21. See Stokes, *Tuskegee Institute, The First Fifty Years*, 33-34, for a list of schools and institutes founded by Tuskegee graduates.

trict." Any people with such "natural sense," said Washington, "could be led to do a great deal towards their own elevation."[7] Thus, he issued an invitation to about seventy-five "representatives of the masses—the bone and sinew of the race—the common, hard working farmers with a few of the best ministers and teachers" to come and spend the day of February 23, 1892 at a Negro Conference on the campus of Tuskegee Normal and Industrial Institute. The purpose of this meeting was to arouse public sentiment among the farmers and create among them a real interest in the common, mundane and practical affairs of life.[8]

To the surprise of Washington over 400 men and women, mostly farmers, "of all grades and conditions," attended the First Tuskegee Negro Conference. In order to find out the "actual industrial, moral and educational condition of the masses," delegates were urged to speak. They spent the morning telling about their problems of owning and renting land, living in one-room log cabins, mortgaging crops, paying debts, educating children, and living a moral and religious life. The farmers reported frankly and simply that four-fifths of them lived on rented land in small one-room cabins and mortgaged their crops for food on which to live. Their three month schools were conducted in "churches or broken down log cabins or under a bush arbor."[9]

The afternoon portion of the conference focused on remedies. After an extensive exchange of views on how "to lift themselves up in their industrial, education, moral and religious life," the delegates adopted a very optimistic ten point declaration which recognized the problems and evil conditions facing rural black people and pledged support to a program of self-improvement:

> The seriousness of our condition lies in that, in the States where the colored people are most numerous, at least 90 percent of them are in the country, they are difficult to reach, and but little is being done for them. Their industrial, educational and moral condition is slowly improving, but among the masses there is still a great amount of poverty and ignorance and much need of moral and religious training.
>
> We urge all to buy land and to cultivate it thoroughly; to raise more food supplies; to build homes with more than one room; to tax themselves to build better school houses, and to extend the school term to at least six months; to give more attention to the character of our leaders, especially ministers and teachers; to keep out of debt; to avoid lawsuits; to treat our women better; and that conferences similar in aim to this one be held in every community where practicable.[10]

[7]Booker T. Washington, "How I Came to Call the First Negro Conference," *A.M.E. Church Review*, XV (April, 1898), 802. See also Max B. Thrasher, *Tuskegee, Its Story and Its Work* (Boston, 1900), 162-163.

[8]*A Negro Conference to Be Held In the Black Belt of Alabama*, handbill, 1892, Box 11, Tuskegee Institute Extension Papers, Tuskegee Institute Archives, Tuskegee, Alabama, Hereafter cites as TIE Papers. Louis R. Harlan, *Booker T. Washington, The Making of a Black Leader* (New York: 1972), 198.

[9]Washington, "How I Came to Call the First Negro Conference," 803-804.

[10]*Ibid.,* 804; for a complete list of the declarations see "Colored People of the Black Belt Pass Resolutions of Interest to Their Race," Montgomery *Advertiser,* February 24, 1892; Birmingham *Age-Herald*, February 24, 1892.

The declaration was in fact an address to the Negro farmers of the South advising them what to do, and such resolutions were adopted each year by the annual conference.

The 1892 conference was highly successful in focusing the attention of the poverty-stricken farmer upon the things they could do in their homes, on their farms, and in their schools and churches for self-improvement. The stories heard at the conference were carried home by the delegates and became a sort of oral literature that spread gradually over the entire black South. The conference drew praise from those farmers and teachers who attended. A teacher from Notasulga, Alabama wrote Washington that the conference had done "untold good . . . among the farmers" of his community and that it had "put new life in our farmer's Club . . . which had been disbanded ever since Jan. 20, 1891." After promising to attend all future conferences at the Institute, the teacher described how his club had appointed a committee to visit the farmers in the district and "advise them to plant more corn, peas, and potatoes, and to find out, as near as possible, the true condition of the farms."[1]

Washington was so overwhelmed by the success of the first Negro Conference that he established it as an annual affair. He saw its continuation as an "opportunity for service and a chance to build a personal machine of support for himself, his school, and his cause."[12] But to the black farmers of Alabama the annual conference was a chance to come once a year "to the Tuskegee Mecca for a new baptism of thrift, industry, and the kindred virtues of sober, contented and decent living."[13]

The second conference in February, 1893 was attended by some 800 persons representing almost every section of Alabama and the South. In 1894 and 1895 the attendance increased to over 1,000 and by 1898 the attendance exceeded 2,000. Because of the growing attendance, Washington held a two day conference in 1894. The first day was the Farmers' Conference and the second day was the Workers' Conference that was composed of teachers from Negro institutions of higher education in the South. The expansion of the conference brought

---

[1] Richard Potts to Booker T. Washington, March 6, 1892, Box 102, BTW Papers. The Farmer's Club in Notasulga was organized in 1885 by Richard Potts who had been a student at Tuskegee Institute. The purpose of the Club was "to better the conditions of the colored farmers . . . in the following ways: To own homes, to take better care of their families; to educate their children; to buy goods in large quantities by wholesale and get them cheaper; to discuss better methods of farming; and to unite the farmers." Tuskegee *Southern Letter*, May, 1897, quoting a letter from R. Potts.

[12] Harlan, *The Making of A Black Leader*, 200.

[13] Emmett J. Scott, "The Tuskegee Negro Conferences," *The Voice of the Negro*, I (May, 1904), 181.

changes in the program: A portion of the meetings was devoted to a Women's Conference; prominent persons from throughout the country spoke at the conferences; and an evening barbecue became a regular feature.[14]

The Tuskegee Negro Conference was one of the most significant projects for black farmers that Washington inaugurated. It was the beginning of agricultural extension work among the Negroes of the South, and out of it grew all of the other extension activities of Tuskegee Institute.[15] The approval and the publicity given to the Negro conferences by the Southern and the Northern press was extremely helpful to Washington in his crusade to spread the "Tuskegee Idea."[16]

From this central conference at Tuskegee grew a large number of state Negro conferences which were organized by black educational institutions from Virginia to Texas. There were hundreds of local conferences which sprang up in the rural areas of Alabama and other states in the South.[17] It is difficult to determine exactly how much the Negro

---

[14]John Q. Johnson, *Report of the Fifth Tuskegee Negro Conference, 1896,* John F. Slater Fund Occasional Papers, No. 8 (Baltimore: 1896); *The Third Tuskegee Negro Conference,* handbill, 1894, Box 11, TIE Papers; Scott, "The Tuskegee Negro Conferences," 179; Colonel J. M. Parker, *The Negro As a Farmer, An Address Delivered at the Annual Tuskegee Negro Conference, January 18, 1910* (Tuskegee Institute: 1910); Tuskegee *Southern Letter,* March, 1898. The Farmers' Conference was still being held at Tuskegee Institute in 1973.

[15]Robert E. Park, "The World's Greatest Mission Station," typescript, *ca.* 1908, Box 992, BTW Papers; "How Tuskegee Helps the Farmer," typescript, *ca.* 1910, Box 979, BTW Papers; Stokes, *Tuskegee Institute, The First Fifty Years,* 35; "History of Extension Work Among Negroes and the Part Played by Tuskegee Institute," typescript, n.d., Box 23, TMC Papers.

[16]Cleveland (Ohio) *Leader,* February 11, 1892, clipping, Box 99, BTW Papers; Montgomery *Advertiser,* February 22, 1894; Francis E. Leupp, *Negro Self-Uplifting,* reprint from New York *Evening Post,* February 19-22, 1902, Box 3, TIE Papers; Hammon Lamont, *Negro Self-Help,* reprint from New York *Evening Post,* February 16-March 1, 1903, Box 7, Edith M. W. Shehee Papers, Tuskegee Institute Archives, Tuskegee, Alabama. Hereafter cites as EMWS Papers. Booker T. Washington to Bulletin Press Association, February 10, 1894, Box 99, BTW Papers.

[17]Roy V. Scott, *The Reluctant Farmer, The Rise of Agricultural Extension to 1914* (Urbana, Ill.: 1970), 115-116; Washington, "How I Came to Call the First Negro Conference," 807; Tuskegee *Southern Letter,* February-March, 1899, quoting a letter from Mattie L. Ovletrea; Tuskegee *Student,* November 18-December 2, 1897, January 27, 1898, June 18, 1904; Martin A. Menafee to George W. Carver, December 18, 1918, Box 5; J. H. Wilson to George W. Carver, November 15, 1918, Box 5; H. C. Dugas to George W. Carver, February 10, 1905, Box 2, George W. Carver Papers, Tuskegee Institute Archives, Tuskegee, Alabama. Hereafter cited as GWC Papers. Booker T. Washington, *The Story of My Life and Work* (New York: 1969), 316-317. The local conferences became the foundation of the farm improvement work of Tuskegee Institute. In 1909 it was reported that there were 93 local conferences in 29 counties of Alabama and two conferences in Georgia. Monroe N. Work to Booker T. Washington, March 1, 1909, Box 604, BTW Papers. In 1914 the National Negro Farmers' Congress

conferences contributed to the progress of the black farmers in the South from 1892 until 1920, but it is a fact that during these three decades the number of Blacks who owned farms doubled the value of their land and buildings from $69,636,420 in 1900 to $522,178,137 in 1920.[18]

The success of the Negro Conference convinced Washington that Tuskegee Institute was the place to establish the nation's best agricultural training center for Negroes. His special emphasis upon agricultural education began in 1896 when he persuaded George W. Carver to accept a position as head of the school's Division of Agriculture. Carver came to Tuskegee in November, 1896, because ". . . it had always been the one great ideal of my life to be of the greatest good to the greatest number of 'my people' possible and to this end I have been preparing myself for these many years; feeling as I do that this line of education is the key to unlock the golden door of freedom to our people."[19]

At the same time that he was luring Carver from Iowa State Agricultural College, Washington was making plans to construct an agricultural building at the Institute and to get the Alabama legislature to create a branch Agricultural Experiment Station at Tuskegee Institute. On February 15, 1897 the governor of Alabama approved an act establishing a "Branch Agricultural Experiment Station and Agricultural School for the colored race" at Tuskegee Institute. The state agreed to pay $1,500 a year for operating and maintaining the station and school, while the Institute provided all the necessary lands and buildings. The station and the school were directed to advance the interest of scientific agriculture through experimentation, to provide "the colored race . . . an opportunity to acquire intelligent practical knowledge of agriculture in all of its branches," and to educate and train Negro students in scientific agriculture.[20] Professor Carver was named director of the new experiment station in 1897, and six members of the school's

---

was organized by Professor P. C. Parks, Director of Agriculture at the A. and M. College, Normal, Alabama. It met in Montgomery, Alabama June 12-14, 1914 with F. L. Blackshear of Prarie View A. and M. College in Texas as president. The meeting, which had the endorsement of Alabama's Governor Emmet O'Neal and many prominent Negro agriculturists of the state, was called "in the interest of better farming, better business and living among the Negro farm workers of Alabama. . . ." Tuskegee *Negro Farmer*, June 6, 1914.

[18]Monroe N. Work, ed., *Negro Year Book, An Annual Encyclopedia of the Negro, 1920-21* (Tuskegee Institute: 1922), 321-327. The number of Negro farmers in the South increased from 732, 362 in 1900 to 915,595 in 1920, but approximately seventy-five per cent of them remained tenant farmers during the two decades.

[19]George W. Carver to Booker T. Washington, April 12, 1896, Box 116, BTW Papers and Box 1, GWC Papers.

[20]*Acts of the General Assembly of Alabama, 1896-1897* (Montgomery: 1897), 945-947.

agricultural faculty were assigned as staff.[21]

Washington's dream of creating at Tuskegee the best Negro agricultural school in the United States approached realization in November, 1897, with the opening of the Armstrong-Slater Memorial Agricultural Building. The two-story brick structure, which contained laboratories, classrooms, and accommodations for the museum, was built especially for Professor Carver's Department of Agriculture and Experiment Station.[22] In dedicating the building, Washington pointed to the eighty-five per cent of his race in the Gulf states that were engaged in some form of agriculture and promised them that they would "not be left to forever endure the serfdom and moral slavery of present farming conditions." The young men of the race, he said, must "learn how to achieve practical results in this line of work, and go out and emancipate the less fortunate ones of the race, who still cling to the broken down plow and the half-fed mule and the little patch of half-cultivated cotton."[23]

Carver lost no time in reaching out to the black farmers and in establishing himself and the Institute's agricultural center as "a powerful factor in the development of the 'New South'."[24] From the time he came to Tuskegee in November, 1896, Carver made week-end trips in his buggy to rural communities where he made talks and gave instructive agricultural demonstrations. Other members of the agricultural faculty, especially Charles W. Greene and John H. Palmer, made horse and buggy trips to the homes and the country churches for the purpose of spreading scientific agricultural knowledge and showing the farmers and their wives how to improve their conditions.[25]

In another effort to reach the black farmers, the first Agricultural

---

[21] The Experiment Station staff included Charles W. Greene, farm manager, Crawford D. Menafee, horticulturist, Wiley W. Holland, head of market gardening, William V. Chambliss, head of the dairy herd, William J. Clayton, head of stock raising, and John H. Palmer, librarian. George W. Carver, "Organization and Work," *Tuskegee Agricultural Experiment Station, Bulletin No. 1*, February, 1898 (Tuskegee Institute: 1898).

[22] Tuskegee *Student,* November 11, 18, 26, 1897. The building cost $10,000 of which the John F. Slater Fund paid half and promised to pay the operating expenses of the new agriculture program. The Institute claimed that this was "the first building ever erected in connection with any of the Negro schools of the South for practical teaching of agriculture alone." *Ibid.,* November 11, 1897.

[23] *Ibid.,* December 2, 1897. About 5,000 people attended the dedication of the new agricultural building which featured Secretary of Agriculture James Wilson and Alabama's Governor Joseph F. Johnston as speakers. Some 500 white farmers of Macon and adjoining counties were present at the gathering.

[24] George W. Carver to Booker T. Washington, May 30, 1898, Box 1, GWC Papers.

[25] Thomas M. Campbell, "George Washington Carver As I Knew Him," typescript of a speech delivered at Carver High School, Hamilton, Georgia, January 16, 1955, Box 22, TMC Papers; Palmer, "Farmer Greene," Box 15, TMC Papers; "How Tuskegee Helps the Farmer," Box 979, BTW Papers.

Farmers' Institute was organized at Tuskegee on November 11, 1897, and Professor Greene was chosen president. At the monthly meetings in the school's agricultural building, simple lectures and demonstrations covering the principles of agriculture were given by the faculty, and the farmers were encouraged to relate their personal experiences in applying these methods and principles. In other words, it was a one-day-a-month schooling for the farmers and their families at no cost to them. Such subjects as the culture and value of sweet potatoes, practical farm economy, the care of young chickens, the value of deep plowing, the proper preparation of corn and cotton land, and woman's helpful influence in the home were discussed at the meetings which attracted from twenty-five to seventy-five farmers from Macon and adjoining counties. Professor Carver occasionally took the farmers on a tour of the grounds of the Experiment Station in order "to stimulate and encourage them."[26]

The idea of Farmers' Institutes gained strength in the South after 1900, and spread to other Negro agricultural colleges in Texas, Mississippi, North Carolina, Florida, Georgia, South Carolina and Louisiana. Professor Carver and other agriculturalists from Tuskegee frequently received invitations to deliver speeches or conduct demonstrations at these institutes.[27]

Out of the Farmers' Institute movement grew community and county fairs which did much to stimulate black farmers to improve their efforts. The first Farmers' Institute fair was held in the fall of 1898 on the campus of Tuskegee Institute. It provided the farmers an opportunity to display their products and show what they had accomplished. At first the farmers' products exhibited at the fair were few and of poor quality. But each fall thereafter the samples of their crops and livestock and of the women's needlework, quilts and canned goods were more abundant and of the best quality and variety. The number of black farmers who came to the fairs increased from a few hundred in 1898 and 1899 to thousands by 1915, and the length of the fair was extended from one day to two or three days in some counties. Many

---

[26]Tuskegee *Student*, November 18, 1897, June 18, 1904; *Thirty-First Annual Catalogue of the Tuskegee Normal and Industrial Institute, 1911-1912* (Tuskegee Institute: 1912), 97; "Farmers' Institute Meeting," typed outline, May 21, 1901, Box 10, TIE Papers; George W. Carver to Booker T. Washington, April 20, 1904, Box 555. BTW Papers; "Farmers Institute Meeting," typescript, March 15, 1904, Box 555, BTW Papers.

[27]Scott, *The Reluctant Farmer*, 114-116; see also John Hamilton, "History of Farmers' Institutes in the United States," United States Office of Experiment Stations. *Bulletin 174* (Washington: 1906); H. C. Dugas to George W. Carver, February 10, 1905, Box 2; J. M. Collums to Carver, June 3, 1910, Box 3, John P. Powell to Carver, July 20, 1910, Box 3; B. T. Crawford to Carver. June 3, 1910, Box 3, GWC Papers.

whites began to take part in the Tuskegee fairs, and in 1911 the Negro
Macon County Fair, which had erected a permanent fair ground away
from the Institute campus in 1906, merged with the white association of
the county under the name of the Macon County Fair Association.[28]

The fairs developed into educational and social gatherings for the
black farmers in each county. They came to the fairs, listened to lectures by experts on agricultural subjects, examined the exhibits, received suggestions about how to improve their farming, watched the
parades, and took part in the races and other amusements that were
available. The growth and success of the Farmers' Fair at Tuskegee
brought Professor Carver an invitation in 1903 to exhibit the agricultural products and works of the Institute in the state capitol at Montgomery. The influence of Carver and his impressive exhibit, the progress of black farmers as demonstrated at the county fairs, and the
recognition and approval of Washington as the leader of his race
caused the Alabama Agricultural Association to establish, in October,
1906, a "Negro Day" at its first annual state fair in Montgomery.
Washington, the Director of the Negro Department of the fair, was
responsible for the "Negro Building" that contained the exhibits of
black farmers from over the state and "a restaurant and other conveni-
ences . . . for the entertainment and comfort of the colored people."
Included in the events of the special "Negro Day," which was the last
day of the fair, were speeches by Washington, Governor William D.
Jelks, and other prominent black leaders and white politicians who
"talked plainly to the negroes of their duty to law, order, and
progress."[29]

Through the influence of Tuskegee Institute the idea of Negro
county fairs spread quickly to other Alabama counties, especially
Lowndes, Dallas, Lee, and Madison. By 1910, fairs were being held in
all parts of the South, and requests came from all directions for Tuskegee Institute's agricultural specialists to speak and demonstrate ag-

---

[28]Tuskegee *Student*, December 24, 1910, clipping, Box 980, BTW Papers; *Tuskegee
To Date, 1915*, 15; Rackham Holt, *George Washington Carver, An American Biography*
(New York: 1943), 163-164; Tuskegee *Student*, November 5, 1904; T. M. Campbell,
"The Relation of Extension Work to the General Economic Conditions of Country
Life," typescript, *ca.* 1908, Box 19, TMC Papers.

[29]R. R. Poole to Booker T. Washington, September 12, 1906, and Booker T. Washing-
ton to George W. Carver, October 3, 1906, Box 2, GWC Papers; Holt, *George
Washington Carver*, 164; G. R. Bridgeforth to Booker T. Washington, July 6, 1910, Box
598, BTW Papers; Tuskegee *Messenger*, October 25, 1907; Tuskegee *Southern Letter*,
December, 1906; Tuskegee *Student*, February 7, November 21, 1903, December 24,
1910; *The Tuskegee Farmers' Institute Fair*, handbill, October 28-29, 1904, Box 551
BTW Papers; Montgomery *Evening Journal*, February 5, 1903; Montgomery *Journal*,
October 25, 27, November 3, 1906; Tuskegee *Messenger*, October 25, 1907.

ricultural equipment.[30]

Another significant outgrowth of the Farmers' Institute and the Negro Farmers' Conference was the "Short Course in Agriculture" which was first held at Tuskegee Institute in January, 1904. The course was designed to provide the farmers in surrounding counties, at the season when most of them were idle, several weeks of study and observation of the school's farm and Experiment Station. The first Short Course in 1904 lasted for six weeks, opened at 10:00 A.M. and closed at 3:00 P.M. each day so that the farmers could ride in for the school and return the same day; the second was only four weeks and all courses after 1905 lasted only two weeks. There was no charge for the course which was taught by Professors Carver and George R. Bridgeforth. Sometimes guest lecturers were brought in from the United States Department of Agriculture, the Georgia Agricultural Experiment Station, and Alabama's agricultural college at Auburn. While the school considered the individual needs of the farmers and tried to help them solve some of their problems, the course program included scheduled classes and lectures on general farming, livestock, dairying, poultry raising, fruit growing, and truck gardening.[31]

The courses given were eminently practical and the school was conducted in the most informal manner. There was no compulsory attendance, and the farmers were free to come and go at any time. Since there were special classes for women and children, entire families frequently attended the Short Course. In 1908 the directors of the Short Course instituted a plan of giving certificates to those persons who had attended for three or five years and were able to pass an examination covering the subjects which they had studied. At the end of the course prizes in amounts from $1.00 to $5.00 were awarded to persons who had made the greatest progress or advancement in specified subjects or fields of study.[32]

The first year of the Short Course brought only eleven students, most of whom were older men. When the second year brought only

[30]"Annual Negro Fair Held," Mongtomery *Advertiser*, December 1, 1911, clipping, Box 983, BTW Papers; "State of Alabama for the Promotion of Agriculture Among Negroes," typescript, *ca.* 1911, Box 984, BTW Papers; "The Great Giles County [Tenn.] Negro Fair," 1910, clipping, Box 7, BTW Papers; Charlotte R. Thorn to George W. Carver, October 14, 1904, Box 1, GWC Papers.

[31]Tuskegee *Student*, December 12, 19, 1903, December 10, 1904, December 24, 1910; Montgomery *Advertiser*, January 10, 14, 17, 1912, clippings, Box 986, BTW Papers; *Tuskegee to Date, 1915*, 14-15.

[32]Monroe N. Work, "A Short Course For Farmers," *The Outlook*, XCI (April 17, 1909), 866-867; *Tuskegee Normal and Industrial Institute Farmers' School*, pamphlet, January 4-18, 1910, BTW Papers; *Short Course in Agriculture*, pamphlet, January 5, 1909, Box 979, BTW Papers; *Short Course Closing Exercises, February 1, 1905*, handbill, Box 559, BTW Papers; Tuskegee *Student*, January 15, 1910.

seventeen farmers, the directors sought to attract younger men and women and farm families from all sections of the state. Arrangements were made for the participants to secure board and lodging near the school for $2.50 a week. The third year brought seventy, the fourth year 490, and by 1912 the enrollment surpassed 1,500.[33] The increased attendance at the Short Course reflected "a real enthusiasm among the farmers . . . for education and progress along agricultural lines." "It seems to me," wrote Booker T. Washington in 1908, "that I can see signs of a general awakening among the masses of the negro farming population."[34] A white visitor at the Short Course, who had lived in the Black Belt of Alabama all of his life, gave some evidence of the progress that the black farmers had made when he said:

> It used to be the case that you could ride along the road and tell by the appearance of the farm whether it was worked by a negro or a white man. Now the negroes are whitewashing and painting their buildings and working their crops so well that it is difficult to tell by looking at a farm what is the color of the skin of the man who worked it.[35]

Prior to 1906 all of Washington's extension activities had centered on bringing the uneducated black farmers to Tuskegee Institute to drink from the fountain of agricultural wisdom. As he rode through the countryside recruiting students for his school, Washington realized that there was little hope of advancement for the isolated farmers unless modern agricultural training was carried to their doorsteps. With this in mind, he questioned Professor Carver in November, 1904 about the possibility of outfitting a wagon to serve as a traveling agricultural school. Carver accepted the idea as "a most excellent one," and quickly returned to Washington a rough sketch of "a light, strong wagon body for either a one or two-horse wagon made to open part way down" that would carry "a small milk separator, churn and complete outfit for making butter and cheese, . . . and large charts on soil building, orcharding, stock raising, and all operations pertaining to the farm." This equipment on the wagon would be used with lectures and demonstrations given by a faculty member from the school. Carver saw this scheme as a means of strengthening his Agriculture Department and at the same time disseminating to the farmers the agricultural

[33]*Twenty-Ninth Annual Catalogue, Tuskegee Normal and Industrial Institute, 1909-10* (Tuskegee Institute: 1910), 97; Work, "A Short Course for Farmers," 866; Montgomery *Advertiser*, January 10, 1912, clipping, Box 986, BTW Papers; *Tuskegee To Date, 1915*, 15; "A School for Farmers," January 9, 1909, clipping, Box 982, BTW Papers.
[34]Booker T. Washington, "Education for the Man Behind the Plow," *The Independent*, LXIV (April 23, 1908), 919.
[35]Monroe N. Work, "Tuskegee's Short Course," typescript, *ca.* 1909, Box 979, BTW Papers.

knowledge he was producing at the Tuskegee Experiment Station.[36]

While Carver and his staff drew the plans and prepared an estimate of the cost of an agricultural wagon, Washington went North to find the money for it. Morris K. Jesup, a New York banker and philanthropist, agreed to provide the $567.00 for the wagon and equipment and to get the John F. Slater Fund to provide money for the wagon operation. On May 24, 1906, the "Jesup Agricultural Wagon" began its trips into the rural areas of the county with George Bridgeforth as the first operator of this "Farmers' College on Wheels." The wagon carried different kinds of plows and planters, a cultivator, a cotton chopper, a variety of seeds, samples of fertilizers, a revolving churn, a butter mold, a cream separator, a milk tester, and other appliances useful in making practical demonstrations, and it had the immense advantage of carrying scientific agriculture directly to the farmers in the fields. After making the rounds of the small and large farms of a community, the "Movable School" located at a central point and conducted an open-air demonstration for a gathering of farmers and their families.[37]

During the summer of 1906, the school on wheels reached over 2,000 people a month and attracted attention all over the state. White farmers began attending the meetings, and some of them who owned large plantations invited the Jesup Wagon to visit their black tenants. It became obvious to Washington that this innovation was one of his greatest and that it would "do much to break through the hard crust of custom and prepare for a new agricultural era."[38]

In the fall of 1906 Dr. Seaman A. Knapp, Special Agent in charge of Farmers' Co-operative Demonstration Work for the United States Department of Agriculture, visited Tuskegee Institute and talked with Carver and his staff about beginning a co-operative demonstration

---

[36]George W. Carver to Booker T. Washington, November 16, 1904, Box 551, BTW Papers. Roscoe C. Bruce, Director of the Academic Department at the Institute, wrote Carver on May 13, 1904, about the small number of farmers from the area who attended the Negro conferences and suggested that the Agricultural Department organize "a system of lectures with agricultural demonstrations to be held in the various towns in the county at stated intervals during the next year." Agricultural schools and colleges in Europe and in the western states were already conducting such classes, he said. Box 551, BTW Papers.

[37]Tuskegee Institute Executive Council Minutes, December 18, 1905, January 11, May 11, 1906, Book 1005, BTW Papers; Booker T. Washington to Morris K. Jesup, March 12, 1906, Box 721; Booker T. Washington to Mrs. Morris K. Jesup, April 24, 1906, Box 721; George W. Carver to Booker T. Washington, May 21, 1906, Box 567, BTW Papers; Booker T. Washington, "A Farmers' College on Wheeles," *World's Work*, XIII (December, 1906), 8352-8353; Felix James, "The Tuskegee Institute Movable School, 1906-1923; *"Agricultural History*, XLV (July, 1971), 201-209.

[38]"Reports of the Jesup Wagon," June-August, 1906, Box 567, BTW Papers; "Schedule of Jesup Wagon, 1906," George Washington, 1906, Box 567, BTW Papers; Washington, "A Farmers' College on Wheels," 8354.

program for the Negro farmers of the South. Washington seized this opportunity to link his successful but financially insecure agricultural extension operations with that of the federal government. Knapp, using funds provided by the General Education Board of New York, and Washington, with money from the Slater Fund, agreed to share the expenses for employing a man to operate the Jesup Wagon and conduct demonstration work in Macon and surrounding counties. On the recommendations of Carver and Bridgeforth, Thomas M. Campbell, a recent graduate in agriculture from Tuskegee, was hired on November 12, 1906, and became the first black demonstration agent in the United States. About a month later, John B. Pierce accepted a similar position for the upper South with headquarters at Hampton Institute in Virginia. The employment of these two men marked the beginning of the United States Department of Agriculture's Negro Extension work.[39]

Campbell spread the demonstration work of the Movable School into all areas of Alabama, Mississippi, and Georgia. In 1909 he turned the Jesup Wagon over to a new Macon County Demonstration Agent because he was promoted to District Agent with the responsibility of supervising and instructing other agents. The success of the Jesup Wagon continued until 1918, when it was replaced by the improved Knapp Agricultural Truck that could cover more territory and carry more equipment. The scheme was pushed further in 1923, with the modern "Booker T. Washington Agricultural School on Wheels." This new truck, which was purchased with funds contributed by 30,000 Negro farmers and friends, carried the most advanced farm equipment and implements, a home demonstration agent, a rural nurse, and a complete motion picture outfit and phonograph. The Movable School continued its operations until World War II.[40]

---

[39] S. A. Knapp to Booker T. Washington, October 4, 1906, October 30, 1906, Box 3, BTW Papers; T. M. Campbell, "The Alabama Movable School," reprinted from *Transactions of the Twenty-sixth Annual Meeting of the National Tuberculosis Association, 1930;* Thomas M. Campbell, *The Movable School Goes to the Negro Farmer* (Tuskegee Institute, 1936), 91-94; King, *King's Agricultural Digest,* 27-33; J. A. Evans, *Recollections of Extension History,* North Carolina Agricultural Extension Circular 224, August, 1938, (Raleigh, North Carolina), 12-13.

[40] Campbell, *The Movable School Goes to the Negro Farmer,* 92-157; Thomas M. Campbell, *U. S. Farm Demonstration Work Among Negroes in the South* (Tuskegee Institute: 1915), 3-7; Booker T. Washington to Trustees of the John F. Slater Fund, October 31, 1908, Box 39, BTW Papers; Washington, "A Farmers' College on Wheels," 8354; Thomas M. Campbell to Dr. S. A. Knapp, January 24, 1908, and Campbell to Booker T. Washington, October 27, 1908, Extension Service Records, RG 33, National Archives, Washington, D.C.; "Demonstration Work Done By Thomas M. Campbell in Macon County, Alabama, Among the Colored Farmers," typescript, November 11, 1908, Extension Service Records, RG 33, National Archives; Harry Simms and Juanita Coleman, *Movable Schools of Agriculture Among Negroes in Alabama,* Alabama

Campbell advanced rapidly from Demonstration Agent of Macon County to Field Agent for seven Southern states. Although he was an employee of the federal government, his office remained on the campus of Tuskegee Institute and he worked closely with the Principal and the agricultural division of the school. It was the work and the influence of Thomas M. Campbell that made Tuskegee Institute the center of Negro Agricultural Extension work in the deep South. While Campbell used his position to spread the ideas of Booker T. Washington, he made his greatest contribution to black farmers and to his race by constantly pressuring the United States Department of Agriculture to hire more Negro extension agents and to expand its extension operations among black farmers. By the time he retired from government service on February 28, 1953, he had become the most prominent black agricultural leader in the New South. The work which Campbell and Pierce began in 1906 had produced 846 Negro extension agents by 1950, and 435,000 Negro families had received benefit from the government's Agricultural Extension Service.[41]

The extension work of Tuskegee Institute included forty different activities that ranged from the Annual Negro Conference to the Tuskegee Town Mothers' Club. Reaching over 100,000 people each year, the extension work endeavored to do two things: To improve the conditions of the masses of the Negroes; and to give them lessons in self-help that would enable them to take the initiative for their own improvement. Washington established the Extension Department of the Institute in 1910, in order to systematize the school's numerous extension activities. One of the department's major responsibilities was the distribution of printed bulletins, circulars, farmers' leaflets and pamphlets that were issued by various departments of the school,

---

Polytechnic Institute Extension Service Circular 39, March, 1920 (Auburn, Ala.: 1920); "Alabama Negro Extension Service Finds That the Movable School Helps the Negro To Help Himself," *Extension Service Review*, VII (September, 1936), 140-141; William J. Maddox, "Wheeled Schools," *Better Crops With Plant Food* (July, 1927), 5-8; Jamestown (New York) *Morning Post*, October 21, 1925, clipping, Box 8, TIE Papers; Thomas M. Campbell to Henry T. Crigler, November 2, 1950, Box 14, TMC Papers.

[41]W. B. Hill, "Extension Service Celebrates 50th Anniversary," typescript, *ca.* 1953, Box 20, TMC Papers; Thomas M. Campbell, "The First Historical Report on Agricultural Extension Work Among Negroes in the States of Alabama, Georgia, Florida, Mississippi, Louisiana, Oklahoma, and Texas," mimeographed, United States Department of Agriculture, Office of Extension Work South, Circular No. 1, December 31, 1920 (Tuskegee Institute); W. B. Mercier, *Extension Work Among Negroes, 1920,* United States Department of Agriculture, Circular 190 (Washington, 1921), 3-20; "Some Data on T. M. Campbell," typescript, July 1, 1949, Box 25, TMC Papers; King, *King's Agricultural Digest*, 30-33; Lewis W. Jones, "The South's Negro Farm Agent," *Journal of Negro Education,* XXII (Winter, 1953), 38-40; Thomas M. Campbell to Henry T. Crigler, November 2, 1950, Box 14, TMC Papers.

especially the Experiment Station. Most of these publications were very elementary and simple in character. They contained information about scientific methods of agriculture such as the rotation of crops, the uses of fertilizers, the advantages of the garden, nature study, and business economy for the farmer. Carver and the Experiment Station issued forty-four *Bulletins* from 1898 to 1943 that dealt with everything from the Farmer's Almanac to the peanut. All of the publications were distributed free to individuals, schools, and local farmers' conferences.[42]

In another attempt to reach the black people of central Alabama, Washington established a newspaper, *The Messenger*, in September, 1905. Edited by Clinton J. Calloway of the extension division of the school, the paper was devoted to "improving the general condition of the people" in Macon and surrounding counties by encouraging the work of the public schools and instructing the farming community in agriculture. It reported all extension activities, advertised farm equipment and farms for sale, and printed "Suggestions to Farmers" written by the school's agriculture faculty. The paper was circulated widely to schools, farmers' institutes, and local Negro conferences. In 1913, however, the paper encountered financial problems and ceased publication.[43]

In January, 1914, a new paper appeared at the Institute. The *Negro Farmer* was founded in the "interest of Negro landowners, tenant

---

[42]Tuskegee *Student*, June 18, 1904; A. C. True to George W. Carver, April 16, 1902, Records of the Office of the Experiment Stations, General Correspondence, RG 164, National Archives, Washington, D.C.; John C. Lehr to George W. Carver, December 16, 1904, Box 1, GWC Papers; C. J. Calloway, "Raising Chickens," *Farmers Leaflet, No. 14*, May, 1906 (Tuskegee Institute, 1906); Mrs. Booker T. Washington, "For Our Women and Children's Circles," *Practical Help Leaflet, No. 3*, n.d., Box 563, BTW papers; "Department of School Extension," typescript, *ca.* 1912, Box 985, BTW Papers; Monroe N. Work, "Extension Work Among the Negroes of Macon County, Alabama," typescript, n.d., Box 3, MNW Papers; Booker T. Washington to Monroe N. Work, March 2, 1910 and Work to Washington, March 1, 1909, Box 604, BTW Papers; "Bulletins of the Agricultural Research Experiment Station," typescript, n.d., Box 1, EMWS Papers; Jessie P. Guzman, *George Washington Carver, A Classified Bibliography*, Records and Research Pamphlet No. 3 (Tuskegee Institute: 1953), 23-24.

[43]Tuskegee *Student*, September 30, 1905; *Twenty-Ninth Annual Catalogue, Tuskegee Normal and Industrial Institute, 1909-1910* (Tuskegee Institute: 1910), 16; Tuskegee *Messenger*, March 2, 1906, January 24, February 7, 1908, August 27, 1909, January 27, December 11, 1911, January 5, 12, 19, 1912. In 1907 the professional agricultural students of the Institute organized the Tuskegee Agricultural Students' Union for the purpose of stimulating "an interest in agricultural activities along all lines." In May, 1908 they began publishing a small paper, *The Tuskegee Agricultural Students' Farm Journal*, which contained articles on trucking, dairying, poultry, fruit growing and other branches of agriculture. *The Tuskegee Agricultural Students' Farm Journal*, May, 1908, Box 583, BTW Papers.

farmers and those who employ Negro labor."[44] It was edited by the talented Isaac Fisher, a graduate of Tuskegee, who sought to encourage the "colored farmers . . . all over the country to improve their farming methods . . . and to produce in an increasingly large degree more of the food which they and their stock consume."[45] Although Washington announced publicly that Tuskegee Institute had "no financial interest or control over this new publication," he and five others from the Institute were among the stockholders of the newspaper.[46] While espousing the "Tuskegee Idea" in its editorials, the *Negro Farmer* proved to be a dictionary of agricultural knowledge as well as a practical guide to farming. Each issue featured a column entitled "Winners from the Soil—Colored Heroes of the Farm," articles written by the agriculture faculty of the Institute, and letters of praise for the newspaper from subscribers. The paper, which was sent all over Alabama and to many surrounding states, claimed a circulation of 3,000 by August, 1914, and the editor proposed to circulate it among "the 2,000,000 black farmers of the United States."[47] The name of the journal was changed in November, 1915 to the *Negro Farmer and Messenger*. In July, 1916 its able editor resigned and went to Fisk University. Circulation and advertisements declined sharply after this and the paper ceased publication in 1918.[48]

Much has been written about Booker T. Washington as a politician, an educator, and a philosopher, but far too little attention has been devoted to him as a leader of the rural life activities of his people. It seems that there was no group in the country whose cause was of more concern and interest to him than that of black farmers. He dedicated much of his life and his school to improve the lives of millions of black farmers in the South. He was responsible for bringing to Tuskegee Institute many black men of great ability to direct his programs for helping the farmers. These men such as Carver, Campbell, Bridgeforth, and Greene accepted the challenge which the masses of rural black people offered and joined Washington's efforts to emancipate the black farmers of the South from agricultural ignorance. Booker T. Washington and the agriculture faculty of Tuskegee Institute educated and influenced the lives of the rural black people in the South from 1881 to 1915, with the Annual Negro Conferences, the Tuskegee Experiment Station, the Agricultural Short Course, the Farmers' Institutes, the Farmers' County Fairs, the Movable School, and the numerous newspapers and other publications.

[44]Tuskegee *Negro Farmer*, March 14, 1914.
[45]Tuskegee *Southern Letter*, April, 1915.
[46]Tuskegee *Negro Farmer*, March 14, June 20, 1914.
[47]*Ibid.*, March 14, 28, April 11, May 9, 23, 1914.
[48]Tuskegee *Negro Farmer and Messenger*, June 3, July 15, 1916, April 7, 1917.

# Progressivism — For Middle-Class Whites Only: North Carolina Education, 1880–1910

By J. Morgan Kousser

"The problem that the South now presents," asserted Walter Hines Page in an *Atlantic Monthly* article in 1902, "has at last become so plain that thoughtful men no longer differ about it. It is no longer obscured by race differences nor by political differences. It is simply the training of the untrained masses." Education, Page was sure, would build a new "democratic order of society" in the South, would, as he had asserted in a famous 1897 speech, "develop the forgotten man . . . . The neglected people will rise," he went on, "and with them will rise all the people."[1]

What are we to make of Page's glorious hopes? Were they merely the pious pronouncements of a "progressive" phrasemonger, or did his predictions reflect reality? There was, to be sure, a massive increase in educational expenditures in the South during the so-called "Progressive Era." But how equitably were the funds distributed and what explains the pattern of distribution? Did the new monies go primarily to the "forgotten men and women," black and white, mainly to the upper and middle classes, or were they divided equally among all classes? Was the creed of the southern educational crusade "equality of opportunity in the schools for all, black and white," as the chief historian of the movement, Charles William Dabney, put it? Or did the campaigns for education lead to greater inequality, to discrimination in the distribution of funds

[1] Page, "The Rebuilding of Old Commonwealths," *Atlantic Monthly,* LXXXIX (May 1902), 659, 661 (first two quotations); and his book of the same title containing his "forgotten man" speech, *The Rebuilding of Old Commonwealths . . .* (New York, 1902), 31, 47 (last two quotations). Research for this article was sponsored by the National Endowment for the Humanities Grant R0-9980-74-140. I presented an earlier version at the American Historical Association meeting in December 1974. I want to thank Allan G. Bogue, Bruce E. Cain, Lance E. Davis, John A. Ferejohn, Morris P. Fiorina, Robert W. Fogel, David M. Grether, Daniel J. Kevles, Allan J. Lichtman, Gary J. Miller, Forrest D. Nelson, and Roger G. Noll for aid in revising the paper. Naturally, neither NEH nor my colleagues bear any responsibility for the conclusions or any errors that remain.

Mr. Kousser is professor of history at California Institute of Technology.

which was, in Louis R. Harlan's phrase, "almost universal, flagrant, and increasing"?[2]

If such historians as Harlan and Horace Mann Bond have concerned themselves with the distribution of expenditures, rarely if ever have students of the past taken up the question of the distribution of taxes. Yet it is obvious that the incidence of the burdens is no less important than the incidence of the benefits of government; government guarantees of equal opportunity or redistribution of society's resources involve taxing as well as spending. Surely, we need to know more about past state tax policies: How progressive or regressive was the state tax structure, and how did it change over time? How did tax rates vary by race and class? Did the combination of taxing and spending for education redistribute the society's resources upward, downward, or not at all? How did the amount of redistribution change over the years?

If there were systematic variations in the distribution of taxes and governmental services across time and geographic areas, then the question of the causes of these variations becomes crucial. Scholars have proposed three basic hypotheses to explain such differences. The first or "progressive" model focuses on differences in the demand for education. According to this view, before the "educational awakening" of the early twentieth century poor whites were indifferent to public education, and rich whites, while seeking education for their own children, often opposed increases in school taxes because some of the benefits would have to go to blacks. Only when the "progressive" elites pushed the recalcitrant masses to increase school taxes did the sentiment for public education become widespread. This induced demand and the beneficence of "educational statesmen" produced an expanded and democratized educational system that offered increasingly equal opportunity to all whites and, some scholars claimed, even to blacks.[3]

The second hypothesis focuses on changes in the structure of politics. What effect did the disfranchisement of large numbers of

[2] Dabney, *Universal Education in the South* (2 vols., Chapel Hill, 1936), I, vii–ix; Louis R. Harlan, *Separate and Unequal: Public School Campaigns and Racism in the Southern Seaboard States 1901–1915* (New York, 1969), 269. See also Horace Mann Bond, *The Education of the Negro in the American Social Order* (New York, 1966). By 1910 even Page realized that in schooling Negroes were either "forgotten" or "deliberately swindled." See George-Anne Willard, "Charles Lee Coon (1868–1927): North Carolina Crusader for Educational Reform" (unpublished Ph.D. dissertation, University of North Carolina, 1974), 248.

[3] Charles W. Dabney, "The Public School Problem in the South," in William T. Harris, *Report of the Commissioner of Education for the Year 1900–1901* (2 vols., Serials 4299–4300, Washington, 1902), I, 1013, 1019–20 (cited hereinafter as Harris, *Report*); Cornelius J. Heatwole, *A History of Education in Virginia* (New York, 1916), xiii–xiv, 321; Edgar W. Knight, *Public School Education in North Carolina* (Boston and Chicago, 1916), 329, 342.

poor whites, as well as practically all the blacks, and the contemporaneous precipitant decline in party competition have on the level and distribution of educational benefits?[4] Was politics, in Charles W. Dabney's words, "The great curse of our public educational system," the removal of which would, he presumed, lead to educational progress? Or, on the other hand, was Vladimir O. Key, Jr., correct in asserting that, at least "over the long run, the have-nots lose . . ." in a political system without organized parties?[5]

Adopting the same general view which Key espoused, Horace Mann Bond and Louis R. Harlan attributed the increased discrimination against Negroes in educational benefits after 1900 to the disfranchisement of blacks. They also believed that blacks had been losing ground steadily since the end of Reconstruction. Despite the thoroughness of their impressionistic research on racial discrimination, however, Bond and Harlan did not investigate changes in taxation practices, employed unsophisticated statistical methods, and largely ignored the possibility that the decline of the Populist and Republican parties and the restrictions placed on the suffrage of poor whites might have led to increases in discrimination against lower class whites as well as the blacks after 1900. Was progressivism "for whites only," or was it for only some whites?[6]

Critics of Key, most notably Thomas R. Dye, have advanced as a third general hypothesis a socioeconomically deterministic explanation of variations in such political "outputs" as public education. Simply stated, Dye's view is that the socioeconomic structure directly or indirectly determines the levels and perhaps the distribution (he is not so categorical on this point) of public services. Permutations of such characteristics of the political structure as turnout and party competition, according to proponents of this hypothesis, have no independent influence upon public policy.[7]

These hypotheses will be tested in this article through an analysis based on approximately 40,000 pieces of county-level economic, social, political, educational, and tax data for each year from 1880 to 1910 for North Carolina. The birthplace of Page, Dabney, and such other famous educational reformers as Edwin Anderson Alderman and Charles Duncan McIver, and the home of the foremost

---

[4] For a more extensive discussion of disfranchisement and the decline in party competition see my book, *The Shaping of Southern Politics: Suffrage Restriction and the Establishment of the One-Party South, 1880–1910* (New Haven and London, 1974).

[5] Dabney, in Harris, *Report*, I, 1018; Key, *Southern Politics in State and Nation* (New York, 1949), 307.

[6] The phrase "progressivism for whites only" comes from C. Vann Woodward, *Origins of the New South, 1877–1913* ([Baton Rouge], 1951), Chap. 14.

[7] Dye, *Understanding Public Policy* (Englewood Cliffs, N. J., 1972), conveniently summarizes Dye's point of view and much of his earlier research.

southern progressive "educational governor," Charles Brantley Aycock, North Carolina has also been perhaps the favorite state of southern historians. Developments in education in North Carolina in the early twentieth century were broadcast throughout the region and even the nation at the time, and they have since been studied intensively by Edgar Wallace Knight and Charles W. Dabney, whose conclusions were revised by Louis R. Harlan. Many other works of biography and political and educational history also treat the evoluation of education in North Carolina.[8]

Most important for a cliometric study, North Carolinians kept the best educational and tax statistics during this period.[9] Consequently, although the research of which this article is a part has not yet progressed far enough to establish conclusively that North Carolina was typical of the South as a whole, the experience of that state

[8] See for example Alan B. Bromberg, " 'Pure Democracy and White Supremacy': The Redeemer Period in North Carolina, 1876–1894" (unpublished Ph.D. dissertation, University of Virginia, 1977); William D. Cotton, "Appalachian North Carolina: A Political Study, 1860–1899" (unpublished Ph.D. dissertation, University of North Carolina, 1955); William E. King, "The Era of Progressive Reform in Southern Education: The Growth of Public Schools in North Carolina, 1885–1910" (unpublished Ph.D. dissertation, Duke University, 1970); Frenise A. Logan, "The Legal Status of Public School Education for Negroes in North Carolina, 1877–1894," *North Carolina Historical Review,* XXXII (July 1955), 346–57; Philip R. Muller, "New South Populism: North Carolina, 1884–1900" (unpublished Ph.D. dissertation, University of North Carolina, 1972); Marcus C. S. Noble, *A History of the Public Schools of North Carolina* (Chapel Hill, 1930); Oliver H. Orr, Jr., "Charles Brantley Aycock: A Biography" (unpublished Ph.D. dissertation, University of North Carolina, 1958); David H. Prince, "A History of the State Department of Public Instruction in North Carolina, 1852–1956" (unpublished Ph.D. dissertation, University of North Carolina, 1959); Richard B. Westin, "The State and Segregated Schools: Negro Public Education in North Carolina, 1863–1923" (unpublished Ph.D. dissertation, Duke University, 1966); Frank H. White, "The Economic and Social Development of Negroes in North Carolina Since 1900" (unpublished Ph.D. dissertation, New York University, 1960); Daniel J. Whitener, "Public Education in North Carolina During Reconstruction, 1865–1876," in Fletcher M. Green, ed., *Essays in Southern History Presented to Joseph Gregoire de Roulhac Hamilton . . .* (Chapel Hill, N.C., 1949), 67–90; Whitener, "The Republican Party and Public Education in North Carolina, 1867–1900," *North Carolina Historical Review,* XXXVII (July 1960), 382–96; Harvey Wish, "Negro Education and the Progressive Movement," *Journal of Negro History,* XLIX (July 1964), 184–200.

[9] All statistics on education, taxes, and wealth during this period are drawn from the relevant published reports of the state superintendents of education and the auditors. Demographic data comes from the published U. S. census reports. For the sources of the political data see Kousser, "The Shaping of Southern Politics: Suffrage Restriction and the Establishment of the One-Party South" (unpublished Ph.D. dissertation, Yale University, 1971), 427–29. Because a great many counties did not report fully on taxes and expenditures in every year, I have collected data for each of the thirty years and averaged all indices over five-year periods—1880–1884, 1885–1890, etc.—thereby eliminating missing data from the averages. This procedure reduced the number of missing counties to three at most in any one period. It also smoothed out the expenditure figures, which after 1900 tended to jump about somewhat because of the nonrecurring capital expenditures involved in increased school construction. I also consolidated counties whose boundaries changed during the period, which reduced the total number of units to a maximum of eighty-eight for any one period.

will remain crucial to any interpretation of the politics of southern education in the late nineteenth century and the early twentieth century. The politics of education, in turn, is central to any discussion of the distribution of government services in the South in this period, for state and local government there provided no other services, except possibly the courts, which directly affected large numbers of people or which could possibly have redistributed societal resources from race to race or class to class.

North Carolina's manner of raising and spending monies for education after 1871 assured that taxes would be regressive and expenditures would correlate closely with wealth. The Radical Reconstructionists, a coalition of whites from poor mountainous counties and lowland ex-slaves, led in educational matters by carpetbagger Samuel S. Ashley, had envisaged education as a device for transforming an inegalitarian social and economic system into one providing equal opportunity. The Radical program set up a uniform property tax collected by the state and distributed to each county in proportion to its school-age population and guaranteed by law that equal amounts would be spent on each child, regardless of race. These devices would ensure, the Radicals hoped, a four-month school term for all the state's children.[10]

Before this system could firmly be established, however, the violent revolution of 1870–1871 by the Klan-led Conservatives upset the Republican legislative majority, impeached Radical governor William Woods Holden, forced Ashley to resign as superintendent of public instruction, gerrymandered legislative districts to prevent a successful counterrevolution, and rewrote the law apportioning educational funds. The 1871 law, which formed the basis of the distribution of school funds in North Carolina for fifty years, kept the school property tax uniform across the state but allowed each county to keep the monies it raised.[11] For the Radical mandate of equal expenditures on each child, in other words, the Democrats

[10] There is no adequate comprehensive history of Reconstruction or the Republican party in North Carolina, but see the two articles by Whitener cited in note 8; Cotton, "Appalachian North Carolina," 167–75, 215, 249, 277–78, 364, 551; *Journal of the Constitutional Convention of the State of North Carolina at Its Session, 1868* (Raleigh, 1868); J. G. de Roulhac Hamilton, *Reconstruction in North Carolina* (New York, 1914), Chaps. 6, 9–14, 16.

[11] On the upheaval see Hamilton, *Reconstruction in North Carolina*, Chaps. 12–15; Allen W. Trelease, *White Terror: The Ku Klux Klan Conspiracy and Southern Reconstruction* (New York, Evanston, and London, 1971), Chaps. 12–13. On the gerrymandering see the maps in John L. Cheney, Jr., ed., *North Carolina Government, 1585–1974; A Narrative and Statistical History . . .* (Raleigh, 1975). On the 1871 law see *Public Laws of the State of North Carolina, 1870–1871 Session . . .* (Raleigh, 1871), 387; North Carolina, Senate, *Journal, 1870–1871* (Raleigh, 1871), 325, 361, 402, 420, 487, 545–46, 559, 610–11, 648; North Carolina, House of Representatives, *Journal, 1870–1871* (Raleigh, 1871), 62, 132, 534, 571–72; Raleigh *Daily Sentinel*, January 23, February 15, 20, 23, March 18, 22, 1871.

TABLE 1

BLACK AND WHITE TAX PAYMENTS AS A PERCENTAGE OF ASSESSED
PROPERTY VALUES
NORTH CAROLINA, 1880–1910

| Period | White Tax Rates | Black Tax Rates | Ratio of Black to White Tax Rate |
|--------|-----------------|-----------------|----------------------------------|
| 1880–1884 | .0019 | .0120 | 6.32 |
| 1885–1890 | .0022 | .0146 | 6.64 |
| 1891–1895 | .0025 | .0128 | 5.12 |
| 1896–1900 | .0030 | .0133 | 4.43 |
| 1901–1905 | .0027 | .0080 | 2.96 |
| 1906–1910 | .0032 | .0082 | 2.56 |

substituted a mode of distribution of funds which favored children
living in wealthy counties at the expense of those residing in poor
areas. Expenditures per capita were therefore necessarily directly
proportional to each county's wealth except for five variations: differences in the number of children per family; a few local taxes
specially authorized by the legislature from time to time before
1905, and a large number thereafter; the collection rate of the poll
tax ("indigents" were legally exempted from paying it, but the definition of indigence was vague);[12] racial discrimination in apportionment of funds; and the school revenue accruing from sources other
than direct taxes, much of which came from tuition fees.[13]

By pegging the statewide poll tax to statewide property tax rates,
the Conservatives who dominated the 1875 constitutional convention guaranteed a regressive tax structure, since the poll tax was
equal for each adult male regardless of wealth.[14] Table 1 summarizes trends at the state level and indicates the effect of the regressivity of the tax system for schools on the almost universally poor

[12] Correlation and regression analyses of the percentage of "indigent" male adults, listed
separately by race, and the percentage blacks in each county failed to reveal any clear patterns. There was no consistent relationship between wealth and poll-tax collection rates for
blacks, nor did blacks in heavily black counties consistently pay a larger or smaller proportion of poll taxes than their counterparts in predominantly white counties. The printed figures on indigents covered the years 1880 through 1900.

[13] This last source of variation really ought to be considered a use tax. Since there are no
accurate figures on the average amount of tuition charged by schools in each county or the
proportion of parents paying such charges, I am forced to treat these indirect revenue sources
as if they were additional direct taxes.

[14] Article V, Section 1, of the 1876 North Carolina constitution set the capitation tax at a
level "equal on each [male between twenty-one and fifty] to the tax on property valued at
three hundred dollars in cash." Francis N. Thorpe, comp., *The Federal and State Constitutions* . . . (7 vols., Washington, 1909), V, 2834. For example, a property tax rate of 15 cents
per $100 would require a statewide poll tax of 45 cents. This could be supplemented by a local
poll tax of up to $1.55, since, by another constitutional provision, the total poll tax could not
exceed a level equal to a property tax of 66 2/3 cents per $100, that is, $2.00.

blacks.[15] In this paper the "tax rate" is defined as the proportion of assessed property paid in property and poll taxes, and "regressivity" means that people with little or no property were taxed at higher rates than those with more property.

White tax rates rose steadily until 1900, after which the largest increases in the assessed value of property since the Civil War allowed expenditures to rise even though tax rates stabilized. Black tax rates showed no clear trend until after 1900, when the poll tax became a suffrage requirement, and many tax collectors appear to have forgone revenue rather than take the chance of expanding the black electorate. Despite the reduction in the ratio of tax rate discrimination from 6.32 to 2.56 over the years, the basic fact is that throughout the period poor blacks paid taxes at much higher rates than the comparatively wealthy whites. To determine whether the tax system was regressive for whites separately and whether the degree of regressivity for blacks varied in counties with different white social structures, one must look at the county-level data.

Since the state supreme court and the legislature prohibited most local property taxes for schools until after the turn of the century, variations in tax rates from county to county chiefly reflected differences in the willingness to support schools through considerable variations in poll-tax collection rates, small deviations in the amount of the local poll tax, and disparities in the ratios of poll taxpayers to property taxpayers.[16] The significant coefficients in all rows of the first two columns of Part A of Table 2 confirm the regressivity of the North Carolina tax system for blacks and whites.[17] That the tax rates became less regressive with the increase in local property levies, stimulated by extensive and repeated "educational campaigns" after 1900, should not draw attention away from the fact that the tax system remained markedly regressive. At the beginning of the period, the white tax rate in a typical poor county was 1.7 times as high as that in a typical rich county; by the end, the ratio had fallen to 1.3, but it was still greater than unity.[18]

[15] Taxes for other purposes are not considered here, but the results would be very similar if they had been, since they were set and collected under the same provisions of the 1876 constitution as were the school taxes.

[16] In *Lane* v. *Stanley*, 65 N.C. 153 (1871), the court prohibited local taxation for schools without a special authorizing act from the legislature, and the legislature passed relatively few such laws until after 1900.

[17] Pearsonian correlation coefficients are statistical measures of association between two or more variables which vary from + 1.0 (strong positive correlation) to − 1.0 (strong negative correlation). They are more precisely defined and further explained in any elementary statistics text; for example, Eric A. Hanushek and John E. Jackson, *Statistical Methods for Social Scientists* (New York, 1977), 19–21.

[18] I defined poor and rich counties from 1880 to 1884 as ones where the white property values per white adult male were $400 and $1,400, respectively; for 1906 to 1910 the figures were raised to $600 and $1,600 because of increased prosperity.

## TABLE 2

COUNTY-LEVEL PEARSONIAN CORRELATIONS OF NORTH CAROLINA
TAX RATES, 1880–1910

| Period | White | Black | Black/White Ratio |
|---|---|---|---|
| A. Correlations by Race Between Wealth per Adult Male, Tax Rates, and Ratios of Tax Rates by Race | | | |
| 1880–1884 | − .720*[1] | − .663*[2] | + .165[3] |
| 1885–1890 | − .860* | − .649* | + .179* |
| 1891–1895 | − .839* | − .564* | + .085 |
| 1896–1900 | − .759* | − .610* | − .058 |
| 1901–1905 | − .393* | − .364* | − .202* |
| 1906–1910 | − .465* | − .335* | + .093 |
| B. Correlations by Race Between Percentage of Black Population, Tax Rates, and Ratios of Tax Rates | | | |
| 1880–1884 | − .638* | − .224* | + .097 |
| 1885–1890 | − .622* | − .158 | + .114 |
| 1891–1895 | − .650* | − .188* | + .101 |
| 1896–1900 | − .624* | − .360* | − .187* |
| 1901–1905 | − .348* | − .205* | − .150 |
| 1906–1910 | − .210* | + .049 | + .257* |

[1] Correlation between white tax rate and white wealth per white adult male. Pre-1890 values of wealth and property taxes by race were estimated by multiplying the nonracially separated 1880-1889 property values by the 1890-1896 proportions of wealth held by each race in each county. Starred coefficients in this and succeeding tables are those significant at the .05 level.

[2] Correlation between black tax rate and black wealth per black adult male. There were two counties with missing data on black taxes during the 1880s and one for the period from 1896-1905.

[3] Correlation between the ratio of black to white tax rate and white wealth per adult male.

This disparity in rates reflected a combination of what appears to have been a greater desire for schools in poor white areas and the political decisions made in 1871 and 1875, which were disproportionately supported by legislators from wealthy counties, to harness the state with a taxing system which discriminated against those with little property.[19]

[19] Strictly speaking, these figures, and others based on data aggregated by county in the paper, do not prove that there was systematic class discrimination among whites in North Carolina, for rich and poor may have lived in the same county, and all these suffered or benefited from the same tax and expenditure rates. I would argue, however, that the aggregate totals strongly imply discrimination between most of the rich and poor in this particular case for four reasons. First, the counties were tiny, averaging only about 2,500 white and 850 black male adults in 1910, and fewer in earlier years. The level of aggregation was thus not very high. Second, North Carolina was at least 86 percent rural during this period, and income and wealth distributions are well known to be distributed in a more egalitarian fashion, at least within races, in rural areas than in large cities. See for example Robert E. Gallman, "Trends in the Size Distribution of Wealth in the Nineteenth Century: Some Spec-

The negative correlations between black tax rates and the percentage of blacks in each county before 1905, given in Part B of Table 2, imply that, before disfranchisement, blacks who controlled enough votes could keep their taxes relatively low. That that correlation was highest (−.36) and that the negative correlation between the ratio of black to white taxes reached statistical significance only during the 1896–1900 period, when North Carolina was controlled by the Populist-Republican fusion movement, suggests that the increased power of the blacks in the heavily Negro counties during those years translated itself into comparatively lower tax rates for blacks. Conversely, the positive correlations between the ratio of black to white tax rates and the proportion Negro in the years from 1906 to 1910 indicate that after disfranchisement black tax rates declined less in counties controlled by rich black-belt whites than in the poor white counties. Since Negroes everywhere had very little wealth, whites in areas where there were few blacks probably thought it not worth the trouble and expense of collecting taxes from blacks. In areas where there were large numbers of Negroes, however, their collective pittances amounted to large sums. Furthermore, racism was probably more virulent in counties where blacks made up enough of the population to appear socially, economically, and, before disfranchisement, politically threatening. Thus, the black-belt whites probably had more desire and certainly more incentive to exploit blacks by raising their taxes, and after disfranchisement they had the ability to ignore the contrary desires of black voters.[20]

The positive correlation between the percentage Negro and the black/white tax ratio is especially striking since the black tax rate

---

ulations," in Lee Soltow, ed., *Six Papers on the Size Distribution of Wealth and Income* (New York and London, 1969), 1–30. Third, though there may have been some indigent whites in rich counties and a few wealthy ones in poor counties, the disparities in average wealth between counties were so great that the counties could not have had many such deviants. In 1880, for instance, the mean white wealth per white male adult by county was $875.44, but the standard deviation by county was nearly half as large, $418.29. Thus, though, there may have been some variation *within* counties, particularly in towns, there was also a very large amount of variance *between* counties. If the ratio of between-county to within-county variance was high, and if the equations are well-specified, regression and correlation coefficients based on aggregate data will not be seriously biased estimates of individual correlations. On this matter see Laura I. Langbein and Allan J. Lichtman, *Ecological Inference* (Beverly Hills and London, 1978). Fourth, I eliminated from the statistics investments in railroads, the largest single corporate property holding, inclusion of which would no doubt have perturbed the relation between individual and aggregated wealth.

[20] That the differences in black and white tax rates across counties did not merely reflect nonracially stiffer or looser collection policies is demonstrated by the fact that the correlations between black and white tax rates by counties varied from +.163 to +.405 and averaged only +.294. The correlations are all positive, and all but one are significant at the .05 level, but they are by no means perfect. There was a great deal of room for local deals between the often scandalously nonprofessional tax collectors and racial voting blocs.

TABLE 3

PEARSONIAN CORRELATIONS BY RACE BETWEEN TAX RATES AND
EXPENDITURES DIVIDED BY SCHOOL POPULATION
NORTH CAROLINA, 1880–1910

| Year | White | Black |
|------|-------|-------|
| 1880–1884 | − .499* | − .103 |
| 1885–1890 | − .607* | − .287* |
| 1891–1895 | − .575* | − .079 |
| 1896–1900 | − .566* | − .382* |
| 1901–1905 | − .273* | + .020 |
| 1906–1910 | − .217* | − .246* |

Starred coefficients were significant at the .05 level.

TABLE 4

STATEWIDE PER CAPITA EXPENDITURES ON EDUCATION BY RACE
NORTH CAROLINA, 1880–1910

| | Expenditure/Population | | |
| | | | Black/White |
| Year | White | Black | Ratio |
|------|-------|-------|-------|
| 1880–1885 | $0.93 | $0.98 | 1.05 |
| 1886–1890 | 1.07 | 0.94 | 0.88 |
| 1891–1895 | 1.17 | 1.02 | 0.87 |
| 1896–1900 | 1.22 | 1.14 | 0.93 |
| 1901–1905 | 1.98 | 1.17 | 0.59 |
| 1906–1910 | 3.70 | 1.49 | 0.40 |

was so largely a function of the proportion paying poll taxes, and it was precisely in the heavily black rich counties that whites had most to fear from an increase in black political participation.[21] This correlation implies that the black-belt whites were so sure of their ability to hold down black voting through literacy tests and extralegal means that they did not hesitate to create potential black voters by collecting their poll taxes.[22]

If the tax structure was regressive, the quality of education these taxes bought was also malapportioned. Inequality in wealth combined with North Carolina's method of distributing school funds to

[21] The correlation between white wealth per white adult male and the percentage of blacks in each county in the 1906–1910 period, for example, was + 0.704.

[22] I also tried to fit several models by regressing the tax rates and ratios, logged tax rates, and changes in the tax rates and ratios on various combinations of the following variables: the percentage of blacks, white wealth per white male adult, an index of party competition, turnout, the percentage for each political party, and changes in each of these variables. The $R^2$s and F ratios were not high, and their inclusion would needlessly extend the discussion in the text, which is more of an attempt to describe initial results on tax rates than to explain them fully.

ensure that high tax rates did not guarantee large expenditures. As Table 3 shows, tax rates for both blacks and whites correlated negatively with expenditures per child in the school-age group in eleven of the twelve cases, and all nine of the statistically significant correlations were negative.

The statewide trends in expenditure per child for blacks, whites, and the ratio between them given in Table 4 are clear enough.[23] Whites and blacks shared scholastic poverty relatively equally until 1900. During the period of fusion rule (1896–1900), the proportion of funds going to blacks increased by 6 percent, but after the restriction of the suffrage, the ratio of black to white expenditures per school-age child dropped by 53 percent in ten years.

Although the statewide figures demonstrate the sudden jump in racial discrimination after 1900, they mask variations in the fortunes of black schools in different counties and reveal little about the patterns of school support among whites. Investigation of these topics requires multiple-regression analyses of county-level data. Table 5 presents the results of three sets of multiple regressions, where the independent variables were wealth per white adult male and the percentage of blacks, and the dependent variables were expenditures per white child (Part A) and per black child (Part B) and the ratio of those expenditures (Part C).[24] Given the system of dis-

[23] I used expenditure per child as a proxy for educational quality because of the unavailability of other measures such as achievement tests; because of the dependence of other measures such as illiteracy on such nonschool factors as family background; because of the variance over time and geography in such criteria as the "grades" of teachers; because variables based on attendance or enrollment were functions not only of the quality but also of the desire for education, as well as the availability of jobs for juveniles; and because various pupil-teacher ratios indicated as much about the size of schools and the ease of transportation (there were often small schools and consequent low pupil-teacher ratios in poor but inaccessible areas) as about the quality of education. A thorough analysis, available on request, of expenditures broken down into salary and nonsalary components, as well as an examination of other related statistics, demonstrates that trends in the discrimination against blacks in expenditures did not merely reflect nonracist responses of school boards to a dual labor market in the private sector.

[24] After attempting to fit several models containing political, social, and economic variables, I decided that a simple equation containing only two independent variables had the advantages of parsimony and clarity of interpretation. Addition of up to nine other independent variables (the percentages for each political party, the electoral turnout, an index of party competition, estimates of turnout among whites, the percentage living in urban areas, the value of black property per black male adult, and tax rates) either did not markedly change the values of the coefficients in Table 6 or were so highly correlated with the percentage of blacks or other independent variables as to raise severe interpretive problems, or, in the case of the percentage urban, did not vary enough to explain much. (Only 7 percent of North Carolina's population lived in towns or cities containing 2,500 or more people in 1890, and only 14 percent did so in 1910, when only two cities exceeded 25,000 in population. There was a similarly small variation in various measures of industrialization during the period.) Moreover, the additional variables barely raised the percentages of variance explained by the two-variable model, and only rarely had significant F ratios. I also performed regressions

## TABLE 5

MULTIPLE-REGRESSION ANALYSIS BY RACE OF COUNTY
VARIATION IN EDUCATION EXPENDITURES
NORTH CAROLINA, 1880–1910

| Period | White Wealth Per White Adult Male (in $1,000) | Percent Black | Constant | $R^2$ |
|--------|------------|------------|----------|-------|
| A. White Expenditure/Child in Population | | | | |
| 1880–1884 | .47* | − .21 | .60 | .35* |
| 1885–1890 | .81* | + .06 | .23 | .58* |
| 1891–1895 | .75* | + .19 | .38 | .54* |
| 1896–1900 | .77* | + .61* | .49 | .54* |
| 1901–1905 | 1.21* | + .86* | .56 | .74* |
| 1906–1910 | 2.72* | + 2.12* | − .05 | .56* |
| B. Black Expenditure/Child in Population | | | | |
| 1880–1884 | .50* | − 1.03* | .84 | .09* |
| 1885–1890 | .43* | − .30 | .54 | .30* |
| 1891–1895 | .39* | − .45* | .71 | .18* |
| 1896–1900 | .41* | − .16 | .74 | .29* |
| 1901–1905 | .44* | − 1.02* | 1.09 | .13* |
| 1906–1910 | 1.09* | − 3.51* | 1.41 | .18* |
| C. Black Expenditure Per Child/White Expenditure Per Child | | | | |
| 1880–1884 | + .02 | − .78 | 1.28 | .07 |
| 1885–1890 | − .11 | − .36* | 1.11 | .19* |
| 1891–1895 | − .10 | − .66* | 1.16 | .25* |
| 1896–1900 | − .03 | − .53* | 1.01 | .29* |
| 1901–1905 | − .12 | − 1.02* | 1.10 | .49* |
| 1906–1910 | + .06 | − 1.83* | 1.01 | .33* |

Starred coefficients were significantly different from zero at the 0.05 level.

tributing school funds, it is not surprising that the most important predictor of expenditures was wealth, which had significant positive coefficients at the .05 level in each of the equations in Parts A and B. With wealth, in effect, controlled for by the regression procedures, the percentage Negro had a significant coefficient in three of the six cases in Part A.

But note that the time trend of the percentage of blacks for the white expenditure section of the table was from coefficients very close to zero to large and significantly positive coefficients and that there was a considerable jump in the value of the coefficients for

---

involving changes over each five-year period in the independent and dependent variables. In general, these equations did not result in as good fits as the static regressions. Especially striking was the decreased explanatory power of the wealth variable—that is, changes in wealth over five-year periods by county were never statistically significant predictions of changes in expenditures at the 0.05 level.

TABLE 6

PREDICTED EXPENDITURES PER CHILD BY RACE AND RATIOS
OF EXPENDITURES IN RICH AND POOR COUNTIES
NORTH CAROLINA, 1880–1910

| Period | Poor | Rich | Difference (Rich-Poor) |
|---|---|---|---|
| A. White | | | |
| 1880–1884 | $ 0.77 | $ 1.15 | $ 0.38 |
| 1896–1900 | $ 0.86 | $ 1.87 | $ 1.01 |
| 1906–1910 | $ 1.79 | $ 5.36 | $ 3.57 |
| B. Black | | | |
| 1880–1884 | $ 0.94 | $ 1.03 | $ 0.09 |
| 1896–1900 | $ 0.89 | $ 1.23 | $ 0.34 |
| 1906–1910 | $ 1.71 | $ 1.40 | − $ 0.31 |
| C. Ratio (Black/White) | | | |
| 1880–1884 | 121% | 92% | 26% |
| 1896–1900 | 95% | 70% | 25% |
| 1906–1910 | 86% | 19% | 67% |

NOTE: Poor counties are defined as those where the average white property value per white male adult was $400 in the first two periods and $600 in the last, and where the percentage of blacks in the population was 10 percent. Rich counties are those where white wealth was $1,400 in the first two periods and $1,600 in the last, and where the percentage of blacks was 50 percent. The estimates here are based on the relevant regression results from Table 5; that is, the predictions in Part A of Table 6 derive from the estimates in Part A of Table 5, and similarly for Parts B and C. Because of rounding errors in the calculation of the regression coefficients, the predictions in Part C do not always equal the ratios of the relevant figures in Part B to those in Part A.

white wealth and the percentage of blacks in the last period. As Table 6, which is based on the results in Table 5, shows, a white child who lived in a poor county which was 90 percent white would have received, on the average, 77 cents per year from 1880 to 1884, while his counterpart in a rich county which was only 50 percent white would have gotten $1.15, a disparity of 38 cents. By 1896–1900 the disparity had grown to $1.01, but the gap widened to an enormous $3.57 ten years later.

The figures for blacks in Tables 5 and 6 contrast sharply with those for whites. Even after taking into account divergences in wealth, whites in heavily black counties benefited from greater expenditures than whites in poor white counties, but black expenditures were negatively associated with the percentage of blacks. More important, consider the combination of the effects of the two variables. In the years before 1900 both whites and blacks who lived in rich, heavily black counties received more money for education than their confrères in poor white counties; but after disfranchisement the whites in rich counties increased their lead over those in poor counties, while the blacks in rich counties actually fell behind their fellows who were fortunate enough to live in counties which had small amounts of wealth and few blacks. As Part C of both tables demonstrates, the relative amounts that went to blacks shifted more dramatically against the black children in black-belt than in hill-country areas after disfranchisement.

While results from the expenditure regressions reveal changes in the patterns of expenditures, they rest, in effect, on a particular notion of justice—that each child, regardless of race or environs or shifts in political structure, has a right to the same education any other child receives. That Radical Republican notion is not the only possible criterion for justice in the distribution of public services. Many North Carolina Democrats, especially after 1900, espoused another, which, because of the richness of the data the state collected, is also quantifiable. Contending that one should receive in proportion to what one pays, these Democrats sought, by constitutional amendments or more informal means, to force black schools to operate on the taxes raised from blacks and, by increasing the proportion of funds for schools raised at the local level, to allow whites living in rich areas to better themselves without sharing their largess with whites who lived in areas where almost everyone was comparatively poor.[25]

In an attempt to quantify at least part of this principle, I have calculated what might be called the "black balance of payments," which is computed by subtracting the proportion of direct taxes blacks paid from the percentage of expenditures in each county which went to black schools.[26] The statewide trend given in Table 7

[25] By encouraging rich localities to raise their own expenditure levels, without having to share with poorer areas, the state supreme court decision in *Collie* v. *Commissioners of Franklin County,* 145 N.C. 170 (1907), actually increased inequality. The case was financed by the Southern Education Board and argued personally by "progressive" governor Charles B. Aycock, who realized at the time that the effect of increasing local taxation would be to benefit wealthy much more than poor areas. See Orr, "Charles Brantley Aycock," 333–34.

[26] Obviously, the "white balance of payments" would be equivalent to the black balance with the sign changed, and the regression coefficients in the text would just have their signs reversed had the dependent variable been calculated for whites instead of blacks. Though school expenditures also derived partially from fines and forfeitures, and indirect taxes on liquor, railroads, merchants, etc., it is impossible to estimate what exact proportion of these taxes blacks paid in each county. In any case, the indirect taxes accounted for an average of only 12 percent of total expenditures, with a standard deviation of 5 percent, over the period. More important, there was no clear trend to an increased or decreased reliance on indirect taxes (they amounted to 14 percent of the total in both 1885 and 1910). And such taxes as those on railroads and merchants cannot be easily allocated to particular counties, since they would have been partially passed on in the form of higher prices to wholesale or retail customers in different counties from those in which the tax was levied. Because I am much more interested in the variations across time and space than in the level of the black balance

## TABLE 7

### STATEWIDE TRENDS IN "BLACK BALANCE OF PAYMENTS" NORTH CAROLINA, 1880–1910

| Period | Balance* | Period | Balance* |
|--------|----------|--------|----------|
| 1880–1884 | .205 | 1896–1900 | .189 |
| 1885–1890 | .177 | 1901–1905 | .097 |
| 1891–1895 | .174 | 1906–1910 | .057 |

*Black proportion of expenditures minus black proportion of property and poll taxes.

shows that while blacks had the ballot their schools were, in effect, substantially subsidized by the whites. As in the case of other measures of their welfare, blacks seem to have done somewhat better under the 1896–1900 fusionist regime than in the years immediately preceding. After 1900, however, the decrease in the proportion of expenditures which went to blacks was so sharp that despite a decline in the proportion of taxes they paid (from 16 percent in 1898 to 11 percent in 1908, for instance), their balance of payments dropped by more than two-thirds in a decade. By 1910 the whites were barely subsidizing black schools at all.

Most interestingly, blacks were able to claim a favorable balance of payments despite the passage of a law in 1885, vigorously resisted by black legislators, which openly invited local school boards to discriminate against black children, and despite a salary-grading system for teachers which local boards might also have used to transfer funds from black to white schools.[27] The pre- and post-1885 figures imply that school boards feared to take much advantage of the opportunity to discriminate until the disfranchisement law changed the shade of the electorate.

This conclusion is strengthened even more by the results of a set of regressions of the black balance of payments on the percentage black, the square of the percentage black, and white wealth (Table 8). By far the most important predictor of the black balance was the percentage Negro, which had highly significant F ratios until 1906. From 1885 to 1900 the coefficients for the percentage of blacks and its square indicate that a variation across counties of 10 percent in

of payments, I have disregarded indirect taxes and fees in calculating the balance here, but see the appendix for a consideration of these matters.

[27] Until 1885 local boards were legally required to distribute all county school funds to subcounty districts strictly in proportion to the school-age population. The 1885 act allowed one-third of the county funds to be distributed so as to equalize the average length of school terms between races. Since black teachers were generally paid somewhat less than the whites per month, black school terms before 1885 had sometimes exceeded those for whites. With the passage of the bill, one-third of the funds were discretionary, and could be used to increase white teachers' annual salaries at the expense of the black teachers. For the protest by three state senators see North Carolina, Senate *Journal* (1885), 520–21.

TABLE 8

MULTIPLE-REGRESSION STATISTICS ON THE SHIFTING "BLACK
BALANCE OF PAYMENTS," NORTH CAROLINA, 1880-1910

| Period | Percent Blacks | Percent Blacks² | White Wealth (in $1,000) | Constant | R² |
|---|---|---|---|---|---|
| 1880-1884 | + 0.54* | − 0.33* | + 0.05* | − .02 | .86* |
| 1885-1890 | + 1.02* | − 1.15* | + 0.02 | − .04 | .75* |
| 1891-1895 | + 0.85* | − 0.87* | + 0.02 | − .02 | .74* |
| 1896-1900 | + 0.85* | − 0.85* | + 0.01 | − .02 | .69* |
| 1901-1905 | + 0.32* | − 0.40* | + 0.09 | − .04 | .53* |
| 1906-1910 | − 0.08 | − 0.01 | + 0.06 | + .01 | .11 |

*Starred coefficients were significant at the .05 level.

TABLE 9

PREDICTED VALUES OF THE "BLACK BALANCE OF PAYMENTS"
IN POOR AND RICH COUNTIES, NORTH CAROLINA, 1880-1910

|  | Poor 10% Black | Rich 50% Black |
|---|---|---|
| 1880-1884 | .051 | .238 |
| 1896-1900 | .061 | .207 |
| 1906-1910 | .038 | .064 |

Definitions of counties are the same as in Table 6.

the percentage Negro was associated with a change in the black balance of payments of 8 or 9 percent.[28] That is to say, the higher the proportion of blacks in the county—and in the electorate—the greater the surplus blacks won. In the period 1901-1905, the change in the surplus dropped to 3 percent for every 10 percent change in the percentage Negro; and in the final period the change in the balance was negatively related to variations in the Negro proportion. The relation between white wealth and the black balance, controlling for the percentage Negro, was very weakly positive, and it was statistically significant only in the first period.

Viewing the results in another way, the subsidies for blacks who lived in poor, heavily white counties were small from the beginning but did not change much after disfranchisement (Table 9). There

[28] The square of the percentage of blacks was introduced into the equation because the scatterplots indicated a significant degree of nonlinearity. The interpretation of the square term in this instance is that before disfranchisement two countervailing forces underlay the relationship between the balance of payments and the percentage of blacks. The first, black political power, increased with the proportion of blacks across counties. The second, white resistance to black demands, also increased as the proportion of blacks rose. Since the two forces were offsetting, the coefficients on the percentage of blacks and its square were of opposite signs until 1906-1910, when black political power, previously much the stronger of the two forces, had vanished and left no trace.

was never very much tax money in such counties, and blacks never enjoyed enough political power there to appropriate it to themselves. On the other hand, the balance of payments in rich black-belt counties was strongly positive before the restriction of the suffrage and dropped markedly afterwards. These figures show that, contrary to the claims of some historians, black political power was real and effective long after Reconstruction ended and that the crucial turning point came only after the passage of the suffrage amendment.[29]

The analysis of the black balance of payments, furthermore, reinforces some little-known impressionistic evidence on the intentions of the "progressives" toward the blacks. Some scholars have made a great deal of the opposition of "progressive" Governor Charles B. Aycock and state school superintendent James Y. Joyner to the movement for a constitutional amendment in North Carolina to limit black school expenditures to the amount paid by Negroes in taxes.[30] It is true that Aycock threatened resignation if such a law passed and that, speaking to the legislature in 1903, he condemned the proposed measure as "unjust, unwise and unconstitutional." Yet in the same address he put greater stress on his view that the act was impolitic than he did on its injustice. The law would invite a challenge in federal court, he believed, and "if it should be made to appear to the Court that in connection with our disfranchisement of the negro we had taken pains for providing to keep him in ignorance, then both amendments [the literacy test and racial separation of taxes] would fall together." In other words, the disfranchisement of the almost unanimously Republican blacks, which was virtually

[29] See for instance Harlan, *Separate and Unequal,* 9, 40; and Richard Bardolph, ed., *The Civil Rights Record: Black Americans and the Law, 1849-1970* (New York, 1970), 58. The legislature's attempts to allow towns to tax themselves and appropriate only black taxes to black schools might have led to greater racial discrimination, but the laws were declared unconstitutional by the state supreme court in *Puitt* v. *Gaston County Commissioners,* 94 N.C. 709 (1886) and *Riggsbee* v. *Town of Durham,* 94 N.C. 800 (1886). Another available means of discrimination grew out of the fact that a state law (never enforced) set different salaries for teachers of first, second, and third "grade." ("Grades" referred to quality, which was usually measured by performance on written or oral tests administered by local superintendents or school boards.) Since before 1900 there was little standardization in grading criteria from county to county (the state took over certification entirely only in 1917), white school boards could easily have redressed the black balance in their favor by downgrading the certificates of black teacher and keeping the same student-teacher ratios, thereby increasing the total funds available to the whites.

[30] Such proposals had been made as early as 1873. Indeed, the collection of data on the taxes paid by members of each race—statistics very crucial to this paper—probably reflected a desire to determine the extent to which whites subsidized black schools. But serious consideration of a general law or amendment of this nature awaited the end of black political power. For the early proposals see Westin, "The State and Segregated Schools," 46-47; Bromberg, " 'Pure Democracy and White Supremacy,' " 82-84; Cotton, "Appalachian North Carolina," 25. For a protest against the proposals by North Carolina blacks see Indianapolis *Freeman,* January 28, 1899.

priceless to the Democrats, would be bartered for the temporary gain of a few extra dollars of the school fund.

Besides, as Aycock went on, under the constitution as he construed it, "both races can be reasonably educated without excessive cost to the white people . . . ." Aycock's ally Joyner, in numerous letters to local superintendents, explained how to save the appearance of equality while discriminating: "The negro schools can be run for much less expense and should be. In most places it does not take more than one fourth as much to run the negro schools as it does to run the white schools for about the same number of children. The salaries paid teachers are very properly much smaller, the houses are cheaper, the number of teachers smaller. . . . if quietly managed, the negroes will give no trouble about it [the discrimination]." Another superintendent, bluntly questioning Joyner, "Can we discriminate vs. the negro?" received assurance that they could. "As a rule," the "progressive" responded, "the funds can be so divided as to give to the negro school practically what the negroes pay [in taxes] . . . ."[31] As Tables 7 through 9 demonstrate, some superintendents took a few years after the restriction of the suffrage to master the technique of "quiet management," but by 1910 the "progressives" had achieved their public aim of avoiding bad publicity, while in many counties exceeding their private goal of balancing white payments.

A third notion of justice, somewhat more comprehensive than the two already treated, is that government ought to foster social mobility by distributing its services in a fashion more egalitarian than the contemporaneous societal distribution of resources. This principle can be operationalized by a device now familiar to historians, the Lorentz curve. Usually employed to compare income distributions, the curve is formed by plotting on Cartesian coordinates the cumulative distribution of, say, income, ordered from lowest to

---

[31] Aycock, in North Carolina, *Public Documents* (Raleigh, 1903), 9–12 of Governor's Message (first quotation); Joyner to Supt. J. E. Debnam of La Grange, N. C., February 3, 1903, quoted in Westin, "The State and Segregated Schools," 198 (second quotation); Joyner to W. M. Pearson, July 23, 1904, quoted in Willard, "Charles Lee Coon," 220–21, n. 15 (third and fourth quotations). For similar letters and a fuller discussion of the impressionistic evidence see Westin, "The State and Segregated Schools," 198–203, 294–95, 468. Joyner was superintendent from 1902 until 1919. Joyner's public position, as stated in North Carolina, *Biennial Report of Superintendent of Public Instruction, 1900–1902* (Raleigh, 1902), vii–xii, differed considerably from his private guidelines on how to discriminate. For a set of letters which, contrary to their editor's gloss, support the interpretation given herein of the "progressives' " private motives, see William E. King, "Charles McIver Fights for the Tarheel Negro's Right to an Education," *North Carolina Historical Review*, XLI (Summer 1964), 360–69. Even Oliver H. Orr's defense of Aycock's actions on Negro education contains evidence that the governor knew that during his administration (1901–1904) that the white subsidy to black schools was very small. See Orr, "Charles Brantley Aycock," 486.

FIGURE 1

LORENTZ CURVE ILLUSTRATING THE IMPACT OF DISFRANCHISEMENT ON
THE DEGREE TO WHICH EDUCATION WAS REDISTRIBUTIVE IN NORTH
CAROLINA, 1880–1910 (BOTH RACES)

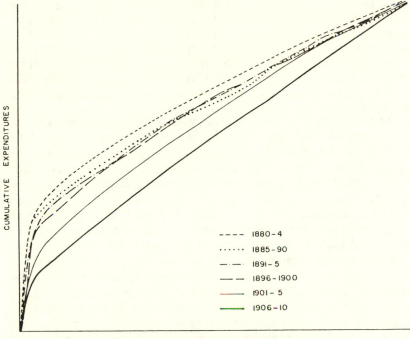

CUMULATIVE WEALTH

highest, against the correspondingly ordered cumulative distribution of population. If everyone had the same income, the curve
would lie on a line which formed a 45 degree angle with each axis;
the extent of inequality is therefore proportionate to the area between the actual curve and the 45 degree line, an area which can be
measured by the Gini coefficient.

Table 10 gives Gini coefficients for the distribution of wealth in
North Carolina during the period. Among whites, the amount of
inequality in property holdings by county declined slightly but fairly
steadily from 1880 to 1910.[32] In the whole population, with the
figures segregated by race in each county, there was of course much

[32] For a discussion of measures of inequality see Anthony B. Atkinson, "On the Measurement of Inequality," *Journal of Economic Theory,* II (September 1970), 244–63. On al-
gorithms for computing the Gini Index see Joseph L. Gastwirth, "The Estimation of the
Lorentz Curve and Gini Index," *Review of Economics and Statistics,* LIV (August 1972),
306–16.

TABLE 10

GINI COEFFICIENTS OF DISTRIBUTION OF REAL AND PERSONAL
PROPERTY BY RACE, NORTH CAROLINA, 1880–1910

| Period | Whites Only | Both Races |
|---|---|---|
| 1880–1884 | .243 (86) | .475 (169) |
| 1885–1890 | .217 (88) | .442 (174) |
| 1891–1895 | .208 (88) | .422 (176) |
| 1896–1900 | .223 (88) | .422 (175) |
| 1901–1905 | .208 (88) | .402 (175) |
| 1906–1910 | .189 (88) | .380 (175) |

The number of counties without missing data is in parentheses. For both races, the number is, in effect, doubled.

more inequality than there was for whites alone, but the tendency was toward a markedly more egalitarian distribution. The Gini coefficient declined from 0.475 in the first period to 0.380 in the last. Had the trend in the distribution of public services reflected that of wealth, as the socioeconomically deterministic theory would seem to require, one would expect to find a *more* equal distribution of expenditures in 1910 than in 1880. But the Gini coefficients on educational spending, not presented here, show much less equality at the end than at the beginning of the thirty-year period.[33]

To determine whether the rich, middle class, or poor benefited most from this decrease in educational equality, cumulative population can be replaced by cumulative wealth on the X axis of the graph. The resulting curves, original with this paper, measure the degree to which government benefits were distributed more or less equitably than the contemporaneous distribution of wealth, and how that relation changed over time. In the Lorentz curves of Figure 1 the lines for the years 1880 to 1900 were rather similar, the drop from 1880 to 1900 reflecting a decline in the redistributiveness of the system mostly among whites. For the last two periods, however, the curves shifted strikingly downwards, especially at the lower end of the wealth spectrum, confirming the fact that the poor received a much smaller proportion of the expenditures after than before the turn of the century.

[33] I did not collect data for the years after 1910 because, first, one has to stop somewhere, and second, financing schemes for public education became increasingly complex and finances increasingly subject to bureaucratic pressure after 1910. Nonetheless, it is clear that inequality between races and across areas continued long after 1910. On these points see Westin, "The State and Segregated Schools," 174–82, 267–76, 295–96, 326–72, 393–483; Samuel L. Smith, *Builders of Goodwill: The Story of the State Agents of Negro Education in the South, 1910 to 1950* (Nashville, 1950), *passim;* A. T. Allen's chapter on education in Paul V. Betters, ed., *State Centralization in North Carolina* (Washington, 1932), 15–59; Samuel H. Thompson, "The Legislative Development of Public School Support in North Carolina" (unpublished Ph.D. dissertation, University of North Carolina, 1926), 390–91, 401–403, 420, 438–39; White, "The Economic and Social Development of Negroes," 158–59; North Carolina State Educational Commission, *Public Education in North Carolina* (New York, 1921), 98–100.

## TABLE 11

### REDISTRIBUTION INDEXES BY RACE, NORTH CAROLINA, 1880–1910

| Period | Whites Only | Both Races |
|--------|-------------|------------|
| 1880–1884 | − .174 | − .435 |
| 1885–1890 | − .091 | − .373 |
| 1891–1895 | − .114 | − .369 |
| 1896–1900 | − .126 | − .353 |
| 1901–1905 | − .120 | − .280 |
| 1906–1910 | − .044 | − .160 |

The redistribution index is proportional to the area between the 45 degree line and a Lorentz curve in which cumulative expenditures by county are plotted on the Y axis and cumulative wealth on the X axis. Both are ordered from the poorest to the richest unit. The numbers of observations are the same as in Table 10.

The extent of the changes in these Lorentz curves can be measured by what might be called the "redistribution index." Just as the usual Lorentz curves relating income to population can be summarized in Gini indexes, the curves of Figure 1 can be related to Gini-like indexes which measure the area between the wealth and expenditure curves and the 45 degree line. If the curve lies wholly above the 45 degree line, government expenditures redistribute the society's resources from top to bottom and the redistribution index is negative; if it lies wholly below the 45 degree line, resources are redistributed from bottom to top and the index is positive; if it lies partly below and partly above the 45 degree line, resources may be shifted in several ways, and the sign of the index is indeterminant.

The index values in column three of Table 11, which correspond to the curves in Figure 1, reveal a slight drop between the earliest and the next three periods, and substantial decreases in the last two periods. From a value of −0.353 in 1896–1900, the index for both races dropped to −.160 ten years later. For whites alone the change was not so substantial (a drop from −0.12 in 1896–1900 to −0.044 in 1906–1910), but it still represented a quite perceptible movement toward a distribution of services which merely reflected the distribution of wealth, rather than moving toward a less inegalitarian one.

One may also use the technique of the Lorentz curve to determine changes in the degree to which the system of educational taxation and expenditure as a whole redistributed society's resources. Table 12 presents a set of what might be called "burden and benefit" indexes, which are proportional to the area between the 45 degree line and a Lorentz curve computed by arraying cumulative expenditures by county on the Y axis and cumulative taxes on the X axis, both ordered from the poorest to the richest units. The separate figures for whites jump around a bit from 1880 to 1900, but the

TABLE 12

INDEXES OF BURDENS AND BENEFITS BY RACE
NORTH CAROLINA, 1880–1910

| Period | Whites Only | Both Races |
|---|---|---|
| 1880–1884 | − .080 | − .225 |
| 1885–1890 | + .002 | − .171 |
| 1891–1895 | − .025 | − .187 |
| 1896–1900 | − .065 | − .197 |
| 1901–1905 | − .055 | − .136 |
| 1906–1910 | − .001 | − .053 |

See the text for a definition of the index. The numbers of observations are the same as in Table 10.

main feature of that column is the change from a mildly redistributive system with an index of −0.065 during the fusion era to a system which did not redistribute resources at all in the period from 1906 to 1910. The column containing figures for both races traces a pattern similar to those in earlier tables. The combination of taxes and spending was highly redistributive at the outset, dropped off slightly, rebounded somewhat during the time of fusion control, and plunged precipitously after 1900.

There is one other idea related to equality and justice which deserves examination here. Those who emphasize what might be termed intergenerational progress might concede increasing inequality in services, but focus on the fact that *absolute* levels of expenditures were growing for all groups in the population. A system in which every child would have a chance to get a better education than his parents might be inegalitarian, but, according to this view, not unprogressive. Despite its appeal to many North Carolinians during the early years of the century and to some scholars since, this notion fundamentally mistakes the nature and function of education in a competitive society. In the struggle for jobs, or, more broadly, for increased economic welfare, it is *relative,* not absolute, levels of education that count. It mattered less to the white mountaineer's or the black-belt Negro's son that he had been to school longer and received instruction from a better teacher than his father than that his white competitors from the towns and lowlands had gotten a considerably better education than he had. Increasing inequality in services, then, inevitably spawned increasing inequality in income and wealth—a peculiar definition of progress.

In 1937 the North Carolina Education Association, disregarding the fact that there was no real free statewide public school system in the state until Reconstruction, presented "an historical pageant and masque commemorating the centennial of public education in North Carolina" on the football field of Duke University. In their sketch of the early twentieth century "educational campaigns," the pageant's authors picture Aycock and Joyner addressing a group, one of whose members, an "illiterate and indignant farmer" comments before hearing the "progressives" that "I'm agin' this so-called Education Campaign . . . . There's enough money being spent on l'arning all ready." Cajoled into listening by "a well dressed man" who encourages the farmer "to see this subject in a broader light," the farmer, along with the rest of the crowd is converted to the cause. The play ends with an original verse:

> One hundred years the state's courageous leaders
> Have carried on their fight for better schools.
> One hundred years the Old North State has kept
> Her sacred pledge to offer every child
> The right to learn at state expense.[34]

Reality differed from the state-fostered "progressive" myth. Because state Democratic leaders established a system of regressive taxation and because the poor, both black and white, seem to have been willing to pay more for public education than the wealthy, school taxes for whites were higher in poor than in relatively rich counties, and much higher among blacks than whites. Moreover, the increased demand for education, fostered by the "progressive" educational campaigns, did not, under their aegis, lead to a more democratized and egalitarian educational system in any but the fourth sense of justice mentioned above. Whether the criterion is service equality, services in proportion to payment, or service redistribution, the fact is that for blacks overwhelmingly and for poor whites to a lesser but still an important extent equality declined after 1900. The rhetorical "progressive" description and explanation of changes in the distribution of educational taxation and expenditures is simply not in accord with the statistics.

Contrary to the socioeconomic determinist model, the distribution of taxes and expenditures and changes in those distributions appear to have reflected political conditions directly. The levels of taxes and expenditures varied systematically with wealth and race, but the direction of that variation changed during the period, and the changes mirrored political, not economic conditions. Whereas wealth was distributed in an increasingly egalitarian fashion, educational equality diminished considerably. Most strikingly, blacks suffered much more discrimination after than before disfranchisement and the establishment of the one-party system, particularly in

[34] North Carolina Education Association, *A Century of Culture: An Historical Pageant and Masque Commemorating the Centennial of Public Education in North Carolina* (Durham, N. C., 1937), 55–61.

the heavily black areas where before 1900 their votes had bought a disproportionately high level of services.

Finally, the distribution of white educational expenditures did not remain roughly constant over the period, nor was there a marked decline in the black-white expenditures ratio before 1900 as the Bond-Harlan "progressivism for whites only" hypothesis stated. Though the post-1900 discrimination against whites in poorer areas was less than that against blacks, which probably reflected the fact that fewer whites than blacks were disfranchised, there was a clear change in the distribution of white expenditures from a relatively equitable pattern before to an increasingly inequitable one after the passage of suffrage restriction laws. And, bearing out C. Vann Woodward's picture of a dramatic increase in racial discrimination around the turn of the century, the major part of the drop-off in relative expenditures for blacks was concentrated in the period immediately following the passage of those laws.[35] In North Carolina education at least, "progressivism" was, as a consequence of disfranchisement, for middle-class whites only.

APPENDIX: TAX SHIFTS AND THE BLACK BALANCE OF PAYMENTS

Since the discussion of the "black balance of payments" in the text focuses on variations across counties, a consideration there of the possibility that taxes levied on white-owned property were passed through to blacks in the form of higher prices and rents would have been distracting. Nevertheless, because of the inherent interest of the concept of the balance, the problem deserves to be treated briefly.

There were two taxes which might have had a substantial effect on the black balance: the tax on white-owned farms tenanted by blacks, which might have been passed through in the form of higher rents, and the tax on the value of the property of railroad, telephone, and telegraph companies, which might have been shifted to consumers. The effect of either of these transfer would have been much less in the earlier than in the later part of the era, for taxes on all forms of property were a much smaller proportion of the total taxes before 1900 than after. In 1880, for example, poll taxes amounted to 58 percent of the total school taxes; in 1889 and 1894, 45 percent; and in 1900, 38 percent. But they dropped to 29 percent of the total by 1904 and to 23 percent in 1909. Any shift of property taxes to renters, tenants, and consumers, therefore, would have a much greater impact on the total tax burden of blacks after 1900 than before, and their effect in the earlier years can for practical purposes be largely disregarded.

The calculation of the impact of tax shifts for 1909 is more tedious than

[35] Woodward, *The Strange Career of Jim Crow* (3d rev. ed., New York, 1974), Chaps. 1–3. Woodward emphasizes the part played by whites—northern liberals, southern conservatives, and southern Populists—in impeding Jim Crow's quick advance. I would put more weight than he does on black politcal power.

complex. The 1910 U. S. census gives the value of property for farms tenanted by blacks on cash or shares as $37,931,340. This land value, however, must be deflated to take into account North Carolina assessment practices. The total value of land in the state in 1909 given in the state auditor's report was $176,881,261; whereas, the census rated the total value as $307,606.620, which yields an implied assessment ratio of 57.5 percent. Let us assume that all farms with black tenants were owned by whites. Since the state property tax rate was 18 cents per $1,000, the state property tax paid on all such land was about $39,259 ($37,931,340 × 0.575 × 0.0018). Similar calculations on the county level for local school taxes yield a value of $34,846.[1]

Blacks received 16.2 percent of the funds for salaries, buildings, and sites in the 1910 school year, when the 1909 taxes would have been spent. If white landlords shifted none of the taxes to black tenants, the blacks would have paid 10.4 percent of the total taxes, which gives a positive black balance of payments of 5.8 percent. If they passed through 50 percent of the taxes, the balance drops to 3.7 percent; if landlords transferred the total burden to croppers and renters, the balance goes to 1.6 percent.

Railroad, telephone, and telegraph taxes were smaller (a total of $161,489 in 1909) and make less difference in the estimate of the balance of payments. Blacks owned 4.67 percent of the property in North Carolina in 1909. There are no income figures at the state level separated by race. If the corporations passed on all these taxes to consumers of freight and passenger services and blacks bought goods and services in proportion to the wealth they held, then the increases in taxes blacks paid would amount to $7,542 (0.0467 × $161,489). Since blacks no doubt received a higher proportion of total income than wealth, this may be an unreasonably low estimate. If they consumed 10 percent of the goods affected by railroad, telephone, and telegraph company tax shifts, the black tax burden would increase by $16,149. Subtracting this arbitrarily chosen figure from the

[1] The total of local taxes was computed in the following fashion: The 1909 state auditor's report gives the total school taxes levied in each county by all districts. Dividing the local school taxes by the value of real and personal property in each county yields a local school-tax rate. The 1910 census lists the number of farms (call it F); the value of their land (V); and the number of black cash and share tenants (T). (T ÷ F) × V gives the best estimate of the value of the land on which blacks were tenants. If we deflate the land value recorded in the census by 0.575, which is the ratio of the state and national assessments, multiply the result by the tax rate in each county, and sum over all counties, we get an estimate of the total local taxes paid on land tenanted by blacks. In equation terms, if "R" represents the tax rate and "L" the total of local taxes on black-tenanted land,

$$L = \Sigma \ (.575) \times (T/F) \times V \times R.$$

The two assumptions embedded in this procedure tend to offset each other. The first, the uniformity of the tax rate in each county, probably overestimates the taxes paid on land where blacks were tenants, since the rates were not really uniform and were undoubtedly higher in urban than in rural school districts. The second, the uniformity of land values in each county, probably underestimates the tax, since the plantation owners who had black tenants almost surely owned comparatively high-priced land. In 1910 the value per acre of land tenanted by blacks was $19.26, while the value of all farms was $15.29 per acre according to the census. Unfortunately, because the data was aggregated at the county level, there is no way to test these two assumptions thoroughly.

black balance computed above gives a balance in favor of the blacks of about 0.3 percent.

Thus, varying assumptions about the shifts in taxes from businesses and landlords to consumers and tenants yield a range of estimates of the black balance of payments in 1909 of from 5.8 percent to 0.3 percent. Though earlier census figures on tenancy are either too sketchy or too unreliable to allow similar estimates, it is clear that the earlier tax transfers must have been much smaller. It is reasonable to conclude, therefore, that while one can be fairly certain about the validity of the figures for the early years in Table 8, the black balance of payments may well have been reduced to little or nothing by 1910.

# Race Differences in Public School Expenditures

## Disfranchisement and School Finance in Louisiana, 1890-1910

ROBERT A. MARGO
*University of Pennsylvania*

**No matter how one measures** its commitment to public education, the South in 1890 lagged far behind the rest of the nation.[1] Twenty years later, southern public schools were still characterized by relative backwardness, but the preceding two decades had seen impressive expansion in absolute terms. Among the salient features of this transformation were sharply increased per pupil expenditures, school terms, and enrollment rates; greater provision of normal schools and related institutions; and high rates of investment in school capital. State legislatures increased their appropriations, limitations on local taxes were abolished, and the number of counties and school districts voting to increase school expenditures skyrocketed.

The fruits of this educational awakening were not, however, distributed equitably between black and white children. Table 1 gives estimates of expenditures on teacher salaries per pupil (black and white) in average daily attendance (in 1890 dollars), and the length of the school year in days for selected states in 1890 and 1910. These data demonstrate that whites shared disproportionately in the expansion that took place. Blacks experienced a

Author's Note: *I would like to thank my thesis advisers, Robert Fogel and Stanley Engerman, for their detailed comments on earlier drafts of this article; seminar participants at Harvard, Rochester, Wisconsin, Northwestern, Prince-*

reduction in per pupil expenditures and lost ground relative to whites—in Louisiana and Florida, absolutely—in the length of the school year. Within states, there was considerable variation, but it was in the black belt where the race differences were starkest (see Table 2).

Perhaps the most famous explanation of these phenomena was provided by Horace Mann Bond (1934, 1939). There were three steps to Bond's argument. First, black political power declined precipitously in the aftermath of Reconstruction. Second, white enrollment in public schools exploded. To meet the growth in demand, various means, legal and otherwise, were devised to shift to white schools some fraction of the funds that the state allocated to county school boards on the basis of the black school population under their jurisdiction, thus limiting the need for local support. Black belt whites benefitted enormously from such schemes since the absolute amount that could be appropriated per white student rose with the black share of the school population. Third, the further enactment of suffrage restrictions in the 1890s, while doing little more than ratifying the status quo, stripped blacks of any remaining power they possessed to check this process. Several years later, Louis Harlan (1958) echoed Bond's arguments in his analysis of public education in the seaboard states during the Progressive era. A further point was made by Gunnar Myrdal (1944). Agreeing that the ability to appropriate state funds favored the black belt, he noted that the same principle applied to locally generated school taxes: "If, for instance, there are twice as many negroes as white children, every (local) dollar per pupil taken from the negro group means two dollars per pupil added to the apportionment for the white group" (Myrdal, 1944: 341).

The view espoused by Bond and others (Key, 1949: 533), that disfranchisement was a fait accompli by 1890, has recently been

*ton, Pennsylvania, and Chicago for useful suggestions; and Richard Freeman for allowing me to use data that he has collected. All errors are my own. This research was supported by Harvard University, the Joint Center for Urban Studies, Harvard-MIT, and the University of Pennsylvania. An earlier version of this article was presented at the 1980 Social Science History Association meetings in Rochester, New York.*

*Table 1*    Race Differences in Expenditures per Pupil and
            and Length of School Year: 1890 and 1910

| STATE | WEXP | BEXP | RATIO | WLT | BLT | RATIO |
|-------|------|------|-------|-----|-----|-------|
| Alabama |  |  |  |  |  |  |
| 1890 | 3.14 | 3.10 | 1.01 | 70.4 | 75.1 | 0.94 |
| 1910 | 10.07 | 2.69 | 3.74 | 131.3 | 97.3 | 1.35 |
| Florida |  |  |  |  |  |  |
| 1890[a] | 9.42 | 4.63 | 2.03 | 99.7 | 99.8 | 0.99 |
| 1910 | 11.58 | 3.11 | 3.72 | 112.4 | 90.8 | 1.24 |
| Louisiana |  |  |  |  |  |  |
| 1890 | 5.85 | 2.92 | 2.00 | 86.8 | 89.5 | 0.97 |
| 1910 | 11.54 | 2.07 | 5.57 | 153.1 | 75.1 | 2.04 |
| N. Carolina |  |  |  |  |  |  |
| 1890 | 2.71 | 2.74 | 0.99 | 60.5 | 62.6 | 0.97 |
| 1910 | 5.20 | 2.52 | 2.06 | 107.0 | 96.0 | 1.11 |
| Virginia |  |  |  |  |  |  |
| 1890 | 7.08 | 4.93 | 1.44 | 115.1 | 123.7 | 0.93 |
| 1910 | 11.59 | 4.10 | 2.83 | 139.1 | 123.8 | 1.12 |

SOURCE: Margo (1982: Ch. 2).

NOTE: Figures are weighted averages of county data. Weight = Average daily attendance in county/Total average daily attendance in state. Price index used to deflate
expenditures figures is Burgess Consumer Price Index (Historical Statistics, 1976:
212).

a. 1893/1894 school year.

WEXP: expenditures on teacher salaries in white schools, per pupil in average daily
attendance (1890 dollars).

BEXP: expenditures on teacher salaries in black schools, per pupil in average daily
attendance (1890 dollars).

WLT: length of school year in days, white schools.

BLT: length of school year in days, black schools.

challenged by Morgan Kousser (1974). Based on an ingenious use
of election statistics, Kousser showed that Democratic hegemony
in the post-Reconstruction era was far more precariously based
than historians had previously believed. Blacks continued to cast
their ballots in support of opposition parties well into the 1890s in

*Table 2*     Ratio of per Pupil Expenditures Within States: 1910

| | PBLK | 0–25% | 25–50% | 50–75% | 75–100% |
|---|---|---|---|---|---|
| STATE | | | | | |
| Alabama | 2.23 | 3.00 | 5.61 | 10.04 |
| Florida | 2.78 | 2.89 | 5.10 | 13.88 |
| Louisiana | 2.21 | 4.72 | 7.36 | 17.45 |
| N. Carolina | 1.42 | 2.36 | 4.16 | – |
| S. Carolina | 3.78 | 3.52 | 5.91 | 7.78 |
| Virginia | 1.66 | 2.99 | 5.47 | – |

SOURCE: Margo (1982, Ch. 2).

NOTE: Figures are ratios of white to black expenditures on teacher salaries per pupil in average daily attendance. The expenditure figures are weighted averages of the county data within county groups (i.e., 0-25%). Weight = Average daily attendance within county/Average daily attendance within county group.

PBLK: Black share of population within county.

some states, but through a combination of selective enforcement of existing suffrage statutes, electoral chicanery, and other dubious activities, black belt Democrats were able to pass suffrage restrictions that effectively eliminated blacks from politics, along with large numbers of poor whites. "At the same time, Southern state and local governments increased their discrimination against blacks in the only important service those governments provided—education. . . . Discrimination in voting, in other words, paralleled discrimination in government services, a condition unlikely to have been coincidental" (Kousser, 1974: 228-229). Further support for this point of view was provided by an analysis of race differences in school expenditures and tax burdens in North Carolina over the period 1880 to 1910. Kousser (1980) found that, prior to disfranchisement in 1900, the black population share was negatively correlated with white per pupil expenditures, and positively correlated with the subsidy that white taxpayers provided to black schools, but that the reverse was true after disfranchisement.

This article has two goals. First, a model of school board behavior is developed that emphasizes the ability of whites to appropriate black school funds while trading off expenditures on white schools and local taxes. The virtue of the model is that it systematically incorporates the relationships between race, school finance mechanisms, and disfranchisement discussed by Bond and others into a framework amenable to econometric testing. Similar models have been widely used by contemporary scholars to analyze the effects of state and federal grants on local government spending and taxes (see Inman, 1979, for a summary of contemporary studies). I argue that the appropriation of state funds earmarked for black schools was similar to an increase in state aid to white parents (in the language of school finance, an unconditional or nonmatching grant). The appropriation of local black taxes, on the other hand, acted to lower the marginal cost of education to whites (a matching grant). Both effects, under plausible behavioral assumptions, led to increased expenditures on white schools and lower school taxes paid by whites. Thus, there was a strong incentive for school boards to minimize expenditures on black schools that was especially powerful wherever the ratio of black to white school children was large, i.e., in black belt counties. Simply put, the disfranchisement hypothesis states that suffrage restriction severely limited blacks' ability to check this process.

The opposite view—that disfranchisement had little or no effect on the racial distribution of school expenditures—can also be supported by qualitative arguments. In particular, the racial distribution of school expenditures may have been chiefly determined by the racial distribution of taxable resources. Whites may have spent more money on their schools, but they were richer and bore a larger share of the tax burden than blacks did, especially in black belt counties. In addition, migration of disgruntled blacks and whites eager to take advantage of better schools or lower local taxes should have tended in the long run to limit any benefits enjoyed by black belt whites arising from the appropriation of black school funds. Thus, whether or not the school finance mechanisms functioned in the manner implied by the model is an empirical issue.

In the second part of the article, the empirical issue is addressed by means of a multiple regression analysis of data on white and black per pupil expenditures and local school taxes for Louisiana in 1890 and 1910. The econometric analysis provides a more thorough examination of the effects of school finance and disfranchisement on the racial distribution of school expenditures and on local taxes than previous work.[2] School finance in the Pelican State fits the model's paradigm; an added advantage is that Louisiana was the only state that reported voter registration by race before and after suffrage restriction. These data are imperfect, but they do allow at least a rudimentary direct test of the disfranchisement hypothesis. The results of the regressions support the notion that disfranchisement reduced expenditures on black schools and enabled whites to use state funds earmarked for black schools to better their own schools and lower local school taxes. The evidence on the appropriation of local black taxes is less clear, but it appears that the racial distribution of expenditures more closely mirrored the racial distribution of taxable resources, particularly wealth, after disfranchisement.

## A MODEL OF A DISCRIMINATING SCHOOL BOARD

In this section, I present a simple model of a discriminating school board that captures the interactions among race, school finance, and disfranchisement discussed above. (The exposition is verbal; for a mathematical treatment, see Margo, 1982.) There is a dual school system segregated by race. Education is produced using labor, capital, and student time. For simplicity, the capital and student time inputs are assumed to be fixed; the basic insights of the model are not sensitive to this assumption. A school board contracts for the labor input; the members of the board are elected to their posts. The budget of the board is equal to state funds (for every child of school age residing in the county, the board receives "s" dollars) and local taxes voted by residents. In allocating these funds between blacks and whites, the board weighs the political support it receives from each group. This need not be the only factor motivating the board's actions, but it is the behavioral postulate that best captures the notion that the distribution of government output mirrors the distribution of political power, which is the heart of the disfranchisement hypothesis.[3] Other factors affecting the board's decisions are discussed below. Blacks are assumed to be disfranchised, so that only the preferences of white voters matter in determining the amount of local school taxes to be levied and the distribution of school funds between the races. Despite their inability to influence local fiscal behavior at the ballot box, however, blacks are required to pay local taxes at the same rate (i.e., per dollar of assessed value or per adult male in the case of a poll tax) as whites.

Initially, the level of spending on white schools should be positively related to white income or wealth, and negatively to the price of labor inputs, i.e., the wage rate of white teachers. Suppose that the school board is able to appropriate some fraction ($a_s$) per dollar of the state subsidy allocated to the board on the basis of the black school population living in the county. If there are θ black children per white pupil, each white resident effectively receives an increase in state aid equal to $a_s s\theta$ per white student. These dollars can be used to purchase additional teachers at the going wage rate or to reduce local school taxes.

The appropriation of local taxes paid by blacks affects white fiscal decisions by lowering the marginal cost of education to whites. To see this, suppose that all local funds are derived from a tax on property. With a fixed level of state support, marginal increases in school expenditures are financed by a marginal increase in the local tax rate. All of the added funds to white schools, but the fraction of the cost per dollar raised borne by whites is equal to the white share of taxable wealth, which is less than one. Thus the "price" of white education, or how much

*Table 3*    Variable Definitions

| VARIABLE | DEFINITION |
|---|---|
| s | Amount of state funds allocated to school board per child of school age |
| $a_s$ | Fraction of every state dollar allocated to the school board on the basis of the black school population appropriated by whites |
| $\phi$ | Black school population, per white child enrolled |
| SPHI (=$s\phi$) | State funds allocated to parish school board on the basis of the black school population, per white pupil enrolled (1890 dollars) |
| WEXP | Expenditures on teacher salaries in white schools, per white pupil enrolled (1890 dollars) |
| BEXP | Expenditures on teacher salaries in black schools, per black pupil enrolled (1890 dollars) |
| LTAX | Local school funds/Total school funds |
| WWPAM | Assessed white wealth per white adult male (1890 dollars) |
| BWPAM | Assessed black wealth per black adult male (1890 dollars) |
| AWMC | White adult males (age 21+) per white pupil enrolled |
| ABMC | Black adult males (age 21+) per black pupil enrolled |
| PCTWW | Percent of total assessed wealth held by whites |
| PCTAWM | Percent of adult males who were white |
| PBVOTE | Fraction of registered voters who were black |
| PBSP | (Current black school population − Black school population if the black share of the current school population remained unchanged from the previous school census)/current white enrollment |
| SPHIPBSP | SPHI times PBSP |
| SPHIBV | SPHI times PBVOTE |
| WWAGE | Daily wage of white teachers (1890 dollars) |
| BWAGE | Daily wage of black teachers (1890 dollars) |
| BB2 | =1 if black share of parish population is between 25% and 50%, 0 otherwise |
| BB3 | =1 if black share of parish population is between 50% and 75%, 0 otherwise |
| BB4 | =1 if black share of parish population is between 75% and 100%, 0 otherwise |

SOURCES: WEXP, BEXP, LTAX, SPHI, WWAGE, BWAGE (Biennial Report of the State Superintendent of Public Education [1892: 158-168; 1912: pt. 2, 3-38]); PBVOTE (Report of the Secretary of State [1902: 553; 1912: 96]); WWPAM, BWPAM (Biennial Report of the Auditor of Public Accounts [1892: 59; 1912: 65]); ABMC, AWMC (U.S. Bureau of the Census [1895: 766-767; 1913: 779-789]).

NOTE: Price index used to deflate WEXP, BEXP, SPHI, WWAGE, BWAGE, WWPAM, and BWPAM is Burgess Consumer Price Index (see note to Table 1).

income whites must give up to acquire an additional unit of labor input, falls. It is generally believed that the demand for any commodity is downward sloping with respect to price, so the fall in price should induce a rise in the quantity of labor inputs demanded by whites. Since the wage of white teachers is unaffected, expenditures on teacher salaries will increase. As long as whites have access to the proceeds of local black taxes (as in the case of property or poll taxes), the preceding arguments apply.[4]

This discussion makes clear that in the absence of any constraints on its behavior, the interest of the school board is served by spending as little as possible on black schools. Why then did school boards spend anything on black schools if they could expect no political support from blacks, as the disfranchisement hypothesis suggests? One answer might be that a modest amount of egalitarianism governed the actions of some boards; individual acts of white philanthropy were common. Some whites may have benefitted from a better educated black labor force, as Freemen (1972) notes. The courts and the federal government were ineffective avenues of redress for blacks after 1890, but probably insured at least a minimal level of expenditures on black schools.

Even if the ballot box had been foreclosed to them, blacks may have voted with their feet to escape discrimination against them by the local government. Black migration from the locality would have reduced the indirect state aid to whites. Since every black student brought at least s dollars in state funds into the school board's coffers, the board might have increased spending on black schools in the hope of attracting additional black students, or to prevent an outflow of existing ones. There is some qualitative evidence indicating that politicians were not only aware of this point, but took it into account in their behavior. "The money allocated to the colored children is spent on the education of white children," wrote a delta cotton superintendent from Louisiana. "We have twice as many colored children of school age as we have white, and we use their money. Colored children are mighty profitable to us here in this parish."[5] In a study of the public schools of East Feliciana Parish, Louisiana, Foote and Robertson (1926: 20-21) summarized the discussion of black schools at one board meeting in the following manner:

That the Negroes are an economic asset would not be challenged. That they have been leaving the parish for the past twenty years has clearly been shown by the data from the census reports. That they emigrate because of meager school conditions cannot be proved but the consensus of opinion among both white and Negro leaders who have studied the problem is that one of the most potent influences that can be brought to bear in retaining them is the provision of reasonably satisfactory school facilities. The opinion was expressed by several thoughtful citizens that the parish must provide better schools and longer terms or the exodus of Negroes will continue, perhaps at an increasing rate. The continued residence of the Negro population has an important bearing on the school revenues, because the Negro educables now bring into the parish from the state school fund $20,000 more than is now expended for Negro education.

White migration may have also affected school board behavior. In appropriating black school funds, whites in one locale make their county more attractive to other whites. But if other whites move in, they reduce the amount of appropriable black school funds per white student and bid up the price of land, making white education more expensive. Economic theory suggests that migration, both black and white, will continue to the point until the benefits (lower rates of appropriation, better schools, or lower local taxes) are exactly offset by the costs of moving to the marginal migrant. One implication of the argument is that the racial distribution of school expenditures will tend toward the racial distribution of the school tax burden. In other words, individuals, black and white, get what they pay for on the margin.

In addition, there may be powerful ideological reasons why those who bore a large share of the tax burden believed they should receive an equivalent share of government output. "The whites pay the taxes and the Negroes go the school" was a common slogan of whites opposed to increases in school taxes because they believed that blacks would acquire a larger share of the funds raised than blacks paid in taxes. One of the results of suffrage restriction may have been that the incidence of school taxes fell more heavily on black taxpayers after disfranchisement. Various measures of the racial burden of school taxes typically show that whites subsidized black schools (at the state and local levels) before disfranchisement, but that the subsidy was reduced afterwards (Smith, 1974; Kousser, 1980).

The racial incidence of school taxes raises complex theoretical and empirical problems, and it is not the intent of the paper to solve them. Rather, the point of the model is that there existed mechanisms by which black belt whites could provide themselves simultaneously with better schools and lower local taxes at the expense of blacks and other whites. The idea that individuals get what they pay for, however, is a useful null hypothesis against which to test for the effects of these mechanisms. In this case, expenditures on white schools should be positively related to the amount of taxable resources held by whites per white student, and to the fraction of total taxable resources held by whites. Once these variables are controlled for, there shoud be no relationship between the appropriable black state subsidy and expenditures on white schools. Similarly, the appropriable black state subsidy should have no effect on local school taxes.

## AN EMPIRICAL TEST: LOUISIANA

In this section, regression analysis is used to investigate race differences in school spending and local taxes in Louisiana for two dates: 1890 and 1910. As previously noted, Louisiana was the only state that reported voter registrations by race before and after the enactment of suffrage restrictions, allowing a direct examination of the effects of disfranchisement on school spending and local taxes. Formal suffrage restrictions in Louisiana were enacted between 1896 and 1898. The effects of these restrictions on black voters were dramatic. In 1890, 50.5% of the state's registered voters were black, but in 1910 only 0.6% were (Louisiana, Secretary of State Report, 1902: 553; 1912: 96).

The regression specification used to test the model is:

$$WEXP = a_0 + a_1 SPHI + a_2 WWPAM + a_3 PCTWW + a_4 AWMC + a_5 PCTAWM + a_6 WWAGE + a_7 PWHSE + a_8 SPHIBV + a_9 SPHIBSP + a_{10} BB2 + a_{11} BB3 + a_{12} BB4 + e_w$$

$$\text{BEXP} = b_0 + b_1\text{SPHI} + b_2\text{WWPAM} + b_3\text{BWPAM} + b_4\text{PCTWW} +$$
$$b_5\text{ABMC} + b_6\text{PCTAWM} + b_7\text{PBVOTE} + b_8\text{BWAGE} +$$
$$b_9\text{BB2} + b_{10}\text{BB3} + b_{11}\text{BB4} + e_b$$

$$\text{LTAX} = c_0 + c_1\text{SPHI} + c_2\text{WWPAM} + c_3\text{BWPAM} = c_4\text{PCTWW} +$$
$$c_5\text{AWMC} + c_6\text{ABMC} + c_7\text{PCTAWM} + c_8\text{WWAGE} +$$
$$c_9\text{BWAGE} + c_{10}\text{PWHSE} + c_{11}\text{SPHIBV} + c_{12}\text{SPHIPBSP}$$
$$+ c_{13}\text{BB2} + c_{14}\text{BB3} + c_{15}\text{BB4} + e_{LT}$$

where the a's, b's, and c's are parameters and the e's are disturbance terms. The regressions were estimated on a cross-section sample of parishes in 1890 and 1910.[6] Data used to construct the dependent and independent variables were drawn from the report of the state superintendent of public education, the state auditor's report (Louisiana Biennial Report, 1892, 1912), the report of the secretary of state of Louisiana (1902, 1912), and the U.S. Census (1895, 1913). For a detailed discussion of the data sources and the problems connected with them, see Margo (1982, Ch. 2 and 4).

The dependent variables are expenditures on teacher salaries, per pupil enrolled, (WEXP for whites and BEXP for blacks) and the share of locally generated funds in total school revenue. Expenditures on teacher salaries were used because more comprehensive measures were not available by race. Teacher salaries accounted for the bulk of school spending, however, and expenditures on plant, equipment, and administration (which accounted for the remainder) were likely to be even more heavily skewed toward white schools, so it is unlikely that much bias is introduced. The local tax share was used rather than local taxes paid by whites because the latter was not available.[7] If whites used black school funds to reduce local school taxes, however, the share of local taxes in total school revenue will necessrily fall, so that the implications of the model with respect to local taxes can still be tested.[8]

The critical independent variables are SPHI, PBVOTE, SPHIBV, and SPHIPBSP. SPHI is the amount of state funds allocated per white pupil to the parish school board on the basis of the black school population residing in the parish. If whites were appropriating black state school funds and using the dollars to buy more education or to reduce local taxes, $a_1$ should be positive and $c_1$ negative. PBVOTE is the black share of registered voters and SPHIBV is SPHI times PBVOTE. If the disfranchisement hypothesis holds, $b_7$ should be positive (the larger the share of registered voters who were black, the larger are expenditures on black schools), $a_8$ negative, and $c_{11}$ positive (the larger PBVOTE, the lower the rate of appropriation of black state funds, i.e. lower expenditures on white schools [a reduction in $a_1$] and a higher local tax share [an increase in $c_1$]). The variable SPHIPBSP is included to assess the effects of black and white migration on school spending and local school taxes. PBSP is equal to the difference between the number of black children enumerated in the current school census (the basis for the distribution of state school funds in any given year), and the number of black children who would have been enumerated had the black share of the school population remained unchanged since the previous school census, per white pupil enrolled. Thus, PBSP measures the net change in the number of black children whose state funds could be appropriated per white pupil. SPHIPBSP is SPHI time PBSP. If $a_9$ is negative and $c_{12}$ positive, migration tended to reduce the positive effect of white appropriation of black state funds on expenditures on white schools and the negative effect on the local tax share.

PCTWW and PCTAWM are, respectively, the white share of taxable wealth and the fraction of adult males who were white. Property and poll taxes (on adult males) furnished most of the funds for public schools at the local level. If whites perceived that an increase in the white share of taxable wealth or in the fraction of adult males who were white raised the marginal cost of education to them, as the model suggests, then $a_3$ and $a_5$ will be negative. It might be, however, that the racial distribution of expenditures explicitly or implicitly reflected the racial distribution of taxable resources. In this case, $a_3$ and $a_5$ will be positive (the larger the share of taxable resources held by whites, the larger are expenditures on white schools), and $b_4$ and $b_6$ negative.

The remaining independent variables are intended to control for other factors that were likely to have influenced school spending and local school taxes.[9] WWPAM, BWPAM, AWMC, and ABMC, are white assessed wealth per white adult male, black assessed wealth per black adult male, the number of white adult males per white pupil enrolled, and the number of black adult males per black pupil enrolled. The available tax base per pupil was directly related to assessed wealth and to the number of adult males per pupil.[10] Furthermore, both variables should be positively correlated with income per pupil. These considerations suggest that $a_2$, $a_4$, $b_3$, $c_2$, and $c_3$ should be positive. It also seems likely that wealthy whites would benefit most from a better educated black labor force, and also could have afforded to be less discriminatory in their behavior, so $b_2$ is predicted to be positive as well. WWAGE and BWAGE are the daily wage rates of white and black teachers. These variables are intended to control for the effects of the price of labor inputs on school spending and local school taxes.[11] PWHSE is the fraction of white students enrolled in high school. It should be positively related to expenditures on white schools since high schools were more expensive to run than common schools. Almost no whites were enrolled in high schools in 1890, so the variable appears only in the 1910 regressions. Outside of New Orleans, there appears to have been no black high schools in Louisiana during the period. BB2, BB3, and BB4 are dummy variables for the black population share in the parish (25-50%, 50-75%, 75-100%). They are included to assess how much of the remaining variation in the dependent variables was due to race.

The mean values of the dependent and independent variables in the sample, and the regression coefficients appear in Tables 4 and 5. The $R^2$ are reasonably good, especially for whites, given the small sample size and the quality of the data.

Several important findings emerge from the 1890 regressions. The appropriable state subsidy (SPHI) was positively related to expenditures on white schools and negatively related to the local tax share; however, $a_1$ was significant at only the 19% level. Moreover, the size of this coefficient implies that a 10% increase in SPHI increased expenditures on white schools by only 1.6%. Thus, while whites apparently used the black state subsidy to better their own schools prior to disfranchisement, the effect was

*Table 4*     1890 Regressions

| VARIABLE | MEAN | WEXP | WEXP | BEXP | LTAX | LTAX |
|---|---|---|---|---|---|---|
| Dependent Variable, Mean | | 7.43 | | 2.33 | 0.52 | |
| CONSTANT | | 6.73 | 5.03 | -12.59 | 0.25 | 0.35 |
| | | (0.44) | (0.34) | (1.36) | (0.24) | (0.30) |
| SPHI | 2.52 | 0.48 | 4.60 | 0.02 | -0.06 | -0.05 |
| | | (1.33) | (2.15) | (0.13) | (4.16) | (0.48) |
| WWPAM | 1240.35 | 0.004 | 0.004 | -0.0001 | 0.00009 | 0.0001 |
| | | (3.61) | (3.43) | (0.33) | (1.83) | (1.47) |
| AWMC | 1.97 | 2.41 | 2.05 | | 0.06 | 0.05 |
| | | (5.04) | (3.94) | | (2.58) | (2.36) |
| PCTWW[a] | 0.93 | -20.12 | -22.48 | 12.88 | 0.45 | 0.33 |
| | | (1.39) | (1.56) | (1.26) | (0.40) | (0.26) |
| PCTAWM | 0.49 | 5.87 | 9.53 | -1.16 | -0.39 | -0.36 |
| | | (0.93) | (1.47) | (0.29) | (1.15) | (0.96) |
| WWAGE | 1.68 | 3.76 | 3.80 | | -0.05 | -0.05 |
| | | (2.45) | (2.54) | | (0.72) | (0.69) |
| SPHIBV | 1.84 | | -4.54 | | | -0.02 |
| | | | (1.91) | | | (0.17) |
| SPHIPBSP | 0.54 | | -0.21 | | | 0.0008 |
| | | | (1.36) | | | (0.12) |
| BWPAM | 76.68 | | | 0.01 | $-3\times10^{-7}$ | -0.00009 |
| | | | | (1.56) | (0.01) | (0.08) |
| ABMC | 2.60 | | | 0.46 | 0.005 | 0.004 |
| | | | | (4.96) | (0.49) | (0.35) |
| BWAGE | 1.37 | | | 0.81 | 0.08 | 0.08 |
| | | | | (1.38) | (1.09) | (1.02) |
| PBVOTE | 0.53 | | | 3.48 | | |
| | | | | (1.09) | | |
| BB2 | 0.30 | -1.36 | -1.39 | -0.32 | -0.06 | -C.06 |
| | | (0.70) | (0.74) | (0.38) | (0.70) | (0.70) |
| BB3 | 0.40 | -0.37 | -0.05 | -2.56 | -0.12 | -0.12 |
| | | (0.13) | (0.02) | (2.16) | (1.01) | (1.00) |
| BB4 | 0.15 | 1.65 | 1.64 | -2.45 | -0.01 | -0.02 |
| | | (0.38) | (0.38) | (1.44) | (0.06) | (0.01) |
| $\bar{R}^2$ | | 0.82 | 0.83 | 0.49 | 0.32 | 0.28 |
| N | | 53 | 53 | 53 | 53 | 53 |

NOTE: The absolute values of the t-statistics are in parentheses.
a. 1891 data. Data for 1890 not available.

modest. SPHIBV was negatively related to expenditures on white schools (significant at the 6% level). The size of the coefficient was large enough to nearly wipe out the appropriation of black state funds by whites in parishes where the black share of registered voters was close to one. Note also that $a_1$ increases dramatically in absolute value once SPHIBV is added to the regression of expenditures on white schools. Thus, one of the effects of the black vote was to strongly limit the degree to which whites appropriated the black state subsidy and spent the proceeds on better schools. SPHIBV had a slightly negative impact on the local

*Table 5*    1910 Regressions

| VARIABLE | MEAN | WEXP | WEXP | BEXP | LTAX | LTAX |
|---|---|---|---|---|---|---|
| Dependent Variable, Mean | | 9.79 | | 1.63 | 0.59 | |
| CONSTANT | | -5.09 | -6.79 | 9.34 | -2.16 | -1.53 |
| | | (0.49) | (0.65) | (1.55) | (1.27) | (0.94) |
| SPHI | 3.60 | 0.75 | 0.83 | -0.02 | -0.02 | -0.03 |
| | | (9.89) | (8.32) | (0.77) | (2.28) | (3.42) |
| WWPAM | 1357.78 | 0.0009 | 0.0009 | 0.0006 | $3 \times 10^{-5}$ | $6 \times 10^{-5}$ |
| | | (2.13) | (1.78) | (3.50) | (0.06) | (1.13) |
| AWMC | 1.26 | 0.53 | 0.84 | | 0.03 | 0.01 |
| | | (0.91) | (1.39) | | (0.55) | (0.20) |
| PCTWW | 0.95 | 8.26 | 8.37 | -10.20 | 2.89 | 2.29 |
| | | (0.73) | (0.73) | (1.58) | (1.54) | (1.26) |
| PCTAWM | 0.52 | -4.32 | -3.02 | 1.18 | -0.55 | -0.58 |
| | | (1.41) | (0.97) | (0.83) | (1.34) | (1.46) |
| WWAGE | 2.00 | 2.59 | 2.71 | | 0.07 | 0.08 |
| | | (2.70) | (2.84) | | (0.61) | (0.80) |
| PWHSE | 0.05 | 9.13 | 10.27 | | 0.43 | 0.09 |
| | | (1.41) | (1.58) | | (0.68) | (0.14) |
| SPHIBV | 0.01 | | -9.97 | | | 0.19 |
| | | | (1.52) | | | (0.32) |
| SPHIPBSP | -0.15 | | -0.08 | | | 0.06 |
| | | | (0.31) | | | (2.14) |
| BWPAM | 56.89 | | | -0.009 | 0.002 | 0.002 |
| | | | | (1.88) | (1.31) | (1.41) |
| ABMC | 2.65 | | | 0.09 | -0.01 | -0.01 |
| | | | | (2.31) | (0.93) | (0.55) |
| BWAGE | 1.05 | | | 1.63 | 0.17 | 0.11 |
| | | | | (5.14) | (1.65) | (1.10) |
| PBVOTE | 0.005 | | | 1.68 | | |
| | | | | (0.33) | | |
| BB2 | 0.43 | -0.71 | -0.55 | -0.72 | -0.07 | -0.08 |
| | | (0.87) | (0.68) | (2.61) | (0.92) | (1.13) |
| BB3 | 0.34 | -1.56 | -1.33 | -0.98 | -0.11 | -0.11 |
| | | (1.18) | (1.02) | (2.26) | (0.88) | (0.94) |
| BB4 | 0.11 | -1.98 | -2.18 | -1.64 | -0.27 | -0.16 |
| | | (1.02) | (1.13) | (2.55) | (1.45) | (0.87) |
| $\bar{R}^2$ | | 0.94 | 0.94 | 0.71 | 0.53 | 0.57 |
| N | | 56 | 56 | 56 | 56 | 56 |

NOTE: The absolute values of the t-statistics are in parentheses.

tax share, insigificantly different from zero, but in contradiction of the model. Whites may have been reluctant to raise funds by means of property or poll taxes if they feared that blacks would reap most of the benefits, a situation most likely in parishes where blacks were in the majority. Consequently, whites in these parishes may have supported their schools by means of contributions or tuition payments. The local tax share, as defined in the regressions, would be unaffected, however, since data on both these sources of funds are lacking.

SPHIPBSP was negatively related to expenditures on white schools and positively related to the local tax share. This suggests that migration did affect spending on white schools and the local tax share in the direction implied by the model, but its impact on either variable was weak and statistically insignificant.

The black share of registered voters (PBVOTE) had a large, positive effect on expenditures on black schools. For example, an increase in the mean value of PBVOTE (0.53) to 0.75 would have added $.77 to the mean value of expenditures on black schools, an increase of 32%. This increase, however, was significantly different from zero at only the 25% level. PBVOTE is not a perfect proxy for black political clout: many blacks who registered probably never voted, others could have been bought off by white politicians, and the registration rolls apparently included an indeterminate number of fictitious blacks in some parishes.[12] In light of these considerations, the size of the impact is strong evidence that the black vote did have a significant effect on expenditures on black schools, in the manner implied by the model.

The white share of taxable wealth (PCTWW) was negatively associated with expenditures on white schools, as the model predicts, but the size of the coefficient seems much too large to be measuring just a price effect on white education. Some insight into this issue is provided by the positive relationship between PCTWW and expenditures on black schools. Evidently the property tax burden of black schools fell largely on white taxpayers. In light of this result, the positive relationship between PCTAWM and expenditures on white schools is puzzling. The regression does not control for the fraction of adult males who actually paid their poll taxes, and PCTAWM may be a poor measure of this fraction. PCTAWM may also capture some element of political power not reflected in the data on voter registrations; the negative relationship between PCTAWM and expenditures on black schools is consistent with this interpretation.

Turning to the 1910 regressions, the appropriable state subsidy (SPHI) continued to display a positive impact on expenditures on white schools and a negative impact on the local tax share, as the model predicts. A 10% increase in SPHI (at the sample mean) increased expenditures on white schools by 2.8%, 72% greater than in 1890. Moreover, a₁ was significantly different from zero (1% level), unlike the 1890 figure. However, a 10% increase in SPHI (at the sample mean) reduced the local tax share by only 1.2%, compared with 3.9% in 1890. Apparently whites preferred to use the bulk of the black state subsidy that they appropriated in 1910 to satisfy their growing demand for education rather than to reduce local taxes. SPHIBV was negatively related to expenditures on white schools, and positively related to the local tax share, as the model predicts. The magnitude of its impact on either variable was very small, however, because the black share of registered voters was nearly zero everywhere in the state. Indeed, had blacks not been disfranchised, the effects of the appropriable state subsidy on expenditures on white schools and the local tax share would have been eliminated.[13] Thus, the reduction in the black vote can account for the entire increase in expenditures on white schools over the period. SPHIPBSP was negatively related to expenditures on white schools and positively related to the local tax share, but neither coefficient was statistically significant. Thus, while migration had the predicted impact on school spending and local taxes, it had an insignificant effect on the appropriation of black state school funds by whites. The black share of registered voters was positively related to expenditures on black schools, but the association was weak and statistically insignificant since so few blacks were registered.

The effects of the "price" variables (PCTWW and PCTAWM) are puzzling. PCTAWM was negatively associated with expenditures on white schools, consistent with the model, but PCTWW was positively associated, which is inconsistent. Again insight is provided by examining the relationship between PCTWW and expenditures on black schools: PCTWW was negatively correlated with BEXP. One of the effects of disfranchisement, therefore, was to make the racial distribution of school expenditures reflect the racial distribution of taxable wealth, as Kousser (1980) found for North Carolina. Evidently Louisiana whites believed, and were able to enforce, that property taxes paid by whites should go to white schools.[14]

The remaining independent variables also influenced school spending and local taxes. White wealth per white adult male and the number of white adult males per white pupil were positively associated with expenditures on white schools and the local tax share in both years. White wealth per white adult male had little impact on expenditures on black schools in 1890, but had a positive effect in 1910. Thus, wealthy whites were evidently motivated to increase expenditures on black schools after disfranchisement. Whether they did so for altruistic or paternalistic reasons, or because they benefited from a better-educated black populace, is a subject for further research, but whatever slack they did pick up was not enough to stem the sharp reduction in expenditures on black schools over the two decades. Black wealth per black adult male had a positive impact on expenditures on black schools in 1890, and a negative impact in 1910. Thus, the root cause of the low level of school spending on blacks in 1910 was not necessarily due to a low level of black assessed wealth. The number of black adult males had a positive and statistically significant effect on expenditures on black schools in both years. But while a 10% increase in ABMC (at the sample mean) increased the mean level of expenditures on black schools by 5.1% in 1890, the corresponding increase in 1910 was only 1.5%. The poll tax was one of several suffrage requirements adopted by the Louisiana Constitutional Convention in 1898. Poor blacks may have simply not paid the tax because they had no way of ensuring that the dollars would be spent for their benefit.

The wage rate of teachers affected school spending in both years. In 1890, a 10% increase in the mean daily wage of white teachers reduced expenditures on white schools by 1.5%, while a 10% increase in the mean daily wage of black teachers reduced expenditures on black schools by 5.2%. In 1910, a 10% increase in the daily wage of white teachers reduced expenditures on white schools by 4.4%, but expenditures on black schools were essentially independent of the wage rate of black teachers. It may be that expenditures on black schools were already so low that no variation in the quantity of black teachers demanded by school boards was possible within the observed variation in the black teacher wage. Despite the small fraction of white students enrolled in high school, PWHSE had a positive effect on expenditures on white schools, significant at the 16% level.

The coefficients of the percent black dummies (BB2-BB4) were generally insignificant in the regressions on expenditures on white schools and the local tax share. Thus, the variables suggested by the model, in particular SPHI and PBVOTE, capture the important effects that racial composition had on expenditures on white schools and the local tax share. However, in both years expenditures on black schools were significantly lower in the black belt even after controlling for other factors. The regressions do not control for the fraction of black males who paid their poll taxes or for black income, both of which were probably lowest in the black belt, resulting in a low level of spending on black schools. Blacks in these parishes were over-whelmingly rural, working as tenant farmers, and children were an important source of labor supply for their families. Fewer days of school attended per year among the children of such families could account for the negative coefficients (see Bullock, 1967: 177-178, for a discussion of this point). Similarly, the crop mix affected the demand for child labor, and thus school attendance and possibly the demand for black teachers. Both these points could be explored by an analysis of attendance patterns at the parish level.

## CONCLUSION

This article has examined the effects of disfranchisement on race differences in school spending and local school taxes in Louisiana for 1890 and 1910. Building on the seminal work of Bond (1934, 1939), Harlan (1958), and Kousser (1974, 1980), a model of school board behavior was developed that emphasized the ability of whites to appropriate state funds earmarked for black schools and local black taxes. Both effects led to increased expenditures on white schools and lower local taxes. Regression analysis was used to test the model, and the results of the regression suggest that disfranchisement reduced expenditures on black schools, enabled whites to take fuller advantage of the fiscal mechanisms outlined above, and led to a racial distribution of school spending that more closely approximated the racial distribution of the taxable resources.

This study leaves open a number of issues for future research. The precise allocation of the school tax burden between blacks and whites needs to be calculated, although a satisfactory theoretical model has yet to be developed. Data for other states, some of which include information on the distribution of investment in school capital by race, and for the post-1910 period, have yet to be exploited. The mix of state and local funds and the types of taxes used to finance education varied dramatically across states, and the determinants of both remain unstudied. The impact of contributions by philanthropic organizations such as the Rosenwald and Jeanes Foundations might be profitably analyzed within the general framework of the model. It is generally believed that these funds stimulated expenditures on black schools. While this is undoubtedly true, it is also possible that these donations may have replaced some fraction of state and local funds that would have been spent on blacks, thus freeing up additional dollars for white schools or for lowering local school taxes.

## NOTES

1. In 1890, the length of the school year averaged 92 days in the South compared with 154 days in the non-South, and current expenditures per pupil enrolled were only 43% of the non-South average. In 1910, the Southern school year averaged 128 days compared with 171 days in the non-South, and current expenditures per pupil enrolled were 49% of the non-South average. In 1890 dollars, expenditures per pupil in the South grew at an average annual rate of 1.9% over the two decades, compared with 1.3% in the non-South (U.S. Office of Education, 1890: 13, 14, 29; 1911: 695, 696, 704).

2. Multivariate statistical techniques were not utilized by Bond, Harlan, or Myrdal in their work. Kousser's (1980) analysis of North Carolina employed multiple regression, but he did not separate out the effects of the school finance mechanisms discussed by Bond from the general effects of race. Gershenberg (1967) analyzed the length of the white school year in Alabama over the period 1880 to 1930, but did not address the school finance issue nor did he analyze the relationship between race and local taxes.

3. Recognition of the idea that governments distribute resources to maximize political support originates with Downs (1957) and is central to the modern economic theory of public choice. See Mueller (1979) for a survey of this theory.

4. There are three assumptions underlying the result in the text. First, the black tax base must be perfectly inelastic with respect to the tax rate. If some types of property are untaxed or not fully assessed, blacks could shift the composition of their wealth to escape appropriation. Second, black and white wealth must be assessed at the same rate. If discrimination is possible, the school board's optimal strategy is to tax blacks so as to maximize black tax payments before imposing any taxes on whites, i.e., convert black taxes into an income supplement to whites. Evidence on race differences in assessment ratios is available for Virginia. Snavely (1916: 75) found that the assessment rate on black real estate exceeded the assessment rate on white real estate by 37%. Part of this difference was due to a tendency to assess less valuable property at a higher rate. Holding the value of property constant, however, blacks were still assessed at a higher rate than whites (by approximately 25%) on properties valued at less than $1000.00 which accounted for 91% of the black and 61% of the white real estate transactions in his sample. Snavely attributed this difference to discrimination in the real estate market against blacks, rather than to discrimination in assessment practices (Snavely, 1916: 77-78). Third, if the costs of collecting the tax are borne by whites, and black wealth is a small fraction of total wealth (as was generally the case), then the benefits of assessing blacks may not be worth the cost. Finally, the model is partial equilibrium in the sense that the wage of white teachers is fixed. But if the demand for white teachers increases as a result of the appropriation of black school funds, the wage of white teachers will likely be bid up, and the effects of appropriation blunted.

5. The quote is taken from Neyland (1958: 100) and originally appeared in Washburne (1942: 114).

6. All parishes with complete data were included in the sample. Parishes excluded in 1890 were Acadia, Jefferson, Orleans, Richland, St. John, and St. Landry. The parishes excluded in 1910 were Avoyelles, Cameron, and Orleans.

7. The 1890 report does not give teacher salaries by race. However, it is possible to estimate them with a high degree of accuracy. The estimating procedure is somewhat involved and will only be sketched here. The number of teachers employed times the length of the school year times the average daily wage of teachers, all of which were reported by race yields an estimate of total salaries. The estimate is adjusted on the basis of a time-series cross-section regression on data for 361 counties from four states (Alabama, North Carolina, Louisiana, and Florida) for the census years 1890, 1900, and 1910, all of which reported total salaries by race and the above series. The true ratio of white to black per pupil expenditures was regressed on the estimated ratio, allowing for various inter-action and dummy variables for time and the percent black in the county. Utilizing the regression coefficients, along with data on total salaries (which was nearly always available), it is possible to estimate white and black expenditures by means of the identity: Total Salaries = Expenditures per white pupil times white pupils plus expenditures per black pupil times black pupils. For further details, see Margo (1982, ch. 2). The primary state funds available to parish school boards included an appropriation based on the number of school age children residing in the parish as enumerated in a school census taken every few years, and a share of the interest on sixteenth section lands, based on the parish holdings. Local funds included an appropriation by the police jury (the local government in Louisiana), poll taxes, and after 1898, local property taxes voted by residents. The poll tax rate was set by the state, but the collection of the tax was left to local officials. There were several minor state and local sources (for example, rent of school lands) that have been

ignored in this analysis. In preliminary work, sixteenth section interest per pupil was included among the independent variables, but since it exhibited little effect, it was excluded from the final runs. Total school revenue includes the state and local funds defined above and is net of any funds accruing over from the previous fiscal year. The local tax share does not include any contributions by patrons or tuition payments. In the late nineteenth-century South, it was common for school boards to extend the school year once public funds were exhausted by charging tuition (Blodgett, 1895: 13-16). Evidently these funds were not generally included among the school board's receipts, although they may have been included in disbursements in some cases. These funds are properly classified as private rather than public, but the appropriation of black school funds by whites might have had a negative effect on white tuition payments. It seems likely, therefore, that $c_i$ is biased downward in absolute value, but a definitive answer awaits the retrieval of additional data.

8. Let A = local school funds, and B = state school funds. Then the local tax share equals $A/(A+B)$. Suppose that whites appropriate black school funds and use some of the dollars to reduce local school taxes, i.e., A falls. Differentiating $A/(A+B)$ with respect to A, $d[A/(A+B)]/dA = [B/(A+B)]dA$. Thus, a fall in A ($dA < 0$) necessarily reduces the local tax share. This result holds even if the rate at which local taxes are assessed differs by race.

9. In an earlier version of the article, the list of independent variables also included measures of urbanization, the relative number of private school pupils, and the growth rate of enrollments. While these variables usually had the appropriate signs (rapid rates of growth of enrollments reduced expenditures, for example), they added little to the $R^2$ and created severe multicollinearity problems. Since the general scope of the results with respect to disfranchisement was robust whether or not these variables were included in the regressions, they were left out of the final runs.

10. Because some adult males were exempt from the poll tax (disabled Confederate veterans, for example) and many who were subject to the tax never paid it, AWMC and ABMC are only proxies for the true tax base (the number of males actually subject to the tax times the fraction paying the tax) per pupil. Data on the racial distribution of poll tax payments in 1890 are unavailable, but are available for 1910. The results of the 1910 regressions were generally insensitive to the method of defining the poll tax variables (but see note 14); in order to simplify the comparison between the two years, only the specification given in the text is reported.

11. This procedure assumes that variations in the wage rate of teachers across parishes represented true price variation rather than reflecting local choices with respect to the qualifications of teachers. The "hedonic" price technique (Antos and Rosen, 1976) corrects for this problem, but cannot be used here because of a lack of data on teacher quality. Modern studies of school spending using the average wage or an hedonic ajusted wage typically find little or no difference in the estimated price elasticities (Bergstrom, Rubinfeld, and Shapiro, 1980: 24).

12. The accuracy of the registration figures has been questioned by one prominent Louisiana historian, William Ivy Hair, who charged that "a real white majority (in 1890) had been transformed into an alleged black majority of almost 4000, through the counting of thousands of fictitious Negroes. . . . Most of the doctoring of registration rolls and election returns was accomplished in the cotton plantation parishes of northern and central Louisiana" (Hair, 1969: 115). The proximate cause of the inflated figures was the method for determining representation at state Democratic conventions. The size of the parish delegation depended directly on the prior Democratic count. By fraudulently filling the lists, black belt Democrats insured control over the state machine. "Only in the sugar growing regions of South Louisiana . . . were black men free to vote for more than one

party" (Hair, 1969: 113). It is possible to incorporate Hair's criticisms into the regression analysis by allowing the coefficients of SPHIBV and PBVOTE to differ for the sugar parishes he identified (see Hair, 1969: ftn. 17, 39). When this is done, however, there is no evidence that the effect of the black vote was more powerful in these parishes.

13. Another way to make this point is to suppose that disfranchisement had taken place in 1886 instead of 1896 by setting the black share of registered voters in 1890 equal to its 1910 value. Then the mean value of expenditures on white schools would have been 12.01 in 1890 instead of 7.43, a 61.6% increase compared with an actual increase of 31.7% over the 1890-1910 period.

14. A series of regressions was estimated for 1910 in which the fraction of poll taxes paid by whites was substituted for the white share of adult males. In these regressions, as was positive in contrast to the result reported in the text. This reinforces the conclusion that the racial distribution of expenditures mirrored the racial distribution of taxes paid after disfranchisement. The coefficients of the other variables were similar.


# REFERENCES

ANTOS, J. R. and S. ROSEN (1975) "Discrimination in the market for public school teachers." J. of Econometrics 3.2 (May): 123-151.

BERGSTROM, T. C., D. RUBINFELD, and P. SHAPIRO (1980) "Micro-based estimates of demand functions for local school expenditures." Prensented at the Center for Research on Economic and Social Theory, Department of Economics, University of Michigan.

BLODGETT, J. H. (1893) Report on Education in the United States at the Eleventh Census: 1890. Washington, DC: Government Printing Office.

BOND, H. M. (1939) Negro Education in Alabama: A Stuay in Cotton and Steel. Washington, DC: Associated.

——— (1934) The Education of the Negro in the American Social Order. New York: Prentice-Hall.

BULLOCK, H. A. (1967) A History of Negro Education in the South from 1619 to the Present. Cambridge, MA: Harvard Univ. Press.

DOWNS, A. (1957) An Economic Theory of Democracy. New York: Harper & Row.

FOOTE, J. M. and M. ROBERTSON (1926) The Public Schools of East Feliciana Parish. Baton Rouge, LA: State Department of Education.

FREEMAN, R. (1972) "Black-white economic differences: why did they last so long?" Department of Economics, University of Chicago. (mimeo)

GERSHENBERG, I. (1967) "Alabama: an analysis of the growth of white public education in a southern state, 1880-1930." Ph.D. dissertation, University of California, Berkeley.

HAIR, W. I. (1969) Bourbonism and Agrarian Protest: Louisiana Politics, 1877-1900. Baton Route, LA: Louisiana State Univ. Press.

HARLAN, L. R. (1958) Separate and Unequal: Public School Campaigns and Racism in the Southern Seaboard States, 1901-1915. Chapel Hill: Univ. of North Carolina Press.

Historical Statistics of the United States, Part 1 (1976). Washington, DC: Government Printing Office.

INMAN, R. P. (1979) "The fiscal performance of local governments: an interpretive review," in P. Mieszkowski and M. Straszheim (eds.) Current Issues in Urban Economics.
Baltimore, MD: John Hopkins Univ. Press.

KEY, V. O. (1949) Southern Politics in State and Nation. New York: Knopf.

KOUSSER, J. M. (1980) "Progressivism - for middle class whites only: North Carolina
education, 1880-1910." J. of Southern History 46 (May): 169-194.

—— (1974) The Shaping of Southern Politics: Suffrage Restriction and the Establishment of the One-Party South, 1880-1910. New Haven and London: Yale Univ. Press.

Louisiana, State of (1912) Biennial Report of the Auditor of Public Accounts for the Years
1910 and 1911. Baton Rouge, LA: Ramires-Jones.

—— (1892) Biennial Report of the Auditor of Public Accounts for the Years 1890 and
1891. New Orleans, LA: E. Marchand.

—— (1912) Biennial Report of the State Superintendent of Public Education to the
Governor and to the General Assembly, School Sessions of 1909-1910 and 1910-1911.
Baton Rouge, LA: Ramires-Jones.

—— (1892) Biennial Report of the State Superintendent of Public Education to the
General Assembly, 1890-1891. Baton Rouge, LA: State Printer.

—— (1912) Report of the Secretary of State to His Excellency the Governor of Louisiana. Baton Rouge, LA: Ramires-Jones.

—— (1902) Report of the Secretary of State to His Excellency the Governor of Louisiana. Baton Rouge, LA: Baton Rouge News.

MARGO, R. A. (1982) "Disfranchisement, school finance, and the economics of segregated schools in the U.S. South, 1890-1910." Ph.D. dissertation, Harvard University.

MUELLER, D. C. (1979) Public Choice. New York: Cambridge Univ. Press.

MYRDAL, G. (1944) An American Dilemma: The Negro Problem and Modern Democracy. New York: Harper & Row.

NEYLAND, L. (1958) "The Negro in Louisiana since 1900: an economic and social
study." Ph.D. dissertation, New York University.

SMITH, R. K. (1973) "The economics of education and discrimination in the United States
South: 1870-1910." Ph.D. dissertation, University of Wisconsin.

SNAVELY, T. R. (1916) The Taxation of Negroes in Virginia. Charlottesville, VA: Mitchie.

U.S. Bureau of the Census (1913) Report on Population of the United States at the Thirteenth Census: 1910. Washington, DC: Government Printing Office.

—— (1895) Report on Population of the United States at the Eleventh Census: 1890.
Washington, DC: Government Printing Office.

U.S. Office of Education (1911) Report of the Commissioner of Education for the year
1910-1911. Washington, DC: Government Printing Office.

—— (1890) Report of the Commissioner of Education for the Year 1889-1890. Washington, DC: Government Printing Office.

WASHBURNE, C. (1942) Louisiana Looks at Its Schools. Baton Rouge, LA: State Department of Education.

*Robert A. Margo is Assistant Professor, Department of Economics, University of Penn-
sylvania. His principal areas of research are the political economy of the postbellum
South, the economics of slavery, nutrition and labor productivity in the nineteenth-century United States, and the economics of education in the early twentieth-century United
States.*

# The American Baptist Home Mission Society and Black Higher Education in the South, 1865-1920

SANDY DWAYNE MARTIN

ONE OF THE MOST INTERESTING AND FASCINATING PHENOMENA of American history is the meteoric rise of blacks from the destitution of slavery to their establishment and management of independent ecclesiastical institutions, in the period 1865-1920. The American Baptist Home Mission Society (ABHMS), the Northern, predominantly white Baptist organization founded in 1832, contributed immensely along these lines. The Civil War had barely come to a successful resolution when the ABHMS began active mission work among the newly freed persons of the South. Among the missionary enterprises was the establishment and maintenance of educational institutions among Southern blacks. In this line of work the Society moved across the South with amazing speed and profound dedication on the part of individual missionaries, Northern and Southern, black and white—but primarily Northern and white.

The chief aim of this article is to provide one interpretation of this chain of events. Special attention shall be devoted to analyzing (a) the crucial role played by the ABHMS in the establishing and growth of black educational institutions and (b) the philosophy and practical results of these enterprises, and finally (c) attempting an assessment of the Society and its missionaries as they related to blacks.

## VIRGINIA UNION UNIVERSITY AND SPELMAN COLLEGE

The 1892 publication *Our Baptist Pulpit and Schools,* by Albert W. Pegues lists at least fifteen colleges, institutes, universities, and seminaries founded and supported by the Society in Washington, D.C., Kentucky, and practically every state of the former Confederacy.[1] At least six of these institutions still exist as

SANDY DWAYNE MARTIN is an assistant professor in the University of North Carolina at Wilmington, North Carolina.

institutions of higher learning today: Benedict College (Columbia, South Carolina), Bishop College (Dallas, Texas), Florida Memorial College (St. Augustine, Florida), Morehouse College and Spelman College (Atlanta, Georgia), Shaw University (Raleigh, North Carolina), and Virginia Union University (Richmond, Virginia).[2]

An account of two of these colleges will serve as a descriptive model of the practice of the Society in the period 1865-1920. The white Baptists of the North early realized that successful efforts to evangelize and materially uplift Southern blacks had to proceed by way of educating their ministers. Virginia Union University of Richmond traces its origins in 1865 to such a goal. The institution has been known successively as Colver Institute, Richmond Institute, Richmond Theological Seminary, and finally, Virginia Union University upon the Society's reorganization of its collegiate activities in Virginia and the merger of the Seminary with Wayland Seminary.[3]

Symbolic of the phenomenal rise of Afro-Americans from slavery to active participation in society, the school began in a building once used to trade in slaves, "Lumpkins Jail." In 1867 Nathaniel Colver, a professor of biblical theology of Chicago Theological Seminary and a former participant in the antislavery movement, assumed control of the school. Contrary to the deduction one might draw from the early minutes of the Society, the early missionary-teachers did meet with considerable suspicion if not opposition from within the black community. Some doubted that Colver was sincere. There were also misgivings about an educated ministry.[4]

But the missionaries and teachers, black and white, continued the work. When Colver resigned in 1868, he was replaced by C. H. Corey who transferred from his mission field in Augusta, Georgia. On February 10, 1876, the school was chartered by the State of Virginia and, interestingly, three of its trustees were black Baptist leaders. Two well-known black Baptists, Joseph Endom Jones and David N. Vassar, also served as members of the faculty during these early years. Pegues reports that between the years 1868 and 1882, the Richmond School had enrolled 771 students, prepared 300 for the ministry, and 200 for teaching. By the time that the school became Richmond Theological Institute in 1886 it had prepared two of the first Post-Civil War black Baptist missionaries for service in Africa, Solomon Cosby and William W. Colley, and was in the process of training others.[5]

Quite significantly, Baptist women made their influence felt in all of these educational efforts. Quite appropriately, Spelman College stands as one of the best examples of this contribution and the concern of the Society for the intellectual advancement of black women in the South.[6] It appeared as an instant answer to the Reverend Frank Quarles, the pastor of Friendship Baptist Church in Atlanta, Georgia, when in April, 1881, two women appeared at his door to establish a school for black women. The Woman's Baptist Home Mission Society had commissioned these women, Sophia B. Packard and Harriet E. Giles, for this purpose. Miss Packard, a former corresponding secretary of the WABHMS, had already surveyed the needs of black women in the South and sought the support of her society in their behalf. The school began on April 11th in the basement of the Church with eleven students, most of whom were ineligible for state education because they were adults.[6]

Instructions began with Bible reading and writing lessons. The women in the overcrowded, uncomfortable basement knelt on the floor using their seats as desks. The teachers vigorously rejected a proposal to unite the school with the ABHMS-supported Atlanta Baptist Seminary (Morehouse College), an all-male institution. The founders felt that female education would best proceed in separation from the males.

Meanwhile Frank Quarles continued in his efforts on behalf of the school, collecting funds among blacks in the area and journeying North for building funds. In 1883 the school acquired a nine-acre campus site. The school also received the support of the famous John D. Rockefeller, who paid off most of the debt on its property. The *Spelman Messenger,* the school paper, was organized in 1886.

The scope of education was broadened over the next several years by the addition of the following departments: nurse training in 1886, missionary training in 1891, and teachers training in 1892.[7] In 1888 the school was chartered by the State of Georgia. Like Virginia Union, some of its first graduates served their racial brothers and sisters in Africa. Miss Nora A. Gordon and Miss Emma B. DeLany were two of these brave and dedicated women. An institution which in 1882 had only two teachers, eleven students, and was meeting in an uncomfortable basement had by 1902 acquired 42 teachers, an enrollment of 700 students, and had possession of a campus site and buildings worth a total of $350,000.

## THE UNIQUE ROLE OF THE ABHMS

In order to carry out effectively any missionary activity among black Southerners at the close of the Civil War a church group needed to match three basic requisites: possession of adequate financial resources for the enormity of the task, a strong commitment to the religious and material benefit and progress of the freed people, and the confidence and respect of the people to be missionized. Baptists of America during the 1865-1900 period were divided into four major ecclesiastical groups: Northern Baptists, black and white; and Baptists of the South, white and, increasingly, black. Of these four groups, Northern, predominantly white, ABHMS had the three basic requisites for successful missionary work.

To be sure, blacks took an aggressive and lively interest in the efforts of evangelization and education. Black Baptist bodies were in full operation during this time on behalf of domestic missionary activities. The American Baptist Missionary Convention, founded in 1840, was in operation mainly in the North prior to the War. So in 1864 black Baptists decided to organize the Southern and Northwestern Convention to cover territory in the West and South. In 1866 these two Conventions merged, forming the Consolidated American Baptist Missionary Convention. Eight years later the New England Baptist Missionary Convention was formed. All of these groups had as their central concern the evangelization and education of blacks to improve the institutional church and uplift the race usually working in close cooperative efforts with each other.[8]

At the very foundation of their educational philosophy was the desire to enhance the educational status of the black ministry. New England Baptists claimed that there existed "a growing demand for an educated ministry" which would work to eradicate "ignorance and superstition" replacing them with true gospel doctrines. Preaching was "teaching in the highest sense," and those who would labor in the office of the ministry needed spiritual *and* intellectual qualifications. The Committee on Education, therefore, recommended "that our churches license no brother who does not manifest evident ability to teach."[9]

But black Baptist interest in education went beyond concern for ministerial training. Black Baptists believed that Christianity *and* education, both spiritual and secular, were of paramount significance for the advancement of the whole race in Africa and the United States. For this reason the Consolidated American Educational Association, a subsidiary of the Consolidated American Baptist Missionary Convention, had as its aim "to diffuse general intelligence, by sustaining secular, systematic and religious education in the South, in Africa, and wherever our unfortunate brothern and fellow-men are found destitute of educational advantages; and to train and qualify persons for teachers and practical life, always having in view the glory of God, and the best good of society."[10]

Besides commitment, black Baptist leaders had the general confidence of their people as evidenced by close cooperative ties among associations across state and sectional lines—a cooperation culminating in the formation of the American National Baptist Convention in 1886 and more importantly the emergence of the National Baptist Convention in 1895.

But though they had the commitment and the confidence of the people, black Baptists, generally speaking, lacked substantial financial resources. If white church groups found money to be scarce during this time, black groups found fund-raising efforts even more sadly disappointing. The Consolidated ABMC's problems were so acute that their educational department was unable to commit themselves to paying their teachers regular salaries. Schools, public and private, from the South had requested the Association to send teachers. Indeed qualified, unemployed teachers, from North and South, had applied to the Association for placement. But the group was unable to send them because of the inadequacy of funds.[11]

Southern white Baptist churches at the end of the War were also often hard pressed for mission funds and often requested the ABHMS' assistance for mission work in the South through their convention. But the Southern Baptist Convention's greatest problem consisted of a combination of a lack of sustained, explicit interest in the well-being of blacks politically and economically combined with a corresponding distrust in the black community of their white neighbors. It is not surprising that black Baptists would be reserved to missionary endeavors of a group which had persistently defended slavery, both morally and actively, and had unashamedly reduced them to segregated, second-class membership in the pre-Civil War church.[12]

As John Lee Eighmy states, the basic thought pattern behind these actions did not dissipate with the emancipation of blacks. Blacks were encouraged to leave churches and to organize separate congregations. Southern Baptists made a point of stating that religious training of blacks in no way was or should be an endorsement of "social equality" or political freedoms—a position which dampened the chances of North-South cooperation. Though the Southern Baptist Convention might occasionally have condemned lynchings and other brutal acts against blacks by white mobs, it nevertheless supported and justified the racism of the South, in such forms as jim crow laws and political disenfranchisement of Afro-Americans.

This is not to say that there were not individual white Southern Baptists who were active supporters of black progress and who even served as missionaries and teachers. Nor do the above observations deny the fact that the SBC cooperated with the ABHMS in certain mission activities. But the strength of black Baptist and ABHMS commitment appears to have been lacking. For though the SBC seriously discussed the establishment of black schools in the 1880's, it was not until the 1920's that concrete and consistent steps were taken to meet that goal. In other words, Southern Baptists' commitment to the political subordination of blacks limited the range of their educational efforts on behalf of their black neighbors.[13]

Thus, the stage was set for a dramatic influence of the ABHMS upon the educational lives of Southern blacks. Their financial means were not unlimited and they too sadly observed the unsuccess of their fund raising campaigns. But their position was much better than black and Southern white Baptists. The ABHMS enjoyed greater confidence among blacks than the SBC. Its pre-War position was *antislavery,* though not substantially and consistently abolitionist. J. M. Pendleton probably approached accuracy when he commented in 1863 that blacks would be inclined to accept missionaries from the Society because its headquarters were in a free state.

This is not to say that the Society never encountered suspicion and distrust. Blacks were not passively naïve and oblivious to the character failings of those who came in their midst. Besides, many black Baptists, like white Baptists, looked askance at the idea of educated ministry. But because of the Society's swift entry into the field of labor, its employment of black missionaries and teachers, and its basic commitment to the advancement of the race, it made considerable inroads into the hearts and minds of the people. Thus, a white missionary could write in 1873 of the ABHMS educational endeavors:

> And *colored* men themselves, who, owing to former misapprehensions, had not worked with us, are beginning now to help. These far-sighted and wise-hearted leaders of both races began to see clearly that these schools are *theirs* in a sense most emphatic. They are theirs in a sense they *never can be ours;* theirs to cherish, theirs ultimately to own and manage, either with or without their Northern brethren; and theirs from which to derive untold benefits. [14]

The major state conventions found no difficulty in claiming these institutions as means to benefit the race and, thus, urging financial support for them. For example, the Virginia Baptist State Convention adopted a report of its Committee on Education which reads in part:

> The Richmond Institute, which has done so much for the mental and moral improvement of the race, has a large claim on this body. An united effort must be made on our part with the [ABHMS] to make said school a still greater blessing by bringing within its bounds our influence and means, and that said institutions may thereby ere long become a college with a theological department second to none in the State. [15]

The ABHMS did in fact move on the mission field in the South quickly and with enthusiasm and dedication. Indeed, their commitment, which impressed or at least reassured many blacks, was an extension of their pre-Civil War antislavery stance. As early as 1863, the Reverend D. B. Purinton addressed the Society concerning its obligation to newly freed blacks. According to Purinton, it had taken war to remove African slavery—that "relic of barbarism" and "scandal of the Christian name." Now that the mistreated and abused sons and daughters of Africa were free, the Baptists of America must not add insult to injury by overlooking their miserable condition of "ignorance and vice." [16]

Purinton maintained that Baptists must be loyal to the command of Christ to spread His gospel to every *creature;* and whatever anyone may think of blacks, "they are at least *'creatures.'"* Baptists had sent missionaries to the colored populations of Asia, why not send them to colored people in America? Missionaries had even been sent and had sacrificed their lives "in well-intentioned but illguided attempts to convert Africans in Africa." Another great challenge faced them now, however, in their own country—the conversion of Africans in America. [17]

Besides the connection between evangelization and pre-War antislavery position, the Society also felt an obligation to Southern blacks because of the large numbers of Baptist church members or those leaning toward the Baptist church among them. Thus, despite the enormity of the task of educating the freed people, the Society had a special obligation. "We have a sympathy for them and interest in them, which can be felt by no other denomination." [18]

Already (1866) the Society had collected over $21,000 during the past year, commissioned 25 whites and 10 blacks as missionaries and 62 other persons as assistant missionaries to the freed people, and had established schools for secular training in over eight cities, including "Washington, Alexandria, Richmond, Petersburg, Fredericksburg, Lynchburg, Newbern, [and] Memphis." [19] The ABHMS, in short, had during these early years the financial resources, the commitment to the improvement of both the spiritual and material aspects of black life, and, comparably speaking, a solid core of black confidence in its motivations and missions.

### EDUCATION: SACRED AND SECULAR

It has been stated that black Baptists and Northern white Baptists perceived education as a means of evangelizing, developing Christian character, and promoting material uplift. Both of these groups insisted on an education which yielded practical results both for the race collectively and for the individuals. E. R. Carter

asked in his book, *Biographical Sketches of Our Pulpit,* "Can the
Negro Attain What Other Races Have?" In the six pages of his
essay he gives the answer as Northern white and black Baptists
had done even in the days of slavery: "Yes, through the means of
Christianity and education." [20]

In the realm of sacred education, the Society believed from
the beginning that the evangelization and moral uplift of the race
must begin with educating the black preacher. Northern white
missionaries and other Baptists took note of the crucial role of the
black preacher as leader in the communities of the freed people.
Besides the family, the church was the only institution which slaves
could call their very own. Now that emancipation had come, that
was still the case. For the most part, black preachers, as the
traditional leaders and spokespersons of blacks, were the ones
occupying the most advantaged positions to assume leadership in
any social and political activities in the post-War South. It was
clear to the Society, as it is clear to American and Afro-American
historians today, that the newly emancipated placed their confidence
in the black preachers—in matters moral, political, social, and
economic.

This arrangement met with the hearty approbation of the Society. Its concern was with the maintenance of this leadership
role—at least in the realm of the ecclesiastical—lest the people
drift into immorality and vice.

> [If] we devote ourselves to educating the youth, neglecting the education
> of the preachers, we elevate the youth to an intellectual plane from which
> they shall look down upon the meagre attainments of their present religious
> teachers. The preachers uneducated will lose much of their religious influ-
> ence over the educated youth. The youth in shunning ignorance and su-
> perstitious religion will be led away to immorality and infidelity. . . .[21]

But the Society was also mindful of the need to train lay
leaders who also would venture among their people to labor.
Though ministerial education received premium attention and support during the very early days of the Society's activities in the
South, there were also substantial efforts made to educate Sunday
school and Bible teachers, deacons, teachers for the youth, and lay
missionaries.[22]

On the other hand, the ABHMS never attempted to provide

a purely "religious" or "industrial" type of curriculum for these students, whether lay or clergy. As early as 1869, C. H. Corey wrote the Society informing it of the type of learning taking place at the Richmond Institute. According to Corey, the students had received instruction in "reading, writing, arithmetic, spelling, geography, and English grammar," the basics. Students had studied portions of the Old and New Testaments and "composition and delivery of sermons as well as "Interpretation and Biblical Antiquities," the ministerial. But they had also been exposed to Latin, Greek, and readings in Caesar. The missionaries and teachers were striving to go beyond the barely essential and doctrinal and "to develop every manly quality."[23]

In later years the Society made more explicit commitments to lay and "secular" education (though it should be borne in mind that the development of Christian character was always a prime objective of all types of education). During the years 1880-1915 there was increasing pressure to channel blacks into curricula of "industrial" education, such as farming, carpentry, and sewing. The rationale, as brilliantly advanced by Booker T. Washington, the President of Tuskegee Institute, maintained that blacks should be equipped with skills they were most likely to employ in the Southern job market. Classical or liberal arts education was derided as a worthwhile undertaking for the masses of black people who would never have a need for Latin and Greek!

The basic position of the ABHMS was analogous to that of most black Baptists, North and South. It lauded the position, influence, and leadership of Washington. It recognized the value of industrial education. But the Society through its spokespersons refused to reduce the options of blacks to the industrial alone, and not excluding liberal arts or professional education. Blacks could be allowed to perform in the same educational labors as whites.

Only three years after Booker T. Washington's famous Atlanta Exposition Address urging blacks to acquiesce to the monopoly of white political rule, George Sale, the white President of Atlanta Baptist College (Morehouse) addressed the white Georgia State Teachers' Association on "The Education of the Negro." Sale disputed the notion that Southern whites were the best judges of the abilities of blacks. Daily, he maintained, blacks were accomplishing things that whites had theorized that they could not. Blacks were increasingly demonstrating that they could hold any and every occupation, regardless of the intellectual demands of that position:

> When you give the Negro what he sometimes calls a white man's chance, he can do what any other man can do, and can learn what any other man can learn, and there is no barrier in structure of the Negro's brain or in the faculties with which he is endowed in the way of the most advanced education.[24]

The Society as a whole could make these statements because much of the black leadership in the South, ecclesiastical and secular, were products of their schools. Albert W. Pegues, black Baptist biographer, Dean of Shaw University, attended Benedict College in South Carolina and graduated from the Richmond Institute in 1882 with honors before graduating as the only black person in 1886 from Bucknell University.[25] Calvin S. Brown after graduating as valedictorian from Shaw University in 1886, founded and served as president of Waters Normal Institute in eastern North Carolina; he edited such Baptist periodicals as the *Samaritan Journal, The Good Samaritan,* and the *Baptist Pilot;* later he assumed leadership of the Lott Carey Baptist Foreign Mission Society founded in 1897.[26]

One of the best examples of the dramatic influences of the ABHMS education on black religious leadership is Joseph Endom Jones. Jones was born a slave on October 15, 1850 in Lynchburg, Virginia. After joining the church in 1868 he attended Richmond Institute, from which he journeyed to Colgate University, graduating in 1876. An ordained minister, Jones served as an instructor in Richmond Theological Seminary. Active in denominational circles, he served as corresponding secretary of the Baptist Foreign Mission Convention (BFMC) (1880-1895), associate editor of the *Baptist Companion,* and the editor of the BFMC organ, *African Missions.*[27]

Furthermore, it should be recalled that black ministers trained by these schools served society in other capacities along with persons specifically trained for medicine, teaching, newspaper working, and politics.

But the ABHMS schools also sought to serve blacks in Africa as well as the United States. A deeply rooted theme in both black and white Christianity in America—born in the days of slavery—

was the notion that this system, though considered evil, was part of God's plan to convert and "civilize" the continent of Africa by means of Afro-Americans who had acquired these blessings of Christianity and western culture. There is evidence that though the Society had primary concern for the Christianization and advancement of blacks in the South, they understood their mission schools to encompass Africans as well. According to the 1871 minutes of the Society it is stated in reference to domestic mission work:

> This noble work, which blesses not only the South, but has in its contemplation the redemption of Africa also.[28]

Even if the Society had considered the parameters of its work limited to the domestic theater, black Baptists would have reminded them that the missionary enthusiasm for Africa, born in pre-Civil War years, still captivated the attention of many black Baptists. The Reverend L. A. Grimes, black ABHMS missionary, wrote of this interest as early as 1866. Writing from Virginia, he remarked:

> The colored men have Africa on their minds. They wish to evangelize that land, and we must get 400 missionaries out of the blacks of this country for Africa. In the name of my oppressed race, I ask for some definite organization to educate the young men just emancipated. . . .[29]

Indeed, black Baptists, especially in the vicinity of Richmond and other portions of Virginia, did hold Africa dear in their hearts. The Virginia Baptist State Convention adopted a constitution at its inaugural meeting in 1867 which set as its goal not only the evangelization of Virginia, but Africa.[30] The Consolidated American Baptist Missionary Convention through its Educational Association before 1869 also included Africa in the orbit of its concern to spread religious and secular education among its black siblings.[31] In 1875 the Consolidated Convention was bemoaning the fact that the zeal for African missions had declined from fifteen years previous! These Convention minutes reveal a reason on the part of black American Baptists to pursue African missions.

> Though of American birth and education, we are nevertheless sons of Africa. God has ordained it. He has written it on our faces, and on the tablets of our hearts, and no political changes, nor no social amalgamation, or rhetorical [verbiage] can blot it out. . . .[32]

The schools of the Society became primary training institutes for would-be African missionaries. It is not surprising in light of the above observation that the Richmond Institute prepared many of the earliest black Baptist missionaries: e.g., W. W. Colley, J. J. Coles, J. H. Presley. In the 1880's James O. Hayes and Lula C. Fleming would go to Africa from Shaw University in Raleigh, North Carolina.

The ABHMS institutions certainly attracted persons who were already persuaded to assume a field of labor in Africa. But in addition to the training provided these persons, the schools also undergirded that missionary concern or in some instances were the means through which that desire was implanted. Spelman College is but one example of the role which these institutions played in the lives of African missions. Nora Antonia Gordon, a native of Columbus, Georgia, initiated a great Spelman tradition in African missions. Converted at the college, she subsequently decided upon Africa as her field of labor, setting sail on March 16, 1889. Over the next eleven years three more Spelmanites followed her to the Motherland: Clara Howard, Ada Jackson Gordon, and, in 1900, Emma B. De Lany.[33]

De Lany reported in 1902 that her interest in African mission work started early in life upon hearing a returned missionary discuss his work. Upon conversion her desire increased, but it was not until her matriculation at Spelman that that "desire" was transformed into "duty." She journeyed first to southern Africa and then to Liberia, always keeping in touch with her Alma Mater whose faculty and students through their local African missions society provided her with substantial financial and material assistance while she remained on the field.[34]

Not only did the ABHMS schools provide a training ground for missionaries, but they also attracted and educated young African men and women. For example, at Spelman alone five African women had enrolled by 1900. The schools, thus, provided a meeting ground both theologically and physically for Afro-Americans and indigenous Africans.[35]

### THE ABHMS AND BLACK BAPTISTS: AN ASSESSMENT

Liberators? Paternalists? Essential racists? How do we, with the advantage of hindsight, assess the educational activities of the Society among Southern blacks? On one hand, we must render it a very high rating. The trials and difficulties of racial progress and black-white relations in this country often cloud the amazing feats accomplished by blacks in the 1865-1920 period. For example, in the ecclesiastical realm, it is astonishing to observe how men and women born in the utter depths of slavery rose to leadership positions in their churches, associations, conventions, and home and foreign mission activities. From a collective perspective, it is surprising to witness black Baptists organizing and effectively managing independent black regional conventions such as the Baptist Foreign Mission Convention and the National Baptist Convention within a mere fifteen to thirty years after the Civil War.

No small amount of credit must be given to the numerous missionaries and teachers who journeyed to the South during this very critical time in the history of black America. In reading the biographical sketches of these missionaries, the minutes of black and white Baptists groups, and the histories of these institutions, it would be difficult not to recognize the bravery, heroism, and persistence of these persons in the midst of deprivation, distrust, suspicion, and opposition. Because the Society had a concern for both the spiritual and material advancement of blacks, it acted in a hostile climate to provide the type of education which not only equipped religious leaders but secular leaders as well. Furthermore, despite the strong desire of Northern white Baptists to cooperate fully with their Southern counterparts and an increasing pressure from many quarters to limit their educational roles to the sphere of the "industrial," the Society never ceased to give its full endorsement to an education which prepared blacks for all kinds of occupations.

To be sure, we cannot judge the academic standards of these schools by the identical criteria that is in use today. But in their time and context, these institutions served their purpose well. This commitment to black higher education continued throughout the period under study. Even if the means were lacking, the will was present. In 1919 the Society still insisted on the need for education with a Christian character—something they believed that the Southern public schools were unable to provide. And, the dedication to *black* education was still strong.

The Northern Baptists have peculiar opportunities and obligations to the Negroes because in every state in the South there are far more colored Baptists than there are members of any other denomination. . . . This fact puts our denomination under special obligation and gives the denomination a remarkable opportunity for service.[36]

The words of the black Virginia Baptist State Convention in 1896 in reference to the Society accurately mirrors the reality of its contributions to black progress.

Immediately after the war representatives of the Society came into the various Southern states as angels of mercy. They endured the hardships and made for themselves and the emancipated slaves a place and they together became a new and potent factor in a new era.[37]

If we give high points to the Society for its establishment and support of black schools, we must, nevertheless, acknowledge a basic weakness in its management of these institutions and relationship with black Baptist leadership. Any missionary endeavor among another people, whether in domestic or foreign efforts, must pass through three stages of development. First, given the rather destitute conditions of the ex-slaves, there had to be a period in which the Society had the overwhelming management of mission affairs. Second, there should be a subsequent period in which the missionaries have a significant if not major input and direction, but where the missionized have taken a far greater, if not equal responsibility in administration of matters. Finally, there comes the period in which the formerly missionized assume complete authority in their affairs.

It would appear that the ABHMS never successfully passed beyond the stage of assuming near total control of the educational institutions. Known as the "cooperation controversy," the series of events that ensued had a chilling effect on both black-white relations and black Baptist unity.

Succinctly put, white Northern Baptists and some black Baptists maintained that the Society did not seek to stifle the independent yearnings of blacks but felt that at that point in history black Baptists were unable to assume independent leadership of the schools. They needed more time under the tutelage of whites. Some supporters of "cooperation," white and black, went even further and suggested or explicitly declared that for blacks to renounce the leadership of whites indicated an ingratitude for the sacrifices that had been made by the Society. The Reverend William M. Moss of Norfolk, Virginia in 1902 addressed the Lott Carey Convention on the subject of "Our Indebtedness":

> We are ungrateful and pay those who have been kind to us in words of harshness and unthankfulness. We are debtors to those who have built schools for us and helped us when we were unable to help ourselves. The summer, fall, winter and spring seek to pay their debts to God of nature. We should settle our debts in the spirit of cheerfulness to God. . . .[38]

The editor of the *African Expositor,* the official organ of Shaw University in Raleigh, North Carolina, reminded black Baptists of that state of the debt they owed the Society. He wondered if they would support the work of James O. Hayes, missionary to Liberia, or if they would "turn a deaf ear, forgetting that when in poverty and friendless that Northern friends came to their relief, and have spent tens of thousands of dollars in North Carolina to advance the cause of education and to build up the Kingdom of Christ."[39]

Perhaps much of the verbiage in the controversy was unnecessary rhetoric, but there were those who saw the movement by blacks to establish and support separate institutions as attempts to promote a "racial" Christianity. Since Christianity should foster interracial fellowship and since the doctrine of salvation was offered to all, then the cooperationists maintained that "cooperation" was the only acceptable alternative.[40]

Of course those blacks who espoused the separates or independent line denied all of these allegations. Beginning in the 1870's and 1880's these Baptists began to demand greater roles, even control of the institutions in their midst. Some blacks even contended that whites, because they were attempting to dominate religious policy, were actually enemies to black progress. In their opinion, the paternalism of whites would actually cause blacks to be dependent on them and thus prevent them from doing what every people should; assume control of their own destiny. Indeed, according to Wesley F. Graham of Richmond, the independent movement was actually a solid American tradition. Hence, blacks were not being ungrateful but merely responding as adults.[41]

The independents also denied that they were promulgating a racial Christianity. First, the control of black institutions did not imply that blacks eschewed genuine fellowship with white Christians. Secondly, the independents claimed that they were simply reacting to the exclusionary policies of Northern white Baptists.

It was at least in part this firm desire for independent control of black institutions which led to the formation of the American National Baptist Convention in 1886, the American Baptist Educational Convention in 1893, and the National Baptist Convention in 1895. But just as the independent line could aid in the unification of blacks, it also caused divisions in their ranks. In Virginia, the Virginia Baptist State Convention divided between those who supported the independent-oriented Virginia Seminary and College founded in 1890 and the splinter group, the Baptist General Association which supported the ABHMS-controlled Virginia Union University and the newly organized Lott Carey Convention, a splinter group from the NBC.

It is unfortunate that an enterprise started so nobly with great sacrifice and dedication met with such rancor and division. Perhaps things would have been much different if the officials of the ABHMS had realized in the late 1870's what George Sale observed in 1898: "The day of white leadership of the Negro is rapidly passing away . . . and if we will do anything for or with the Negro, we must do it through Negro men. . . ."[42]

On the other hand, the contributions of the Society to blacks in one of the periods of greatest needs and thereafter profoundly overshadow the "fallout" of the cooperationist controversy. And besides, the insistence of blacks for a greater control of their institutions ironically indicated the veracity of a proposition always advanced by the Society—that blacks had the will and native ability to match the accomplishments of any other people.

1. Albert W. Pegues, *Our Baptist Pulpit and Schools* (Springfield, Mass.: Wiley & Co., 1892) 28.
2. Robert G. Torbet, *A History of the Baptists* (3rd Edition, Valley Forge: Judson Press, 1973) 547.
3. Adolph H. Grundman, "Northern Baptists and the Founding of Virginia Union University: The Perils of Paternalism," *Journal of Negro History*, Volume 63, January 1978, p. 26.
4. *Ibid.*, 26-9.
5. See Pegues, *Pulpit*, 567-9, for a sketch of Virginia Union University.
6. *Ibid.*, 607-17 gives a description of Spelman College.
7. *Spelman Messenger*, Volume 18 (January 1902) p. 1.
8. For an account of the rise of independent black conventions, see James M. Washington, "The Origins and Emergence of Black Baptist Separatism, 1863-1897" (Unpublished Ph.D. dissertation, Yale University, 1979).
9. *Annual Minutes*, New England Baptist Missionary Convention, 1878, p. 17.

10. See Article II of the Constitution, *Annual Minutes,* Consolidated American Education Association, 1869, p. 7.
11. *Annual Minutes,* Consolidated American Baptist Convention, 1877, p. 31.
12. For accounts of the Southern Baptist Convention and its stance toward blacks in the postwar era, see John Lee Eighmy, *Churches in Cultural Captivity: A History of the Social Attitudes of Southern Baptists* (Knoxville: The University of Tennessee Press, 1972) 25-40; and Rufus B. Spain, *At Ease in Zion: Social History of Southern Baptists, 1865-1900* (Nashville: Vanderbilt University Press, 1967) especially 44-126.
13. Torbet, *Baptists,* pp. 371, 378-9; see also Sydney A. Ahlstrom, *A Religious History of the American People* (New Haven: Yale University Press, 1974) 720, including note number 10.
14. *Annual Minutes,* American Baptist Home Mission Society (ABHMS), 1873, p. 36.
15. *Annual Minutes,* Virginia Baptist State Convention (VBSC), 1882, p. 19.
16. *Annual Minutes,* ABHMS, 1863, pp. 32-33.
17. *Ibid.*
18. *Annual Minutes,* ABHMS, 1866, p. 17.
19. *Ibid.,* 16.
20. E. R. Carter, Writer and Collater, *Biographical Sketches of Our Pulpit* (Chicago: Afro-AM Press, 1969; Reprint of 1888 edition) 80-85.
21. *Annual Minutes,* ABHMS, 1866, pp. 17-18.
22. *Annual Minutes,* ABHMS, 1867, pp. 17-18.
23. *Annual Minutes,* ABHMS, 1869, pp. 39-40.
24. *The Advance,* Volume 7, November 1898, p. 2.
25. See introduction of Pegues, *Pulpit,* by C. L. Purce, 8-15.
26. *Ibid.,* 95-98, for a biographical sketch of Brown.
27. *Ibid.,* 299-304; sketch of Jones.
28. *Annual Minutes,* ABHMS, 1871, p. 23.
29. *Annual Minutes,* ABHMS, 1866, p. 34.
30. *Annual Minutes,* VBSC, 1878, P. 4.
31. *Annual Minutes,* Consolidated American Education Association. 1869, p. 7.
32. *Annual Minutes,* Consolidated American Baptist Missionary Convention, 1877, p. 31.
33. *Spelman Messenger,* Volume 36 (November 1919) 2-3.
34. *Spelman Messenger,* Volume 18 (February 1902) 5.
35. *Ibid.,* 3.
36. *Annual Minutes,* ABHMS, 1919, p. 71.
37. *Annual Minutes,* VBSC, 1896, p. 15.
38. *Annual Minutes,* Lott Carey Baptist Foreign Mission Convention, 1902, p. 9.
39. *African Expositor,* Volume 11, January 1888, p. 4.
40. See Edward M. Brawley, "The Duty of Colored Baptists in View of the Past, the Present, and the Future,": in his edited work, *The Negro Baptist Pulpit: A Collection of Sermons and Paper on Baptist Doctrine and Missionary and Educational Work by Colored Baptist Minister* (Philadelphia: American Baptist Publication Society, 1890) 287-300.
41. See James T. Tyms, *The Rise of Religious Education Among Negro Baptists* (New York Exposition Press, 1965) 150-53; and Grundman, "Northern Baptists . . . ," 27, 35.
42. *The Advance,* Volume 7 (November 1898) 2.

# White Liberals and Black Power in Negro Education, 1865-1915

JAMES M. MCPHERSON

ALTHOUGH the phrase "black power" is of recent origin and has acquired ambivalent and emotional overtones, the issue is in some respects not new. Reduced to its lowest common denominator, the concept of black power means greater control by Negroes themselves of the major institutions and processes that shape their lives. During the two generations after the Civil War there were many disputes over control of the freedmen's schools and colleges founded and supported by Northern abolitionists, missionaries, and other "white liberals" interested in advancing the Negro's status and improving race relations through education. Many Negroes desired a larger role in managing these schools; their demands produced clashes that foreshadowed some current racial controversies in the field of education. The earlier black-power drive did not aim toward a restructuring of the methods, content, or purposes of education; Negroes desired not to change the system but to achieve greater participation in it as teachers, deans, presidents, and trustees.[1] While retaining considerable control over the schools they had founded, white liberal educators three-quarters of a century ago began gradually to yield most faculty and administrative posts to blacks. This article will try to describe and evaluate that transition.

The freedmen's aid societies of Northern Protestant churches established more than a hundred institutions of college and secondary education for Negroes after the Civil War[2] (see table following text). The foremost of these societies was the American Missionary Association (AMA), organized in 1846 by abolitionists protesting the lack of antislavery zeal in existing Congregational mission societies. In 1861 the AMA committed most of its resources to freedmen's education; the Northern branches of the Methodist, Baptist, and Presbyterian churches soon joined the effort by setting up freedmen's aid societies or adding a freedmen's department to an established home mission body. The schools founded

▶ An associate professor of history at Princeton University, Mr. McPherson's major interest is black history and race relations in the United States, 1820–1920. Mr. McPherson received the doctorate in 1963 from The Johns Hopkins University, where he was a student of C. Vann Woodward, and he is the author of The Struggle for Equality: Abolitionists and the Negro in the Civil War and Reconstruction (Princeton, 1964). The author wishes to thank the National Endowment for the Humanities, the John Simon Guggenheim Foundation, and the Princeton University Research Fund for grants that made possible part of the research for this article.

[1] The major curricular debate in Negro education three-quarters of a century ago concerned the relative merits of academic versus industrial education. This issue was unrelated to the "black-power" controversy treated in this article.

[2] A few of these schools were originally founded by the freedmen themselves but were soon adopted, at the request of Negroes, by Northern mission societies.

by these churches (plus a few supported by Quakers and minor sects) provided nearly all the college education and most of the high school training for Southern Negroes until well into the twentieth century. This was the "finest thing in American history, and one of the few things untainted by sordid greed and cheap vainglory," wrote W. E. B. Du Bois, a graduate of the AMA's Fisk University.

The teachers in these institutions came not to keep the Negroes in their place, but to raise them out of the defilement of the places where slavery had wallowed them. The Colleges . . . were social settlements; homes where the best of the sons of the freedmen came in close and sympathetic touch with the best traditions of New England.[3]

But all was not well in this educational Zion. Some Negroes resented the patronizing attitude often expressed in the missionary rationale for freedmen's education. "The colored people are yet children, and need to be taught every thing," proclaimed the secretary of the Methodist Freedmen's Aid Society in 1874. "They need that those more favored should take them by the hand and lead them . . . up from debasement and misery into purity and joy." Frederick Douglass was angered by such statements. "We have been injured more than we have been helped by men who have professed to be our friends," he told a black audience in 1875. "We must stop these men from begging for us. . . . We must stop begging ourselves. If we build churches don't ask white people to pay for them. If we have banks, colleges and papers, do not ask other people to support them. Be independent. . . . I am here to-day to offer and sign a declaration of independence for the colored people of these United States."[4]

Though Douglass soon receded from this rhetorical venture into separatism, some Negro leaders turned increasingly to the concept of independent, black-owned institutions as the overthrow of Reconstruction and the onset of reaction blocked access to power and achievement in white American society. "There is not as bright and glorious a future before a Negro in a white institution as there is for him in his own," E. K. Love told the National Baptist Convention (the body representing black Baptist churches) in 1896.

We can better marshal our forces and develop our people in enterprises manned by us. We can more thoroughly fill our people with race pride . . . by presenting to them

---

[3] W. E. B. Du Bois, *The Souls of Black Folk* (New York, 1903), 100. In the 1920's Du Bois became critical of white teachers and administrators at some Negro colleges, including his alma mater. In 1924 he accused Fisk of humiliating students and curbing their aspirations by authoritarian restrictions; he demanded the hiring of more black faculty and the installation of black presidents at colleges still headed by whites. Francis L. Broderick, *W. E. B. DuBois: Negro Leader in a Time of Crisis* (Stanford, 1959), 163–64. But when Du Bois published his autobiography in 1940, he recalled with fondness and gratitude his own student days at Fisk (1885–88, when all faculty members but one were white): "The three years at Fisk were years of growth and development. . . . My personal contact with my teachers was inspiring and beneficial. . . . I knew the President, Erastus Cravath, to be honest and sincere." Du Bois, *Dusk of Dawn: An Essay Toward an Autobiography of a Race Concept* (New York, 1940), 30–31. Du Bois reiterated this praise of Fisk in the later version of his autobiography, written near the end of his long life. *Du Bois, The Autobiography of W. E. B. Du Bois,* ed. Herbert Aptheker (New York, 1968), 112–13.

[4] *Seventh Annual Report of the Freedmen's Aid Society of the Methodist Episcopal Church* (Cincinnati, 1874), 8–9; Douglass quoted by New York *Tribune,* July 7, 1875, and *Weekly Louisianian,* July 17, 1875.

for their support enterprises that are wholly ours. . . . The world recognizes men for the power they have to affect it. . . . Negro brain should shape and control Negro thought.[5]

This impulse toward self-help and race pride did lead to the founding by the AME (African Methodist Episcopal) and AME Zion churches of several colleges supported and controlled entirely by Negroes.[6] But the black community lacked the financial resources to sustain major projects, and most of these schools were poor in quality and starved for funds. The colored A & M colleges established by Southern states to provide Negroes with their share of the appropriations from the Morrill Land-Grant Act afforded another quasi-separatist outlet for black ambitions. In 1870 a district secretary of the AMA reported that some Negroes in Mississippi, dissatisfied with white control of Tougaloo College, were pressing the state legislature for the creation of a college "of *their own*" where nobody "but themselves run their machine."[7] The legislature established Alcorn College the next year. Similar pressures were brought to bear in other states. At the South Carolina constitutional convention in 1895, black delegates urged the withdrawal of the state appropriation from Claflin University (controlled by Northern Methodists) and the creation of a school for blacks in which the "professors and instructors shall be of the negro race." Benjamin Tillman supported the proposal for a separate Negro college, and at his behest the convention authorized the establishment of the Colored Normal, Industrial, Agricultural and Mechanical College of South Carolina. By the end of the century every Southern state supported some kind of institution of higher education for Negroes. Most presidents of these schools and all but a handful of teachers were Negroes, presenting a facade of black control.[8] The reality of black power in such institutions was dubious, however, since their faculties and administrations were beholden to state legislatures. All the state Negro colleges in this period were woefully under-financed and devoid of genuine college-level offerings. The major institutions of higher education for Negroes were and are those founded by Northern missionaries. The struggle for black power and against white paternalism in education, therefore, took place primarily within the schools established and supported largely by Northern whites, not outside them.

As the Negro colleges began turning out graduates who were denied positions of authority and influence in a Jim Crow society, the schools themselves

[5] Lewis G. Jordan, *Negro Baptist History, U.S.A., 1750–1930* (Nashville, 1930), 124.

[6] The AME colleges were Wilberforce University (Wilberforce, Ohio); Morris Brown College (Atlanta); Allen University (Columbia, S. C.); and Paul Quinn College (Waco, Texas). The AME Zion school was Livingstone College (Salisbury, N. C.). Wilberforce had been founded by Northern white Methodists in 1856; it was sold to the AME Church in 1863. The AME and AME Zion churches also established elementary and secondary schools.

[7] Edward P. Smith to Oliver O. Howard, Apr. 2, 1870, AMA Archives, Fisk University Library.

[8] George B. Tindall, *South Carolina Negroes, 1877–1900* (Columbia, S. C., 1952), 229–30; *Journal of the Constitutional Convention of the State of South Carolina* (Columbia, S. C., 1895), 580–81; Clarence A. Bacote, "The Story of Atlanta University: A Century of Service, 1865–1965," unpublished manuscript generously lent by the author, 128–30; Earl Edgar Dawson, "The Negro Teacher in the South," unpublished M.A. thesis, University of Iowa, 1931, pp. 74–75.

became the focus of black ambitions. Despite their professed and, in most cases, sincere belief in racial equality, white missionaries yielded only gradually and sometimes reluctantly to black demands for greater control of schools. There were both subjective and objective reasons for this gradualism. Subjectively, some missionaries shared (perhaps subconsciously) the widespread conviction that black people were deficient in organizational and executive skills. They were especially hesitant to entrust Negroes with outright control of funds contributed by Northern philanthropy. Moreover, many teachers were slow to believe that the "grown-up children" for whom the schools were founded had matured to the point of readiness for adult responsibilities. Objectively, the first and even second generations of freedmen could not produce enough able teachers to staff the schools with personnel equal in average ability and training to Northern teachers, who came from middle-class, New England-oriented backgrounds that stressed education and achievement. A genuine concern for maintaining the highest possible standards for freedmen's schools was a major reason for the slowness to supplant white teachers and administrators with blacks. Indeed, two contemporary experts on education thought that some mission societies yielded too readily to demands for black power and that the quality of many schools suffered as a result.[9] Black communities served by mission schools were themselves frequently divided on the question; many Negroes, especially parents of students, considered white teachers superior to black instructors and were opposed to the drive for black control of schools. The interplay of these various attitudes produced smoldering tensions in several schools.

The issue first surfaced on the question of hiring black teachers. From 1865 to 1870 the freedmen's aid societies operated several hundred elementary schools with support from the Freedmen's Bureau. Perhaps one-fourth of the teachers in these schools were black. But when the Bureau's educational work ceased in 1870, most of the common schools were absorbed into the South's new public school system and the mission societies began to concentrate their resources on a smaller number of secondary schools and colleges. At first nearly all the teachers in these higher schools were white, even though the societies often did try to employ black teachers when they were qualified. The American Missionary Association's Avery Institute in Charleston, for example, had an interracial faculty headed by a black principal in the 1860's. The trustees of Howard University made an effort to recruit black professors, and four Negroes were on the staff in the early 1870's. The Methodist Freedmen's Aid Society stated in 1878 that "as rapidly as we have been able to prepare our own students, we have introduced them . . . as teachers in our schools."[10]

[9] Amory D. Mayo, "The Work of Certain Northern Churches in the Education of the Freedmen, 1861–1900," in *Report of the U.S. Commissioner of Education for the Year 1901–02* (Washington, 1903), I, 312; *Negro Education: A Study of the Private and Higher Schools for Colored People in the United States*, ed. Thomas Jesse Jones (Washington, 1917), *passim*.

[10] South Carolina file, 1865–68, AMA Archives; William J. Wilson to George Whipple, Aug. 13, 1869, AMA Archives; Walter Dyson, *Howard University: The Capstone of Negro Education* (Wash-

But by 1880 there was still only a handful of black teachers in the better missionary schools, a sore point in several Negro communities. A black minister in an AMA church at Mobile reported disaffection among his flock because the Association's school had no Negro teachers. "This is the great reason for all the prejudice that exists," he wrote. "The employment of a colored teacher would increase the influence of the school and the church" and "shut the mouths of those who are murmuring." A Negro educator in Virginia wrote a paper in 1876 entitled "Colored Teachers for Colored Schools," which sharply criticized Hampton Institute for its shortage of black instructors. The paper was endorsed by the Virginia Educational and Historical Association, a Negro organization. A black lawyer in South Carolina went the whole way in 1883 and demanded that "Negro teachers exclusively be employed to teach Negro schools."[11]

This drive for more black faculty met a mixed response from white philanthropists. Some urged a crash program to recruit and train Negro teachers. The secretary of the Baptist Home Mission Society wrote to the president of Richmond Institute: "You do not know how resolutely colored leaders have pressed us to employ and pay colored teachers. . . . I pray you take your strongest and ablest students . . . and drill them, and *drill* them, and DRILL them privately" until they are competent to join the faculty. This policy was carried out, and when Richmond Institute became Virginia Union University in 1899, half the faculty was black. The white principal of the AMA's Storrs School in Atlanta advised the Association's secretary to yield to black pressure: "It will be well for them to try to manage the school for they will never be satisfied until they do," she wrote, and if the board "is wise in its selection of teachers I think they will do well. Certainly we are not the ones to oppose them, for it is for this work that we have been educating them. I only condemn the ungrateful spirit exhibited by many."[12]

Other white administrators counseled a cautious policy in hiring black teachers on the ground that few Negroes were yet qualified. Laura Towne, founder of Penn School on St. Helena Island in South Carolina, wrote in 1873 that schools taught by Negroes on the sea islands "are always in confusion, grief, & utter want of everything. It is hard to imagine schools doing so little good." Miss Towne kept white teachers at Penn School until their black replacements were thoroughly trained. The president of Straight University (a forerunner of Dillard) in New Orleans urged the AMA not to employ black teachers in the law and theological departments just because of "this clamor for colored teach-

ington, 1941), 348, 371; *Eleventh Annual Report of the Freedmen's Aid Society of the Methodist Episcopal Church* (Cincinnati, 1878), 19-20.

[11] William H. Ash to Michael E. Strieby, Feb. 26, Mar. 13, 1878, AMA Archives; *People's Advocate*, Aug. 26, 1876; Augustus Straker, in New York *Globe*, Oct. 13, 1883.

[12] James B. Simmons to Charles H. Corey, Dec. 27, 1872, in Charles H. Corey, *A History of the Richmond Theological Seminary, with Reminiscences of Thirty Years' Work among the Colored People of the South* (Richmond, 1895), 97-98, 173-79; Amy Williams to Mrs. Thomas Chase, quoted in Thomas Chase to Michael E. Strieby, Mar. 19, 1878, AMA Archives.

ers. . . . We can't have any humbug about this department for the sake of color.
. . . Colored teachers are not generally successful."[13]

Some black leaders discounted the argument that educational quality would
suffer if Negro teachers were employed too soon; they insisted that Anglo-
Saxon academic standards should not be the only criteria for hiring teachers.
Francis Grimké declared in 1885 that the development of race pride should be a
major objective of Negro education. The low self-image with which the black man
had emerged from slavery was perpetuated by schools with white faculties,
Grimké complained. "The intellects of our young people are being educated at
the expense of their manhood. In the classroom they see only white professors,"
which leads them "to associate these places and the idea of fitness for them only
with white men." In their slowness to appoint black professors, the schools "are
failing to use one of the most effective means in their power, of helping on this
race." J. Willis Menard, who had been the first Negro elected to Congress, asserted in 1885 that while many white teachers were sincere and dedicated, others
were selfish hypocrites, and in any case, no white teacher could achieve the
rapport and empathy with black students that a Negro teacher could. "We demand educated colored teachers for colored schools," wrote Menard, "because their color identity makes them more interested in the advancement of
colored children than white teachers, and because colored pupils need the social
*contact* of colored teachers."[14]

But Negroes were not united behind this viewpoint. A black woman, herself
a teacher, condemned as a "peculiar error" the argument that Negroes should be
given jobs "without due regard to their fitness." She did not want "the standard
of excellence lowered for us. To admit the necessity is to insult the Negro. Our
youth have the right to the best possible training, and we should not allow a mistaken race pride to cause us to impose upon them inferior teachers." A Negro in
Atlanta pleaded with the AMA to retain control of Storrs School "with the understanding that we have Northern teachers." The school inspector for the AMA
reported in 1878 that blacks in Atlanta "have again, as last year, arrayed themselves on both sides of the question and each party has petitioned . . . one for colored teachers & the other for Northern whites." There was "no doubt," the inspector stated, that in most cities where the AMA maintained schools the "parents prefer
to send their children to Northern white teachers instead of colored." In a few
cases after the mission societies had turned their schools over to Negro teachers,
the deterioration in quality prompted black leaders to ask for the return of whites.
"Since the cessation of your work among us," wrote one Negro to a white

[13] Laura Towne to William C. Gannett, Feb. 9, Dec. 14, 1873, William C. Gannett Papers, Rochester University Library; James A. Adams to Erastus M. Cravath, Nov. 17, 1874, Jan. 11, 1875, AMA
Archives.
[14] Francis Grimké, "Colored Men as Professors in Colored Institutions," *A.M.E. Church Review*,
II (Oct. 1885), 142–44; Florida *News*, Dec. 5, 1885, clipping in the American Baptist Home Mission
Society (hereafter ABHMS) Archives, American Baptist Historical Society, Rochester-Colgate Theological Seminary. Menard was editor of Florida *News*.

educator, "the schools have degenerated, and the system as operated here is a mere farce."[15]

Because of divided opinion among both races on the issue of black teachers, the AMA decided at a conference in 1877 to "make haste slowly in this regard." In subsequent years the AMA emphasized "slowly" more than "haste." As late as 1895 only twelve of 141 teachers in the Association's seventeen secondary schools were blacks; only four of 110 faculty members in its five colleges were Negroes. A black journalist stated in 1901 that the AMA's small percentage of Negro teachers had long been an "eyesore" to the race, and that "only the splendid work of the association has kept down an agitation of this matter."[16]

It was not only the high quality of AMA schools but also the tiny black constituency of the Congregational Church that minimized Negro criticism of the Association. The Baptist and Methodist societies, on the other hand, were under greater pressure from the large black memberships of their denominations. By the mid-1890's approximately half the teachers in the schools of these societies were black. The Presbyterians and most of the small denominations also moved faster than the AMA in the appointment of Negro teachers. In 1895 there were ninety-four schools for Negroes of nominal high school or college grade in the South established by the abolitionist-missionary impulse and largely supported by Northern Protestants. In the ninety institutions for which statistics are available there were 1,046 teachers, of whom 370 (thirty-six per cent) were black.[17]

Viewed in one way, this represented significant progress. A race barely one generation away from slavery and illiteracy had advanced to the point of supplying more than one-third of the teachers for the higher schools founded or supported mainly by the missionary efforts of another race. Yet progress was less impressive than it appeared on the surface. Most students in the ninety-four schools, including the "universities," were in elementary grades, and at least ninety per cent of the black faculty were teaching these grades rather than secondary or college classes. Even in schools with a sizable Negro faculty, major policy decisions were normally made by whites. Power flowed from the purse; Northern whites contributed most of the money, and Northern whites occupied the major

[15] Josephine Turpin, "Teaching as a Profession," *A.M.E. Church Review*, V (Oct. 1888), 108; Junius Alexander to Michael E. Strieby, July 7, 1878, AMA Archives; Thomas N. Chase to Michael E. Strieby, July 5, 1878, Nov. 26, 1877, AMA Archives; Henry L. Shrewsbury to Ednah D. Cheney, Feb. 19, 1886, Ednah D. Cheney Papers, Boston Public Library.

[16] Thomas N. Chase to Michael E. Strieby, Nov. 26, 1877, AMA Archives; Cleveland *Gazette*, Jan. 19, 1901. The AMA required higher qualifications for its teachers than the other mission societies, which was one reason for its relatively small number of black teachers and for the superior reputation of its schools. Many of the students in AMA schools were Baptists or Methodists who had left the schools of their own denominations for the better education offered in AMA institutions.

[17] In 1894–95 there were twenty-nine colleges and professional schools and sixty-five secondary schools. For details, see table. Bennett College was not ranked as a college-level institution in 1894–95, which places the percentage of black faculty in Methodist colleges lower than indicated in the table. The missionary societies maintained many elementary schools in the South not included in these statistics. The statistics also do not include schools supported by the Roman Catholic and Protestant Episcopal churches, nearly all of which were parochial elementary schools sustained by local parishes or dioceses in the South rather than by Northern mission societies. Nor do the figures include independent institutions like Tuskegee, which were founded and conducted by Negroes, even though they received most of their support from the North.

administrative posts of the mission societies and colleges. Although Negroes were represented on the local boards of trustees of most schools and colleges, these boards usually had little power; ultimate control rested with the mission societies. Most Negroes who benefited from these schools accepted the fact that the greater administrative experience and financial resources of white philanthropists made a large degree of white control inevitable, at least for a time. Some felt differently. Virtually from 1870 on a black minority struggled behind the scenes for greater influence in the management of some schools.

Occasionally these conflicts broke into the open, as in the search for a successor to General Oliver O. Howard as president of Howard University in 1874–75. Black trustees and students supported John Mercer Langston, dean of the law school and vice-president of the university, for the job. But the white Congregationalists (most of them members of the AMA) who had founded the institution and dominated its board of trustees felt that Langston, despite his Oberlin degree and eminence as a black leader, lacked talent as a fund raiser and "was not the man to hold the institution to the religious and moral ideas on which it was founded."[18] The board offered the presidency to three white men in succession; two of them declined and the other died before he could fully assume office. Embittered by what he considered the paternalism, prejudice, and religious narrowness of white trustees, Langston resigned from the university and denounced the AMA, which "relieve[s] the object of their sympathy of the pressure of responsibility and the honor due its efficient discharge, and thus weaken[s] him, as an over-affectionate and indulgent father does his son." The black man, concluded Langston, "seeks release from such associations and their self-assumed control of his affairs." In an editorial reply that unwittingly conceded the partial truth of Langston's charges, the AMA's monthly magazine declared that some friends of Negro education might be tempted to say, "If this is all the thanks we get, we will waste no more on such a people." But "we intend to go on with our efforts for the colored race. . . . With the abolitionists we endured persecution for the slave, and, now that he is free, we shall toil for his elevation and happiness, as undeterred by his fault-finding as we formerly were by the opposition of his foes."[19]

While the trustees were agonizing over the selection of a president, Howard University, which had been in serious financial straits since the cessation of Freed-

---

[18] *The Congregationalist*, XXVII (July 1, 1875), 204. See also Edward P. Smith to Oliver O. Howard, Nov. 23, 1874, Apr. 13, June 9, July 16, Nov. 5, Dec. 1, 20, 1875, Jan. 14, 1876, Oliver O. Howard Papers, Bowdoin College Library; Rayford W. Logan, *Howard University: The First Hundred Years, 1867–1967* (New York, 1969), 59–62, 71–76.

[19] Logan, *Howard University*, 77–79; Dyson, *Howard University*, 58–59; John Mercer Langston, *Emancipation and Citizenship. The Work of the Republican Party, Address at Chillicothe, Ohio* (Washington, 1875), 7–8; *American Missionary*, XIX (Sept. 1875), 197–98. Though the AMA did not control Howard University, it played an important role in the school's affairs. Howard was an independent institution governed by its own board of trustees, but all presidents until 1903 were Congregational ministers (except General Howard, 1869–74, who was an active layman in the church), and the Association at various times provided financial support to the normal and theological departments of the university and paid part of the president's salary.

men's Bureau support and the panic of 1873, was on the verge of collapse. Believing that only a white man of prominence and administrative experience
could tap the springs of Northern philanthropy and save the school, black and
white trustees finally joined to elect William W. Patton president of Howard in
1877. Patton was a Congregational minister, a veteran abolitionist, and former
district secretary of the AMA. He was a good administrator, but his relations
with the black community were strained. He raised money in the North, persuaded Congress to make annual appropriations for the school, brought the university from the brink of disaster, and built it into a major institution. But Patton ran Howard with a strong and sometimes domineering hand. Some black
trustees and alumni disliked his "overbearing ways," and there were periodic
demands for his resignation. The *People's Advocate*, a Negro newspaper in
Washington, declared in 1883 that "there are very few *white* men who possess the
qualifications of a president of a college where *colored* men principally are educated," and concluded that Patton was not one of the few.[20]

Negro criticism of Patton intensified in 1885 when the president forced
through the appointment of a white professor of Greek instead of a black candidate whom Negroes on the board of trustees thought was at least as well qualified as the white man. Francis Grimké, a member of the board, published an
angry article blasting Patton as a "hypocrite" and a "pseudo-friend" of the black
man. "If this is philanthropy," declared Grimké, "then I, for one, think we have
had quite enough of it. If this is the treatment we are to continue to receive from
our friends, then it is time for us to begin to pray to be delivered from our
friends."[21]

Regarded by many Negroes as their national university, Howard continued to
be a center of controversy. When Patton retired in 1889 black trustees wanted
Jeremiah E. Rankin as his successor. A white man, Rankin was a former abolitionist and pastor of the integrated First Congregational Church in Washington
who had won the unanimous respect of the Negro community. Frederick Douglass believed that Rankin had "done more to secure the rights of my race than all
the legislation of Congress." Black leaders were pleased when Rankin was elected
to the post; Richard Greener considered Rankin "the grandest type of man ever
connected with the Institution." But faculty politics, rumor, and Rankin's own

[20] District of Columbia file, 1874–78, AMA Archives; *Advance*, X (May 3, 1877), 9; Logan,
*Howard University*, 83; Dyson, *Howard University*, 301–06, 386–88; *People's Advocate*, June 9, 1883;
for the reference to Patton's "overbearing ways," see Jeremiah E. Rankin to Oliver O. Howard, Oct.
15, 1889, Howard Papers.

[21] Grimké, "Colored Men as Professors in Colored Institutions," 147–48. Negroes who criticized
Patton on this matter may have had a good case. The black candidate for the professorship was William S. Scarborough, the author of a Greek textbook and the possessor of a modest reputation as a
classical scholar. Scarborough later became president of Wilberforce University. The white man who
won the professorship was Carlos Kenaston, a relatively obscure member of the Ripon College faculty
who happened to be the son-in-law of James H. Fairchild, president of Oberlin College and a friend
of Patton. A major factor in Scarborough's failure to get the job was a letter of recommendation from
Fairchild that damned him with faint praise. Carlos Kenaston to James H. Fairchild, Mar. 19, 27,
1885, J. B. Johnson to Kenaston, June 6, 1885, James H. Fairchild Papers, Oberlin College Library;
Francis Grimké to William S. Scarborough, June 16, 1885, Scarborough Papers, Wilberforce University Library.

mistakes in judgment dissipated much of this good will and provoked a verbal attack on the president by black leaders, particularly Calvin Chase of the Washington *Bee*. Even though Rankin tripled the number of black teachers during his administration (1890–1903), Negroes were angry when he appointed his own daughter and several other whites to staff positions sought by Negroes. The president's alleged vendetta against a black professor stirred up a storm, and Calvin Chase asked angrily, "What claim has Dr. Rankin to the presidency of that institution? Is it not set apart for colored people?" But when Rankin retired in 1903 the *Bee* apologized for earlier attacks based on misinformation and praised the retiring president for having "done more . . . for the negro" than any other man in the country. "You have been a faithful public servant," Chase told Rankin, "and to you the negroes owe a debt of gratitude."[22]

By the first decade of the twentieth century several black deans at Howard had carved out spheres of power within their colleges or departments. Rankin's successor as president, a white Presbyterian minister named John Gordon, moved to restrict the growing autonomy of the Teachers College under Dean Lewis B. Moore and the "Commercial Department" under Dean George W. Cook. The *Bee* supported Gordon because of its editor's declared conviction that inefficiency and intrigue in these departments had grown to scandalous proportions (Chase's role in this affair may also have been related to feuds among Washington's Negro leaders). The attempt to reform the departments led to a bitter power struggle that, though not specifically racial in origin, took on racial overtones as it became a showdown between a white president and two black deans. Moore and Cook rallied many students behind them, but the *Bee* continued to back Gordon and charged that "personal pique . . . selfishness, cupidity and ambition" motivated the deans' recalcitrance. When a hundred students demonstrated against Gordon and called for his resignation, the *Bee* urged the expulsion of the students and the firing of the "teachers who encouraged or inaugurated that disgraceful scene." Also supporting the white president, another black newspaper declared that "a negro mob in college looks, to the *Independent*, just like a white mob around a stake burning a negro. . . . Colleges were never intended to create and organize mobs. They were instituted for the purpose of disseminating Christian education."[23]

Instead of expelling the students, the shaken and exhausted president submitted his own resignation. A battle for succession shaped up amid demands that a Negro be appointed to the position. In a reversal of his stand a decade earlier, Calvin Chase of the *Bee* ridiculed the intrigues among black aspirants for the presidency. Alluding to alleged power struggles, backstabbing, and cor-

[22] Washington *Bee*, Jan. 4, 1890, Sept. 7, 1895, July 3, 1897, Jan. 13, 1900, Feb. 28, 1903; Richard T. Greener to Francis J. Grimké, Dec. 27, 1890, in *The Works of Francis James Grimké*, ed. Carter G. Woodson (Washington, 1942), IV, 25. Greener, a prominent Washington Negro, was former dean of the Howard Law School. For the support of Rankin by black leaders, see J. M. Gregory to Oliver O. Howard, June 8, 1889, L. Deane to Howard, July 2, 5, 1889, Rankin to Howard, Oct. 15, 1889, Howard Papers.
[23] Dyson, *Howard University*, 64–65; Washington *Bee*, Nov. 18, 25, Dec. 9, 16, 30, 1905, Jan. 27, 1906; Atlanta *Independent*, quoted in Washington *Bee*, Feb. 10, 1906.

ruption in the Negro public schools of Washington under a black superin-tendent, Chase predicted that a similar situation would prevail at Howard under a Negro president. To the advocates of a "colored president for a colored school," the *Bee* stated: "If the existence of Howard University depended upon the col-ored people, the institution could not exist a day. . . . White men have done far more to ameliorate the condition of the negro, and to elevate him in the social scale than negroes themselves have ever done."[24]

After several months of discussion, the Howard board of trustees unanimously elected as president Wilbur P. Thirkield, a white Methodist minister and former secretary of the Methodist Freedmen's Aid Society. An able and sensitive ad-ministrator, Thirkield retained the confidence of all parties. But when he was elected a bishop of the Methodist Episcopal Church in 1912, an "unholy scram-ble"[25] for his job took place between Moore, Cook, and Kelly Miller. (Miller had been dean of the College of Arts and Sciences since 1907.) Each faction of the black community, including the *Bee* (which favored Miller), backed one of the deans. Surprisingly, only two of the eight Negro trustees supported any of the black candidates, while a majority of white trustees desired the election of a Negro president. If any two of the three deans had withdrawn from the con-test in favor of the third, a black man would have ·been elected president of Howard in 1912. Since each of them preferred a white man to one of his rivals for the presidency, a white president was finally elected.[26] Though two-thirds of the faculty was black by this time, another fourteen years passed before Howard had a Negro president.

Events at Howard received wide publicity in the Negro press, but the black-power struggle in Methodist and Baptist institutions was in some respects even more intense. Black militancy reached high tide in these two churches between 1880 and 1900, as the frustration born of the failure of Reconstruction and the intensification of Jim Crow produced compensatory strivings toward self-help, race pride, and separatism among Negroes and focused these strivings on two of the institutions in American society that offered some access to power, the school and the church. Since more than ninety per cent of Negro church mem-bers were Baptists or Methodists, the schools of these denominations became major arenas of conflict.

The Methodist Episcopal Church (Northern branch of the denomination) moved aggressively into the South after the war and recruited a black member-ship of nearly a quarter of a million by 1890. Under the leadership of Methodist abolitionists, the church established a Freedmen's Aid Society that by 1890 was maintaining twenty-two schools for freedmen, ten of them nominally colleges or professional schools. These institutions had interracial boards of trustees, and a few of the boards had a *de facto* black majority because some Northern

---

[24] Washington *Bee*, Dec. 30, 1905, Jan. 27, 1906.
[25] *Ibid.*, June 1, 1912.
[26] Dyson, *Howard University*, 65, 375; Washington *Bee*, June 8, 15, 22, July 6, 13, Aug. 3, 1912.

trustees rarely attended meetings. Since real control was exercised by the Freedmen's Aid Society and white college presidents, however, tension mounted until it broke into the open after the Society overruled the trustees of Claflin University and Atlanta's Clark University in matters concerning Negro professors in 1890.

The white presidents of both schools were unpopular with a part of the black community, a situation that added fuel to the controversy. The president of Claflin, exasperated by Negro criticism, said privately: "I do not suppose that it is wrong for them to aspire to teach their own schools and manage their own concerns, but unfortunately for them not one in 1,000 has enough executive ability to manage the concerns of his own household successfully. It is not really their fault, as they have had but little experience in independent management." The president feared that "an effort will be made to tear up things at our next trustee meeting. But they must not be allowed to have their own way in this matter. Until they furnish a considerable proportion of the funds necessary to conduct the school, they should be content to allow others to manage it." When a refractory black professor was fired from Clark University in 1890, a local Negro leader deplored this "attempt to crush down negro manhood" and denounced the president of Clark as a "cheap and incompetent" man who had come to Atlanta "to boss southern negroes."[27]

Black militants urged their fellow Methodists to leave the Northern church and join the AME or AME Zion denominations. While the school controversy plus the unwillingness of the Northern church to elect a Negro bishop caused a small exodus to the black denominations, most Negro members of the Northern church rejected separatism. "The M.E. Church is doing more for the moral, educational, and religious elevation of the colored people," wrote one black minister, "than all the different colored bodies presided over by colored Bishops and all other colored churches in the United States. . . . What little I have learned was taught to me by the agencies of white people."[28] Another moderate pointed out that most of the AME and AME Zion leaders had themselves been educated in Methodist Episcopal schools at the expense of Northern whites. The foremost Negro minister in the Methodist Episcopal Church, E. W. S. Hammond, was opposed to the drive for separatism even though his disappointment at the church's failure to elect him bishop had tempted him in that direction. "I can conceive of no calamity so appalling," said Hammond, "so calculated to blast the hopes and retard progress in the great struggle for manhood, as to be let alone," cut off from white help.[29]

[27] L. M. Dunton to William Claflin, Mar. 24, 1890, William Claflin Papers, Rutherford B. Hayes Library, Fremont, Ohio; letter from R. T. Adams in the Atlanta *Times,* undated clipping in the Joseph C. Hartzell Papers, Drew University Library.
[28] Letter from B. J. Dennell in *Southwestern Christian Advocate,* XVIII (Apr. 5, 1883), 1. *Southwestern* was the organ of the Negro conferences of the Methodist Episcopal Church. It usually took a moderate stand on the black-power issue, perhaps because its editor was elected every four years by the General Conference.
[29] A. E. P. Albert's editorial in *ibid.,* XXIII (Aug. 9, 1888), 4; *Christian Educator,* II (Apr. 1891), 106–08.

Despite the loyalty of moderates, the Freedmen's Aid Society was under increasing pressure to concede more power to Negroes. In 1891 the Society responded by appointing M. C. B. Mason, a talented black minister, as a field agent. This appointment reduced but did not end criticism.[30] The impotence of local boards of trustees remained a festering issue. One black trustee said in 1895 that "we are no more than figure-heads. . . . It is only a question of time when there will be revolt. . . . We believe in distribution of authority, and not centralization."[31]

"Home rule for our colored schools" had become a powerful slogan by 1895. But one Northern Methodist editor, an old abolitionist, advised caution in granting greater power to local boards. The Freedmen's Aid Society had been successful in raising money, he said, because contributors had confidence in the Society. There would be no such confidence in twenty-two separate boards of trustees. "Liberal Methodists" in the North, he asserted, "will not risk $300,000 annually to the tender mercies of the rhythmical phrase, 'Home rule for our colored schools in the south.' They will give cash confidently [only] so long as the cash is wisely expended." Decentralization might lead to "educational calamity." A black leader replied that proponents of "home rule" did not demand entire control of the schools; they wanted more authority in "the appointment of teachers and other matters pertaining to the local management of our schools," but were willing to leave financial affairs in the hands of the Freedmen's Aid Society.[32] Here was the troublesome point: Southern Negroes considered the mission schools "our schools" because they served the black community; Northern whites were reluctant to relinquish control of these schools, which they had founded and still supported. It was an example of the difficult, delicate relationship between benefactor and client that creates tensions not easily resolved to the complete satisfaction of both parties.

In 1895 the Freedmen's Aid Society committed itself in principle to decentralization. It decided to grant enlarged powers to local boards in proportion to increased financial support by Negroes themselves for "their" schools, with the ultimate aim of transferring ownership of the institutions to local boards when they became largely self-supporting.[33] The amount of money contributed by black Methodists to the schools grew from about fifteen per cent of the total income (not counting tuition, room, and board) in the 1890's to one-third of the total by 1916. The authority of local boards rose in rough proportion to this growth

30 The *Southwestern* reacted with a "thrill of joy" to Mason's appointment, announced that this "flattering recognition" showed "what comes to loyal and patient merit," and asserted that it "sternly rebukes the turbulent disposition of those who argue that the way to ecclesiastical recognition is by intriguing to overthrow those who happen, by virtue of age and experience, to be just before them." *Southwestern Christian Advocate*, XXVI (July 23, 1891), 4. This reaction seems a bit over-enthusiastic in view of the modest responsibilities of Mason's job—the raising and disbursing of education funds in the Negro conferences of the church.

31 *Western Christian Advocate*, quoted in *Southwestern Christian Advocate*, XXX (July 25, 1895), 1.

32 *Northwestern Christian Advocate*, XLIII (Aug. 7, 1895), 1 (Aug. 21, 1895), 1. (Arthur Edwards was editor of the *Northwestern*.) *Southwestern Christian Advocate*, XXX (Aug. 29, 1895), 4.

33 *Ibid.*, XXX (July 25, 1895), 1; *Christian Educator*, VII (June-July, 1896), 88.

of self-support, but in 1916 the Society still owned and controlled most of the schools. That black dissatisfaction with this situation declined after 1896 was due to the appointment of M. C. B. Mason as one of the two executive secretaries of the Society in that year and to the increasing number of black teachers and administrators in Methodist schools (see table). By 1915 six of the twelve colleges and professional schools had black presidents. Although the schools were not yet wholly under Negro leadership, the movement in that direction appeared steady enough to moderate the black-power controversy in the church.[34]

It was in the Baptist schools that the drive for black autonomy produced the greatest discord. After the Civil War the American Baptist Home Mission Society sent missionaries to the South to help organize Negro churches and state Baptist conventions. These churches and conventions were independent of Northern control, but some were dependent upon missionary aid in the early years. The Home Mission Society also founded thirteen Negro schools of secondary or college level in the South, which were supported mainly by Northern money and owned by the Society. In addition, the local black churches and state conventions established nearly fifty schools, mostly of elementary grade, by 1895. At the same time that these institutions were owned by Negroes, fifteen of the higher-grade schools received aid and supervision from the Home Mission Society.

The younger generation of black leaders that emerged in the 1880's became restless in the leading strings of missionary and educational agencies controlled by Northern Baptists and demanded greater power in these agencies or advocated total separation for black churches and schools. As E. M. Brawley, the foremost Negro Baptist minister in South Carolina, who tried to lead a revolt against the white president of Benedict Institute in Columbia, put it in 1882: "[We] do not wish any longer to be treated like children but like men." D. Augustus Straker, a lawyer and teacher, wrote in 1883 that

we are willing to return thanks to the many friends who have assisted us in educating ourselves thus far, but we have now reached the point where we desire to endeavor to educate ourselves, to build school houses, churches, colleges and universities, by our own efforts . . . ere we sacrifice our manhood.[35]

The issue was exacerbated by the ineptness or unpopularity of white administrators at four Home Mission Society schools between 1882 and 1891. The

[24] Statistics on the increase of Negro support for the schools can be found in various issues of the *Christian Educator*, the magazine of the Methodist Freedmen's Aid Society, and in Frank K. Pool, "The Southern Negro in the Methodist Episcopal Church," unpublished doctoral dissertation, Cornell University, 1939, 130–31. Because of the Society's method of reporting various categories of income and expenditure under a single head, it is impossible to be precise about the proportion of black support. If tuition and room and board are included, Negroes had contributed nearly forty per cent of the cost of their education in Methodist schools down to 1908. Richard R. Wright, *Self-Help in Negro Education* (Cheyney, Penn., 1908), 14–15. Information on ownership and control of various Methodist schools can be found in *Negro Education*, ed. Jones, II, *passim*.

[35] Brawley quoted in C. E. Becker to Henry L. Morehouse, Nov. 27, 1882, ABHMS Archives; Straker quoted in New York *Globe*, Jan. 20, 1883. For discussions of growing militancy and separatism among Negro Baptists in the 1880's and 1890's, see Carter G. Woodson, *The History of the*

worst flareup occurred at Roger Williams University in Nashville, where a threatened student strike in 1887 brought the forced retirement of the president and the bursar, the expulsion of several students, and the angry resignation of four black trustees who resented the Home Mission Society's action against the students. At the height of the controversy, the hapless president and bursar received anonymous notes from students warning that "this is our house and you dirty pup we will kick your ass out if you do not act better" and informing the bursar that "[your] daughter makes love to one of us niggers."[36]

The issue of separation versus continuing cooperation with the Home Mission Society split black Baptists into two factions. In an effort to conciliate the separatists and strengthen the cooperationists, the Society moved in 1883 to share some power with its black constituency by creating local boards of trustees for its schools to prepare for the time when Negroes "may maintain and manage these institutions for themselves." The Society also increased its support for several schools owned entirely by black Baptists. Such support involved a degree of supervision, however, and one militant separatist announced that "if Negro schools cannot get money from the Home Mission Society without making cowards and bootlicks of all the men connected with them it were far better that they never get a dime."[37] The black-power rhetoric of such separatists as Harvey Johnson of Baltimore, Walter Brooks of Washington, and R. H. Boyd of San Antonio generated great enthusiasm in some Negro Baptist circles, but financial agents for independent schools and mission organizations complained that these institutions could not exist on enthusiasm alone. Two of the most influential cooperationists, both of them presidents of black-owned schools that survived only with help from the Home Mission Society, pointed out the perils of rejecting white help. "I state from positive knowledge that the colored people are not able to support the schools now maintained in the South," wrote William B. Simmons of Kentucky Institute. "Don't for want of discretion destroy our friends' interest in us, by biting off more than we can chew." Charles L. Purce of Selma University ridiculed the claim that blacks could sustain their own schools: "How many have we supported ourselves that have attained to anything of importance? . . . It is all nonsense for any of us to say we can support them, and then will not do it." In Georgia one of the leading Baptist advocates of black power, E. K. Love, was disillusioned by his failure to raise funds for a separate, black-owned institution to rival Atlanta Baptist Seminary, and confessed in 1887 that "we are simply attempting too much. . . . We are poorly

---

*Negro Church* (2d. ed., Washington, 1945), 235–41; and James D. Tyms, *The Rise of Religious Education Among Negro Baptists* (New York, 1965), 150–66.

[36] The anonymous notes are in the Roger Williams file, ABHMS Archives. The other three schools where trouble occurred between students and presidents were Benedict Institute, Wayland Seminary, and Bishop College. Correspondence, memoranda, and newspaper clippings on all of these developments are in the ABHMS Archives.

[37] *Home Mission Monthly*, V (Feb. 1883), 35; undated clipping of *The Christian Organizer* in the ABHMS Archives.

prepared to control and manage high schools financially and intellectually. Graduation is not a sufficient guarantee that one is prepared to manage the school from which he graduates."[38]

The struggle between separatists and cooperationists intensified in the 1890's and was a major cause of the formal division of the Negro Baptists of Texas and Georgia into rival state conventions. The Home Mission Society came under increasing pressure from separatists and cooperationists alike, pressure that prompted the secretary of the Society, Thomas J. Morgan, a former abolitionist and commander of Negro troops in the Civil War, to explain in 1894 why the Society could not yet turn over its thirteen academies and colleges to black control. Negroes had shown commendable initiative in establishing many small schools on their own, wrote Morgan, but "it must be said . . . that the management of these schools is not in every case what it should be." Funds had been stolen, teachers were unskilled, principals incompetent. The blacks, said Morgan, had not yet acquired the experience necessary to manage larger schools effectively without white assistance. Relinquishment of control by the Society, he feared, would "result in a rapid retrograde movement, if not the immediate ruin of the schools."[39]

In an effort to head off a renewed attempt by Georgia separatists to found their own college, Morgan proposed a plan under which the two state conventions would jointly form an education association to work with the Home Mission Society in the coordination of all educational efforts in Georgia. The board of trustees of Atlanta Baptist College would then be enlarged by the addition of more black members and given increased powers. If this was unsatisfactory, Morgan suggested as an alternative the lease of the college to the state's black Baptists for one dollar per year, provided they would assume its entire financial support. This suggestion may have been a bluff; if so, the Georgia militants failed to call it. The majority of Negro Baptists did not wish to drive the Home Mission Society from the state, and the two conventions agreed to Morgan's first proposal in 1897.[40]

The idea of an education association seemed to work out so well in Georgia that the Society helped black Baptist conventions in other states establish similar cooperative associations. But the Georgia accord almost broke down in 1899 when the separatists, resentful of the Negroes' continued subordinate position on the reorganized board of Atlanta Baptist College and only token representation on the Spelman board, carried out their threat to found a rival in-

[38] *People's Advocate*, July 28, 1883; *Home Mission Monthly*, X (Dec. 1888), 348; clipping of a letter from Love published in the Georgia *Baptist*, Nov. 24, 1887, ABHMS Archives. Love later resumed his separatist efforts.
[39] *Home Mission Monthly*, XVI (Aug. 1894), 321–22. In the archives of the ABHMS there is some evidence—part of it from black sources—to back Morgan's charges of dishonesty or incompetency against a few black missionaries, principals, and financial agents.
[40] *Home Mission Monthly*, XIX (June 1897), 237–38 (July 1897), 271–72 (Oct. 1897), 342–43, XX (Jan. 1898), 27–30 (Apr. 1898), 109–17; Benjamin Brawley, *A History of Morehouse College* (Atlanta, 1917), 88–92.

stitution, Central City College at Macon. Hailed as a grand new venture in self-help and independence, Central City College failed to receive adequate financial support and existed essentially as a marginal secondary school.[41] Most black Baptists in Georgia remained loyal to the Home Mission Society and its schools. Atlanta Baptist College (renamed Morehouse College in 1913) and Spelman grew under the Society's guiding hand to become two of the best Negro colleges in the South.[42]

A dissident group of black Baptists in Virginia also denounced the Home Mission Society as paternalistic, demanded more influence in the running of Virginia Union University, carried a majority of the state Baptist convention with them in 1899, and disassociated the Negro-owned Virginia Seminary at Lynchburg from Virginia Union when the Society declined to make the required concessions (whereupon the cooperationists seceded to form their own convention). Shrill rhetoric by militants in Virginia and other states caused Morgan to deplore "a spirit of unreasoning racism" among Negroes and to charge that a "few noisy, ignorant, ambitious, self-seeking would-be leaders" were trying to turn the race against its Northern friends. R. H. Boyd replied to Morgan's outburst with an assertion that

the race movement which you so much dread and stigmatize . . . is simply a determination on the part of the Negroes to assume control of their race life and evolve along such lines and such ways as their spirit and genius may dictate and unfold, and not as the Anglo-Saxon may outline. . . . Hitherto the Home Mission Society has led and the Negroes have followed; henceforth the Negroes must lead and the Home Mission Society may follow . . . if it will.[43]

Fearful that anti-white tirades by black radicals would dry up Northern support for Baptist schools, Negro moderates rallied to the defense of the Home Mission Society. The president of a school receiving aid from the Society said the militants were motivated only by a "greed for office. . . . The fellow that makes the bitterest race speech gets the most applause, and he is honored as a champion of the rights of the race." This black educator believed in self-help, "but it is possible to separate self help from self foolishness; it is possible to practice self help and yet receive the generous aid of able friends." Black independence did not mean that Negroes can "take all we can get from the whites and abuse them as much as we please." He hoped the militants' conduct would not "discourage our white friends who have stood by us so loyally during the dark and bitter past." In 1902 the president of the National Baptist Convention, E. C. Morris, who had once leaned toward the separatists, expressed his desire

[41] A government survey of Negro education in 1915 found Central City College operating on a budget of about $1,700 a year with only sixty-five students, all in elementary and secondary grades, and plagued by "poor equipment and ineffective management." *Negro Education*, ed. Jones, II, 194-95. E. K. Love led the movement to found Central City College.

[42] Willard Range, *The Rise and Progress of Negro Colleges in Georgia, 1865-1949* (Athens, Ga., 1951), 109-10; Ridgely Torrence, *The Story of John Hope* (New York, 1948), 137-38.

[43] *Home Mission Monthly*, XX (Aug. 1898), 254, XXI (July 1899), 264; clipping of an open letter from Boyd to Morgan, published in the *Christian Banner*, Dec. 22, 1899, ABHMS Archives.

that "all of the misunderstandings cease and all the hard sayings indulged be left in the forgotten past."[44]

The Society reciprocated these signs of good will by stepping up efforts to bring Negroes into posts of greater responsibility. "I am not at all prepared to admit the false philosophy that a white man cannot teach a Negro," wrote Morgan in 1900, but "I recognize that race feeling is very strong, and that other things being equal, a Negro will have more influence upon his race than a white man." Atlanta Baptist College hired more black faculty and began grooming John Hope for its presidency. Hope assumed the office in 1907, the first Negro president of a Home Mission Society college. By 1915 nearly half the faculty in the Society's nine colleges was black, and three of the college presidents were Negroes.[45]

Though the Northern Presbyterians had only a small black membership in the South, the church's Board of Missions for the Freedmen was also confronted by the black-power issue. In 1888 the white secretary of the Board, Henry N. Payne, urged a positive response to black demands for greater power and responsibility in the schools. Because of the effects of slavery, said Payne, Negroes "have been weak and dependent; only in this way can they be made strong and self-reliant."[46] The Board decided to begin phasing out white teachers earlier than any other mission society, and in 1891 Daniel J. Sanders, born a slave, was installed as president of Biddle University (later renamed Johnson C. Smith University). Several new Negro faculty members were also appointed in 1891, and within three years the Biddle faculty was entirely black. Some Presbyterians criticized this development as a "rash experiment"; the Board of Missions for the Freedmen conceded that it was a "bold experiment," but hoped it would not turn out to be rash. In 1893 the Board pronounced the venture a success; administrative control of Biddle was thenceforth in black hands, though major financial and policy decisions were still made by the Northern Board.[47]

The other major Presbyterian college, Lincoln University (the only white-supported Negro college outside former slave territory), took a radically different position on the issue of black teachers and administrators. Lincoln's faculty and board of trustees were virtually one hundred per cent white until the 1930's (a few Negroes were appointed earlier as instructors or assistants, but none as professors). This caused considerable dissatisfaction among Lincoln alumni and students. In 1916 Francis Grimké, an alumnus, said that Lincoln's lily-white

[44] C. S. Brown, president of Waters Institute, Winton, N. C., to Thomas J. Morgan, in *Home Mission Monthly*, XXII (Apr. 1900), 123–24; pamphlet copy of Morris' address to the National Baptist Convention, 1902, ABHMS Archives.

[45] *Home Mission Monthly*, XXII (Dec. 1900), 336, XXX (Nov. 1908), 439–40; Brawley, *Morehouse*, 95; Torrence, *John Hope*, 142–57, 164, 185. See table for 1914–15 statistics. The figure of nine colleges for 1915 includes Jackson College, not classified by the Jones report as a full-fledged collegiate institution. Several of its secondary students were taking college courses in 1914–15, and shortly thereafter the school became a four-year college. *Negro Education*, ed. Jones, II, 355–56.

[46] *Church at Home and Abroad*, III (Mar. 1888), 270.

[47] Andrew E. Murray, *Presbyterians and the Negro—A History* (Philadelphia, 1966), 188–89; *Church at Home and Abroad*, VI (Dec. 1889), 549, IX (Mar. 1891), 248, XIII (Apr. 1893), 208–09.

policy was "a standing argument against the professed friendship and Christian character of the men who have permitted this condition of things to continue as long as it has."[48] Lincoln was entirely unconnected with the Board of Missions that supervised freedmen's education in the South; it had been founded before the Civil War by the Old School Presbyterians (most of the antislavery sentiment in the denomination was concentrated in the New School faction) and was governed by an independent board of trustees.

All the mission societies rapidly increased the ratio of Negro faculty and administration in the first decade of the twentieth century, an increase that helped reduce the intensity of the black-power controversy in education. (The issue remained alive, however, and flared up again in the 1920's.) The change was most dramatic in the secondary schools of the American Missionary Association. In 1895 only nine per cent of the teachers in these institutions were black; by 1905 the proportion had risen to fifty-three per cent, and seven of the twenty-one principals of AMA high schools were Negroes.[49] This change was in part the result of a deliberate policy decision to begin an orderly transition of "mission" schools to "native" control, but it was also a pragmatic response to continuing black pressure. In AMA schools with interracial faculties, young Negro teachers were often impatient with the continued presence of white veterans who blocked their promotions. One black male teacher wrote in a private letter: "If that old bitch from Massachusetts would ever die or get through here, I could begin to live."[50]

Not all Negroes connected with AMA schools favored the conversion to black faculties. In fact, resistance from parents of students helped bring a virtual halt for several years to the relative increase of black teachers in AMA secondary schools, and in 1915 the percentage of Negro faculty was about the same as it had been in 1905. Many Negro parents believed that white teachers were better than black; some of them said privately, "My child shall not go to school to a nigger." The AMA's assistant superintendent of education reported that when Negro teachers replaced whites in some communities, enrollment decreased and parents complained that "their Harvard was being taken from them and they were being pushed back into the log cabin school." On more than one occasion parents formed a "Committee to Save Our School" and obtained hundreds of signatures on petitions urging retention of white teachers.[51] This phenomenon was perhaps less an objective index of the relative quality of white and black teachers than a reflection of the self-distrust and self-hatred ingrained into many Negroes by centuries of white supremacy. In any case, the cross-pressures between

[48] Grimké to George Johnson, dean of Lincoln University, Mar. 25, 1916, in *The Works of Grimké*, ed. Woodson, I, 530–31.
[49] *Report of the U.S. Commissioner of Education for the Year 1905* (Washington, 1906), 1310–17; *American Missionary*, LVIII (Feb. 1904), 35.
[50] Quoted by Lura Beam, in *He Called Them by the Lightning: A Teacher's Odyssey in the Negro South, 1908–1919* (Indianapolis, 1967), 153–54. Lura Beam was the AMA's assistant superintendent of education from 1910 to 1919, after having taught for two years in AMA schools.
[51] *Ibid.*, 150–52.

younger Negroes ambitious for places in the schools and parents who wanted white teachers to stay caused many headaches for officials of the AMA.

A set of factors related to broad developments in American education had some impact on the changing ratios of white and black teachers in Negro schools. In the two decades before 1900 an "academic revolution" diminished the role of the nineteenth-century Christian college, whose .curriculum emphasized the classics, moral philosophy, and theology, and led to the rise of the modern university, which has emphasized physical sciences, social sciences, vocational-professional training, and a commitment to secularism. An important part of this revolution was the increasingly self-conscious professional status of teachers at both the secondary and college level. Normal schools became teachers' colleges, which granted bachelor's degrees to prospective high school teachers; colleges were increasingly staffed by Ph.D.'s or at least M.A.'s instead of B.D.'s.[52]

Negro colleges and secondary schools were not unaffected by these changes. By the second decade of the twentieth century the AMA (whose standards were higher than those of the other mission societies) required a college degree for its secondary school teachers and post-graduate training for its college instructors.[53] As teaching qualifications, missionary zeal counted less and professional education more than in earlier days. Curiously, this development did not lead to an improvement in the quality of white teachers; indeed, the opposite seems to have occurred. It was generally agreed by contemporaries and alumni that the first generation of missionary teachers, who had a genuine humanitarian commitment to their work, were more effective than the later, more professional generations, who were less interested in helping the poor than in getting a job. There was an unfortunate and growing tendency among discards from Northern colleges to go South to teach in Negro colleges. As racism in white America hardened, some whites attached a stigma to teaching in a black school. Thus one reason for the partial conversion to Negro faculties was a relative decline of willing and able white teachers.

This factor should not, however, be overemphasized. Secularism and professionalism were slow to penetrate Negro education. Missionary and humanitarian motives remained the most important ones impelling Northern whites to teach at Negro schools, at least before 1915. Of course there is no necessary contradiction between thorough professional training and missionary dedication; many white teachers successfully combined both. And while the percentage of white faculty in the schools covered by this study declined between 1895 and 1915, the actual number of white teachers increased at a rate almost equal to the growth of the middle-class Protestant population from which most of these teachers came. The most important reason for the rising percentage of black

[52] Lawrence R. Veysey, *The Emergence of the American University* (Chicago, 1965); Lawrence A. Cremin, *The Transformation of the School: Progressivism in American Education, 1876–1957* (New York, 1961), especially 168–76; Richard Hofstadter and Walter P. Metzger, *The Development of Academic Freedom in the United States* (New York, 1955), especially 277–479. The phrase "academic revolution" is from Veysey, 267.
[53] Beam, *He Called Them by the Lightning*, 140.

teachers in the schools was not a relative shortage of white teachers, but pressure from strong segments of the black community coupled with the conscientious desire by many officials of mission societies to transfer responsibility to their former protégés.

By 1915 sixty per cent of the teachers in all secondary schools and colleges founded by or receiving support from Northern missionary sources were black. The proportion of Negro faculty in the colleges alone had nearly doubled from twenty-seven per cent in 1895 to fifty-one per cent in 1915. Nine of the thirty college presidents were black, while fifty-two of the eighty-five secondary schools had Negro principals. But most of the schools and colleges, including those with black administrations, were still governed mainly by the mission societies or by independent boards on which white trustees predominated.

In 1915, a half century after the beginnings of Negro education in the South, white influence was still paramount in the major institutions of higher learning. This was doubtless due in part to the paternalism inherent in all mission enterprises and to a reluctance by those in authority to give up power, but it was due also to a desire to maintain high standards and to a continued dependence on Northern financial support. Adam Clayton Powell, Sr., recognized the importance of this last factor in 1930 when he estimated that "Negroes have paid only 10 per cent of the cost of their [higher] education during the last sixty-five years. . . . There are only two worth-while educational institutions in America receiving their chief financial support from Negroes." Powell said that black people owed "our white friends a unanimous vote of thanks," but that "this kind of charity cannot and should not go on forever"; the Negro should do more to support his own institutions.[54]

Of course, white sponsorship did not necessarily preclude black control of finances, though it was on precisely this point that the mission societies were most reluctant to yield authority. At the same time that the societies moved steadily forward with the appointment of Negro teachers and administrators, they maintained a close watch over funds and general policy. This was perhaps the result of an unjustified and patronizing distrust of the Negro's competence to manage things for himself. Nevertheless, several black leaders, admitting their lack of experience, urged the mission boards and white trustees to continue their supervision of Negro colleges. Kelly Miller lamented as late as 1933 the "failure of Negroes to handle successfully practical projects which they had assumed" and stated that "the race is not yet sufficiently experienced . . . to justify assuming complete guardianship of higher institutions of learning. . . . This is not a race question, nor one of discrimination, but only one of common sense and prudence."[55]

An important government survey of Negro education in 1915 concluded that

[54] Article by Powell in Jordan, *Negro Baptist History*, 306. Powell's estimate of ten per cent probably understated the Negro's actual contribution to his higher education.

[55] Kelly Miller, "The Past, Present, and Future of the Negro College," *Journal of Negro Education*, II (July 1933), 418–19.

some of the mission boards had actually been premature in promoting black teachers and appointing black presidents. The Methodist and Presbyterian schools had the highest percentage of Negro faculty and administrators; the survey declared that in many of these institutions "the standards of administration and educational work" had "not been satisfactory." In several Methodist colleges the change from white to black faculties "has been too rapid for the good of the schools." At the Presbyterians' Biddle University, the first mission college to have a Negro president, "the work is poorly organized and the large plant is ineffectively used." The experience of this and other schools "shows clearly that the white boards render their best service when they send not only their money but also their capable men and women to have a vital part in the instruction of colored youth." On the whole the weakest schools, according to the survey, were those controlled entirely by Negro denominations—the Baptist state conventions and the AME and AME Zion churches—while the strongest were those founded by the American Missionary Association, in which white influence prevailed longest.[56]

This evaluation, by a white educator, could perhaps be dismissed as the product of white racism.[57] It was, however, echoed several years later by Kelly Miller, who asserted that the transition from white to black faculties "was too sharp and sudden. It was a misfortune barely short of a calamity." As white teachers were replaced by blacks the "colleges were shifted from a Puritan to a pagan basis" and the "moral stamina" of the first generation of Negro education declined. (E. Franklin Frazier made a similar point in *Black Bourgeoisie*.) "Painful observation," wrote Miller, "convinces us that the later crop of college output falls lamentably short of their elder brothers in this respect. The inducing process was cut short before the induction had become permanently effective."[58]

It may be impossible to reach a consensus on whether the transition of power from white to black in Negro colleges was too fast, just right, or not fast enough. Evidence regarding administrative efficiency and the ability to impart skills and mastery of subject matter seems to indicate that white administrators and teachers were better qualified than their black colleagues, at least before 1900 or 1910.

[56] *Negro Education*, ed. Jones, I, 15, 17, 135, 139–40, 143–45, 151–52, II, 424. It should be noted, however, that Morehouse College and Wiley University, with Negro presidents and about ninety per cent black faculties, were among the best Negro colleges in 1915. And a major factor in the superiority of the schools owned by the AMA and other mission societies to the institutions owned by black denominations was the greater financial resources of the former. The degree of support by Negroes themselves for the Baptist, Methodist, and Presbyterian schools was greater than for the AMA schools; there were very few Negroes in the Congregational Church, so nearly all the denominational support for AMA institutions still came from the North. This was a significant factor in the longer persistence of white influence in these schools; the AMA remained a "mission" enterprise longer than any of the other societies.

[57] The director of the survey, Thomas Jesse Jones of the US Bureau of Education, was basically more in sympathy with the Hampton-Tuskegee program of industrial education than with the academic orientation of Fisk, Atlanta, and other colleges, and was thus somewhere to the right of center in the spectrum of friendly white attitudes toward Negro higher education. Nevertheless, he praised the work of the academic colleges when he thought their program was of high quality.

[58] Miller, "The Past, Present, and Future of the Negro College," 414; see also E. Franklin Frazier, *Black Bourgeoisie* (Collier Books ed., New York, 1962), 73–76.

On the other hand, proficiency in these areas may have been purchased at the cost of restricting the development of black initiative, self-reliance, and pride. It is not easy to say which objectives should have been uppermost in Negro education. It can be said, however, that the schools and colleges discussed in this article could not have been sustained by pride alone. Despite discord, these institutions survived and grew, keeping Negro higher education alive through difficult times. From the viewpoint of today's black-power movement, persistent white influence in Negro education perpetuated the blacks' colonial dependence on white liberals. But without this educational "colonialism" there would have been little higher education for Negroes; there would have been no Howard, no Fisk, no Lincoln, no Morehouse, no Spelman, no Atlanta University. From the schools founded by whites were graduated many twentieth-century leaders of the black community, including W. E. B. Du Bois (Fisk), James Weldon Johnson and Walter White (Atlanta), James Farmer (Wiley), Martin Luther King (Morehouse), Thurgood Marshall (Lincoln University and Howard Law School), and Stokely Carmichael (Howard). This was their main bequest to our generation. It was no mean legacy.

SOUTHERN NEGRO COLLEGES AND SECONDARY SCHOOLS ESTABLISHED BY NORTHERN MISSION SOCIETIES

| Mission Societies and Schools | 1894–95 | | | | | | | | | 1914–15 | | | | | | | | | |
| --- | --- | --- | --- | --- | --- | --- | --- | --- | --- | --- | --- | --- | --- | --- | --- | --- | --- | --- | --- |
| | Faculty and Administration | | | | | Students | | | | Faculty and Administration[b] | | | | | Students[e] | | | | |
| | Total | Negro | White | % Negro | President or Principal | Total | Elementary | Secondary | College and Professional | Total | Negro | White | % Negro | President or Principal | Total | Attendance[d] | Elementary[d] | Secondary[d] | College and Professional[d] |
| American Missionary Association: Colleges | | | | | | | | | | | | | | | | | | | |
| Fisk University, Nashville, Tenn.[c] | 31 | 1 | 30 | 3% | White | 539 | 221 | 263 | 55 | 45 | 14 | 31 | 31% | White | 505 | 505 | 112 | 205 | 188 |
| Straight University, New Orleans, La. | 24 | 2 | 22 | 8% | White | 569 | 367 | 152 | 50 | 30 | 13 | 17 | 43% | White | 758 | 578 | 364 | 203 | 11 |
| Talladega College, Talladega, Ala. | 20 | 1 | 19 | 5% | White | 581 | 509 | 66 | 6 | 41 | 12 | 29 | 29% | White | 668 | 561 | 382 | 124 | 55 |
| Tillotson College, Austin, Tex. | 13 | 0 | 13 | 0% | White | 193 | 153 | 40 | 0 | 20 | 6 | 14 | 30% | White | 314 | 223 | 135 | 70 | 18 |
| Tougaloo College, Tougaloo, Miss. | 22 | 0 | 22 | 0% | White | 377 | 332 | 45 | 0 | 31 | 2 | 29 | 6% | White | 455 | 444 | 275 | 149 | 20 |
| Total | 110 | 4 | 106 | 4% | Black: 0 White: 5 | 2,259 | 1,582 | 566 | 111 | 167 | 47 | 126 | 28% | Black: 0 White: 5 | 2,700 | 2,311 | 1,268 | 751 | 292 |

| Institution | 1895 | | | | | | | | | 1915 | | | | | | | | | |
|---|---|---|---|---|---|---|---|---|---|---|---|---|---|---|---|---|---|---|---|
| AMA Secondary Schools: 1895 (17); 1915 (22)[f] | 141 | 12 | 129 | 9% | Black: 1; White: 16 | 4,327 | 3,743 | 584 | 111 | 246 | 132 | 114 | 54% | Black: 10; White: 12 | 5,977 | 4,743 | 3,892 | 851 | 292 |
| Total: All AMA Schools[f] | 251 | 16 | 235 | 6% | Black: 1; White: 21 | 6,586 | 5,325 | 1,150 | 413 | 179 | 234 | | 43% | Black: 10; White: 17 | 8,677 | 7,054 | 5,160 | 1,602 | |
| Freedmen's Aid Society of the Methodist Episcopal Church: Colleges[f] | | | | | | | | | | | | | | | | | | | |
| Bennett College, Greensboro, N. C. | 10 | 10 | 0 | 100% | Black | 203 | 198 | 5 | 0 | 15 | 12 | 3 | 80% | Black | 312 | 312 | 235 | 67 | 10 |
| Clark University, Atlanta, Ga. | 19 | 8 | 11 | 42% | White | 341 | 246 | 91 | 4 | 24 | 14 | 10 | 58% | Black | 304 | 304 | 128 | 144 | 32 |
| Claflin College, Orangeburg, S. C. | 20 | 10 | 10 | 50% | White | 570 | 473 | 74 | 23 | 27 | 21 | 6 | 78% | Black | 866 | 814 | 597 | 191 | 26 |
| Gammon Theological Seminary, Atlanta, Ga. | 4 | 1 | 3 | 25% | White | 84 | 0 | 0 | 84 | 6 | 2 | 4 | 33% | White | 78 | 78 | 0 | 0 | 78 |
| Meharry Medical College, Nashville, Tenn.[f] | | | | | White | | | | | 30 | 28 | 2 | 93% | White | 505 | 505 | 0 | 0 | 505 |
| Morgan College, Baltimore, Md. | 9 | 2 | 7 | 22% | White | 160 | 96 | 3 | 61 | 11 | 4 | 7 | 36% | White | 128 | 81 | 0 | 55 | 26 |
| New Orleans University, New Orleans, La. | 24 | 12 | 12 | 50% | White | 603 | 531 | 65 | 7 | 24 | 11 | 13 | 46% | White | 557 | 432 | 298 | 125 | 9 |
| Philander Smith College, Little Rock, Ark. | 15 | 4 | 11 | 27% | White | 312 | 259 | 37 | 16 | 18 | 17 | 1 | 94% | Black | 491 | 439 | 268 | 132 | 39 |
| Rust College, Holly Springs, Miss. | 10 | 4 | 6 | 40% | White | 230 | 127 | 97 | 6 | 18 | 10 | 8 | 56% | White | 378 | 196 | 128 | 60 | 8 |
| Samuel Huston College, Austin, Tex. | Founded in 1900 | | | | | | | | | 20 | 19 | 1 | 95% | Black | 405 | 377 | 267 | 92 | 18 |

SOUTHERN NEGRO COLLEGES AND SECONDARY SCHOOLS ESTABLISHED BY NORTHERN MISSION SOCIETIES[a] (Continued)

| Mission Societies and Schools | 1894-95 | | | | | | | | | 1914-15 | | | | | | | | | |
|---|---|---|---|---|---|---|---|---|---|---|---|---|---|---|---|---|---|---|---|
| | Faculty and Administration | | | | | Students | | | | Faculty and Administration[b] | | | | | Students[c] | | | | |
| | Total | Negro | White | % Negro | President or Principal | Total | Elementary | Secondary | College and Professional | Total | Negro | White | % Negro | President or Principal | Total | Attendance[d] | Elementary[d] | Secondary[d] | College and Professional[d] |
| Central Tennessee College, Nashville, Tenn.[g] | 11 | 2 | 9 | 18% | White | 326 | 115 | 158 | 53 | 17 | 8 | 9 | 47% | Black | 107 | 107 | 30 | 77 | 0 |
| Wiley University, Marshall, Tex. | 12 | 3 | 9 | 25% | Black | 284 | 89 | 139 | 56 | 30 | 28 | 2 | 93% | Black | 439 | 384 | 176 | 170 | 38 |
| Total | 134 | 56 | 78 | 42% | Black: 2 White: 9 | 3,113 | 2,134 | 669 | 310 | 240 | 174 | 66 | 73% | Black: 6 White: 6 | 4,570 | 4,029 | 2,127 | 1,113 | 789 |
| Methodist Secondary Schools: 1895 (11); 1915 (11)[f] | 72 | 35 | 19 | 72% | Black: 4 White: 4 Unknown: 3 | 1,650 | 1,203 | 447 | | 135 | 94 | 41 | 70% | Black: 5 White: 6 | 2,493 | 2,401 | 1,864 | 537 | |
| Total: All Methodist Schools[f] | 206 | 91 | 97 | 48% | Black: 6 White: 13 Unknown: 3 | 4,763 | 3,337 | 1,116 | 310 | 375 | 268 | 107 | 71% | Black: 11 White: 12 | 7,063 | 6,430 | 3,991 | 1,650 | 789 |
| American Baptist Mission Society: Colleges | | | | | | | | | | | | | | | | | | | |
| Benedict College, Columbia, S. C. | 8 | 1 | 7 | 13% | White | 135 | 0 | 135 | 0 | 30 | 12 | 18 | 40% | White | 595 | 507 | 254 | 205 | 48 |

272

| Institution | | | | | | | | | | | | | | | | | | | |
|---|---|---|---|---|---|---|---|---|---|---|---|---|---|---|---|---|---|---|---|
| Bishop College, Marshall, Tex. | 18 | 7 | 11 | 39% | White | 368 | 270 | 65 | 33 | 22 | 10 | 12 | 45% | White | 421 | 371 | 176 | 153 | 42 |
| Hartshorn Memorial College, Richmond, Va. | 9 | 2 | 7 | 22% | White | 97 | 22 | 75 | 0 | 15 | 3 | 12 | 20% | White | 188 | 169 | 73 | 96 | 0[h] |
| Morehouse College, Atlanta, Ga.[j] | 11 | 6 | 5 | 55% | White | 150 | 72 | 50 | 28 | 19 | 17 | 2 | 89% | Black | 277 | 277 | 110 | 111 | 56 |
| Richmond Theological Seminary, Richmond, Va. | 4 | 2 | 2 | 50% | White | 50 | 0 | 0 | 50 | Merged with Wayland Seminary in 1899 to form Virginia Union University | | | | | | | | | |
| Roger Williams University, Nashville, Tenn.[j] | 16 | 7 | 9 | 44% | White | 227 | 141 | 67 | 19 | 17 | 17 | 0 | 100% | Black | 123 | 107 | 27 | 80 | 0 |
| Shaw University, Raleigh, N.C. | 26 | 10 | 16 | 38% | White | 362 | 129 | 175 | 58 | 30 | 16 | 14 | 53% | White | 291 | 221 | 52 | 123 | 46 |
| Spelman Seminary, Atlanta, Ga.[k] | 38 | 4 | 34 | 11% | White | 491 | 416 | 52 | 23 | 51 | 3 | 48 | 6% | White | 631 | 595 | 330 | 254 | 11 |
| Virginia Union University, Richmond, Va. | Formed in 1899 of merger between Wayland Seminary and Richmond Theological Seminary | | | | | | | | | 16 | 7 | 9 | 44% | White | 265 | 255 | 35 | 145 | 75 |
| Total | 130 | 39 | 91 | 30% | Black: 0 White: 8 | 1,880 | 1,050 | 619 | 211 | 200 | 85 | 115 | 43% | Black: 2 White: 6 | 2,791 | 2,502 | 1,057 | 1,167 | 278 |
| Baptist Secondary Schools: 1895 (20); 1915 (16)[l] | 122 | 97 | 25 | 80% | Black: 15 White: 5 | 2,483 | 1,951 | 441 | | 208 | 195 | 13 | 94% | Black: 15 White: 1 | 4,040 | 3,009 | 2,243 | 766 | |
| Total: All Baptist Schools[f] | 252 | 136 | 116 | 54% | Black: 15 White: 13 | 4,363 | 3,001 | 1,060 | 211 | 408 | 280 | 128 | 69% | Black: 17 White: 7 | 6,831 | 5,511 | 3,300 | 1,933 | 278 |
| Presbyterian College: Biddle University, Charlotte, N.C. | 11 | 11 | 0 | 100% | Black | 260 | 19 | 172 | 69 | 16 | 16 | 0 | 100% | Black | 221 | 207 | 24 | 131 | 52 |

SOUTHERN NEGRO COLLEGES AND SECONDARY SCHOOLS ESTABLISHED BY NORTHERN MISSION SOCIETIES[a] (Continued)

| Mission Societies and Schools | 1894–95 Faculty and Administration[b] | | | | | 1894–95 Students | | | | 1914–15 Faculty and Administration[b] | | | | | 1914–15 Students[c] | | | | |
|---|---|---|---|---|---|---|---|---|---|---|---|---|---|---|---|---|---|---|---|
| | Total | Negro | White | % Negro | President or Principal | Total | Elementary | Secondary | College and Professional | Total | Negro | White | % Negro | President or Principal | Total | Attendance[d] | Elementary[d] | Secondary[d] | College and Professional[d] |
| Presbyterian Secondary Schools: 1895 (7); 1915 (20)[f] | 75 | 41 | 34 | 55% | Black: 4 White: 3 | 1,515 | 953 | 562 | | 218 | 173 | 45 | 75% | Black: 16 White: 4 | 4,798 | 4,197 | 3,516 | 681 | |
| Total: All Board of Missions for Freedmen, Presbyterian Church in the U. S. A., Schools[f] | 86 | 52 | 34 | 60% | Black: 5 White: 3 | 1,775 | 972 | 734 | 69 | 234 | 189 | 45 | 81% | Black: 17 White: 4 | 5,019 | 4,404 | 3,540 | 812 | 52 |
| United Presbyterian College: Knoxville College, Knoxville, Tenn. | 21 | 0 | 21 | 0% | White | 317 | 186 | 108 | 23 | 29 | 5 | 24 | 17% | White | 327 | 327 | 187 | 110 | 30 |
| United Presbyterian Secondary Schools: 1895 (1); 1915 (5) | 14 | 3 | 11 | 22% | White | 686 | 622 | 64 | | 77 | 57 | 20 | 74% | Black: 3 White: 2 | 1,726 | 1,344 | 1,137 | 207 | |
| Total: All Board of Freedmen's Missions, United Presbyterian Church, Schools | 35 | 3 | 32 | 9% | Black: 0 White: 2 | 1,003 | 808 | 172 | 23 | 106 | 62 | 44 | 58% | Black: 3 White: 3 | 2,653 | 1,671 | 1,324 | 317 | 30 |
| Quakers: Secondary Schools: 1895 (3); 1915 (4) | 37 | 20 | 17 | 54% | Black: 0 White: 2 Unknown: 1 | 655 | 297 | 358 | | 64 | 54 | 10 | 84% | Black: 2 White: 2 | 1,464 | 1,243 | 924[m] | 94[m] | 30 |

| Institution / Schools | | | | | | | | | | | | | | | | | | | |
|---|---|---|---|---|---|---|---|---|---|---|---|---|---|---|---|---|---|---|---|
| Other Denominations[n] Secondary Schools: 1895 (3); 1915 (4) | 16 | 8 | 8 | 50% | Black: 1 White: 2 | 379 | 259 | 120 | | 64 | 30 | 34 | 47% | Black: 1 White: 3 | 917 | 862 | 614[m] | 142[m] | |
| Independent, Nondenominational Colleges | | | | | | | | | | | | | | | | | | | |
| Atlanta University, Atlanta, Ga. | 16 | 0 | 16 | 0% | White | 217 | 149 | 48 | 20 | 33 | 4 | 29 | 12% | White | 586 | 586 | 182 | 360 | 44 |
| Howard University, Washington, D. C. | 64 | 21 | 43 | 33% | White | 587 | 129 | 126 | 332 | 106 | 73 | 33 | 69% | White | 1,401 | 1,401 | 0 | 373 | 1,028 |
| Leland University, New Orleans, La.[o] | 13 | 4 | 9 | 31% | White | 439 | 357 | 59 | 23 | 14 | 4 | 10 | 29% | White | 298 | 298 | 203 | 91 | 4 |
| Total | 93 | 25 | 68 | 27% | Black: 0 White: 3 | 1,243 | 635 | 233 | 375 | 153 | 81 | 72 | 53% | Black: 0 White: 3 | 2,285 | 2,285 | 385 | 824 | 1,076 |
| Independent Secondary Schools (including Hampton Institute):[p] 1895 (2); 1915 (3) | 70 | 19 | 51 | 27% | Black: 0 White: 2 | 1,067 | 751 | 316 | | 250 | 93 | 157 | 37% | Black: 0 White: 3 | 1,167 | 1,115 | 710 | 405 | |
| Total: All Independent Schools | 163 | 44 | 119 | 27% | Black: 0 White: 5 | 2,310 | 1,386 | 549 | 375 | 403 | 174 | 229 | 43% | Black: 0 White: 6 | 3,452 | 3,400 | 1,095 | 1,229 | 1,076 |
| All Colleges and Professional Schools[q] | 499 | 135 | 364 | 27% | Black: 3 White: 26 | 9,072 | 5,606 | 2,367 | 1,099 | 805 | 408 | 397 | 51% | Black: 8 White: 21 | 12,894 | 11,661 | 5,048 | 4,096 | 2,517 |
| All Secondary Schools[q] | 547 | 235 | 294 | 44% | Black: 25 White: 35 Unknown: 4 | 12,762 | 9,779 | 2,892 | | 1,262 | 828 | 434 | 66% | Black: 52 White: 33 | 22,582 | 18,914 | 14,840 | 3,683 | |
| Total: All Schools[q] | 1,046 | 370 | 658 | 36% | Black: 28 White: 61 Unknown: 4 | 21,834 | 15,395 | 5,291 | 1,099 | 2,067 | 1,236 | 831 | 60% | Black: 61 White: 54 | 35,476 | 30,575 | 19,948 | 7,773 | 2,517 |

[a] These statistics have been garnered from *The Report of the U. S. Commissioner of Education for the Year 1894-95* (Washington, 1896), 1338-45, and from *Negro Education: A Study of the Private and Higher Schools for the Colored People in the United States*, ed. Thomas Jesse Jones (Washington, 1917). *passim.* The government

figures for 1894–95 are not wholly reliable and have been checked and supplemented whenever possible by the scattered statistics available in the annual reports and other materials published by the mission societies. The statistics in this table do not include elementary schools.

[b] Includes clerical staff for a few schools.

[c] The Jones report applied stricter criteria for classifying students in secondary or college classes than the earlier reports of the Commissioner of Education, so there are fewer students listed in the higher grades than if earlier standards had been applied.

[d] Students in attendance on day of visit.

[e] Acquired an independent status in 1909.

[f] Statistics incomplete for 1894–95.

[g] Name changed to Walden University in 1900.

[h] Hartshorn was the girls' college of Virginia Union University; several students took college courses at Virginia Union.

[i] Named Atlanta Baptist Seminary until 1897, Atlanta Baptist College 1897–1913.

[j] Taken over by the state Negro Baptist convention in 1908; continued to receive some Home Mission Society aid.

[k] Supported mainly by the Woman's American Baptist Home Mission Society, an affiliate of the American Baptist Home Mission Society.

[l] Fifteen Baptist secondary schools in 1894–95 and fourteen in 1914–15 were owned by Negro state Baptist conventions and partly supported and supervised by the Home Mission Society.

[m] Statistics on students incomplete.

[n] Christian Missionary Society; American Christian Convention; Free Baptist Church; Reformed Presbyterian Church.

[o] Partly supported and controlled by the American Baptist Home Mission Society until 1887. Leland always maintained close ties with the Baptist Church.

[p] Hampton Institute was founded by the American Missionary Association, which continued to appropriate some funds to the school until 1894.

[q] Statistics on faculty incomplete or not available for one of the colleges and three of the secondary schools in 1894–95; statistics on students incomplete for one of the colleges and six of the secondary schools in 1894–95, and for two of the secondary schools in 1914–15.

# EXPERIMENT IN INTERRACIAL EDUCATION AT BEREA COLLEGE, 1858-1908

*by*
## PAUL DAVID NELSON

The story of the interracial program of Berea College, a school located in the heart of Kentucky directly between the Cumberland Mountains and the Bluegrass, is filled with the drama of great men achieving great things in black-white relations in higher education. It also includes the actions of those who would compel Berea to compromise its racial ideals in order to conform to the vicissitudes of national racial policy. The founders of the college, radical abolitionists such as preacher John G. Fee and educators J. A. R. Rogers and E. Henry Fairchild, insisted that their educational program (in effect from 1858 until 1892) must incorporate as basic racial principles the total equality of the Negro and a fifty-fifty ratio of black and white students. To these bedrock ideals Fee and his colleagues tenaciously clung, through Reconstruction, through the sectional compromise of 1877, through pressure from the Ku Klux Klan and hostile state legislatures, through lean years of financial hardship. The historical records contained in the Berea College archives substantiate the assertion that the founders were successful in their educational aims.

However, Berea's racial program began to change rapidly with the inauguration in 1892 of a new president, William G. Frost. While Fee and his colleagues had maintained an even racial balance in the school and had seemed to understand and cater to the desires of the black constituency, President Frost began early in his administration to concentrate on a new field of endeavor—the Southern Appalachian Mountains—and seemed more sensitive to the needs of whites than to Negroes. In shifting emphasis, Frost was following national white attitudes on the question of race, for Americans north and south by the 1890's were turning more and more toward public segregation of blacks as a "solution" to its racial problems. Having never been fully committed, even during Reconstruction, to racial integration in the South, the white people of the United States were entering in the last decade of the nineteenth century a period of heightened antagonism toward blacks.[1] Berea, surrounded by whites who favored segregation, and

Paul David Nelson is Assistant Professor of History in Berea College. He wishes to thank Berea College for financial assistance in writing this article. He is also grateful to Sherman Gibbs and George Moore, Berea students, who unselfishly provided him with certain documents from their own research.

[1] See, for example, Carter G. Woodson, *The Negro in our History* (Washington, 1922); Rembert W. Patrick, *The Reconstruction of the Nation* (New York, 1967), 278;

now under the leadership of a man who was not opposed to dominant national intellectual currents that portrayed Negroes as racially inferior, could not—perhaps did not want to—remain above this growing national intolerance.

This change in policy and attitude at Berea brought cries of sadness, anger and disgust from elements of Berea's black population and their supporters, Negro and white, on and off campus. Statements written by militant blacks pointed out to Frost both the degradation the authors saw falling upon their race and the moral compromise they believed was taking place at Berea in order to bring the college into conformity with racist national patterns. Many of their statements contain echoes of present day arguments by blacks who contend that America in the latter half of the twentieth century is dominated by similar failures of program and purpose. This paper, by examining Berea's attitudes under Fee, and how they changed under Frost, will argue that President Frost thwarted the purposes of the founders, in the process perpetrating injustices on black Bereans; and that black student discontents at the college, until now shrugged off as invalid, even by those who have known they existed, were very real and justifiable.

Berea's remarkable interracial history began in 1858, five years after John G. Fee had accepted an invitation from Cassius M. Clay, an influential Kentucky landowner, politician and emancipationist, to found an antislavery church and school in southern Madison County, Kentucky. Although Fee and Clay both opposed slavery, it was soon apparent that the two men did not agree on how the "peculiar institution" should be abolished or what the role of Negroes would be in Kentucky society and politics once they were freed. Fee, a "higher law" man, argued the moral position that slavery was contrary to the word of God and should be exised immediately from American life. Moreover, once the black man was free, he must have complete civil and political equality. Clay, on the other hand, not only was opposed to immediate abolition—he favored a consitutional amendment (either state or national) which would guarantee the slaveowner gradual emancipation, with compensation for his property—but also had no intention of incorporating freed Negroes into society as equals of whites.[2] Differences between these two strong willed men would soon

---

John Hope Franklin, *From Slavery to Freedom: A History of American Negroes* (2nd. ed., New York, 1956), 320-38, 426-42, and *Reconstruction After the Civil War* (Chicago, 1961), 226-27; C. Vann Woodward, *The Strange Career of Jim Crow* (New York, 1957), "The Birth of Jim Crow," *American Heritage*, XV (April, 1964), 52-55, 100-103, and *Origins of the New South, 1877-1913* (Baton Rouge, 1951); Rayford W. Logan, *The Negro in American Life and Thought: The Nadir, 1877-1901* (New York, 1954), and *The Betrayal of the Negro* (New York, 1965).

[2] John G. Fee, *Autobiography* (Chicago, 1891), 102-05, 126-32. Compare the foregoing with Cassius M. Clay, *The Life of Cassius Marcellus Clay: Memoirs, Writings, and Speeches* (Cincinnati, 1886), 212, 571-72.

lead them into personal quarrels.

In 1858 Fee and J.A.R. Rogers, who had joined the little Berea community and school that year, decided to write a constitution for an interracial college—in the heart of pro-slavery Kentucky! That Fee and Rogers made clear their intentions can not be doubted; Clay certainly felt so. The second by-law of the constitution laid the basis for mixed education of the races in the new school when it declared that the college "shall be under an influence strictly Christian, and as such, opposed to sectarianism, slaveholding, caste, and every other wrong institution or practice."[3] "Opposition to caste," declared Fee, with Rogers' full approbation, "meant the co-education of the (so-called) 'races.' "[4] The position of Fee and Rogers on integration was for 1858 a remarkably advanced view of the direction black-white relations should take in America. Merely to oppose slavery at that time—much less to favor interracial education—was to jump ahead of the thinking of the vast majority of white Americans, both North and South.

When the founders petitioned Clay to join their board of trustees, he adamantly refused. For he totally opposed the direction in which Fee and Rogers were going. His action caused three other prominent Kentuckians to withdraw their support from the school, and so under state law there remained insufficient members of the board to secure a corporate charter. Fee sadly wrote, "Thus the caste issue sifted the very board of trustees themselves [sic];" some "friends of liberty who could assent to the general principles of justice and love thought it not expedient to make a literal, specific application of them."[5]

As Clay turned his face from the small antislavery community on the edge of the Bluegrass, it became known in Madison County that he no longer extended his personal protection to Fee. Soon the abolitionist preacher fell under both physical and verbal attack. Mobbed, threatened, cajoled, his friends whipped by rowdies and his own life in danger, Fee never flinched from his assault upon slavery.[6] Proslavery parents around Berea, unable to bear the merest hint that Rogers' small grade school might integrate, withdrew their children from his care. Yet, declared Fee, "We had then no sufficient precedent to guide, and no theory to maintain, save that it is always safe to do right, follow Christ. . . The incorporation of the principle of impartial conduct to all, in institutions for the public good, was to the founders of Berea College the only course at once Christian, patriotic, and philanthropic."[7]

---

[3] Elisabeth S. Peck, *Berea's First Century, 1855-1955* (Lexington, Kentucky, 1955), 13.

[4] Fee, *Autobiography*, 138; J. A. R. Rogers, *Birth of Berea College: A Story of Providence* (Philadelphia, 1904), 63-65.

[5] Fee, *Autobiography*, 138.

[6] *Ibid.*, 97-101, 107-20, 122, 24; Peck, *Berea's First Century*, 10, 14.

[7] Fee, *Autobiography*, 131.

Despite Fee's brave words, worse trouble soon befell his community. In October, 1859, there occurred at Harpers Ferry, Virginia, a raid by John Brown against slavery, an incident that would have repercussions in Berea. For Brown's foray caused Kentucky slaveowners to lose whatever equanimity they had toward their abolitionist neighbors. Fee's activities also created trouble. When Brown's raid took place, Fee was in the East on a fund raising tour, and in one of his speeches the preacher commented, "We need more John Browns." Although he hastened to add that he did not condone Brown's violence, only his purpose, the damage was done. Kentucky's newspapers quoted only the first part of Fee's comments, and soon there was great unrest toward Berea in Madison County. Slave owners looked with mounting suspicion toward the Berea ridge and commented on its strategic location for raids into the Bluegrass, should the people of Berea wish to try such a stunt.

Their fears were increased when rumors spread that the small anti-slavery community was stocking up on rifles. Although these horror stories were totally without basis, the situation became so tense that crates with Berea mailing labels were seized and opened in Richmond, the county seat, for fear that Fee's followers were receiving "Beecher's bibles" through the mail. One package, according to a few excited enthusiasts, was found to contain "infernal machines" —nothing more dangerous than candlesticks as it turned out. Finally, the slaveowners organized a citizens' group to force the followers of Fee from their homes. In December, 1859, the Bereans were compelled by a *posse* to give up their homes and seek shelter across the Ohio River.[8] Thus driven from Kentucky, they spent the long years of the Civil War in exile.

In 1865, the Bereans, a tenacious lot, converged once more on their adopted home. Fee and Rogers, fulfilling their prewar dream, now reorganized their college, collected enough like minded souls for a board of trustees, and immediately declared their intention of running an interracial school. On March 1, 1866, three black students were taken into Rogers' classes. According to E. Henry Fairchild, who in 1869 would be appointed president of the college, the Negroes' presence was not lightly accepted by the whites. "The morning that those three harmless youths walked in," he reported, "half the school walked out."[9] Yet, since there were few schools in southern Madison County at the time and many whites realized that their choice was either to follow the path of right as seen by Fee and Rogers or receive no education, many of them soon drifted back. Even after the number

---

[8] Mrs. J. A. R. Rogers, "Personal History of Berea College," Chapter 12, Berea College Archives.

[9] E. Henry Fairchild, *Berea College, Ky., An Interesting History* (Cincinnati, 1875), 41.

of Negro students was augmented in April, 1866 by the enrollment of several adults, veterans of the Union army whom Fee had met during his teaching and preaching service to them during the war at Camp Nelson on the Kentucky River, white enrollment remained stable.[10]

Under President Fairchild's enlightened administration, and with Reverend Fee serving as chairman of the board of trustees, Berea College in the 1870's and 1880's adhered mightily to its interracial program. In his inaugural address, Fairchild argued that Berea must remain "a school for all races of men, without distinction." Such an educational establishment was not one merely of taste but of strong principle. "We are aware," he said, "that this feature of the school fails to meet the approbation of many of our fellow citizens;" but he did not "doubt that in the end this characteristic . . . will be most highly approved and popular." He assumed "that negroes [sic] are to have, and ought to have, the same civil and political rights as white men, and the sooner and more thoroughly both classes adapt themselves to this idea, the better for all . . . We have had nearly two hundred students at a time, about half white and half colored, . . . and no collisions have occurred."[11] It was no accident, then, that for two decades under President Fairchild the racial balance of Berea was fairly even. In fact, the year before Frost arrived at Berea to assume his duties as president, Fee proudly proclaimed that the college's policy had always been to accept Negroes in "equal numbers with equal opportunities." This, he said, was "the design of the founders of the institution when they founded it. . . ."[12] In 1866, there were 96 Negroes enrolled, 91 whites; by 1875, 143 blacks and 94 whites attended Berea's classes. In 1889, the last year of Fairchild's administration, Berea's total enrollment was 334, of whom 177 were Negro, 157 white. In only one year between 1866 and 1894 (1877) did whites outnumber blacks at Berea; statistics for that year gave a 129-144 ratio.[13]

During those years, a time when Berea was as close as it ever got to a "golden age" of interracial education, Negro and white students came to Berea because they were willing to integrate. According to a white student who attended the school during Fairchild's years, the person who enrolled in the nineteenth century said to himself, "I am willing to come to a school like that"—one in which whites were given to understand by official policy that blacks would be present in such numbers as to stamp their own life style on college society. No white student was encouraged to attend if he were not willing to abide by this definition of integration.[14] By action of the board of trustees, the ad-

---

[10] Peck, *Berea's First Century*, 24; *Berea Evangelist*, II (March, 15, 1886), Berea College Archives.

[11] E. Henry Fairchild, "Inaugural Address," 11-12, Berea College Archives.

[12] Fee, "The Education of the Negro," *Digest* (April, 1891), Berea College Archives.

[13] Berea College, *Catalogues*, various dates, Berea College Archives; Peck, *Berea's First Century*, 42.

[14] Ernest G. Dodge to William G. Frost, April 11, 1925, Berea College Archives.

Aside from personal factors, powerful forces were operating upon Frost as he took over his new responsibilities, forces that were to change the basic direction of Berea's interracial commitment. First, the new president was a product of his intellectual and social times, and he seemed to accept national white opinion on Negro racial inferiority. He had studied for his Ph.D. at Harvard and was later intimate with many members of the school's staff who accepted as fact the intellectual inferiority of blacks. President Charles Eliot, who segregated Harvard's dormitories in the early twentieth century, was a supporter of Frost's segregationist activities at Berea.[20] Another advocate of the new president's policies was Nathaniel S. Shaler, professor of geology at Harvard.[21] Of Shaler a recent authority has said, he "helped to rationalize the century's belief in the physical and mental diversity of races in order to justify contemporary racial thought."[22] In raising funds for Berea, President Frost also went for assistance to national political figures like Theodore Roosevelt and Woodrow Wilson, men who openly expressed attitudes of racial superiority in their efforts to achieve political office.[23]

Second, President Frost began to concentrate the efforts of the college toward education of Appalachian whites. In 1895, he claimed discovery of "Appalachian America" (apparently he coined the phrase), a "new pioneer region in the mountains of the central south."[24] Immediately he began to bend his efforts to increasing the number of white Appalachians in the school. In 1892, when he arrived at Berea, total enrollment had been 354, of whom 184 were Negro. By 1903, there were 961 students in attendance, but only 157 were black. The vast bulk of the new white students were from the Appalachian South.[25] Much talk began to be heard around Berea of a "seven-to-one" white-black ratio of students, the same ratio of races as was found in Kentucky's population. Moreover, President Frost began referring to Berea's "unique work" in terms not of interracial education, as Fee had insisted in 1891, but of "effacing sectional lines" between North and South. He began to assert openly that he was creating a "newly made program" and years later proudly declared that "in my own time we frankly shifted emphasis, appealing more for the

---

[20] President Charles Eliot to *Boston Herald*, February 15, 1907, clipping in Berea College Archives. See Nell Painter, "Jim Crow at Harvard: 1923," *The New England Historical Quarterly*, XLIV, no. 4 (December, 1971), 627-34.

[21] Peck, *Berea's First Century*, 71.

[22] John S. Haller, Jr., *Outcasts From Evolution: Scientific Attitudes toward Racial Inferiority, 1859-1900* (Urbana, Illinois, 1971), 153-54. Today Berea College has an endowed professorship in geology and chemistry dedicated to the memory of Shaler. See *Berea College Bulletin: College Catalogue Issue, 1972-73* (Berea, Kentucky, 1972), 35.

[23] Peck, *Berea's First Century*, 147-49.

[24] Cited in *ibid.*, 70.

[25] Berea College, *Catalogues*, 1893-1904, Berea College Archives.

ministration even declared in 1872 that it was not opposed to interracial dating.[15] Black students, with the support of two black faculty members, Miss Julia Britton and Mr. James S. Hathaway, apparently responded favorably to the liberal Fee-Fairchild policy.

Berea's neighbors, however, did not take to the school's racial program. As Kentuckians lived through post war readjustments, they favored neither national policy on reconstruction nor its remarkable manifestation within their midst. Attacks, both verbal and physical, were directed against Berea during these years. One news account, President Fairchild disgustedly reported in 1875, had called Berea "a stench in the nostrils of all true Kentuckians." Worse, the militant Ku Klux Klan, taking the law into its own hands, attacked and harassed the school. "Rumors of raids came from far," said Fairchild, "and rowdyism sometimes disgraced itself very near. Pistols were discharged by drunken idiots racing through the streets, and occasionally were fired into buildings."[16]

Yet, Fee, Rogers, and Fairchild had faced worse, and they persevered. With the assistance of northern supporters, Berea College during reconstruction gained in economic and moral strength. Benefactors such as Dr. D. K. Pearsons, George Washington Cable, and General O. O. Howard helped build a pleasant physical plant and establish an endowment of $200,000 for the support of Berea's unique interracial program.[17] If many whites despised the college, others saw in it a model that would teach racial justice to the rest of the nation. Negroes in Kentucky supported the school with every means they had within their limited grasp.[18]

Such was the situation when in 1892 William G. Frost, professor of Greek at Oberlin, became president of the college. Frost's administration, which over the years proved controversial on the question of Berea's educational and racial aims, was born in controversy. When President Fairchild died in 1889, he was replaced by William B. Stewart, the personal choice of Fee. However, Stewart turned a number of trustees against him, and even Fee's support was not enough to ward off an assault upon the new president's position. In 1892, the board met, chose two new members who were opposed to Stewart and Fee, and proceeded to force Stewart's resignation. The board then elected Frost president, over the opposition of Fee and his friends.[19] From the beginning of their relationship, then, Fee and Frost were on poor terms with each other.

---

[15] Action of the board of trustees, July 2, 1872, "Minutes of the Board of Trustees," Berea College Archives; Fairchild, *Berea College*, 44-45.

[16] Fairchild, *Berea College*, 41.

[17] Peck, *Berea's First Century*, 34, 71, 141-42.

[18] Rogers, *Birth of Berea College*, 96, 99.

[19] Peck, *Berea's First Century*, 143-44; *Berea College Reporter*, IV (June, 1892), Berea College Archives.

mountaineers.''[26]

While the school's major commitment was undergoing this radical alteration, campus social life was changing dramatically. President Frost was imposing racial segregation upon the college's black community. One of his first official acts was to have the board of trustees rescind its resolution of 1872, allowing interracial dating on campus.[27] Later, in his memoirs, the president remarked that early in his tenure students "did the proper thing" by separating themselves by race in their eating and living habits. Soon, he declared, Berea was "respectable." It was his contention, then, that segregation occurred with the approbation of both races.[28] Yet at the time he made these changes, the evidence indicates he had no support from many Negroes. Moreover, it appears that he was *saying* one thing and *doing* another. In 1902, for instance, he explained his policy to the college faculty and trustees by declaring, "It is no unimportant part of a white boy's education to see the Negro treated as a man."[29] Yet at the same time he was writing prospective white students who had evinced interest in Berea but who were afraid of intermingling with Negroes: "It is quite possible for people to attend school at Berea and have no more to do with the colored people than at their home. White and colored students never room together and seldom board at the same places."[30] This was not the only time (as will be seen) that President Frost evinced contradictory policies in regard to black Bereans.

Negroes at the school, already "sensitive," according to a white student, "willing to see any real or suspected slight,"[31] viewed Frost's activities as a sellout to prejudice and began to complain about his new educational emphasis. Their anguish rose to a peak in 1895 when J. S. Hathaway, Berea's only Negro instructor (Miss Britton had left years before), applied for a professorship and was turned down by Frost and the faculty. Hathaway and some of his black friends at Berea (J. T. Robinson, J. W. Hughes, and Frank L. Williams), incensed by the college's action, wrote a scathing pamphlet indicting Frost as a racist and appealing to the board of trustees to reverse the decision. Entitled "Save Berea College for Christ and Humanity," the pamphlet opened with praise for "Brother" Fee's labors in the Negro's behalf. "Time," declared the writers, "has certainly verified his position of 'the gospel of impartial love versus expediency and policy.'" The new president, by changing Fee's emphasis, had created "perils that overhang this

---

[26] William G. Frost, *For the Mountains* (New York, 1937), 99; Frost to G. W. Mallow, May 11, 1907, Berea College Archives.

[27] "Minutes of the Board of Trustees," Berea College Archives.

[28] Frost, *For the Mountains*, 63-65.

[29] *Annual Report, 1902*, 66, Berea College Archives.

[30] For example: Frost to Miss Melissa Parkerson, March 6, 1901, Berea College Archives.

[31] Ernest G. Dodge to Frost, April 11, 1925, Berea College Archives.

institution, . . . permitting ambition and vanity to override individual right and justice." Said the pamphlet, Frost had allowed an appeal to the public for funds to educate only whites; and he had distorted in college publicity the reasons why others had contributed money—even when the donors expressly declared their intention that the funds were for co-education of the races. "The assumption [of Frost]"—so different from that of the founders—"that white persons should control Berea, on a white basis, has grown into a 'color policy,' with caste tendencies, and makes clear the necessity for fuller recognition of the colored people's rights . . ."

"It will be observed," the writers noted, "that [President Frost] is influenced by one controlling assumption, namely, that a white majority is necessary to abolish caste . . . This toadying fallacy is in itself a plea for caste . . . The management is pursuing an interpretation of the design and mission of Berea College in conformity with the prevailing sentiment, and not the spirit and principles of the college . . . We believe," they declared, "Pres. Frost is conscientious in his convictions; that he has the good of the colored people at heart (from his standpoint of what is for their good) but those convictions are based on false conceptions of religious obligation. . . ."[32]

Despite their petition, supporters of Hathaway were to see the board of trustees uphold Frost's decision. For their pains, Negroes at Berea who had spoken so passionately for their cause received from Frost not denial of their charges but epithets. One writer the president labeled a "monomaniac," another he called a "reckless individual," a third he said was "incompetent."[33] Negro militants on the campus were quick to point out, "It is a sure sign of an indefensible position when the slander of character is resorted to as a defense."[34] In another place, however, Frost did make this explanation: "A professorship is not the best place in which to demonstrate the powers of the Negro . . . We shall do [him] poor service . . . if for the sake of having colored professors we lose our chance to instruct mountain youth."[35] But a few years later, in testimony before a state legislative committee, Frost was effusive in his praise for Hathaway.[36] The president had evinced once more a confusion of statement that lent credence to black suspicions of his dedication to their welfare. Perhaps one more vignette could be added here to indicate his racial attitudes. At the height of campus tensions over Hathaway's non-promotion, President Frost planned to return late one night to the campus from a fund raising trip. Fearful for his safety, his wife wrote him and urged that he arrange to

---

[32] J. S. Hathaway, et al., "Save Berea College for Christ and Humanity," passim, Berea College Archives.

[33] Frost to [?], September 10, 1895, Berea College Archives.

[34] Hathaway, et al., "Save Berea College," 2.

[35] Frost, For the Mountains, 91.

[36] Transcript of President Frost's testimony, Berea College Archives.

arrive during daylight hours. Replied Frost, "No darkie has nerve enough to be an assassin. . . ."[37]

The evidence indicates that Negro fears of Frost were well founded. Many blacks certainly were appalled that he could believe his actions were benefitting them. Apparently he reasoned that in "effacing sectional lines" at Berea, a completely equalitarian policy would work to the detriment of Negroes in the long run by scaring whites from the campus. If southern whites did not come, they could not be wrung from their racism by having contacts with blacks. If he reasoned thus, Negroes were correct in believing that such a program was "in itself a plea for caste." For it would necessitate an entirely new attitude at Berea, one which would view whites as the benefactors of the school and Negroes as hardly more than tools for white uplift—certainly a change from Fee's beliefs. It would foreclose any possibility that blacks could stamp their culture on the college, because they were to be placed in a perpetual minority. By moving rapidly to segregation at Berea, Frost created a situation that allowed whites on the campus to view their Negro colleagues as inferiors.

That is exactly what happened. Whites soon were petitioning Frost to eliminate Negroes from every aspect of college life. Already segregation was a fact in dormitories, dining halls, sports, and the school band. Now some whites wanted blacks out of classrooms as well.[38] The prevailing attitude had become, whatever Frost had believed it would be, "Berea's a good school and surely has taught me a lot, but it's really a shame that I [have] to stoop to reciting with darkies in order to get its advantages."[39] By 1907, the Kentucky State Teacher's Association (which was composed largely of Negro men and women educated at Berea) passed a resolution at the instigation of Frank L. Williams, a former Berean who in 1904 had been given an honorary degree by his *alma mater,* entitled "President Frost's Betrayal of the Colored People in his Administration of Berea College." Indicting Frost's policies as a sellout to prejudice, Williams and his colleagues, A. W. Titus of Berea, J. C. Jackson and Dr. Mary Britton of Lexington, underscored the point that the president's program had almost inevitably led to white segregationist militancy at Berea.[40]

Through these wrenching years, John G. Fee, old and tired (he died in 1901), fought desperately to keep the school wedded to its original commitment. To the college convocation he argued early in Frost's administration, "You ask how shall we make a financial success. I answer by a speedy return to the original purposes of Berea College

---

[37] Frost to Mrs. Frost, December 19, 1894, Berea College Archives.

[38] Students of Model School, Petition to Faculty, [n. d.], Berea College Archives.

[39] Ernest G. Dodge to Frost, April 11, 1925, Berea College Archives.

[40] Frank L. Williams, *et al.,* "President Frost's Betrayal of the Colored People in his Administration of Berea College," *passim,* Berea College Archives. Williams later served as a high school principal in St. Louis, Missouri.

. . . Vigorous efforts have been made during the last year to bring in white students from the mountains . . . We would like to see an equal effort to bring in the colored for the sake of demonstrating the possibility and practicability of the education of colored and white . . . ., a fair percentage of each . . . The tendency now in Berea is to run down to a mere white school. Berea College will then be no more than thousands of other schools in the South. Ichabod will be written upon the face of Berea College . . .; the glory is departed—that of maintaining into fair proportion the policy of educating the brotherhood of the race."[41] In 1895 he asserted in *The Standard*, a Negro newspaper in Lexington: "I have no sympathy with the policy that would bring in from North or South a white majority. Such a policy would not meet the design of the founders of the institution." If a program like that were promulgated, he sadly noted, the early stalwarts of Berea would "rise from their graves as Rachel of old and weep because their cherished design was not carried out."[42] Finally, he argued in 1899, "Let me say that the unique work of Berea College is not 'effacing sectional lines' . . . and helping white people ('contemporary ancestors in the southern mountains') [as Frost had declared] but effacing the barbarous spirit of caste between colored and white at home. Let the friends of Berea College demand faithfulness to the original design of the college . . . Much more is being done here to bring in white students than colored. This the colored know and feel. . . ."[43]

Fee's entreaties fell on deaf ears. Soon Berea's white militants were working actively not only upon the campus but also throughout the state to coerce by law the total exclusion of blacks from the college. Following national racial patterns at the turn of the century, Kentucky in 1891 had barred by constitutional amendment all interracial education in public schools. Before long a movement was building in the state, led (some people believed) primarily by white Berea graduates, for the passage of a state law that would bar Negroes and whites from attending private schools together. Since only Berea had Negro students, clearly the mounting agitation applied specifically to the one school. In 1900, Tennessee had barred interracial education at Maryville College, and as President Frost wrote a friend in 1901, "This event happening so near us is occasioning a great deal of 'talk' in Kentucky." He added that if such a law were proposed in his state, Berea would fight it "to the very end."[44]

In 1904 he had to begin the struggle when Representative Carl Day introduced a bill in the Kentucky legislature calling for an end to interracial education in privately owned schools in the state. President Frost and the teachers of Berea petitioned the legislature and put in

---

[41] Fee, "A Word to the Convocation," (circa 1893), Berea College Archives.
[42] Fee to Lexington *Standard*, [n. d.], 1895, clipping in Berea College Archives.
[43] Fee to Springfield *Republican*, [n. d.], 1899, clipping in Berea College Archives.
[44] Frost to N.D.H., October 12, 1901, Berea College Archives.

personal appearances in Frankfort in opposition to the measure. Frost's major point of argument against the bill, as seen in his correspondence with legislators, was not its constitutionality or justice but the fact that, given Berea's totally segregated nature, it was wholly unnecessary.[45] Despite all efforts the bill became law, and the college trustees, at the suggestion of President Frost, decided to test the measure in the courts. When the law went to trial, the Kentucky Court of Appeals accepted a defense argument that the legislature had a right to police private institutions under its power to grant corporate charters; hence, the law was upheld. But the court invalidated one part of the law, that requiring any all-Negro school that Berea might decide to build to be located at least twenty-five miles from the campus.[46] Finally, in 1908 the United States Supreme Court handed down a decision that, while skirting many constitutional issues, completely affirmed the lower court's decision.

As the Day law wended its way through the courts, President Frost did not remain idle. Quickly he laid plans to move all Negro students off campus. That the races must be completely separated was apparent, for fines imposed by the law upon the college and its members soon would have bankrupted everyone at Berea. Yet many blacks immediately raised a question about Frost's action: why did Negroes have to leave Berea? Why not whites? "It would seem," declared Williams, Titus, Jackson, and Dr. Britton, "that in the name of justice, to say nothing of humanity, [the school] should have been given to the colored people. Had it not been for the colored people, there would have been no Berea College . . . We feel . . . they have been robbed of their birthright."[47] President Frost insisted in his memoirs that in order to do justice for black Bereans his first impulse had been to "[go] himself with the colored school." In fact, he said, "Had this separation occurred ten years earlier, the crusader" would have done precisely that. Probably Frost's remark was intended as a justification for his action; but if read another way, it could be construed as an open admission that his racial views had changed in the decade since he had come to Berea. In any case, he now made the decision that the Negroes must go, because despite his love for the race and his wish that black Bereans not be hurt, still they had schools such as Fisk and Tuskeegee in which they could matriculate, while white Appalachians had nowhere to go.[48]

Negroes were not impressed by this argument. Declared Williams and his colleagues in their anti-Frost pamphlet, "In the state of Kentucky there are a number of well equipped colleges all of which are

---

[45] Numerous letters from Frost to legislators, now housed in Berea College Archives, support this contention.

[46] Peck, *Berea's First Century*, 51-53; Frost, *For the Mountains*, 178.

[47] Williams, *et al.*, "President Frost's Betrayal," 11.

[48] Frost, *For the Mountains*, 176, 178-79, 184-85.

open to the mountain whites and many [with specific programs] for the mountain whites. The colored people of the state have NOT ONE COLLEGE . . .''[49] Soon Negroes had other arguments against Frost, for in 1906, *two years before the Supreme Court's final decision on the Day law*, the president began plans to establish a separate *technical and vocational school* for Negroes in Kentucky, *but not in Berea*. This action raised more questions in the minds of blacks about Frost's regard for their welfare. If Negroes had so many schools to go to, why build another one? And why must the proposed school be oriented toward vocational rather than liberal arts education? Was it because the president felt blacks incapable of intellectual pursuit? Why was the elimination of blacks from Berea becoming permanent in Frost's mind before the Day law had been upheld by the courts? And why was the new school to be located outside the town of Berea, miles away from the now all-white campus?[50] The evidence again indicates that Negro fears had real basis. Once again President Frost was saying one thing and doing another. But whatever his motives, he worked out a generous plan for the division of Berea's property, and a grant of $400,000 was set aside to found Lincoln Institute near Louisville as an all-Negro school.[51]

Many Kentucky blacks now came to distrust Frost completely. ''Thinking colored people of the state,'' said Williams and his friends, ''have no confidence in him.''[52] No wonder that James Bond, distinguished educator, alumnus and trustee of Berea College, a dedicated fund raiser during this time, wrote heart rending messages to Frost —coldly received—about his difficulties in collecting money from Kentucky's black community for Lincoln Institute.[53] Finally, Bond noted sadly to the president, ''Clearly you do not understand the Negro.''[54] Also no wonder that Carter G. Woodson, Berea's most famous alumnus, later a prolific scholar and founder of the Association for the Study of Negro Life and History, had few warm feelings toward either President Frost or the college.[55]

---

[49] Williams, *et al.*, ''President Frost's Betrayal,'' 11.

[50] *Ibid., passim.*

[51] Peck, *Berea's First Century*, 55-56.

[52] Williams, *et al.*, ''President Frost's Betrayal,'' 12.

[53] Berea's historian, Mrs. Peck (*Berea's First Century*, 56), argued that opposition to Frost came from a ''vocal minority, both Negro and white.'' Talk from these groups, said she, was ''sinister'' and ''insulting'' to the president. If Mr. Bond's experience was any indication of the attitudes of black Kentuckians, perhaps Mrs. Peck underestimated the opposition to Frost and his new programs. Moreover, in making this assertion, Mrs. Peck completely ignored the dismay expressed by Reverend Fee and his supporters.

[54] Bond to Frost, [n. d.], 1909, Berea College Archives.

[55] Woodson's correspondence with college officials, now located in the college archives, conveys a tone of muted anger toward Berea. One letter questions whether Woodson was given a degree commensurate with his work while at the school (Woodson to ''the President of Berea College, Berea, Ky.,'' [n. d.], Berea College Archives).

To many friends of Berea, both black and white, it had been evident for years that the school's policy under Frost had thwarted the rights of Negroes. Hence, probably inevitably, rumors began to circulate that he had helped draft the Day bill, that he had fought the law in court only because he strongly believed it would be upheld despite his opposition, and that his actions had been a good cover for baser designs. While the evidence indicates that he may have been capable of such activity, it does not prove that he actually was involved in writing, or surreptitiously supporting, the Day law.[56] From 1892 until 1904, while President Frost's time had been spent in expanding white enrollments at Berea; while he decided that the interracial commitment was to take a decidedly secondary position to this main thrust; and while he encouraged segregation on the Berea campus in order to achieve his ends, still it seemed that he was absolutely sincere in wanting to keep a complaisant Negro enrollment at around one-seventh of the college population. His aim, as he made clear, was not immediate uplift for blacks; indeed, Negro Bereans were to be hardly more than guinea pigs used for the improvement of white Appalachians. Yet in the long run, he felt (or at least publicly declared) that his program would help both races. Curiously, he did not seem to foresee that his scheme, by its very nature, rather than eliminating prejudice from whites would only exacerbate already existing prejudices.

If this had been President Frost's policy in 1904, two years later he had changed his mind. For by 1906 he was perfectly willing to see blacks permanently barred from Berea College and had entered the camp of Representative Day. In some respects, Frost went even farther toward racial intolerance after 1906 than the Day law required. Specifically, he barred Negroes from the nondenominational Church of Christ, Union, which was affiliated with the college, and he eliminated from the Alumni Association rolls the names of all black graduates.[57] As a capstone to his endeavors, in 1911 President Frost helped rewrite the constitution of Berea in order to change the stated basic commitment from co-education of the races to education of poor white mountaineers.[58] Ever since, as Mrs. Elisabeth Peck, college historian, correctly pointed out, ". . . Berea has remained an institution especially devoted to the mountain people."[59]

Even after all these events, a large number of Negro Bereans did not believe Frost unjust. If he received criticism from some blacks, others gave him their support. In 1908, a number of former students of the school passed a resolution "affirm[ing] our faith in President Frost and the Board of Trustees." They also were disgusted at the activities of

---

[56] See Richard A. Heckman and Betty Jean Hall, "Berea College and the Day Law," *Register of the Kentucky Historical Society*, LXVI (January, 1968), 51-52.

[57] Ernest G. Dodge to Frost, April 11, 1925, Berea College Archives.

[58] Peck, *Berea's First Century*, 79.

[59] *Ibid*, 61.

their brothers who were opposing Berea's policies. "[We] deprecate," they declared, "the bitter and . . . unjust and unwise criticism . . . in some quarters and council our people to exercise patience and charity in the matter. . . ."[60] Seemingly, national arguments between black leaders W. E. B. DuBois and Booker T. Washington about the proper role for Afro-Americans in this time of racial crisis had had an impact at Berea. The black community at the school certainly had divided between those who preached accommodation with racist whites (the Washington position) and those who urged no compromise with injustice (the DuBois attitude). In any case, these arguments among Negroes made little difference at Berea during the Frost years. Regardless of how they felt, blacks seemed to be for the president little more than objects to be manipulated for the betterment of mountain whites. Negro voices, whether conservative or radical, went largely unheeded.

In summation, President William G. Frost by 1908 had remade Berea College into an institution quite different in purpose than it had been under John G. Fee. In rejecting interracial education, Frost had subverted the Founder's dream and had wrought damage upon black Bereans. While Negro Americans' pleas for justice were ignored, it seems clear that they had a strong argument against supporters of Berea's new direction and purpose. Perhaps Frost felt he had no choice but to carry out the program he did. Perhaps he did not want to. But the evidence shows the opposite. In contradicting himself so often on what his purposes were, in saying one thing and doing another, he laid himself open for blacks to accuse him of racial prejudice. In conforming to unjust national racial policies, in befriending educators, scientists, and politicians who also expressed feelings of superiority over black Americans, he was far from the nobility that Fee had shown years before in standing up, despite all adversity, for what he believed was right. Admirers of the old Berea must have remembered during these bitter years words written by Fee in an attempt to counteract Frost's new policies. For, as the patriarch had feared, "Ichabod [had been] written upon the face of Berea College," and the old glory had departed. Surely the founders now had cause to "rise from their graves as Rachel of old [and] weep because their cherished design was not carried out."

---

[60] Resolution, April, 1908, Berea College Archives.

# Northern Philanthropy and the Emergence of Black Higher Education—Do-Gooders, Compromisers, or Co-Conspirators?

J. M. Stephen Peeps, *Assistant to the President, Stanford University**

## INTRODUCTION

This is an account of organized northern philanthropy and the telltale role it played in shaping the emergence of private black colleges after America's Civil War. As is often the case, one account inspires another, and that is precisely the effect Jencks and Riesman's *The Academic Revolution* had on this investigation. Its authors earned quick and considerable notoriety at the close of the 1960s for condemning contemporary black colleges as "academic disaster areas." That phrase alone was enough to inspire a torrent of rebuttal from scholars—primarily black—who felt the basic mission and value of historically Negro colleges had been both undervalued and misunderstood. Yet what inspires this essay's much narrower slant is the tense relationship between two other strident observations made about black aspirations and white responsibilities for higher education. On the one hand we are told that, "the Negro college of the 1950's was usually an ill-financed, ill-staffed caricature of white higher education,"[1] as if to suggest that blacks ought to have succeeded better at emulating the white college model. On the other we are told, *despite* acknowledgement that "the private Negro colleges were for the most part financed by white philanthropists, controlled by white boards of trustees . . .," "it is easy to misunderstand or exaggerate the extent to which white control shaped these private colleges."[2]

---

*At the time this article was written, the author was a graduate student in Administration, Planning and Social Policy at the Harvard Graduate School of Education—ED.

[1]Christopher Jencks and David Riesman, *The Academic Revolution* (Garden City: Doubleday, 1969), p. 425.

[2]Ibid., p. 418.

*Journal of Negro Education*, Vol. 50, No. 3 (1981)
Copyright © 1981, Howard University

The implication lingers that blacks have themselves to blame for running second best to their white role models. Indeed, Jencks and Riesman ultimately conclude that:

> In any event, we do not believe the basic character of the private Negro colleges was determined primarily by the prejudices or self-interest of their white trustees, any more than the basic character of other colleges has been. Rather, the Negro college was molded by the circumstances in which it found itself locally.[3]

In this manner certain white hands are washed of responsibility for the retarded evolution of black private education. Still it is hard not to sense potential contradiction in what Jencks and Riesman claim. It seems ironic that more than a century after their founding and financing by white philanthropists, Negro colleges should lag so far behind their white counterparts. It was, after all, white philanthropists who presided so centrally over the conception, birth, and early childhood of most private black colleges. Given such a commanding presence, it appears odd that white control—particularly if born of strong philanthropic sentiment—would have had so little influence on long-range development. That is the outcome one might expect had black colleges been launched under black control. Yet Jencks and Riesman state otherwise. Thus another possibility arises. This one suggests that northern white philanthropy did indeed exert influence but that it sometimes ran a course contrary to what we would expect from their good intentions. The history of post-bellum southern education, particularly as it relates to America's new freedmen, provides more than enough evidence to pay that more sinister possibility some close attention.

## PHILANTHROPY'S FIRST PHASE:
## EGALITARIAN BEGINNINGS

Alan Pifer, President of the Carnegie Corporation, precedes his historical review of black higher education with the following observation:

> Understandably, the development of higher education for blacks during Reconstruction and its aftermath was conditioned by . . . military, political, and social developments . . . . Indeed the history of higher education for blacks in the latter part of the 19th century is mainly a chapter in Southern history.[4]

Pifer's point is well taken. To understand both progressive and repressive developments in the black college movement after the Civil War it is important that those developments be placed within

[3]Ibid., p. 419.
[4]Alan Pifer, "The Higher Education of Blacks in the United States," Reprint of the Alfred and Winifred Hoernle Memorial Lecture for 1973, South African Institute of Race Relations, Johannesburg, 1 Aug. 1973, p. 11.

context of that divisive historical era. When the "conflict" ended in 1865, some four million slaves suddenly became free men. Stephen J. Wright and other historians estimate that as many as 96 percent of their number were illiterate.[5] Though that condition seems alarming in contemporary terms, it is really not so surprising in light of the South's pre-war white supremacist society. All Southern states employed statutes called the Black Codes which strictly forbade the schooling of black slaves. Supremacist thinking was patently simple. Any sort of education promised to poison the slave mentality. Southern whites were not about to grant their slaves "access to such pernicious ideas as those expressed in our Declaration of Independence, namely, that all men are created equal and have certain inalienable rights. In short, education was dangerous."[6]

Reconstruction, that period of just twelve short years after the War, introduced this repressive notion to some rather remarkable reforms and, as far as white southerners were concerned, some bitter impositions at the hands of northern politicians, carpetbaggers, and Christian missionaries. The missionaries must certainly be considered the educational philanthropists of that era, predecessors to the great philanthropic foundations which were to make their own quite different mark on black higher education toward the end of the century. The situation the missionaries faced in terms of bringing higher education to the freedmen can only be described as close to hopeless. Quite apart from southern white doubt about *any* level of educability of blacks, Stephen Wright observes that there were simply no elementary or secondary schools to prepare students for college in any case.[7] Of all the southern states prior to 1860, only Kentucky and North Carolina had anything which even approached a system of public schools.[8]

That dire situation aside, several northern denominational groups set about establishing a number of bona fide colleges for blacks. Our perspective a century later suggests that attempts at higher education may have been beyond the bounds of the newly emancipated. Yet a variety of factors clearly convinced the missionaries otherwise, and they quickly embarked on their more progressive course. One inspiration was the prosperous existence of two northern missionary colleges established for blacks before the War's end—Lincoln University of Pennsylvania by the Presbyterian

---

[5]Stephen J. Wright, "The Negro College in America," *Harvard Educational Review*, 30 (1960), 280.

[6]Pifer, p. 8.

[7]Wright, p. 280.

[8]Frank Bowles and Frank A. De Costa, *Between Two Worlds: A Profile of Negro Higher Education* (New York: McGraw-Hill, 1971), p. 27.

*The Journal of Negro Education*    253

Church in 1854 and Wilberforce of Ohio in 1856 by the Methodist Episcopal denomination. This early demonstration of faith in blacks' higher educability proved well-founded over the rest of the century, for as St. Clair Drake points out:

> The founders of Lincoln may have been paternalistic, but they never had any doubt about the ability of black men to master the standard liberal arts curriculum of the day. By 1900, Lincoln had graduated six hundred men (five times more than any of the thirty-three other black degree-granting institutions then in existence). They had been subjected to a heavy dose of Greek, Latin, and the Holy Scriptures, but had also been exposed to . . . elementary sociology and political economy, as well as some algebra, geometry, trigonometry, geology, chemistry, physiology, and psychology.[9]

It is only reasonable, of course, to acknowledge that the trend at Lincoln was an isolated example of remarkable success. Most of the so-called "colleges" pioneered for southern blacks were admittedly little more than secondary schools. Nonetheless, Pifer reports that a half dozen or more institutions for blacks had genuine collegiate departments as early as 1872 which would by 1895 produce more than eleven hundred graduates bound for careers in teaching, the ministry, and other service professions.[10] The point is not to overemphasize the quality of what was then passing as black higher education, but simply to stress the missionaries' formative faith in the capacity of blacks to be college educated. Theirs was a belief which ran sharply and explosively counter to the thinking of most white southerners, both before and after the War Between the States. As explained by Browning and Williams in *Black Colleges in America*:

> Education in the liberal arts was, for the missionaries, a means of remaking blacks into the image of the ideal American citizen . . . What distinguishes missionaries' work from other social reforms of the period and from that which followed was a belief, at least stated, that blacks were equal to whites but for the debilitating effects of slavery.[11]

Hence the philanthropists of the Reconstruction era might fairly be labeled abolitionist egalitarians. Yet as Stephen Wright points out, there were pragmatic motivations as well. Given the assumption that beyond the basic necessity of life an education was the first need of the newly emancipated, there existed an urgent need for black teachers and a literate black ministry to carry education down to the millions of freedmen and children so sorely in need of rudimentary learning. In top-down fashion, the missionaries thus

[9]St. Clair Drake, "The Black University in the American Social Order," *Daedalus*, 100 (1966), 836.

[10]Pifer, p. 12.

[11]Jane E. Smith Browning and John B. Williams, "History and Goals of Black Institutions of Higher Learning," in *Black Colleges in America: Challenge, Development, Survival*, ed. Charles V. Willie and Ronald R. Edmonds (New York: Teachers College Press, 1978), p. 91.

254    *The Journal of Negro Education*

created their black colleges largely as teacher training institutions to hasten the overall process of educating a mass of illiterates.[12]

Whatever the combination of motives, northern missionaries are rightfully credited with launching an extraordinary spate of southern black institutions of higher learning modeled largely on the academic liberal arts format common to white higher education in the North. Their denominations included northern Baptist and their American Baptist Home Mission Society, the Congregationalists' American Missionary Association (AMA), the Episcopalians' Freedmen's Aid Society, and a number of others. As early as 1870 the AMA alone had overseen the founding of Howard, Fisk, Atlanta University, and Talladega College. And there was to be no shortage of clientele. For a population historically deprived of any opportunity for formal learning, education represented nothing less than a "badge of freedom."[13] As John Hope Franklin put it in his epic work *From Slavery to Freedom:*

> The pursuit of education, therefore, came to be one of the great preoccupations of Negroes; and enlightenment was viewed by many as the greatest single opportunity to escape the proscriptions and indignities that whites were heaping upon blacks.[14]

The attempt by northern missionaries to institute a traditional liberal arts form of higher learning for ex-slaves has not escaped some harsh and legitimate criticism. Such philanthropic progressivism is seen in hindsight as more the product of zeal and pity than as legitimate appraisal of the needs and circumstances of ex-slaves. Missionaries are sometimes portrayed as bullheadedly idealistic in their attempt to impose an essentially classic college curriculum on "scarcely literate" students. One highly respected historian, Merle Curti, caps such incisive criticism with his observation that "zealous northern philanthropy had clearly undertaken too much too soon."[15]

There is no questioning the basis of Curti's appraisal. Yet much like Jencks and Riesman's, his verdict fails to gauge adequately the profound opening influence white philanthropic control exerted on the emergence of black higher education. There essentially was no such thing prior to 1865. By the end of Reconstruction, a staggering increase had occurred. More important, at that time those rudimentary black colleges were perhaps more akin to their white models than were their counterparts a century later when condemned in *The Academic Revolution* as "academic dis-

[12]Wright, p. 281.
[13]Martin Carnoy, *Education as Cultural Imperialism* (New York: David McKay Company, 1974), p. 284.
[14]John H. Franklin, *From Slavery to Freedom* (New York: Knopf, 1974), p. 271.
[15]Merle C. Curti and Roderick Nash, *Philanthropy in the Shaping of American Higher Education* (New Brunswick: Rutgers University Press, 1965), p. 174.

aster areas." And again contrary to what Jencks and Riesman imply, Fisk, Howard, and Atlanta Universities were indeed deeply shaped by a brand of northern white philanthropy destined all too soon to disappear. As Holmes observed in 1934:

> . . . it is likely that if there had been no Northern philanthropy there would have been no Negro college in the South until a transformation had taken place in the attitude of the white South on this subject . . . . The point is clear, at any rate, that however mistaken the Northern denominational bodies may have been in their educational theories, without their zeal the Negro race would have been lacking the leadership which the first generation out of slavery furnished.[16]

## "FOR HUMBLE SERVICE IN THE BACKWATERS"[17]

Sociologist Charles Willie reminds us again that the continuing story of black colleges and their benefactors cannot be appraised outside its time.[18] For example, that peculiarly progressive era called Reconstruction must be understood as a clear aberration in southern history. As such, the Reconstruction phenomenon was just as responsible for the emergence of academic black colleges as was missionary egalitarianism. The latter simply could not have existed within any other context. Thus it is very important to remember that the reforms which ruled southern whites during Reconstruction were anything but enduring or homespun.

Early northern benevolence on behalf of the freedmen so chafed at certain southern sensibilities that the era of backlash which followed now appears inevitable. So it was that Reconstruction's demise took with it the missionaries and that abiding faith in black higher educability which so characterized the initial development of Negro colleges. In its place emerged the credo of new black benefactors. These were powerful white men who must still be considered philanthropists, even though they were born of an industrial rather than missionary way of thinking. Their influence on black college development appears no less profound in retrospect than that of their missionary predecessors. Yet what so distinguishes this second philanthropic phase is its tendency to accommodate the wishes of reemerging white supremacy. Historian Henry Allan Bullock holds the new philanthropists' posture in part responsible for the "Great Detour" which Negro education and the Negro colleges were soon to take from America's educa-

[16]Dwight O. W. Holmes, *The Evolution of the Negro College* (New York: Arno Press and the New York Times, 1969), p. 70.

[17]Raymond Wolters, *The New Negro on Campus: Black College Rebellions of the 1920s* (Princeton: Princeton University Press, 1975), p. 16.

[18]Charles V. Willie, "Racism, Black Education, and the Sociology of Knowledge," in *Black Colleges in America: Challenge, Development, Survival*, ed. Charles V. Willie and Ronald R. Edmonds (New York: Teachers College Press, 1978), p. 4.

tional mainstream.[19] But to understand Bullock's indictment, it is first important to review the new historical context in which educational changes were taking place.

Just twelve tumultuous years after the Confederacy's surrender, northern industrialists and a compromise president, Rutherford B. Hayes, relinquished control of the South to its planters and white supremacists. Reprisals against ex-slaves were thus quick and uncompromising, for the withdrawal of federal troops "ushered in a period of general repressiveness in Southern society."[20] The Emancipation Proclamation may forever have spared black Americans the resurgence of slavery, but it did nothing to stem the emergence of a new caste system which Martin Carnoy describes as "only legally different from slavery."[21]

Out with the Union troops went the progressive Reconstruction legislatures which had made possible the mercurial equality of black men from 1865 to 1877. In their wake spewed all the pent up hostility of a subdued supremacist society which had too long endured unwanted parity for a race so recently at white command. The post-Reconstruction mood of most white southerners was thus quite explosive, at least intent on dismantling whatever formal structures black equality had assumed in recent years. This new era of white supremacy gathered momentum in the first post-Reconstruction decade, and by 1890 is described by Pifer as "the most virulent spate of 'Negrophobia' that has ever engulfed the United States."[22]

In actual fact, the Reconstruction era had not given America's ex-slaves all that much to show for their freedom. Real gains were small in material terms, but immense in symbolic significance to hostile white supremacists. Near the top of the list was the freedman's newly acquired access to education, particularly at the higher education level to which northern missionaries had pushed black aspirations. Repressing education, along with income, was immediately regarded as crucial to maintenance of the new caste system which was to replace outright slavery.[23]

The intense fear with which most white southerners viewed anything beyond elementary education of blacks is something well

[19]Henry A. Bullock, *A History of Negro Education in the South* (Cambridge: Harvard University Press, 1967), pp. 60-88.

[20]Browning and Williams, p. 72.

[21]Carnoy, p. 273.

[22]Pifer, pp. 14-15. Historian James McPherson gives an even clearer picture of the times: "The year 1890 marked a turning point in race relations. . . . During the [1890s] Southern States enacted a host of Jim Crow laws that segregated blacks in virtually every aspect of public life. . . . Lynching reached its worst level in the 1890s and became increasingly a racial and Southern phenomenon. See: James McPherson, *The Abolitionist Legacy: From Reconstruction to the NAACP* (Princeton: Princeton University Press, 1975), p. 299.

[23]Drake, p. 839.

chronicled by historian Raymond Wolters, whose work reveals strong southern sentiment that higher learning would not only lead blacks to increased dissatisfaction with their inferior status, but in turn would render Negroes less submissive, less deferential, and unwilling to labor in the fields. As Wolters succinctly defines the situation, "Southerners intuitively recognized that no aristocracy—whether caste or class—could maintain its privileges in the face of an egalitarian educational system."[24]

Accompanying that basic racist vindictiveness was a new quasi-scientific movement called Social Darwinism. Its physiological thesis was uncomplicated; blacks were simply thought to be a genetically inferior race. The movement's tenets approached the level of scientific axiom during the latter part of the century. McPherson reports that, "weighty tomes based on research in physical and social sciences offered apparently irrefutable evidence of racial differences."[25] Naturally, accepting the theory made it a good deal easier to rationalize repression of Negro college education. Indeed, even if one harbored no fear of dangerous, black "uppityness," there was little sense in supporting higher learning for a race which was "by birth and natural capacity fitted only for manual labor."[26]

However strong these sentiments ran against the freedmen and their newly acquired opportunities for college training, even southern racists held no hope for a reversion all the way back to the Black Codes of earlier years. The War *had* been lost, after all, and both northern sentiment and federal legislation remained on the side of emancipation. Yet the white South strove for some less pernicious means of regaining the upper hand in their bi-racial society. Fully enforced illiteracy may no longer have been an option, yet the twin forces of racism and Social Darwinism found a fully acceptable target in the missionaries'. academically oriented, classical model for higher education of blacks. More significant, in the very same stroke a much-to-be-debated alternative was to be broached, the term for which was industrial education. As Raymond Wolters puts it:

> The prevailing view of the post-Reconstruction era held that if blacks were not innately inferior they were, at the very least, at a relatively primitive state of cultural evolution and thus incapable of mastering the liberal arts . . . . Thus it was inevitable that the white South, when it returned to power after Reconstruction, would limit Negro college education to the preparation of the few professionals needed to insure a hermetic caste system . . . . In this way vocational training became a corollary of white su-

[24]Wolters, *The New Negro on Campus*, p. 5.
[25]McPherson, p. 339.
[26]Ibid., p. 219.

premacy, with black men and women expected to learn the elementary lessons of carpentry, gardening, and homemaking that would make them useful helots.[27]

## THE EDUCATIONAL CHOICE

The history of the industrial versus classical conflict over Negro higher education covers a. time span from the 1880s through to the First World War. It has consumed the fulltime attention of countless educational historians. The conflict is perhaps most often thought of as a fierce ideological struggle between two black leaders, Booker T. Washington and W. E. B. Du Bois, each of whom took antithetical stands on what level of education was in the best interests of America's new black citizen. The choice made between their philosophies was to have a profound effect on the nature of private black colleges in the upcoming century.

Tuskegee Institute's Booker T. Washington was, in a sense, one of those "few professionals needed to insure a hermetic caste system" whom Wolters refers to above. For lack of a better label, Washington is regarded by many contemporary historians as an arch accommodationist to the dictates of southern white supremacy. If indeed he had high long-term aspirations for his people, they were to be attained pacifistically and from ground up. In essence, Washington, a disciple of Hampton Institute's founder, Samuel Chapman Armstrong, advocated almost total acquiescence to the regressive educational notions of white southerners. By pursuing immediately useful vocational training, Washington felt blacks might more quickly establish an acceptable (and non-threatening) economic foothold from which gradually to attain a position of power and equality in the South.[28]

There was clearly little room yet in this educational game plan for what Washington called "mere book learning."[29] Instead, Washington advocated what was a low-level sort of vocational training and did little to encourage the sort of educational aspirations earlier promoted in the missionary brand of higher education learning. In all likelihood, Washington genuinely saw this industrial avenue leading his people slowly but surely to a level of parity and brotherhood that for now he cautioned them to defer. The irony, as John Hope Franklin explains, was that:

> The particular type of industrial education that Washington emphasized was outmoded at the time he enunciated it . . . Many of the occupations that Washington was urging Negroes to enter were disappearing altogether. As training grounds for industrial workers, the curriculums and the institutions urged by Washington were not at all satisfactory . . . He therefore utterly

[27]Wolters, p. 7.
[28]Franklin, p. 286.
[29]Wolters, p. 20.

failed to see the relation of the laboring class to the Industrial Revolution and counseled an approach that had the effect of perpetuating the master-slave tradition.[30]

Blacks and new northern philanthropists of the post-Reconstruction era certainly had the choice of an optional philosophy, this one embodied by W. E. B. Du Bois. Unlike Washington, Du Bois had been educated in classical fashion, first at Fisk, a black institution which prided itself on its academic orientation, and then at predominantly white Harvard. It is really enough to say that Du Bois argued for everything Washington argued against. An ardent believer in liberal arts college training, Du Bois was convinced that black equality meant developing black leadership (his "Talented Tenth") to the same level of intellectual, social, and political education as whites. Nothing like that was attainable through Washington's industrial model. In fact, quite the opposite seemed likely. As Browning and Williams put it, "For Du Bois, industrial education required blacks to give up political power, abandon their insistence on civil rights, and withdraw demands for the education of black youth."[31]

So it was that despite any good intentions behind its introduction, industrial education was seen by some blacks and many progressive whites as a dangerous new weapon to keep the Negro caste-bound. What was purported to be a bona fide technical education comparable to the utilitarian movement in the American college mainstream quickly degenerated to a symbolic brand of inferior training. Naturally, white supremacists seized on the industrial college model as a design to maintain blacks at the lowest rungs of the economic ladder.[32] Alan Pifer points out that what was elsewhere regarded as skilled education for America's modernizing economy became at many of the South's best-supported Negro colleges a "pre-industrial" curriculum of simple crafts, gardening, and the like. Far from preparing students for more responsible roles in the expanding economy, this distorted model divorced the Negro from any sort of social mobility. It was instead a caste education meant to delineate the college-educated black from the college-educated white and thereby to keep the former in "his proper place."

## "GREAT DETOUR" GUILT: FACT OR IMPLICATION?

Clearly, the dramatic political and sociological reversals following Reconstruction tend best to explain how black industrial education, that so-called "Great Detour" from mainstream opportuni-

[30]Franklin, p. 290.
[31]Browning and Williams, p. 77.
[32]Ibid., pp. 72-75.

ty, came to loom on the southern horizon. In its shadow stood the future well-being of the private Negro college. Just as the peculiar historical context of post-War years had allowed early northern philanthropy to introduce a progressive brand of academic higher education for blacks, so now the return of supremacist ideology stood poised to snuff it out.

The important thing to remember is that a choice did remain for those in a position to influence the education of Negroes. On the one hand stood the Washington model and on the other stood those black institutions which identified themselves with Du Bois and more liberal learning. Emerging simultaneously was the powerful new prototype of northern philanthropy. This was the richly endowed educational foundation, backed by the personal fortunes of such great northern industrialists as George Peabody, John D. Rockefeller, and Andrew Carnegie. Though their influence was to be less ideological and more financial than that of their missionary predecessors, even in the late 1800s there was no question that the allocation of philanthropic dollars represented an endorsement of one educational philosophy over another.

History's ballots have now been collected, and the judgment on philanthropy leans heavily toward its complicity in the "Great Detour." As Martin Carnoy sums it up:

> The position taken toward white supremacy by these Northern capitalists, who may have been genuinely concerned about the social and economic constraints placed on blacks by Southern whites, was completely consistent with their views on white racial and ethnic superiority as practiced in the North.[33]

Just what is the nature of the evidence against the new northern philanthropists and what can be said about the ramifications of their support for the vocational detour? In a nutshell, the consequence of their primarily industrial orientation was fiscal disinterest in Negro colleges that promoted liberal education and more generous attention to the recognized industrial institutions.[34] More often than not, the general agents of philanthropic foundations went first to Booker T. Washington for advice, and the not-so-surprising result was an outpouring of dollars for preeminent vocational models like Hampton and Tuskegee. Simultaneously, even the best of the Du Bois-style liberal arts colleges began to show the signs of philanthropic malnourishment. St. Clair Drake observes that:

> During the last twenty years of the nineteenth century the matter was settled as to what kind of education was deemed 'best' for most ex-slaves and as to how limited financial resources would be allocated . . . .

[33]Carnoy, p. 292.
[34]Pifer, p. 16.

... A group of Northern industrialists ... threw its support behind institutions that stressed Booker T. Washington's concept of 'industrial education. Institutions concerned with developing a Talented Tenth became the stepchildren of the philanthropists: the Tuskegee-Hampton approach dominated the education of black people in the South until after World War I. Hampton and Tuskegee, *not* Howard, Fisk, and Atlanta, secured the large endowment funds and the money needed for rapid physical expansion.[35]

These are not just subjective indictments. They are supported by historical fact. Ledgers of foundation appropriations show that most philanthropic dollars did indeed turn up at the two institutions most often identified with Washington. By 1915 Hampton's and Tuskegee's respective endowments of $2.7 and $1.9 million were by far the heaviest of all black colleges, representing over half the entire endowment of America's black private institutions. In poignant contrast stood Lincoln University, then the oldest and best-endowed liberal arts college, with its nest egg of but $700,000.[36] The situation was not to change over the next decade. By 1925, Hampton, "which actively solicited the assistance of Northern philanthropies that deferred to the white South on the proper education of Negroes," was still philanthropy's shining example with an $8.5 million endowment. That not only placed Hampton first among black schools, but seventeenth among only 176 American colleges then possessing endowments of more than seven million dollars.[37]

Subtler evidence of philanthropy's "cold reception to Negro colleges designed on the standard American pattern of higher education"[38] was the inclination of those colleges to apply a new vocational blackface. Stephen Wright observes that such compromises to attract philanthropic favor "tended to give an industrial-vocational character to many of the colleges for Negroes."[39] Even Fisk, when faced with dire economic circumstances near the turn of the century, offered to establish an applied science department. That concession proved profitable, for within the year Booker T. Washington encouraged two prominent foundations to come forward with funding.[40]

These indictments lack no sting, yet so far they are general enough to preserve the anonymity of individual offenders. As might be expected, a closer look at specific philanthropic foundations suggests a rogue's gallery to some critics. George F. Peabody

[35]Drake, p. 840.
[36]Sherman J. Jones and George B. Weathersby, "Financing the Black College," in *Black Colleges in America: Challenge, Development, Survival,* ed. Charles V. Willie and Ronald R. Edmonds (New York: Teachers College Press, 1978), p. 111.
[37]Wolters, p. 231.
[38]Louis R. Harlan, *Separate and Unequal* (New York: Atheneum, 1968), p. 86.
[39]Wright, p. 286.
[40]Jones and Weathersby, p. 112.

established America's first exclusively educational foundation in 1867, and as such the Fund concentrated on public industrial education at primary and secondary levels. The Fund's two-fold significance for private Negro colleges was Peabody's trend-setting philosophy toward Negro educability and the enduring influence of one of that philosophy's framers, Jabez L. M. Curry. Merle Curti notes that:

> The agents selected to administer the Peabody Fund, first Barnas Sears and in 1892 Jabez L. M. Curry, followed the policy of cooperating with Southern opinion. This meant that segregation was maintained, vocational training promoted, a policy of inequity established in allocation of funds . . . and control of the institutions kept out of Negro hands.[41]

Curry's attitude is important because it later came to bear on the activities of two other post-Reconstruction giants, the Slater Fund and the General Education Board (GEB). John F. Slater launched his foundation in 1882 as the first to provide exclusively for Negro education. True to Peabody's precedent, Slater money was from the start restricted to those Negro institutions that conformed to southern white insistence on industrial education for the freedmen.[42] And although Atticus G. Haygood preceded J. L. M. Curry as the Fund's first "general agent," his convictions were the same and were not lost on the struggling black colleges. Writing in 1934 about Haygood and the Fund, Dwight O. W. Holmes observed:

> As a result of this attitude on the part of the general agent, it became the policy of the Fund to aid only those schools which offered industrial training. Because of the financial strain under which all schools for Negroes were working, many of them adjusted their curricula to qualify for aid from the Fund, among them being most of the Negro colleges.[43]

Things changed little during Curry's subsequent twelve-year term as the Fund's general agent (1891-1903). An ardent admirer of the Hampton-Tuskegee model, he so influenced the Slater board to support these two institutions that during the last three-year period of the Curry administration some 50.3 percent of all Slater appropriations went into their coffers.[44]

The last philanthropic giant to exercise great reformative influence over the post-Reconstruction Negro college was John D. Rockefeller's General Education Board, established in 1902. The GEB's founding earns special note as a major event in the history of American philanthropy, for as Curti observes, "no other agency, public or private, exerted a comparable force in shaping Negro

---

[41]Curti and Nash, p. 175.
[42]Harlan, p. 8.
[43]Holmes, pp. 167-168.
[44]Ibid., p. 169.

higher education."[45] Given that degree of influence, the language of the Board's incorporating charter takes on special importance, for it foreshadows precisely what the GEB's opening influence on black higher education would be:

> ... the said corporation shall have power to build, improve, enlarge, or equip, or to aid others to build, improve, enlarge or equip, buildings for ... industrial schools, technical schools, normal schools, schools for training teachers ... or for higher institutions of learning, or, in connection therewith, libraries, *workshops, gardens, kitchens* [emphasis added] or other educational accessories.[46]

At least from 1902-1914, the Board stuck closely to that credo by channeling its appropriations to colleges which emphasized agricultural and industrial education. Excellent documentation of that trend is provided in Barbara Powell's study of black colleges and northern philanthropy.[47]

Perhaps the combined influence of Rockefeller's GEB and Booker T. Washington also accounts for the quite similar approach pursued by Andrew Carnegie in directing his own philanthropic efforts from 1900 through 1919. Carnegie is described by Pifer as an "enthusiastic convert"[48] for what Washington, the black accommodationist, had to say about Negro higher education. As Powell once again shows, his keen approval was reflected in exclusive personal support for Tuskegee and Hampton from 1900 to 1910. During that span, Carnegie shelled out no less than $741,000 of his own income for those two schools, and those alone.[49] Even in the decade after 1911 when his corporation was formally established with ostensibly wider horizons, Carnegie appropriations to liberal arts colleges like Fisk and Lincoln were to prove few and far between.

## OF MOTIVES AND MALICE

So go the facts of northern philanthropic complicity, and there are many more to be found within documented studies like Barbara Powell's. Yet even this limited evidence suggests that Jencks and Riesman's assertion deserved such scrutiny. Their claim that the character of private Negro colleges was not significantly shaped by "the prejudices or self-interest of their white trustees" seems an understatement when measured against the halcyon days of missionary influence or the industrial "detour" which foundations

[45]Curti and Nash, p. 173.
[46]General Education Board, *The General Education Board: An Account of its Activities, 1902-1914* (New York: The General Education Board, 1915), pp. 212-213.
[47]Barbara J. Powell, *The Impact of Philanthropy on the Development of Private Black Institutions of Higher Education*, Qualifying Paper, Harvard University Graduate School of Education (Cambridge, 1978), p. 20.
[48]Pifer, p. 17.
[49]Powell, p. 26.

later supported. White control was predominant during both eras, and at least around the turn of this century did much to define the retarded condition of private black colleges in years to come.

This article's main objective was to show that a providential link existed between early white philanthropy and black higher education, the sort which *The Academic Revolution* encouraged us not to "exaggerate." Having confronted that objective, the mission nears its end. Still, one important question follows from that relationship and it has to do with "why?" What motives prompted the leaders of America's first great educational foundations to reject so significantly the progressive example of their missionary predecessors? Probably the best agenda of interwoven motivations is Louis Harlan's, whose *Separate But Not Equal* concluded that:

> The failure of Northern emancipators and their sons to resist effectively the Southern wave of racism may be explained by many changes in Northern attitudes since Reconstruction. The Northeast and West wooed the South politically. Northern liberals conciliated Southern whites in the hope of reciprocal support for reform measures. Others had long since laid down the burden of the freedman to turn without restraint to the pursuit of economic gain, which proved more exciting and rewarding. A less direct, but pervasive influence on Northern attitudes was the climate of Social Darwinism in which the progressive movement flourished.[50]

From this synopsis tumble most of the prevailing explanations for northern complicity in the years after Reconstruction. Key among them are that philanthropists: (1) had no better choice than to accommodate southern sentiment; (2) displayed a belief in racial control and Social Darwinism that was really little different from the southern white supremacist's; and (3) were openly inspired by the promise of industrial exploitation. Because latter day analysts fall on all sides of these theories, a capsule of each seems essential to completing this narrative.

The need to "accommodate" is at once the kindest and most common explanation for the behavior of post-Reconstruction philanthropists. At its heart is the claim that anything more progressive than what Peabody, Slater, and the GEB promoted would have incurred white supremacist vengeance. That in turn would have sacrificed even the very little which Negro higher education came to stand for after Reconstruction. The accommodationists' defense seems best stated by Raymond Fosdick, retired head of the GEB, who wrote in 1962 that:

> ... the Board was aware from the start of the dangers inherent in a Northern institution working in the highly charged emotional atmosphere of a biracial South.... A single misstep could be disastrous.... Consequently its role was marked with caution and modesty....

[50]Harlan, p. 43.

... That the philosophy of Buttrick [longtime head of the GEB] and his contemporaries was based on the idea of 'gradualism' cannot be denied. But this was the thinking of the time . . . . Their strategy was strongly pragmatic. To raise the level of education in the South . . . it was necessary to work through the race in power. Sixty years ago there was no alternative to this approach; there was no public opinion to support any other cause.[51]

Other historians generally agree with Fosdick's premise, even if they do not go so far to excuse the foundations for their efforts. Raymond Wolters concedes that "the new vocationalism was dictated by considerations of expediency."[52] Merle Curti acknowledges that the GEB in particular felt a need to respect southern white feelings, and points out that "Buttrick hesitated to support any bold innovation in behalf of the Negro for fear of alienating Southern opinion."[53]

Unfortunately, from other quarters came appraisals far less sympathetic to the philanthropists' bind. Instead, considerable evidence is offered to show that many philanthropists were just as narrow-minded about Negro rights and educability as their southern white counterparts. Even well-intentioned George F. Peabody betrayed a limited belief in black capabilities by insisting that his Hampton benefactees continue singing plantation songs. Peabody had serious misgivings about Negro suitability for "so-called academic education" and shared them with other Hampton trustees who resisted college-level studies there.[54]

If Peabody appears suspect, then the men who headed the General Education Board look downright sinister. Waldemar Nielsen's comprehensive history of organized philanthropy paints a startling picture of GEB racial attitudes—and all in the words of the white men who ran it. Nielsen quotes William H. Baldwin, Jr., the Board's first chairman, as saying in 1899:

The Negro should not be educated out of his environment. Industrial work is his salvation; he must work . . . at trades and on the land . . . . Except in the rarest of instances, I am bitterly opposed to the so-called higher education of Negroes.[55]

Similarly, J. L. M. Curry, who has proven himself prominent in several different foundations, is shown to have written:

The white people are to be the leaders, to have the initiative, to have the directive control in all matters pertaining to civilization and the highest interests of our beloved land. History demonstrates that the Caucasian will

---

[51]Raymond B. Fosdick, *Adventure in Giving: The Story of the General Education Board* (New York: Harper and Row, 1962), pp. 320-323.

[52]Wolters, p. 11.

[53]Curti and Nash, p. 175.

[54]Wolters, p. 252.

[55]Waldemar A. Nielsen, *The Big Foundations* (New York: Columbia University Press, 1972), p. 335.

rule. He ought to rule. This white supremacy does not mean hostility to the Negro, but friendship for him.[56]

Finally, Nielsen chronicles a meeting between Tennessee school superintendents and Dr. Wallace Buttrick, then the newly appointed executive head of the GEB, in which Buttrick proclaimed that "The Negro is an inferior race . . . . The Anglo-Saxon is superior. There cannot be any question about that."[57] No doubt an element of forced conciliation colored every message that these men conveyed to their southern white audience. Moreover, Fosdick reminds us that "a vast revolution of ideas and social habits has swept over the decades since," and that "in many respects they [GEB leaders] were the prisoners of their times."[58] Yet all this aside, there is still unmistakeable meaning in their words. It is that which makes the question of philanthropic racism an issue we cannot easily dismiss.

By far the harshest motive assigned to post-Reconstruction philanthropists is that they were industrialists disguised in benefactors' clothing. Du Bois is said to have considered the early 1900s one of the most critical periods in Negro history precisely because he witnessed then a "new Trinity," the coming together of white supremacy, black subordination, and industrial progress.[59] DuBois's cynicism inclined him to define philanthropic accommodationism quite specifically as "an antecedent condition for American economic growth" that was taking place at that time.[60]

A few contemporary observers, in particular certain neo-Marxist historians, embrace Du Bois's suspicions, and suggest that at least some northern money for black vocational institutions was consciously intended to help train a semi-skilled black labor force for industrial development. Philanthropy represented a respectable way to do that, and the accommodationist excuse for not imposing anything more threatening than industrial training served as a convenient alibi for more selfish intentions. The leading spokesman for this severe interpretation is Martin Carnoy, whose book, *Education as Cultural Imperialism*, includes a biting chapter on northern foundations and philanthropic misrepresentation. Writes Carnoy of the men behind philanthropy:

> . . . While Northern capitalism has been associated with humanitarian treatment of the black—and it must be conceded that a humanitarian element was present in philanthropic efforts during Reconstruction and around the end of the century—humanitarianism was always secondary to capitalists' economic needs . . . . Unfortunately for blacks, Northern capitalists were much

[56]Ibid., p. 335.
[57]Ibid., p. 335.
[58]Fosdick, p. 11.
[59]Wolters, p. 25.
[60]Ibid., p. 63.

more interested in exploiting Southern resources than in promoting black liberation . . . .

. . . Northern capitalists were interested in Southern economic development —achieved by the training of a large skilled labor force—an economic development in which progressive industrialists from both the North and South could participate. They were already opposed to class or racial equality before they headed South.[61]

Each of these theories tarnishes the already sullied image of post-Reconstruction northern philanthropy. Thus, it might seem to matter little which explanation holds most water. After all, the major point remains that northern foundations did more to promote a regressive trend in black higher education than they did to stem it.

Still, there is merit to such analysis, and it is of an enduring sort. Fully understanding the motives behind past events often helps to keep history from repeating itself. However, that more difficult analysis extends beyond the scope of this study and into the domain of professional historians. Suffice it to say that the extent of research already invested in "why" philanthropists promoted education's "Great Detour" serves as further evidence that a shaping relationship did in fact exist between white control and the private black college.

## CONCLUSIONS

This article's first objective was to establish the relationship just mentioned. As it emerged, the story of white philanthropic influence on black college destiny broke down into two distinct opening chapters. The first one, written by Reconstruction's egalitarian-minded missionaries, proved short-lived but inspirational. It embraced the ideal of liberal education for the freedmen, and based it on true faith in black educability. The second chapter, rewritten in large part by post-Reconstruction industrialists, proved pragmatic but repressive. In its time frame the great vocational "detour" was taken, from which black higher education still seems to be finding its way back home to the ideal of liberal education.

Enroute to these conclusions, a more important principle was reinforced. It is that educational change can never be explained outside the complete historical context in which it takes place. Quite evidently—and whether for better or worse—early philanthropic influence on private black colleges was a child of particular and peculiar times.

Like any investigation, this one has its deficiencies. Most obvious is that it stops short. Tours of history tend to do that. This one, for example, chooses not to extend itself to the 1920s in

[61]Carnoy, pp. 273, 286, 292.

which a new breed of philanthropic egalitarians is seen struggling "to regain the ascendancy they had enjoyed during the era of Reconstruction."[62] Only one additional decade and it is claimed that

> ... by the late 1930s sustained large-scale philanthropy had remedied many of the shortcomings from earlier giving. . . . The old idea of confining Negro education to agriculture and vocational training was clearly a thing of the past.[63]

[62]Wolters, p. 31.
[63]Curti, pp. 123-124.

# Half a Loaf: The Shift from White to Black Teachers in the Negro Schools of the Urban South, 1865–1890

By Howard N. Rabinowitz

By 1890 FOUR MAJOR DECISIONS HAD BEEN MADE CONCERNING public education in the South. The first involved the very acceptance of state-supported public school systems. The second and third meant that blacks as well as whites were to be among the students, although the two races would be strictly segregated. And the final decision, well on its way to widespread implementation, was that blacks rather than whites would teach the black pupils.

It is common knowledge that by the end of the century education in the South was less advanced than in the rest of the country and that for blacks it was both separate and unequal.[1] Less attention, however, has been paid to the change from white to black teachers in the Negro public schools.[2] It is worth noting that there was a shift to black faculties during the period 1865 to 1890 and that it was the blacks themselves who forced this change.

[1] See for example Louis R. Harlan, *Separate and Unequal: Public School Campaigns and Racism in the Southern Seaboard States 1901–1915* (Chapel Hill, 1958); Henry A. Bullock, *A History of Negro Education in the South from 1619 to the Present* (New York, 1970).

[2] The demand for black teachers in the colleges run by the northern societies, however, is ably covered in James M. McPherson, "White Liberals and Black Power in Negro Education, 1865–1915," *American Historical Review*, LXXV (June 1970), 1357–86. Only a few of the numerous state studies of Negroes during and after Reconstruction mention, and then only briefly, the interest of blacks in replacing white teachers. See for example George B. Tindall, *South Carolina Negroes, 1877–1900* (Baton Rouge, 1966), 220–21; Charles E. Wynes, *Race Relations in Virginia, 1870–1902* (Charlottesville, 1961), 126–28; Frenise A. Logan, *The Negro in North Carolina, 1876–1894* (Chapel Hill, 1964), 146; Lawrence D. Rice, *The Negro in Texas, 1874–1900* (Baton Rouge, 1971), 221–22.

Mr. Rabinowitz is assistant professor of history at the University of New Mexico. He wishes to acknowledge assistance and criticism from Professor Arthur Mann of the University of Chicago and financial aid from the Center for Urban Studies at the University of Chicago.

The Journal of Southern History
Vol. XL, No. 4, November 1974

There was a pronounced succession in the kinds of people who taught blacks in the quarter century following the Civil War. First, there were the idealistic Yankee schoolmarms who came south as representatives of the northern missionary societies; they were replaced by southern whites unable to win positions in the white schools; they in turn were succeeded by black graduates of local colleges and normal schools. This progression and the reasons for it reveal much about the nature of Negro education in the urban South and the expectations and responses of both blacks and whites. Though occurring throughout the South this shift can be traced in the following cities: Atlanta, Georgia; Raleigh, North Carolina; Nashville, Tennessee; Montgomery, Alabama; and Richmond, Virginia. Educational developments in these cities mirrored those taking place elsewhere in the region, and together they provide an urban cross section in terms of the level of educational provisions for blacks, and in their size, location, and political background.

Geographically, the cities encompass the Atlantic Seaboard, Deep South, and the border states. In attitudes towards blacks, the states they represent range from Virginia and North Carolina, commonly identified as moderate, to Alabama, usually considered more restrictive. Like the states, the cities were affected differently by so-called Radical Reconstruction. The Radicals never controlled Atlanta and enjoyed only a short hegemony in Nashville, Richmond, and Montgomery. In Raleigh, however, the city administration was in Radical hands from 1868 to 1875, one of the few instances in which a southern city remained under the Radicals for more than two municipal elections. Negroes were still serving on city councils in Richmond and Raleigh in 1890, while such black representation ended in Atlanta in 1871, Montgomery in 1875, and Nashville in 1885. In the matter of size, Montgomery and Raleigh were among the smaller southern cities, having populations of 21,883 and 12,678 respectively in 1890. Richmond and Nashville had already been relatively large cities before the war, and by 1890 the former had a population of 81,388 and the latter, 76,168. Atlanta with fewer than 10,000 in 1860 grew to 65,533 by 1890. All were distribution centers and, as befitted their roles as capitals, administrative centers as well; Richmond and, to a lesser extent, Nashville also had manufacturing bases. The percentage of Negro population in 1890 for Atlanta was 43 percent; Nashville, 39 percent; Raleigh, 50.1 percent; Richmond, 40 percent; and Montgomery, 59 percent. The provisions made for the education of blacks in Richmond were among the best in the South; those in Montgomery, among the worst.[3]

As towns fell under the control of Union forces, representatives from northern philanthropic societies arrived to bring education and religion to the enthusiastic freedmen. Aided by the Freedmen's Bureau, these societies, particularly the American Missionary Association (AMA) and the American Freedmen's and Union Commission, played the leading role in educating blacks during the first five years after the war. It was a formidable task made even more difficult by the local hostility to their efforts.[4] To some extent the freedmen had prepared the way by establishing schools without outside support. The first three teachers sent to Raleigh by the AMA in July 1865 assumed control of a school for black children founded and taught by blacks at an African Methodist Episcopal church.[5] The AMA teachers who arrived in Atlanta the same year found a small school organized by two ex-slaves in the basement of an old church.[6] The blacks, however, had limited financial resources and soon came to rely primarily on the aid of their northern friends.[7]

With the Freedmen's Bureau supplying the buildings and the missionary societies paying the teachers, the number of blacks enrolled in classes mushroomed. Shortly after Nashville was occupied by Federal forces in 1863 there were 1,200 pupils in the freedmen schools. By 1867 schools run by four societies served

[3] U. S. Bureau of the Census, *Compendium of the Eleventh Census: 1890*, I: *Population* (Washington, 1892), 434, 448, 450, 667, 673, 719, 739, 743.

[4] For opposition to the education of blacks by northerners see Richmond *Dispatch*, May 8, 1866; Atlanta *Constitution*, May 1, 1869; see also the following letters from society officials and teachers: E. B. Adams, agent of the American Freedmen's and Union Commission for Georgia, *American Freedman*, I (June 1866), 44; R. M. Manly, superintendent of freedmen's schools in Richmond, *ibid.*, I (August 1866), 75–76; Reverend W[illiam] G. Hawkins, Raleigh teacher, *National Freedman*, I (September 15, 1865), 276; Anna F. Clarke, Raleigh teacher, *Freedmen's Record*, I (November 1865), 181.

[5] Letter of the Reverend W. G. Hawkins, *National Freedman*, I (September 15, 1865), 276.

[6] Franklin M. Garrett, *Atlanta and Environs: A Chronicle of Its People and Events* (3 vols., New York, 1954), I, 741–42.

[7] Northerners paid the board of AMA teachers in Atlanta and contributed money to the fuel fund of the New England branch of the American Freedmen's and Union Commission school in Richmond. Appeal of the Reverend Mr. Ware, *American Missionary*, XI (October 1867), 224; letter of Horace W. Hovey, December 5, 1866, *Freedmen's Record*, III (January 1867), 21. In all the schools students paid as much of the tuition as they could afford.

approximately 3,000 students.[8] In Montgomery the AMA's Swayne School had begun in October 1866 with an enrollment of 210; after eight months the number had grown to 700.[9] By 1868, 700 of the 800 or 900 Negro children of school age in Raleigh were enrolled in the schools of the AMA and the American Baptist Home Mission Society.[10] Each city had lists of youngsters eager to attend but denied admission because of lack of room or an insufficient number of instructors.

Teachers in these schools were mostly white women from the Midwest and New England. Although they had a variety of reasons for coming, it seems clear that hostility towards the South or crass political motives carried little weight. The majority were imbued with strong antislavery beliefs, humanitarian impulses, and burning religious fervor.[11] Some, like a teacher at Atlanta's Storrs School, were perhaps atoning for past sins. "I am ashamed every day to think I was ever guilty of being a democrat," she wrote in 1870, "and [I] ask God [to] forgive me for ever having sympathy, in the least, with them who would keep these people in slavery."[12] As for the typical reason, Raleigh's Lucy Dow expressed it best: "Our great hope lies in the children. They must be taught habits of industry, economy, personal and household cleanliness and much more besides book learning."[13]

Yet book learning was important, and the teachers hoped their pupils would go on to instruct others of their own race, especially in the countryside where the northern societies had not penetrated. An AMA teacher in Atlanta proudly told of a student

[8] Letter of the Reverend David Chapman, army chaplain stationed in Nashville, to George Whipple, November 18, 1863, American Missionary Association Archives (Amistad Research Center, Dillard University, New Orleans, La.); Nashville *Daily Press and Times,* June 14, 1867.

[9] Letter of W[illiam] T. Richardson, superintendent of schools for the Cleveland Aid Commission, July 1, 1867, *American Missionary,* XI (September 1867), 205–206.

[10] Charles L. Coon, "The Beginnings of the North Carolina City Schools, 1867–1887," *South Atlantic Quarterly,* XII (July 1913), 237.

[11] This conclusion is drawn from an examination of letters in the American Missionary Association Archives and those reprinted in the *American Missionary,* the *Freedmen's Record,* the *American Freedman,* and the *National Freedman.* For a specific denial that the teachers came south "to fill the minds of our pupils with hatred," see letter of MBS [Mary B. Slade], *Freedmen's Record,* VII (January 1871), 98. Only two teachers played a prominent role in the political life of any of the five cities, John Silsby in Montgomery and R. M. Manly in Richmond. For a different view of the primary motivation of the teachers see Henry L. Swint, *The Northern Teacher in the South, 1862–1870* (Nashville, 1941), 140–42 and *passim.*

[12] Unsigned letter, *American Missionary,* XIV (January 1870), 7.

[13] Letter, November 29, 1866, *Freedmen's Record,* III (January 1867), 5.

who roomed in the city and walked six miles every day to teach in a rural school.[14] In Raleigh the Washington and Lincoln Schools of the AMA had produced five teachers by 1867.[15] By 1871 fourteen of the students who had been educated by the New England Branch of the Freedmen's and Union Commission in Richmond were teaching in the vicinity.[16] The pioneer among the society's Negro teachers had been Peter H. Woolfolk, one of the handful of black instructors employed by the northern societies. Given his own class after graduating from the society's normal school in 1868, he was frequently visited by officials who remarked favorably on his ability.[17]

Despite their normal school divisions, however, the primary schools could not meet the pressing need for able black teachers. The societies realized this and soon founded more advanced schools. Though called colleges or universities, they were at first little more than high schools. Prior to 1870 most of them had primary and secondary departments, which permitted poorly prepared students to work their way up to collegiate or normal school divisions. Some institutions were founded in rural areas or in smaller towns, but as with the primary schools, the benevolent societies concentrated most of their efforts in the larger cities, where the impact could be greater and more visible. The result was so successful that no city tour for important visitors was complete without an inspection of "the colored college." The two most influential schools were Fisk University in Nashville and Atlanta University. Others, however, included Central Tennessee College and the Nashville Normal and Theological Institute (later Roger Williams University) in the Tennessee capital; Shaw Collegiate Institute and St. Augustine's Normal School and Collegiate Institute in Raleigh; Clark University, Spelman College, and Atlanta Baptist Seminary (later Morehouse College) in the Georgia capital; and Richmond Institute.

By 1870 the missionary societies were thus shifting their priorities with the intention of improving their advanced schools and of turning over primary education to southern officials. From the

[14] Letter of "A Teacher," September 23, 1870, *American Missionary*, XIV (November 1870), 247.

[15] John W. Alvord, *Semi-Annual Report on Schools and Finances of Freedmen* (Washington, 1868), 17.

[16] Letter of B[essie] L. Canedy, March 4, 1871, *Freedmen's Record*, VII (April 1871), 111.

[17] Letter of "EDC," October 17, 1868, *ibid.*, IV (November 1868), 175–76. Woolfolk became a prominent figure in Negro political and economic life in the city.

beginning the societies had expected public authorities to assume responsibility in this area,[18] but the whites during Presidential Reconstruction had dragged their feet. Although prompted largely by anti-Negro attitudes, the delay was due partly to the disrepute in which public education had long been held in the South. Alone among the five cities providing the core of this study, Nashville had operated a public school system before the war, but its pupils were considered charity cases. On the state level only North Carolina had made any signifiicant antebellum progress in the field of public education. Whatever had been done, of course, had been strictly for whites. After the war Negroes complicated the problem.

The initial southern response was to ignore the blacks and to move haltingly towards the education of white children at public expense. Under the administration of Governor Jonathan Worth, North Carolina initially abolished its state-supported public schools to prevent the enrollment of blacks.[19] Yet this policy could not be followed long in the face of the northern societies' success in educating Negroes. "The effort to educate the colored people of the State has given an impulse to education among all classes," wrote a Freedmen's Bureau official from Alabama in 1867.[20] Similarly, a growing protest in North Carolina that Negroes had adequate schools while the whites allegedly had none forced the Conservatives in February 1867 to establish a system of public education for white children between the ages of six and twenty-one. No provision was made for blacks, thus continuing the antebellum policy of exclusion.[21]

Georgia had previously enacted legislation in December 1866 approving education for "any free white inhabitant" between six

[18] See for example letter of the Reverend D[avid] Burt, superintendent of education of the Freedmen's Bureau in Tennessee, to the editor, Nashville *Union and Dispatch*, October 29, 1867.

[19] North Carolina, *Public Laws, 1866* (Raleigh, 1866), 87. For Worth's belief that "the Com. School system had better be discouraged, for a time, and thus avoid the question as to educating negroes," see letter to William A. Graham, January 12, 1866, J. G. de Roulhac Hamilton, ed., *The Correspondence of Jonathan Worth* (2 vols., Raleigh, 1909), I, 467.

[20] Excerpt from the report of the Freedmen's Bureau's superintendent of schools, *American Missionary*, XI (November 1867), 248.

[21] North Carolina, *Public Laws, 1866–1867* (Raleigh, 1867), 17–20. Among those objecting to the advantage which black children seemed to have over whites was the Raleigh *Daily Sentinel*. The October 29, 1866, issue, for example, estimated there were at least twice as many black children as white youngsters attending school in the city.

and twenty-one and any "disabled or indigent" soldier under thirty.[22] The act merely permitted the education; it did nothing to make it possible. Frequent complaints by Atlantans that local whites went without schooling while blacks received excellent education from northern invaders led the Committee on Public Schools of the City Council in November 1869 to urge the opening of public schools for whites. They admitted it would be wise for the Board of Education to provide for blacks as well, but provisions were already being made for them "through the aid of the Freedmen's Bureau and voluntary contributions from various sources." Clearly then, "the wants of the white children are more immediate and pressing."[23] As late as February 1872 all 1,200 pupils in Atlanta's public schools were white.[24]

Unlike other states, Tennessee early went on record in favor of schools for children of both races. An 1866 statute authorized public schools for all youngsters but required that the races be taught separately.[25] As elsewhere, passage of the law did not mean that the schools were built or that provisions were necessarily made for both races. Such action, although limited, was taken on the state level because at the time Tennessee was the only southern state in which the Republicans were in control of the government. Tennessee Republicans thus expressed the policy later to be followed by members of the party throughout the South in education as well as in many other spheres of life affecting blacks. The earlier policy of exclusion would be replaced, but by segregation rather than integration.

Nashville, however, was still in the hands of Conservatives who, while providing schools for the whites, used the existence

[22] Georgia, *Acts, 1866* (Macon, 1867), 59.

[23] Atlanta, *Report of the Committee on Public Schools to the City Council of Atlanta, Georgia* (Atlanta, 1869), 11. For complaints of the disregard for white education while blacks were in school see W. I. Mansfield to the editor, Atlanta *Constitution,* April 15, 1869; letter of Elizabeth Sterchi to Bishop George F. Bannson, January 14, 1869, Adelaide Fries, ed., "The Elizabeth Sterchi Letters," *Atlanta Historical Bulletin,* V (July 1940), 202. For the reaction of teachers of white children to the advantage blacks had over whites in 1867 in a state not covered in this study see Joe M. Richardson, *The Negro in the Reconstruction of Florida, 1865–1877* (Tallahassee, 1965), 108. Even by the end of the period Georgians believed that Negroes had an unfair advantage over whites because of the support of northern philanthropists. See for example remarks of the chancellor of the University of Georgia, Atlanta *Constitution,* July 26, 1889; letter to the editor, *ibid.,* August 25, 1889.

[24] Atlanta, Board of Education, Minutes, January 30, 1872 (Atlanta Board of Education Building, Atlanta, Ga.).

[25] Tennessee, *Laws, 1865–1866* (Nashville, 1866), 65.

of freedmen schools to defend the lack of facilities for Negroes. By the summer of 1867 the city fathers were ready to change their policy. Several factors, mostly negative, influenced this decision: the dislike of having blacks educated by northerners, the fear that impending Republican control of the council would result in integrated schools, and the possibility of noneducated Negroes becoming "thieves and scoundrels."[26] Soon afterward the Board of Education informed the assistant commissioner of the Freedmen's Bureau of the city's decision to educate blacks. Though the schools would be separate, selection and certification of teachers, grading of pupils, and the rest of the organization would be "in all the respects the same" as the whites received. In a sideswipe at the societies, the board also stated that "nothing of a sectional, political or partisan nature in social or religious matters shall be included in these schools."[27] The authorities relied on the federal government and the benevolent societies to house these students. The two original schools, Bell View and Lincoln, which opened in September 1867, and the two that opened the following year, McKee and the Gun Factory Building, were either rented or purchased from the "northern invaders" and all had previously been used for freedmen schools.[28]

Elsewhere Negro public education was absent until Congressional Reconstruction brought Radical governments to power. In their Reconstruction constitutions Alabama, Virginia, North Carolina, and Georgia acknowledged for the first time the state's obligation to educate blacks. Although Negroes were to be educated at public expense, the Radicals, if indeed they desired otherwise, were careful not to go entirely against the grain of southern opinion. Negro education was to be equal to white education, but it was to be separate. Neither segregation nor integration was specified in the constitutions, but the position on this question was clarified in the laws passed by Radical-controlled legislatures. In North Carolina, for example, former provisional governor William Woods Holden sought to allay fears that the state constitutional convention had provided for the

[26] The debate over the issue is reported in full in the Nashville *Daily Press and Times*, June 14, 1867.

[27] I. M. Hoyt, secretary of the board, to Major General William Passmore Carlin, July 27, 1867, Nashville, Board of Education, Minutes, July 27, 1867, Box 25, James Emerick Nagy Nashville Public School Collection (Tennessee State Library and Archives, Nashville, Tenn.). These minutes will hereinafter be cited as such along with the appropriate box number.

[28] *Ibid.*, September 4, 1867; April 1, 1868, Box 25.

teaching of white children by black teachers. He voiced a view common among southern Radicals.

There will be schools for white children to themselves, with white teachers; and schools for the colored children to themselves, with colored teachers. . . . but there will be no difference as to rights and responsibility . . . . If the white child gets a dollar for its education the colored child will get a dollar also. If the white child is provided with a good teacher, so will the colored child.[29]

On its concluding day members of the convention sought further to ease troubled minds. Part of the resolution proposed by a Negro member and unanimously adopted stated that "it is the sense of this Convention that . . . the interests and happiness of the two races would be best promoted by the establishment of separate schools."[30] The school law drafted in 1869 clearly enunciated the principle of separate but equal education.[31] Similarly, Georgia guaranteed separate schools in 1870, but its statute ordered that local officials "shall provide the same facilities for each [race], both as regards school houses and fixtures, and the attainments and abilities of teachers, length of term-time, etc."[32] In Alabama, however, mixed schools with "the unanimous consent of the parents and guardians of such children" (an unlikely possibility) were permitted by an 1868 law.[33]

Individual cities proceeded at different speeds to make public education a reality. Everywhere, however, the Radicals prodded others to action, and the former missionary schools served as the nuclei for the new black systems. Richmond public schools actually antedated the beginning of the state system. Although the state constitution had made no mention of racial segregation in public education, the Radical-controlled Richmond City Council clearly spelled out its policy in an 1869 ordinance: ". . . the public schools herein provided for shall be kept separate and apart for white and colored children."[34] In order to start the Negro schools the Board of Education relied heavily upon the Freedmen's

[29] Raleigh *Daily Standard,* March 7, 1868.

[30] Marcus C. S. Noble, *A History of the Public Schools of North Carolina* (Chapel Hill, 1930), 296.

[31] *Ibid.,* 314–15.

[32] Georgia, *Acts and Resolutions, 1870* (Atlanta, 1870), 57.

[33] Alabama, *Acts, 1868* (Montgomery, 1868), 148.

[34] Richmond, *The Charter and Ordinances . . . with Amendments to the Charter* (Richmond, 1869), 251.

Bureau and the northern societies. During the first year of operation the bureau contributed most of the buildings rent free and
supplied without charge two-thirds of the furniture while the
northern societies provided the teachers and paid half their salaries. The Board of Education appropriated $15,000 each for the
white and black schools. At the end of the year the bureau ceased
paying the rent and sold all its property, much of it to the city.[35]
Other freedmen schools such as the Bakery and Navy Hill properties were sold by the northern societies. Still others, like the
Richmond Colored High and Normal School, were not turned
over completely until 1876.[36]

It was not until 1877 that the Raleigh school system officially
began. Prior to that date in the case of the Johnson School and
until 1875 for the Washington School the city's two main Negro
educational facilities received most of their funds from the AMA
and remained under its direction. Once the system began the
whites were taught in the old public schoolhouses while the
Negroes continued to meet in churches and the buildings erected
by the Freedmen's Bureau and benevolent societies.[37]

Frequently the system of dual support for the Negro public
schools persisted several years after the initiation of the citywide school system. A source of continual dispute, however, was
the composition of the teaching staffs. As late as 1882 the AMA
contributed almost $3,000 to the Montgomery Negro schools.[38]
Until 1884 the society made available the Swayne School building
and nominated the teachers, who were paid by the Board of
City School Commissioners. Disagreements over hiring practices

[35] Richmond, Board of Education, Minutes, September 30, 1869 (Richmond
Board of Education Building, Richmond, Va.); Richmond, Superintendent of
the Public Schools, *Third Annual Report . . . for the Scholastic Year Ending
July 31, 1871* (Richmond 1871), 7. These published annual reports will hereinafter be cited as Richmond, *Annual Report of the . . . Public Schools*, with the
appropriate years.

[36] Richmond, Board of Education, Minutes, January 16, May 22, 1871; Richmond, *Annual Report of the . . . Public Schools, 1876–1877* (Richmond, 1878),
222–23; *ibid., 1875–1876* (Richmond, 1877), 68–70.

[37] Raleigh, *Annual Reports of the Mayor and Officers . . . 1877* (Raleigh, 1877),
222–23. For background of the 1877 state act which provided for a system of
city graded schools supported by special local taxes see Coon, "The Beginnings
of the North Carolina City School," 239, 243. Until 1877 the only public revenue
given local schools came from a statewide common school fund.

[38] Ruth M. Vines, "The Contributions of Negroes in Providing School Facilities
in the Montgomery, Alabama City Schools" (unpublished M.A. thesis, Montgomery State Teachers College, 1943), 21.

resulted in the school's finally being turned over to the city.[39] In Atlanta, Radicals led by former Negro councilman William Finch finally secured black schools in February 1872. One school, Summer Hill, was rented free of charge from the Northern Methodist Missionary Society, with the city assuming the cost of its support. This arrangement continued until the Board of Education voted to purchase the building and the lot in 1876. The other school, Storrs, was also rented free of charge from the AMA, which nominated the teachers whose salaries were paid by the board.[40] As in Montgomery, however, disputes raged over who would have the final authority in hiring the faculty, and in 1878 the agreement was terminated. Storrs then became a private school which enjoyed an excellent reputation among members of the black community.[41] Although the schools themselves did not always provide a continuity with the original period of missionary fervor, some of the teachers did. Lizzie Stevenson in Atlanta, Louise L. Dorr in Raleigh, Lizzie Knoles in Richmond, and Teresa McKeon in Nashville were only a few of the many who stayed to teach in the public schools after the phasing out of the missionary endeavors.[42]

The continuation of the link with the northern societies was greeted with mixed emotion by the Redeemers when they replaced the Radical city administrators. On the one hand the supply of rent-free buildings was attractive to officials chronically plagued with monetary worries; on the other, as long as this tie

[39] See for example Montgomery, Board of City School Commissioners, Minutes, September 16, 1879; June 5, 1882 (Montgomery County Board of Education Building, Montgomery, Ala.). The transfer of control to the city is mentioned in H. G. McCall, *A Sketch, Historical and Statistical of the City of Montgomery* (Montgomery, 1885), 20.

[40] Atlanta, Board of Education, Minutes, December 30, 1871; January 25, 30, 1872; December 13, 1876.

[41] For friction between the Board of Education and the American Missionary Association see *ibid.*, July 5, 1872; July 24, August 28, 1873; July 27, 1876; July 1, 3, August 22, 1878. On the school's later history under a corps of American Missionary Association veterans who still went north during the summer see Atlanta *Constitution*, June 28, 1879; untitled article by Ella E. Roper, *American Missionary*, XLIV (July 1890), 212–14; American Missionary Association, *44th Annual Report . . . and Proceedings of the Annual Meeting . . . 1890* (New York, 1890), 53.

[42] All but Miss McKeon remained in the Negro schools. At first she taught in black schools, but by 1881 she was teaching fourth grade at the white Hume School. Eight years later she was one of the school's two principals. Nashville *Banner*, September 10, 1881; September 7, 1889. It would be profitable to know more about the post-Reconstruction lives of such teachers.

persisted, whether through teachers or money, there would exist
a formidable alternative to southern white control over the minds
of the Negroes. One of the first orders of business for the Redeemers, therefore, was to hire only local residents as teachers.
In addition to weeding out the northerners, this action would
supply jobs to local whites who were unable to secure positions
in the white schools.[43] John Watson Alvord, the Freedmen's
Bureau superintendent of schools, reported that Nashville teachers
had been told their schools might not resume after the 1869
Christmas vacation. "It was thought this would induce these
devoted Northern ladies to leave . . . ," but most remained and
about half were employed when classes resumed.[44] Having failed
with subtlety, the following summer the City Council over-
whelmingly passed a bill providing that faculty members in public schools had to reside permanently within the corporation limits
of Nashville.[45] Shortly thereafter the Richmond City Council refused an offer of the Friends' Freedmen Association of New York
to provide twelve instructors and pay one-fourth of their salaries.
At the end of the school year the Board of Education resolved
that "this board will employ no teachers who are not permanent
residents of this city or State." One of the two dissenting votes
came from Rabsa Morse Manly, head of the Richmond Education
Association, which ran the Colored High and Normal School.[46]

But the Redeemers had to tread carefully. Upon their return
to power they found the lines on education firmly drawn. They
might trim at the edges, but they had to respect the ground rules
of the basic Radical policy as expressed in state constitutions,
educational statutes, and city ordinances. The threat of federal
intervention still hung over their heads, and conscious of this
fact, they announced that the gains won by blacks would not
be jeopardized. The shift from exclusion to segregation would be

[43] When the Atlanta Board of Education terminated its agreement with the
American Missionary Association, a letter from "Many Citizens" in the Atlanta
*Constitution*, August 29, 1877, rejoiced: "It is neither just nor patriotic to tax
southerners for the education of the colored people among us, and then employ
northern teachers, while there are so many southern men and women who need
the situations, who are amply qualified and better understand the idiosyncrasies
of the African race."

[44] Alvord to O[liver] O[tis] Howard, January 26, 1870, Alvord, *Letters from
the South Relating to the Condition of Freedmen Addressed to Major General
O. O. Howard* (Washington, 1870), 21.

[45] Nashville, Board of Aldermen, Minutes, July 28, 1870 (Davidson County
Building and Nashville City Hall, Nashville, Tenn.). This motion had been
tabled on June 23, 1870.

[46] Richmond, Board of Education, Minutes, August 8, 1870; June 12, 1871.

maintained, but more important, the Radical policy of separate but equal treatment would be continued.[47]

The Redeemers also made clear their determination to continue staffing the black schools with white teachers, although of course seeking to replace any remaining northerners with southerners. Increasingly, however, this policy was challenged by local blacks who pushed for the appointment of Negroes. In 1887 when Atlanta Negroes were seeking to get a black faculty at Summer Hill School, the last facility with white instructors, the Atlanta *Constitution* assured northerners "that the white people are not trying to force colored teachers upon them [the Negroes], for it is their own notion and desire . . . to put colored teachers in the Summer Hill school . . . ." The newspaper added that Nashville Negroes were making similar demands, as had those in Augusta, Athens, and other cities.[48] As early as 1881 the Colored Press Association convention in Louisville had gone on record calling for Negro staffs in Negro schools.[49] The following year a black newspaper in Richmond, the *Virginia Star*, presented the case for control by blacks of their schools:

The *Star* and all the better thinking people of our race in the city and the state are asking for a Normal School *proper*. One where boys and girls can be instructed by teachers of their own race, who could be able to fit them in every particular to fill their part in the great dance of life. Give us a High and Normal School where our young people may be instructed by those who have their interests at heart. We are tired of having the treadles of all the machines run by the whites. Noble descendants of Ham stand up for pride of race.[50]

In the same issue the editor reported favorably on his visit to the Navy Hill School, then run by an all-Negro staff. In the

---

[47] See for example the report on the hygiene of the public schools, Nashville, Board of Health, *Third Annual Report* . . . *1878* (Nashville, 1879), 260–61; Atlanta, Board of Education, *Seventh Annual Report* . . . *1878* (Atlanta, 1878), 7–8; Atlanta *Constitution*, September 3, 1878; Atlanta, *Annual Reports of the Mayor and Officers* . . . *1888* (Atlanta, 1889), 13. The annual reports of the Atlanta Board of Education will hereinafter be cited as such with the appropriate years.

[48] Atlanta *Constitution*, June 18, 1887.

[49] Montgomery *Advance*, September 3, 1881.

[50] Richmond *Virginia Star*, November 18, 1882; italics in original. In a similar manner, the editor of the Montgomery *Alabama Guide* in the October 1884 issue recommended Tuskegee Institute because "If there is any place in the whole state that our people should patronize in the way of educating their children in the way of race pride, it is certainly at this point, for the school is managed and controlled by our race."

interest of "justice and common sense," he said, school authorities should note "that it is best for all concerned" to appoint blacks to teach members of their own race. The pleas were continued the next month and supported by references to the successful substitution of Negro teachers for whites in all the Virginia Negro schools of Lynchburg, Petersburg, Norfolk, Hampton, Danville, Charlottesville, and Manchester. More than racial pride was involved, since the editor argued that in all these places the experiment had shown great improvement over the old system. The few cases in Richmond offered further proof. According to the reports of the superintendent, "attendance, scholarship, punctuality and deportment in colored schools taught by colored teachers" were markedly better than in those taught by white instructors.[51] In a subsequent letter to the editor "F" endorsed the newspaper's position. "The American colored man will never be satisfied until he has all the rights of any other American citizen," he wrote. "We want a good honest government that does not make a difference on account of the color of the skin." His proposals imply that segregated schools were not necessarily seen as a betrayal of Negro rights. Although the writer called for the end of the ban against intermarriage and the end of segregation in churches, he cited the major need in school policy as the hiring of black teachers in the black schools.[52] Negro faculty members were therefore seen as more than merely making the best of a bad situation.

The reasons for wanting black instructors varied. Racial pride, of course, was important, but still more so were the attitudes and qualifications of the white teachers. In cities such as Nashville, certain white teachers forbade their Negro pupils to recognize them in public.[53] Of greater consequence was the fact that after the northern societies surrendered their power to appoint the faculties, the Negro schools served as the dumping grounds for the rejects from the white institutions. For the 1871–1872 session, for example, the Richmond Board of Education needed twelve teachers for the white and fifteen for the Negro schools. The individuals with the highest scores on the teacher's examination were sent to the white schools. Those with the next highest scores were assigned to the black schools if they were willing

[51] Richmond *Virginia Star,* December 9, 1882.
[52] *Ibid.,* December 16, 1882.
[53] William W. Brown, *My Southern Home: or, The South and Its People* (Boston, 1880), 215; see also an interview with a white teacher, Nashville *Banner,* January 29, 1884.

to teach black children. Since many whites refused to work with blacks, the remaining positions had to be filled with applicants "whose standard was lower than heretofore enumerated."[54] Throughout the period it seemed that any incompetent white teacher ended up in a Negro school. Mrs. M. C. P. Bennett, for example, having failed to get reappointment to the white schools, argued her case in a series of four letters to the Richmond Board in 1876 and was finally assigned to a black institution.[55]

But black teachers were seen by blacks as preferable even to qualified whites. Some blacks, including a group of preachers in Nashville, wanted Negro teachers because they would mingle socially with the families of the pupils, assisting in the elevation of the race.[56] Others, agreeing with the northern visitor William Wells Brown, were upset that excellent black instructors were being produced by schools such as Fisk, Central Tennessee, Atlanta, and Howard and had no potential employers.[57] Most would have agreed with James H. Harris, Raleigh's leading Negro politician, who called for the hiring of black teachers because "no one can enter so fully into the sympathy of the negro's condition as the negro himself."[58]

Whatever their reasons, Negroes sought to convince the authorities of the need for black instructors. More petitions were presented to boards of education and city councils on this matter than on any other of concern to Negroes. Although such petitions appeared as early as 1869 in Nashville and 1873 in Atlanta, the great increase in the movement for black faculties came after 1875. This was due in part to the failure of the Civil Rights Act of that year to forbid segregated schools. This omission convinced Negroes that segregated schools would be a long-term reality. Then, too, the growing number of graduates from black colleges provided a pool of candidates who were ready to teach other members of their race and who clearly had no chance of teaching white children.[59] Thus, less than five months after passage of the Civil Rights Act four Negroes petitioned the Richmond School Board. After profusely thanking the board for maintaining public

[54] Richmond, Board of Education, Minutes, September 5, 1871.
[55] *Ibid.*, September 21, 26, 1876.
[56] Nashville *Daily American,* April 7, 1877.
[57] Brown, *My Southern Home,* 215.
[58] Raleigh *Register,* March 27, 1878.
[59] See for example letters of the Reverend L. M. Hapgood to the editor, Nashville *Banner,* May 23, June 13, 1883; account of a black protest meeting, *ibid.,* June 9, 1883; interview of the Reverend Wesley John Gaines, Atlanta *Constitution,* June 16, 1887.

schools for blacks, they cited "the necessity of employing *more colored teachers in the colored schools.*" They pointed out that black teachers had been in the school system since its inception and that on numerous occasions their performances had been praised by the superintendent. Nevertheless, they said,

of the thirty-three colored schools [classes] of the city of Richmond only seven are instructed by colored teachers while there is not one colored principle [*sic*] in the entire city. It does not appear to us that there is any valid reason for this small proportion of colored teachers in colored schools, we, therefore kindly petition you, as a matter of justice to us, as citizens of this Commonwealth to give us a more equitable proportion of teachers and principals in the colored schools of the city of Richmond.[60]

Similar declarations continued to be sent in Richmond and the other cities. In general the approach of this early petition was followed: the Negroes thanked whites for what good had been done but respectfully asked that further improvement be bestowed through the appointment of Negro teachers. In the words of an 1878 appeal presented to the Atlanta Board of Education by the Reverend Frank Quarles and a group of "leading citizens of the city":

Our highest gratitude for the kindness you extended to us in the appointment of two colored teachers in one of the public schools in the year 1877. And as they have met the highest approbation of the parents of the children, and we believe have given satisfaction to all your requirements, we ask you for the appointment of colored teachers in all the colored public schools of the city, if they can be found competent in every respect.[61]

In 1877 a white veteran of the missionary movement in Raleigh complained to the governor that "there was an attempt made by certain of the colored people to throw out all the northern teachers from my school . . . and to put all colored teachers in."[62]

---

[60] Richmond, Board of Education, Minutes, June 24, 1875; emphasis in original.

[61] Atlanta, Board of Education, Minutes, June 13, 1878. A petition of four job-seeking Negroes two years earlier had paved the way for the initial appointments. Speaking for themselves and others interested in a teaching career, they informed the board that "We have finished our studies, having passed through the preparatory and collegiate course. We had considerable experience in teaching during the summer months." *Ibid.*, April 27, 1876.

[62] Louise L. Dorr to Governor Zebulon B. Vance, August 17, 1877, Governors' Papers (North Carolina Division of Archives and History, Raleigh, N. C.). The Reverend Wesley John Gaines, a prominent Atlanta Negro, also expressed dissatisfaction with his city's northern teachers. Interview in Atlanta *Constitution,*

The effort was thwarted, but there as elsewhere it did not signal any loss of Negro interest in the matter.

Individual school boards and city administrators reacted differently to the requests for black instructors. As already noted, from the beginning Richmond assigned Negro teachers to Navy Hill, a black school under the direction of a white principal. The other cities, however, proved more reluctant to hire blacks. One of the major obstacles was the possibility that this step would lead to integrated faculties. Even when the decision was made to permit the entry of Negroes into the system, qualification examinations and teacher-preparation classes were held at different hours or even days for the two races.[63] By the end of the period only Raleigh still had integrated staffs in Negro schools. Montgomery had permitted this practice in the AMA Swayne School, but when the school became totally subject to public decisions in the mid-1880s only blacks were employed.[64] The three other cities avoided racial mixing with the exception of one year at Atlanta's Storrs School. Richmond, however, believed it was necessary to have white principals in control of the Negro teachers and continued this policy into the twentieth century. Atlanta and especially Nashville, on the other hand, made it clear that schools would be turned over to black faculties only when there were enough qualified applicants to fill all the positions including that of principal.

While it has been the purpose of the [Nashville] Board to organize a corps of colored teachers as early as practicable, the Board can not recommend the passage of the resolution [of the City Council calling for employment of black teachers] as the effect would be to make it

---

June 16, 1887; letter to the editor, *ibid.*, June 21, 1887. For additional petitions requesting black teachers see Atlanta, Board of Education, Minutes, August 22, 1874; July 10, 1876; Nashville, Board of Education, Minutes, March 6, April 3, 1877; June 12, 1883, Box 26. At the meeting called to draw up the Nashville petition of June 12, 1883, William H. Young, a black lawyer and politician, proposed that blacks should withdraw their children from the schools if the petition was rejected. More moderate leaders prevailed, however, and Nashville was spared what would have been one of the first southern school boycotts. Nashville *Banner*, June 12, 1883.

[63] See for example Nashville, Board of Education, Minutes, June 15, 1887, Box 26; Atlanta, Board of Education, *Annual Report, 1884* (Atlanta, 1885), 17; Atlanta, Board of Education, Minutes, October 9, 1877; Montgomery, Board of City School Commissioners, Minutes, August 19, 1882; Richmond, Board of Education, Minutes, September 7, 1870.

[64] Compare the lists of teachers in Joel Davis, comp., *Montgomery Directory, 1883-1884* (Montgomery, 1883), 22; and C. J. Allardt, comp., *Montgomery City Directory for 1888* (Montgomery, 1888), 16.

compulsory upon the Board to employ all or even one colored teacher who might upon examination prove competent which would inevitably result in having a mixed corps of teachers, some white and some colored. This state of affairs, in the opinion of the Board, would lead to serious embarrassments and should by all means be avoided.[65]

The problem of securing a sufficient number of competent Negroes to staff an entire school was the most frequent of the many excuses offered to forestall black demands. Sometimes the boards simply explained that it was inadvisable to take such action at that time or that the plan constituted an unnecessary experiment. Unstated was the feared loss of control over the Negro students. On one occasion the Richmond board refused on the unsupported grounds that most of the black parents preferred white teachers and that acquiescence would serve only to extend further the color line in race relations.[66] Another consideration, whether explicit or implicit, was never absent from the minds of board members. "I am perfectly willing for colored teachers to have colored schools," said an Atlanta board member, "but the colored schools in Atlanta have been served faithfully by white ladies, all of whom, except one, are southern born. I am not willing to see them turned off without notice."[67]

By the time black instructors were finally given control of Negro schools, this problem of what to do with the white teachers had been settled by their retirement or reassignment to newly built white schools.[68] There were other factors as well which accounted for the final surrender of the city boards to the wishes of the Negroes. Clearly, the unending array of petitions played an important role as did the pressure brought by such Negro politicians as James Carroll Napier, the prominent lawyer and Nashville city councilman.[69] Perhaps foremost in the minds of many whites was the matter of economy; as a member of the Atlanta Board of Education pointed out, it was cheaper to hire black teachers.[70] The comparative salaries of blacks and whites bore him out.

[65] Nashville, Board of Education, Minutes, November 5, 1878, Box 26.

[66] Richmond, Board of Education, Minutes, June 30, 1880.

[67] Atlanta *Constitution,* June 25, 1887; see also similar reasons given for the rejection of a Negro petition in Richmond, Board of Education, Minutes, June 30, 1880.

[68] See for example the decision to turn over Nashville's Bell View School to black teachers. Nashville, Board of Education, Minutes, June 12, 1883, Box 26.

[69] See for example accounts of the Nashville Common Council meetings, Nashville *Daily American,* August 29, 1879; Nashville *Banner,* May 26, 1882.

[70] Atlanta, Board of Education, Minutes, July 26, 1877.

Even though it was sometimes unclear if the discrepancy between the salaries of whites and blacks was a reflection of differences in abilities or merely due to prejudice, every city by the end of the period showed a widening gap in the salaries paid to the two sets of instructors.[71] Due to the lingering influence of the missionary societies and the continued employment of whites in the Negro schools, the salaries for teachers in the respective schools were initially comparable and at least theoretically based on merit. As late as August 1874 the salaries of teachers (all of whom were Caucasian) in Atlanta's white and Negro schools were similar, although the staffs in the black schools were already earning somewhat less.[72] By 1891, however, when all the principals and teachers in the Negro institutions were black, the gap in salaries became a chasm. Negro principals earned $650 annually; only one of the thirteen white principals received such a small amount, and all but three of the remainder were being paid more than $1,200. One teacher in each black school made $400 and the others, either $350 or $375; in the white schools the lowest salary was $500, and most of the instructors earned at least $550.[73]

This discrepancy in salaries was challenged in 1893 by the Reverend Edward R. Carter, a moderate Atlanta Negro leader. In his view, "This one fact makes a wide difference between the white and colored schools of Atlanta."[74] No better example could be given than the Summer Hill School. In 1885, when it was the only Negro school staffed by whites, its teachers received $400, less than at white schools but more than the high of $350 then being paid to Negro teachers at the other institutions. In 1887, when the school was turned over to black teachers, salaries dropped into the $300–$350 range.[75] A majority of the Negro faculty members were graduates of Atlanta University and were by no means unqualified to take over instruction of

[71] At the same time pupil-teacher ratios were higher in the black schools. Again the differences were least in Richmond and greatest in Montgomery. For the 1890–1891 school year the ratio in Richmond was 39:1 in the white schools and 43:1 in the black schools. Richmond, *Annual Report of the . . . Public Schools, 1890–1891* (Richmond, 1892), 5–6. For the 1885–1886 school year in Montgomery the ratios were 42:1 and 73:1 respectively. Montgomery, *Annual Message of the Mayor . . . and Reports . . . 1886* (Montgomery, 1886), 76–77.

[72] Atlanta, Board of Education, *Annual Report, 1873–1874* (Atlanta, 1874), 6–7.

[73] *Ibid., 1891* (Atlanta, 1892), 267–71.

[74] Carter, *The Black Side. A Partial History of the Business, Religious, and Educational Side of the Negro in Atlanta, Ga.* (Atlanta, 1893), 235–36.

[75] Atlanta, Board of Education, *Annual Report, 1885* (Atlanta, 1886), 5; *ibid., 1887* (Atlanta, 1888), 148.

their race. Even if a number were poorly trained, however, it is inconceivable that the best among them were no better than the worst among the white teachers. The Board of Education saw an easy way to save money, regardless of whether or not the reductions were merited.

Atlanta seems to have been in the middle in its attitude towards salaries of black and white employees in Negro schools. The scant information available for Raleigh suggests that teachers of white pupils enjoyed a slight edge, though not as great as in Atlanta.[76] The more extensive data for Richmond suggests the same pattern. In its first discussion of the matter in 1874 the Richmond Board of Education set fixed salaries based on the level of instruction and length of time in service.[77] During the next few years there was no indication of discriminatory compensation. However, when a Board of Education dominated by Readjusters took over in 1883 it passed a resolution ordering that salaries of teachers in the black schools be the same as those of similarly qualified instructors in the white schools.[78] The only previous indication of distinctions came in a request from the white principal of the Colored High and Normal School in 1881 that her salary be raised from $75 to $100 per month. Since her duties and responsibilities were the same as other principals, she believed she deserved the same compensation. The board raised her salary to $90 and also raised those of her first and second assistants.[79] The successor to the Readjuster board reiterated this ideal of equal pay for equal qualifications, and in 1888 the salary of principals in all schools was placed at $150 per month.[80] By 1891 teachers in the white schools made slightly more than their black counterparts in the black institutions, but there was clearly an effort to reward on the basis of qualifications. Whereas 62.9 percent of the whites made $500 per year or less, the figure in the Negro schools was 63.4 percent. The principals of the primary schools, all of whom were white, were paid equally, as were

[76] This was due primarily to the large number of whites teaching Negro pupils. In the white Centennial Graded School one teacher received $50 per month and the others, $40 per month; in the Negro schools two teachers received $30 and the rest, $40. Raleigh, *Annual Reports of the Mayor and Officers . . . 1883–1884* (Raleigh, 1884), 52–57.

[77] Richmond, *Annual Report of the . . . Public Schools, 1874–1875* (Richmond, 1876), 351.

[78] Richmond, Board of Education, Minutes, July 26, 1883.

[79] *Ibid.*, July 1, 1881.

[80] *Ibid.*, September 25, 1884; September 24, 1888.

the heads of the Negro and white high schools. The only significant difference in salaries actually favored the blacks. Only 10.8 percent of the blacks were making the minimum monthly salary of $33 as compared to 14.3 percent of the whites.[81]

Nashville, which maintained a roughly equal pay scale throughout most of the 1880s, moved in the direction of inequality with the appearance of its first schedule of salaries for white schools in 1889. In September 1891 new schedules were made for both the white and Negro schools. They marked a severe decline in the status of the teachers and principals in the black schools, all of whom were Negroes. Whereas white instructors in grades 1 to 7 were to receive from $35 to $55 monthly based on years of experience, the comparable range for blacks was $25 to $41. The highest figure for blacks was reached after eleven years, while a white teacher in his second year made $40. For eighth-grade teachers the range was $55 to $60 for whites and $25 to $45 for blacks. The same inequality characterized the salaries of administrators, where the monthly gap between equally qualified Negroes and whites was at no time less than $80. At times it was as great as $110. There was a strong reaction to these discrepancies, however, and in December 1891 the schedule for Negro schools was revised upwards. Nevertheless, in all cases a minimum difference of at least $5 per month still reflected the dual standard for teachers; the monthly gap between white and black administrators now ranged from $40 to $100.[82]

Montgomery officials had no compunction against furthering the divergence of salaries in their two sets of schools. While the arrangement with the AMA was in force, the wages were approximately the same. By 1875, however, the white school principal was earning $150, and the staff members, between $50 and $75; the Negro school principal received $100, and his teachers, $35 to $60, with only one in the highest category. By 1880 the average white school teacher was making $60 a month, and his Negro school counterpart, $49. Ten years later the white teachers had maintained their earlier salary level, but individuals in black schools (by now all Negroes) had been reduced to $38. By 1893 no black teacher was making more than $320 per year, while the lowest salary for whites was $400.[83]

[81] Richmond, *Annual Report of the . . . Public Schools, 1890–1891*, pp. 38–39.
[82] Nashville, Salary Schedules, Box 51, Nagy Collection.
[83] Montgomery, City Council, Minutes, December 5, 1870 (Alabama Depart-

Ironically, the shift from white to black teachers was made easier by the earlier neglect of black facilities. When new schools for blacks were finally opened in the 1880s it seemed natural to appoint Negroes because of black demands, the absence of white teachers to be displaced, and the lower salaries of blacks. Such considerations, for example, accounted for the appointment of blacks in the Knowles School in Nashville and the East End School in Richmond.[84] Yet the innovation would have still been impossible had there not been competent Negroes available to fill the positions. Favorable reports from other cities about the quality of black appointees led an Atlanta Board of Education member, for example, to base his support partly on the precedents set in Augusta, Savannah, and Macon.[85] The growing numbers of such qualified individuals by the late 1880s thus nullified the charge that inexperienced or incompetent blacks would be replacing whites. Whereas in 1884 only five of the twenty-four Negro applicants passed Nashville's teacher examination, by 1887 this was true of nineteen of forty-two. More significantly, two of the top three scores, including the highest, were achieved by Negroes. Seventh in the city was a young Fisk student named William Edward Burghardt Du Bois.[86]

Despite such arguments in favor of the black demands, the transition was a slow process, usually spread over several years and confronted by staunch resistance. The Pearl School, the last black facility in Nashville to be staffed by Negroes, had to wait until 1887.[87] In that year Summer Hill School achieved the same distinction in Atlanta, thanks to the tie-breaking vote

---

ment of Archives and History, Montgomery, Ala.); Montgomery, Board of Education, Minutes, December 31, 1875; July 1, 1893; Alabama, Superintendent of Education, *Report . . . 1880* (Montgomery, 1880), 19; *ibid., 1890–1891* (Montgomery, 1891), 162.

[84] Nashville, Board of Education, Minutes, October 7, 1879, Box 26; Richmond, *Annual Report of the . . . Public Schools, 1881–1882* (Richmond, 1883), 22.

[85] Atlanta, Board of Education, Minutes, July 26, 1877.

[86] Nashville, Board of Education, Minutes, May 26, 1884; May 30, 1887, Box 26. The Nashville *Daily American* on May 26, 1880, exaggerating the achievements in Nashville and underestimating conditions elsewhere, had argued that "Nashville is the only Southern city where the colored schools are up to the same standard as the white schools in discipline, scholarship and attendance. Nearly all the other cities have colored teachers in the colored schools." The Nashville *Banner* of June 11, 1883, based part of its opposition to black teachers on the fact that only two of thirty-two black applicants had passed that year's teacher's examination.

[87] Nashville, Board of Education, Minutes, June 14, 15, 1887, Box 26. The change was made because the performance of blacks in that year's teacher's examination could not be ignored.

of the president of the Board of Education.[88] In Richmond black teachers were placed in all the Negro schools only after the Readjuster-controlled Board of Education was appointed. The new board hired Negro principals and teachers for every black school except the high school. When the Democrats returned to power they replaced the principals with whites but retained the black instructors. The Colored High and Normal School, however, remained entirely in the hands of whites until 1924.[89]

Having finally acted, the boards of education seemed pleased with the performances of the black faculty members. "I believe the Board found the key to the problem of the education of our colored population when competent colored teachers were put in charge of Houston Street School," wrote the Atlanta superintendent of education in 1881. They "have demonstrated the fact that they understand their own race, and can discipline and teach to the satisfaction of their patrons."[90] His counterpart in Montgomery reported that the Negro instructors "have done very well," although he modified his praise by observing that "it would not be very easy to find teachers among the blacks that would succeed better."[91] Commenting on the recent change in Richmond whereby white principals and white teachers had been replaced by blacks, the superintendent noted that while he had expected much trouble, "in justice to the principals and teachers I must say the schools were conducted with good order and with few complaints from patrons and pupils, and when it is taken into consideration that the principals were inexperienced and had 27 teachers new to the system, the conduct of the schools was very satisfactory."[92]

Satisfaction with the new system was partly due to the fact that most of the new faculty members were considered "safe"; the boards and the white citizens at large believed that the students would not be exposed to ideas that would threaten the status quo in race relations. When the Atlanta Board of

[88] Atlanta *Constitution*, June 25, 1887. The next day, when the time came to elect the Negro teachers, two councilmen were still in opposition. One said he wanted "no niggers" in the school. *Ibid.*, June 28, 1887. The chief stumbling block was the absence of sufficient available positions for the white teachers.

[89] Richmond, Board of Education, Minutes, March 7, June 28, 1883; June 26, 27, 1884. The Readjusters, however, were dedicated to the principle of separate (though equal) schools. See *ibid.*, March 7, 1883.

[90] Atlanta, Board of Education, *Annual Report, 1880–1881* (Atlanta, 1882), 8.

[91] Montgomery, Board of City School Commissioners, Minutes, June 8, 1889.

[92] Richmond, Board of Education, Minutes, June 26, 1884; see also *ibid.*, October 26, 1885.

Education initially considered the appointment of Negro teachers in 1877, one of the requirements was that they be natives of the South and residents of Georgia; ten years later one of the main arguments in favor of turning the last school over to black instructors was the existence of a sufficient number of competent graduates of southern institutions.[93] In 1887 twenty-four of the Negro teachers employed by the city had received their training at Atlanta University; by 1910 more than three-quarters of the faculty members in the black schools were its alumni.[94] A Nashville newspaper applauded the appointment of two local graduates as that city's first Negro teachers. "This is right," proclaimed the *Daily American.* "In employing colored teachers the Board of Education could scarcely find any better prepared than those trained from the beginning in the schools where they are to teach."[95] Indeed, not only did most of the teachers graduate from neighborhood colleges or normal schools, but many came up through the local public school system. Consider Mabel Beatrice Johnson. Although born in rural Georgia, she grew up in Atlanta, where she attended three of the public schools and later graduated with honors from Spelman College. First selected as a supernumerary, she was finally chosen as a regular teacher in 1888 and was rapidly promoted.[96] Of the 84 Negro instructors employed in 1890 by the Richmond school system 80 had attended the Negro high school, as compared to only 87 graduates of the white high school among the 154 teachers in the white schools.[97]

[93] Atlanta, Board of Education, Minutes, October 2, 1877; June 25, 1887.

[94] Atlanta *Constitution,* December 23, 1887; William N. Hartshorn, *An Era of Progress and Promise, 1863–1910: The Religious, Moral and Educational Development of the American Negro Since His Emancipation* (Boston, 1910), 88–89.

[95] Nashville *Daily American,* October 10, 1879.

[96] Carter, *The Black Side,* 101–103. In 1894 four of the black teachers in the city were former pupils of the Mitchell Street School. *Ibid.,* 240.

[97] Richmond, *Annual Report of the . . . Public Schools, 1889–1890* (Richmond, 1891), 13. Even "home-grown" talent could prove difficult. See for example accounts of the disciplinary problems at the Colored High and Normal School. Richmond, Board of Education, Minutes, December 28, 1885; July 2, 1886. School officials also had difficulties with individual black teachers and principals. Antoine A. Graves, a graduate of Atlanta University and principal of Atlanta's Gate City School, resigned after school children were dismissed for a celebration to honor Jefferson Davis. Carter, *The Black Side,* 233–34. Graves's successor, L. M. Hershaw, was fired after making a speech in which he criticized southern educational policy towards Negroes and compared the region unfavorably to the North. He was reinstated after writing a contrite apology. See Atlanta *Constitution,* July 26, August 30, 1889. Daniel B. Williams, a Richmond teacher,

But what of the schools in which blacks now taught? Despite Redeemer assurances that education would be both separate and equal, an ever-widening gap in the distribution of funds for the two races came to replace the relatively equal treatment accorded by the Radicals. The differences ranged from the expenditure per enrolled child in Richmond during 1890–1891 of $10.25 for whites and $9.50 for blacks to the $5.58 per white child and $3.47 per black youngster in Montgomery in 1880, the last year for which figures are available. The sums for the Alabama capital represented an investment of $1.17 for each white of school age and only 44 cents for each school-age Negro.[98]

Conditions in the schools reflected these differences. In every city there was a shortage of space for blacks wishing to attend school. During the 1875 academic year Richmond educators lacked accommodations for 117 more white than Negro students, but 600 Negroes and only 200 whites were denied entrance in 1888. Worse still from the standpoint of the blacks, the whites would soon have seats thanks to the opening of additional rooms in Springfield and Elba schools, but the blacks would have to wait for new facilities until funds were available "in the near future."[99]

Such assurances about finding accommodations for the Negroes "in the near future" came to have a hollow ring. When more room was planned for whites, it was sought through the erection of new buildings. When dealing with black needs, however, renting or subdividing older buildings was preferred; if new construction was decided upon, sites were carefully chosen so as to hinder the dispersal of Negroes. Improvements in space

---

was dismissed after a clash with his white principal over the school's promotion policy. He was encouraged to reapply for his position by the Board of Education and having done so, saw his request unanimously denied. Richmond, Board of Education, Minutes, February 22, March 22, 1883.

[98] Richmond, *Annual Report of the . . . Public Schools, 1890–1891,* pp. 38–39; Alabama, Superintendent of Education, *Report . . . 1879–1880* (Montgomery, 1880), 28. The sums for Richmond in 1880–1881 were $12.60 per white and $11.11 per black pupil. Richmond, *Annual Report of the . . . Public Schools, 1880–1881* (Richmond, 1882), 14. Under the Radicals in 1870–1871 Montgomery had spent $11.51 on each white and $11.44 on each black student. Montgomery, City Council, Minutes, September 4, 1871.

[99] Richmond, Board of Education, Minutes, November 25, 1875; September 24, 1888. The excess of rejected black over white applicants was already evident in the 1877–1878 school year when 150 white and 525 black children were initially denied admission to the public schools because of lack of room. It was expected that at least 40 of the whites would be accepted later in the year. *Ibid.,* September 27, 1877.

for blacks were often delayed while better provisions were made as quickly as financially possible for whites. With such occasional exceptions as the Moore Street School in Richmond or the Gray Street School in Atlanta, both built after 1887, the Negro schools were generally older, less favorably located, and of inferior construction.[100] In 1876 the Richmond superintendent recommended closing the Navy Hill School, since it was in very bad repair and "very unfit for school purposes"; in 1891 the building was still in use. By 1891 only two of the six Negro schools in good or very good condition as compared to nine of the ten white schools.[101] The Cemetery Hill School completed in Montgomery in 1887 was a frame building that provided blacks with "greater school facilities and much more comfort than they have had heretofore." On the other hand, a white school opened the previous year was an "elegant and commodious brick building," with a capacity of 405 students, more than twice that of the Negro school.[102] The Lawrence School built for blacks in 1890 indicated Nashville's attitude towards black needs. In an age when wooden schools were anachronistic and when several hundred black students were without accommodations, the city erected a one-story, five-room frame structure with seats for only 214.[103]

The principle of separate but equal also went largely unheeded in the number of advanced grades provided for Negro pupils. With the exception of Raleigh, all the cities had high schools for their white children at an early date, but only Richmond and Nashville had established such facilities for their blacks by the end of the period. And in Nashville the black high school was organized by adding grades to a grammar school, thus seriously increasing overcrowding.[104] Even more damaging was

[100] For an extended discussion of the Gray School see Carter, *The Black Side*, 224–26; on the Moore Street School see Richmond, *Annual Report of the . . . Public Schools, 1890–1891*, p. 44.

[101] Richmond, *Annual Report of the . . . Public Schools, 1875–1876*, p. 367; *ibid., 1890–1891*, pp. 84–85.

[102] Montgomery, *Annual Message of the Mayor . . . and Reports . . . 1887* (Montgomery, 1887), 57.

[103] Nashville, Lawrence School Notes, Box 57, Nagy Collection. The way in which a new Negro school was furnished ten years earlier also demonstrated the attitude of whites and was perhaps a regular procedure for black schools. According to the Nashville *Daily American*, November 1, 1879, "All the furniture for it was obtained from the various other school buildings in the city, and has not cost the city a cent."

[104] See for example Nashville, Board of Education, Minutes, September 29,

the absence of completely graded grammar schools. In Raleigh in 1884 only Johnson offered classes in all seven grades as did the white institutions. After it was closed at the end of 1885 Negro students were limited to the first five grades.[105] Even in Richmond, where black students received the best treatment, progress was often blocked by insufficient provisions for more advanced work. In 1891 eight of the nine white elementary schools offered classes in one of the two highest grades as compared to four of their seven Negro counterparts.[106]

Groups of Negroes, many of whom had fought for black teachers, sought to spur local lawmakers to improve the quality of Negro education. Rather than pushing for an end to segregation, the blacks fought for the ideal of truly equal, though separate, Negro schools; and most of the limited improvements can be traced directly to these pressures. In January 1874 the Nashville Board of Education acknowledged that "the colored people are demanding more convenient accommodations in the central and western portions of the city." Nine months later the board's request for additional facilities for blacks in West Nashville was approved by the Board of Aldermen.[107] Petitions from Atlanta Negroes in 1880 and 1888 led the Board of Education after a slight delay to construct the Houston Street and Gray Street schools.[108]

More often the petitions were tabled, bottled up in committee, or rejected outright. Unlike black demands for black teachers, the crusade for better black schools found white and

---

1884; June 29, 1885; September 15, 1886, Box 26. In Richmond the high school program of whites was more rigorous and extensive than that of blacks. For the schedule of students see Richmond, *Annual Report of the . . . Public Schools, 1879–1880* (Richmond, 1881), 41, 43; *ibid., 1890–1891*, pp. 56, 61.

[105] Raleigh, *Annual Reports of the Mayor and Officers . . . 1885–1886* (Raleigh, 1886), 87.

[106] Expressed another way, 7.6 percent of the enrolled white students and 4.5 percent of the blacks were in the two highest grammar school grades. Richmond, *Annual Report of the . . . Public Schools, 1890–1891*, pp. 36–37. By the end of the period Richmond and Atlanta also operated night schools only for whites.

[107] Nashville, Board of Education, Minutes, January 6, 1874, Box 26; Nashville, Board of Aldermen, Minutes, October 20, 1874. Typically, the new accommodations were to be in a rented rather than a specially constructed building. Eight years later Negro councilman J. C. Napier successfully led the fight to construct two new black schools after receiving numerous requests from blacks. "It is cheaper," he said, "to take care of colored children in schools than in prisons." Nashville *Banner*, May 26, 1882.

[108] Atlanta, Board of Education, Minutes, April 29, September 3, 1880; March 22, November 22, 1888.

black aims in conflict. Rather than easing the financial burdens of the local boards, the building of new black schools and the improvement of old ones would require massive appropriations. Twice during 1873 Atlanta officials cited the lack of funds in rejecting black pleas for additional schools.[109] A petition signed by seventy-seven Richmond Negroes in 1878 complained that "all the public schools of this city for the education of colored youth lie within a space of five blocks by fifteen . . . and that long since the seating capacity of these has been entirely exhausted." Students had to travel great distances to attend Valley School which was practically inaccessible during the winter months. The board's proposal to enlarge Valley was therefore seen as unsatisfactory. Instead, the petitioners called for new schools in Church Hill and Rocketts "for the sake of . . . those who so anxiously desire and so urgently need the benefits of education." The board responded that it sympathized heartily with the desire for more accommodations but could take no action due to lack of funds.[110]

Two years later a different group of thirty-four Richmond Negroes reiterated the demand for increased accommodations in the eastern section of the city. The plans to enlarge Valley School still had not been implemented, and the petitioners took the opportunity to criticize the site further and to endorse again a policy of dispersal rather than concentration. Of particular concern was the location of the school, which was not only at a great distance from the prospective pupils but was "in a bottom near a creek into which the filth of the other side of the city is drained." The petition was tabled.[111] Four months later the board also rejected a recommendation that the Nicholson School property in the east end be set aside for blacks. At the same meeting the members voted to purchase a lot in that area for construction of a white school. Shortly afterward the board had second thoughts and ordered the Nicholson property to be sold, with the proceeds going towards erection of Negro facilities. In the face of pressure from white parents, however, the board once again reversed itself. The Nicholson property was retained and used as a school for whites.[112] Montgomery

---

[109] *Ibid.*, January 3, October 28, 1873; for similar rejections see *ibid.*, October 30, 1875; June 26, 1880.

[110] The petition and the board's response can be found in Richmond, Board of Education, Minutes, February 28, 1878.

[111] *Ibid.*, March 25, 1880.

[112] *Ibid.*, June 30, September 23, October 6, 1880.

Negroes, who underwent similar experiences with their petitions, finally got the board to erect a new building in 1888, but only after raising $500 towards its construction.[113]

Blacks were equally unsuccessful in securing appointments to boards of education. Demands such as those made in 1883 by two Atlanta Negroes, politician Columbus C. Wimbish and Richard H. Carter, principal of the Houston Street School, at the Georgia State Educational Convention for Colored Men bore little fruit, nor were the numerous petitions any more effective.[114] Here again, the contrast with demands for black teachers was marked, for much more was at stake. As the Richmond *Dispatch* put it, blacks should not be allowed to exercise control over white children, teachers, and taxpayers. It also feared that mixed schools would result and besides, it said, "where and when did the negro become possessed of the notion that he was the equal of the white man."[115] Only when Republicans or Readjusters, as in Richmond, were in power did Negroes have the opportunity to serve on local boards. Alfred Menefee served on Nashville's board in 1867, Richmond G. Forrester and R. A. Paul on the Richmond board in 1883, and Holland Thompson on the Montgomery board from 1870 to 1873. Along with their white Republican colleagues, they lost their positions when the city councils reverted to Democratic control.[116] The boards on which these men served

[113] For petitions of Negro churches to have their buildings used as public schools see Montgomery, Board of City School Commissioners, Minutes, February 7, August 14, 1876. For the role of Negro contributions in 1888 see Vines, "The Contributions of Negroes," 21. For evidence of continued difficulty in getting positive responses to petitions in Nashville see letter of W. H. Young to the editor, Nashville *Banner*, November 29, 1889.

[114] See Atlanta *Constitution*, December 14, 1883, for the remarks of Wimbish and Carter. Petitions calling for black representation on boards of education are mentioned in Nashville, Board of Aldermen, Minutes, November 21, 1876; Atlanta, City Council, Minutes, December 5, 1887 (Atlanta City Hall, Atlanta, Ga.).

[115] Richmond *Dispatch*, May 26, 1883; see also *ibid.*, May 25, 1883.

[116] Nashville *Union and Dispatch*, December 17, 1867; Nashville, Board of Aldermen, Minutes, October 30, 1869; William A. Christian, *Richmond, Her Past and Present* (Richmond, 1912), 382, 387; Montgomery, City Council, Minutes, September 19, 1870; January 10, 1873. There may have been a second Negro who served on the Montgomery Board of City School Commissioners. W. J. Stevens was elected by a Republican-controlled council in January 1874 to represent the heavily Negro Fifth Ward. Montgomery *Alabama State Journal*, January 20, 1874. Although he is not identified by race, "Stevens" may actually have been Wash Stephens, a local black politician. A check of the voter registration list for the 1875 municipal election published in the Montgomery *Daily*

were the most favorable to the cause of Negro education. The Readjusters during their brief hegemony in Richmond, for example, not only appointed black principals and teachers to all the Negro grammar schools but added needed classroom space by making Moore Street Industrial School, a previously private Negro institution, a part of the public system and by constructing a twelve-room building in the neglected eastern part of the city. In the long run the board probably had the greatest influence on the decision of its successors to accord blacks the best treatment of any of the five cities.[117] Of all the Negro members, however, the most influential in the five capitals and perhaps in the entire South was Holland Thompson. Montgomery's leading black politician, former delegate to the state constitutional convention, and four-term city councilman, Thompson was appointed to the city's first school board by the Republican council of which he was a prominent member. He was instrumental in helping to organize the system and in defending the right of Negro schools to equal appropriations.[118]

The protests from local blacks thus resulted primarily in the replacing of white instructors with blacks. This early display of black power had its cost, however. Blacks accommodated themselves to the system of segregated schools and produced a group with a vested interest in its continuation. Some blacks accepted the view of those white Radicals and Redeemers who said schools could be separate and equal; others no doubt decided that half a loaf in the form of black faculties was better than nothing; still others probably believed that black teachers were more important than integrated schools and saw this as a prelude to greater control over the education of their children. In the end, of course, the gap between white and black schools widened. And, ironically, by accepting segregation blacks had made it easier for whites to discriminate. Finally, by stressing the need for black instructors, black representatives on the boards of education, and better black schools rather than integration, Negroes helped to convince any doubting whites that the blacks themselves really did want segregation.

---

*Advertiser*, April 18, 1875, found no Stevens or Stephens listed among the whites in the Fifth Ward, but Wash Stephens was listed among the blacks. When the Democrats regained control of the council a white Democrat replaced Stevens. *Ibid.*, January 4, 1876.

[117] See for example Richmond, Board of Education, Minutes, September 23, 1883.

[118] See for example Montgomery, City Council, Minutes, September 5, 1870.

# Francis L. Cardozo: Black Educator During Reconstruction

Joe M. Richardson, *Department of History, The Florida State University*

In August 1865 a tall, fair and elegantly tailored young Black man returned to Charleston, South Carolina, after being away for several years. Francis Louis Cardozo had come home to educate his recently emancipated brethren. Born January 1, 1837, of a Jewish businessman father and a free Black mother, Cardozo received his early education in Charleston schools for free Blacks. At age twelve he was withdrawn from school and became an apprentice carpenter. He served as an apprentice for five years and then worked for four years as a journeyman carpenter. When he was twenty-one he renounced the carpenter's trade and sailed for Glasgow, Scotland, to pursue a college education. Cardozo's aim in going to Europe was to prepare for the ministry. While working part time as a carpenter to support his education, Cardozo completed his studies and graduated from the University of Glasgow with honors, winning prizes in Latin and Greek. He studied three additional years at Presbyterian seminaries in London and Edinburgh before returning to the United States in May 1864. Upon his return, he became pastor of the Temple Street Congregational Church located in New Haven, Connecticut.[1]

However, believing that he could be of more value to his race as the principal of a normal school than as a minister, in June 1865 Cardozo offered his services to the American Missionary Association, the most important of the many northern benevolent societies engaged in educational work with southern Blacks.[2] The As-

---

[1] Marina Wikramanayake, *A World in Shadow: The Free Black in Antebellum South Carolina* (Columbia, 1973), p. 16; Lerone Bennett, Jr., *Black Power U.S.A., The Human Side of Reconstruction, 1867-1877* (Chicago, 1967), pp. 9, 136, 138-9; William J. Simmons, *Men of Mark: Eminent, Progressive and Rising* (Cleveland, 1887), pp. 428-29; F. L. Cardozo to M. E. Strieby, August 13, 1866, American Missionary Association Archives, Amistad Research Center, Dillard University, New Orleans, Louisiana (cited hereafter as AMAA).

[2] The American Missionary Association had been organized September 3, 1846, as a protest against the silence of northern churches concerning slavery. The Association was not created as an educational society but its funds and organization permitted it to respond to the needs of destitute Blacks at the outbreak of the Civil War. The Association sent missionaries to Fortress Monroe, Virginia, as early as September 1861. By 1866 it employed more than 350 persons in southern schools and churches. The AMA had been active in South Carolina since 1862.

73

sociation, eager to send well trained Black people South, immediately invited Cardozo for an interview.[3] Cardozo was accepted as an AMA teacher and, at his request, was sent to Charleston.[4]

Unfortunately, Cardozo's first duty in Charleston was to report on the activities of his brother, Thomas W. Cardozo. Thomas had arrived in Charleston April 1865 to establish an AMA school. He immediately employed five Black Charleston teachers, all former classmates, and began the Lewis Tappan Night School, with about one hundred students.[5] Within a short time, Thomas Cardozo, who was described as "a gentleman, educated, intelligent, discreet and faithful," had a school which "reflected great credit upon all persons connected with it. . . ."[6] Thomas' efforts gained him the respect of his faculty and the Black community. However, things changed when a rumor about Thomas concerning some personal activity caused the AMA to begin an investigation of its Charleston agent. While teaching in Flushing, New York, Thomas had encountered an "immodestly" inclined older female student and, in his words, "in a moment when I was unguarded, I fell!" He promised AMA officials that he would avoid "such temptations hereafter and *never no never* allow myself to be thrown in the way of them upon the most earnest solicitations." The unimpressed officials asked F. L. Cardozo for a report. Cardozo believed that his brother's conduct had shown "a *weakness* of moral and religious principle, and a thoughtlessness. . . ." He was convinced that the incident had humbled Thomas and that he would thereafter be a "more humble and devoted Christian." F. L. Cardozo added that because Thomas' accomplishments had been beneficial, the AMA should forgive him.[7] Unimpressed by this argument, AMA officers fired Thomas.[8] Following this incident, F. L. Cardozo took charge of AMA work in Charleston.

[3]Jonathan Jasper Wright, Black state senator and South Carolina Supreme Court Justice, like Cardozo, was sent South to Beaufort, by the American Missionary Association. J. J. Wright to M. E. Strieby, July 27, August 15, September 6, 1865, AMAA.

[4]Cardozo was highly recommended by such well-known men as Henry Ward Beecher. Henry Ward Beecher to Mansfield French, April 17, 1865, Carter G. Woodson Collection of Negro Papers and Related Documents, Library of Congress, Washington, D.C.

[5]The five Black teachers were: William O. Weston, thirty, married with two children, formerly a bookkeeper for a tailoring firm, and an exhorter in the Methodist Church; Francis Rollin, twenty-two and educated at the Institute for Colored Youth in Philadelphia; Mary Weston, twenty-six, had taught in schools for free Blacks for the last several years; Amelia A. Shrewsbury, twenty-four and Margaret Sasportas, twenty-one. T. W. Cardozo to W. E. Whiting, April 11, 1865; T. W. Cardozo to M. E. Strieby, April 29; June 16, 1865, AMAA.

[6]M. French to M. E. Strieby, April 24, 1865; R. Tomlinson to G. Whipple, June 14, 1865; T. W. Cardozo to M. E. Strieby, April 29, 1865, AMAA.

[7]T. W. Cardozo to My Dear Friends in the Rooms, August 17, 1865; F. L. Cardozo to G. Whipple and M. E. Strieby, August 18, 1865, AMAA.

[8]After being relieved by the AMA, Thomas Cardozo "engaged in mercantile pursuits" in Charleston until his store was burned (he thought by incendiaries) in December 1865. Later, he went to Mississippi where he became State Superintendent of Education. T. W. Cardozo to G. Whipple, December 27, 1865, AMAA.

When Cardozo arrived in Charleston he planned to become a professional educator. He had no desire to enter the "turbulent political arena," and though he would continue to preach occasionally he had abandoned the occupation for which he had been trained. Firmly convinced of the importance of training Black youth, he had forsaken "the *exclusive* duties of the ministry" to become a leader in education.[9] In his interview with George Whipple, corresponding Secretary of the AMA, Cardozo emphasized that his objective in going South was to establish a Normal School. But when he reached Charleston he discovered that students were not yet ready for normal training; therefore, he determined to establish the best possible common school.[10]

Saxton School opened in early October in a building that was formerly the state normal school. By November there were 1000 students, divided into 19 classes, and 21 teachers, including Cardozo. Cardozo's school attracted considerable attention both because of its size and its management. Reuben Tomlinson, Bureau Superintendent of Schools for South Carolina, visited Saxton School. He was impressed by Cardozo's effective administration. It would be difficult, Tomlinson said, to find a northern school "conducted with more system and intelligence than are displayed" in the management of Saxton School.[11]

Cardozo's first major concern was securing and retaining effective teachers. However, he had little control over selection. Instructors were sent by the Association. If he objected to a teacher that was sent, AMA officials generally ignored his objections.

Cardozo had no anxiety about color. Competency was more important to him than race. As a rule, he preferred northern teachers, Black or white, because he thought them better trained; but Cardozo recruited most of his Black teachers from among local talent.[12] Free Blacks in Charleston had operated schools for themselves for years and Cardozo selected the most experienced and able local teachers for his school.[13]

At Cardozo's request, the AMA sent two northern Black women teachers, Amanda Wall and J. L. Alexander, in November 1865.

[9]F. L. Cardozo to G. Whipple, October 21, 1865, AMAA.

[10]F. L. Cardozo to M. E. Strieby, August 13, 1866, AMAA.

[11]R. Tomlinson to E. Hawks, October 7, 1865, J. M. and Esther Hawks Papers, Library of Congress, Washington, D.C.; Reuben Tomlinson, South Carolina School Report, October 4, 1865, December 10, 1866, Records of the Bureau of Refugees, Freedmen and Abandoned Lands, Educational Division, National Archives, Washington, D.C.; F. L. Cardozo to S. Hunt, December 2, 1865, AMAA.

[12]Black Charlestonians who taught in Saxton School in 1865–1866 were: William O. Weston, Richard S. Holloway, Catherine Winslow, Amelia Ann Shrewbury, Harriet Holloway, Rosabella Fields and Charlotte Johnson.

[13]For a description of free Black education in antebellum South Carolina see: Wikramanayake, *A World in Shadow, op. cit.,* pp. 32, 49, 73, 80, 85-87, 116, 127, 167-68.

In December Cardozo wrote the AMA requesting that his sister Mrs. C. L. McKinney and her husband C. C. McKinney be sent to assist him. They had lived and taught in Flushing, New York, for several years. Cardozo proposed the McKinneys as excellent examples of Blacks who had proved themselves to be "intellectually fitted." With some reluctance, the AMA honored Cardozo's request and the McKinneys arrived in Charleston in January 1866.[14] As long as Cardozo was principal of the school there were comparable numbers of Black and white teachers.[15] However, Black teachers usually held lower and less responsible positions.

Cardozo not only taught several classes and supervised Saxton School, he was also responsible for watching over the "mission home,"—buying food for the "family" and giving religious direction to students. The AMA provided special living facilities for the Saxton faculty since Charleston whites tended to oppose Black education and northern teachers were ostracized and occasionally threatened.[16]

During Cardozo's tenure as principal, there was remarkable harmony in the "family."[17] There were very little racial problems among the faculty. Cardozo's prior association with whites coupled with his innate attachment to the Black community and his dedication to improving Black education enabled him to preside over both the school and home with dignity, intelligence, and fairness.

While Cardozo got along well with his faculty and students, he was engaged in a continuous battle with certain AMA officials, especially Samuel Hunt, superintendent of schools. Hunt tried to influence the faculty to develop negative attitudes against Cardozo.[18] He showed a lack of respect for Blacks[19] and constantly harassed

[14]F. L. Cardozo to S. Hunt, December 2, 1865, January 13, 1866, November 3, 1866; F. L. Cardozo to G. Whipple and M. E. Strieby, December 2, 1865, AMAA.

[15]Whether deliberately or not, Samuel Hunt, AMA superintendent of schools, 1864–1866, created unpleasant feelings against Cardozo among Black teachers sent from the North. Misses Wall and Alexander were told by Hunt, before departing for Charleston, that Cardozo had requested that no Black teachers be sent. Cardozo wrote Hunt that he was mistaken and asked Hunt for a written statement to that effect. "I am sure you would not willingly do me the injustice of supposing me guilty of such unchristian conduct as requesting competent persons be denied positions on account of their *color*," Cardozo wrote. "And indeed," Cardozo added, "such conduct would be specially foolish and suicidal on my part." Hunt's motives are unexplained though he seems to have had reservations about using Black teachers. Fortunately for the Association, Hunt remained in the position for only two years. F. L. Cardozo to S. Hunt, December 2, 1865, AMAA.

[16]The local Black teachers did not board in the home.

[17]C. F. Aitken to S. Hunt, October 24, 1865; P. A. Alcott to S. Hunt, March 27, 1866, AMAA.

[18]In the fall of 1866, Hunt sent teachers who, in Cardozo's view, were inferior. He told Hunt so. Hunt did not withdraw the teachers, but sent them a letter saying that Cardozo was disappointed in them. Cardozo was puzzled by Hunt's actions since the teachers were not being withdrawn and such a statement would only make them unhappy in the situation. F. L. Cardozo to S. Hunt, October 30, 1866, AMAA.

[19]Hunt had reservations about the moral fitness of Blacks for AMA work. He apparently agreed, even if reluctantly, of the propriety of having Black workers, but it was almost impossible to find Blacks suitable to Hunt. F. L. Cardozo to S. Hunt, January 13, 1866, AMAA.

Cardozo about money. Hunt claimed that the Charleston operation was too costly and asked Cardozo to relieve some of his teachers to save money. However, Cardozo refused. Some faculty members came to Cardozo's defense. Phebe A. Alcott recounted how hard the teachers worked, how little they ate, how sparsely furnished the mission home was and how badly all the teachers were needed. She further praised Cardozo and expressed regret that Hunt "should perhaps unwittingly depress or depreciate a good man working faithfully and intelligently in our cause."[20] Despite this support, the sparring between Cardozo and Hunt continued. Fortunately for Cardozo and the AMA, Hunt was replaced in 1866 by Edward P. Smith. Cardozo and Smith quickly became fast friends.

Cardozo never had to speculate about the views of a majority of Charleston whites in 1865. He knew that their initial response to his project was negative. Bureau Superintendent Tomlinson claimed that whites were not merely indifferent but completely opposed to Black education.[21] Cardozo's close observations of white attitudes and behavior caused him to be pessimistic. In October 1865 he wrote that South Carolina whites were being entrusted with power too quickly. He believed they were, at heart, still disloyal and "most treacherous." "The feeling of hate and revenge toward the colored people," Cardozo added, "seems to me fiendish." Whites threw every possible obstacle in the way of Black progress, Cardozo thought, and then pointed to a lack of advancement as an argument for treating Blacks differently. Cardozo anticipated trouble when civil law was fully restored because he was convinced that Blacks were "determined not to submit so tamely as they did before the war."[22] Cardozo was never subservient, but he vigorously sought southern white support for Black education.

Despite white opposition and lingering economic problems, Cardozo had good reason to be proud of his first year's work. He had collected a racially mixed group of efficient, dedicated teachers who worked together harmoniously in leading Saxton students to remarkable advancement.

George A. Trenholm, former secretary of treasury of the Confederacy, and several other native whites, visited Saxton School in March 1866. They were impressed with both the teachers and scholars. Saxton School was widely acclaimed as the outstanding

---

[20]P. A. Alcott to S. Hunt, March 27, 1866; P. A. Alcott to G. Whipple, December 28, 1865, AMAA.

[21]Joel Williamson, *After Slavery: The Negro in South Carolina During Reconstruction, 1861-1877* (Chapel Hill, 1965), p. 213.

[22]F. L. Cardozo to G. Whipple, October 21, 1865, AMAA.

school for Black youth in South Carolina,[23] and one of the superior schools in the South.

While Cardozo was a superb administrator with an able faculty, the students must also be acknowledged for contributing to the success of Saxton School. They were eager to study and learn. A number of the students were young men and women who were preparing themselves for careers as teachers or in other professions. Approximately 25 per cent of the students came from free Charleston families that had enjoyed some educational advantages before the Civil War. The Charleston *Daily News* referred to those students as "an aristocracy of color" and warned that the school was not a fair representation of Black education in Charleston.

Though Cardozo was a free-born and mulatto, he showed no preference for this class in his school. However, fair skinned students seemed to predominate, especially in the advanced classes. Since Cardozo's ambition was to create a normal school, he sought the best available student talent; and circumstances so dictated that a large number of those with prior training happened to be light skinned and free-born. Cardozo ridiculed the notion that mulattos learned more quickly than darker students. He stated that there was "no difference in the capacity of *freemen and freedmen*. . . Indeed the difference would not be known if it were not for the more advanced condition of the former, on account of previous advantages."[24]

Spring exams in May 1866, marked the end of Cardozo's first year as principal in Charleston. It had been a year filled with both frustrations and rewards, but the faculty had worked together well, students had made commendable progress and the Black community, both the poor and the prosperous, had accepted Saxton School as their own. There even seemed to be a grudging recognition by local whites of the school's efficiency and importance.

Cardozo spent his summer vacation enlisting new support for Saxton and trying to convince AMA officials that there should be a normal school in Charleston. Cardozo had little expectation of receiving financial aid from native whites, but he hoped to secure the endorsement of several influential people. He felt that if some of Charleston's "first families" approved his school, it might partially allay white opposition. Cardozo was basically cautious and conciliatory. He was determined to maintain good relations with influential whites without sacrificing his principles. He refused to

[23]Martin Abbott, *The Freedmen's Bureau in South Carolina* (Chapel Hill, 1967), p. 92; S. C. Hale to S. Hunt, June 11, 1866, AMAA.

[24]Cardozo quoted in *Twenty-First Annual Report of the American Missionary Association and the Proceedings at the Annual Meeting . . . October 17th and 18th, 1867* (N.Y., 1867), p. 33.

preach at the Black mission sponsored by Reverend Thomas Smyth of the Second Presbyterian Church even though Smyth was a man of great local influence because, as Cardozo wrote, "I could not possibly cooperate with men holding such views as he does." Still, Cardozo was able to get Reverend Smyth's signature approving his school. Cardozo was especially pleased with the endorsement of P. G. Gaillard, a Confederate hero and Mayor of Charleston. "I thought it a most singular thing," Cardozo wrote, "that I should hold the document for a one-armed Confederate officer to sign to educate and elevate the men for whose perpetual enslavement he had lost an arm." Other signatures secured by Cardozo included Governor James L. Orr, State Senator Henry Buist, Lieutenant Governor W. Porter, and Thomas T. Simons, editor of the Charleston *Courier.*

That Cardozo could secure the endorsement of South Carolina whites without subservience or loss of principle seemed remarkable to some observers. In November 1866, Bureau Superintendent Tomlinson said that the few prominent individuals who favored Black education lacked the courage to express their views because there was no "locality in the state in which there was *public opinion* favorable" to educating Blacks.[25] During his first two years in Charleston, Cardozo was unusually successful in communicating with three major classes: the antebellum free Black community, former slaves, and wealthy or otherwise influential whites. When he became actively involved in politics, his relations with the third group quickly became strained.

While Cardozo was securing signatures in support of Black education, he was also reminding AMA officials that he had gone to Charleston to establish a normal school. "It is the object for which I left all the superior advantages and privileges of the North and came South," he wrote. "It is the object for which I have labored during the past year and for which I am willing to *remain* here and make this place my home." Cardozo estimated that he had 200 students now ready for normal school. Most of them had been free before the war and had received some education before going to Saxton School. Reverend Edward P. Smith, field secretary for the Association, 1866–1870, visited Cardozo in mid-1866 and was impressed by both the man and his plan. "His normal school project is now his highest aim and he is willing to make it his life work," Smith wrote.[26] Since AMA officials already believed that

[25]F. L. Cardozo to E. P. Smith, October 23, 1866, AMAA; *American Missionary,* X (December, 1866), 271; R. Tomlinson, South Carolina School Report, November 3, 1866, Bureau Records, Educational Division.

[26]E. P. Smith to G. Whipple, September 26, 1866, AMAA.

Blacks eventually would be required to furnish their own teachers, it was relatively easy to convince them that a normal school was needed in Charleston.[27] Hence, Saxton School became a normal school in the fall of 1866. Cardozo, apparently, was satisfied that he would spend the remainder of his life as a normal school educator.

The fall, 1866, school term began inauspiciously. Although Cardozo was the principal, he was not permitted to choose his own teachers. As with other AMA schools, the Association's officials in New York made the selection. Cardozo had been pleased with his teachers of the previous year and during the summer, had repeatedly requested that he be sent another set of first-rate people. When the teachers finally arrived, he was disappointed. He felt that the teachers were inferior to those of the previous year; he needed superior teachers as the school was now more advanced. One of the white teachers was so uncivil that Cardozo had to request that she be removed.[28]

Despite Cardozo's dissatisfaction with the teachers, he managed to operate an efficient, effective school. There were approximately 1000 students enrolled. Among the students, Bureau Superintendent Tomlinson observed, were "children of the most intelligent and cultivated parents in the state." Those actually taking normal training tended to be from the financially more secure families. As during the previous year, a majority of the advanced students had been free before the war. The preponderance of traditionally free students resulted in charges that Cardozo and the school favored mulatto over darker and freemen over freedmen students. The charges were untrue; those students simply had received greater advantages.[29]

In spite of Cardozo's white father, free status, and European education, he elected to go South and identify with Blacks as his people. He harbored no racial prejudice. There is no indication that he believed his light skin made him superior to his darker brethren, as did many of that day. He was as concerned with the Blacks as with the mulatto students.

Cardozo was an extremely religious man, but had little sympathy for the southern Black church. He believed religious teach-

[27]Augustus F. Beard, *A Crusade of Brotherhood: A History of the American Missionary Association* (Boston, 1909), p. 168.
[28]F. L. Cardozo to S. Hunt, October 16, 1866; F. L. Cardozo to E. P. Smith, December 24, 1866, January 10, 1867, S. W. Stansbury to E. P. Smith, December 24, 1866; T. W. Cardozo to S. Hunt, June 23, 1865, AMAA.
[29]R. Tomlinson, South Carolina School Report, July 1, 1867, Bureau Records, Educational Division; J. A. Van Allen to E. P. Smith, February 16, 1867, AMAA; Luther P. Jackson, "The Educational Efforts of the Freedmen's Bureau and Freedmen's Aid Societies in South Carolina, 1862–1872," *Journal of Negro History*, VIII (January, 1923), 25.

ing should be a part of normal training, but he preferred that the religion be congregational or, at least, nondemonstrative. In 1867, he wrote requesting congregationalist teachers for the next year. Of the fourteen day-school teachers he now had, Cardozo said, only two worked in the Sabbath School. "And it does seem to me a great pity," he added, "to see so many of our promising scholars going over to the ignorant and fanatical methodists for the want of a good Sabbath School and good teachers in our church."[30] Cardozo was, of course, speaking of the Black Methodists.

While Cardozo was training future teachers, he was also becoming involved in politics, something that would eventually take him away from the educational field for many years. Although he genuinely seemed to have no personal desire to hold political office, he believed that Blacks must have political power to gain protection. He had long been aware of the political situation in South Carolina, and Congressional Reconstruction in 1867, which enfranchised Blacks, made it difficult for him not to become involved in politics. Cardozo had lost none of his interest in educating his people, but his intelligence, prominence, wide range of acquaintances and willingness to stand up for principles made him a natural leader. More and more, Black Charlestonians looked to Cardozo for political guidance. In the Spring, 1866, General Daniel E. Sickles, military commander of South Carolina, asked Cardozo if he would become a member of the board of advisors to suggest rules and regulations for the proper execution of voter registration. Cardozo believed it his responsibility to work with the Board, but he still had no desire to run the office. His major concern in mid-1867 was to secure a new building for his school, for he believed he could never have a model school until he had the proper building.[31]

Cardozo and his wife spent the summer vacation of 1867 visiting friends in Cleveland, New York, Philadelphia and New Haven. He seemed totally unconcerned with South Carolina politics. In September, 1867, he sent a telegram to AMA headquarters in New York asking that teachers be sent immediately to Saxton School. During October, he was occupied with getting his students and faculty organized. He reduced the number of students in 1867 to concentrate on teacher training. In November he reported 65 students in primary classes, 281 in intermediate classes and 92 in the advanced class. It was necessary to have some primary pupils to provide teaching practice to advanced students. He fretted about

[30]F. L. Cardozo to E. P. Smith, June 8, 1867, AMAA.
[31]C. Thurston Chase to E. P. Smith, March 22, 1867, F. L. Cardozo to E. P. Smith, June 8, December 7, 1867, AMAA.

the slowness in constructing his new school building—which was supposed to have been ready for occupancy at the beginning of the fall, 1867, term.

During this time, while Cardozo was laboring in the school, he was persuaded by friends to become a candidate for the Constitutional Convention. After much urging, he agreed to run, more "from a sense of duty, than from choice, for I have no desire for the turbulent political arena, but being the *only educated colored* man here my friends thought it my duty to go if elected, and I consented to do so." Cardozo asked AMA officials to send him a copy of the constitutions of all the states so he could be prepared if elected, and promised that if he went to the convention he would see that the school did not suffer while he was gone.[32]

After Cardozo was elected delegate to the Constitutional Convention, he continued to direct his energies toward developing the school. He lacked a strong instinct for political power, and apparently preferred teaching and administration. When he learned that the convention would meet in Charleston, Cardozo agreed that he could still superintend the school even though he could not teach. A visitor to Charleston in December 1867 wrote that Cardozo was happy with his school, but, the visitor believed, the young educator would "make his mark in the future of this state and ere long will represent her in the national council." Cardozo, the visitor added, had "grown and developed in character by his political associations."[33]

Whether or not he realized it at the time, Cardozo's election as a delegate to the Constitutional Convention marked the close of his career as a South Carolina educator.[34] The same characteristics that made him an excellent principal resulted in his becoming an effective politician. He continued to superintend his school, but more and more this interest became secondary. His prominence in the convention led to his being elected Secretary of State; whereupon he tendered his resignation to the AMA effective May 1, 1868.[35] He continued to support his former school but he had been transformed from professional educator to professional politician.

[32] *Teacher's Monthly School Report*, November, 1867; F. L. Cardozo to E. P. Smith, November 4, December 7, 1867, AMAA.

[33] C. Thurston Chase to E. P. Smith, December 26, 1867; F. L. Cardozo to E. P. Smith, November 4, December 25, 1867, January 2, 1868, AMAA.

[34] AMA officials, though concerned about losing a first rate principal, encouraged Cardozo's political activity after his election to the constitutional convention. They hoped that he would be elected to the United States Congress. Reverend E. P. Smith said that Charleston Blacks were "bent on having this aristocratic district represented by a [coloured] man and Cardoso [sic] is really the only one fit for it." E. P. Smith to G. Whipple, February 5, 1868, AMAA.

[35] F. L. Cardozo to E. P. Smith, March 9, May 1, June 22, 1868, AMAA.

Before resigning, Cardozo changed the name of his school and moved it into a new building. For more than a year, he had negotiated for a more efficient physical plant. In spring 1868, with the assistance of the Freedmen's Bureau and a $10,000 grant from Charles Avery of Philadelphia, Cardozo transferred his students to the new two-story brick building and placed his faculty in a new mission home.[36] The new school was dedicated on May 7, 1868, as Avery Institute. For the next several years, Avery Institute would be considered the premier Black school in South Carolina and would furnish many of the teachers for Black schools in the state. Much of Avery Institute's later success was a direct result of the firm foundation laid by Cardozo.

In 1867–68, E. L. Boring travelled throughout the South in the interest of the New School Presbyterian Church. In his travels Boring examined scores of schools and he awarded Cardozo "the preeminence as principal." Cardozo's every movement, Boring stated, was characterized by "promptness, order and system. . . ." Furthermore, Boring found himself "moving in a much brighter sphere of social, intellectual and moral attainment," at Cardozo's school than he had "met with elsewhere."[37]

Boring's assessment of Cardozo's ability was accurate. Though he was principal of Avery for less than three years, and is best remembered for being Secretary of State and Secretary of the Treasury, Cardozo had an important impact on the education of Blacks in South Carolina.

[36] Avery's donation paid for the land and the mission home. The Freedmen's Bureau constructed the school building at a cost of $17,000. H. Heide to J. W. Alvord, December 4, 1868, Bureau Records, Educational Division; *American Missionary*, XII (July, 1868), 148.

[37] E. L. Boring to E. P. Smith, January 13, 1868, AMAA.

# Joseph Carter Corbin and Negro Education in the University of Arkansas

By THOMAS ROTHROCK*

Springdale

THE NAME JOSEPH CARTER CORBIN IS INDELIBLY STAMPED upon the pages of the early history of Arkansas Industrial University, now the University of Arkansas. This Ohio Negro arrived in Arkansas in 1872, served as a reporter for the Little Rock *Arkansas Republican,* ran for and won election as state superintendent of public instruction, and by virtue of that office was president of the board of trustees of Arkansas Industrial University. When the trustees, in 1873, awarded a contract for the construction of University Hall (Old Main), Joseph Carter Corbin, as board president, signed the document on behalf of the trustees. In the Age of Jim Crow that followed Reconstruction in Arkansas, white writers on the history of the segregated university noted with curiosity that a Negro had signed the contract for Old Main. Today, in the Age of Black Militancy, young Arkansas Negroes at the integrated university take pride in the fact that a member of their race was president of the board of trustees and signed the contract for the construction of the building which black and white alike think of when they mention the name University of Arkansas.

*Editor's Note: As a contribution to the events commemorating the centennial of the University of Arkansas, in 1971-1972, Mr. Rothrock has undertaken, in this the first of two articles on the history of Branch Normal College, to fill an important gap in the story of the university's first century.

Who was this man?[1] He was born in Chillicothe, Ohio, on March 26, 1833, of free Negro parents, William and Susan Corbin. In this northern town, where the Jim Crow system was in effect, Negro children were not permitted to attend white public schools, and there were no public schools for blacks. Consequently, young Jim Corbin's parents, determined he should be educated, enrolled him in private tuition schools in the winters. He studied diligently, advanced as far as the "single rule of three" in these elementary schools, read much on his own, and at age sixteen went to Louisville, Kentucky, and entered a private school attended by both free and slave students. Here he apparently prepared himself for college by studying, in Latin, Caesar and Cicero, and, in mathematics, through analytical geometry.

Having saved sufficient funds to enter college, he won acceptance at Ohio University at Athens in 1850 when he was seventeen. Three years later he received his bachelor's degree in arts, and three years after that, in 1856, took a master of arts degree. According to the *Ohio Bulletin,* an alumni magazine of Ohio University, an honorary doctorate was later conferred on Corbin by an unknown "Baptist institution in the South." His success as a public speaker was attributed to the experience he gained at Ohio University in the work of the Philomathean Society, a student literary and debating organization.

Although the chronology is not clear, young Corbin seemingly left Ohio University in about 1853 to work as a messenger and clerk in the Bank of the Ohio Valley at Cincinnati. He also taught school at Louisville, returning to Cincinnati at the outbreak of the Civil War. At Cincinnati during the war years he edited and published a newspaper, *The Colored Citizen.* He married in 1866 Miss Mary Jane

---

[1]Biographical facts on Corbin's early life are from Ohio University *Ohio Bulletin* (Athens, 1909), 26-27; John Hugh Reynolds and David Yancey Thomas, *History of the University of Arkansas* (Fayetteville, 1910), 356-357; obituaries in Pine Bluff *Daily Graphic* and Little Rock *Arkansas Gazette,* both Jan. 10, 1911.

**Joseph Carter Corbin**

Ward, who bore him six children, two of whom, a son Will and a daughter Louisa, survived the father.

Corbin moved in 1872 to Little Rock, where he became a reporter on Powell Clayton's party organ the *Daily Republican*. He rose swiftly in the ranks of the Clayton party, was secretary of the Republican state convention in August 1872 and was nominated by that convention for the state office of superintendent of public instruction.[2] Heading the Republican ticket in 1872 was Elisha Baxter, who defeated dissident Republican Joseph Brooks in the famous disputed election of that year.

Corbin's opponent in 1872 was the incumbent Dr. Thomas Smith, a Union Army doctor who had served in

[2]Little Rock *Daily Republican*, Aug. 22, 23, 1872.

Arkansas and afterwards settled at Helena. Dr. Smith as a Republican leader had done yoeman service in setting up Arkansas's first tax-supported public school system, but had become a political liability to the Claytonites in his open attacks on the handling of school funds at the county level and on the political conduct of the circuit superintendents set up under Arkansas's first school law. Consequently, the Claytonites had dumped Dr. Smith in 1872, but the Brooksites had nominated him on their state ticket.[3]

Corbin in 1872 stumped the state in behalf of the national and state regular Republican ticket. He seemingly had nothing personal to say against Dr. Smith, but tagged the entire Brooks slate as disloyal "Liberal Republicans," a reference to the anti-Grant coalition of 1872. Most of the references to Corbin during the campaign were clippings from Cincinnati papers reprinted in the Little Rock *Daily Republican.* The editors of the Cincinnati papers were proud of Corbin's success in Arkansas in being nominated for superintendent of the state's schools. "Mr. Corbin is an educated gentleman of fine natural talents," said the *Cincinnati Gazette,* "and would fill the position with credit to himself and profit to the state."[4]

Corbin was on the side of political power in 1872, and his faction had the means at hand to count themselves into office no matter what the results at the polls on election day. To be sure, there was corruption on both sides as the Claytonites and Brooksites battled for supremacy. When the legislature convened, January 6, 1873, the Claytonites were in control. They found that, although Dr. Smith had carried thirty-five counties to Corbin's twenty-six, Corbin had received a total of 40,010 votes to Smith's 39,295 and was elected. The Claytonites had dumped the controversial Dr. Smith.[5]

Very little is known about Superintendent Corbin's

---

[3]Clara B. Kennan, "Dr. Thomas Smith, Forgotten Man of Arkansas Education," *Arkansas Historical Quarterly,* XX (Winter, 1961), 303-317.
[4]*Daily Republican,* Sept. 6-7, 28, 1872.
[5]*Ibid.,* Jan. 7, 1873.

administration. He was in office less than two years when Augustus Hill Garland led the Arkansas Redeemers in the final overthrow of the warring Republican factions, wrote the Constitution of 1874, and supplanted the Baxter forces in Little Rock in the late fall of that year. Departing Little Rock, Corbin went to Jefferson City, Missouri, where he had accepted a teaching position in the Lincoln Institute.[6]

While serving as superintendent of public instruction, Corbin had, however, helped lay the foundation for establishing for Negroes "a branch Normal college" of Arkansas Industrial University. The university, founded in 1871 and opened in 1872, was a Federal Land Grant College under the Morrell Act of 1862 and was not, therefore, a segregated institution. Yet the university located at Fayetteville in the far northwest corner of the state, had, indeed, treated its handful of Negro students on a segregated, separate basis, and was on the opposite side of the state from the center of Arkansas's Negro population. Since the university afforded practically no opportunity for Negro higher education, there had been agitation almost from the beginning for a separate branch for Negroes to be located somewhere in the center of the state's black population.[7]

Taking office in 1873, Corbin not only was sympathetic with the needs of the Negroes but was in a position to help them. As state superintendent of public instruction, he was ex officio president of the university board of trustees, and at a board meeting in Little Rock on March 5, 1873, Professor M. W. Martin of Pine Bluff and Mrs. Alida Clark of Helena, white missionary teachers of Arkansas Negroes, appeared and spoke. They deplored the almost total lack of facilities for training Negro teachers in the state, and requested the board of trustees to do what it could to secure from the legislature, which was then in session, an

---

[6]Reynolds and Thomas, *University of Arkansas,* 357.

[7]Guerdon D. Nichols, "Breaking the Color Barrier at the Universitiy of Arkansas," *Arkansas Historical Quarterly,* XXVII (Spring, 1968), 3-4; University of Arkansas Trustee Minutes, Jan. 17, 1872, Book A, 72, in University Archives, Special Collections, University of Arkansas Library (hereafter cited Trustee Minutes).

act creating and locating in eastern Arkansas a Negro branch of the university. What was needed, they told the board, was "a normal school for the education and fitting of persons as colored teachers."[8]

The board readily agreed to act on the request of Martin and Mrs. Clark, and President Corbin appointed a committee of three to draw up a bill and present it to the legislature. The three trustees named were loyal Claytonites, two of them justices on the supreme court (Judges John Emory Bennett and Elhanan J. Searle) and the third a state senator from Jefferson County, John Middleton Clayton, a brother of United States Senator Powell Clayton. State Senator Clayton promptly introduced a bill authorizing the university board of trustees "to select a suitable site and locate thereon a branch Normal college, which location—owing to the principal college being located in the northwest portion of the state—shall be made southeast or east or south of the county of Pulaski." Interestingly, no mention was made of race in the bill, although the language did stipulate that the board, in locating the school, "take into consideration the interests of the state, and especially the convenience and well-being of the poorer classes. . . ."[9]

Other features were that the "said branch Normal college" would be "under the care and management" of the university board of trustees; that the branch college should "in all things be governed by the same rules and regulations" as the main university and "of Normal department therein" at Fayetteville; that the board of trustees should have the same admission standards, the same quality of fac-

---

[8]Trustee Minutes, March 5, 1873, Book A, 74; there were three women and a man named Clark all teaching at or near Helena in 1873, but the only married woman was Mrs. Alida Clark, a Quaker missionary teacher to Arkansas freedmen. A list of teachers in the freedmen schools in Arkansas is in Larry Wesley Pearce, *The American Missionary Association and the Freedmen in Arkansas, 1863-1878* (unpublished History honor's paper, Hendrix College, April 20, 1970), 146. Martin was an American Missionary Association teacher at Pine Bluff, and from Ripon, Wisconsin. *Ibid.*, 149.

[9]Trustee Minutes, March 5, 1873, Book A, 74; *Arkansas Acts*, 1873, pp. 231-233.

ulty, and the same books, courses of study, and "like training and proficiency" as "adopted and required" on the Fayetteville campus. The bill authorized the trustees "to receive aid in money, property or other valuable effects" for the benefit of the branch college "from any and all individuals, towns or other communities or corporations, and all gifts, devises and donations that can be had to secure the location, or to aid in erecting or maintaining said branch college." Which was an involved way of saying they could accept competitive bids for the location of the school at any given site. Finally, the bill appropriated $25,000 "out of any money in the treasury not otherwise appropriated" to be used by the university trustees for the purchase of a site, the erection of college buildings, the improvement of the grounds, the purchase of necessary furniture, the organization of the college, and "the payment of professors and teachers for two years commencing with the fall term" of 1873.[10]

Clayton's bill became a law on April 25, 1873, and at a board of trustees's meeting in July President Corbin appointed Clayton, Judge Bennett, and H. A. Millen a committee to "take steps similar in character to secure a location for said College, as was taken to secure that of the main College at Fayetteville. . . ." Six months later, in January 1874, the committee reported that because of the country-wide financial panic and the "consequent low price of script" that it had decided to incur no expense whatever in advertising and receiving bids for the location of the college.[11]

The year 1874 witnessed the overthrow of the Reconstruction regime, the adoption of the new constitution, the inauguration of a new Democratic regime, the exodus to Missouri of Dr. Corbin, and the replacement of the university board of trustees in its entirety. A new committee of the board, composed of Governor Garland, Dudley Emerson

---

[10]*Arkansas Acts,* 1873, pp. 231-233.
[11]Trustee Minutes, July 1-3, 1873, Jan. 14, 1874, Book A, 123, 130, 150, 161.

Jones, a Little Rock businessman, and Professor Wood E. Thompson of Monticello, an educator who was afterwards to be superintendent of public instruction, acted in the summer of 1875 to carry out the provisions of the act of 1873. Their instruction from the board was to locate the "Branch Normal School . . . temporarily at Pine Bluff, Jefferson County. . . ." Governor Garland, as chairman of the committee, was authorized to draw vouchers on the Branch Normal College fund for "organizing and conducting" the college.[12]

The Garland committee executed its work by employing Corbin as their agent for establishing Branch Normal College. Corbin arrived from Missouri in late June 1875 and spent a week in Pine Bluff conferring with its citizens and conducting a public meeting in the courthouse. He found he could secure a suitable building for the use of the school, and, returning to Little Rock, wrote a report to the Garland committee. The committee approved renting from Colonel M. L. Bell a house that stood on a quarter block of land at the southwest corner of Lindsay and Sevier Streets. It was a one-story, ell-shaped frame house facing north on Lindsay Street and with porches along the entire front and across the back to the ell. A small frame building, ten by twelve feet in dimension, stood on Sevier Street in front of the ell.[13]

Hired as "principal" of Branch Normal College on August 18, 1875, Corbin returned to Pine Bluff. Colonel Bell agreed to remodel and repair the house, which Corbin leased for a year at $300. Corbin then busied himself ordering school furniture and supplies, and in spreading word among Arkansas's Negroes of their new school.[14] Typical of the announcement disseminated at this time was an article in the *Pine Bluff Republican* which sketched the brief history of the school, Corbin's role in locating it, and his

---

[12]*Ibid.*, June 21, 1875, Book A, 226, 227.

[13]The report of the Branch Normal College Committee is in Universiy of Arkansas *Fourth Catalogue*, 1876, pp. 122-123; an abstract of Corbin's report for 1875-1876, is in *ibid.*, 124-134.

[14]University of Arkansas *Fourth Catalogue*, 1876, pp. 128-129.

plans for opening the school on September 6th, the appointed day for opening of the university in Fayetteville.

> Tuition in the school will be free, the beneficiary is, however, required to enter into a written obligation to teach for two years in the schools of the state in consideration of three years tuition. The regulation applies also to such beneficiaries of the preparatory department as will be able, after one year's tuition, to enter the normal. The school will be opened upon rather a small scale at first, but additions to the number of teachers, etc., will be made from time to time, as the necessities of the case may demand. As the school is supported by the state, it is, of course, open to citizens generally, and we hope to see a large number of our colored youth avail themselves of its advantage.[15]

Corbin's wish to open his school on the 6th of September was not realized. Sickness among the workmen engaged by Colonel Bell in remodeling the building and the sinking of the steamboat which carried his school furniture, slating, and other materials enroute from Chicago, combined to prevent him from opening his school until the 27th of the month, when seven Negro students, four from Drew County and three from Jefferson County, presented themselves for registration and began classes.[16]

At the end of the first year, in June 1876, Professor Corbin reported to the university board of trustees on "the progress" made in "establishing a Normal School for the direct benefit of the colored population of the State."[17] Recounting the history of his role in establishing the school, his election as principal, and the delay in getting the school open, Corbin described a year of frustration mixed with hope. He had found it difficult to find Negro students of the proper age, qualifications, and necessary means for attending. Governor Garland, as chairman of the board committee on Branch Normal, had authorized Corbin to enroll

---

[15]*Arkansas Gazette,* Sept. 2, 1875, quoting Pine Bluff *Republican,* n.d.
[16]University of Arkansas *Fourth Catalogue,* 1876, p. 129.
[17]All information on the year 1875-1876 is from *ibid.,* 124-134, unless otherwise noted.

as beneficiaries all students who turned up, so long as the total number allowed (237) was not exceeded and so long as no county's quota was denied. The school began, then, as an elementary school, worked up to the high school level, and, before 1900, largely ignored both the "normal" and the "collegiate" features for which the school was intended.

Corbin reported a total of seventy-five students enrolled during the year 1875-1876, but his manuscript rosters render it impossible to determine how many were enrolled.[18] One roster for 1875-1876 lists twenty students enrolled in the "Normal Department" and fifty-one in the "Preparatory Department," with twelve of the seventy-one listed as "beneficiaries." Another roster shows his enrollment by "grades," that is, two "Third Grades" of sixteen and seventeen respectively and a "Second Grade" of eighteen.

Attendance was bad, as reflected by available records for April-May 1876. The April roster showed fifty-five students enrolled, ranging in age from eight to twenty-eight. Seventeen had perfect attendance, but the remainder had from one to ten and a half absences. Curiously, Corbin explained on the roster what had happened: "A picnic of the public schools and a protracted meeting that has been going on three weeks in the Baptist church which holds to as late an hour at night as 2 o'clock are the causes of much of the absence." The roster for May 1876 found forty-one students enrolled and with good attendance. Twenty had perfect records.

Struggling to organize his school, Corbin began by classifying his students generally according to their reading ability. This done, he labored patiently to equalize their "unequal" attainments: to teach, first of all, good reading, good writing, and good drawing; to do, secondly, what he could to strengthen and equalize their arithmetic; and to

---

[18]These rosters are in "Records Pertaining to Branch Normal College, 1876-1895," University Archives, Board of Trustees, Special Collections, University of Arkansas Library; they apparently accompanied Corbin's handwritten "Narrative Report" for 1875-1876, which has been either lost or misfiled. (Hereafter cited Branch Normal College Records.)

introduce them, thirdly, to the elements of vocal music. The result was, as we have seen, the organization of his students into a school of "three" grades arranged roughly according to their reading ability. Actually, he had two "Third Grades" and one "Second Grade."

It will be well to point out that Corbin was using the "grading" method common to his day in Arkansas and in the rest of the country, and not the "grading" system with which we are familiar today. In the average ten-grade school system of Corbin's day, the "First Grade" was the senior year of high school, the "Second Grade" the junior year, etc., down to the "Tenth Grade," which was the first year of "primary school." But, to complicate matters slightly, the McGuffey's Readers then commonly used, as well as the popular Appleton's Readers, were graded from "First" through the "Fourth" from bottom to top. The First through Fourth Readers were used in the Tenth to Third Grades, with the harder Fifth Reader, when used, being employed sometimes in the Third and Second Grades. In the parlance of the day, a student who had advanced to the level of and mastered the Fourth Reader was ready for the final two years of high school or "prep" school, that is, the Latin, algebra, geometry, trigonometry, history, English grammar and composition, etc., required to pass the entrance examinations for college work.[19]

None of Corbin's students in 1875-1876 were of college level. One "Third Grade" was reading *McGuffey's Fifth Reader*, studying Guyot's Intermediate Geography, and using Ray's Third Arithmetic—all "primary" and "intermediate" subjects of the Fifth upward to the Third Grade. His other "Third Grade" was so poorly prepared as to fall back to *McGuffey's Third Reader* and "oral lessons in arith-

---

[19]An example of a "graded" public school together with textbooks can be found in T. M. Stinnett and Clara B. Kennan, *All This and Tomorrow Too, the Evolving and Continuing History of the Arkansas Education Association—A Century and Beyond* (Little Rock, 1969), 63, which is an advertisement for Josiah B. Shinn's "Russellville Public School," a ten-grade school.

metic, language and geography." His final class, the "Second Grade" read in *McGuffey's Fourth Reader*, had oral lessons in geography and language, and studied "mental and practical arithmetic." He had only one student in the entire school, Rufus Daugherty, eighteen, who had come to him from Chamberville, Calhoun County, who could work in algebra, but Daugherty was a "Third Grader" reading in *McGuffey's Fifth Reader*.

Corbin was quick to admit that it had been more difficult to grade the school in arithmetic than in reading, "the qualifications of the students being so unequal." He had heard Rufus Daugherty and another student, W. Bland, recite in advanced arithmetic and algebra after school hours, and they in return had assisted him some "in teaching the lower classes." Corbin was proud of the fact that the rest of his best Third Graders had "gone as far as fractions in arithmetic."

Some of the students Corbin enrolled that first year were below the prescribed age for either preparatory or normal collegiate work. He justified this on the grounds that the university regulations were written for white students, that the regulations were out of touch with reality insofar as the situation of black students and black public schools in the state were concerned, and that to have adhered to the rules was "impossible without imperiling the very existence of the school."

He had had to contend, he reported, with many "false rumors" about the regulations and objects of Branch Normal College. He had advertised widely among the Negroes that the object of the school was to train Negro teachers, and, with Governor Garland's approval, that free tuition would be given to such as applied for admission upon signing a pledge obligating themselves to teach for a term of at least two years in the public schools of the state. In the same announcements he had explained that in connection with the "normal school proper" a preparatory department was attached which might be attended by such youth as might be enabled after a year's tuition, to enter the normal school.

For one reason and another many Negroes refused to believe Corbin. Some said the establishment of the college was "a political trick," an "experiment" with no guarantee of permanence, and that it would cost five dollars a month to attend. Such rumors not only had reduced attendance, but also had rendered it difficult for him to collect the matriculation fee of $5.00 required by university regulations of every student who enrolled, the $5.00 fee authorizing a student to attend for four years. Tuition and board were, of course, in addition to that, but tuition was not required of "beneficiaries," that is, those needy but promising students sent by quotas from the different counties and unable to pay. The university permitted 237 beneficiaries, each certified by his respective county judge, to attend the collegiate department, and the same number to attend the normal department.[20] Corbin interpreted the regulations to mean that he could admit up to 237 to Branch Normal, and since the blacks were concentrated in the counties of the southeast he winked at the county-quota list used at the Fayetteville campus. Branch Normal had been founded for the education of the "poorer classes," he reasoned. Therefore, he treated nearly all his students who enrolled in the early years as "normal beneficiaries," collecting very little in tuition and matriculation fees and beseiging the board with petitions that he not collect any at all. While the board never agreed to such a double standard for Corbin's students, they failed, in the early years, to pay much attention to his business methods and his record keeping. This is not to say he did not collect some matriculation and tuition fees; indeed, for 1875-1876 he reported collecting $125.00 in tuition and matriculation fees, a figure hardly in line with the number enrolled. If he had collected the required $5.00 matriculation fee from the seventy-one students on his roster of 1875-1876, the figure alone would have come to $355.

In addition to his problems of grading his school, col-

---

[20]University of Arkansas *Fourth Catalogue,* 1876, pp. 17-31.

lecting fees, dispelling rumors, and deciding how far university regulations in respect to standards and to beneficiaries applied to his school, Corbin served as janitor of "the barracks," a name his students quickly applied to the Bell house in which the school had opened. The building, he reported in 1876, was on ground so low that it stood in water during heavy rains. He recommended that money be appropriated for drainage and constructing walks, for opening the "east and west end rooms" of the house for school rooms, and for purchasing a new supply of wall slating, which, because of the "atmospheric changes" of the school grounds and the building, was "constantly vibrating from tight to loose."

The university committee on Branch Normal College reported to the board of trustees in June 1876 that they were pleased with Professor Corbin's work. He had organized and taken charge of the school, and had it operating "better than could have been expected under the circumstances."[21] Accordingly, Corbin agreed to stay on for a second year.

We infer from Corbin's "Narrative Report" for that second year, 1876-1877, that he was not happy with the "condition, progress, and prospects" of Branch Normal College.[22] Whereas he had spent the first year in grading his school and in introducing the proper textbooks, he spent the second year in "reducing to an equality the attainments of students from various schools who had been taught in a most heterogeneous way by various teachers." And he further refined his process of grading the school, reporting a "First Grade" of fourteen members, a "Second Grade" of forty-one, and a "Third Grade" of twenty-eight. A perusal of the readers and of other textbooks used reveals that the

---

[21]*Ibid.,* 122.

[22]"Narrative Report" for 1876-1877 in Branch Normal College Records. This is a thirteen-page manuscript, undated, in Corbin's handwriting: internal evidence shows it was written in the spring of 1877, when the school had "done about nineteen months work," but some librarian or clerk has erroneously dated it 1875-1876.

school very plainly was operating at the primary and intermediate level rather than at the preparatory or collegiate level of the normal department at Fayetteville.

Irregular attendance continued, in 1876-1877, to be a problem. Sickness, bad weather, and "want of means" had caused legitimate absences, but these were few compared to those resulting from "the habits of the people generally" in the plantaton belt. The opening of farming in the spring and the opening of public schools in late fall-early winter, when many of his students left to take up school teaching, always witnessed an exodus from his school. He had considered changing the schedule of the college but, on consulting the students, had decided it would do little good insofar as his own school's enrollment was concerned and the school's service to the Negro community. He cited his rosters as proof that Pine Bluff residents were the worst offenders in unnecessary absences.

Applicants under the prescribed age continued to plague him. He had rejected these, and the only students of "non-age" still on his rosters in 1877 were those in attendance at the close of school in 1876. He retained these simply because he did not wish them "to lose the benefit of previous training."

Student conduct had been good with hardly any "serious cases" to dispose of, and "none of public disorder." In two or three cases, where he had "good reason to suspect females of immoral conduct," he had "quietly notified them to leave the school." He had also refused to admit several other women students "for the same reason," and considered himself "fortunate enough to effect the desired purpose without serious difficulty."

A religious and highly moral man, Corbin encouraged his students to attend and work in the Pine Bluff churches, and he, not unlike his counterpart on the Fayetteville campus, President General Daniel Harvey Hill, made religion a part of each day's "programme." The "opening exercises" at Corbin's school each morning included twenty minutes devoted to an International Bible Lesson, a hymn, and a prayer, accompanied by a music lesson. He proudly reported in the spring of 1877 that the three large Negro Sunday Schools in the three Negro churches of Pine Bluff were a direct result of the teaching of his students.

That Corbin was unhappy with the Pine Bluff location, the inadequate school building, the lack of help in teaching, the unjust fee system, the teacher certification system of the state, and the lack of a separate Branch Normal College catalogue were obvious in his report. He hoped, he said in discussing these subjects, that the board of trustees had it in contemplation "to increase the attraction of the school" as soon as possible. Moreover, he hoped the board would submit a "well-digested plan" to the next legislature. "If the legislature could be induced to make the necessary appropriation," he believed it would be for the advantage of the college "and much increase its efficiency," if certain "recommendations" could be carried out.

He then numerated and defended his recommendations. First, to secure a more suitable school building, a necessity that needed no defense. Second, to seek an amendment to the Branch Normal act so that the college could be moved permanently to Little Rock, where the public schools were superior to those of Pine Bluff and where the college could secure a supply of better material for students. Third, to increase the number of teachers, a need so apparent that it needed no argument to sustain it. Fourth, to make changes in the matriculation fee system whereby the school might better be adapted to the "necessities of its class of students," especially a reduction of the matriculation fee for students who planned to attend for a period of less than four years. Fifth, to provide by law, as in other states, "that a proper certificate from the Normal Department" should be equivalent to an examiner's license and entitle its holder to teach in the public schools of the state "without having to submit to the county examinations." Sixth, to publish separately "a circular and catalogue relating specifically to the Normal Branch," copy for which he enclosed in his report with the request that "not less than Five Hundred copies" be printed.

At its meeting in Fayetteville, June 15, 1877, the board responded, one after another, to Corbin's six requests:

> 1st.   We deem it impracticable with the funds at the command of the Board to secure for the Branch Normal School a more suitable building at present.
> 2nd.   We recommend that the Branch Normal School be not removed to Little Rock.
> 3rd.   When the number of students of the required age & possessing the requisite qualifications has reached forty we would recommend the employment of an assistant.
> 4th.   We think it inexpedient to make any change in the matriculation fee, as it would offer a premium to students to enter for short terms and the present fee is cheap tuition for a single term.
> 5th.   We think that the products of our Normal Schools should not be excepted from the requirement to procure certificates from County Superintendents or examiners.
> 6th. We concur in his recommendation that a separate circular should be issued representing the interests of the Branch Normal School provided the amount of matter printed be limited to the giving [of] such information as is absolutely needed by the Patrons of the school.[23]

Corbin had his answers: no new building, no removal to Little Rock, no assistant teacher, no change in the matriculation fee. Not only that, but he had received a mild reprimand for underaged and unqualified students and for requesting exemption of his students from the certifying examination given in the respective counties. His only victory, a very thin slice of the loaf requested, was a separate "circular" for his college.

More than anything else, Corbin desired a new school building and a new location in Pine Bluff for his school. Indeed, he was determined to have it, and the very next year, in 1878, a depression year of great severity in the country

---

[23]Trustee Minutes, June 15, 1877, Book A, 296-297.

The Branch Normal College Building as it appeared sometime arter Corbin opened school in it in 1882. Corbin personally cleared much of the twenty acres of woodland surrounding the structure.

at large, he opened his campaign with the board of trustees. Knowing that the Land Grant College Fund monies, which were used to operate Branch Normal College, could not be used to purchase land or erect buildings, he asked the board if the matriculation and tuition fees could not be set aside for such purposes. They either could not or were so small that the board ruled out such a possibility.[24]

But Corbin continued to remind them of the need, and, at last, in June 1880 the board responded by appropriating $3,000 of state funds for purchasing land and erecting a building. The Branch Normal College committee, consisting of university trustees Governor William R. Miller, William E. Thompson, and Grandison D. Royston, were directed to select the land and contract for the building. The committee went to Pine Bluff and purchased for $700 twenty acres of woodland at the western edge of the city. But finding there was not enough money on hand for constructing an adequate building, they went no farther than engaging an architect and having suitable plans drawn. In 1881 the board appealed to the legislature on behalf of Branch Normal and received a grant of $10,000 for erecting a building and "for furnishing the same."[25]

With plans already at hand and with renewed authority from the board at its June meeting in 1881 the Branch Normal Committee of the board immediately took bids and awarded the contract to Harding and Bailey, a Little Rock construction company.[26] The plans called for a two-story brick building with four rooms below and an assembly hall above, the structure to be crowned by a bell tower, or "steeple," and faced by a pavilion projecting in the center of the front, with tripple windows at the second level and a portico at the first level of the pavilion. The rooms on the first floor had ceilings of twelve feet, the hall above, forty-

[24]"Narrative Report" for the year ending June 14, 1878, in Branch Normal College Records.
[25]Trustee Minutes, June 10, 1880, June 8, 1881, Book A, 374, 388; *Arkansas Acts,* 1881, p. 20.
[26]Trustee Minutes, June 8, 14, 1881, Book A, 413, June 9, 1882 Book A, 429, 432.

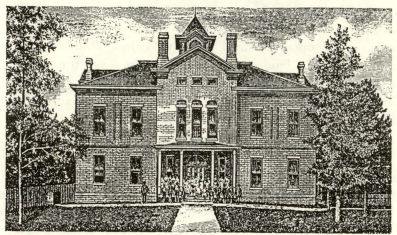

Branch Normal College building, Pine Bluff.

by-fifty feet in size, had a ceiling of sixteen feet.

It was a small building, costing $9,930, but it was new and was ready for occupancy in almost six months. Nearby the committee had a hand-dug well sunk and lined with brick to furnish water for the school. A plank fence enclosed the small area occupied by the building and well, and new furniture was purchased for the school.[27]

Corbin opened school in the new building on January 30, 1882, as his spring report of the same year revealed:

> A heavy snow covered the ground at the time, and the building was still very damp, unenclosed, and without the necessary outbuildings, blackboard, furniture, &c, &c. Still, we managed to get along with a reasonable degree of comfort, and have found by actual trial that it is very well adapted for the purpose designated; being well lighted, easily warmed and freely ventilated.[28]

Looking back on his first seventeen years at Branch Normal College, Corbin, in 1893, remarked on the primitive conditions at the new campus in 1882. The success of the school at the old Bell house, "the barracks," had, he said, induced the state to purchase in 1880 the twenty acres

[27]*Ibid.,* June 9, 1882, Book A, 432.
[28]"Narrative Report" for 1881-1882, in Branch Normal College Records.

on which the "new school" had been built. It was, he wrote,

> a wild tract of land, in about the same condition as when Columbus discovered America, with only one house within a distance of a quarter of a mile. With my own hands, I cleared away the forest, burned the brush and chopped the trees for fuel in the school, thus relieving the state of a considerable expense. The grounds are now valued by competent judges at about $25,000 and are surrounded by a large settlement of respectable people.[29]

Over the years, between 1882 and 1893, Corbin had confronted and dealt with many problems connected with the new physical plant and grounds. The ground was marshy and so low and level that it could not be drained; his remedy for the dampness was to recommend filling in and building walks. Surface water drained through the brick lining of the hand-dug shallow well; he recommended a coating of "hydraulic cement" to seal out the contaminating seepage.[30] Trespassing on the unfenced and thickly wooded grounds was a problem, which he solved by fencing the entire twenty acres and thinning out the trees and brush so "that guilty parties could be detected more readily." The fence served, also, to "prevent wagon roads from being cut all over the grounds."[31]

The removal of the school to the far western border of the city had created serious housing and boarding problems for the black students. Accordingly, Corbin urged the board of trustees to build a men's dormitory and a women's "Boarding Hall." He was especially concerned, as he reported in the spring of 1884, about the lack of suitable facilities for women students. Boys apparently found it easy to find places in Pine Bluff homes as servants, but not girls. "Under existing circumstances," he said, "female students

---

[29]"Narrative Report," May 1893, in Branch Normal College Records.
[30]"Narrative Report," for 1881-1882, in Branch Normal College Records.
[31]"Narrative Report," for 1883-1884, in Branch Normal College Records; this report is undated but the *Trustee Minutes,* June 1884, Book A, p. 495, reveal that it was for the year ending in June 1884 and was considered by the trustees at their June 1884 meeting.

find it very difficult to obtain suitable homes, and are free entirely from supervision during the greatest part of their time." He had, he reported elsewhere in his report, "declined receiving one female student on account of her boarding in what I regarded as an improper place, and dismissed one of the same sex, privately, having strong reason to suspect her of immoral character, without sufficient proof to sustain my suspicions as charges."[32]

The trustees were sympathetic to Corbin's request but were not moved to speedy action. He persisted, however, and in 1887 the board appealed to the legislature for funds for Branch Normal, getting $5,000 for a girl's dormitory, $500 for repairs on the college building, $90 for purchasing stoves, $200 for new desks, $300 for improving and repairing the "library room," and $300 for buying coal.[33]

In November 1887 the board, with plans and specifications at hand, advertised for bids on the women's dormitory. The building, to cost no more than $4,500 was to be of brick with a "first class tin roof well painted."[34] When the dormitory was completed the committee on Branch Normal was, said Corbin, "much perplexed about finding suitable persons to take charge of it." Corbin relieved them of the problem

> by agreeing to move my wife from Little Rock and to take charge of it myself. As they wished to secure persons without male children, and my sons had completed their course at the Branch Normal and were going away to study professions elsewhere, I was able to comply with their request and take charge, receiving no compensation for either myself or wife and assuming the entire responsibility for fuel, light and provisions, charging for board, light and fuel, $8.00 per month.[35]

The dormitory at Pine Bluff was the first one for women authorized by the university board, for Carnall Hall

---

[32]*Ibid.,* 1883-1884.
[33]*Arkansas Acts,* 1877, pp. 193-194.
[34]Trustees Minutes, Nov. 17, 1887, Book A, 595.
[35]"Narrative Report," for May 1893, in Branch Normal College Records.

for women at Fayetteville was not authorized until 1905. Accordingly, the Branch Normal committee, in Corbin's opinion, "regarded the opening of the Dormitory as somewhat of an experiment" and were unwilling "to spend much money in its outfit." He heated the rooms by using three or four old wood stoves which he had salvaged when moving from the Bell house to the new campus, and he made the building look respectable by placing in it a thousand dollars' worth of his own furniture which he moved with his wife from Little Rock. At last, in 1889, the trustees authorized $1,000 to furnish the dormitory.[36]

For the convenience of the women students, and to help in keeping down expenses, Corbin built a wash-house for them and put up chicken-houses in the rear of the dormitory. The lumber for these he had salvaged from the original wooden fence surrounding the college building.[37]

From 1875 until 1882 Corbin had done all the teaching except for what free help he had had from student assistants. His persistent annual request for a full time paid assistant teacher was not honored until 1883. That year the trustees authorized employment of an assistant teacher at a salary of thirty dollars a month but required Corbin to collect a dollar a month from each non-beneficiary student with which to pay the salary. Corbin hired as assistant, James C. Smith, one of his own students, and two years later, in 1885, got Smith's salary increased to sixty dollars a month. By then Corbin had hired Alice Sizemore as second assistant. In 1893, when the trustees ordered Corbin to organize the Branch Normal teaching staff into "a faculty," there were five members: Corbin, chairman; W. S. Harris, secretary; A. E. Smith, T. G. Childress, and James C. Smith, members.[38]

---

[36]*Ibid.;* Reynolds and Thomas, *University of Arkansas,* 302.

[37]"Narrative Report," for May 1893, Branch Normal College Records.

[38]See "Narrative Reports," for 1876-1877 and 1881-1882 (when he asks permission to hire his student James C. Smith as assistant teacher for $40 a month); Trustee Minutes, June 9, 1882, Book A, p. 429, in which the Branch Normal Committee recommended the employment of Smith as advised by Corbin; Trustee Minutes, June 9, 1883, Book A, 463, instructing

Corbin at first not only taught all the subjects in a demanding academic schedule, but fell heir to the additional burden of "the custody of the building, cleaning two stories and the care of from four to eight large stoves."[39] Asking in 1884 for custodial help, which was ignored by the board, he narrated:

> I have not only attended personally to all these things from the commencement of the school [in 1875], but have also attended to the preparing of the fuel. During cold weather, this extra labor has consumed almost my entire time outside of regular school hours and a large amount of energy that could be more profitably expended in other directions. While the institution was in an experimental condition and the labor comparatively light, my interest in its welfare prompted me to do anything in my power to aid us making it a success, but I think that it has now reached a stage where some provision should be made for relieving me of so great a burden.[40]

The act of 1873 required the university board of trustees to operate Branch Normal College in accordance with the identical requirements and standards laid down for the normal department at Fayetteville. But they seemingly gave Corbin a free hand in setting admission standards, enforcing the quota system for beneficiaries, collecting student fees, and adjusting the course offerings to the needs and abilities of his students.

In setting admission standards, Corbin followed the rule that any black applicant who could read the fourth reader and who had "some acquaintance with the fundamental rules in arithmetic and a corresponding standing in Penmanship and Geography" should be allowed to ma-

---

Corbin to collect one dollar a month from each non-beneficiary student and to use the funds collected for an assistant teacher at no more than $30 a month; W. S. Harris to Board of Trustees, Pine Bluff, report for the year Sept. 4, 1893-June 7, 1894, relating the story of the organization of the faculty, in Branch Normal College Records.

[39]"Narrative Report," for 1883-1884, in Branch Normal College Records.
[40]*Ibid.*

triculate.[41] This was less than was generally required of entering normal students at Fayetteville after 1875, but the trustees, though they complained, never really demanded that Corbin adhere to the Fayetteville standards.[42]

The same policy was followed in the matter of enforcing the quota system for beneficiaries. Under this system each county judge was permitted to appoint a limited number of tuition-free students, there being allowed some 237 for the seventy-odd counties. Since Corbin's black students were concentrated in the counties of eastern Arkansas, he ignored the system altogether and treated almost all, if not all, his students as beneficiaries. If a student came to him without an appointment, he would write off, say, to a friendly county judge and ask for a letter appointing the student. When some judges violated their quota by appointing every student who requested it, Corbin accepted them apparently without protest, except to explain to the board of trustees that it was impossible for him to "regulate" the matter of appointments.[43]

His annual report for 1883-1884 contained a clear statement of his dilemma over the apportionment of beneficiaries as it affected Branch Normal College:

> The present apportionment of students is based upon the total white and colored population of the various counties. Under its operation counties, such as Benton, which are almost destitute of colored people, are entitled to six or eight beneficiaries and send none [to Pine Bluff]; while many counties with a large colored population are entitled to only one or two. I would suggest that an apportionment based on the respective white and colored population would be a probable advantage to both Fayetteville and Pine Bluff; and if the provisions of the law do not preclude the adoption

---

[41]"Narrative Report," for May 1893, in Branch Normal College Records.

[42]Reynolds and Thomas, *University of Arkansas*, 205-207, 307-311; Trustee Minutes, June 7, 1881, Book A, 387.

[43]University of Arkansas *Fourth Catalogue*, 1876, pp. 17-25; "Narrative Report," for 1876-1877, 1878, 1883-1884, 1893, in Branch Normal College Records; "Report of Committee to Visit the Branch Normal School at Pine Bluff," 1893, in Branch Normal College Records.

of such a plan, it would, perhaps, be good policy for your honorable body to take the matter under consideration. In my opinion such is the real spirit of the law.[44]

The spirit of the law was what he followed, though the board of trustees apparently never sanctioned it.[45] Governor Garland had told him in 1875 to treat all applicants from Arkansas as beneficiaries, and, thereafter, when the trustees or snoopy-nosed legislators complained about black counties having more beneficiaries than their quota called for, Corbin cited Garland as his authority for circumventing the regulation. In Democratic Arkansas after 1875 he could have had no better authority to cite.[46]

The question of the matriculation fee was different. This was a $5.00 entrance fee required of every student who enrolled in the university. Paid but once, it entitled one to matriculate for four years, but was required of beneficiaries as well as tuition-paying students.[47] Since practically all of Corbin's students were beneficiaries, he often erroneously called the matriculation fee a "tuition fee" and he complained eternally that it, like the quota system for beneficiaries, was a burden to his poor students. He hounded the trustees to reduce the fee, to allow it to be paid on installments, or to abolish it.[48]

His report of 1893, explaining to the board his trouble in collecting fees and in regulating the appointment of beneficiaries, revealed how he operated and was permitted to

---

[44]"Narrative Report," 1884, in Branch Normal College Records.

[45]Curiously in 1881 the Board adopted a motion requesting Professor Francis LeRoy Harvey "to prepare a circular letter for the information and guidance of County Judges in the appointment of Beneficiaries to the University, said requirements not to be enforced in regard to the Normal Branch College at Pine Bluff." If the trustees intended this as an exemption for Branch Normal from the onerous quota system it was not so enforced nor was Corbin so informed. Trustee Minutes, June 13, 1881, Book A, 398.

[46]"Report of Committee to Visit the Branch Normal School," 1893, in Branch Normal College Records; "Narrative Report," for May 1893, in Branch Normal College Records.

[47]University of Arkansas *Fourth Catalogue,* 1876, p. 17.

[48]"Narrative Report," 1877, 1884, 1893, 1895, in Branch Normal College Records.

operate. It was a depression year and had been "very hard" for him to collect the matriculation fees

> simply because our people have been impoverished and a rigid insistance upon payment would have depleted the school. Several families now reside in Pine Bluff whose children were appointed from Arkansas, Monroe, Woodruff and other counties where they formerly resided. It is a matter of absolute impossibility to comply with the regulation regulating appointments and the county judges pay no attention to it whatever, but appoint all who apply. Very few students are able to attend the session during the entire ten months; the greater number are able to do so only five or six months, the exceptions being those from Pine Bluff, and it is very difficult to decide upon the course proper under such circumstances. It would be of great advantage to the institution could the whole system be abolished and a small monthly tuition fee be collected or the institution made absolutely free.[49]

In the matter of the curriculum, Corbin felt that the normal course at Fayetteville was too loaded with Latin and mathematics. He was permitted, in 1881, to drop descriptive geomtery, differential and integral calculus, and logic; and, in 1883, to drop Latin.[50] But his normal curriculum remained largely a short course in arts and sciences with some education subjects and, after 1891, some industrial work added.[51]

While Corbin reported in 1884 that he had "three Preparatory and three Normal grades" at Branch Normal, it was obvious that the school operated more at a high school than at a college level.[52] A legislative committee visiting

---

[49]*Ibid.*, for May 1893, in Branch Normal College Records.

[50]Trustee Minutes, June 7, 1881, June 9, 1883, Book A, pp. 387, 463.

[51]*Ibid.*, June 9, 1883, Book A, 463, contains a complete list of subjects studied in the "modified" normal course at Branch Normal; it was a two-year course, which when completed entitled the student to "a certificate of scholarship showing the work done," but those who completed the full course "as published" in the university catalogue at Fayetteville would be "entitled" to the "Normal Diploma." See Reynolds and Thomas, *University of Arkansas*, 205-209, for the many changes made in the normal course at Fayetteville.

[52]"Narrative Report," for 1884, in Branch Normal College Records.

and investigating the school in 1893 reported that the "normal features are in a large measure ignored."[53] In fairness to Corbin, it might have been added that the average white public school teacher of the time was not the product of a "normal college," but the product of a "high school" or of "self study" which made them capable of passing a county examiner's certification test. Corbin's students did quite well on these county tests, although he himself, in 1878, was chagrined that: "Many of the students think that sufficient education to secure a certificate is enough for their needs." That same year, the third year of his school's operation, he had as county examiner for Negro teachers in Jefferson County issued one first-, nine second-, and four third-grade certificates to students of Branch Normal; and he had letters telling him that twenty other Branch Normal students had been certified in other counties of the state.[54]

The board of trustees expressed great confidence in Corbin, praising, as in 1886, his "capacity, efficiency, and fidelity."[55] The legislature seemingly shared the board's feeling. When a joint committee of the house and senate visited the campus in 1891 to inspect the college, they described the principal as "a very zealous and successful teacher. We find that he commands the utmost respect not only from all of his pupils and teachers, but from all of the citizens of Pine Bluff."[56]

Two years later, in 1893, Corbin's world crumbled and fell in upon him. That year the legislature sent a not so friendly committee to Pine Bluff to investigate Branch Normal College and to report on its condition. It had been

---

[53]"Report of the Committee to Visit the Branch Normal School," 1893, in Branch Normal College Records; "Narrative Report," for May 1893, in Branch Normal College Records, contain a good reply to the half-truths of the "Report of the Committee."

[54]"Narrative Report," for 1878, in Branch Normal College Records. In the last quarter of the nineteenth century the university was roundly criticized for its failure to furnish leadership in "normal education." See Stinnett and Kennan, *Arkansas Education Association*, 57-61, 72-73, 76-80, 82-87.

[55]University of Arkansas *Biennial Report*, 1886, p. 7.

[56]*Arkansas Senate Journal*, 1891, p. 399.

charged by Democrats in Jefferson County that back in 1888 Corbin, a Republican, had "voted" his male students against the Democratic Congressman Clifton R. Breckinridge and for John M. Clayton. Clayton had been defeated, but, seeking to unseat his opponent, set out on a trip from Pine Bluff to gather evidence of election frauds. At Plumerville, on the night of January 29, 1889, he was assassinated, shot from ambush while he sat near a window of his hotel. Breckinridge was ousted from Congress in 1890 but was triumphantly reelected the same year. The 1893 investigation of Branch Normal College seemed, therefore, to be mere political harassment of Corbin by Jefferson County white enemies.[57]

The committee visited the campus and looked at the buildings.[58] They found that "the college building was in need of some repairs," reported the dormitory to be in good condition, were much impressed with the new brick shop building of the "mechanical department," but found the grounds "not as clean and well kept as they should be." The committee next "rigidly examined" the students, reporting that in some of the "higher grades" the students "stood a very creditable examination," that not so much could be said for "the primary branches," and that "the normal features are in a large measure ignored."

Finally, the committee looked at Corbin's school roster and financial records. They found 206 students enrolled but a much smaller number in actual attendance. Of the number enrolled, they reported sixteen out-of-state students and seventy-two from Jefferson County, a number which they declared to be "largely in excess of the number of

---

[57]"Narrative Report," for 1893 in Branch Normal College Records; "Report of Committee to Visit the Branch Normal School at Pine Bluff," 1893, in Branch Normal College Records; David Y. Thomas, *Arkansas and Its People*, I (New York, 1930), 219, 229.

[58]The account of the Committee investigation that follows is from: *Arkansas Senate Journal*, 1893, pp. 40, 114, 145, 164, 185, 792-793, 849; *Arkansas House Journal*, 1893, p. 231; "Report of Committee to Visit the Branch Normal School at Pine Bluff," 1893, in Branch Normal College Records.

beneficiaries allowed that county." Other counties also had had more than their quota of beneficiaries, which Corbin explained was a policy permitted by Governor Garland, chairman in 1875 of the board of trustees and of the Branch Normal College Committee, and followed since the beginning. They learned from Corbin that he charged out-of-state students a dollar a month; that this money, together with the matriculation fee of beneficiaries, he "collected and disbursed himself;" that it had been more than six months since he had reported to the board his receipts and expenditures; that he now had in hand $275 which he had been advised by Trustee William Henry Langford, chairman of the Branch Normal committee, to use in paying for ditching of the grounds around the dormitory and for insurance on one of the buildings.

The committee, finding all the business records relating to Branch Normal College to be in the hands of the university treasurer at Fayetteville, summoned that official with all Branch Normal papers to Little Rock. They found everything in order, complimented the white treasurer for his careful methods and his "intelligent and thorough knowledge of his books and papers," and ignored completely to report that Corbin and the Branch Normal committee had sent him all the papers in his possession. They recommended that Corbin emulate the white bookkeeper by keeping as complete records at Pine Bluff, a requirement the board of trustees had never demanded of him.

The committee apparently had considerable difficulty agreeing on a report. One member wanted to abolish the college, sell the land and "fixtures," and use the money for the "common school education" of Negroes. A majority wished to retain the college but fire Corbin, but two of the majority, while they wished to recommend changes in the business management of the college, refused to assent to the removal of Corbin. One of the two dissented on grounds that Corbin's dismissal was a duty of the university board of trustees.

When the committee, reporting back to the legislature in early April 1893, submitted their majority report, they asked that the eighteen-year old school be continued as an experiment in "educating the colored race," declared that it "must be arranged on a better primary line" and administered on a "more economical" basis, and recommended that Corbin be fired. The professor, they said,

> stands fair among the people of Pine Bluff, and is considered a good and moral man, with a finished education, but in view of the fact that he has been so long connected with the institution, and his failure or neglect to give more attention to the normal features of the school and his carelessness in business methods, a change should be made. Therefore your committee recommend that he be displaced and some well qualified educator of his race, a man of good executive ability, and a man who understands and appreciates the normal features of the institution be secured.[59]

The committee understood neither the law creating Branch Normal College, the relationship between the school and the university, the policies of the board of trustees for the school, the long, arduous years of service by Corbin, nor the sympathy of the principal for the poor blacks who sought education at the school. The committee was not interested in history. They wanted Corbin fired, and they drew up what they believed were good enough charges to accomplish their purpose.

It hardly mattered to them that the charges were unfair and based on half-truths. Yes, Corbin had not given much emphasis to the primary grades but it was because he had neither the teaching force nor the power to do it. Yes, he had emphasized the higher grades and not the normal collegiate years, but it was because Negro students came to him so poorly equipped, had to be prepared in the work of the higher grades, and frequently left to teach before entering the normal years. Yes, he was heedless of good business methods, of careful collection of matriculation and

---

[59]"Report of the Committee to Visit the Branch Normal School at Pine Bluff," 1893, in Branch Normal College Records.

tuition fees, but it was not because he was a thief but rather because his heart went out to the poor who came to him. He neglected to collect fees from them when he could, helped impoverished students get appointments as beneficiaries wherever and whenever he could, and almost annually requested the board of trustees to alter or abolish the fee system.[60]

Obviously realizing that his position was in jeopardy, Corbin knew that he could depend now only on the integrity and loyalty of the board of trustees. His annual report to them in May 1893 was an eloquent but subtle reply to the vicious implications of the legislature's charges, as well as a reminder that if there were shortcomings or grounds for complaint the blame was not his alone. If he had violated the quota system for beneficiaries, if he had permitted matriculation wihout payment, if he had collected and spent fees locally, he had never attempted, as he reminded the board, to hide a single act of his; and the board had by eighteen years of approval acquiesced in his methods for managing the school.[61]

The trustees at their June meeting in 1893 did not fire the sixty-year-old Corbin; neither did they have the courage nor the decency to defend him. They compromised by keeping him on as principal, but humiliated him by robbing him of nearly all power over the school and the students. Into the hands of the white foreman of the industrial shops, William Stephen Harris, the graduate of Virginia's Manual Training School, went all responsibility for admitting students, collecting fees, and reporting to the board of trustees. It was an act in keeping with the rising Age of Jim Crow in Arkansas, to place this white "treasurer" in charge of the Negro school, but it was, nonetheless, as ruthless a piece of ingratitude and as cowardly a compromise as the trustees ever perpetrated.[62]

---

[60] *Ibid.;* "Narrative Report," for May 1893, November 1893, in Branch Normal College Records.

[61] "Narrative Report," for May 1893, in Branch Normal College Records.

[62] Trustee Minutes, June 6, 1893, Book B, 43-47.

Courtesy UA Library

## William H. Langford

From 1893 on, Corbin watched Harris, who signed himself "Local Superintendent" in his reports to the board of trustees, gradually assume command of the school.[63] Corbin was not passive. He resented Harris's power and the new "cash basis" on which the white "treasurer" operated the school. He regretted that many poor students were turned away, and, in 1895, wrote the board that he thought "the Principal or faculty should be allowed some discretion" in the matter of admitting those without money. In the same report he first put into writing his appraisal of Harris's character:

> It would be somewhat more convenient to send students, at once to the shops to settle accounts, but as the office is in the shops, I know that to allow female students to get in the habit of going there would certainly give rise to scandals and, for that reason do not allow them to go there except by special permission.[64]

If there was any doubt about what Corbin meant, it

[63] See Harris's two reports to board of trustees, for Sept. 4, 1893-June 8, 1894, in Branch Normal College Records.
[64] "Narrative Report," for 1895, in Branch Normal College Records.

could not have been lost on the board of trustees. Harris's office was in the shop building, where he taught manual training to the male students and where Corbin suspected him of practicing seduction of the female students. Corbin's suspicions doubtlessly had a sound basis, but the board, in 1895, either ignored or disbelieved him.

The power behind Harris in these years was William H. Langford, the white Pine Bluff trustee-in-residence, who served eighteen years on the board from 1889 to 1907 and came to look on Branch Normal College as *his* school. A graduate of the university in Fayetteville, Class of 1880, Langford practiced law, dabbled in politics, and became a highly successful businessman in Pine Bluff. He was president of the Citizens Bank, owner of a corn mill and grain elevator, a large stockholder in two giant cotton-seed oil mills, a promoter of the Pine Bluff and Arkansas River Railway, founder of the city's street railroad, and a large land holder in Jefferson County and other counties of the state.[65]

Langford took a great interest in the development of the Negro college after his appointment to the board of trustees in 1889. He was instrumental in 1891 in getting state funds for building and equipping the industrial shops, for sinking a deep well and putting in the school's first water and sewer system, and for staffing the "mechanical department." In 1892 he selected Harris to take charge of the shops at a salary of $1,400, within $200 of Corbin's, explaining to the board that mechanics of Harris's ability "have no trouble in finding positions." At the same time he got the board of trustees to hire an assistant to Harris, "a smith or machinist," at a salary of $900 while Corbin's first assistant, James C. Smith, with two college degrees drew but $700. By 1899 Harris's salary was the same as Corbin's—$1,800.[66]

---

[65]Reynolds and Thomas, *University of Arkansas*, 401-402.
[66]*Arkansas Senate Journal*, 1891, pp. 399-400; *Arkansas Acts*, 1891, pp. 192-193, 219-220, 319; Trustee Minutes, July 2, Dec. 3, 1891, Book B, pp. 3, 22, Nov. 28, 1892, Book B, pp. 27ff., Dec. 1, 1892, Book B, p. 31, June 1899, Book B, p. 154ff.

Langford was much impressed with the need for industrial education at the school, was a strong admirer of Booker T. Washington's philosophy at Tuskegee, and was ambitious to convert Branch Normal into an "Arkansas Tuskegee." He was, therefore, more impressed with Harris's mechanical skills than he was with Corbin's scholarly attainments, and he obviously felt no remorse whatever about pushing industrial education at the expense of teacher education.[67]

Langford ran the school, and the white shop instructor Harris was his "man on campus." For years he either winked at stories of Harris's immoral relations with the female students or refused to believe the stories were any more than Corbin's attempts "to smut" Harris's character. At last, in 1901-1902, Langford warned Corbin that he could not be reelected, recruited a black replacement from Tuskegee, and in June 1902 got the old man "unceremoniously dropped" by the board of trustees.[68]

According to Corbin's successor, Isaac Fisher, the Negroes of Pine Bluff believed that Langford had replaced Corbin in order to protect Harris. While Langford's motives were undoubtedly much broader than that—his desire, for example, of bringing in a black Tuskegee man to help further the concept of industrial education—there is little doubt how the black community felt. Fisher, in a letter to Booker T. Washington, explained their attitude toward Harris:

> Our Treasurer, who is a white man [,] is not popular with the Negroes of this town because it is felt that he is immoral, and that he has debauched several of the stu-

---

[67]Isaac Fisher to Booker T. Washington, Pine Bluff, Aug. 2, 4, 18, 1902, Booker T. Washington Papers, Library of Congress, on microfilm in University of Arkansas Library (hereafter cited Washington Papers). "Hon. W. H. Langford told me," wrote Fisher on August 18, "that he wanted me to give the state of Arkansas another Tuskegee—this in face of the fact that the Negroes are raising a great hue and cry that they don't want their school brought down (?) to Tuskegee's level."

[68]Fisher to Washington, Montgomery, Ala., May 24, Jersey City, N. J., June 28, July 4, Pine Bluff, Aug. 2, 4, Sept. 6, Oct. 10, 1902, Nov. 2, 1903, *ibid.*

Courtesy UA Library

Isaac Fisher

dents of this school. It was claimed that the former principal was deposed because he took cognizance of certain immoral relations said to exist between this man and a student. You can see that it would be expected that I would be a mere puppet here, since the Treasurer, and not the Principal is really the executive head of the school under Hon. Langford.[69]

Had Corbin been Fisher's friend, he could have told the young man that Harris did, indeed, head the school "under Hon. Langford." But Corbin, waging a battle to get himself reinstated as principal, did not speak to Fisher, leaving the young teacher to discover for himself the facts of life at Branch Normal.[70]

[69]Fisher to Washington, Pine Bluff, Oct. 10, 1902, *ibid.*
[70]Fisher to Washington, Pine Bluff, Nov. 2, 1903, *ibid.,* revealed that

Thus Corbin did not "retire" gracefully, though it is difficult to say whether it was Corbin or his Negro friends who resented most his deposition and did the most to seek his reinstatement. Corbin may have been behind the movement, as Fisher believed he was, but, whatever the truth in the matter, it failed. The attack, whether Corbin's or Corbin's friends, was waged against Fisher, who was sustained by Langford and the board and reelected in 1903. Poor Fisher, whose story will be told in a later article, had triumphed over Corbin, or Corbin's friends, only to become the black puppet of Langford and of Langford's white manager Harris. The inscrutable Harris was destined, as it turned out, to survive them all—Corbin, Langford, and Fisher.[71]

Losing his appeal for reinstatement, Corbin continued to live in Pine Bluff, where he became principal of the Merrill High School. In the years between 1902 and his death in Pine Bluff on January 9, 1911, he was active in the Negro life of the state. He served as president of the Colored Teachers Association in 1902-1903. A prominent Freemason, he served as Grand Master of the Negro Grand Lodge of Arkansas, as secretary of the Grand Lodge for some twenty-five years, and, in 1903, was a leader in the building at Pine Bluff of a four-story brick temple for the Negro Grand Lodge. At his death he left considerable property to his sur-

---

Fisher had discovered Harris's true power: "My treasurer, nominally my inferior but virtually my superior, has me on a 'dead center'—I won't retreat and the power which he holds will not allow me to advance. His mechanical department is almost ideal in equipment—my [normal] department is, comparatively speaking, a disgrace to the state; he can make bills for anything for his department—I am dependent on his moods for $1 for school necessities, and his enmity means my head."

[71]Fisher to Washington, Pine Bluff, Aug. 2, 4, 19, 1902, March 22, April 1, June 19 (two letters), Little Rock, June 24, 25, 30, East Lake, Ala., July 5, 17, 20, 23, 28, 31, Aug. 1, *ibid.;* Fisher to Board of Trustees of the University of Arkansas, East Lake, Ala., July 22, 1903, *ibid.;* Fisher, "A Memorial to the Board of Trustees of the University of Arkansas, Little Rock, Arkansas, July, 1903," *ibid.;* Pine Bluff *Daily Graphic,* June 24, July 12, 15, 1902; Pine Bluff *Semi-Weekly Graphic,* June 20, 25, 27, Aug. 1, 1902; Pine Bluff *Weekly Commercial,* June 28, 1902; Pine Bluff *Weekly Graphic,* March 21, 25, 28, July 4, 14, 29, 1903.

viving son and daughter, who had his body taken to Chicago for burial.[72]

[72]Reynolds and Thomas, *University of Arkansas*, 356-357; Little Rock *Arkansas Gazette*, Jan. 10, 1911; Pine Bluff *Press-Eagle*, Jan. 24, 1911; Pine Bluff *Daily Graphic*, June 22, 1902, Jan. 10, 1911; Pine Bluff *Semi-Weekly Graphic*, June 25, Aug. 9, 13, 16, Dec. 31, 1902; Pine Bluff *Weekly Graphic*, July 6, Aug. 12, 1903; Pine Bluff *Weekly Commercial*, June 6, Oct. 10, 1903.

# The Harris Brothers: Black Northern Teachers in the Reconstruction South

Earle H. West, *School of Education, Howard University*

Hard on the heels of the Union armies as they advanced into the South were the Yankee school teachers. Based upon official reports whose interpretation is subject to some uncertainty, the number of teachers in schools for freedmen rose from 972 in January, 1867, to a high of 9,502 in July, 1869.[1] Although the latter figure is described as being composed of "white and colored" teachers, there is no way by which the respective proportions can be fixed. Professor Swint's careful and interesting treatment of northern teachers in the South treats the entire group as if all were white. The only explicit reference to black teachers occurs in certain quotations documenting the qualifications and motives of teachers. Although certainly not intentional, the result is that the sole references to black teachers picture them as illiterate and conniving for money.[2]

While no correction of the neglect of black teachers is possible in statistical terms, the purpose of this paper is to ameliorate the picture somewhat by tracing the course of three northern black teachers who joined the trek to the South during Reconstruction. Although black contributions to the reconstruction of various states have been described, still it is impossible to determine the extent to which the Harris brothers were typical of northern black teachers who went South. We shall use Swint's portrayal of the northern white teachers as a framework within which to examine these black teachers.

## CHRONOLOGY

The story began when the Harris family emigrated from North Carolina to Ohio in 1850. They settled first in Chillicothe, then

---

[1]Henry L. Swint, *The Northern Teacher in the South, 1862-1870* (Nashville: Vanderbilt University Press, 1941), p. 6.
[2]*Ibid.*, pp. 7, 8.

moved to Cleveland where they settled permanently.[3] The oldest son, William D. Harris, married and moved to Delaware, Ohio. In 1864, William wrote to the American Missionary Association (hereafter, AMA) requesting an appointment as teacher in eastern Virginia or North Carolina. The letter mentioned that he had been a plasterer for 17 years, but that he had taught school for two years in North Carolina before going to Ohio.[4] He enclosed two letters of recommendation. One from Colonel N. P. Reid spoke of Harris as an "industrious, energetic, and highly respected citizen" with "much more than ordinary education, talents and judgment."[5] The recommendation from E. Thomson, editor of the *Advocate and Journal*, declared Harris to be "of unblemished moral and religious character" who might safely be "entrusted with the management and instruction of youth."[6] The application was quickly accepted and within less than a month, Harris was in Portsmouth, Virginia, busily occupied with teaching.[7]

During the summer of 1864, William's brother, Robert Harris, also applied for a teaching position in the South. Robert lived in Cleveland with his widowed mother and younger brothers and sisters whom he supported by working for the railroad, although he was a plasterer by trade as was his brother. His letter of application indicated that his only experience in teaching had been privately teaching slaves in North Carolina.[8] His pastor in the Cleveland African Methodist Episcopal Church (AME) wrote a strong recommendation, describing Robert as a "model young man . . . with but one great object in view, the glory of God and the prosperity of Mankind."[9] By November, Robert had received a teaching appointment and arrived in Portsmouth, Virginia to assist William.[10]

During the usual summer vacation trip back to Ohio, William Harris received a call to become pastor of the AME church in Richmond, Virginia. Since the church could not supply full salary, the approval of the AMA was necessary. In support of his request

[3]*Annual Report of the Superintendent of Public Instruction of North Carolina for the Fiscal Year Ending September 1, 1880* (Raleigh: P. M. Hale and Edwards, Broughton and Company, 1881), p. 42. Hereafter references to reports in this series will be referred to as *Annual Report of the Superintendent*, with appropriate date.

[4]Manuscript letter, February 13, 1864, #86867 in the American Missionary Association Archives, Amistad Research Collection, Dillard University, New Orleans. These materials were at Fisk University when examined by the author. Hereafter all manuscript letters from this collection will be referred to by date and AMA number only.

[5]January 30, 1864, AMA 111540.

[6]E. Thomson, "To Whom It May Concern," February 13, 1864, AMA.

[7]March 1, 1864, AMA H 1-5416.

[8]August 26, 1864, AMA 111897.

[9]July 29, 1864, AMA 111840.

[10]November 29, 1864, AMA 1116368.

for approval, Harris pointed out that the AMA school was conducted in the church building where he would be pastor and that he supposed a missionary society would not care whether an employee were a preacher or a teacher, the "distinction being so fine in my mind."[11] In late August, 1865, Harris was ordained by the Central Ohio Yearly Conference of the Wesleyan Methodist Church and thus was eligible to fill the role of pastor.[12] A month later, he was in Richmond and had taken charge of the 600-member AME church. In addition to the usual pastoral duties, Harris was active in promoting a night school and various benevolent efforts to relieve the great suffering among the freedmen.

Meanwhile, Robert Harris continued teaching school in and around Norfolk. He wrote the AMA recommending that his younger brother, Cicero, be given an appointment. Apparently the appointment was delayed for it was not until the winter term of 1867 that Cicero was mentioned again. By then, Robert had moved to Fayetteville, North Carolina, and was joined by Cicero.[13] Their school developed rapidly and soon came to be known as the "best in the state" according to the state superintendent.[14] The building was erected by the Freedmen's Bureau on land bought by the freedmen themselves. A further testimony to the stability and quality of the school is found in the fact that the Peabody Education Fund adopted the school and made regular contributions for several years. In view of the relatively high standards imposed by the Fund and the fact that few black schools were ever aided by the Fund, Robert Harris' school must have been of unusual quality indeed.[15]

In 1877, the state legislature created a normal school for black teachers in Fayetteville. When it opened in September, 1877, Robert Harris was the first principal. He was followed in this position by Charles W. Chesnutt, the well-known black writer, who remained as principal until 1883. Robert Harris died in 1880.

William Harris never returned to teaching after assuming pastoral duties. In 1867, he moved from Richmond to Georgetown, D.C. Two years later he took a similar post in Columbia, S.C., and by 1875 was in Groton, Connecticut, having left both teaching and the South.[16]

Against this brief background of events, the motives, impressions, experiences and activities of the Harris brothers as they

[11]August, 1865, AMA 112627.
[12]September 3, 1865, AMA 112642.
[13]July 26, 1865, AMA 112642.
[14]Annual Report of the Superintendent, 1870, p. 276.
[15]Correspondence, Superintendent of Public Instruction, Raleigh, N.C., August 19, 1875.
[16]January 22, 1875, AMA 13946.

worked in the South will be examined. In making this analysis, comparisons will be made with the motives, impressions, experiences and activities of the white northern teachers as described by Professor Swint.

## MOTIVATION

Swint found that the principal motive underlying the work of the northern white teacher in the South was "religious and humanitarian interest."[17] The AMA specified that its teachers must be persons of "fervent piety," and Swint asserted that many bordered on religious fanaticism. Less important motives were the hope of improvement of health by a move to the South, the desire for financial improvement, and the love of adventure.

What were the motives of these black teachers from the North who went South? Their letters to the AMA reflect the dominant religious motives characteristic of the typical white teacher. William's letter of application in 1864 expressed the feeling that "it is the Spirit of the Savior that influences me to engage in this work." He viewed the opportunity to teach in the South as an answer to his prayers for "the abolition of Slavery and the elevation of the Oppressed and the extension of the Redeemer's kingdom."[18] Apparently, Robert shared his brother's religious concern, but often added expressions indicating the desire to contribute to racial advancement. In fact, this motive was listed first in his letter of application where he described himself as desirous of "assisting in the noble work of elevating and evangelizing our oppressed and long abused race, and of promoting the interest of Christ's spiritual kingdom on Earth."[19] Although racial advancement was frequently mentioned by both brothers, neither expressed racial motivation significantly different from the expressions one would find among the white teachers. After having been in the field a short while, Robert Harris reported that his experiences had "only increased my desire to labor among them, relieving their wants, and teaching them the way of salvation."[20]

After a year's service, Robert expressed the fervent desire to be reappointed so he could continue to work "for the elevation of these long despised people, and for the advancement of Christ's kingdom on earth."[21] He later reported to the AMA Superintendent of Education that he kept it clear to his pupils that he was laboring "for their conversion as well as for their enlighten-

[17]Swint, op. cit., p. 36.
[18]February 13, 1864, AMA 86867.
[19]August 26, 1864, AMA 111897.
[20]November 29, 1864, AMA 1116369.
[21]June 28, 1865, AMA 1117343.

ment."[22] After recounting the hardships under which he labored, he insisted that "all this I count as nothing if I am counted worthy to labor in the vineyard of Him who has suffered and died for me."[23] The Harris brothers thus experienced the same happiness in their work which marked the white teachers. William considered that even angels would "esteem it a privilege" to be engaged in his work.[24] Nor did time diminish the sense of exhilaration. After having been in the South five years, Robert exclaimed: "O! What joy there is among us to see so many coming home to God! Rejoice with us, brother, for the work of the Lord is glorious!"[25]

## ACTIVITIES

How did the missionary teachers spend their time? What occupied a typical day or week? Swint pointed out that in addition to their teaching and religious work, the northern teachers were quite active politically and that this was a major cause of friction with native whites.

Although the major objective was teaching in an area of great educational destitution, one is hardly prepared for the heavy workload which they experienced. When William Harris arrived in Portsmouth, Virginia, in 1864, he took charge of a school in which he taught four days a week, with two sessions each day and an average of 62 students per session.[26] A year later, the school had doubled in size and Harris had two women assistants.[27] He also opened a night school for adults. Evening schools were apparently a common activity for both Harris brothers, although such schools were quite ephemeral. Shortly after his arrival in Virginia, William reported assisting with an evening school which enrolled 700 students,[28] yet, by the end of April no school was in session "due to religious efforts."[29] Apparently this expression referred to the frequent revival meetings. In the Spring, 1865, William reported that his evening school met only two weeks out of the month because the building had been appropriated for other uses. Various other considerations led him to believe the school should remain closed. The night air was considered unwholesome; it was dangerous for teachers to be out at night following the assassination of President Lincoln and the return of many "Rebel" prisioners.[30]

[22]March 1, 1866, AMA 1118435.
[23]December, 1865, AMA 1117979.
[24]March 1, 1864, AMA H 1-5416.
[25]August 5, 1869, AMA 102529.
[26]April 1, 1864, AMA H 1-5552.
[27]May 1, 1865, AMA 1117062.
[28]March 1, 1864, AMA H 1-5416.
[29]April 30, 1864, AMA H 1-5663.
[30]May 1, 1865, AMA 1117062.

Not content with inactivity, William conducted what he called "a little family school" in place of the usual evening school.[31]

Robert was no less active and busy. Upon arrival in Virginia, he arranged an evening class which enrolled fifteen persons at his residence.[32] After moving to North Carolina, he once again organized an evening school, this time with 51 students. Since these evening classes usually lasted three hours, after two three-hour sessions during the day, it is not surprising that Robert found it "excessively wearisome teaching night and day." Nevertheless, their efforts apparently did not flag, and they trusted God would give them strength to carry on.[33]

After a week of such diligent work, these teachers could not even count Sunday as a day of rest. Sabbath School was as much a part of the work week as secular school. William Harris reported his Sunday schedule required him to be at Whitehead Farm near Norfolk by 8:15 A.M. for a school of 100 students. Then at 10:00 A.M. he met with about 50 soldiers of the 2nd U.S. Colored Battery encamped nearby. Finally, at 2:00 P.M. he had a school for 125 students at the community of Gosport.[34] Although the passing of time diminished the energies and enthusiasm of the white teachers, this was not true of these black teachers. Five years later, Robert reported from North Carolina that he was engaged in two Sabbath Schools each Sunday, and that he was "content and happy to be thus busily employed" in the vineyard of the Lord.[35] Considering the fact that the fulfilling of these varied responsibilities usually involved walking several miles to the different locations, it is clear that the experience of being a teacher was not a holiday. Years later, while principal of the state normal school, Robert Harris conducted Sunday School as an adjunct to the normal, using the same teachers to teach the International lessons to the normal pupils.[36]

As one might expect, the letters from the Harris brothers to their sponsoring missionary society emphasize their teaching, both secular and religious. Still there are sufficient hints of other activities to indicate that their concerns for racial development were conceived rather broadly. Both men described themselves as busily occupied with considerable visitation to the homes of people in their communities. William reported on one occasion that he averaged visiting two families per night; another report gave a

[31]June 1, 1865, AMA 1117228.
[32]February 3, 1865, AMA 1116683.
[33]January 1, 1868, AMA 101621.
[34]August 31, 1864, AMA 1116042.
[35]September 4, 1869, AMA 102538.
[36]*Annual Report of the Superintendent*, 1878, p. 44.

*The Journal of Negro Education* 131

total of 31 families visited in a month's time.[37] Much of the visitation was to convince parents to send their children to school, or was to carry out the equivalent of "pastoral" visits to the sick; yet, many other humanitarian and social purposes were in view. In one of his earliest observations made outside the strictly educational and religious sphere, William urged the AMA to use its influence to "secure homes and permanent homesteads for the people ... as the basis for their future usefulness and well-being."[38] No doubt such matters were topics for discussion in these home visitations.

Robert carried his concern for economic advancement a bit further. He reported forming "an association whose ultimate object is the purchase of tracts of land for Homesteads." Members of the association agreed to deposit their savings in a bank until sufficient money had accumulated to buy land. Although poverty made it difficult to amass considerable savings, Harris expressed the intention of using "all my influence" to promote the project.[39]

The AMA sent not only packages of food and clothing for distribution by the teachers, but on one occasion Robert acknowledged receipt of garden seeds which he distributed.[40] William's efforts seem somewhat less concrete. He reported usually finding a room full of people waiting for him at 9:00 A.M. each day seeking relief packages or recommendations. He would "hold prayers and lecture them briefly on economy and self-reliance and refer them to the inexhaustible and bountiful spiritual rations."[41]

Another common activity for missionary teachers, marginal between the secular and the religious, was the promotion of temperance and related associations. Having found in North Carolina the use of tobacco and other "iniquitous substances" to be nearly universal, Robert used the Christmas holiday period in 1868 to organize a "Band of Hope" society among his pupils. Sixty-nine of them took the pledge to "abstain from the use of intoxicating drinks, from the use of tobacco in any form, and from all profane and vulgar language."[42] By April, the "band" had increased to 136 and was "marching on."[43] To supply the group with proper encouragement, Robert requested fifty copies of "The Youth's Temperance Banner" to be sent at half price since they were too poor to pay full price.[44] Ten years later, the Total

[37]April 29, 1865, AMA 1117036.
[38]July 14, 1864, AMA H 1-5931.
[39]December, 1865, AMA 1117979.
[40]April 15, 1867, AMA 101153.
[41]February 18, 1867, AMA 1119770.
[42]December 5, 1868, AMA 102084.
[43]April 7, 1869, AMA 102346.
[44]January 15, 1872, AMA 102956.

Abstinence Society was an important adjunct to the state normal school.

Robert Harris was also concerned with promoting general cultural development in the community. He organized a Literary Society in connection with the normal school. Functioning much as a lyceum, the society met weekly for declamations, readings, lectures. In 1879, the society featured a debate on the question of emigration for black people.[45]

All of these activities suggest one of the major differences between the black and white missionary teachers. Certainly both groups of teachers were busy day and night; both were involved in school and church teaching. Yet, the black teachers apparently became more deeply involved and permanently intertwined with the black community than was true or possible for white teachers. Robert Harris omitted his usual summer vacation trip to Cleveland in 1869 because he was "so connected with the educational, religious, social and industrial affairs of the people that we cannot well be spared."[46]

A study of the activities of the black teachers suggests one other major difference as compared to the white teachers, a difference which may be related to the one just mentioned. According to Swint, the northern teacher used the classroom as well as other community contacts to promote the northern Republican political philosophy, and this more than anything else, was the basis of southern hatred for the Yankee teacher.[47] That the Harris brothers agreed with their white counterparts in political sentiment is clear enough from their letters, but the letters give absolutely no indication that political indoctrination was any part of their teaching. This lack of emphasis on politics seems to be confirmed by reports in their letters that they themselves were well received by the white community and that initial hostility had changed to appreciation. The esteem of the larger white community for the work of Robert Harris is given independent testimony in the reports of the North Carolina Superintendent of Public Instruction.

It would seem that the intimate involvement of the black teachers in the whole life of the black community made it possible for them to express their political views outside the schoolroom and thus maintain the school relatively neutral politically, whereas the white teachers, because they were outside both the southern white as well as black communities, had no other potent means

[45]*Annual Report of the Superintendent*, 1879, pp. 39, 40.
[46]June 10, 1869, AMA 102476.
[47]Swint, *op. cit.*, p. 59 and *passim*.

of political influence beside the classroom. Thus, they made political indoctrination an important part of their teaching.

## ISSUES AND OPINIONS

According to Swint, the two principal issues among the missionary teachers and associations were (1) segregation, and (2) whether schools should educate or convert.[48] A scanning of their letters and reports indicates that considerable interest was also manifested by the teachers in making observations respecting racial traits with a view to confirming or rejecting the typical racial stereotypes. We now raise the question as to whether or not and to what degree the black teachers were concerned with these issues, and what stand they took.

By virtue of their racial identity, it might be expected that the black teachers would exhibit less curiosity about racial traits than the white teachers. One is struck quickly by the absence in the Harris letters of the kind of observations which occurred frequently in the white teachers' letters respecting the rapidity with which black children learned, especially in comparision with white northern children. It was as if the liberal philosophy of the white teachers had led them to expect it, but that they were surprised to find it really true. Naturally, the Harris brothers had undergone different experiences and, therefore, made relatively few comments on this topic. In the entire collection of letters, there is only a single comment on race and ability. William, shortly after arriving in Virginia, noted that the "light complexion seem to be the most apt to learn on the average." But to compensate for this possibly derogatory observation, he quickly added that the "smartest scholar among the girls, and also among the boys, is quite dark."[49] The only other racially oriented remarks appearing in the Harris letters were occasional observations intended to refute accusations that the freedmen were lazy. Robert found in Virginia "no signs of laziness."[50] Two months later, he confirmed his earlier impression, reporting that he had "failed to discover any who are idle or unwilling to work. On the contrary, the men, women, and children are industriously engaged in tilling the soil."[51]

But what of the segregation issue? The missionary associations, including the AMA, took the position that segregation would not be countenanced. The Harris brothers expressed them-

[48]*Ibid.*, pp. 19, 20.
[49]April 1, 1864, AMA 1115552.
[50]April 29, 1865, AMA 1117036.
[51]June 28, 1865, AMA 1117343.

selves as fully agreeing with this in principle. William emphatically "opposed making *any* distinctions on account of Color, as a general principle." While this was a rigid principle with abolitionists and the associations, the Harris brothers apparently recognized a need for expediency and flexibility. When a proposal was being discussed to install all colored teachers in a colored school near Portsmouth, Virginia, William was willing to make an exception to his rule, provided (1) the people desire and prefer it, (2) good, efficient teachers be employed, and (3) the facilities be equal to other schools. By asking whether the "people desire or prefer it," Harris was not speaking of the southern whites, but of the native black population whose wishes must be respected. In setting up the criteria of good teachers and equal facilities, Harris was exhibiting accurate prescience at a date preceding by about twenty years the emergence of discriminatory policies in financing and facilities for black schools.

The question of education versus religion was probably more an issue among the associations than it was among the teachers. Most of the teachers probably joined themselves to the society whose philosophy was most compatible with their own, and thus relatively little discussion of this issue appears in their letters. The views of the Harris brothers were consistent with that of the AMA which held that education of the freedmen should be based on religion.[52] William Harris, though he had a personal interest in the matter since he was seeking AMA approval to move from teaching to preaching, was surely expressing his true views when he argued that "teachers and preachers must go together or the education of the freedmen and the evangelization of the South will be incomplete if not a failure."[53]

There was little discussion among the white northern teachers about the kind of education needed by the freedmen. It was assumed that the northern pattern of academic, classical education, more specifically the New England pattern, was best for the freedmen. Confronted by the massive need for literacy education, it is not surprising that the issue might not be raised for several years and might, therefore, not loom large in the letters of the missionary teachers. Discussion of this topic appeared only once in the Harris brothers' letters. William mentioned Hampton Institute where he had sent his daughter, Charlotte, and noted that it "must commend itself to the cooperation of the philanthropic and benevolent who know best the wants of the Southern people."

[52]Swint, *op. cit.*, p. 38.
[53]February 18, 1867, AMA 1119770.

He noted, as Douglass had done earlier and as Washington was to do later, that slavery had led the freedmen to believe education and labor were incompatible. He declared that he hoped this "erroneous and aristocratic idea" would be "bombarded effectually from Hampton."[54]

## EDUCATIONAL CONTRIBUTIONS

What educational contributions did the black teachers make? Of course, this is most difficult to assess. Apparently their methods of teaching were little different from methods generally in use; nor is there reason to expect otherwise. The monitorial method of teaching was used by both Robert and William. William reported that he spent most of his time instructing the 13 monitors (all girls; ages 15-17) who could "spell tolerably well," were in the Third Reader, and were also studying arithmetic and geography.[55] William described a typical session of his night school as involving scripture reading, singing a hymn, prayers, reading a portion of the Constitution in concert, then spelling and defining the words (sometimes a portion of the Congressional Proceedings was used for this purpose), then singing the multiplication tables.[56]

Robert made more frequent comments on his methods than did William. In 1866, he had noted in a magazine which he did not name, the advisability of dividing elementary schools into primary and intermediate divisions, and so introduced this innovation into his school.[57] He found little difficulty in controlling the children, and reported that most instances of punishment were for *out* of school behavior. He found the use of the birch to be effective, along with depriving them of recess, compelling them to stand a long time, and above all, the use of ridicule.[58]

Some issues are apparently timeless. Robert commented that learning to read was, with his pupils, like learning a new language, "so different is their language from that in the books." His response was to have an "exercise in articulation at every recitation."[59]

Perhaps the most important educational contribution to come from the work of the Harris brothers was in teacher education. After Robert moved to Fayetteville, North Carolina, he began to organize satellite schools in the outlying areas in the country from his city school, and to dispatch his older students to these schools

[54]January 25, 1868, AMA 17508.
[55]October, 1864, AMA 1116160.
[56]April 9, 1866, AMA 1118694A.
[57]December 5, 1866, AMA 100769.
[58]January 1, 1866, AMA 1117975.
[59]February 2, 1866, AMA 1118220.

as teachers. In 1868, he described the opening of a school twelve miles out in the country which would be supported by the local people, aided by the Freedmen's Bureau, and taught by one of his advanced pupils. This teacher was the sixth to be sent from his school.[60] A month later, he reported plans to send several more teachers into outlying districts so that schools would be kept open throughout the summer.[61] Apparently Robert's efforts in this direction generated much self-help within the black community, perhaps to a far greater degree than would have been true of schools under different leadership. As a result, Robert could describe the opening of a new school house in Fayetteville as the first building specifically erected for black students in that county.[62] These efforts all culminated in the opening of the Fayetteville Normal School, the first such school in North Carolina, with Robert Harris as principal. At a time when the University of North Carolina normal course consisted of five- to six-week summer sessions, Robert Harris was presiding over a three-year, nine-month course of teacher education.[63]

Something of Robert Harris' philosophy of teacher education is contained in the following report on the Fayetteville Normal embedded in the Annual Report of the State Superintendent:

> We aim to prepare better teachers for the public schools; teachers who will know more of the nature of children and their proper development; teachers who understand the subjects to be taught, and good methods for teaching them; teachers who will learn and practice good methods of study and discipline; and, above all, teachers who will, by precept and example, teach the rising generation those principles of virtue and piety by which good characters are formed for time and eternity. Character-building is the teacher's main work, and skill in communicating knowledge and developing the intellectual and moral faculties is one of the most important qualifications of the teacher.[64]

A person must finally be evaluated in terms of what he intended to do and what he accomplished rather than in terms of what others think he should have done. In this light, the Harris brothers certainly made a contribution by teaching many people, by organizing and inspiring the communities in which they worked, by training teachers, by encouraging self-help. While they certainly intended to do these things, nevertheless they aimed at a larger goal and it is in terms of this goal that their work must ultimately be judged. William expressed it well early in his career

[60]May 2, 1868, AMA 101868.
[61]June 1, 1868, AMA 101915.
[62]April 7, 1869, AMA 102346.
[63]*Annual Report of the Superintendent*, 1880, p. 37.
[64]*Annual Report of the Superintendent*, 1879, p. 38.

when he reported "a firm, unwavering trust, that the final triumph of truth, Liberty, Justice, and righteousness is certain. Thank God for what he has done through Congress, Maryland, Missouri, Tennessee, etc. The Lord indeed reigneth. Let the people rejoice."[65]

Thus, for the Harris brothers, education was more than a means of making a living, more than the means by which an individual child would be equipped to get ahead in the world, and even more than the most effective means for racial advancement. Education was viewed as linking the teacher with cosmic forces and cosmic purposes that transcended a single school term, a generation of children, or even the individual lifetime of the teacher. They saw the teacher as being a co-worker with God, and as laboring for the realization of divine purposes. In this hope, such teachers as the Harris brothers worked with confidence that despite human frailty, despite temporary defeats, despite the intransigence of the opposition, triumph was certain.

[65]February 1, 1865, AMA 1116653.

138   *The Journal of Negro Education*

# The Peabody Education Fund and Negro Education, 1867-1880

## EARLE H. WEST

AID TO THE "SUFFERING SOUTH," especially educational aid, was the concern of many groups after the Civil War. Alongside the agents of the Freedmen's Bureau and the Yankee schoolmarms was the Peabody Education Fund, first of the major educational foundations in this country. After the soldiers, agents, and missionaries had gone, the Peabody Fund remained an influence upon southern education for nearly fifty years.

If the South was the forgotten region until Franklin Roosevelt pronounced it the nation's number one economic problem, the Negro was the South's forgotten man. Whether equality of educational opportunity was ever intended or seriously attempted may be debatable, but that systematic discrimination became woven into southern education has been thoroughly demonstrated.

What role did the Peabody Education Fund have in the development of the southern pattern of education? George Peabody, the donor, Robert C. Winthrop, the chairman of the trustees, and Barnas Sears, the general agent from 1867-1880, were natives of Massachusetts. A majority of the trustees were northern men. And yet the Peabody Fund has been described as having cooperated enthusiastically in the development of a segregated and inferior education for the Negro. (1)

The purpose of this paper is to describe the work of the Peabody Education Fund in behalf of Negro education and to interpret it in the light of the educational thought, policies, and purposes of the persons associated with the fund.

### ESTABLISHMENT OF THE FUND

George Peabody established the Peabody Education Fund in 1867 with a gift of one million dollars and charged his trustees with encouraging

*Mr. West is Assistant Professor of Education at Howard University.*

education in the South. That the fund would, in some measure, aid in the education of Negroes had been settled by the donor, who asked that the benefits "be distributed among the entire population, without other distinction than their needs and the opportunities of usefulness to them." (2)

In March 1867, the trustees selected as their general agent, Barnas Sears, president of Brown University during the Civil War, successor to Horace Mann as Secretary of the Massachusetts Board of Education, well-known Baptist minister, and classicist. Sears administered the fund until his death in 1880 and distributed a total of about 1.2 million dollars. Of this sum, about 6.5 percent, or $75,750 was given to schools specifically designated as Negro schools.

Until about 1876, the Peabody Fund emphasized aid to elementary schools. For the first few years, Sears made most of the arrangements for aid by personal tours through the South to confer with civic leaders in cities and towns. Gradually, specific decisions as to which schools to aid were left to the state superintendents of education. After 1875, the emphasis shifted to teacher preparation through encouraging the establishment of state normal schools.

## PEABODY FUND POLICY

It is the thesis of this paper that the role of the Peabody Fund in the development of Negro education cannot be correctly understood solely from a racial breakdown of its gifts, or from its support of a white, private school system in Louisiana, or from its opposition to civil rights legislation in Congress. These specific actions were expressions of an educational philosophy, a particular view of the purpose of the fund, and a policy evolved to achieve that purpose.

There were three major determinants of Peabody Fund policy: the donor, the trustees, and the general agent. Three key criteria for giving aid were suggested by Mr. Peabody in transmitting the original gift: (a) need, (b) opportunity for usefulness, and (c) aid to the states in their exertions. (3) From this last criterion it was clear that the Fund was not to be a wholly charitable enterprise. Just how the other criteria were to be defined and applied, Mr. Peabody left for the trustees to decide.

The influence of the trustees upon the development of policy was relatively minor. The board had been deliberately constituted of nearly equal numbers of northern and southern men, but with a northern majority. (4) As the board approached a March 1867 meeting at which some mode of operation would have to be decided, no clear plan had emerged. Chairman Winthrop looked to the southern trustees to indicate what they wished (5), and it was, therefore, assumed that schools for the indigent would be opened. (6) Some southern trustees, moved by the economic prostration of the South, begged impassionately that Peabody money be used to feed and clothe the population, while others hoped it would be restricted to the children of those formerly wealthy men who had been ruined by the war. (7) A flood of suggestions came from the public, ranging from William Carey Crane asking for funds to resuscitate Baylor University, to a forlorn lady whose husband had never "been able to make at anything." (8) While the northern trustees did not approve the proposals of the southern trustees, their inability to agree upon a workable alternative probably meant that the Fund would have become little more than an adjunct to southern pauper schools had it not been for the fortuitous introduction of the third determinant of policy.

On a brief visit to Boston in early March, 1867, Barnas Sears, then president of Brown University, was invited to visit with the Wednesday Evening Club at the home of Robert C. Winthrop. As a friend of long standing, Winthrop sought Sears's advice on the Peabody donation. Sears put his recommendations into a letter which Winthrop read to the trustees at their March meeting. So well were the ideas received that Sears was appointed general agent and his policies as expressed in the letter and further developed over the next twelve years became the official policies of the fund.

Among Mr. Peabody's criteria, Sears placed greatest emphasis upon "opportunity for usefulness." He was a true son of Massachusetts in his commitment to education. Thus, "usefulness" not only demanded education, but state systems of public education. Rejecting all suggestions that special schools for the poor be opened, Sears insisted upon using Peabody money only to assist others in their efforts, and only in such efforts as would lead toward systems of schools publicly supported and publicly controlled. Millions were in need. It would have been an easy matter to spend the entire resources of the fund without substantially benefiting the individuals aided or leaving any permanent influence upon the region. "Let good schools," he wrote, "spring-ing upon the soil, growing out of the wants of the people, and meeting those wants, be sprinkled all over the South as examples, and be made nuclei for others, and let them be established and controlled as far as possible by the people themselves, and they will, in time, grow into state systems." (9)

It is important, however, to see Sears's policies as the outgrowth of years of development rather than ad hoc policies devised to placate the Bourbon South. His concern with the relation between schools, the law, and popular sentiment extended backward twenty-five years to his appointment by Governor Briggs to the Massachusetts State Board of Education. He served on the board's executive committee until his appointment in the fall of 1848 to succeed Horace Mann as Secretary of the Board of Education.

Sears viewed the development of state systems of education as com-ing about in one of two ways. In some states there had been systematic efforts to enlighten people and create a demand for a good school law. In other states, there had been legislation in advance of public opinion; this required strenuous efforts to make the schools of such excellence as to command the respect and support of the people. (10) True social progress, he felt, came not by legislation imposed upon people, but by "the spirit of a whole people feeling out its path, and manifesting itself in different degrees in many minds." (11) Unless legislation followed rather than led public sentiment, the result would often be rash experi-ments that by causing negative public reaction would hinder educa-tional progress even more than ignorance itself. (12)

Sears felt that Mr. Mann had erred in precisely this regard. Thus, when Mann resigned, he left several substantial segments of people in the state alienated from the school system. Sears saw his work as Mann's successor more that of developing greater confidence in the system among the people than "perfecting the system theoreti-cally." (13)

Another aspect of Sears's background that affected Peabody Fund policy was his attitude toward the Negro and racial issues. As early as 1838 in Biblical theology classes at Newton Theological Institution, he was affirming the unity of the human race in opposition to racist theories. (14) Thirty years later he taught the seniors at Brown Uni-versity that each human being has within himself an end for which he exists and ought never be forced to the level of being used merely as means to the ends of others. Whatever freedoms were enjoyed by, or restrictions were imposed upon, one man were to be the same as those upon all other men. (15)

Education was intimately intertwined with these beliefs. Rejecting social classes as in any way reflecting divine will, Sears found the "nature and necessities of man" to be universal and, therefore, education should be universal. "Society cannot afford to sacrifice," he argued, "one-half or three-fourths of the best men of its population by allowing that portion of the people to go uneducated." (16) Clearly, then, for Sears there could be no such thing as a distinctive "Negro education" or "place" in Christian American society.

Despite the definiteness of his beliefs in respect to the implications of Christianity for the race question, Sears had long been a moderate in promoting those views. Amory D. Mayo was surely judging by the letter rather than the spirit of the man when he described Sears as "a New England man, obnoxious to the leading southern people on every line of his political creed, an eminent leader of a rival religious sect, proposing a system of universal popular education." (17) During the tortuous maneuverings of the 1840's, which resulted in a sectional split within the Baptist church, Sears was a member of the boards of both the foreign and home missionary societies when the decisions were rendered respecting the appointment of slave-holding missionaries. He voted with the majority in refusing to "be a party to any arrangements which would imply approbation of slavery," but preferred that it not be announced as public policy. This neutralist position would, he hoped, permit the radical abolitionists to separate and leave the main body of Baptists intact. (18)

Constitutionally, Sears felt that the question of slavery belonged to each state to decide for itself. The extension of slavery belonged to Congress. Disagreements beyond these areas should be settled by the Supreme Court. The long-range solution to all such problems would not come, he believed, by legal or physical compulsion but by the "intellectual and moral progress of the race." Christian principles planted in the hearts of men, though imperfectly and inconsistently put into practice, would eventually work themselves out into the required social reforms. (19)

In sum, what we have said to this point is that Barnas Sears was the chief architect of Peabody Education Fund policy from its beginning in 1867 until 1880. Sears's policy for the Peabody Fund was grounded in his Christian view of fundamental equality among men and the duty of the state to provide universal education. Slavery was morally wrong, but the problems arising therefrom should be solved by the moral development of the people. Educationally, Sears favored local initiative above legal enactment. Whatever the Peabody Education Fund did in the South for Negro education must be interpreted in the light of these deeply held beliefs of the general agent. Against this background, let us turn to an examination of Peabody Fund activities in relation to Negro education in the South.

## AID TO NEGRO EDUCATION: PUBLIC SCHOOL PHASE

In his earliest observations of conditions in the South, Sears frequently remarked that in terms of need, at least, white children deserved more help than Negro children. In town after town he reported that the combined efforts of the Freedmen's Bureau and missionary societies had resulted in more Negro children attending classes in better school buildings than was true of white children. His report after visiting Charleston, South Carolina, was typical when he reported of the Negro children that "it cannot be said that they are in want of the means of education." (20) Although Horace Mann Bond has agreed that this was indeed true in some instances, (21) this situation was clearly not representative of the total condition. Sears's view of the relative needs of whites and Negroes did not, of course, take into consideration the highly contingent, almost ephemeral, quality of many missionary schools, nor the educational gap between the two racial populations. In what would seem to be a concession to the inevitability of fact, Sears did not continue this line of reasoning as justification for devoting the major part of the fund to white schools.

It has been pointed out that Sears's long range objective was to use Peabody money in such a way that there would develop in the South state systems of public education supported by a favorable public opinion. The strategy for reaching this goal was to select cities or towns likely to influence other areas, then make an offer of Peabody aid provided certain conditions were met. Although the conditions were somewhat flexible and were gradually raised as schools were improved, two were almost universally applied: (1) the communities were required to raise an amount of money three or four times the amount to be contributed by the Peabody Fund, and (2) the schools were required to be under some form of public control. The first would, Sears felt, pave the way for acceptance of school taxes. The second would remove the schools from private or sectarian control and pave the way for state supervision. (22)

During the first year of operation, Sears found so few places able and willing to meet these terms that he could report to the trustees offers of assistance totalling only $11,000 to thirteen towns in five states. Although none of these offers were to specifically designated Negro schools, in five of the thirteen towns Sears stipulated that educational opportunity be provided for "all children." It was understood that there would be separate schools for the two races. (23)

During the first half of 1868, offers for the next school year were made to seventy-four towns and in seven instances it was required that children of both races be supplied with schools. In one instance, the aid was designated for a Negro school. The requirement that towns provide schools for both races continued to be common. In 1869, for example, Huntsville and Montgomery, Alabama, were each offered $2,000 if they would enroll at least 500 white and 700 Negro pupils. Beaufort, South Carolina, was to receive $600 if it would "give education to all children." However, in many more instances towns were required to provide only for white children. (24)

Negro communities could seldom be found that were able to meet the conditions outlined. Widespread poverty made it almost impossible for them to raise two-thirds or three-fourths of the cost of school operation, especially if it were required to be a free school as Sears usually stipulated. Negroes owned or provided school buildings in many localities, but judging from Freedmen's Bureau records they were nearly always church buildings and, therefore, under church trustees, which would compromise Sears's insistence upon nonsectarian control. Finally, there were apparently few communities with a Negro leadership capable of overseeing schools. This was, at least, Sears's perception, which he reported to the Peabody trustees. Negro schools, he said, were subject to the "fitful activity and irregularity of this class of our population." (25) In both Louisiana and Texas, circulars were distributed offering aid to Negro schools "after they come into existence, and the provisions of their organization and support shall be fully known." (26) Sears wrote the Freedmen's Bureau superintendent for Georgia that assistance to Negro schools had been intentionally postponed "till I could adopt some system. We cannot give money to irresponsible parties." (27) Thus, given a noncharitable conception of the Peabody Fund, the relative neglect of Negro education seemed inevitable.

It would, of course, be proper to evaluate for accuracy Sears's impressions of Negro communities and schools. The existence of some educational leadership is indicated from the fact that Negroes served as state superintendents for brief periods in Florida, Arkansas, Mississippi, and Louisiana. A Negro served as assistant superintendent of education in North Carolina for several years. Negroes served on education committees in many state legislatures and revisionist interpretations of Reconstruction seem to suggest that a more positive evaluation of their contributions may be appropriate.

Leadership at the state level does not necessarily provide an adequate picture of local conditions. One approach to an understanding of these local conditions is through the monthly reports of the subassistant commissioners of the Freedmen's Bureau. These officers were required to answer a list of questions including how much money could be raised among the freedmen, how long northern charitable aid would be needed, and whether it would be possible to organize local school committees to carry on the schools. Extensive sampling of these monthly reports indicates that relatively few Bureau agents would have challenged Sears's observations. The report of Alfred Thomas of Lumberton, North Carolina, is representative. As to the amount of money that could be raised among freedmen, Thomas reported it "impossible to say, as money with the Freedmen is a very scarce article." Northern charitable aid, he felt, would be required until the state "inaugurates the free school system," since the freedmen were too "poor and impoverished to sustain schools." No local school committee of freedmen was possible, he declared, "under existing circumstances." (28)

Sears and the Peabody trustees apparently felt pressure to do something for Negro schools and consequently began to explore ways of giving aid. It was no doubt an embarrassment to have the fund described by a southern newspaper as "an important adjunct to the cause of education among the white people." (29) Although it had been Sears's policy to work independently of other organizations and agencies, he concluded that the Freedmen's Bureau would provide at least a minimum of supervision. The commissioners in Virginia, North Carolina, and Georgia were willing to serve as Peabody agents. Accordingly, $1,000 was set aside for Negro schools in each of these states during 1868-1869. The amount was increased to $4,000 for the following year. Largely because of this aid, contributions to Negro education reached 18 percent of Peabody contributions during that year.

Aid channeled through the Freedmen's Bureau was not subject to the requirements imposed elsewhere. Since the schools were principally staffed by northern missionary teachers, Sears felt little hope that they would grow toward a public school system. Nevertheless, he did encourage Bureau officers to use Peabody money to stimulate even small contributions from the Negro population and thus avoid developing the impression that it was a charitable dole. The North Carolina superintendent reported that he was requiring a payment of twenty-five cents per scholar and the Georgia superintendent declared that Peabody aid had helped draw out "aid from the colored people that could not have been obtained in any other way." (30)

Congressional appropriations for the Freedmen's Bureau expired in July 1870, and systematic efforts of the Peabody Fund to aid Negro education ended at the same time. Thereafter, such aid as was given to Negro schools was given in the same manner and on similar terms as to white schools. Normally, a white school enrolling the minimum of one hundred students would receive $300 with proportionately greater amounts for a larger enrollment. However, Negro schools of the minimum size received only $200 on the grounds that "it costs less to maintain schools for the colored children than for the white." (31) Although the largest racial disparities did not develop for two decades, Sears's statement was essentially correct if one judges cost in terms of teacher salaries and pupil-teacher ratios. (32)

## AID TO NEGRO EDUCATION: NORMAL SCHOOL PHASE

The earliest policy statements by the Peabody trustees envisioned major attention to teacher education. Although some aid had been given for this purpose all along, there was a definite shift in emphasis from elementary schools to normal schools about 1875. Negro normal schools fared much better than the elementary schools. Over the entire thirteen year period, about 18 percent of all contributions for teacher education went to Negro schools, but the proportion reached above 30 percent several years.

With some exceptions, Peabody Fund aid for teacher education was mainly in the form of tuition payments assigned to specific schools as scholarships. Sears wrote to General Howard for advice in aiding the preparation of Negro teachers. He told the General that "persons wholly supported by others are apt to be passive, inefficient and helpless." Therefore, Peabody contributions should be considered "aid" rather than "support" so as to encourage greater self-reliance. Negro teachers would have to be "very industrious and economical" in their work and, therefore, should not be spoiled by ease and indulgence during their period of preparation. (33)

General Howard was anxious to have the Peabody Fund adopt Howard University as its central training school for Negro teachers. He recommended scholarships of $100 annually for female students and $150 for male students. (34) Sears finally decided to restrict Peabody aid to southern schools and also to regular normal schools rather than schools that proposed to add a normal department in order to receive funds. Contributions on a sustaining basis were made to Hampton, Fisk, and Atlanta University as well as to several normal schools of lower quality. The rate of scholarship aid was $50 per student per year and was the same for both white and Negro students.

Negro normal schools did not share in the substantially increased aid to normal schools that became the new Peabody Fund policy after 1876. Most of the increase went directly or indirectly to the Nashville Normal to which Negroes were not admitted. The plan, of course, was for the Nashville school not only to be adopted by the state, but for it to be a sort of regional model at the college level and thus stimulate the entire region in upgrading normal schools. Various states over the South were assigned scholarship quotas and the level of aid was raised from $50 to $200 per student. Despite the critical need for competent Negro teachers, no effort was made to develop a similar, high-level, regional normal school for Negroes. As early as 1870, Sears had assigned some scholarships for Virginia residents at Hampton Agricultural and Industrial College. Later, students from South Carolina and occasionally other states were admitted on Peabody scholarships but the amount remained at $50. For white students, the amount given was estimated as being "sufficient to meet all necessary expenses"; whereas, Negro students were obviously forced to work for additional support. (35)

## THE MIXED-SCHOOL ISSUE

In his travels and contacts over the South, Sears found many factors hindering the development of education. Financial prostration, opposition to taxation, legal uncertainties, widespread discouragement, all loomed large. One of the most disturbing questions, however, was that of racially mixed schools arising both from fear as to what the radical state constitutions might require and as to the provisions of federal civil rights legislation. The Peabody Fund was confronted with this problem wherever it operated but became intensely involved with it in the state of Louisiana and in an effort at congressional lobbying during late 1873.

When the Peabody Fund was initiated, various persons inquired about its policy as to racially mixed schools. Sears reiterated his belief in the importance of indigenous schools, a belief that he had acquired twenty-five years earlier under circumstances devoid of racial overtones. Accordingly, John E. Amos of Georgia after going North to interview Sears reported that the fund would "in no wise conflict with any sentiment, institution, or custom peculiar to us." (36) Sears's position was that the mixing or separation of the races in school was a matter for the people to decide themselves. The Peabody Fund would be happy to cooperate either with a system that separated the races, or a system that put the races together, provided that the schools were supported by the people and were, in fact, generally attended by the children. (37)

An interesting, and to the Peabody Fund an embarrassing, test of this position occurred in Louisiana, where the radical constitution required integrated public schools. Because it was in this state that the Peabody Fund became most deeply involved in racial controversies, Sears's work here deserves special attention.

Barnas Sears visited Louisiana in 1867 during the waning days of conservative control under presidential reconstruction. He discussed with Robert Mills Lusher, State Superintendent of Education, the new constitution soon to go into effect. Lusher had been presiding over a public school system exclusively for whites, but would soon leave office because he had declined to run for reelection to an office in which he would have to administer racially mixed schools. (38)

As Sears considered how the fund could aid education in Louisiana, various alternatives were considered. Negro children were being provided for by the Freedmen's Bureau and these schools would be brought into the state system when the new constitution went into effect. The white children, since they would refuse to attend mixed schools, would be shut out from public schools and would, therefore, be the destitute group. Adopting a policy unlike that used in any other state, Sears decided to offer aid to schools for white children operated on a private basis. (39) Deposed as state superintendent, Lusher became the Peabody agent for the state and in effect the unofficial superintendent of a system of private white schools conducted with Peabody Fund aid. Sears dealt with him exactly as he did with state superintendents elsewhere. Lusher selected the schools to be aided and certified that they met Peabody Fund conditions. When new schools were organized, they were placed under trustees appointed by Lusher. Total Peabody money available to Lusher each year was about equal in amount to the state apportionment before the war when public schools were maintained for white children in principal towns. (40)

Although it was a cardinal objective with Sears to eschew political debates, nevertheless, Lusher's antagonism toward Republican rule inevitably involved the fund in unpleasant controversy. From private exchanges, it erupted into the newspapers and the published reports of the superintendents. The fund was charged with being an "engine of oppression" that was "mailing the heel of caste." (41) No doubt it was disconcerting to have the hue and cry taken up by a Baltimore paper, a city with which Mr. Peabody had particularly close connections. (42) What was perhaps the most decisive criticism so far as Sears was concerned was the fact that the Peabody Fund in sustaining a private system of schools was strangely allied with those elements in the state that, even with the racial issue aside, were opposed to a state-supported school system. Although this could not be said of Lusher himself, yet the racial issue gathered into common alliance many persons who could agree on little else. This is well illustrated by the editorial position of the New Orleans *Daily Picayune*, that, while defending Sears against Republican attacks, also called for a quick return "to the beneficial system that prevailed over the South before the war, when the public fund was used as an auxiliary to private schools." (43)

Sears had clearly underestimated many things about the Louisiana situation: the strength of radical insistence on mixed schools, the duration of reconstruction in the state, and the degree of opposition to public schools among the patrons of Lusher's private schools. The Peabody Fund was being placed in a false light. Private schools were multiplying and Peabody money was actually fostering the movement. Accordingly, aid to Louisiana was terminated in October 1875 and was acknowledged as perhaps the greatest failure of all fund efforts. (44)

To his Republican critics in Louisiana, Sears insisted that if somehow conditions were reversed and the Negro children refused to attend schools provided for them, then the fund "should just as readily aid them." (45) There were, of course, no states whose constitutions required mixed schools but which Negroes refused to attend. There were, however, state systems from which Negroes were effectively excluded for other reasons but where the Peabody Fund made no contributions specifically for Negro education.

Such was the situation in Kentucky. In 1874 a system went into effect whereby Negro education was supported by Negro taxes. This provided "wholly inadequate" funds according to the state superintendent. (46) Here, then, was a state included by Mr. Peabody in the list of southern states for which the fund was intended, and in which there was a systematic neglect of Negro children in the public school system. Yet no funds were contributed either for white or Negro schools.

Perhaps the grounds on which Sears justified these actions become clearer from an examination of activities related to pending civil rights legislation in Congress. So strongly did Sears feel about the issue that in December 1873 he visited Washington to lobby against the mixed schools provision of the proposed civil rights bill. In company with John Eaton, Sears called upon General Butler who was guiding the bill in the House, upon several senators, and finally upon President Grant. Two days after debate on the bill had begun, Butler withdrew it, expressing doubts as to the provisions for mixed schools. (47) The bill was finally passed in 1875 minus the clause pertaining to the schools.

Apparently, Sears was not opposed to civil rights legislation per se but only to that part relating to the schools. Nor did he object to legislation requiring equal privileges in the schools. But to require racially mixed schools would, he felt, destroy the emerging state school systems by alienating the people whose support and leadership were required for the system to function successfully.

This point of view was given wide publicity in an *Atlantic Monthly* article. From his travels over the South, Sears asserted that opinion respecting public education was delicately balanced with about one third opposed, a third favorable, and a third undecided. If racially mixed schools were to be forced, he was certain that it would swing the balance away from public education and the region would revert to its traditional private school system. An influential Baptist paper was calling for that very thing. (48) The Peabody Fund debacle in Louisiana seemed to show conclusively what would happen. Perhaps Sears was also thinking of experiences in New England four decades earlier when opposition to state supervision was so strong that legislatures might abolish in one session what had been created in a previous session. The South, as he saw it, was at this same critical juncture. With public education itself in the balance, it was folly to force an issue that would ensure its defeat. (49)

Sears's main concern, of course, was in the development of public education. To those whose principal concern was the welfare of the Negro, Sears argued that to require mixed schools would only harm. Adequate education for Negroes required state supported systems of education. If zeal for the freedman's needs caused the South to revert to private schools, it would be the Negro and the poor white that would suffer. Northern philanthropy had nearly ceased; the Freedmen's Bureau had come to an end eighteen months before. Therefore, Sears concluded, "any measure, no matter how plausible in theory, which shall in fact take the light of knowledge from the Negroes of the South, will come with an ill grace from those who have given them the boon of liberty." (50) Nor was this, he felt, just a white man's view. His contacts among Negro leaders in the South (not, as he said, Sumner's "trained Negroes") enabled him to say that adequate educational opportunity, not mixed schools, was the thing desired by Negroes themselves. (51)

The assumption underlying this whole line of argument was that if state educational systems were firmly established, genuine educational opportunity would be granted the Negro. This faith was, Sears felt, well grounded. First, the existing state laws called for equal educational opportunity for all. The political power of the Negro would guarantee that these laws would be observed. Second, because of its deep Christian commitment, the South "must, in the end, adopt and carry out the same rule for both races." (52)

The slow pace of economic recovery was apparently the only cloud Sears saw to mar the dawning of justice and equality in Southern education. By 1877, after ten years of intimate contact with the region, Sears felt compelled to urge federal assistance. Avoiding reference to any particular piece of legislation, though he favored the Hoar bill, Sears's eleventh annual report called attention to the financial inability of the South to provide adequate schools for the entire population. (53) So strongly did Sears and the trustees feel that he visited Washington again in the spring of 1878 to confer with the chairmen of committees on education and labor, and with other influential men on "the condition of the South." (54) In the last board meeting before Sears's death, Robert C. Winthrop announced that the Peabody trustees would be glad to "occupy this special field" of Negro education if their funds were "rendered adequate by any public or private endowment." Perhaps this was an oblique bid for federal money since the trustees agreed that nothing short of the "wealth and power of the Federal Government" would be adequate. (55)

Sears did not feel the inconsistency, which has been laid upon him by one historian of Negro education, in his opposition to civil rights legislation on the grounds that equal facilities would come naturally and in then petitioning Congress to make federal grants for Negro education on the grounds that the South could not adequately provide for its Negro population. (56) Civil rights legislation involved the will of the southern people, while federal aid involved their ability to educate the Negro. Respecting the former, Sears was honestly confident that the South was then, and would continue to be, willing to provide equality of educational opportunity for all citizens. That subsequent events may have proved him wrong, or at least overly optimistic, does not detract from the sincerity with which the conviction was held. As touching the ability of the South to educate the Negro, it seems clear that Sears seriously underestimated the problems involved in the economic recovery of the region so that it was not until the very last years of his work with the Peabody Fund that he came to feel that federal aid was required.

## CONCLUSION

Between 1867 and 1880, Barnas Sears was chiefly responsible for the policy and administration of the Peabody Education Fund, a philanthropic enterprise that influenced educational development in the South during a critical period in its history. Negro schools received a disproportionately small share of Peabody money, especially in view of the fact that its purposes embraced both races equally. The support of a private system of white schools in Louisiana and opposition to federal civil rights legislation as applied to schools suggest discrimination against Negroes.

These activities related to Negro education must be interpreted in the light of Sears's educational views and the purposes of the Peabody Fund. Sears was deeply committed to the belief that social progress required universal education. Such systems, however, must not be imposed by legislation but must be the natural outgrowth of popular sentiment. This led Sears to regard the favor and support of southern whites, especially the leadership class, as essential. Temporary discrimination toward the Negro could, therefore, be justified in order to achieve long range justice. That justice would be done, Sears entertained a sincere, if naïve, faith based principally upon the ultimate demands of Christianity.

That Sears and the Peabody Education Fund lent their influence to the white South in its efforts to make the Negro a second-class citizen appears undeniable, even while granting that it was unintentional. Sears's compromise with the conservative South appears to have been a forerunner of the compromise most northern clergymen and politicians had reached by the turn of the century, except that Sears specifically rejected the racist assumptions that others appeared to accept. (57) Perhaps his compromise also helps one to understand how so much of the history of Negro education, even that education provided by their friends, has so often been an education in despair.

## Notes

1. John Hope Franklin, "Jim Crow Goes to School: The Genesis of Legal Segregation in Southern Schools, " *South Atlantic Quarterly*, LVIII (Spring 1959), 232.
2. *Proceedings of the Trustees of the Peabody Education Fund*, I (Boston: John Wilson and Son, 1875), 3. Hereafter cited as *Peabody Proceedings*.
3. *Ibid.*, pp. 1-7.
4. John H. Clifford to Robert C. Winthrop, October 18, 1874. ALS in the John H. Clifford Letters, Massachusetts Historical Society.
5. Robert C. Winthrop to William A. Graham, January 26, 1867, and February 21, 1867. ALS in the William A. Graham Papers, North Carolina Department of Archives and History, Raleigh, North Carolina.
6. William C. Rives, "Resolutions Submitted to the Peabody Trustees, April 1867." MSS in the Rives Papers, Library of Congress.
7. John Eaton, *Grant, Lincoln and The Freedmen* (New York: Longmans, Green and Company, 1907), pp. 257, 258.
8. M. L. Upjohn to William C. Rives, May 14, 1867. ALS in the Rives Papers, Library of Congress. Also Barnas Sears to William Carey Crane, April 25, 1867. ALS in the William Carey Crane Collection, Southern Baptist Convention Historical Commission, Nashville, Tennessee.
9. Barnas Sears to Robert C. Winthrop, March 14, 1867. ALS in the J. L. M. Curry Papers, Library of Congress.
10. *Peabody Proceedings*, I, 362.
11. Massachusetts Board of Education, *Thirteenth Annual Report of the Board of Education* (Boston: Dutton and Wentworth, 1850), p. 29.
12. *Ibid.*, p. 51.
13. *Ibid.*, p. 28.
14. Charles W. Reding, "Class Notebook containing lectures on Biblical Theology by Barnas Sears at Newton Theological Institution, 1838," p. 68. MSS in the Andover Newton Theological Library, Newton Centre, Massachusetts.
15. Henry H. Earl, "Class Notebook containing lectures on Mental and Moral Philosophy by Barnas Sears at Brown University, 1866." Unpaged. MSS in Brown University Library, Providence, Rhode Island.
16. *Peabody Proceedings*, I, 63-65.
17. Amory Dwight Mayo, "Robert Charles Winthrop and the Peabody Education Fund for the South," *Report of the Commissioner of Education for the Year 1893-94*, I (Washington: Government Printing Office, 1896), 754.
18. *Baptist Missionary Magazine*, XXV (August 1845), 220, 221; Basil

Manly, Jr. to Basil Manly, Sr., March 25 and 28, 1845. ALS in Basil Manly Letters, Southern Baptist Convention Historical Commission, Nashville, Tennessee.

19. Barnas Sears, "The Moral and Religious Value of Our National Union," *Bibliotheca Sacra*, XX (January 1863), 137-39.

20. *Peabody Proceedings*, I, 51-53.

21. Horace Mann Bond, *The Education of the Negro in the American Social Order* (New York: Prentice-Hall, Inc., 1934), p. 63; also, Horace Mann Bond, *Negro Education in Alabama* (Washington: The Associated Publishers, 1939), p. 104.

22. Barnas Sears to Robert C. Winthrop, March 14, 1867. ALS in the J. L. M. Curry Papers, Library of Congress.

23. *Peabody Proceedings*, I, 38-57.

24. *Ibid.*, pp. 187-221.

25. *Ibid.*, p. 94.

26. "The Peabody Education Fund," December 14, 1867. Card in the Lusher Scrapbook, New Orleans Public Library.

27. Barnas Sears to E. A. Ware, July 10, 1868. ALS in the records of the Bureau of Refugees, Freedmen, and Abandoned Lands, National Archives.

28. "School Report of Alfred Thomas, Lumberton, North Carolina, April 30, 1868." MSS in School Reports, North Carolina Superintendent of Education, Records of the Bureau of Refugees, Freedmen, and Abandoned Lands, National Archives. Conclusions expressed about Negro educational leadership are based on an unpublished study carried out in 1964-1965, under a Washington *Evening Star* research grant.

29. *The Alexandrian Democrat* (Louisiana), August 25, 1869.

30. H. C. Vogel to John W. Alvord, October 27, 1867; Report of J. R. Lewis to John W. Alvord, June 23, 1869. MSS in Educational Division, Records of Refugees, Freedmen, and Abandoned Lands, National Archives.

31. Barnas Sears to Robert C. Winthrop, September 21, 1869. ALS in the J. L. M. Curry Papers, Library of Congress.

32. *See*, for example, *First Annual Report of the State School Commissioner of the State of Georgia, 1871*, p. 59. Data from several states are reported in Horace Mann Bond, *The Education of the Negro in the American Social Order*, pp. 157-59.

33. Barnas Sears to Oliver O. Howard, April 22, 1867. ALS in the Oliver O. Howard Collection, Bowdoin College.

34. Oliver O. Howard to Barnas Sears, May 7, 1867. ALS in the Oliver O. Howard Collection, Bowdoin College.

35. *Eleventh Annual Report of the Superintendent of Education of South Carolina, 1879*, p. 39.

36. *Southern Recorder* (Milledgeville, Georgia), April 9, 1867.

37. Barnas Sears to Robert M. Lusher, August 28, 1869, cited by Robert M.

Lusher, "Public Instruction in the South," circular in the Lusher Scrapbook, New Orleans Public Library.

38. Howard Turner, "Robert Mills Lusher, Louisiana Educator" (unpublished doctoral dissertation, Louisiana State University, 1944), pp. 103, 148-51.

39. *Peabody Proceedings*, I, 90, 91.

40. *Ibid.*, pp. 262-63; also, "The Peabody Education Fund for Louisiana, May 1, 1868," circular in Lusher Scrapbook, New Orleans Public Library.

41. *Annual Report of the Louisiana State Superintendent of Public Education for 1870*, pp. 33-38.

42. *Baltimore Gazette*, January 25, 1869.

43. *Daily Picayune* (New Orleans), February 28, 1869.

44. *Peabody Proceedings*, II, 14, 15.

45. Barnas Sears to Robert M. Lusher, August 28, 1869, quoted by Robert M. Lusher, "Public Instruction in the South," circular in Lusher Scrapbook, New Orleans Public Library.

46. *Common School Report for the School Year Ending June 30, 1875* (Frankfort, Ky.: James A. Hodges, 1875), p. 105; *Initial Report of H. A. M. Henderson, Superintendent of Public Instruction, to the Governor and Legislature of Kentucky* (Frankfort, Ky.: S. I. M. Major, 1871), p. 24.

47. *Congressional Record*, 43d Cong., 1st Sess., p. 457.

48. *Religious Herald* (Richmond), IX (January 8, 1874), 2.

49. Barnas Sears, "Education in the South," *Atlantic Monthly*, XXXIV (September 1874), 382.

50. *Ibid.*

51. Barnas Sears to Robert C. Winthrop, January 8, 1874. ALS in the J. L. M. Curry Papers, Library of Congress.

52. *Peabody Proceedings*, I, 404-12; also Barnas Sears, "Education in the South," *Atlantic Monthly*, XXXIV (September 1874), pp. 381-82.

53. *Peabody Proceedings*, II, 127, 128.

54. Barnas Sears to Robert O. Winthrop, March 24, 1878. ALS in the J. L. M. Curry Papers, Library of Congress.

55. *Peabody Proceedings*, II, 202, 203, 270-98.

56. Horace Mann Bond, *The Education of the Negro in the American Social Order* (Washington: The Associated Publishers, 1929), p. 132.

57. David M. Reimers, *White Protestantism and the Negro* (New York: Oxford University Press, 1965), pp. 51-83.

# Black Schooling during Reconstruction

## Bertram Wyatt-Brown

Despite a recent outpouring of books and articles on southern educational history, especially with regard to race relations, most of these works have a narrowly institutional cast. There is nothing wrong with that. Yet the "new social history," although no longer really new, offers an opportunity that educational historians should seize. The purpose for applying cultural approaches would not be to conform to intellectual fashions of the moment. Rather, the prospect would be to grapple with some of the knotty problems in black educational history that institutional studies have not altogether explained.

Chief among these issues is the question of why black Americans so often have failed to reach their intellectual potential. By and large, scholars are agreed that the chief handicap has always been white racism and the consequently meager institutional, financial, and political support given to those involved in black education. Indeed, who would quarrel with so just an assessment? After all, racism not only withered freedmen's hopes 120 or more years ago but continues to poison life in the modern-day ghetto, the rural black community, and wherever poverty and government neglect help to stunt intellectual growth.[1]

The objective of this essay is to combine some traditional findings with ones borrowed from anthropology and sociology, so that we move from the tragically familiar but always significant problems of white class and racial bias to more subtle obstacles lying in the path of the black school-child during Reconstruction and, by implication at least, in our own lifetime. The subject, why blacks learned less than they might have, falls into three interconnected categories: (1) the most visible problems: white sectional and racial arrogance of which both native southerners and Yankee teachers were grievously guilty; material and financial deficiencies; inter-

146

nal bickerings among teachers and administrators; classroom bias affecting teachers' attitudes toward children and parents; (2) methodological and cultural confusions, including the limitations of the white teachers' methods of teaching the three R's; and (3) the unfortunate but all too understandable resistance of the black community to advanced individualistic learning as opposed to forms of group learning to which oral traditions and community life were amenable.

In regard to the first issue, so much historical investigation has appeared in print that only a brief review need be included here to show the interaction with the other two areas.[2] Former rebels were in no welcoming mood when a petticoat invasion began even before the guns fell silent. "It is heaping coals of anguish—to have sent among us a lot of ignorant, narrow-minded, bigoted fanatics," wrote a Norfolk editor in 1866, "just as if we were Feejee Islanders and worshippers of African fetish gods, snakes, toads, and terrapins." In the lower South, the *Tuscaloosa Observer* echoed the unpleasant refrain: "False calves, palpitating bosoms and plimpers are all the rage now in the land of wooden hams among the poor slab sided old maids who are coming South to teach the Negroes to lie and steal." Even that debunker of cherished southern myths, W. J. Cash, could not resist the stereotype of the "Yankee schoolma'am" who, "horsefaced, bespectacled, and spare of frame," seemed to him "at best a comic character, at worst a dangerous fool, playing with explosive forces which she did not understand."[3] Indeed, the female missionaries, like Rachel, stood amid the alien corn and cotton, with little hope of gaining a place on the proverbial southern pedestal reserved for native specimens of the gender.

Nevertheless, by 1870 the Yankee "schoolma'ams" and others had reached a total of 9,503, and more than 200,000 black scholars were enrolled. That figure represented about 12 percent of the 1.7 million black school-age children, a healthy though small beginning for a people barred for centuries from access to education by law and custom. White mission agencies such as the venerable antislavery American Missionary Association (AMA), largest in the field, sustained 1,388 teachers. Other agencies, including the Freedmen's Bureau educational branch, raised the total of Yankee-born instructors to nearly 5,000 during the peak of Radical Reconstruction.[4] Although most attention has focused on their work, one should bear in mind, as James D. Anderson, educational historian, stresses, that freedmen themselves organized and paid for teachers (about 1,000 in 1870) from their own community without outside support. Also, the black churches enrolled 107,109 pupils in 1869, a figure that

147

427

increased to 200,000 by 1885.[5] These weekly schools undertook basic instruction in reading and writing for religious purposes, thus reinforcing the daily studies at regular schools. Some of the Yankee teachers were themselves black. Especially noteworthy were those trained at antislavery Oberlin College, which supplied a large number of teachers for the evangelical American Missionary Association.

All missionaries, regardless of color, encountered bitter reprisals. A typical example of southern intimidation was the case of the Reverend John Bardwell, who had sought to open a school in Grenada, Mississippi. He and a group of spirited freedmen moved a small cabin from a nearby military camp and placed it in the midst of the black quarter of town. A Colonel Adams, CSA, accused him of "stealing a house," and Bardwell prepared to defend himself before the bench. While conferring with his attorney, he was violently struck down by a drunken town alderman who had rushed into the lawyer's office. "I have received no martyrdom," Bardwell declared while nursing gashes about his head, "but if it comes I shall not shun it, if God grants me the grace sufficient unto the day."[6]

Courageous and dedicated though they were, the missionaries brought some of the antagonisms upon themselves. Many of them had very little appreciation of southern white values and social habits. Certainly the nineteenth century was not an epoch of cultural relativism. It is hardly a wonder, then, that Ariadne Warren at the AMA school in Meridian, Mississippi, urged Bardwell, her supervisor, to get a "good revolver" after the Grenada incident: "My private opinion is that the powers of darkness are let loose upon this God-forsaken, distracted, demoralized half-civilized country."[7] Such thoughts were hardly a matter of private opinion: they had been disseminated for well over thirty years, in antislavery publications, the halls of Congress, the churches, and public lecture rooms throughout the North.

As this credo was applied to the freedmen, it took a form expressed by Samuel F. Porter, a teacher in Vicksburg, Mississippi. In 1864, he argued in typical fashion that educational and religious instruction required that slaves, like heathens anywhere, had to be "taken by the hand." Porter was typical of most missionaries, who had not come from well-appointed homes; they knew near poverty themselves. They, like white southerners, were often an agrarian people with a basic earthiness and hard-eyed view of life, which Victorian formality and rigid self-discipline held somewhat from open expression. As a result, they considered their message of uplift an outgrowth of personal experience, not an imposition of social control to replace the chains of bondage. They had discovered self-mastery over "sin" by sheer dint of will. Others—slaves and possibly even southern rebels—should be able to do likewise.[8]

148

Several internal problems also dogged the operations of the missionary agencies and may have affected classroom instruction in ways hard to determine. A common situation was the attitude of male supervisors toward the female teachers who constituted two-thirds of the American Missionary Association's contingent. Single women—"giddy girls," scoffed the Reverend Selah Wright, an AMA functionary—were crowding into the field. The evangelical supervisors fretted about how to handle them. Lively and bright, Oberlin-trained women were especially troublesome. Though often Oberlin alumni themselves, the men were unaccustomed to independent thinking from females. Bardwell in Mississippi, for instance, complained that Adriadne ("Addie") Warren, at Meridian, "has never been satisfied that she was not made a *Man*. She wants to be very independent."[9] She got her wish for freedom when transferred from the safety of Meridian to the federally unoccupied Grenada station.

Another major issue was the relationship of white and black agents sent to the South. Admittedly, the problem was complicated. On the one hand, there was a recognition that the presence of well-dressed, accomplished, young black northern women would set fine examples before the children. On the other hand, success partly depended upon provoking native whites as little as possible. But there was also a genuine dislike of black coadjutors within missionary ranks. The Mississippi case of Blanche B. Harris, age twenty-three, her twelve-year-old sister Elizabeth, and Clara P. Freeman, twenty-two, represented in microcosm the volatility and inherent bigotries that scarred the early mission enterprise. On the way from Oberlin to Natchez, Mississippi, the three women had enraged white passengers by mingling freely in the general company aboard the steamboat. Selah Wright, a former missionary to the Minnesota Obijways, was in charge of the expedition. Wright informed AMA headquarters that "I think it folly to send" such teachers South. Their presence made the trip "unpleasant for all of us."[10]

But the initial difficulties were minor compared with the tendency of black teachers to ally with local blacks who wished to run schools to suit themselves, regardless of white interests. Having been forced to find lodgings in the black quarters of Natchez, the Harris sisters and Clara Freeman naturally had access to pupils who eluded the white instructors. So dangerous was the countryside that teachers tended to congregate wherever town life and military protection were available. As a result, there was a maldistribution of the schoolkeepers, who then had to compete among themselves for the children in the vicinity.

The black teachers had a clear advantage, and in places like Natchez the administrators sought to move the inconvenient supernumeraries elsewhere. "Colored teachers should not be sent to places where there are

149

white teachers," the Reverend Palmer Litts, Natchez supervisor, complained to AMA officials in New York in 1866. He had observed that freedmen selected "as their instructors and leading minds those who . . . are surrounded by the same cloud of ignorance" as themselves. The local black preachers, he reported, were "bombastic and vociferous" and all too ready to conspire with the young black teachers to "prejudice the people against those who would teach them the more perfect way." The classes that the Harris girls and Clara Freeman ran were half again as large as those of the white teachers. Blanche Harris's drew more than one hundred. Yet Litts could not prove his charge of deliberate proselytizing from the white teachers' rolls. In fact, Bardwell conceded in a report to New York City that even little "Lizzie" Harris, the teenager, met the criteria for good teaching and all three maintained "good order in school." Perhaps, he mused, "there has been a little too much yielding to the spirit of caste" in the Natchez contingent.[11]

In addition to Yankee biases carried into the field, the risks of the enterprise set the missionaries on edge at times. Sporadic battles over personalities, wages, sectarian prejudices, missionary jurisdictions, and other matters erupted from time to time, and such distractions were bound to affect the quality of instruction. Also, school supplies were always limited, and disputes arose about favoritism and deliberate neglect. Moreover, teachers feuded over living quarters, which were usually cramped and uncomfortable. The climate bothered those unaccustomed to the heat, and many were unused to the swarms of bugs for which the South was renowned. Discomfort led to discord and hindered teacher cooperation even in the choicest posts. Worse yet, the lower pay women teachers received for the same work as the men aroused resentments and led to poor morale. Anna Snowden of Connecticut had to be fired from the Atlanta station in 1869 because of her "mercenary" attitude. She had protested low female wages and thereby violated a taboo in a cause that insisted upon self-sacrifice. The hothouse atmosphere of teachers' lives, separated as they were from white southern society, created its special strains. On the whole, the schoolchildren were not drawn into these troubles. Yet the disputes no doubt prevented teachers from doing their best work.[12]

Another factor, the subtle signs of discrimination that the children might have quickly perceived, is somewhat harder to document in the classroom itself. One suspects, however, that one reason why black parents so often preferred schoolteachers of their own color was a consequence of conscious as well as unconscious white condescension. Part of the problem was the institutional character of missionary work. It had

150

always been official policy that evangelical agents, wherever their location, should hold themselves aloof from the subjects of their labors. The reason was not solely an arrogant sense of moral superiority but also a deep worry about "going native," that is, taking up drink and other bad habits. It happened every once in awhile, to the horror of pious observers. Dread of losing self-command impelled missionaries to insist upon every social observance that promoted respectability. Besides, obedience to proprieties was thought to encourage virtues of a higher order. The southern enterprise was no different from other missions in this respect. The Reverend A. D. Olds, for example, was a veteran from the pre–Civil War AMA station in Jamaica. "The similarity of the fields is most striking," he reported. Even though he found American blacks readier subjects for uplift than those left behind in the West Indies, neither he nor others thought that intermingling would be wise.[13]

Even though teachers and the black community were supposed to keep a respectful distance between them, the missionaries' leaders up North enjoined them to have no doubts about the educability of the black schoolchildren. Much has already been written about this matter. The record is clear: some missionaries were almost as bigoted as native southern whites, but most, after some seasoning in the classroom, grew cautiously optimistic just as their supervisors expected. Otherwise, their own morale would have atrophied. As one teacher said, "Our trials bring us into sympathy with them." On the whole, teachers concluded that both adults and children who were full-blooded blacks were as qualified to learn as those with some white mixture, a conclusion reached through experience as well as long-standing abolitionist dogma. Mission bodies soon dropped questions about the differences between mulattoes and full-bloods.

Nevertheless, white teachers labored under impressions closely allied with their ambivalent views of black religion. For instance, an almost unanimous verdict was that black pupils fared better in Sabbath schools than in daily classwork because the religious "part of their nature," Lydia Thompson, a white instructor, asserted, "has been the most cultivated."[14] These currents of attitudes outside the classroom doubtless were transmitted inside the school. Missionaries strove for professional ideals, motives that mitigated the effects of their cultural preconceptions. Yet try as they might, white teachers were scarcely immune from the prejudices of their generation.

Sometimes the teachers misinterpreted the signs of progress that they were making because their charges were eager to please, as children generally are, even when they may have missed the major point of the in-

151

struction. An example of black attentiveness to white feelings was given in a report of Anna Somers, a Mississippi AMA teacher. She observed that "when their slates or copy books were passed on to me for examination, my face was eagerly watched, to find therein approval or disapproval (they were quick to read the human countenance) and if a word of praise fell from my lips, a look of triumph would so light up their sable faces as to make even them look beautiful."[15] (The last phrase betrayed her. Like so many teachers, she gave the children similarly inadverdent evaluations, whether about racial appearance or mental attribute.)

Indeed, the vitality of black oral tradition did offer advantages in the early steps of learning. For instance, children were remarkably quick-witted about such assignments as memorizing the alphabet, numbers, simple spellings, and short passages of verse and scripture suitable for singing and recital. Recognizing and building upon the observed reaction of northern white children to perform similar tasks, American educators had successfully learned how to make these achievements relatively satisfying and even fun for the pupils. At certain ages, children are particularly eager to absorb facts that lend themselves to group participation. Naming objects, concrete and visible, could be done even in overcrowded classrooms so long as the routine was not mechanical and impersonal. From teachers' reports, it appeared that the first months of education passed relatively smoothly, though the young children were unaccustomed to the prolonged sitting and concentrating.[16]

The group character of early learning was evident when children repeated daily lessons at home. For instance, spelling "the simplest words," observed Anna Harwood, "is a new and apparently inexhaustible source of pleasure and interest to occupy their leisure hours. Parents and children about equally skilled in literature are lost in absorbed attention as they together spell our the wonderful story of A-n-n h-a-d a fast dog." Likewise, Martha L. Jarvis, a black Oberlinite at Meridian, Mississippi, boasted that one pupil had recited twelve biblical verses "without the least hesitation."[17] Phonetic spelling was the method used, so that the children could repeat in unison the proper sound for the syllables. One suspects that even at this level problems arose because of the characteristics of black speech in which the hard "t," "d," and "th" at the end of words was and still is dropped, a vestige of African linguistic habit. The subject has been carefully examined by William Labov, William A. Stewart, David Dalby, and others, but historians have not discussed the stigmatizing effects of these differences nor shown how they affected perceptions of blacks in the past.[18]

152

But despite these and other cultural problems, the northern school-keepers were optimistic that they could be quickly rooted out. From Port Royal, on the South Carolina Sea Islands, where Gullah dialect made communications more difficult than elsewhere, Mrs. Mansfield French reported to the public in 1863, "You would like to see the men and wo-men 'fighting with the letters,' as they say, so that they may not be 'made ashamed' by their children, who are learning fast." At Craney Island, Virginia, "E.C." remarked, "Our instruction is necessarily mostly oral, as much time would be lost if we trained pupils singly. The little things give us almost undivided attention, and are much stimulated by recitations in concert."[19] Buoyed by these signs of initial mastery, blacks among them-selves chided the laggards, a reinforcement for competitive performance that probably stimulated learning. One black girl was overheard to tell a beginner at reading, " 'If I could read as well as you can, I would not say *gwine* for going, *specially* when the white folks take so much pains with you.' "[20]

In imparting how to read, however, teachers soon discovered an unex-pected problem, ironically arising from the blacks' ability at quick recall, by which these early triumphs were achieved. S. M. Pearson at New Bern, North Carolina, found that his students "knew by heart the lessons in the 'Picture Primer' which they had and would tell me how much of a book they knew, while in fact they knew not one word."[21] On the other hand, Henrietta Baldwin reported exuberantly from Arkansas that after only seventeen days of instruction her class, with just twenty minutes devoted to any topic, had completed the *National First Reader,* a popular item in pedagogy, and "could write legibly without copy; could numerate; and one of them could write any number less than a thousand."[22]

Whether pleased or confounded, teachers met quick disappointment with the next stage of intellectual development. One disillusioned teacher in Union-occupied New Bern, North Carolina, explained in 1864: "The principal obstacle I encounter is the want of the power of application" in nearly all students. "They will listen greedily to any instruction given them and would gladly spend the whole session writing on their slates, or copying from the blackboard but appear to have but a very slight idea of acquiring knowledge by studying" and working out problems them-selves.[23]

Some of the problems were clearly mechanical. Primary among them was the size of the classes—as high as eighty-eight in some cases. Large enrollments had not mattered so much in group exercises on the lower levels. But for the more advanced work in cognition, arithmetic, and composition, the disadvantages and inevitable disciplining distractions of

153

overcrowded classes would be obvious. In addition, the materials were poorly suited to the narrow agrarian world in which the pupils lived. Even at the primary level, the books were often much too advanced. The American Baptist Publication Society, for instance, put out a special *First Reader for Freedmen,* advising teachers to have pupils read "by the eye, without spelling." The abecedarians, the author noted, would name the words "in successive paragraphs." Spelling would come later. It was sound pedagogical practice, but the rural black children must have been mystified by pictures of Xerxes for the letter "X" and "newsboy" for "N". The first assignment alone had eighty-two separate words to be learned.[24] For the more advanced classes, the work was still more out of touch with the experiences available to the youngsters fresh from fields and cabins.[25]

American pedagogy at midcentury was totally unsuited to the rural and penurious character of black life. Assignments to be done at home presented no problems for children living in homes with ample privacy, good lighting, and parental guidance. With chores to perform as well, the farm youngster, though, was at serious disadvantage. Indeed, school attendance itself was necessarily much more irregular in the country and always had been in southern life. Teachers constantly complained that, though class size might remain constant, the membership varied decisively, making it hard even to know the enrollees' names.

In addition, abstract concepts required a special concentration for which the rural setting and black styles of thought were uncongenial. A further problem was that the pedagogy for handling abstractions had not been thoroughly mastered by the mid-nineteenth century. Precision, regularity, and grammatical accuracy as rule, not usage or simple logic, were the demands of the day, but the most efficient means for making them habitual had escaped the American instructors. In prior centuries, even the most sophisticated thinkers had spelled words, for instance, as they saw fit. Contemporaneous white southerners, including judges and generals, were often accustomed to follow the irregular orthographies of the past. How much less prepared were the newly freed slaves with Afro-American dialect to add further complications? Correct spelling and grammar were only the beginnings of pedagogical abstraction.[26]

The capability of applying one set of conditions or rules to make sense of another complex of factors is a cultural function. As a group of educational anthropologists recently concluded, there must be a congruence between the problems that customarily arise in a society and the cognitive skills necessary to meet them. In the world of the rural black schoolchild, very little of what was taught and of its presentation had

154

much relationship to daily existence.[27] The drudgery of manual labor, the lively conversations in the black people's cabins, and the generally nonliterate nature of southern living for both races had almost nothing to do with what instructors talked about, once the concrete naming of things had passed. No wonder black pupils preferred group learning, not individual reflection; concrete experience, not cogitation; copying, not composition; parable, anecdote, and story, not categories, formulas, and abstract rules. Unwittingly then (as now), the child from an affective, noninstrumental environment found in the classroom "a symbolic system" appropriate, perhaps, for middle-class village and city life, but not one that bridged, as two modern linguists surmise, the instructional and linguistic distance "between the house and the school."[28]

Naturally, teachers noted the change in academic morale. Lydia Thompson at Vicksburg remarked, "I find many learn very rapidly for awhile, then seem to fall into a stupid, indifferent state." Particularly troublesome was the introduction of arithmetic. The subject was divided between "mental" and "written" forms. The latter was the older, eighteenth-century style whereby "pupils had to apply their skills to elaborate, supposedly commercial problems," says Daniel Calhoun. Victorian mental arithmetic, however, required reason-giving. Teachers, especially those with little training and innate ability, were often "completely nonplussed in any attempt to explain what they have done," said one critic in 1851, "or analyze the principles upon which it is performed." Mental arithmetic was the first that ought to be mastered, according to convention, though it was in some ways the harder because the rules had to be taken on faith. An earlier generation of masters had taught children to think by "reckoning in their heads," a style that conformed with aptitudes arising from rural life. By the 1860s, though, the topic had become very abstract. Some vainly urged a return to the older ways of "sensible arithmetic," that is, said one, "the addition, subtraction, multiplication, &c, of fingers, corn, beans, apples, blocks, and other sensible or tangible objects."[29] Southern black children were not taught now to cipher with such familiar objects as cotton bales and watermelons.

In fact, the entire discipline of arithmetic, written or mental, was fairly consistently avoided. The teachers' reports tell the story. The well-educated black instructors seemed to do best. Clara Freeman, one of the black teachers of Natchez, for instance, taught forty-four pupils in reading and spelling, fifteen in mental arithmetic, and none in written arithmetic. In one of her classrooms, Blanche Harris, the most accomplished teacher in Natchez, taught thirty-three students in mental arithmetic, seven in written arithmetic, and thirty-six in reading and spelling. Elsie

Spees, a white teacher in Natchez, however, taught no children in either branch of the elementary subject. Instead, she set forty students to reading and spelling. Mary Baker's reports revealed the same disproportions as Elsie Spees's. A check of other statistics from Mississippi shows the same pattern. One must suspect that it was a general phenomenon, though no scholar so far has quantified curricular problems. Charles Stearns, in Augusta, Georgia, generalized: "It seems well nigh an impossibility to teach arithmetic" even to scholars excellent in other respects because they were "deficient in memory." All matters regarding "size, weight, number, order, color, eventuality and individuality" were beyond their comprehension, in contrast to their highly proficient *"reflective"* and oratorical faculties.[30]

In public pronouncements, Freedmen's Bureau supervisors and others did not dwell on these alleged deficiencies. Funds were increasingly hard to obtain from Congress or the public as war enthusiasms diminished. Nonetheless, John W. Alvord, head of the bureau's educational division, admitted that the southern blacks did not "excel in the inventive power, or abstract science, perhaps not in mathematics, though we have seen very commendable ciphering" now and then. Instead, like Stearns, he praised them for having "emotional, imitative, and affectionate" natures with aptitude for "graphic and figurative language" and strong "conceptions of beauty and song." Teachers and administrators, then as now, were not given to self-criticism. It did not occur to them that the deficiency lay at least partly in white method, not in black attribute alone.[31]

Like adults, children everywhere perform those tasks best that mesh with their social and economic experiences. They imitate and aspire for proficiency in adult routines. Other activities, especially classwork that represents a different set of criteria and orientations, are seldom easy to grasp. When white teachers discovered the limitations of black advance in abstract conceptualization, particularly in mathematical subjects, most instructors assumed that the deficiency was racially determined. After all, blacks were supposed to be as docile, imitative, and unreflective as females. "It is sometimes said," declared abolitionist Theodore Tilton, editor of the evangelical *New York Independent,* "the the negro race is the feminine race of the world. This is not only because of his social and affectionate nature, but because he possesses that strange moral, instinctive insight that belongs more to women than to men." This misperception was common in antislavery circles. Science, though, was allegedly "masculine," bold, and thoroughly Anglo-Saxon. This interpretation was often combined with the presumed deleterious effects of slavery, which discouraged deductive reasoning. In addition, there was the natural ten-

156

dency of simple folk and children to take the easy course, according to current sentiments about the hierarchies of civilizations. As a result, all agreed, blacks simply did not have the mental stamina and "application" to master tough subjects like mathematics.[32]

A recent experiment in Liberia, however, offers a more satisfactory explanation. It illuminates exactly what took place so many years ago in the freedmen's classrooms. An anthropological team asked a group of Peace Corps volunteers to estimate how many cups of uncooked rice would be necessary to fill a particular bowl. All answers were overestimations by at least 35 percent. Giving much speedier replies, members of the Kpelle tribe, in contrast, made guesses only 8 percent from the mark or better. But in the sorting of geometric patterns on a set of different colored cards, the Peace Corps volunteers quickly provided three separate and correct arrangements, as requested, whereas nearly all the Kpelle tribesmen were unable to complete the task without errors about color, shape, and spatial relations, the very specialties in which Stearns had found black deficiency in 1866. The experiment demonstrated that Africans or any other nonliterate group were not hopelessly ignorant children, but rather that abstract conceptualization must conform with cultural exigencies. Using insights from Jean Piaget and others, the anthropologists put aside Western methodologies and devised a form of instruction that built upon the mathematical experiences indigenous to life in central Liberia, a rice-growing region.

Needless to say, Yankees in the Reconstruction South were hardly equipped to undertake such a mission. The same philosophy of cultural imperialism that had sent these folk southward to punish rebels and elevate blacks to New England standards made it unthinkable to bend pedagogy to meet the needs of a basically peasant society with a strong heritage of nonliterate ways of thinking. As the anthropologists conclude about their Liberian investigation, "It is not the case that the noneducated African is incapable of concept-based thinking nor that he never combines sub-instances to obtain a general solution to a problem. Instead, we have to conclude that the situation in which he applies general, concept-based modes of solution are different and perhaps more restricted than the situations in which his educated age mate will apply such solutions." Educational psychology, however, is still in its infancy. Meantime, white cultural assumptions, no less today than yesterday, dominate the manner of instruction, often to the detriment of the black child's self-confidence and intellectual development.[33]

Carter G. Woodson, famed pioneer in Afro-American history, was one of the few American scholars, black or white, to assail the educational

157

curriculum used in the black people's South. In 1933, Woodson argued that Anglo-American pedagogy had long been "an antiquated process which does not hit the mark even in the case of the needs of the white man himself." In addition, he criticized the examples used in black schoolrooms, which denigrated African and slave contributions to history and economic life and celebrated white heroes and tendencies. But above all, he took special aim at the training of blacks in the rudiments of mathematical sciences:

> Even in the certitude of science or mathematics it has been unfortunate that the approach to the Negro has been borrowed from a "foreign" method. For example, the teaching of arithmetic in the fifth grade in a backward county of Mississippi should mean one thing in the Negro school and a decidedly different thing in the white school. The Negro children, as a rule, come from the homes of tenants and peons who have to migrate annually from plantation to plantation, looking for light which they have never seen. The children from the homes of white planters and merchants live permanently in the midst of calculations, family budgets, and the like, which enable them sometimes to learn more by contact than the Negro can acquire in school. Instead of teaching such Negro children less arithmetic, they should be taught much more of it than white children.[34]

The teachers' neglect of mathematics, the single most unmet need of black education, resulted in mass innumeracy, as tragic as illiteracy, a deficiency that has received more attention.[35] It was not planned or calculated as a hidden means of holding back the race. Had blacks done well at arithmetic and poorly at reading, the instructors would have quickly touted the successes, flattering themselves and the students. Nor was it a natural reluctance on the educators' part to pursue difficult topics when demonstrable results could be quickly obtained from easy work with letters. These were indeed factors but, even so, it foundered because the North was not yet prepared for the industrial age, and educational methods had not made the transition successfully. Pedagogy was still shackled to the primary goal of developing moral character, especially for the black race, which was regarded as very backward in that respect. Frugality, precision, initiative, punctuality, honesty, and steadiness of purpose were culturally associated with reading and writing, much less so with the exact sciences in that still unspecialized and religiously minded age. These and other virtues, currently called "bourgeois," were deemed essential to black advance no less than to white accomplishment.[36] Reformist though the missionary teachers were, they could no more break out of their cultural habits and caste expectations than white southerners

158

could from theirs. Moreover, how would it have been possible for Yankee schoolkeepers, most of them females trained in literary and hortatory modes and prevented by customs of gender from developing mathematical skills, to compensate in the classroom for the scientific deficiencies (by white standards) of black children in the rural South? It was a gloomy situation. Only a few instructors, such as Emma Stickney, Clara Anna Harwood, and "Addie" Warren, who promoted mental arithmetic, made much of an effort—at risk to their own reputation as "submissive" females. Others did less. How much more fruitful it seemed to the leaders at Hampton Institute, for instance, to introduce the Negro to "logic and the subjection of feeling to reason" and to "exercise his curiosity, his love of the marvelous, and his imagination as means of sustaining his enthusiasm."[37] Yet as preparation for opportunities, even the minimal ones available to sharecroppers and laborers, learning to keep accounts and do small calculations was just as important as reading and writing, if not more so.

From the black children's perspective, the hidden agenda was how to cope, a task involving much role-playing and craftiness. Exasperated with constant classroom interruptions, implausible alibis for lateness, mind-wandering, or disruption, one missionary in North Carolina complained that "you never know at what point you may expect to find them clear or stark blind," because there was "the most free-and-easy defiance of all rules of discipline or self-regulation." Another exclaimed that the children were "too easily amused," laughed "at trifles," and found almost any excuse for not paying mind to business at hand. These antics were not merely normal reactions of children anywhere.[38] Rather, the obstacles to attentive learning were themselves learning experiences in the children's oral, physical world, which white folks ruled. Knowing when and how to act out or hide feelings, how to provoke authority without going too far—these and other extracurricular doings were the subjects pupils learned at school, though not printed in the *National Reader* or *Sanders' Speller*. Far from understanding the causes of class mischief, teachers thought in terms of a possibly forgivable "manly" reaction to former bondage.[39]

The most unfortunate but least discussed factor in black education has been the natural desire of the blacks to retain a culture and personal autonomy distinctly separate from the white world. Such hopes of the poor have long bedeviled the intrusive evangels of the dominant culture, be they mountain whites, native Americans, or immigrants from abroad. For the blacks, to become well educated was to leave the familiar sur-

159

roundings of home and community and to risk rebuff and bigotry, all the more galling because of the increased sensitivity that education brings. Even during Reconstruction, when possibilities for advance and recognition were at best slim, black children learned a hidden message: meet your community rules for survival and do not get bleached in the Yankee teacher's educational washroom. You will cut yourself off from your own circle but never be admitted to theirs. Evidence for this drain upon self-confidence cannot be easily found because blacks' conversations among themselves were seldom recorded.

The warnings were given through behavior more often than in words anyway. But occasionally adult blacks voiced the fear of being outdone by the young ones who would learn to despise their parents' country ways. Elizabeth Botume, the great black educator, observed that parents on the sea islands urged their youngsters to school, but the best scholars refused to go back to fieldwork. "This was a serious offense to the old people. 'Do they think I am to hoe with them folks that don't know anything!' exclaimed one of the older boys. 'I know too much for that. . . .' 'Them children discountenance we,' groaned the parents. 'They is too smart; they knows too much.' " Also, inequalities in knowledge among the pupils acted to discourage advance. When some town blacks competed at Elizabeth Botume's school, they boasted of mastering " 'algeeber,' " a subject she did not think her charges ready to tackle. The class was most unhappy to have been so humiliated. Botume complained that the parents were at fault because "home discipline and home instruction" were beyond the simple folks' capacity. She knew that they could not help it, but it was nonetheless their fault.[40]

Yet despite the difficulties, advances were made. Whether evangelicals, black and white, set standards of black educational performance too low or too high, they persisted with all their customary tenacity. Illiteracy in Georgia, for instance, was reduced from 95 to 97 percent in 1860 to 77.3 percent by 1880. Class attendance rates rose from 5 percent in 1870 to 40 percent a decade later in the same state. Similar improvements were made throughout the rest of the South as well. In the District of Columbia, by 1880 only about a quarter of all blacks between ages fifteen and twenty were illiterate. Percentages elsewhere were less dramatically reduced, but in Maryland, for instance, over half the population in the same age group could read and write. Even in South Carolina 26.4 percent had mastered the skills.[41]

Given the high barriers that isolated each participant in the northern teaching enterprise—male and female, Negro and Caucasian, southern and northern—a later age can only marvel that so much was achieved,

160

not how little. The vexations were enormous. The neglect of mathematics was disastrous but probably inescapable. Certainly the complicated task of bringing a race out of slavery was beyond the capacity, knowledge, and intention of that generation of American whites. But the nineteenth-century code of personal heroics, will, and responsibility had ordained that the advocates of emancipation before the war should attempt to fulfill the obligation afterward. Courageous and timid, narrow and visionary, radical and hopelessly conventional, the Yankee missionaries of both races did the best they could. They helped to widen southern black horizons in a world beset with misapprehensions, violent inhumanity, arrogance, and fear. The children knew that domain and its fierce dangers better than their instructors and acted accordingly with valor and persistence that have yet to be appreciated. It may be that those who attended schools against the jeers and violence of white detractors gained more than books alone could give them. Some future historian, one may hope, will find similar marks of achievement in the struggles of teachers and students during the current era. But with more sophisticated means of judging than those available a hundred years ago, what will that historical verdict be?

# Notes

1. See John W. Ogbu, *Minority Education and Caste: The American System in Cross-Cultural Perspective* (New York: Academic Press, 1978); Alvin Poussaint and Carolyn Atkinson, "Black Youth and Motivation," in Edgar G. Epps, ed., *Race Relations: Current Perspectives* (Cambridge, Mass.: Winthrop, 1973), pp. 167–77. No current scholars have treated the black child in the Reconstruction classroom, but Ronald E. Butchart, *Northern Schools, Southern Blacks, and Reconstruction: Freedmen's Education* (Westport, Conn.: Greenwood Press, 1980), p. xiii, promises to do so in a forthcoming study.

2. Robert Church and Michael W. Sedlak, *Education in the United States: An Interpretive History* (New York: Free Press, 1976), pp. 117–53; Butchart, *Northern Schools, Southern Blacks, and Reconstruction;* Robert L. Morris, *Reading, 'Riting, and Reconstruction: The Education of the Freedmen in the South, 1861–1870* (Chicago: University of Chicago Press, 1981).

3. Norfolk, Va., editorial, July 2, 1866, quoted in *American Missionary* 10 (August 1866): 174; *Tuscaloosa Observer,* quoted in John B. Myers, "The Education of the Alabama Freedmen during Presidential Reconstruction, 1865–1867," *Journal of Negro Education* 40 (Spring 1971): 169; Wilbur J. Cash, *The Mind of the South* (New York: Knopf, 1941), p. 140.

4. James M. McPherson, *Ordeal by Fire: The Civil War and Reconstruction* (New York: Knopf, 1982), p. 574; William Preston Vaughan, *Schools for All:*

161

*The Blacks and Public Education in the South, 1865–1877* (Lexington: University Press of Kentucky, 1974), p. 13.

5. James D. Anderson, "Ex-Slaves and the Rise of Universal Education in the New South, 1860–1880," in Ronald K. Goodenow and Arthur O. White, eds., *Education and the Rise of the New South* (Boston: G. K. Hall, 1981), p. 9.

6. John P. Bardwell to George Whipple, April 28, May 4, 21, 26 (quotation), 1866, Mississippi, American Missionary Association MSS (microfilm), Dillard University, New Orleans (hereafter Miss., AMA MSS).

7. Ariadne Warren to Bardwell, May 6, 1866, Miss., AMA MSS. See also Bardwell, letter to editor, *American Missionary* 10 (June 1866): 138, and Anna Clara Harwood to Whipple, April 30, 1866, Miss., AMA MSS.

8. Samuel F. Porter to Whipple, April 5, 1864, Miss., AMA MSS; James M. McPherson, *The Abolitionist Legacy: From Reconstruction to the NAACP* (Princeton: Princeton University Press, 1975); and on missionary backgrounds, see Oberlin College Alumni Files, Oberlin College Archives.

9. Bardwell to Whipple, March 10, 1866, Wright to Whipple, March 19, 1866, "Addie" Warren to Whipple, March 26, May 6, 1866, Joseph Warren to Whipple, May 15, 1866, and Major Jonathan J. Knox to Samuel Hunt, May 25, 1866, Miss., AMA MSS; Sandra E. Small, "The Yankee Schoolmarm in Freedmen's School: An Analysis of Attitudes," *Journal of Southern History* 45 (August 1979): 381; Morris, *Reading, 'Riting, and Reconstruction,* pp. 54–84.

10. Wright to Whipple, April 7, 1866, Miss., AMA MSS. But see Rupert S. Holland, ed., *Letters of Laura M. Towne* . . . (Cambridge, Mass.: Riverside, 1912), p. 146; Small, "Yankee Schoolmarm," 391–92.

11. Palmer Litts to Whipple, 1865, March 7, April 27, 1866, Litts to Samuel Hunt, April 2, 1866, Wright to Whipple, November 11, 1865, April 27, 1866, Bardwell to Whipple, March 2, 1866, Blanche V. Harris to Michael E. Strieby, June 24, 1864, Harris to Whipple, January 23, March 10, 1866, Miss., AMA MSS; Teachers' Monthly Reports, October 1865–March 1866, ibid. For biographies of these individuals, see Oberlin College Alumni Files.

12. Jacqueline Jones, *Soldiers of Light and Love: Northern Teachers and Georgia Blacks* (Chapel Hill: University of North Carolina Press, 1980), pp. 173–83; Willie Lee Rose, *Rehearsal for Reconstruction: The Port Royal Experiment* (Indianapolis: Bobbs Merrill, 1964), pp. 229–35, 372–74; Small, "Yankee Schoolmarm," pp. 381–402.

13. A. D. Olds to Whipple, April 16 (quotation), June 1, July 22, 1863, A. B. Harwell to Whipple, January 19, July 6, 1864, Anna M. Keen to J. R. Shipherd, February 4, 1868, Miss., AMA MSS.

14. Litts to Whipple, July 11, 1865, Wright to Strieby, November 20, 1865 (quotation), Mary O. Baker to Whipple, September 6, 1864, Bardwell to Whipple, March 26, 1866, Anna M. Keen to Shipherd, February 4, 1868, ibid.; Wright, letter, December 10, 1865, in *American Missionary* 10 (January 1866): 37–38; Joel R. Williamson, "Black Self-Assertion before and after Emancipation," in Nathan I. Huggins, Martin Kilson, and Daniel M. Fox, eds., *Key Issues in the Afro-American Experience* (New York: Harcourt Brace Jovanovich,

162

1971), pp. 213–19; Lydia Thompson, May 1864 (quotation), Teachers' Monthly Report, Miss., AMA MSS.

15. Anna Somers to Hunt, June 1, 1866, Miss., AMA MSS; see also Daniel Calhoun, *The Intelligence of a People* (Princeton: Princeton University Press, 1973), p. 75; Jack Goody and Ian Watts, "The Consequences of Literacy," in Jack Goody, ed., *Literacy in Traditional Societies* (Cambridge: Cambridge University Press, 1968), pp. 56–68; David Riesman, *The Oral Tradition, the Written Word and the Screen Image* (Yellow Springs, Ohio: Antioch College Press, 1956); Daniel F. McCall, "Literacy and Social Structures," *History of Education Quarterly* 11 (Spring 1971): 85–92.

16. See Litts to Whipple, July 11, 1866; "The Condol School Exhibition," enclosure in Nathan T. Condol to Whipple, April 21, 1866, Bardwell to Whipple, June 30, 1866, Wright to Bardwell, November 11, 1865, Helen M. Jones to Wright, January 13, 1866, Miss., AMA MSS; Rose, *Rehearsal for Reconstruction,* p. 230.

17. Anna C. Harwood to Whipple, February 1, 1866, Martha L. Jarvis to Whipple, June 30, 1866, Miss., AMA MSS.

18. See William Labov, "The Logic of Nonstructured English," in Frederick Williams, ed., *Language and Poverty: Perspectives on a Theme* (Chicago: Markham, 1970), pp. 153–89, and William A. Stewart, "Toward a History of American Negro Dialect," ibid., pp. 351–79; David Dalby, "Black through White: Patterns of Communication in Africa and the New World," in Walt Wolfram and Mona E. Clark, eds., *Black-White Speech Relationships* (Washington, D.C.: Center for Applied Linguistics, 1971), pp. 99–137; Thomas Kochman, "Toward an Ethnography of Black American Speech Behavior," in Norman E. Whitten, Jr., and John F. Szwed, eds., *Afro-American Anthropology: Contemporary Perspectives* (New York: Free Press, 1970), pp. 149–55.

19. Letters, "E.H.F.," May 15, 1863, "E.C.," March 16, 1863, in *Third Series of Extracts from Letters Received by the Educational Commission for Freedmen, from Teachers and Superintendents at Port Royal and Its Vicinity* (Boston: John Wilson & Son, 1863), pp. 2–3 (hereafter *Extracts,* with date).

20. C. E. Croome to James Horace James, November 23, 1863, in *Extracts* (1864), p. 10.

21. Pearson to James, December 22, 1863, ibid., pp. 10, 11.

22. *Second Annual Report of the Western Freedmen's Aid Commission* (Cincinnati: A. P. Thompson, 1865), p. 38.

23. Letter, "A.C.G.C.," March 1864, in *Extracts* (1864), p. 12.

24. *The First Reader for Freedmen* (Philadelphia: American Baptist Publication Society, 1866), pp. 11, 12.

25. See, for instance, Charles W. Sanders, *Sanders' New Speller, Definer and Analyzer . . .* (Chicago: S. C. Griggs, 1861), a text with 429 exercises. Other books employed were Charles W. Sanders, *The School Reader; McGuffey's Reader; The National Reader; Webster's Reader;* and Arnold H. Guyot, *Physical Geography* (New York: Armstrong, 1866).

26. Calhoun, *Intelligence of a People,* pp. 87–88, 123.

163

27. Michael Cole et al., *The Cultural Context of Learning and Thinking: An Exploration in Experimental Anthropology* (New York: Basic Books, 1971), pp. 230–33.

28. See Eleanor R. Leacock, "Abstract versus Concrete Speech: A False Dichotomy," in Courtney B. Cazden et al., eds., *Functions of Language in the Classroom* (New York: Teachers College Press, 1972), pp. 111–34; Basil B. Bernstein, "A Critique of the Concept of Compensatory Education," in ibid., pp. 135–51; and Basil B. Bernstein and Dorothy Henderson, "Social Class Differences in the Relevance of Language to Socialization," *Sociology* 3 (January 1969): 17 (quotation). See also Calhoun, *Intelligence of a People,* pp. 116–17, and for overview of recent investigations, Michael Cole and Barbara Means, *Comparative Studies of How People Think: An Introduction* (Cambridge, Mass.: Harvard University Press, 1981), esp. pp. 49–51.

29. These quotations and arguments are all from Calhoun, *Intelligence of a People,* pp. 103–6.

30. Charles Stearns, *The Black Man of the South and the Rebels . . .* (New York: American News Co., 1872), p. 394. See Teachers' Monthly Reports for 1865–66, Miss., AMA MSS; Elsie Spees's report, February 20, 1863 (1864?), and Mary Baker, May 1, 1864, ibid. The subject of geography was also greatly neglected.

31. John W. Alvord, *First Semi-Annual Report on Schools and Finances of Freedmen, January 1, 1866* (Washington, D.C.: U.S. Government Printing Office, 1868), p. 11.

32. Tilton, quoted in George M. Fredrickson, *The Black Image in the White Mind: The Debate on Afro-American Character and Destiny, 1817–1914* (New York: Harper & Row, 1971), p. 115; Stearns, *Black Man,* pp. 190–91; Calhoun, *Intelligence of a People,* pp. 23, 124, 199–200, 201, 334.

33. Michael Cole and John Gay, *The New Mathematics and an Old Culture: A Study of Learning among the Kpelle of Liberia* (New York: Holt, Rinehart, and Winston, 1967), p. 1; Cole et al., *Cultural Context of Learning,* p. 225 (quotation); see also Gordon W. Allport and Thomas F. Pettigrew, "The Trapezoidal Illusion among Zulus," in Ihsan Al-Isa and Wayne Dennis, eds., *Cross-Cultural Studies of Behavior* (New York: Holt, Rinehart, and Winston, 1970), pp. 30–48.

34. Carter G. Woodson, *The Mis-Education of the American Negro* (Washington, D.C.: Associated Publishers, 1933), pp. xii, 4. Of course, there were always notable black geniuses in all fields, including mathematics.

35. But see Patricia Cline Cohen, *A Calculating People: The Spread of Numeracy in Early America* (Chicago: University of Chicago Press, 1983).

36. See Barbara L. Finkelstein, "Pedagogy as Intrusion: Teaching Values in Popular Primary Schools in Nineteenth-Century America," *History of Childhood Quarterly* 1 (Winter 1974): 349–78; "The Moral Dimensions of Pedagogy: Teaching Behavior in Popular Primary Schools in Nineteenth-Century America," *American Studies* 15 (Fall 1974): 79–89.

164

37. *Hampton Institute: Catalogue of the Hampton Normal and Agricultural Institute for the Academical Year 1870–71* (Boston: T. R. Marvin, 1871), p. 22, Anna Clara Harwood, September 1865, Teachers' Report, Natchez: 24 mental arithmetic, o written arithmetic; 78 reading and writing; Ariadne Warren, 5 mental arithmetic, o written arithmetic; Emma Stickney, 5 written arithmetic, 38 mental arithmetic, December 1865. Totals for Natchez were 170 reading and spelling; 10 mental arithmetic; 15 written arithmetic; 44 geography. See Miss., AMA MSS.

38. "W.F.A." (probably William F. Allen), April 1, 1864, in *Extracts* (1864), p. 15. See Rose, *Rehearsal for Reconstruction*, pp. 115, 265–67, 313–14; Stickney to Whipple, March 14, 1866, Litts to Whipple, July 11, 25, 1865, Harwood to Whipple, September 1, 1866, Warren to Whipple, January 29, 1866, Martha L. Jarvis to Whipple, January 31, 1866, John Eaton to Whipple, September 11, 1863, Miss., AMA MSS; Eugene D. Genovese, *Roll, Jordan, Roll: The World the Slaves Made* (New York: Pantheon, 1974), p. 167; Elizabeth Botume, *First Days amongst the Contraband* (Boston: Lee & Shephard, 1893), p. 104.

39. Bardwell to Strieby, December 24, 1864, Miss., AMA MSS; letters, "M.G.K.," June (?), 1864, and "W.F.A.," April 1, 1864, in *Extracts* (1864), p. 15.

40. Botume, *First Days*, pp. 274–76.

41. Jones, *Soldiers of Light and Love*, p. 229. Unfortunately, the 1870 census did not give percentage figures for illiteracy. See *Ninth Census of the United States* (1870), pp. 452–57, but see *Tenth Census* (1880), *Compendium*, pt. 2, pp. 1650–53.

165

# ACKNOWLEDGMENTS

Burnside, Jacqueline G. "Suspicion Versus Faith: Negro Criticisms of Berea College in the Nineteenth Century." *Register of the Kentucky Historical Society* 83 (1985): 237-66. Reprinted with the permission of the Kentucky Historical Society. Courtesy of the Kentucky Historical Society.

Butchart, Ronald E. "'We Can Best Instruct Our Own People': New York African Americans in the Freedmen's Schools, 1861–1875." *Afro-Americans in New York Life and History* 12 (1988): 27-49. Reprinted with the permission of the Afro-American Historical Association of the Niagara Frontier. Courtesy of the Afro-American Historical Association of Niagara Frontier, Inc.

Christensen, Lawrence O. "Schools for Blacks: J. Milton Turner in Reconstruction Missouri." *Missouri Historical Review* 76 (1982): 121-35. Reprinted with the permission of the State Historical Society of Missouri. Courtesy of Yale University Sterling Memorial Library.

Finkenbine, Roy E. "'Our Little Circle': Benevolent Reformers, the Slater Fund, and the Argument for Black Industrial Education, 1882–1908." *Hayes Historical Journal* 6 (1986): 6-22. Reprinted with the permission of the Hayes Presidential Center. Courtesy of *Hayes Historical Journal*.

Harris, Carl V. "Stability and Change in Discrimination Against Black Public Schools: Birmingham, Alabama, 1871–1931." *Journal of Southern History* 51 (1985): 375-416. Copyright (1985) by the Southern Historical Association. Reprinted by permission of the Managing Editor. Courtesy of Yale University Sterling Memorial Library.

Hine, Darlene Clark. "The Anatomy of Failure: Medical Education Reform and the Leonard Medical School of Shaw University, 1882–1920." *Journal of Negro Education* 54 (1985): 512-25. Reprinted with the permission of Howard University. Courtesy of Yale University Seeley G. Mudd Library.

Johnson, Whittington B. "A Black Teacher and Her School In

Reconstruction Darien: The Correspondence of Hettie Sabattie and J. Murray Hoag, 1868–1869." *Georgia Historical Quarterly* 75 (1991): 90–105. Reprinted with the permission of the Georgia Historical Society. Courtesy of Yale University Sterling Memorial Library.

Jones, Allen W. "The Role of Tuskegee Institute in the Education of Black Farmers." *Journal of Negro History* 60 (1975): 252-67. Reprinted with the permission of the Association for the Study of Afro-American History. Courtesy of Yale University Sterling Memorial Library.

Kousser, J. Morgan. "Progressivism—For Middle-Class Whites Only: North Carolina Education, 1880–1910." *Journal of Southern History* 46 (1980): 169-94. Copyright (1980) by the Southern Historical Association. Reprinted by permission of the Managing Editor. Courtesy of Yale University Sterling Memorial Library.

Margo, Robert A. "Race Differences in Public School Expenditures: Disfranchisement and School Finance in Louisiana, 1890–1910." *Social Science History* 6 (1982): 9-33. Reprinted with the permission of Duke University Press. Courtesy of Yale University Sterling Memorial Library.

Martin, Sandy Dwayne. "The American Baptist Home Mission Society and Black Higher Education in the South, 1865–1920." *Foundations* 24 (1981): 310-27. Reprinted with the permission of the American Baptist Quarterly. Courtesy of Yale University Divinity Library.

McPherson, James M. "White Liberals and Black Power in Negro Education, 1865–1915." *American Historical Review* 75 (1970): 1357-86. Reprinted with the permission of the author. Courtesy of Yale University Sterling Memorial Library.

Nelson, Paul David. "Experiment in Interracial Education at Berea College, 1858–1908." *Journal of Negro History* 59 (1974): 13-27. Reprinted with the permission of the Association for the Study of Afro-American History. Courtesy of Yale University Sterling Memorial Library.

Peeps, J.M. Stephen. "Northern Philanthropy and the Emergence of Black Higher Education—Do-Gooders, Compromisers, or Co-Conspirators?" *Journal of Negro Education* 50 (1981): 251-69. Reprinted with the permission of Howard University. Courtesy of Yale University Seeley G. Mudd Library.

Rabinowitz, Howard N. "Half a Loaf: The Shift from White to Black Teachers in the Negro Schools of the Urban South, 1865–1890." *Journal of Southern History* 40 (1974): 565-94. Copyright (1974) by the Southern Historical Association. Reprinted by permission of the Managing Editor. Courtesy of Yale University Sterling Memorial Library.

Richardson, Joe M. "Francis L. Cardozo: Black Educator During Reconstruction." *Journal of Negro Education* 48 (1979): 73-83. Reprinted with the permission of Howard University. Courtesy of Yale University Seeley G. Mudd Library.

Rothrock, Thomas. "Joseph Carter Corbin and Negro Education in the University of Arkansas." *Arkansas Historical Quarterly* 30 (1971): 277-314. Reprinted with the permission of the Arkansas Historical Association. Courtesy of Yale University Sterling Memorial Library.

West, Earle H. "The Harris Brothers: Black Northern Teachers in the Reconstruction South." *Journal of Negro Education* 48 (1979): 126-38. Reprinted with the permission of Howard University. Courtesy of Yale University Seeley G. Mudd Library.

West, Earle H. "The Peabody Education Fund and Negro Education, 1867–1880." *History of Education Quarterly* 6 (1966): 3-21. Reprinted with the permission of the author. Courtesy of Yale University Seeley G. Mudd Library.

Wyatt-Brown, Bertram. "Black Schooling During Reconstruction." In Walter L. Fraser, Jr., R. Frank Saunders, Jr., Jon L. Wakelyn, eds., *The Web of Southern Social Relations: Women, Family, and Education* (Athens, GA: University of Georgia Press, 1985): 146-65. Copyright 1985, reprinted with the permission of the University of Georgia Press. Courtesy of Yale University Cross Campus Library.